This volume is the second updating of  Design of Tall Buildings that was publ sequentially between 1978 and 1981. T developments and the state-of-the-art Council on Tall Buildings and Urban I of the Monograph and its Chapters is as

lings

PC PLANNING AND ENVIRONMENTAL CRITERIA FOR TALL BUILDINGS

1. Philosophy of Tall Buildings
2. History of Tall Buildings
3. Social Effects of the Environment
4. Sociopolitical Influences
5. Economics
6. Architecture
7. Interference and Environmental Effects
8. Urban Planning and Design
9. External Transportation
10. Parking
11. Operation, Maintenance, and Ownership
12. Energy Conservation
13. Motion Perception and Tolerance
14. Project Management
15. Application of Systems Methodology

SC TALL BUILDING SYSTEMS AND CONCEPTS

1. Structural Systems
2. Mechanical and Service Systems
3. Electrical Systems
4. Vertical and Horizontal Transportation
5. Cladding
6. Partitions, Walls, and Ceilings
7. Foundation Systems
8. Construction Systems

CL TALL BUILDING CRITERIA AND LOADING

1. Gravity Loads and Temperature Effects
2. Earthquake Loading and Response
3. Wind Loading and Wind Effects
4. Fire
5. Accidental Loading
6. Quality Criteria
7. Structural Safety and Probabilistic Methods

SB STRUCTURAL DESIGN OF TALL STEEL BUILDINGS

1. Commentary on Structural Steel Design
2. Elastic Analysis and Design
3. Plastic Analysis and Design
4. Stability
5. Stiffness
6. Fatigue and Fracture
7. Connections
8. Load and Resistance Factor Design (Limit States Design)
9. Mixed Construction

CB STRUCTURAL DESIGN OF TALL CONCRETE AND MASONRY BUILDINGS

1. Characteristics of Concrete and Masonry Tall Buildings
2. Design Criteria and Safety Provisions
3. Concrete Framing Systems for Tall Buildings
4. Optimization of Tall Concrete Buildings
5. Elastic Analysis
6. Nonlinear Behavior and Analysis
7. Model Analysis
8. Stability
9. Stiffness, Deflections, and Cracking
10. Creep, Shrinkage, and Temperature Effects
11. Design of Cast-in-place Concrete
12. Design of Structures with Precast Concrete Elements
13. Design of Masonry Structures

The material contained in this volume is organized to generally correspond with the chapters listed above. This volume and the entire Monograph set can be ordered by writing to the Council.

Council Headquarters
Building 13
Lehigh University
Bethlehem, Pennsylvania 18015
USA

Advances in
Tall Buildings

Advances in Tall Buildings

Council on Tall Buildings
and Urban Habitat

Lynn S. Beedle, Editor-in-Chief

VNR VAN NOSTRAND REINHOLD COMPANY
New York

Manufactured in the United States of America.

Published by Van Nostrand Reinhold Company Inc.
115 Fifth Avenue
New York, New York 10003

Van Nostrand Reinhold Company Limited
Molly Millars Lane
Wokingham, Berkshire RG11 2PY, England

Van Nostrand Reinhold
480 Latrobe Street
Melbourne, Victoria 3000, Australia

Macmillan of Canada
Division of Gage Publishing Limited
164 Commander Boulevard
Agincourt, Ontario MIS 3C7, Canada

15 14 13 12 11 10 9 8 7 6 5 4 3 2 1

Library of Congress Cataloging-in-Publication Data
Main entry under title:
Advances in tall buildings.
  Bibliography: p.
  Includes indexes.
    1. Tall buildings—Addresses, essays, lectures.   2. Structural
engineering—Addresses, essays, lectures. I. Beedle, Lynn S.
II. Council on Tall Buildings and Urban Habitat.
TH845.A45 1986   721'.042   85-17826
ISBN 0-442-21599-1

Contents

Criteria and Loading

Structural Design of Tall Steel Buildings

Structural Design of Tall Concrete and Masonry Buildings

Appendix

Nomenclature

References/Bibliography

Building Index

Name Index

Subject Index

Preface

The age of telecommuting may not yet be with us, but there is no doubt that the computer is radically changing the architectural and engineering approach to tall building design. Structural engineering can still produce economical designs in spite of the revolution going on in architectural form. Cities are recognizing their power to control tall building development and even the design of their skyline; but in many cases the developer is still able to create the desired image.

One reads less about the demise of the city and more about successful revitalization efforts, the results of which are bringing business and residence back to the central city.

We have come to a time in the United States when, after experiencing a plateau in building in some of the older cities, things are beginning to pick up. A 68-story near-duplicate of Chicago's Water Tower Place is being built only two blocks from the original. A comment of "look at all the cranes" from residents in Tampa has accompanied an explosion of construction. Overseas, there are some places where the pace never slowed down, such as in Kuala Lumpur and Singapore. In other parts of the world there is virtually no tall building construction (as in West Europe).

How much of deciding whether to build or what to build depends on the architect and engineer, and how much depends on the developer, the client, or the owner? There is probably as much variety in the answer to that question as there is in the buildings. In the case of the Onterie Center, Fazlur Khan's last design (for which there is a project description in this book), the design follows closely what began as a student thesis some years ago. The location chosen was the result of good market research.

Tall building architecture, as well, is going through a dramatic change. More and more cities are reflecting the application of what some refer to as "post-modernism."

There is no question in our minds that the structure of buildings will be able to keep pace with the new architectural forms. But the important thing is that it can do it economically. Concretes are available with strengths at service loading up to 10,000 psi. Steels are largely unchanged, but design philosophy is going through a time of transition in the United States. AISC's LRFD (limit states) draft specification, for example, is out for review and comment.

One reads less about energy, but one reads more about computer-directed control systems. (It is reported that the installation of automatic light switches can save as much as 50% in the lighting bill.) It's part of the effort of "service engineering" to make the best possible use of the computer. While it may be "hype" to feature and advertise buildings as "intelligent" or "smart," there is no doubt that we will see more of them in the future.

Tall building research has made new strides as well. In the US-Japan earthquake program, both steel and concrete buildings seven stories in height (as tall as can be tested in the present facility) are hoped to produce evidence for safer and yet more economical design. The late 1983 hurricane in Houston taught a dramatic lesson on the importance of controlling the use of gravel on roof tops at lower levels. The question that remains is what the code committees will do about it.

Will more office workers work from their homes? Will our personal computer be the means of cutting down on travel? In other words will we telecommunicate instead of riding the car, bus, or train?

We don't know. From the few experiments in teleconferences, the computer can help, but it's not going to be the complete replacement for conferences and face-to-face bargaining. If not working at home, can office workers congregate at subcenters — separate office buildings located closer to residential accommodations? Some experiments along these lines resulted in less absenteeism, but others resulted in loss of worker morale (because the workplace was not the headquarters building—"where the action is").

These are but a few of the high-rise trends that can be seen, some of which are reflected in the pages of this book.

It is important to take stock. The Council's Third International Conference in Chicago will provide that opportunity and enrich the tall building experience. Celebrating the 100th anniversary of the skyscraper (William LeBaron Jenney's Home Insurance Building in Chicago) will give the opportunity to take a look ahead at the second century of the skyscraper.

A recent (1983) *Engineering News Record* round-table session looked at future height limits. The conclusion was that eventually a new world's tallest building probably would be built in this century; it will be evolutionary (120 to 150 stories in height); it will be of mixed construction and will be multiuse; and it will probably be built outside of the USA, perhaps in Asia (although some New York and Chicago enthusiasts believe otherwise).

It will be interesting to see what happens.

This volume represents a continuation of the efforts of the Council on Tall Buildings and Urban Habitat to provide meaningful research and development information on tall buildings in one comprehensive source. *Advances in Tall Buildings*, as did *Developments in Tall Buildings — 1983*, brings together the recent works of professionals in the field of tall buildings and offers them to the reader in a format that closely follows that of the Council's five-volume Monograph on the Planning and Design of Tall Buildings, published from 1978 to 1981.

This particular volume originated from the Second Annual Council Meeting, held in Chicago in October, 1982. Many of the articles included here were first presented at that meeting, then discussed and written in their present form. The invitation for additional written contributions resulted in a substantial number of new papers. Thus, this volume takes on the flavor of its Chicago setting, while still maintaining an international perspective.

The Council on Tall Buildings and Urban Habitat, first organized in 1969, took on the goal of producing the five-volume Monograph in 1972. The release of the final volume in 1981 represented a culmination of the intense work of over a hundred people to provide their fellow architects, engineers, planners, and designers with an in-depth source of information on tall buildings.

Concerned that all of that hard work not be subject to the ravages of time and become "obsolete," it was decided to release at appropriate intervals update volumes designed to put the original material into today's perspective. *Advances in Tall Buildings* attempts to do just that, picking up where the 1983 volume left off.

Unlike the Monograph, which was heavily edited by Council topical committees, the papers in this volume are authored by individuals who are specialists in the field. They were reviewed by the committees for their appropriateness to the volume.

The material is divided into chapters according to their topical matter, grouped under five general divisions that correspond to the original volumes of the Monograph:

Planning and Environmental Criteria (PC)
Systems and Concepts (SC)
Criteria and Loading (CL)
Structural Design of Tall Steel Buildings (SB)
Structural Design of Tall Concrete and Masonry Buildings (CB)

Each section begins with an introductory statement by the coordinator of that group, briefly touching on the material contained within that section. According to the open nature of the opportunity for submission of material, some topics have several contributions, while others have none.

Each individual article is followed by a list of references, which likewise appear in the comprehensive bibliography at the end of the volume.

Why devote so much time and energy to tall buildings? The answer to that question revolves around the Council's concern for the totality of the urban experience, of which the high-rise is an integral part. The Council believes that there is a need to closely and continuously examine all aspects of the high-rise, stemming from the following:

- the ever-growing world population, creating an increased demand for living space—which in the urban area equates to the high-rise
- the consequent requirement of economy in construction
- the frequent neglect of human factors in design, at the expense of livability and the quality of life
- the new research required in the field, and the necessity of awareness of that research as well as stimulation of that research

Acknowledgement

The Council is, first of all, indebted to Joe Fitzgerald and the Chicago Committee on High-Rise Buildings, whose efforts in organizing the Second Council Meeting were outstanding. Without them, the initiation of this volume would not have been possible.

We also thank the group leaders whose editorial guidance facilitated the completion of this volume. They include Yona Friedman and Leslie E. Robertson (PC), John Rankine and Walter P. Moore (SC), Takeo Naka and Alan Davenport (CL), William McGuire and Leo Finzi (SB), and Ignacio Martin and Troels Brondum-Nielsen (CB).

The committee chairpeople, vice chairpeople, and editors also deserve commendations for their careful review and editing of the material.

We thank the National Science Foundation for its support of research as well as the collection of needed documentation and of technical workshops and meetings that led to this volume.

The sponsors of the Council are:

American Institute of Steel Construction, Chicago
Office of Irwin G. Cantor, P. C., New York
Cheung Kong (Hldgs.) Ltd., Hong Kong
Gammon Building Const., Ltd., Hong Kong
GCE International, Inc., St. Louis
Hip Hing Const. Co., Hong Kong
Jaros, Baum & Bolles, New York
JDC/Chevalier Joint Venture, Kowloon
Kai Tai Construction & Engineering Co. Ltd., Hong Kong
M & R Buildings (TVL) Pty. Ltd., Elandsfontein
Ahmad Moharram, Cairo
Walter P. Moore and Associates, Inc., Houston
National Science Foundation, Washington, D.C.
Otis Elevator Co., Farmington

Ove Arup Partnership, London
Roberston, Fowler & Associates, P. C., New York
Skidmore, Owings & Merrill, Chicago
Skilling Ward Rogers Barkshire Inc., Seattle
Westinghouse Elevator Co., Short Hills
Wing Tai Const. & Engr. Co., Hong Kong

The contribuors to the Council are:
Acme Metal Works Lt., Hong Kong
Albertis-Dimopoulos Engineers, Athens
Allison, McCormac and Nickolaus, Rockville
Alfred Benesch and Company, Chicago
The Benham Group, Oklahoma City
Boundary Layer Wind Tunnel Laboratory (U. Western Ontario), Ontario
Brandow & Johnston Associates, Los Angeles
Capacete-Martin & Associates, San Juan
CBM Engineers Inc., Houston
Century Development Corp., Houston
Cermak/Peterka & Assoc., Inc., Fort Collins
H. K. Cheng & Associates, Hong Kong
Chin & Hensolt Engineers, Inc., San Francisco
Civil & Civic Pty. Ltd., Sydney
Collyer Associates, New York
Concrete Constructions Pty. Ltd., Potts Point
Conseil Nat'l De La Recherche Scientifique, Beirut
Cosentini Associates, New York
Dao Kee Construction Co. Ltd., Kowloon
DeSimone, Chaplin & Associates, New York
Deutscher Beton-Verein E. V., Wiesbaden
B. M. Dornblatt and Associates, Inc., New Orleans
Dragages et Travaux Publics, Hong Kong
Eggers Group, P. C., New York
Englekirk & Hart, Inc., Los Angeles
Gervais F. Favrot, New Orleans
Franki Contractors Ltd., Kowloon Tong
Fujikawa Johnson and Assocs., Chicago
George A. Fuller Co., New York
Gammon India Limited, Bombay
The Hammerson Group of Companies, Sydney
Hayakawa Associates, Los Angeles
Hentrich-Petschnigg & Partner KG, Dusseldorf
Howard Needles Tammen & Bergendoff, New York
The George Hyman Construction Co., Bethesda
Hsin-Chong Const. Co., Ltd., Hong Kong

Iffland Kavanagh Waterbury, P. C., New York
International City Holdings, Ltd., Hong Kong
International Iron & Steel Institute, Brussels
Kadri Consultants, Pvt., Ltd., Bombay
Kerr Construction Inc., Clifton
Ketchum-Konkel-Barrett-Nickel-Austin, Inc., Wheat Ridge
Kitchell Contractors, Phoenix
Victor F. Leabu, Southfield
Lehr Associates, Cons. Engr., New York
Leighton Holdings Ltd., Crows Nest
LeMessurier Associates/SCI, Cambridge
Leung Cheng Piling & Const. Co. Ltd., Kowloon
Lev Zetlin Associates, Inc., New York
Lidell Construction Co., Ltd., Hong Kong
Liebenberg & Stander Conslt. Engrs., Capetown
Stanley D. Lindsey & Assoc., Nashville
John Lok & Partners, Ltd., Hong Kong
Mahendra Raj Consultants Private Limited, New Delhi
Albert C. Martin & Associates, Los Angeles
Maunsell Consultants Asia, Hong Kong
McClelland Engineers, Inc., Houston
McWilliam & Partners Pty. Ltd., Brisbane
W. L. Meinhardt & Partners Pty. Ltd., Melbourne
Meltzer Management, New Orleans
Jorge Metacos, Valencia
Morrison, Hershfield, Ltd., Guelph
Mueser Rutledge Consulting Engineers, New York
Multiplex Construction Pty. Ltd., Sydney
Nan Fung Development Ltd., Hong Kong
On Lee Gen. Contractors Ltd., Hong Kong
Ove Arup & Partners, Sydney
Paramatta Investment Co., Ltd., Hong Kong
C. L. Peck Contractor, Los Angeles
John Portman & Associates, Atlanta
PSM International, Chicago
Ranhill Bersekutu, Kuala Lumpur
Rankine & Hill Pty. Ltd., Sydney
Ratti-Fossati Associates, P.S., Seattle
RFB Consulting Architects, Saxonwold
Rice & Daubney, North Sydney
Rhodes-Harrison, Fee & Bold, Architects, Saxonwold
Mr. & Mrs. Leslie E. Robertson, New York
Robert Rosenwasser, Associates, P.C., New York
Emery Roth & Sons P.C., Architects, New York

RTKL Associates Inc., Baltimore
Office of James Ruderman, New York
Ryoden Electric Engr. Co., Ltd., Hong Kong
Schindler Management A. G., Luzern
Martin Selig Real Estate, Seattle
Sepakat Setia Perunding (Sdn.) Bhd., Kuala Lumpur
Duiliu Sfintesco, Lamorlaye
Shui On Const. Co. Ltd., Kwun Tong
Robert Sobel/Emery Roth & Sons Inc., Houston
South African Institute of Steel Construction, Johannesburg
Mr. & Mrs. Matthew J. Stacom, Greenwich
Steen Consultants Pte. Ltd., Singapore
Tishman Construction Corp. of N. Y., New York
Tishman Research Corp., New York
Tishman Speyer Properties, New York
Turner Construction Co., New York
Urban Investment & Development Co., Chicago
B.A. Vavaroutas Constr. Engineers, Athens
Voss & Partners, West Germany
Harry Weese & Associates, Chicago
Weidlinger Associates, New York
Weiskopf and Pickworth, New York
Wellform Const. Co. Ltd., Hong Kong
Willey Construction & Engr. Co., Hong Kong
Wiss, Janney, Elstner and Associates, Northbrook
Wong & Ouyang & Associates, Hong Kong
Woodward-Clyde Consultants, New York
M. S. Yolles & Partners Limited, Ontario
Zaldastani Associates, Inc., Boston

Many on the Lehigh University staff have contributed in a significant way to this effort, in particular Group Secretaries Le-Wu Lu and Ti Huang. Special thanks are due to Dolores Rice, publications associate on the Fritz Lab staff, whose editing skill and attention to detail made possible the production of this volume.

Lynn S. Beedle
Editor-in-Chief

Lehigh University
Bethlehem, Pennsylvania
1985

Contributors

The following list acknowledges those who have contributed material for this volume. The names, affiliations, and countries of each contributor are given.

Some contributions were a direct result of the second annual Council meeting, and some were received from professionals in the field.

Albinger, J. M., Material Service Corporation, Chicago, Illinois, USA
Amrhein, J. E., Masonry Institute of America, Los Angeles, California, USA
Arciszewski, T., Wayne State University, Ann Arbor, Michigan, USA

Baker, C. N., STS Consultants, Northbrook, Illinois, USA
Barber, E. J., Northern Virginia Transportation Commission, Fairfax, Virginia, USA
Beedle, L. S., Lehigh University, Bethlehem, Pennsylvania, USA
Bondada, M. V. A., Gannatt Fleming, Engineers and Planners, Harrisburg, Pennsylvania, USA

Chen, W. F., Purdue University, West Lafayette, Indiana, USA
Colaco, J. P., CBM Engineers Inc., Houston, Texas, USA
Corotis, R. B., The Johns Hopkins University, Baltimore, Maryland, USA

Davenport, A., University of Western Ontario, London, Ontario, Canada
Dayaratnam, P., Indian Institute of Technology, Kanpur, India
Derecho, A. T., Wiss, Janney, Elstner & Associates, Northbrook, Illinois, USA
Dietz, R. J., Gannatt Fleming, Engineers and Planners, Harrisburg, Pennsylvania, USA
DiRenzo, J. F., Peat, Marwick, Mitchell & Co., Washington, D.C., USA

Eisenberger, M., Israel Institute of Technology, Haifa, Israel
Ellis, R. H., Peat, Marwick, Mitchell & Co., Washington, D.C., USA
Elnimeiri, M. M., Skidmore, Owings & Merrill, Chicago, Illinois, USA
Engelen, R. E., Barton-Aschman Associates, Inc., Evanston, Illinois, USA

Fintel, M., Portland Cement Association, Skokie, Illinois, USA

Ghosh, S. K., Portland Cement Association, Skokie, Illinois, USA
Glover, M., Ove Arup & Partners, London, England
Gouwens, A. J., Packer Engineering Associates, Inc., Naperville, Illinois, USA
Gregorian, Z. B., Consulting Engineer P.E., Belmont, Massachusetts, USA
Gutman, A., Lev Zetlin Associates, Inc., New York, New York, USA

Haber, G. M., University of the District of Columbia, Washington, D.C., USA
Harder, D. A., O'Hare Associates, Chicago, Illinois, USA
Hocking, R. J., Barton-Aschman Associates, Inc., Evanston, Illinois, USA
Hodson, K. E., University of Nevada, Reno, Nevada, USA

Iffland, J. S. B., Iffland Kavanagh Waterbury, P.C., New York, New York, USA
Iqbal, M., Carl Walker and Associates, Kalamazoo, Michigan, USA
Iyengar, S. H., Skidmore, Owings and Merrill, Chicago, Illinois, USA

Jayachandran, P., Worcester Polytechnic Institute, Worcester, Massachusetts, USA
Jensen, R., Rolf Jensen & Associates, Deerfield, Illinois, USA
Joseph, L., Lev Zetlin Associates, Inc., New York, New York, USA

Kallman, R. G., Urbs in Horto, Chicago, Illinois, USA
Karnikova, I. Czechoslovakia Technical University, Prague, Czechoslovakia
Kowalczyk, R., UNESCO, Amman, Jordan

Lew, P. I., Lev Zetlin Associates, Inc., New York, New York, USA
Livorsi, R., Schal Associates, Chicago, Illinois, USA
Lubinski, M., Warsaw Technical University, Warsaw, Poland
Lui, E. M., Purdue University, West Lafayette, Indiana, USA

Marek, P., Czechoslovakia Technical University, Prague, Czechoslovakia
Martín, I., Capacete, Martín & Associates, San Juan, Puerto Rico
Mathur, G. C., National Buildings Organisation, Government of India, New Dehli,
    India
McGuire, W., Cornell University, Ithaca, New York, USA
Meckler, G., Haines Lundberg Waehler, New York, New York, USA
Moore, W. P., W. P. Moore & Associates, Houston, Texas, USA
Moudon, A. V., University of Washington, Seattle, Washington, USA

Nejman, T., Warsaw Technical University, Warsaw, Poland

Pawlowski, Z., Warsaw Technical University, Warsaw, Poland
Pirner, M., Czechoslovakia Technical University, Prague, Czechoslovakia

Robertson, L. E., Robertson, Fowler & Associates, P.C., New York, New York, USA
Rokicki, W., Warsaw Technical University, Warsaw, Poland
Ruchelman, L. I., Old Dominion University, Norfolk, Virginia, USA
Rutenberg, A., Israel Institute of Technology, Haifa, Israel

Saiidi, M., University of Nevada, Reno, Nevada, USA
Sato, K., Kajima Corporation, Tokyo, Japan
Sieczkowski, J., Warsaw Technical University, Warsaw, Poland
Skaloud, M., Czechoslovakia Technical University, Prague, Czechoslovakia

Tichy, M., Czechoslovakia Technical University, Prague, Czechoslovakia
Tomasetti, R. L., Lev Zetlin Associates, Inc., New York, New York, USA

Zunz, J., Ove Arup & Partners, London, England

Advances in
Tall Buildings

Planning and Environmental Criteria

Introductory Review

Anne Vernez-Moudon

A substantial part of new building development in the world is in the form of high-rise complexes. These complexes bring large concentrations of people to our downtowns and to selected areas of our cities. These concentrations are both exciting and problematic for our cities: They bring in the large crowds necessary for a lively environment, but they also create stresses to the existing sociophysical fabric.

Most of the contributions to *Advances in Tall Buildings* examine the means of fitting large and tall buildings into our cities; they assess the impacts of concentrated growth on such things as transportation, parking, land use distribution, tax levies, and they propose ways of circumventing the disadvantages that arise. These are important aspects of the development of tall buildings, but we cannot overlook the radical ways in which tall buildings, as they proliferate, also change the character of our cities, so that we experience cities in a different manner.

NOT ONLY TALL BUT LARGE

The character of our cities is modified by new buildings that are not only increasingly tall but also increasingly large. In the United States particularly, we are witnessing the development of bulky, multi-use structures that become "towns-within-towns," complete with business, commercial, residential, and

1

recreational facilities. The Renaissance Center in Detroit is an example of such a singularly gigantic development. Downtown Atlanta provides many examples of smaller but still substantial complexes.

PRIVATE, INTERIOR CITIES

In these new projects, activities are internalized at the expense of life in the street, or more generally, life in the public realm. Gone are the hordes of people shopping, meeting, or simply walking the streets. Instead, once they have reached these new developments, people stay within them, because the all-encompassing character of the development caters to most of their needs: cars are parked within them, rapid transit or public transit transfers can be made within them, and shopping, eating, recreational, and employment facilities are also provided from within. The effects of these changes on the way we experience the city and its character have been well described by Allan Jacobs in his *They're Locking The Doors to Downtown* (1980). It is important to study the phenomenon before it completely takes over our cities.

The process of formation of interior, private cities can be documented. Table 1 records the size of some new developments; their large coverage at ground, which often encompasses entire city blocks, is the first indication of their impact on the character of the city environment. But more importantly, the limited number of accesses from the streets, as means of interaction between the private and the public realms, points to the deliberate efforts to keep people in. These figures are particularly revealing when compared to the characteristics of previous development. In the case of the Portland Building in Portland, Oregon, the 60 by 60 m (200 by 200 ft) block now has three pedestrian entries to the building, six shops accessible from an off-street arcade, and one parking access—but the old block is estimated to have had originally as many as six 8- and 15-m (25- and 50-ft) wide parcels. There, each parcel, if developed, would have one entry to the upper floors and one entry to a shop at the ground floor, for a total of 32 points of interaction between the private and the public realms (Fig. 1).

In the case of the Transamerica Building in San Francisco, shops have been completely eliminated, and the single lobby entry replaces as many as 12 parcels, or according to the above estimation, 24 points of access. These can still be seen in the old adjacent blocks (Fig. 2).

These and other examples shown in Table 1 and Fig. 3 are small developments compared, for instance, with the Renaissance Center in Detroit. As a result we now face the following dilemma: The number of people using redeveloped sites is larger than before, but the opportunity to interact in the public realm is greatly reduced.

BRINGING THE PEDESTRIAN BACK IN
THE PUBLIC REALM

We cannot afford to internalize and privatize our cities. Downtowns and commercial areas are some of the few remaining refuges in our cities where people of mixed backgrounds can come in contact with each other; preserving this mix and reinforcing life in the public realm go hand in hand. Furthermore, concentrated use and habitation patterns of our cities are sustained by the pedestrian; this essential ingredient of a lively environment must be supported, courted, and pampered. Fortunately, there are many ways to keep pedestrians in the public realm and even add to their number.

Table 1 Some indicators of the impacts of new developments on the use and character of streets *(Note: figures are approximate, for comparative purposes only)*

	Ground coverage (Square Foot)	Street frontage (Lin. Ft)	Number of principal pedestrian entries	Number of shops accessible from street	Number of car entries	Number of entries for 50' lot front[f]
Willamette Center Portland, Oregon	120,000	2,400	14	6	—	48
Portland Building Portland, Oregon	40,000	800	3[a]	6[d]	1	16
Transamerica Building San Francisco, California	60,000	800	1	—	—	24
Hyatt Regency Hotel San Francisco, California	50,000	950	1[b]	1[e]	—	20
Peach Tree Center Plaza Hotel Atlanta, Georgia	60,000	700	1	—	2	20
AT&T Building New York, New York	36,000	560	1	2[d]	—	16
Olympic Tower New York, New York	25,000	340	3[c]	3	—	9

[a]One main entry, 2 side entries
[b]And one other, 1 flight up
[c]Two office entries, 1 apartment entry
[d]Accessible by arcade
[e]A restaurant
[f]Or equivalent (50 × 180 typical parcels)

Separate Transit Transfers

Pushkarev and Zupan (1975) showed that much of the pedestrian traffic (approximately 60%) in downtowns is due to the trip from work to home. This journey is usually a 10–15 minutes transfer from the workplace to transportation, be it a car, a bus, or a train. Convenience and ease take primary importance in it, and unnecessary stress must be avoided. Things to be reduced are overcrowding, long distances, and extreme temperatures; the advantages of this journey are the opportunities it affords for a change of pace and atmosphere from the home or office environment, for people watching, looking at trees or advertisements, enjoying the fresh air, and the like.

The location and design of the environments of this walk are important both for the commuter and for the animation of public space. This is why the location and design of transit transfer points must be carefully engineered. It

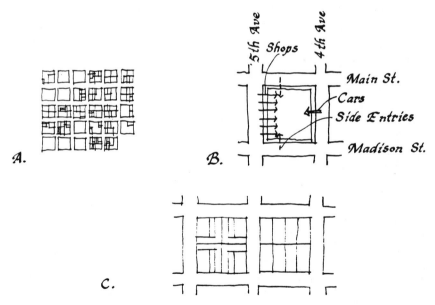

Fig. 1 The Portland Building. (A) Land subdivision in downtown Portland. Blocks are 200 × 200 ft (redrawn from *Downtown Guidelines,* City of Portland, Oregon, Dec. 1980). (B) Site plan of the Portland Building by Michael Graves and Emery Roth, Architects, for the city of Portland, Oregon. The building occupies the entire 200 × 200 ft block. There are two service entries to the building on the north and south sides (Main and Madison Streets), one main entry to the parking garage along Fourth Avenue, and a low, dark arcade fronts Fifth Avenue, essentially separating the few shops from the street itself. Note that stairs pick up the differences in level from the street to the shopping arcade. (C) Hypothetical subdivision of Portland block into small 25 and 50 ft frontage lots.

is counter-productive to join them within large centers of employment. We know, for instance, that in the World Trade Center, pedestrian densities are concentrated to the point of overcrowding, and people are funneled away from public territory and shielded from non-workers, shoppers, and inhabitants of adjacent developments.

So it is better to make major transit points separate from major employment centers, linking them by streets or other public territory. Pedestrians can thus be collected from a mix of both major and minor employment centers and from residential, commercial, and recreational facilities. The few transit malls developed in small- and medium-size cities are good examples of solutions appropriate to the transition between work and transportation, and to mixing the different kinds of downtown users.

Decentralized Land Uses

The other 40% of pedestrian trips in central cities is generated by commercial retail shops and private homes. If these are connected to public territory, then pedestrian traffic in the street can be expected to be substantial. For these pedestrians, too, therefore, decentralized and outwardly directed development will be beneficial.

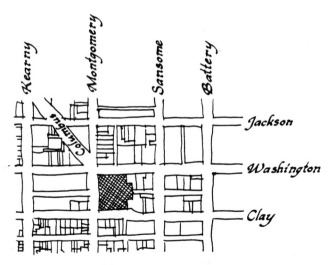

Fig. 2 The Transamerica Building and its surrounding fabric. Blocks are 275 by 412.5 ft.
(Jacobs, 1978)

KEEPING THE PEDESTRIAN IN THE PUBLIC REALM

If increased densities, coupled with decentralized designs, contribute to the life of our public spaces, a careful distribution of land uses and a proper design of street environment will keep pedestrians in these spaces.

Proper Land Uses

Pedestrians can be attracted to and kept in those parts of cities where activities are diverse. Thus residential uses have been encouraged and even mandated by law in many cities for several years now in the traditionally

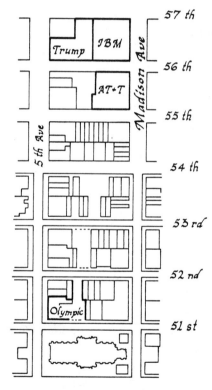

Fig. 3 AT&T Building and Olympic Tower Site Plan: New large-scale development in midtown Manhattan including the AT&T Building and Olympic Place. Blocks are 200 by 400 ft. In the Olympic Place project the L-shaped lot helps to create an interior street between 51st and 52nd Streets. There is one entry to the interior street on both side streets. An additional entry on East 51st Street leads to the apartments. The three shops along Fifth Avenue are covered mostly by the dark curtain wall which enrobes the entire tower: only tiny windows and "coordinated" entries break the ± 100 ft of facade along the Avenue.

business-oriented zones; for instance, the term "CBD" (central business district) is no longer favored; it is generally replaced by the word "downtown". The shortening of the work trip for many downtown workers is just as important as the 24-hour use of the downtown.

Proper Design: The Concept of the Number of Noticeable Differences

Too often, we forget that proper design can also contribute to people's interest, slow them down, and even keep them in special places. While environments cannot force certain behaviors, they can reinforce them (Rapoport, 1977). Rapoport talks about increasing the pleasure of walking by stimulating exploratory activity. Such activity is certainly what we need in our central cities. He argues that as the pedestrian processes information about his environment, the complexity of the information keeps him interested, and eventually gives him pleasure. Complexity is in turn related to the rate at which the information is received, measured by the number of "noticeable differences" perceived in that environment per unit of time. Noticeable differences relate directly to speed of travel and differ, therefore, for the motorist and the pedestrian. It follows, Rapoport says, that

> an environment comfortably stimulating from a car becomes monotonously boring on foot, while what is interesting on foot becomes chaotic in a car . . . more generally, the medieval city is pedestrian, [while] the Ville Radieuse and its progeny [are] for the motorist . . .
> [adding that] ". . . pedestrians can use, and desire, much more acute and abrupt transitions—spatial, kinesthetic, in light levels, sounds, and all other sense modalities. Only they notice, react to and respond to the variety of stimuli which can be used in a rich, opulent environment" (Moudon and Laconte, 1983).

The complexity that sustains a person's interest at pedestrian speed consists of different things to see, smell and hear, perceived at a high rate of change. This supports what we know empirically as true; long monolithic walls are designed for the motorist; the large-scale and bulky designs used in contemporary high-rise developments cannot sustain the interest of the pedestrian.

Proper Design: Transparency and Modulation

Building on the concept proposed by Rapoport, let us briefly review how the pedestrian's sensory experience can be enriched. The crux of this experience, characterized by the "number of noticeable differences perceived in the environment," lies in the relative transparency of the wall separating him from interior space. It is important that he "feel through" into the ground floor of buildings, through windows, doorways, and openings of varying kinds. Seeing through the boundary between the inside and the outside affords multisensory contact with a multitude of people and objects. For example, people, vehicles, and goods move back and forth from building to street and vice-versa. Varying smells come into the street as buildings are penetrated. Hot or cold air gusts into the public way, and seasonal variations are also important.

To afford a rich experience, the street wall itself needs to have a variety of not only land uses but also physical elements supporting its transparency, for instance, entries, lobbies (to apartments, parking garages, shops, offices, etc.), mostly at street level but sometimes above; windows for shops, small industries, and the like; openings for alleys, passages, covered or uncovered, of varying dimensions; yards, open spaces, in the form of courtyards or parks; steps up or down into buildings, generally changes in levels; stoops; varied materials, textures, patterns, and so on. For a list of elements that can be found on or below the street space itself, please refer to Turnipseed, 1982.

Along the streets of older cities, such elements recur at regular intervals that can be as small as 3.5 m (12 ft), based on typical lot widths. The latter are indeed very important in defining both the rhythm of this pattern and the variety that can be found in the way the elements are detailed. Doorways appear regularly, but each of them differs, if ever so slightly, from the others, because they were designed or built at different times by different people.

It is this modulation (repetition, rhythm and variety) that we have now lost with the prevalence of large lots, some of which are as long and wide as city blocks of 60 m (200 ft) or more. These elements define the texture of the urban fabric. We are now mostly faced with rather coarse-grained fabrics that are unsupportive of pedestrian activity.

TALL BUT SMALL

But large lots have no necessary connection with tall buildings. In a city like Rio de Janeiro, for example, high-rise development has occurred within lots that are as small as those of the original colonial land structure, with 6 to 15 m (20 to 50 ft) frontages (Fig. 4). The result, particularly in areas such as Copacabana, is tall but slender buildings providing, at the street level at least, a fine-grained fabric: the rhythm of activities and supporting physical elements along Copacabana's streets is quick, so that movement at slow speed is pleasant and supported by a great variety of experiences (Fig. 5). There are several ways for planners to retain or regain such high-rise environments. One is to encourage smaller development, following the example of a few cities where the building permit process has been simplified, and requirements for the construction of smaller projects changed, to reduce substantially their construction costs (Moudon, 1983). In a recent article, Skidmore, Owings & Merrill's urban designer John Lund Kriken (1983) argues the economic benefits of reducing the scale (not necessarily the height, however) of urban development. Kriken's proposals are extremely challenging; his documentation of large but incremental development offers a view into the future that is very different from the monoliths of the present. We can only encourage more work to be done in this area.

Yet another approach is to try, by design, to break the scale of large developments and to force them to decentralize. For instance, it is not unreasonable to suggest that repeated street-level entries be required for tall

Fig. 4 In Rio de Janeiro's Copacabana district, Avenida Atlantica is lined with narrow increments of building.

buildings at regular and short intervals. In San Francisco, the planning code, which controls development in the residential areas, already calls for building entries to occur at least every 10 m (35 ft), regardless of the size of the building or of its lot. Similarly, breaks in the treatment of the street facade and roof line are required for every increment of 10 m (35 ft) of building along the public way. These requirements are based on preserving the characteristics of the existing nineteenth-century fabric. Similar requirements could be made in any part of any city, especially in those areas where old buildings remain numerous and prominent. Cities need to search into the past and rediscover what streets used to be like before tall buildings were developed. As they assess how much has changed, they will be able to determine the extent to which design can support pedestrian activity.

In areas where old development is no longer prevalent, the establishment of a rhythm in the various elements occurring along the street can be done in a more casual way, not for preservation of old buildings but for the pedestrian's environment. The ways in which entries, facade detailing and the like need to change can then be established so that the interest of the curious pedestrian may be stimulated. Here again work is needed to develop principles of small and fine-grain design for tall buildings.

Fig. 5 On Rio de Janeiro's Avenida Atlantica, activities and land uses alternate at regular and small intervals.

REFERENCES/BIBLIOGRAPHY

Jacobs, A. B., 1978
 MAKING CITY PLANNING WORK, American Society of Planning Officials.
Jacobs, A. B., 1980
 THEY'RE LOCKING THE DOORS TO DOWNTOWN, Urban Design International, Vol. 1, No. 5, July/August.

Kriken, J. L., 1983
 WHAT'S WRONG WITH SMALL PROJECTS, Urban Design Review, Vol. 6, No. (2), 3, Spring, June.

Moudon, A. V., 1983
 CITY FORM AND TALL BUILDINGS: CATHEDRALS, PALAZZI, TALL DOWNTOWNS AND TALL CITIES, Developments in Tall Buildings— 1983, Council on Tall Buildings, Hutchinson Ross Publishing Company, Stroudsburg.
Moudon, A. V. and Laconte, P., 1983
 STREETS AS PUBLIC PROPERTY, Opportunities for Public/Private Interaction in Planning and Design, College of Architecture and Urban Planning, University of Washington, Seattle.

Rapoport, A., 1977
 HUMAN ASPECTS OF URBAN FORM, Pergamon Press.

Turnipseed, S. P., 1982
 URBAN STREET DESIGN ELEMENTS, Department of Environmental Design, Texas A & M University, for the U.S. Department of Transportation Federal Highway Administration, January.

Sociopolitical Influences

Observations on Sociopolitical Impacts of High-Rise Buildings

Dennis A. Harder

As American cities built tall, their downtown areas became characterized and identified by their high-rise structures. Edward K. Muller (1980) observed,

> By the early-20th century, skyscrapers dominated downtown's skyline. . . . Corporations built upwards . . . .The Wisdom of collecting office workers in one building and renting excess space had been demonstrated . . . .Soon corporations, especially in New York and Chicago, competed for architectural distinctions as well as for profits.

As Muller observed, high-rise buildings probably were first produced in quantity in response to the corporate need for both face-to-face communication and expansion of business operations. Businessmen understood the need for proximity and personal communications, and quickly recognized the value of "going up" within a compact business core in the central city. This philosophy has remained despite the extraordinary technical advances made over the last 35 years in both transportation and telecommunications.

The corporation is not the only beneficiary of high-rise development; often other enterprises that serve corporate business or its employees also locate in high rise structures. Offices for lawyers, accountants and other

13

business-related professionals are established in close proximity to the corporations—often being located in the same building. Medical and dental practices open where they can capture and serve office workers as well as the general urban population from a central location. Even where the structure bears a corporate name and was built specifically for a corporate tenant, today's high-rises usually contain a variety of tenants.

The city itself benefits from the concentration of business space and business activity that high-rise development generates. Land values are greater in the downtown areas of cities and at other locations that are highly attractive, and high-rise structures further increase those values. In most cities, high-rises have evolved in concentrations, and those concentrations generate the highest tax returns to local government. For example in Chicago, approximately one-third of the city's real estate tax return comes from the greater downtown area covering less than 7% of the total area of the city.

High-rise buildings and the uses that occupy them usually return more revenue (benefits) to local governments than they require in services (costs) from them. This positive cost–benefit ratio is often used as a measure of the attractiveness of a development. Thus, intensively developed areas of a city have come to provide resources (surplus revenues) to fund improvements and services for other parts of the city where costs exceed revenues.

Fig. 1 New office and hotel accommodations constructed as part of the Illinois Central R. R. Air Rights development. The project also includes residential buildings and ultimately will incorporate a park. *(Photo by Willie Schmidt)*

One final influence of the high-rise structure should be cited here—the influence on city form and organization. As city centers formed in this country, it was the coincidence of concentrated high-rise development and focused transporation networks that proved to be the prime determinents of form. Ernest Burgess (Park et al., 1925) and Homer Hoyt (1939), who analyzed American cities and society, and propounded their theories at the University of Chicago earlier in this century, noted that the patterns of city growth and evolution formed "rings" around the denser central or downtown area with certain understandable variations due to such circumstances as elevated terrain and waterfront areas. The "center zone" of the city and the "zones of variation" subsequently became the locations of most of the high-rise development and, as noted previously, contributed a significant portion of

Fig. 2 The John Hancock Building and the adjacent Water Tower Place are examples of mixed-use development. Although the upper stories of both buildings house residential units, the lower floors of the Hancock Building are reserved for office and retail space while Water Tower Place includes hotel use as well. *(Photo by Willie Schmidt)*

the city's land value and tax revenue. With nonmanufacturing business operations and other uses concentrated in high-rises, the relatively scarce land in the remainder of the city can be devoted to other uses such as open space and lower density residential and related functions.

In terms of form and visual impact, high-rises have come to symbolize the American city and its business interests. Architectural art has been carried to the general population through these structures. Today the high-rise building is often as much a fine piece of sculpture as it is a functional format for use or habitation.

High-rise buildings have established an efficient setting for corporate business enterprise, a significant source of revenue for local government, and a business focus for the entire metropolitan area. When applied to residential or manufacturing uses, however, high-rises have thus far had limited success.

High-rise development has not been universally or consistently successful. At one time, manufacturing operations were placed into multi-story structures in and around the downtown in an attempt to reap for manufacturing industry the benefits which were successful for office uses. However, manufacturing entrepreneurs found that high-rise structures were not readily modernized or expanded and that land values (and taxes) had increased to the point that the viability of their operations were jeopardized. The movement of manufacturing operations away from the high-rise has generated a pattern of reuse for some structures, often after a period of vacancy or gross underutilization. Now these buildings, which range from lofts to major high-rise structures, are being rehabilitated for both office and residential uses.

Residential uses in high-rises have resulted in both success and failure. Tall apartment buildings have successfully fulfilled the needs of lower-income senior citizens and middle- and upper-income occupants in cities and retirement developments, but they are no longer being built for low-income family occupancy. High–rise "public housing projects" were generally unsuccessful, often generating whole communities of "problem" families. These families were forced to live in structures with which they felt neither comfortable nor familiar, and in which their children were separated from recreation areas on the ground and from effective parental supervision. The demolition of the Pruitt-Igoe buildings in St. Louis is the most dramatic statement of failure of the high-rise solution to public housing.

It is clear that the high-rise building has been and will continue to be a strong urban influence. Generally, the challenge in future high-rise development is not likely to emerge from either building technology constraints, or from pressures to decentralize because of advancing technology in computers and telecommunications. However, the challenge is already upon us to make the environment in and around the core area of the city — and within that the individual land parcels and structures—as attractive and hospitable as possible for all users of tall buildings, whether they are shoppers, tourists, residents, or workers.

REFERENCES/BIBLIOGRAPHY

Hoyt, H., 1939
  THE STRUCTURE AND GROWTH OF RESIDENTIAL NEIGHBORHOODS IN AMERICAN CITIES, Federal Housing Administration, Washington, D.C.

Muller, E. K., 1980
  DISTINCTIVE DOWNTOWN, Geographical Magazine, Vol. 52, August, pp. 745-755.

Park, R. E., Burgess, E. W., and McKenzie, R. D., 1925
  THE GROWTH OF THE CITY: AN INTRODUCTION TO A RESEARCH PROJECT, In The City, University of Chicago Press, Chicago, Illinois, p. 47-62.

Sociopolitical Influences

Public-Private Partnerships and Tall Building Development

Leonard Ruchelman

Because of their great size and height, the development of tall buildings usually involves more active interaction of public and private decision-makers than would ordinarily be the case. Public and private interests tend to be greater where skyscrapers are concerned. In many cities, public-private interaction in tall building development has often been adversarial in nature, focusing on questions of who gains and who loses from such forms of construction. For example, opponents typically argue that downtown high-rise districts usually return fewer dollars than they cost in supporting services, and that they detract from the environment. Proponents tend to argue that the benefits in increased revenues, open space and business opportunity exceed the costs of servicing tall buildings. Opponents usually insist on stringent government controls that often serve to discourage high-rise development. (Council on Tall Buildings, Group PC, 1981).

Of particular interest is that the 1980s have heralded a new era of positive relations that have reduced the level of conflict substantially. This can be seen in news accounts of how local governments are forming new cooperative relationships with corporations, foundations, and local businesses for the improvement of the community. The new buzzword describing this is *public-private partnership*.

Much of this is in response to real needs that are confronting communities and particularly big cities. Local governments are encountering significant financial burdens because of the reduction or removal of State and Federal funding supports and because of public resistance to tax increases. Trying to make do with less is challenging communities to unearth new resources for community development projects.

According to the Committee for Economic Development, a respected organization of business executives and educators, the purpose of public-private partnerships is "to link these dimensions in such a way that the participants contribute to the benefit of the broader community, while promoting their own individual or organizational interests" (Committee for Economic Development, 1982). This is another way of saying, "you scratch my back, and I'll scratch yours" if, in the end, we shall achieve a common goal.

The purpose of the present article is to report on some of the more successful partnerships as measured by improvements in the physical development of the community (Fosler and Berger, 1982). In all cases, tall buildings are major features of such developments, particularly where there is interest in revitalizing the downtown central business districts of cities. Each of the cities profiled below represents examples of successful civic leadership that could be emulated in other places.

PITTSBURGH

Pittsburgh has experienced two periods of extensive development: what is called Renaissance I, from 1945 to 1969, and Renaissance II, which began in 1978 and is currently in progress. Performing a key role through most of this has been the Allegheny Conference on Community Development (ACCD), an organization of prominent business and civic leaders. Established in 1944 as a nonprofit research and planning organization, the ACCD provided the planning agenda and implementation support for the redevelopment of the Golden Triangle and the construction of Gateway Center and the Mellon Square complex during Renaissance I. Coordinating with such corporations as U.S. Steel and PPG Industries, the ACCD also laid the groundwork for major new office towers during Renaissance II. Providing leadership in the public sector was Mayor David P. Lawrence in the initial phase, and Mayor Richard Caliguiri in the second phase.

BALTIMORE

The Greater Baltimore Committee (GBC), a group of executives from the area's largest corporations, has been the key organization for mobilizing business initiative in support of downtown renewal efforts. In the late 1950s, the GBC and the Committee for Downtown (an outgrowth of the Retail Merchants Association) raised funds and contracted with a professional planning group for the development of a master plan for downtown renewal. The result was the development of Charles Center, a unified complex of office buildings, apartments, hotels, and a theater connected by pedestrian plazas. More spectacular has been the Inner Harbor development consisting of mixed-income housing, office buildings, cultural facilities, and waterfront recreational development including Harbor Place and an aquarium. These projects have become models for redevelopment in other cities. On the public sector side, Mayor William Donald Schaeffer has provided the necessary resources and leadership to complement the activities of the business sector (Fig. 1) (Schaeffer, 1983).

CHICAGO

The center of initiative for Chicago's redevelopment has been the Loop, the part of downtown in which corporate headquarters are located. Of special importance in this regard has been the Chicago Central Area Committee, which was established in the 1950s when businessmen decided to organize to

Fig. 1 Buildings in downtown Baltimore.

reverse the retail activity decline in the central business district. The committee secured the services of the architectural firm of Skidmore, Owings
and Merrill to prepare a plan for the central business district. This came to be
known as the Chicago 21 Plan. (This is described in Chapter PC-8 of the
Monograph, p. 523.) Since the plan's inception in 1973, 19 of 32 projects have
either been completed or are underway. These include housing development
and rehabilitation, improved transportation systems, and pedestrian malls.
The plan is based on the premise that the central business district should
serve as the transportation hub, seat of government, office and business
center, and central marketplace (Council on Tall Buildings, Committee 31,
1981). A critical factor supporting the planning process was the political
stability afforded by the regime of Mayor Richard Daley. Daley could assure
coordination among a variety of Federal, State and local agencies to overcome
bureaucratic obstacles. This has since suffered somewhat as reflected by the
rather high turnover of persons in the Mayor's office since Daley's death in
1975 (Gove and Masotti, 1982).

DALLAS

A leading example of private sector initiative in urban development has
been the Dallas Citizens Council (DCC), which was formed in 1937 to raise
funds for the Texas centennial celebration. Membership in this organization
consists of the chief executives of the largest corporations in the city. The
DCC has continued to promote cooperation between the city's business and
public organizations to the present time. The Reunion Project is an important
demonstration of such cooperation. This public-private effort has resulted in
the development of a major hotel, a fifty-story tower topped by an observation
deck, a public park, a municipal activities center, a road network with
parking facilities, and a 17,000-seat sports complex. City Manager George
Schrader has assured the necessary support from the public sector.

ATLANTA

During the 1960s, Atlanta launched its greatest building boom under a
Chamber of Commerce promotion program called Forward Atlanta. Architect
John Portman's Hyatt Regency Hotel in his downtown Peachtree Center won
acclaim for Atlanta as the Skyscraper Capital of the South. As the central
business district developed beyond its traditional boundaries, it became
apparent that the city could be better served by a consolidation of existing
business and civic organizations serving the area. Consequently in 1967, the
Central Atlanta Improvement Association and the Uptown Association were
merged to form Central Atlanta Progress (CAP), a private, nonprofit cor-

poration. CAP soon became the base of business power in the city, working closely with Mayor Ivan Allen and the City Council.

In the 1970s, relations with Mayor Maynard Jackson became less cordial, constraining development. Nevertheless, some impressive projects could still be noted, including new office towers and hotels in the central business district, downtown housing for moderate- and upper-income families, mass transit, and expansion of the World Congress Center for the convening of meetings and conferences. In addition, Portman's 1.2 million-ft^2 Atlanta Apparel Mart opened in November 1979, adjacent to the Merchandise Mart, further enlarging Atlanta's role as a regional and national commercial center.

Since being elected mayor in 1981, Andrew Young has been working to develop Atlanta as an international trading center. This may result in additional high-rise construction in the future.

CONCLUSIONS

The five cities just profiled were selected on the evidence of successful public-private collaboration in revitalizing the urban environment. However, somewhat different patterns of collaboration could be noted for each of the cities. Chicago and Baltimore illustrate the efficacy of well-organized and resourceful business groups interacting with an equally vigorous public sector. Pittsburgh and Dallas, on the other hand, show powerful business coalitions working with a city government that has defined its role as being essentially facilitative. In Atlanta, the initiative appears to have shifted from the private to the public sector. But irrespective of who shows more leadership and who shows less, business organizations with civic vision need government and vice versa.

A major aspect of the plans and strategies utilized to strengthen the cities has been revitalization of their central business districts. Thus, tall building development in the form of office towers, hotels, and residential apartment buildings has become a critical part of such revitalization.

As we have noted, however, tall buildings do not stand alone. The cities reviewed have strived to integrate them into the city fabric so as to complement other structures and facilities, both public and private. More than any other arrangement, tall-building development is likely to be most successful where public-private partnerships are strong and viable.

REFERENCES/BIBLIOGRAPHY

Committee for Economic Development, 1982
    PUBLIC-PRIVATE PARTNERSHIP, AN OPPORTUNITY FOR URBAN COMMUNITIES, Committee for Economic Development, New York.

Council on Tall Buildings, Committee 31, 1981
    URBAN PLANNING AND DESIGN, Chapter PC-8, Volume PC of Monograph on Planning and
    Design of Tall Buildings, ASCE, New York.
Council on Tall Buildings, Group PC, 1981
    PLANNING AND ENVIRONMENTAL CRITERIA FOR TALL BUILDINGS, Volume PC of Monograph
    on Planning and Design of Tall Buildings, ASCE, New York.

Fosler, S. and Berger, R. A., eds., 1982
    PUBLIC-PRIVATE PARTNERSHIP IN AMERICAN CITIES: SEVEN CASE STUDIES, Lexington
    Books, Lexington, Mass.

Gove, S. K. and Masotti, L. H., eds., 1982
    AFTER DALEY: CHICAGO POLITICS IN TRANSITION, University of Illinois Press, Urban, Ill.

Schaeffer, W. D., 1983
    RENAISSANCE OF OUR CITIES—A CIVIL ENGINEERING CHALLENGE, Developments in Tall
    Buildings—1982, Council on Tall Buildings, Hutchinson Ross Publishing Company, Stroudsburg.

Economics

Impact of High-Rise Development on Land Values in India

G. C. Mathur

RAPID URBANIZATION

During the last two decades, metropolitan cities have attempted to expand vertically to meet the building requirements of large influxes of population into urban areas. As in advanced countries, in India also tall buildings are becoming the landmarks of big cities.

The increase in the urban population of India has been of a high order, as Table 1 shows.

The growth of urban centers in India has been phenomenal. According to census figures, the increase in the number of cities and towns having a population of more than one lakh (one hundred thousand), has also increased greatly, as Table 2 demonstrates.

TALL BUILDINGS

Thus faced with the problems of urban population explosion, scarcity of land, spiralling land prices, and unwieldly sprawl of cities and towns, some bold attempts have been made in our major cities to provide more built-up space vertically for both working and living.

The trends in the construction of tall buildings in India during the last three decades are shown in Fig. 1.

Table 1 Urban population increases in India since 1951

Year	Urban population in millions
1951	62.4
1961	78.9
1971	108.8
1981	162.3

Table 2 Increase in number of cities and towns in India since 1951

Year	Number of cities having more than 1 lakh (hundred thousand) population
1951	75
1961	113
1971	142
1981	220

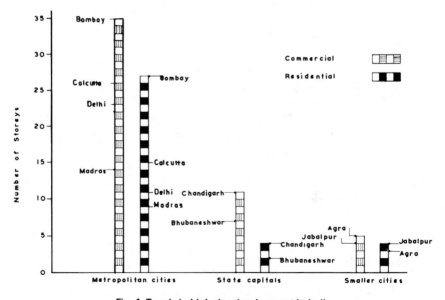

Fig. 1 Trends in high-rise development in India

Up until now the tallest building in India (35 stories) has been erected at Bombay for a hotel project; it is being built in the conventional manner with a reinforced concrete scheme. Plans for the construction of 39-story buildings at Bombay and Delhi have also been made.

For residential purposes, construction of multi-story buildings has been gaining ground. In hot and humid climates like those of Bombay and Calcutta, tall residential buildings have been built for the last three decades. In Bombay, buildings of up to 27 stories, and in Calcutta of up to 13 stories, have been built. In Delhi, which has hot and dry climate, a number of 8-story residential buildings have been built in addition to a few buildings having 8 to 11 stories. High-rise buildings for residential purposes are being seriously considered to provide an answer to urban housing problems. How far this is tenable, in the context of conditions prevailing in developing countries, must be studied in great depth before we adopt high rise buildings for residential purposes in a major way. This form of development, it is believed, has helped the advanced countries in the solution of their housing problem.

High rise development has come in vogue not only in metropolitan cities like Bombay, Calcutta, Delhi, and Madras but also in large cities like Chandigarh, Bhubaneswar, Agra, and Jaipur.

Broadly speaking, two types of high-rise buildings are constructed: (a) institutional buildings including Government and commercial office buildings, hotels, and hospitals; and (b) residential buildings, particularly for middle and high income groups.

LAND USE ECONOMY

High-rise buildings are constructed to ensure economical use of land in areas where land is scarce and its cost is high. The maximum height of buildings and the number of stories that can be constructed are regulated by the floor area ratio (FAR) stipulated for a given area and permissible coverage of land. It is, therefore, obvious that the stipulation of the FAR encourages construction of high rise buildings and is a crucial factor in the increase of land values.

The pressure on urban land has been increasing in the wake of the fast pace of urbanization. There is, therefore, great demand for land in the central parts of cities, which results in high land values and the consequent high-rise development. In this manner a vicious cycle of taller and taller buildings as a consequence of higher and higher land prices takes place. Trends in land prices (residential) in Delhi are depicted in Fig. 2.

Individual plot holders can save a lot of land by going in for multi-story buildings. However, the savings in a given sector of land depend on the gross densities and number of dwellings per hectare including the land required for common amenities like parks, playgrounds, schools, shops, roads, and parking places.

CAPITAL INTENSIVE DEVELOPMENT

High investment in high-rise development is necessary for reasons of structural safety and for the provision of essential mechanical and electrical services such as lifts, elevators, fire safety devices, and air conditioning. In addition to this, the construction of high rise buildings entails disproportionately high costs of construction, which increase with the number of stories as shown in Fig. 3.

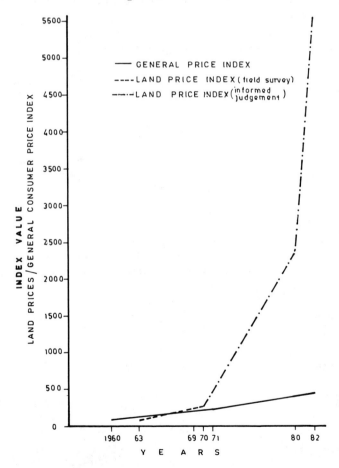

Fig. 2 Trends in land prices (residential) and the consumer price index in Delhi 1960/63–1982 *(Shafi, 1982)*

In addition to the high initial investment of capital in high-rise development, heavy recurring investment is required for their operation and maintenance. Thus it is obvious that to obtain the maximum return of heavy investment both in land and building structure and services, height of buildings must fully take advantage of the permissible FAR. This results in the trend to construct taller and taller high rise buildings.

Speculation in urban land prices has become a common phenomenon that in turn has resulted in speculation in the price of built-up accommodation, and subsequently an overall high rate of escalation in the price of real estate development in the vicinity of high-rise development.

In the case of high-rise buildings constructed for commercial use, such as hotels, banks, and offices, the return in investment made in land and

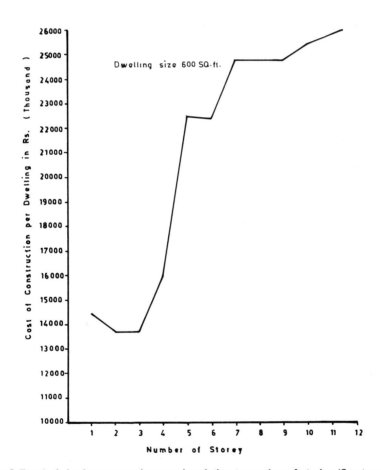

Fig. 3 **Trend of rise in construction cost in relation to number of stories** *(Courtesy: B. B. Garg, CBRI)*

construction is much higher than with such buildings put up for residential purposes. The situation has become abnormal in some metropolitan
cities. Only high-income families can afford to purchase accommodation
in high-rise buildings, and even they find the prices high.

Because the cost of high-rise buildings is disproportionately larger, a
monopolistic situation has developed, where only those few real estate
operators having sufficient financial resources can function.

Therefore, in order that the economies of high-rise development are not
vitiated beyond incorrigible limits, adequate social measures should be
evolved. Then they should be effectively implemented to regulate high-rise
development, particularly for preventing speculation in land values in
developing countries.

Preventing speculation in land value should be one of the major areas
of thrust in the national policy of urbanization. Appropriate measures have
to be devised, including (a) land use planning for the city as a whole and
not for the individual land pockets therein; and (b) land use planning for
an economic region and not merely for the cities and towns in a hierarchy
of interrelated settlements.

Developing countries could greatly benefit from the experiences of advanced countries in preventing speculation in land values in the wake of
the trend toward construction of taller high-rise buildings.

REFERENCES/BIBLIOGRAPHY

Shafi, S. S. and Dutta, S. S., 1982
  URBAN LAND POLICY IN DELHI: A CRITIQUE, Presented at the Seminar on Land in Metropolitan
  Development, Times Research Foundation, Calcutta, India, April.

Tall Buildings and Urbanization in India

Pasala Dayaratnam

Before the industrial revolution, India was predominantly a rural country, with more than 80% of its population living in villages and surviving on agriculture. There has been a constant migration of population since then, and today more than 30% of the population lives in urban areas. A host of new problems has arisen due to this migration, of which housing in urban areas is a pressing one.

Cities in India can be divided into three major groups. The first group consists of four major metropolitan areas: Calcutta, Bombay, Delhi, and Madras. The population of these cities ranges between 9.2 and 4.3 million. The second group of three cities has a population in the range of 2.5 to 3 million. The third group of five cities has a population in the range of 1.0 to 1.7 million, and they are in the process of rapid growth.

The traditions of the people in urban areas have undergone only minor changes, as they have been determined by the religious and cultural background of the population. This paper presents the growth of constructional activity of tall buildings in different cities and its relation to India's cultural, social, economic, and historical background. This paper also presents some of the main problems faced in the design of tall buildings.

31

TALL BUILDINGS IN THE FOUR LARGEST CITIES

Calcutta

Calcutta, situated on the east coast of the Indian subcontinent is the largest and one of the oldest cities in the country. Now in a densely populated region, it developed rapidly during the eighteenth and nineteenth centuries. The East India Company there had extensive business between East and West, giving a boost to the industrial growth of the city.

Electric street cars were introduced in the city in the early stage of its development and they continue to dominate the Calcutta traffic scene even today. Though they are being replaced by faster transportation in all other parts of the country, there is considerable resistance on the part of Calcutta's residents to do away with them.

There has been very little tendency from the beginning to build tall buildings in Calcutta. Even today the rate of construction of tall buildings in this city can be considered minimal when compared with that of other major cities. It appears that builders have little choice of building tall in a city of this type of cultural background, constrained by the slow mode of transporation and frequent traffic jams. A rapid transit metro is under construction with the aid of the World Bank, and it is hoped that the traffic congestion common in the city will then be reduced.

Many of the tall buildings that were constructed in Calcutta during the 1970s and 1980s are in the range of 8 to 15 stories. The soil in the region is soft clay, however, and this is not particularly suitable for the construction of taller buildings.

Bombay

Bombay has grown to be the second largest city in India with a population of 8.2 million. It is called the Gateway of India, since it dominates both national and international trade. It is situated on an island and is attached to the mainland on the west coast. Bombay is a relatively new city that developed over the last two centuries. Industrial growth around the region has also taken place during the last century.

Because the expansion of the city is constrained by the coast line around the island, Bombay can either build tall buildings or build a new city on the mainland. The tall buildings option was taken up first with development on the reclaimed part of the shore, while a new Bombay was being planned for the mainland. The availability of rocky soil along the shore has facilitated economical construction of foundations.

Bombay's modern traditions have brought a good transporation system through trains and buses and rapid growth of tall buildings. The maximum

number of floors of tall buildings constructed during 1940s–50s was eight. In
the 1970s the rate of growth of construction of tall buildings was the highest,
and the number of stories in buildings during this period reached thirty-two.
A typical tall building of Bombay is shown in Fig. 1.

Fig. 1 Typical tall building in Bombay

Presently, tall buildings in the city include apartment buildings, hotels and offices. The city of Bombay can be considered a pace setter in the construction of apartment buildings in India, as other major cities in India have not tended toward construction of apartments in quite the same scale.

Delhi

Delhi is divided into two parts, old Delhi and New Delhi. Old Delhi, which is also called the walled city, has been in existence for many centuries with narrow and congested lanes. During the later part of nineteenth century, the British, then rulers of India, felt the need for a more spacious city. Consequently New Delhi was planned and constructed during early part of twentieth century, and continues to grow very rapidly due, in part, to its wide and spacious roads. The rate of expansion of the city during the last 40 years has been phenomenal, moving it from the fourth largest city to the third.

The concept of satellite towns was introduced about twenty years ago by building a number of small industrial complexes around Delhi at a distance of about 20 to 30 km (12 to 18.5 mi) from the heart of the city. It was envisaged that the industrial complexes around the city would grow into small towns and provide shelter to many of the people who worked not only in the industrial complexes, but also in the city.

It was hoped that the people would live in the satellite towns and commute to work to the city. Unfortunately the reverse has taken place. People who work in the industrial complexes around the city live in the city and go out to work in the satellite towns. Lack of development of facilities such as schools, hospitals, public utilities, shopping, and transportation in the satellite towns has forced working people to remain in Delhi, swelling its population to 5.22 million.

There has thus been a rapid growth in construction of tall buildings in Delhi during the 1970s, lagging only slightly behind that of Bombay. The number of floors of the tall buildings is generally restricted to around twenty. Tall buildings constructed in the city are mainly for hotels and offices, as many people prefer independent units for living rather than apartments. The main mode of public transportation in Delhi is a publicly operated bus system. A rapid transit system is now under construction.

Old Delhi, which was developed before and during the nineteenth century, still has very narrow roads. These roads were designed to allow for slow-moving vehicles such as hand-pulled and horse-drawn carts. Many of the old streets are not even capable of accommodating a modern heavy truck. The height of the buildings on either side of the streets ranges from two to three stories and very rarely to a fourth story.

The main business district in old Delhi is rather congested, because the roads have a maximum of two lanes. Looking at the density of population and business operation of the old city, one wonders how traffic moves at all in this district. Yet trade and business continue to grow and attract many customers in old Delhi in spite of newly developed business districts in the New Delhi area.

The planners of New Delhi, on the other hand, have liberally provided very wide roads and large circular intersections, facilitating the smooth flow of traffic. Despite its manifold growth of population during the last 60 years, there is smooth traffic flow with a minimum of traffic jams. Future plans for construction of tall buildings in New Delhi hinge on the development of a rapid transit system. The construction of one 35-story building was postponed in view of the limited transportation available.

Madras

The city of Madras, which is situated on the southeastern coast, is the fourth largest city in India with a population of 4.27 million people. A fourteen-story office building constructed in 1956 was considered to be the tallest building in the country for almost a decade.

Madras was a small fishing town until the beginning of the eighteenth century, and has grown rapidly since then. The influence of the British during this period has helped in developing a reasonably planned city with wide roads. Electric trains introduced in the 1940s and 1950s have provided mass transportation in the city. Few tall buildings have been constructed; the ones that were are primarily used for offices rather than apartments and hotels, and the number of stories is only to eight to fourteen. This is a typical feature of the city. The rates of construction of tall buildings in Madras and Calcutta are about the same—rather slow when compared with those in Bombay and Delhi.

TALL BUILDINGS IN THE THREE NEXT-LARGEST CITIES

The three next-largest cities, Bangalore, Hyderabad, and Ahmedabad, are relatively new and have grown very rapidly during the last 40 years. They have attracted large industries and are relatively stable for industrial investments.

Tall buildings construction in these cities is usually limited to 8 to 16 stories. Most of the tall buildings house offices and some hotels.

Tall building seems related to the age of the city: The older the city, the smaller the number of tall buildings. Cities such as Varanasi, Kanpur, Agra, Nagpur, and Jaipur, which have been in existence for many centuries, have congested business centers, so that even though they have planned for expansion, the planning of the new areas did not envisage concentration of high-rise construction. The cultural background and the business and social habits of the people make it difficult to control and organize the growth of such cities. There is continual construction of unauthorized buildings and encroachment into the spaces earmarked for public use. The over-loading and blockage of water and sewage lines is a chronic problem. The business districts are overcrowded, and transportation and public facilities have been overused beyond their normal capacities. As a result, the construction of tall buildings in the extension areas is not common. The growth in the new areas is usually restricted to residential, office, and school accommodations, with most buildings having four or fewer floors because of the requirement that any building having more than four floors have an elevator.

Tall buildings constructed in the five cities of Lucknow, Jaipur, Nagpur, Pune, and Kanpur, each with a population of 1.0 to 2.5 million, are primarily for offices. There are one or two tall hotels constructed in each of the cities, but hardly any high-rise apartments. Typical structural frames of tall buildings under construction are shown in Figs. 2 to 4.

MATERIALS USED IN CONSTRUCTION
OF TALL BUILDINGS

Construction in India is labor-intensive and uses reinforced concrete construction extensively. Steel is expensive when compared with concrete, the cost ratio ranging from 60 to 90, whereas the corresponding strength ratio is from 15 to 20. Practically all tall buildings constructed in any part of the country are of reinforced concrete using high-yield strength deformed bars. The strength of the concrete used varies from M15 to M25 and the strength of the reinforcement bars is 415 N/mm^2 (60 ksi). Except for the columns in the lower floors of tall buildings, the percentage of reinforcement used in most of the elements of the buildings is less than 2%. The percentage of reinforcement in beams and slabs is around 1%.

GENERAL PLANNING OF TALL BUILDINGS

Invariably all tall buildings in India have a basement floor that houses machinery, the air conditioning plant, parking of vehicles, and storage space. The basement is taken to 2.5 m to 3 m (8 to 10 ft) below ground level and provided with reinforced concrete floors and walls. A part of the ground floor is also used for car parking or an open plaza. Spacing of the columns usually varies from 5.5 m to 8 m (18 to 26 ft), and occasionally goes up to 10 m. The normal height of floors is about 3.2 m. Most buildings are provided with two elevators except in case of large buildings in which four elevators are provided. The capacity of the elevators varies from six to fifteen.

Partitions in many parts of the country are made of brick masonry. The strength of the brick in the northern and Gangetic plains is about 15 to 30 N/mm^2 (2 to 4 ksi) whereas it is only 3.5 to 10 N/mm^2 (0.5 to 1.5 ksi) in the southern part of the country. The walls and concrete columns are invariably painted with cement paints.

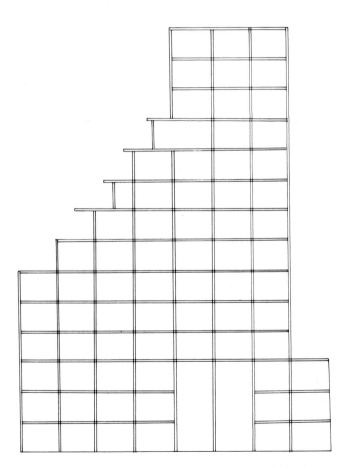

Fig. 2 Building framework, Lucknow Development Authority

TYPICAL PROBLEMS IN TALL
BUILDING CONSTRUCTION

Water supply

Even though the planning of water supply systems has been perfected, many of the small builders continue to have questions about the water distribution system within the building. The questions that are often asked are the following: How accurately can one estimate the peak water demand in a tall building, even if the per capita consumption is assumed? How can the number and levels of storage water tanks be provided so as to optimize the energy consumption in pumping of water and minimize the wear of water line connections and fittings? What is the optimal capacity of the storage reservoir for fire-fighting, and what are the uses of the water in the reservoir for purposes other than fire-fighting?

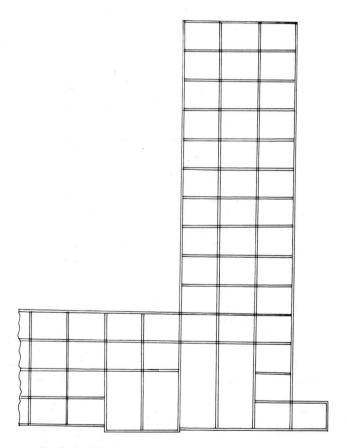

Fig. 3 Building framework, Lucknow Development Authority

Codes of practice do recommend certain norms for the above problems. However, the designer has to make several decisions, because some of the recommendations appear to affect the economy of the building to an appreciable extent both in construction and in maintenance. It is well known that fire-fighting is a special problem in all buildings, and it becomes more acute in countries like India where the equipment and devices in fire detection and control are not developed to a satisfactory level. Since the number of tall buildings constructed is not very large, the industry is not fully prepared to provide dependable equipment at a reasonable cost.

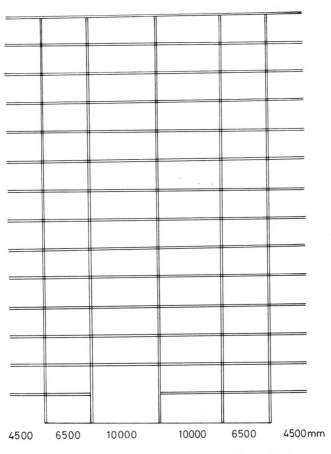

4500   6500   10000   10000   6500   4500mm

Fig. 4 Long span cantilever framework, Yojana Bhavan Lucknow

Maintenance

The maintenance of tall buildings can be divided into two categories: annual maintenance, such as cleaning and painting, and repairs and replacements made necessary by wear and tear of the components. Annual maintenance of tall buildings in India consists of the painting of cladding, doors, windows etc. Depending upon the location of the building, the painting is usually done once in 2 to 4 years. Often it tends to 3 to 6 years. Many of the tall buildings constructed in smaller cities, however, belong to government or public sector undertakings, which bogs down maintenance with procedural problems. Routine maintenance in private buildings is faster.

Construction of tall buildings appears to be far easier than the proper maintenance of the buildings in India. Users of the buildings experience a host of inconveniences due to delay in repairs and maintenance arising out of normal wear and tear. The wear and tear of a building depends, of course, upon the quality of the original construction, the quality of usage, and the sensitivity and quality of repair.

The quality of construction is usually governed by the architectural specifications and the quality of the available material. The quality of structural materials used in tall building construction is usually good, whereas the quality of the fixtures and finishes varies considerably. India being a seller's market, one cannot be very choosy, because the availability of dependable supplies of good quality fixtures is limited.

The quality of the usage of the building depends on the user and his habits. Many of the public buildings are overused either because of the lack of adquate facilities or because of public indifference to the property. Social habits, religious customs, and economic levels determine the quality of usage of such public buildings.

Further, prompt repairs and maintenance are not very easy, as the building inhabitants depend on another department for maintenance. Even though some of the owners do have small maintenance crews, the problems of maintenance in a tall building are many, and prompt repairs are not easily achieved. Effective maintenance of tall buildings, especially in the public sector, is a major challenge to the engineer. There is a great need to develop an optimal way of maintenance of tall buildings considering all the aspects.

CONCLUSIONS

The industrial growth and development of educational and health facilities in the urban areas have influenced a variety of rural people to migrate to cities. The affluent rural population, though small in number, is also moving into urban areas not only for the reasons stated above but also for social and security needs. Poor people are migrating into large cities as a labor force for variety of activities. Building construction, especially tall building construction, is influenced by several factors such as the age of the city, the availability of wide roads and fast transportation facilities, and the customs and habits of the people of the region.

Even though cities in India are absorbing surrounding land, tall building construction usually occurs in and around the main business district, not in the newly developed areas. Tall buildings in all cities are used primarily for offices and hotels, and to a limited extent as apartments.

Technical know-how in structural design and construction is at satisfactory and dependable levels; however, the supply of durable plumbing and architectural materials needs research and expansion. The construction activity is labor-intensive, and the rate of construction is influenced more by the availability of materials and transport than by the technology or the labor force. Educational and research institutes have concentrated their activities in structural engineering. In the present day the need of the building industry is mostly in the area of plumbing and architectural materials and their products.

The rate and quality of construction of tall buildings is far ahead of the maintenance aspects of the buildings. Routine maintenance and repair of the buildings is at a low level, reflecting not only the levels of technical skills in such areas but also the resource allocations and habits of people. The need is to develop an integrated approach to improving the quality of maintenance of the buildings, considering several factors such as the quality of construction, the provision of maintenance-free fixtures and finishes, technical training, social education, and management.

The Development of a Low-Rise Urban Housing Alternative

Roger G. Kallman

A group of Chicago architects, planners, and other professionals has begun an investigation into what they believe is an effective alternative to the high-rise model of urban housing. This group, known as Urbs in Horto, adopted its name from Chicago's motto, which means "City in a Garden" and reflects the aspirations of a significant segment of the urban population concerning the kind of environment in which they want to live. Urbs in Horto came together in response to a challenge set forth in March of 1981 by Peter Land, an architect and educator, who called for undertaking the planning and building of a different urban habitat to demonstrate new ideas and point the way for housing in the future. The Urbs in Horto group shares with the Council on Tall Buildings and Urban Habitat an enormous regard for high-rise building development and acknowledges that the technological achievements in this area have enabled the viability of cities to be maintained. Chicago has been a proving-ground and showcase of the world's most impressive concentration of tall buildings, many of which have served as prototypes for structures throughout the world. From William Le Baron Jenney's Home Insurance building of 1885, technology has evolved to permit the construction of far more lofty structures including the tallest—Chicago's Sears Tower.

From the extraordinary vantage point afforded by these buildings, another perspective emerges — the physical decay of surrounding urban areas and the urgent need to reverse their deterioration. But from this same vantage point, a major opportunity is also recognizable — the chance to vitalize vast stretches of underutilized land through the creation of a new urban habitat. Urbs in Horto has chosen to focus on Chicago to test the viability of this idea — the renewal of neighborhoods through low-rise housing that has the benefits of high-rise density. Successfully tested in Chicago, the concept could then be adapted to other urban areas worldwide.

Despite a population loss of over 600,000 in the course of the past 20 years, Chicago has a shortage of housing, particularly of dwelling units suited to moderate-income households. A significant percentage of existing stock is either in need of major upgrading or must be replaced altogether. The inadequate supply of housing of the type required in urban neighborhoods today has resulted in continued migration to the suburbs and further deterioration of inner city areas. The result is continued dwindling of an already eroded tax base yet a higher valuation of fallow land based on the expectation of extremely high-density renewal. The rehabilitation of inner city neighborhoods will depend on the response to the challenge of providing alternative types of affordable housing. And, economic pressure has never been a stronger impetus.

Bearing this sense of urgency in mind, Urbs in Horto has begun an investigation of one possible solution to this housing problem. Great strides in high-rise technology have made the modern high-rise building an affordable and practicable solution; nevertheless, the public-at-large seeks a variety of housing options. Currently, there are few viable alternatives within the inner areas of cities. Comparable research in other types of high-density housing has been limited to date, but recent studies indicate that there are housing types that have the potential for achieving densities that equal those provided by many high-rise buildings (Fig. 1). It is the pursuit of one building type as an urban housing option to which Urbs in Horto presently addresses itself.

The first major objective of the group is to advance the state of knowledge concerning low-rise, high-density housing — to bring it up to date with the art and technology of its high-rise counterpart. This will require the cooperation of professionals from many disciplines: architecture, engineering, urban planning, finance, building technology, law, sociology, psychology, and others. Urbs in Horto has begun to examine this approach to the housing problem, but a great deal of work remains to be accomplished.

The goals that the group is striving to achieve in the design of low-rise, high-density housing are numerous and certainly include the accommodation of lifestyles not well suited to the high-rise building. As observed by Donn Logan, "The new urbanism in housing design relies on diversity, the pluralism of lifestyles" (Logan, 1977). It is necessary to examine how design can advance this goal more fully and how it can facilitate personal expression in the face of significant constraints.

In responding to the requirements of inner city neighborhoods, low-rise housing must be truly economical and efficient. Initial indications of the group's work suggest that structures would need to be two-, three-, and four-story walk-up units clustered together in combinations adapted to the Chicago grid (Fig. 2). Floorplan layouts would probably be simple, with flexible living areas and more compact and efficient bedrooms and bathroom facilities. The allocation of space is a reflection of usage—of lifestyle by the occupants. The clustering of units could also produce economic benefits in the form of energy savings—a particularly urgent requirement today. Units could be planned and designed to utilize the benefits of sun and wind in providing natural lighting, solar heating, as well as cross-ventilation. Building materials will need to be studied, as well as prefabrication techniques, if substantial economies are to be realized. In order to meet changing needs, the adaptability of units will prove to be an important factor in the long-term economy of low-rise, high-density structures. The aspects of housing that have been identified above are typical of many areas requiring research.

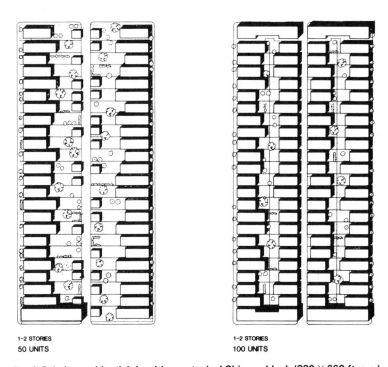

1-2 STORIES
50 UNITS

1-2 STORIES
100 UNITS

Fig. 1 Existing residential densities on typical Chicago block (330 × 660 ft. o.c.)

The second major objective of the group is to study methods of integrating this type of housing into the existing pattern of Chicago neighborhoods. In view of the lack of success in this area over the last several decades, this is an especially important purpose. The goal of creating innovative moderate-income housing must be pursued with the objective of revitalizing total neighborhoods. Historically, large blocks of land have been cleared (Fig. 3) to accommodate wholly new building types erected with little sensitivity to the surrounding community. Recent efforts have been more sensitive but have failed to address the scale of the problem in satisfying housing demand. In the future, it will be necessary to give more thought and attention to both alternative housing types and neighborhood environment.

In order to be realized, the second major objective of the group will also require extensive and coordinated research across the varied disciplines represented in the Council today. In the last several years, there has emerged some evidence of both interest and research into aspects of the housing problem. But there remains a crucial need to expand on these efforts, and to apply the conclusions to the conditions in Chicago.

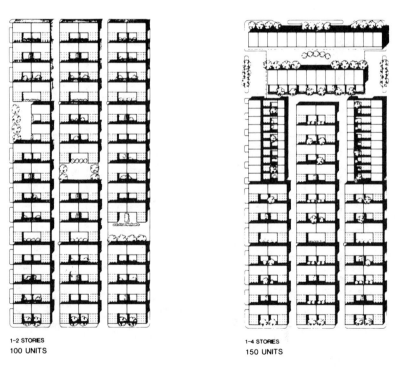

1-2 STORIES
100 UNITS

1-4 STORIES
150 UNITS

Fig. 2 Alternate residential studies for garden houses on typical Chicago block (330 × 660 ft. o.c.)

It is premature at this stage to try to identify specific Chicago neighborhoods where the proposed mode of housing could be successfully incorporated and tested. The neighborhoods investigated should, however, satisfy several fundamental conditions. They should be viable communities in need of new housing with essential infrastructure and service in place, including public transportation, schools, hospitals, recreation facilities, and the like. Neighborhoods without some or most of these ingredients could jeopardize the success of the project regardless of the merit of the housing prototypes themselves.

The importance of integrating new and existing development cannot be overestimated and merits in-depth study. Low-rise, high-density housing can be the key ingredient in rehabilitating viable neighborhoods, but the neighborhoods must be preserved. For it is the neighborhoods that ultimately supply the life of the community and determine the prospects for the success of housing.

The third objective of Urbs in Horto is to go beyond merely theoretical studies to the building of an actual neighborhood. An actual neighborhood would demonstrate in built form high-density, walk-up living as a viable housing alternative. The question remains why the concept must be studied at the scale of a neighborhood. The new urban habitat must be of a size that will permit it to be a competitive form of housing with respect to other options. At this time, the group believes an appropriate site area in Chicago to be twelve to fifteen blocks, but the size may vary after further investigation.

Fig. 3 Vacant land near downtown Chicago

Chicago is a logical place to initiate a project of this scope. Large tracts of underutilized and vacant land exist near viable neighborhoods around the central area. In addition, the proposed 1992 World's Fair, the "Age of Discovery," is slated for Chicago providing added impetus and a possible vehicle for creating a demonstration neighborhood. Furthermore, Chicago has the necessary leadership in both public and private sectors to turn these opportunities into realities. Chicago is a city where great ideas and great achievements are traditions, from rebuilding the entire city from the ashes and rubble of the fire of 1871 to the specific buildings that exhibit bold and ingenious advances in architecture, planning and engineering — innovations that in turn have spread worldwide. A neighborhood prototype developed in Chicago can have a similar effect.

The goals of Urbs in Horto focus on the achievement of a new kind of habitat that is suited to urban areas and that complements high-rise housing. The group has now proposed a strategy for realizing these goals. Research and new prototype housing designs for low-rise, high-density neighborhoods must be carried out; ways to integrate this housing within viable, existing communities must be explored; and a demonstration project to confirm the validity of the concept needs to be implemented.

Urbs in Horto recognizes the talents and achievements represented by the Council on Tall Buildings and Urban Habitat, particularly with regard to the quality and extent of the Council's recent contributions to the study of high-rise housing. Clearly, the Council members' experience and knowledge could also be of the utmost benefit in the development of a low-rise, high-density housing.

REFERENCES/BIBLIOGRAPHY

Land, P., 1981
    ECONOMIC GARDEN HOUSES NEIGHBORHOODS, Presented at the Chicago AIA Design Committee Seminar on Housing, Chicago, Illinois, March, 1981.
Logan, D., 1977
    HOUSING AND URBANISM, The Form of Housing, Van Nostrand Reinhold Company, Cincinnati.

Meeting the Pedestrian Access Needs of Tall Buildings

Rodney E. Engelen

The development of tall buildings may provide both the need and the opportunity to make significant improvements in the pedestrian movement systems of central business districts and activity centers. In such situations, they generate large amounts of pedestrian traffic, which can be beneficial, but which can also create problems and costs. The purpose of this paper is to identify the pedestrian movement needs of large buildings and to explore ways in which these needs can be met in typical activity center or central business district settings. If ways can be found better to meet the movement needs of pedestrians, then problems of vehicular movement, parking, and land availability for development will also be reduced.

The access needs (or pedestrian generation) of tall buildings will vary rather substantially depending upon their location. Three types of locations that must be considered are: (1) those within central business district (CBD) or activity center settings, (2) those near but not within the CBD core, and (3) freestanding outlying locations. Characteristics of movement will vary substantially in these areas. For example, identical buildings in each of these environments will generate different volumes of movement, and methods of movement and trip length will vary. In general, buildings located within

49

larger, more intense CBD environments will generate fewer trips overall. More of these trips will be in the pedestrian mode, and pedestrian trips will have a greater average length than from buildings located within freestanding or peripheral locations (Pushkarev and Zupan, 1975).

Table 1 indicates the median length of pedestrian trips in various locations. It is evident from these data that persons will walk considerable distances to accomplish their objectives. Much of the data collected in smaller U.S. cities suggests that people are willing to walk only a block or two for most trip purposes. However, this may be not so much a reflection of the unwillingness of pedestrians to walk as it is the lack of a need (or ability) to walk longer distances to achieve trip objectives. Most destinations are either not accessible on foot or are not far enough apart to generate longer pedestrian trips.

Table 2 indicates the volume of pedestrian traffic that may be generated by various activities commonly located in tall buildings. In an intense CBD environment, nearly 40,000 pedestrian trips would be generated each day from a mixed-use development containing 92,900 m² (one million ft²) of office space, 9290 m² (100,000 ft²) of retail space, a 400-room hotel, and 1858 m² (20,000 ft²) of restaurant space. About 60% of this movement would be related to the basic home-work trip; 40% would be for other purposes. However, rain reduces the number of shopping trips by about one-half and business trips by about one-quarter. Rain also reduces the length of midday trips by about one-quarter and cold weather also reduces the volume and length of non-home-work trips. On the other hand, a pleasant environment is said to en-

Table 1 Typical trip length (Pushkarev and Zupan, 1975)

City	Median trip length
Smaller city (Seattle, Edmonton)	121.9 m (400 ft)
Chicago	304.8 m (1,000 ft)
Manhattan	335.3 m (1,100 ft)
London	640.1 m (2,100 ft)
Average walking time (Manhattan), five to six minutes, 68.6 to 106.7 m/min (225 to 350 fpm)	

Table 2 Typical trip generation*

Example	Trips per day
92,900 m² (1 million ft²) offices	17,000
9290 m² (100,000 ft²) retail	15,000
400-room hotel	3,200
1858 m² (20,000 ft²) restaurant	3,600
Total	38,800

[a]Estimated based on generation rates cited in Pushkarev and Zupan (1975)

courage walking distances up to 30% greater than the norm (Pushkarev and Zupan, 1975).

Trip purposes vary substantially by time of day. As shown in Table 3, the principal trip purposes during the noon hour are to move from work to eating place and from shop to shop (43% each), and from home to eating place, home to work, and home to business. On the other hand, by far the largest single movement in the evening peak hour is from work to home.

Almost 50% of daily total movement within a shopping area occurs between 12:00 and 2:30 p.m. On the other hand, peak movement within an office area is between 5:00 and 5:30 when 12% of total daily travel occurs (Pushkarev and Zupan, 1975).

Cumulative movement in areas occupied intensively by tall buildings can be substantial. Figure 1 indicates a hypothetical isolated corridor occupied

Table 3 Pedestrian trip origins and destinations (Barton-Aschman Associates, 1974)

	Work	Home	Shop	Business	Eat	Other
Noon hour						
Work	9	6	15	21	43	6
Home	30	10	0	20	40	0
Shop	14	9	43	9	18	7
P.M. peak hour						
Work	7	77	3	9	1	3
Home	50	0	38	0	0	12
Shop	17	42	25	4	4	8

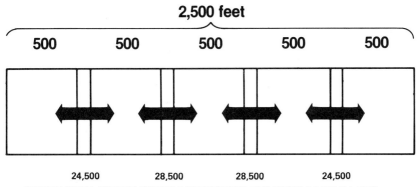

ASSUME EQUAL FOUR-WAY TRIP DISTRIBUTION, BUILDINGS OF EQUAL SIZE, GROSS FAR OF 9.0, NET 14, MANHATTAN-TYPE TRIP LENGTHS AND GENERATION.

Fig. 1 Hypothetical corridor pedestrian volumes

by buildings with a net floor area ratio (F.A.R.) of 14 and with an equal distribution of movement in four directions from each block. An estimate of trips based on assumed building size shows from 24,000 to 28,000 movements through most of the length of the corridor in a 12-hr period. If this corridor were to be paralleled by other intensive development, volumes would be even higher. Checks of data in major cities confirm that such volumes are quite common and are often exceeded. For example in 1972, counts in Chicago showed volumes on numerous office-oriented streets between 8:00 a.m. and 7:00 p.m. in the range of 16,000 to 45,000 person movements (City of Chicago, 1973). Numerous streets in New York City carry even higher volumes. Much of Fifth Avenue, for example, carries 20,000 or more pedestrians *per hour* during both midday and late afternoon hours (Pushkarev and Zupan, 1975).

Aggregate pedestrian movement within intensively developed areas is very great. For example, within a large CBD such as Houston, there may be as many as 2.6 million pedestrian movements each day. For the Chicago Loop, this number may exceed 4 million (Rouse, 1980). Thus on an overall basis, there is a tremendous need to accommodate and facilitate pedestrian movement, which often exceeds normal street and sidewalk capacity, and which can generate substantial conflicts with traffic.

TRANSIT USAGE POTENTIALS

One of the first assumptions regarding pedestrian movements in an intensively developed area is that some form of transit or *people mover* would be helpful to accommodate them. How true is this?

In most situations, the potential for using transit to assist in a large proportion of internal movement is quite limited. Most people will walk up to 0.3 mi (70% of trips are shorter than this) (Pushkarev and Zupan, 1975). Moreover, it is difficult to save a significant amount of time on a typical pedestrian trip by switching to some form of transit or vehicular movement. Table 4 indicates the time that would be taken in a typical CBD setting to make a comparable trip by various travel modes. As can be seen from this

Table 4 Trip time for typical trip within a central business district (Rouse, 1980)

Mode	Minutes of trip time
Pedestrian	30
Auto	22
Streetcar	23
Moving walkway	26
PRT	19

table, the magnitude of time savings over walking for various movement systems is relatively low. As a result, in this situation only a very small percentage of people can normally be attracted to use some form of transit. Analysis suggests that even with a system of high performance facilities with frequent service, no more than about 10% of trips could be attracted to the transit mode (Rouse, 1980).

Nevertheless, in areas of high density and with large numbers of tall buildings, the amount of transit use could be substantial. Table 5 indicates the number of passengers that might be attracted to some rather simple and limited people-mover systems (Fig. 2). As can be seen, volumes could exceed 100,000 person-trips per day for certain transit modes in a large CBD, and would be over 50,000 trips per day in a medium sized CBD. With a somewhat more versatile *figure-eight* configuration, volumes could reach 160,000 and 90,000 passengers per day in the same settings. If such systems were to be complemented with coordinated, high density development and good systems of pedestrian walkways, they could attract even higher levels of use.

With these high volumes of movement and the significant potential for specialized transit usage, more attention, as well as investment, is justified toward ways of capturing and accommodating such movement. A variety of other techniques may be (and are being) employed to facilitate pedestrian movement, including skywalks, tunnels, and other grade separations; pedestrian malls; and limited devices such as escalators and moving sidewalks.

MEETING TRANSIT AND PEDESTRIAN FACILITY NEEDS

Techniques to be used in meeting pedestrian needs will depend significantly on cost. Typical capital costs of providing certain types of transit are shown in Table 6. Assuming usage levels shown in Table 5, aggregate costs per passenger-mile (capital and operating) for various technologies may be as shown on Table 7. Can such costs be justified? What types of facilities should be considered and under what circumstances? How do the answers to these questions relate to the construction of tall or large buildings?

Table 5 Anticipated transit usage of central business district—people-mover systems (Rouse, 1980)

Kind of CBD	Daily passengers (thousands)
Large city CBD	30–120
Large activity center	8–50
Medium CBD	13–70
Transit could generate "induced" travel of 15 to 25%	

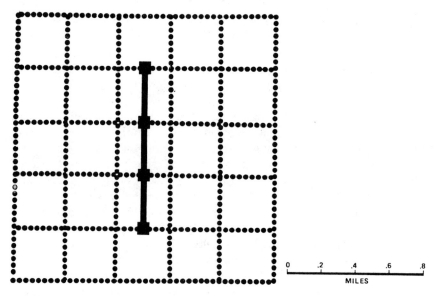

SINGLE-SPINE TRANSIT CONFIGURATION

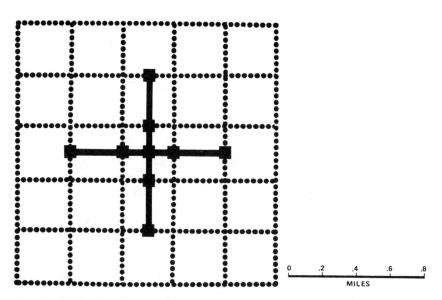

DOUBLE-SPINE TRANSIT CONFIGURATION

Fig. 2 Schematic single and double-spine transit configurations

The justification of investments in transit and pedestrian facilities can be developed in several ways. Where public subsidies are involved, it can include the assignment of a general *value* to the availability and use of transit. Past practice in building transit facilities in the United States places this value at around $1,250 for each passenger mile of weekday usage (Regional Plan Association, 1980). In other words, public policy has determined that the achievement of public objectives through the development of transit is worth this level of investment. At this level, a usage of 5,000 passenger-miles per day would support an investment of $6 million per mile for construction. Presumably embodied in this figure are a whole range of public benefits, including accommodating the movement of those who cannot travel by auto, reducing the need for parking, reducing air pollution, and permitting increases in development density.

Where public investment is not available, is harder to achieve, or must be more thoroughly justified, a somewhat more focused effort must be made to measure the value of pedestrian or transit facilities. This involves estimating either cost savings, or the additional amounts that persons would be willing to pay for added comfort and convenience. Other factors that may be considered include reductions in pedestrian and vehicular conflicts, costs avoided in the provision of parking, and greater efficiencies that may be achieved in the use of land. For example, in Minneapolis and St. Paul, building owners are able to identify higher rent levels and increased retail

Table 6 Generalized costs of various people-mover technologies

Technology	Cost per mile[a]
Trolleybus	$ 2.1 million
Streetcar	7.0 million
Moving sidewalk	9.0 million
SLT	18.0 million
PRT	30.0 million
Skyway	$3,500–5,000/lineal foot of bridge[b]

[a]Source: Rouse, 1980
[b]Source: Barton-Aschman Associates, 1982a

Table 7 Total annual cost per passenger-mile of anticipated use (cents) (Rouse, 1980)

	Moving walkway	Mini-bus	Streetcar	High-tech
Large city CBD	26	18	19	20–110
Large activity center	–	13–22	–	43–78
Medium CBD	–	20–26	–	31–83

sales as benefits of connection to pedestrian skyways (Barton-Aschman Associates, 1976).

Studies in Des Moines, Iowa suggest that the *value* of separating one movement of a pedestrian from the surface crossing of a street would be over 10¢ (Barton-Aschman Associates, 1982b). In more congested areas, this figure could be higher. This accounts for time and energy savings from reduced delay on the part of both pedestrians and vehicle operators. However, it does not include the value of reduced accidents. Other studies suggest that time which can be saved from that spent in walking is valued at from 10 to 48¢/min (Barton-Aschman Associates, 1978). Developers and building owners are also increasingly willing to spend $250,000 to $1 million or more for a bridge or tunnel to span a street or other obstruction to connect to other property or to parking. Studies of pedestrian walkway and people-mover systems also suggest that substantial new development may be induced by such systems and this is frequently considered a major benefit.

Based on the foregoing, and assuming ridership levels shown in Table 5, it should be possible to justify the development of one or more forms of transit and pedestrian movement facilities in many downtowns and in some activity centers. The particular type of system will depend on the density and configuration of development. For example, a linear pattern of very high density development may be able to support a high capacity, high technology system. A compact area might be better served by a fine-grained pedestrian skyway or tunnel system. And more conventional technologies, such as trolleys and streetcars, may be appropriate in other settings.

THE IMPACT OF TALL BUILDINGS

The development of a tall building can either aggravate problems of pedestrian movement or, perhaps, be part of the solution. Because of the scale of ameliorating measures that it can support, a tall building could be more acceptable in some situations than a much smaller one.

One key to the generation of a positive impact from a tall building is its location. In most situations, the lack of specialized pedestrian and/or transit facilities can be traced at least in part to a lack of concentration, focus, or organization in patterns of movement. In some instances, the volumes of movement simply may not be high enough to support the required investment in transit or pedestrian facilities. A tall building, strategically located to reinforce present patterns of movement or to create new movement in an appropriate corridor, may provide the impetus required to produce the needed access investment. This may be true whether the building is located within or near an intensive concentration of business activity.

However, if pedestrian benefits are to be achieved, several conditions must be met. First, priority must be given to developing a good system for movement *within* the existing activity core. This may consist of some combination of transit, grade-separated pedestrianways, or pedestrian precincts or malls. The important condition is that existing functions be strongly linked to each other. New development can later connect via this linkage, and the access to markets and services will make location within or near the central area or activity center valuable.

Justification for the system lies in a fundamental need for good linkage in the area, and does not necessarily depend on new development. However, as indicated above, new development can be the catalyst by which the desired facility or sevice can be achieved.

Second, the ability of a movement system to provide access to lower-cost peripheral land accommodating parking and/or development should be exploited. A large building or complex may be able to utilize effectively and justify the development of a movement system extending outside of the present pattern of intensive activity. Such an extension may reduce costs, minimize pollution and access problems, and bring attractive but less accessible sites into use. Still, with a strong connection, the advantages of proximity and interconnection can be maintained.

Third, existing core development and/or the proposed new development must include a variety of uses—office, retail, and services. Unless a mix of uses is available, the need for interaction between areas will probably not be large enough to generate the level of interchange required to sustain a useful linkage. Excluding the home–work trip, over 70% of pedestrian trips are for non-business purposes (Pushkarev and Zupan, 1975). Thus the availability of shopping, restaurants, and consumer services is important to the extended use of pedestrian or related facilities.

To achieve these conditions, and to assure that the access needs of large concentrations of development can be met, a three-part strategy should be employed.

The improvement of facilities for pedestrians in existing areas of concentrated activity should receive first priority. Even if extensive investments can be made in transit and people-movement systems, good pedestrian facilities will be required (most trips are too short for transit). One of the most effective ways to improve the environment for pedestrians is to create auto-restricted or auto-free zones involving precincts of several blocks in which pedestrian movements are given preference. Additional techniques include the provision of pedestrian and transit malls and the redesign of streets to improve pedestrian amenities. Quantified justification of such improvements in the United States is not readily available. However, the success of such improvements is readily observable in many situations, particularly in Europe.

The provision of grade-separated walkways represents still another level of investment to improve pedestrian movement systems. Ideally, such walkways should be provided as part of a system which extends through many blocks of an area or which connects several auto-restricted precincts. A large, intense development frequently can provide the basis for initiating or extending the development of such a system. Relatively modest volumes of movement can justify the construction of a typical bridge. Assuming a benefit of 10¢ per use, less than 3,000 crossings per business day would pay for the span across a normal street, plus the costs of stairs and other vertical connections to grade.

Grade-separated walkway systems should be developed in most situations involving high densities of activity (in other words, tall buildings), where extensive pedestrian–vehicular conflicts may be expected. Even for a single building they can do much to spread the load of pedestrian movement and to facilitate the high quantities and proportions of short trips.

Plan a people-mover system and reserve a location and right-of-way. This is most important in providing a transit facility. Once a right-of-way is established, buildings, streets, pedestrian facilities, and other features can be adjusted gradually to reflect and reinforce the transit plan. These adjustments will help assure the success of the transit facility when it is provided, and should help reduce its cost.

In most situations, it will be important to keep the system simple. Complex design or hardware concepts should be avoided. Plans selected should be capable of incremental implementation using readily available technology. Costly or elaborate schemes may not be implemented, and may be difficult to justify and finance. Simple shuttle systems, such as that installed at the Tampa Airport, or light rail (trolley) systems are examples of what may be most appropriate. Plans should include lines (and right-of-way reservations) which extend outward from built-up areas which have major potential for development, peripheral parking, or similar use.

Large developments should be located and planned to help implement plans for both pedestrian systems and transit. Large developments at least should help to create, extend and provide continuity to pedestrian movement systems. They should also be located and designed to connect into any transit system, planned or existing. And consideration should be given to using such systems as an integral part of development, to meet the need for essential connections between the development and other features of the area, parking, and the like. As indicated in Table 2, a large, mixed-use development can be expected to generate 40,000 or more pedestrian trips per day. About 60% or 24,000 of these, are in movement between home and work. Sixteen thousand involve other origins or destinations. If no more than 10,000 of these trips were to use transit each business day with a benefit per ride of 30¢, this would generate annual revenues (or benefits) of over $660,000. If half of this were available to cover debt service, this could support a capital investment of up to $4 million. An investment at this level would pay for a significant extension of a trolley or street car line, which could not only meet movement needs but open up lower cost land for parking or for development.

Obviously, different assumptions regarding benefit, operating costs, usage and other factors would produce different results. The point is that it is conceivable for the benefits to a large development of providing transit or people-mover service to outweigh costs. There is a good chance that the expenditure of $5–10 million (in project budgets of $100–200 million) could generate savings in land and parking costs that would offset the capital investments required. Moreover, investments at this level could provide a significant part of a downtown or activity center movement system.

CONCLUSION

The opportunity to build a portion of a transit or people-mover system in connection with a major development may seem remote. However, as cities and developers struggle with problems of access, parking, and pollution, they may find that the type of coordination of land and transportation planning described above may be a solution. Certainly additional study of this approach and application of the principles described above are warranted.

REFERENCES/BIBLIOGRAPHY

Barton-Aschman Associates, 1974
    THE CIRCULATION OF PEOPLE IN THE ST. PAUL CENTRAL AREA, prepared for the City of St. Paul Department of Public Works, March, St. Paul, Minnesota.
Barton-Aschman Associates, 1976
    SKYWAYS IN MINNEAPOLIS/ST. PAUL: PROTOTYPES FOR THE NATION?, July.
Barton-Aschman Associates, 1978
    TRANSPORTATION ANALYSIS OF THE PROPOSED DES MOINES SKYWAY SYSTEM, City of Des Moines, Iowa, August.
Barton-Aschman Associates, 1982a
    FEASIBILITY ANALYSIS AND PLAN FOR A SECOND LEVEL WALKWAY SYSTEM IN DOWN-DOWN ROCHESTER, NEW YORK, City of Rochester, New York, July.
Barton-Aschman Associates, 1982b
    PLAN FOR A SKYWAY SYSTEM, MILWAUKEE, WISCONSIN, June.
Branbilla, R. and Longo, G., 1977
    FOR PEDESTRIANS ONLY: PLANNING DESIGN AND MANAGEMENT OF TRAFFIC FREE ZONES, Whitney Library of Design.

City of Chicago, 1973
    CHICAGO LOOP PEDESTRIAN MOVEMENT STUDY, Pedestrian Mall Task Force, Chicago.

Fruin, J.J., 1974
    PEDESTRIAN PLANNING AND DESIGN, Metropolitan Association of Urban Designers and Environmental Planners, Inc.

Kuhnemann, G. and Witherspoon, R., 1972
    TRAFFIC FREE ZONES IN GERMAN CITIES, Organization for Economic Cooperation and Development, Paris.

Malls Committee of the Institute for Transportation 1979
  PLANNING AND CONSTRUCTION OF MUNICIPAL MALLS, American Public Works Association,
  APWA, Report No. 46, July.
Metropolitan Association of Urban Designers and Environmental Planners, Inc., 1973
  PROCEEDINGS OF THE PEDESTRIAN/BICYCLE PLANNING AND DESIGN SEMINAR, (Pro-
  ceedings of Conference held in San Francisco, 1972) The Institute of Transportation and Traffic
  Engineering, University of California-Berkeley.

Price, B. T., et al, 1970
  TRANSPORTATION SYSTEMS FOR MAJOR ACTIVITY CENTERS, Organization for Economic
  Cooperation and Development, April, Paris.
Project for Public Spaces, Inc. 1982
  DESIGNING EFFECTIVE PEDESTRIAN IMPROVEMENTS IN BUSINESS DISTRICTS, American
  Planning Association, Planning Advisory Service Report No. 368, May.
Pushkarev, B. and Zupan, J. M., 1975
  URBAN SPACE FOR PEDESTRIANS, the MIT Press, Cambridge, Massachusetts.

Regional Plan Association, 1980
  URBAN RAIL IN AMERICA: AN EXPLORATION OF CRITERIA FOR FIXED GUIDEWAY TRANSIT,
  Urban Mass Transportation Administration, Washington, D. C., November, Page 157.

W. V. Rouse & Co., 1980
  GENERIC ALTERNATIVES ANALYSIS: FINAL REPORT, Volume 2, U. S. Department of Transportation, UTMA, June.

Automated People Mover
and Tall Buildings

Murthy V. A. Bondada
Robert J. Dietz

INTRODUCTION

The downtowns of our cities are, simply, clusters of tall buildings. With the advent of innovative structural designs of high-rise buildings, especially since the 1960s, these downtowns have further intensified as tall buildings change the skylines of our central business districts (CBD). Tall buildings with several thousand ft^2 of floor space in each floor form mini-downtowns within these downtowns. The designs of these structures provide efficient, convenient, and esthetic internal pedestrian circulation systems consisting of passageways, ramps, elevators, escalators, atriums, lobbies, and the like. Access or connection to these buildings from various activities of the CBD is of paramount importance in realizing the advantages of the tall buildings. If these external transportation facilities are not efficient and convenient, however well designed the internal circulation systems are, tall buildings will not serve their desired function. In several instances, new and modern tall buildings built in peripheral areas of the downtowns have not realized the expected returns because of the lack of convenient connection to other activities in the CBD.

In a U.S. city of more than one million population, the average size of the downtown area is 1.76 mi^2 (4.51 km^2). The high density core, which is a cluster of the tall buildings, is limited to an average size of 0.45 mi^2 (1.15 km^2), which is about one-fourth of the CBD. New tall buildings in the CBDs are built by replacing the old buildings or using available vacant lots of the CBD. The existing street system, which is already clogged with pedestrians and vehicles, must then accommodate the increased volumes of pedestrian and vehicular traffic.

Parking, a low-return land use, cannot compete for sites with high-rise office, hotel, and retail buildings in the core area and thus often is located on the periphery of the core area. Auto users have to walk long distances from peripheral parking facilities to tall buildings located in the core area. Buses have difficulty penetrating into and moving efficiently through the core area because of congested streets. Pedestrians encounter many traffic lights, and cross streets with heavy vehicular traffic. Thus auto users, bus users, and pedestrians all are subjected to severe inconveniences in accessing buildings in the downtown core.

Efficient circulation systems are needed to interconnect various downtown activities. These external circulation systems, moving people horizontally, must connect to the vertical internal circulation systems of tall buildings to provide convenient, comfortable, safe, and fast travel among CBD activities.

AUTOMATED PEOPLE MOVERS IN DOWNTOWN

Automated People Movers (APM) are the most logical and state-of-the-art external circulation systems in major downtowns with concentrations of tall buildings. The APM is a proven technology in controlled environments such as airports, shopping centers, and zoos. The APM provides the level of service compatible with the internal circulation systems available in modern tall buildings. The APM is a form of transportation in which computer-controlled unmanned vehicles are operated on a fixed guideway along an exclusive right-of-way. Based on system capabilities and vehicle capacities, APMs can be classified in different ways. Such a system's complexity depends on the headway (minimum allowable time or distance between successive vehicles) at which the vehicles can be operated, on the switching capability, and on station configurations (on-line or off-line). Figure 1 shows the existing hardware for people mover systems with revenue experience in the United States.

APMs in downtowns provide convenient transportation among tall buildings and other activities including parking, depending upon the locations of stations. APMs not only save travel time but also can protect riders from inclement weather if stations are integrated with buildings. Trips within the dense downtown can be made without the necessity of long walks or rides in vehicles (auto or bus). APM systems are expected to reduce congestion on downtown streets, especially during the peak travel periods.

Recognizing the importance of APMs as efficient circulation systems and also as catalysts for economic development and renewal of downtowns of major U.S. cities, the Urban Mass Transportation Administration (UMTA) initiated a Downtown People Mover (DPM) demonstration program in 1976. Detroit and Miami are the first U.S. cities to implement their DPMs. The

UNIMOBIL/HABEGGER TYPE II —
Hersheypark,Pennsylvania
(*Universal Mobility,Inc.,1969*)

AIRTRANS—Dallas/Fort Worth
Regional Airport, Texas (*Vought*
Corporation,1974)

WEDway PEOPLE MOVER— Disney
World,Orlando,Florida (*Community*
Transportation Services,1975)

TRANSIT EXPRESSWAY—*Busch*
Gardens,Williamsburg,Virginia
(*Westinghouse Electric Corporation,1975*)

MORGANTOWN PEOPLE MOVER—
West Virginia University
(*Boeing Corporation,1975*)

Fig. 1 Available hardware for people mover system with revenue service experience in the United States

routes of the DPMs were chosen to serve as many activities as possible by connecting with major buildings. To realize the major advantages and maximize patronage, the Detroit and Miami DPMs are being integrated with selected tall buildings, the major trip generators of the downtowns. This paper discusses the integration aspects of APMs with tall buildings through case studies from the two U.S. cities (Detroit and Miami) that are building downtown people movers.

GENERAL GUIDELINES IN INTEGRATING APMs AND TALL BUILDINGS

Structural Integration

Structural integration is clearly the most difficult aspect of integrating an APM into an existing urban center. It is also one of the most important aspects if the APM is to serve effectively as a convenient horizontal transportation mode. Success of APM installation will, to a great extent, depend upon the designers' ability to provide ease of transfer between the horizontal people mover and the major buildings within an urban center. Ideally, such transfer should be accomplished within a totally controlled environment free from the vagaries of the weather.

To date, the best example of such integration of building facilities and APMs has occurred in airports. Here, designers have had the luxury of a self-contained site where all facilities are built simultaneously. Probably the best non-airport example is the Fairlane Development in Dearborn, Michigan. Here, the Ford Motor Company integrated its ACT people mover system within the Fairlane Shopping Center at one end and within the Hyatt Regency Hotel at the other end of a shuttle-track alignment. This demonstrates the potential for direct interface between automated people movers and major buildings. Again, in this instance, both the people mover and the buildings were constructed simultaneously.

When installing people movers within already-developed urban centers as in the current programs in Miami and Detroit, the structural integration issue becomes much more challenging. The ease with which such integration can take place depends upon the type and age of building, and is as follows, going from the easiest to the most difficult:

1. Buildings constructed simultaneously with the APM

2. Recent new buildings, preferably built with future APM connections in mind

3. Recent modern buildings with architecture compatible with current APM guideway designs

4. Older buildings where external architecture and internal structural configuration and HVAC systems create significant challenges to complete integration

5. Historic structures

The real key to structural integration is one of timing. Since APMs are generally publicly funded and major buildings are privately developed, the interface becomes extremely difficult. Once the private portion of a development is designed and funded, the developer must move without delay. Frequently, his schedule will be incompatible with the normal public design and bidding process imposed on the APM. Moreover, because APMs are still in the developmental stage, many private building developers are skeptical of them until the last moment. Once it is finally recognized that the APM will be built, attitudes change significantly. Nevertheless, perhaps the greatest challenge to the designer is not one posed by structural issues but one centered on political and programming issues to coordinate design and construction of such facilities.

Esthetic Integration

Esthetic integration is a major challenge in existing urban centers. The APM guideway often is an imposing structure that must be woven into the fabric of the city. This can only be accomplished through a comprehensive urban design analysis that takes into account not only the route alignment and station locations dictated by service requirements but also the building facades, urban vistas, and similar environmental and esthetic concerns throughout the urban center. Frequently, final guideway and station location — both horizontal and vertical — will be dictated by these environmental and esthetic concerns. Previous design studies identified the specific elevations on the facade of each building through which the guideway passes. Similarly, specific locations for columns were established to match vertical features on building faces.

Esthetic integration at station areas is even more of a challenge. This is particularly true if the station is to be integrated within buildings such as those planned for several locations in Detroit. Each solution is necessarily site specific.

Noise/Vibration

Generally, noise is not a major concern with APMs because of the relatively low speeds (less than 30 mph) and the fact that most systems have demonstrated extremely favorable noise characteristics. A potentially greater concern is vibration isolation, although even this is not usually a major issue because of the low speeds involved. In certain specific instances, isolation of the APM guideway from the adjacent building structure may be required. But this does not represent a significant concern or cost item.

Security

Security is a major concern for both the APM owner and the building owner. While complete integration of a station facility within the building is desirable from a service standpoint, the internal station configuration must provide for operation of the APM even during those hours when the building is normally closed. This frequently means the provision of separate vertical circulation and access directly to street level. Again, each solution is necessarily site-specific, and must be dealt with in the conceptual design phase.

Safety

The major safety concern is protection of normal building occupants and visitors who may be unfamiliar users of automated guideway transportation. A primary concern is one of inadvertent encroachment onto the guideway. Current solutions range from detailed closed circuit television (CCTV) surveillance of the platform and guideway area to complete enclosure of the platform area with elevator-type doors that operate only when a vehicle is in the station. From a building owner's standpoint, platform doors are a major maintenance problem. It is anticipated that high-volume systems such as those now under construction in Detroit and Miami, which are examined later, will operate without platform doors. Partial screens are proposed to limit the amount of platform edge space and to provide a warning to users of the dangers of encroachment on the guideway. Other systems, including most airport installations, use complete enclosure with bi-parting doors. The final decision on how future systems will be configured is still in question.

Integration with Other Transportation Modes

External Modes. It is desirable that the APM be closely coordinated with local bus, regional rail, and other semipublic transportation modes such as taxis. Of particular importance is regional rail integration because of the potential for large numbers of transferring passengers. Such connections are not easy and are frequently a function of the fare collection policy of the operating authorities. (In other words, is free transfer desirable between the regional system and the APM?) Again, solutions are site-specific, as with the integration of the APM and the regional rail systems in Detroit and Miami.

Internal Integration.   Within tall buildings, the APM station must be located to facilitate movement between the other vertical circulation modes of the building. Ideally, the APM should open into a major elevator lobby when speed of circulation is the goal. If the tall building contains a major retail center, it may be most advantageous to funnel APM passengers into the normal circulation systems of the building to increase retail exposure.

CASE STUDY: THE DETROIT CENTRAL AUTOMATED TRANSIT SYSTEM AND RENAISSANCE CENTER

The Detroit Central Automated Transit System (CATS) is a 3.1-mile single-track loop circulating through downtown Detroit. The system is currently planned to have 13 stations. Five of these will be integrated with existing or new buildings. Since the system has a single track, station integration is more straightforward than with a double-track system such as Miami.

The case study under discussion is the integration of the Detroit CATS with the Renaissance Center, which is a major office, hotel, and retail building development on the Detroit riverfront. The Center includes a 70-story circular hotel and six office towers providing over 3 million ft^2 of office space. Extensive commercial development is also included. Figure 2 shows the Detroit Renaissance Center.

Structural Integration

The Renaissance Center has a precast concrete berm structure located on the city side of the complex, which houses all mechanical HVAC equipment. The berm was intended to accept a people mover along the top of the structure at a future date. The current CATS plan calls for the guideway to rest on one of the two berms with approximately 90° turns at both ends. The CATS station will straddle the berm and be connected with one of the office towers by a new pedestrian bridge (Fig. 3). A knockout panel has been provided in the office tower to accommodate this. A thorough analysis of loads imposed upon the berm by the people mover system has indicated some potential problems. The technology selected for Detroit utilizes steel wheels running on steel rail. Welded steel rail generates significant thermal stresses that are translated into both longitudinal and lateral forces on the berm structure. The lateral forces, coupled with soil forces on the berm foundation,

Fig. 2 Renaissance Center, Detroit, Michigan. Architects: John Portman & Assoc.
(Courtesy: Tishman Const. Co.; photo by Win Brunner)

may lead to overstress situations. As a result, structural integration will certainly be more costly than originally anticipated. The designers are currently examining several alternatives for strengthening the berm foundation structure to accept the guideway and the other loads.

Esthetic Integration

Because of the modern, basically precast concrete and glass treatment for the Renaissance Center, the concrete guideway presents no major problems. Similarly, the pedestrian bridge will be identical to another bridge planned to cross an adjacent street at the westernmost office tower.

Noise/Vibration

Because the guideway and station are adjacent to one of the busier downtown streets, it is not anticipated that the CATS will result in any increased noise level for the Renaissance Center.

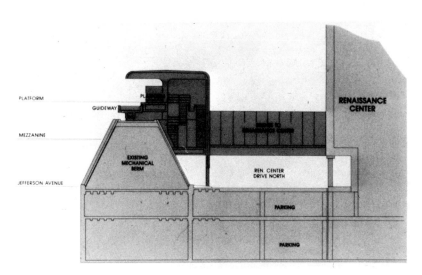

Fig. 3 Renaissance Center Station

Security

Security is a prime consideration with the Renaissance Center. Management of building and system security is facilitated because the station is actually a freestanding structure immediately in front of the office tower. It will, therefore, be possible to isolate the CATS station whenever necessary.

Safety

Because of the high volume of passengers and frequent service of the CATS system, and because of the desire to minimize operating and maintenance costs, the CATS station will not have station platform doors. However, fixed partitions with openings opposite the vehicle door locations will be provided along all station edges together with comprehensive closed-circuit TV surveillance.

Integration with Other Transportation Modes

The Grand Trunk Western Railroad commuter rail station is immediately adjacent to the Renaissance Center. By giving the CATS station a direct connection into the Renaissance Center, it will be possible for commuters to move from the commuter trains to the CATS system using the pedestrian network within the Renaissance Center. This was a prime consideration in the location of the CATS system.

CASE STUDY: THE MIAMI METRO-LOOP AND WORLD TRADE CENTER

The Miami Metro-Loop is a two-mile double-track loop circulating through downtown Miami. The system is planned to have ten stations. The case studied is the integration of the Miami Metro-Loop with the World Trade Center building, shown in Fig. 4. The World Trade Center consists of a 35-story office tower with 600,000 ft^2 of floor area located above an 11-story parking garage with 1,450 spaces. Retail space, access to Metro-Loop and an open-air pedestrian arcade are located at the street level.

Structural Integration

Structural integration of the APM with the World Trade Center became very simple because the building is planned, designed, and presently under construction simultaneously with the guideway and station facility of the Metro-Loop. Both the office tower and the parking garage are reinforced concrete structures. The parking structure consists of ten levels of double-ramp parking with the roof (podium), which is the base of the tower, used as an open garden. The Metro-Loop Station is located on the fourth and fifth levels of the parking garage. An open-air pedestrian arcade at the street level connects the Metro-Loop Station through escalators and an elevator. The parking structure also serves the Miami Convention Center located across Interstate-95. A pedestrian walkway at the arcade level under I-95 off-ramps connects the garage under the World Trade Center with the Miami Convention Center. As a result of the simultaneous design and construction of the APM and the new building, better structural integration is achieved.

Esthetic Integration

The planners of the Miami Metro-Loop selected rubber-tired vehicles running on a concrete guideway. The concrete office tower above the parking structure is clad in alternating horizontal bands of aluminum panel and reflective glass. The modern precast concrete structure of the parking garage esthetically matches the concrete guideway. One track of the guideway is

Fig. 4 Miami World Trade Center *(Courtesy: I. M. Pei Partners/Spillis Candela & Partners; photo by N. Lieberman)*

supported on extended horizontal beams of the garage projecting over the sidewalk. The other track runs through the garage supported by the horizontal beams of the structure (Fig. 5). The station, its access facilities, and its guideway are designed as a part of the total development instead of as a later add-on; this results in good esthetic integration between the APM and the World Trade Center.

Noise/Vibration

Because the guideway and station are within the parking garage and the vehicles are rubber tired, it is not anticipated that the Metro-Loop will result in any increase in noise level for the World Trade Center or any nearby sensitive areas.

Security

Management of building and system security is facilitated because the station serves as a free-standing station attached to the parking garage. The only access to the station is from the pedestrian arcade at the street level. Hence, the Metro-Loop users come to the street level pedestrian arcade then proceed toward the office tower, convention center, or along sidewalks to places nearby.

Safety

Because of the high volume of passengers and frequent service of the Metro-Loop System, and the desire to minimize operating and maintenance costs, as well as to be compatible with the regional rapid transit system under construction, the Metro-Loop Stations will not have station platform doors. A niche under the platform edge provides space for a passenger who has accidentally fallen on the guideway away from the vehicle. The station safety features applicable to the regional rapid transit stations are also being adapted to the Metro-Loop Stations.

Integration with Other Transportation Modes

The location of a station within the 1,450-space parking structure next to the I-95 off-ramps provides an excellent integration with the auto mode. The Government Center Stations of the regional rapid transit and the Metro-Loop

Fig. 5 Extended horizontal beams to support one track and entrance for the other track of the people mover system (under construction)

systems connect to each other, facilitating easy transfers between the two systems. The World Trade Center Station is the second station from the Government Center Station in the counter-clockwise direction of the double-track loop. Thus fast movement between the World Trade Center Station and the regional rapid transit system is available through the transfer at the Government Center Station.

CONCLUSIONS

The integration of APMs and tall buildings is desirable if APM service is to be maximized. Moreover, such integration permits the opportunity for increased rental revenue and retail exposure for building owners. This in turn can be an opportunity for outside income to the authority operating the APM.

The major obstacle to integration of APMs and tall buildings is one of timing credibility. Frequently, building owners refuse to believe that the APM will be constructed and are unwilling to enter into serious discussions. Once the reality of the system is established, there is still hesitancy because there are no precedents for such systems. It is hoped that this situation will improve once the Miami and Detroit installations are operable.

Integration within existing buildings presents numerous structural and architectural challenges. The newer the building, the easier this challenge generally is. But significant obstacles will arise on a site-by-site basis. As evidenced by the Renaissance Center, even new facilities designed with a future people mover in mind may not be compatible with the technology ultimately selected.

The best potential for integration is with totally new buildings that are built simultaneously with the people mover. Unfortunately, timing is frequently an insurmountable obstacle. Developers move very quickly once financing is arranged. Unless the APM program can keep pace, it is not practical to have extensive physical integration.

Renaissance Center, Detroit, USA.

Architects: John Portman & Assoc. *(Courtesy: Tishman Const. Co.; photo by Win Brunner)*

Shared Parking Considerations of Tall Buildings

Richard J. Hocking

Tall buildings represent major concentrations of human activity and correspondingly high levels of trip generation. For a significant number of tall building projects, these person-trips are auto trips that result in the need for parking space. The amount of parking space varies by location as a function of walk-in access and availability of public transportation. The latter needs to be clarified in that while transit services have increased in most urban areas during the past 15 years, and more trips are made by transit, the ability to accommodate the private auto is an essential requirement for the large majority of tall building developments.

In addition to recognizing the continuing importance of parking service, tall buildings generally involve mixed or multiple land-uses. Water Tower Place in Chicago, Illinois is a prime example; it creates a unique parking demand. Each individual land-use or activity within a tall building development has a different parking demand characteristic, measured in terms of the maximum number of spaces needed per unit of land-use and by when the peak needs occur (by time of day, day of week, and season).

The mixed uses could merely be "convenient cohabitants" of a tall building or interactive uses with direct functional relationships. Under either condition, their inclusion in a tall building creates the potential for shared use of parking facilities.

DEFINITION AND BENEFITS

By definition, shared parking is space that can be mutually used by more than one land-use or activity without conflict or encroachment. The underlying objective in identifying shared-use is its specific generation, that is, causing it to happen rather than merely allowing it to happen as in the case of the concept of simple multiple-use of parking. It implies a more rigorous management approach to parking facilities. Because shared use is not intended as a casual activity, it should be institutionalized via the planning process, codes, and regulations.

The benefits of shared parking can be understood in terms of several potentials or opportunities. As such, the benefits are not guaranteed or automatic, but can be realized if appropriate plans, designs, and operations are adopted.

Potential benefits are summarized as follows.

Reduced Project Cost.   Shared parking reduces the amount of space needed. With current capital costs (exclusive of land) of garage space ranging from $4,500 to $7,500 per space, potential reductions of even 10% can produce savings of several million dollars. Furthermore, reduced supply decreases the operating cost. With annual O & M costs of garages in the $150 to $400 (or more) per space range, the present value of reduced space is significant. It is possible that the reduced parking costs could make the difference between a feasible and an infeasible development.

Reallocation of Project Budget.   The reduction of parking cost could be transferred into increased budgets for other elements of tall building projects. This would not include more activity space (i.e., rentable floor area), but could include amenity items or increased construction quality or other special features.

Increased Leasable Space.   If the parking element were sized (and budgeted for) according to traditional demand analysis methods, rather than reducing supply for shared-use reasons, the larger supply level could be used to support more trip generation or more leasable activity space.

Improved Site Plan   This benefit is the most speculative, but reducing the amount of site volume could produce design improvements. This would be most evident in a constrained or small site.

LAND-USE COMBINATIONS

The shared parking concept has varying applications. Opportunities and benefits depend principally on the land-uses involved and the locational situation. Land-use combinations affect parking characteristics associated with time and multiple trip purposes. Location affects the absolute value of peak parking demand factors (for example, high transit availability versus low transit).

Based on a limited survey (Barton-Aschman, 1981) of developers and local planning agencies, the mixed-use projects that are being developed tend to concentrate in the following combinations:

1. Office—hotel.

2. Office—restaurant/entertainment.

3. Office—residential.

4. Regional retail—residential.

5. Regional retail—restaurant/entertainment.

6. Hotel—restaurant/entertainment.

This list identifies only two land-uses in combination, where in fact, projects tend to have combinations of three to five of the individual land-uses listed.

The potential for shared parking exists because of the inherent differences in the activities generated by these land-uses. The key difference is the time when peak parking demands are generated, that is, these times are offset from one another so that the aggregate peak is less than the sum total of individual peaks.

Further, shared parking is possible because of functional relationships between land-uses. Of the five land-uses included in the above list, office, hotel, and residential would be considered basic activities. They generate trips to the area; these trips are normally principal trip purposes for the people involved. Restaurant/entertainment and regional retail can be basic activities but also can be support activities in many cases. For example, shoppers and restaurant patrons are employees in nearby offices or guests in nearby hotels. The extent to which the support relationship exists creates the opportunity for shared parking. Market studies in some downtowns, for example, indicate that at least 20 to 30% of retail customers are downtown employees.

Finally, there are other land-uses or activity combinations that generate shared parking potentials. These are less frequent. Activities include mass public event facilities (arenas, auditoriums, convention centers), theaters, and transportation terminals.

ANALYSIS OF SHARED PARKING POTENTIAL

To describe more specifically the potential of shared parking, the results of various parking surveys have been summarized and applied to a prototypical tall building or mixed-use project. To make this analysis, the parking characteristics of individual land-uses are identified.

Figure 1 illustrates the time pattern for an average weekday for several land-uses. This depicts the usual change in parking demand for individual activities showing the significant offsets. In examining these graphs, two analysis periods would be picked, midday (1:00–2:00 p.m.) and evening (7:00–8:00 p.m.). For these times, the percent of peak parking demand generated is estimated as in Table 1.

Associated with the time accumulation is the actual peak parking demand factor. Table 2 summarizes these factors for two situations, one with low transit service and usage and another with high transit service and usage. The low transit situation is typical of suburban and midtown locations where

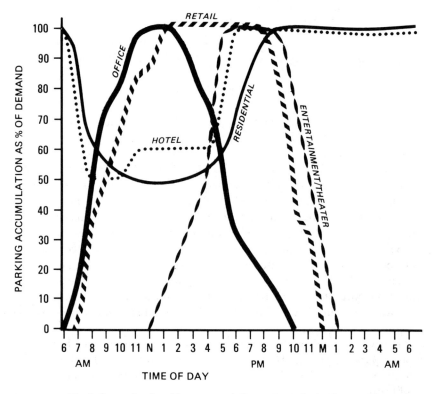

Fig. 1 Generalized parking accumulation patterns by land use

transit use is 10%. The high transit case is typical of the Chicago central area where peak-hour transit use is 80 to 90%.

To show the order of magnitude of shared parking potential, the preceding data has been applied to a prototypical project. The results are as follows.

1. Development program
   500,000 ft^2 office
   1,000 rooms hotel
   10,000 ft^2 restaurant
   1,000 seats movie theatres

2. Low transit situation
   a. Traditional demand method
      Peak parking demand = 3,200 spaces
   b. Shared parking method
      Peak midday = 2,270 spaces
      Peak evening = 2,000 spaces
   c. Potential space reduction
      3,200–2,270 = 930 spaces (29%)

Table 1 Peak parking demand for various kinds of buildings by time of day

	Midday (percentage)	Evening (percentage)
Office	100	10 to 20
Regional retail	100	Up to 80
Hotel	35	100
Restaurant	70	100
Theater	70	100
Residential	85	100

Table 2 Peak parking demand factors

Land-use	Land-use unit	Peak Spaces per land-use unit	
		Low transit	High transit
Office	1,000 ft^2 (GLA)	3.0	0.75
Hotel[a]	Room	1.2	0.5
Restaurant	1,000 ft^2 (GLA)	20.0	6.0
Theater	Seats	0.30[b]	0.20[b]
Regional retail	1,000 ft^2 (GLA)	5.0[b]	1.5[b]

[a] Assumes some restaurant and services included.
[b] These ratios are applicable to weekend day conditions.

3. High transit situation
   a. Traditional demand method
      Peak parking demand = 1,135 spaces
   b. Shared parking method
      Peak midday = 732 spaces
      Peak evening = 835 spaces
   c. Potential space reduction
      1,135–835 = 300 spaces (26%)

The results indicate that space reductions can be significant. The absolute number of spaces used is, of course, greater in those urban areas where transit use is low.

The analysis also indicates that the shared parking potential is sensitive to the relative mix and proportion of land-uses in the project. In order to determine whether specific relationships exist that describe the mix of land-uses, the demand compilation was tested as follows.

Let M be the maximum parking demand using this traditional method; let D be the midday demand using the shared parking concept; let E be the evening demand using the shared parking concept. Then applying the peak factors summarized in Table 2 for low transit cases,

$$M = 3.0(O) + 20.0(R) + 1.2(H) + 0.30(T) \tag{1}$$

$$D = 3.0(O) + 14.0(R) + 0.42(H) \tag{2}$$

$$E = 0.6(O) + 20.0(R) + 1.2(H) + 0.30(T), \tag{3}$$

where (O) is office space, (R) is restaurant space, (H) is hotel rooms, and (T) is theater seats. For high transit cases,

$$M = 0.75(O) + 6.0(R) + 0.5(H) + 0.20(T) \tag{4}$$

$$D = 0.75(O) + 4.2(R) + 0.18(H) \tag{5}$$

$$E = 0.15(O) + 6.0(R) + 0.5(H) + 0.20(T). \tag{6}$$

The reduction in parking space is computed as

$$P_1 = \text{reduced space midday} = M - D \tag{7}$$

$$P_2 = \text{reduced space evening} = M - E. \tag{8}$$

By substituting the terms in the above equations, the resulting relationships are, for low transit cases,

$$P_1 = 6.0(R) + 0.78(H) + 0.30(T) \tag{9}$$

$$P_2 = 2.4(O), \tag{10}$$

and for high transit cases,

$$P_1 = 1.8(R) + 0.32(H) + 0.20(T) \tag{11}$$

$$P_2 = 0.60(O). \tag{12}$$

In the analysis of P_1 and P_2, the governing value is the smaller or lesser of the two. This describes the practical limit expected in reduced parking during the typical day (7:00 a.m. to midnight). Moreover, by making $P_1 = P_2$, the most efficient situation would exist. In this case, the amount of office would be related to the aggregate amount of hotel, restaurant, and theater, so that the space reduction is the same for midday and evening rather than having too much parking for one of these time periods.

Thus, for low transit situations, the relationship is

$$(O) = 2.5(R) + 0.33(H) + 0.13(T), \tag{13}$$

and for high transit situations, it is

$$(O) = 3.0(R) + 0.53(H) + 0.33(T). \tag{14}$$

These relationships can be used to develop programs that maximize shared parking efficiency. It should be noted that these are general equations; specific applications need to be analyzed individually.

The above analysis deals only with time offset factors. As noted earlier, there are other land-use relationships that produce further shared parking effects. If 50% of a restaurant's patrons in midday were office employees in the same mixed-use development, the parking factor would be so discounted in the values summarized in Table 2. The basic-to-support land-use linkages are difficult to document. They are also different for midday versus evening peaks. Much more data is needed before concrete analysis is possible.

OTHER CONSIDERATIONS

Besides the demand or quantitative considerations, shared parking involves important planning and design considerations. These are summarized in the following paragraphs as issues (Gibson and Liddicoat, 1981).

Planning Issues

Compatibility. For shared parking within mixed-use developments to work, it must be recognized that all land-uses do not lend themselves to shared parking. Some land-uses have parking demands that peak at the same time. If developers have this information when they are initially planning a mixed-use development, it might influence the recommended mix of land-uses.

Exclusivity. Even if the land-uses peak at different times, it is probable that some land-uses will demand reserved spaces all day long regardless of their peaking characteristics. If this occurs, obviously the advantages of shared parking are lost. Some examples of exclusive parking demands are reserved spaces for residential dwelling units within a mixed-use development, doctor's reserved parking at hospitals or medical office buildings, VIP or executive parking office or industrial parking areas, and so on.

The determination of shared parking potential requires that a realistic assessment of the actual need for exclusive, reserved parking spaces within a parking facility be made at the outset of the planning.

Location. If the mixed-use development covers a large land area or if the land-uses within that mixed-use development are spread over a wide area, then the location of available spaces becomes important. If the only available spaces to be shared are so remote that the walking distances may be unacceptable for retail customers, then the effectiveness of shared parking will be dramatically reduced.

Shared parking within the mixed-use development may be easy to justify on an accounting or a mathematical basis, but it must be realistic in terms of its practicality if the viability of the entire mixed-use development is to be maintained (Fig. 2).

Local Agency Concerns. Probably the most difficult obstacle to shared parking within a mixed-use development is the local agency zoning ordinance. Most ordinances do not even recognize shared parking as an acceptable planning tool. Approximately 60% of the parking ordinances in the United States do not even define shared parking. Of the 40% that do, most make shared parking an acceptable planning tool only as a variant to their parking ordinance. (Based on a sample of 41 municipalilities in several regions across the U.S., including Chicago, Washington D.C., Houston, Los Angeles, and Minneapolis.)

This means, of course, that every new development must engage in extensive documentation of shared parking potential, and it must do this without any guidelines to the acceptability of those data once presented. Further, the approval of shared parking under a variance procedure puts the developer and the mixed-use development totally at the mercy of the zoning variance board's mood on a particular night. Since this is such a risky business, many developers have either stayed away from mixed-use development or not bothered to take advantage of the potential for shared parking. Over-supply of parking has resulted, along with an increase in construction and operating costs.

The city is typically concerned only that enough parking be provided for each new development so as not to be a burden on the city's transportation and parking system. Because very little research on shared parking is available, cities find it much easier to rely on existing zoning ordinances that treat every land use as a freestanding facility.

Developer Concerns. Developer opinions were gathered from a sample of 34 major development companies located throughout the United States. These reflected experience with mixed-use projects in California, Colorado, Illinois, Indiana, Kansas, Maryland, Massachusetts, Michigan, Minnesota, Missouri, Nebraska, New York, Ohio, Pennsylvania, Texas, Virginia, Wisconsin, and the District of Columbia (Barton-Aschman, 1981).

No developer wants to build more parking than is financially feasible for

Fig. 2 A 900-plus space garage built as part of a downtown shopping mall in Wausau, Wisconsin. Because of its location, this garage has multiple use for shoppers, employees, restaurant patrons, and theater patrons.

his project. Most developers do not want to build more parking supply than they will actually use on-site.

However, there are cases when the developer does not want to be competitive with other projects within his market area. Even when it can be shown that shared parking would work on a particular mixed-use development, some developers are reluctant to provide less parking for a retail facility or for an office building than the competition down the block.

Again, because shared parking within mixed-use developments is a relatively new phenomenon, many developers are reluctant to implement it, because so little documentation exists.

Tenant Concerns. The prospective tenants of a mixed-use development want to be assured that sufficient parking will be available at all times for their employees and customers. Solid documentation of parking usage by hour of the day is needed to convince tenants that adequate parking will be available. Examples of operating, comparable mixed-use developments are needed.

Tenants are also concerned about the desirability and location of parking spaces within the proposed parking facility, and many tenants will want to know about reserved or exclusive parking spaces.

Last, knowledgeable tenants are very concerned about the resulting parking costs (both direct and indirect), and the cost savings associated with shared parking need to be documented and shown to prospective tenants.

Lender Concerns. The financial backers of major mixed-use developments are obviously concerned that enough parking space be provided to make the project successful. Again, a detailed breakdown of parking demand by hour is needed to assure the lenders that sufficient parking is being planned as part of the development.

The lenders, too, will want the proposed parking supply to be compared with that of competitive projects within the development's market area, because their concern is the protection of the leasability of the proposed project.

Operator Concerns. In many shared parking or joint parking plans, one population of parkers from a particular land-use fills the parking spaces during a particular period of the day and then vacates those spaces so that they can be used again by patrons or employees of another land-use within the project. For example, office parkers may use the parking spaces during the day, go home at the end of the afternoon, and the entertainment and restaurant functions within the project generate activity so that the spaces are used again in the evening. From the operator's standpoint, the overlap of these two functions is a key concern: the garages must be operated so as to minimize any problems associated with overlapping peak parking demands.

Design Issues

In addition to planning issues described above, there are a number of design and operational issues that should be considered in the planning of shared parking.

Usage Monitoring.   If the shared parking portion of the parking supply is to function efficiently, the operator must know who is using the parking facility and when. This knowledge of parking use is critical to the determination of parking fees, garage operation, entrance/exit requirements, and so on.

Outside Parkers.   If the on-site project parking supply has been designed only just to accommodate the project demands, then non-project parkers could drastically alter the parking characteristics on-site. If, for example, office workers from the whole area park within the project, then the middday peaking characteristics could be much different from the peaking characteristics of the project itself. Shared parking benefits may, therefore, be lost because of outside parkers. One of the ways to control the usage of the facility by outside parkers is through the fee structure. Outside parkers could be controlled through heavy parking fees, which may require the land-uses within the project to adopt an on-site validation system. If vehicles that do not have business within the project are parked within the project parking area, they would not receive parking validation stickers and, therefore, their parking rates would be very high.

Enforcement.   If shared parking is to be successful, the enforcement of reserved spaces, special zones or areas, loading zones, fire lanes, curb spaces, and so on may be needed.

In some mixed-use developments and even in some large-scale retail developments, customer spaces are protected by closing entire areas of the parking structure or parking lot to employees. This is done by only opening certain parking entrances before the stores are open. Thus, employees coming to the site are forced to park in the employee parking area. A number of urban and suburban shopping centers are forcing their employees to park in the least desirable customer parking spaces through the use of early morning parking controls (in other words, physically chaining off sections of the parking lot or particular floors of parking structures).

Other mixed-use and retail facilities have taken a somewhat softer approach by using different colors of paint striping within the parking lots. Some developments use white spaces for customer parking and yellow space for customer or employee parking. This is relatively easy to enforce because all early morning parkers are assumed to be employees and therefore no white-striped spaces should be filled in the morning.

The key to the operation of these systems is the enforcement of the reserved or special spaces. In Irvine, California, major office developments have actually had to resort to towing vehicles out of reserved spaces. This is obviously more dangerous (from a marketing standpoint) to do with customers than with employees. In most cases, employees know where they are supposed to park and know that they run the risk of having their vehicle towed if they park in the wrong areas.

Design Flexibility. The actual internal design of parking lots and parking structures for mixed-use developments is more important than ever. This is because the parking facility is likely to be used by different types of parkers during different time periods of the day.

If the shared parking facility is intended to serve different land-uses within the mixed-use project, then a number of parking design techniques must be considered. Such items as tandem parking, percentage of compact stalls, and even the size of stalls themselves may be appropriate at one time of day and inappropriate at others. Likewise, the in/out gate control may have to be changed for different types of users—which means that it may have to be changed for different times of the day.

The designers of the parking facility must recognize that different populations will be using the facility at varying times of the day or week. The actual operation of the parking facility will likewise have to reflect these potential fluctuations (Fig. 3).

Fig. 3 The Grand Avenue garage in Milwaukee. Overhead auto ramp connection to an adjoining 500-plus space garage allows the two garages to function as a unit.

IMPLEMENTATION

The concept of shared parking is becoming recognized by the planning and development community. But because it is not standard, the applications are challenging and difficult. A recent survey of over 30 developers indicated that 80% tried shared parking and had problems, while 50% said that parking demand analysis did not recognize shared-use potentials; but 50% again said that there were some incentives to consider shared parking. The same survey contacted 40 local planning agencies; 30% did not permit space reductions due to shared parking, but 60% provided incentives to consider shared parking.

The institutionalizing of the concept is still in the future. More data and research are needed to document and describe shared parking relationships. One such effort has been recently completed by The Urban Land Institute. A detailed survey of nearly 150 development projects across the country was completed. Data has been analyzed in a manner to establish the relationship and set the stage for establishing new standards. The shared parking project has now proceeded into the implementation phase.

REFERENCES/BIBLIOGRAPHY

Barton-Aschman Associates, 1981
     PHASE I-STUDY DESIGN, The Urban Land Institute, Washington, D.C.
Barton-Aschman Associates, 1983
     SHARED PARKING STUDY, The Urban Land Institute, Washington, D.C.

Gibson, P. A. and Liddicoat, N. K., 1981
     SHARED PARKING IN MIXED USE DEVELOPMENTS, Barton-Aschman Associates, April.

Tall Buildings in Central Business Districts: Management of Parking Needs

Raymond H. Ellis
John F. DiRenzo
Edward J. Barber

INTRODUCTION

Policies to manage downtown parking supply and location are receiving renewed attention from many older cities seeking to revitalize their central business districts (CBDs) as well as newer cities that are actively shaping their development. The traditional approach to CBD parking is a zoning require-ment on developers to provide a minimum number of spaces, depending upon the size of the building. However, limitations on the number of automobiles that can be accommodated in a CBD without serious congestion and pollution problems have prompted many cities to manage automobile usage by controlling parking opportunities.

This paper examines the policies adopted by several North American cities to regulate the supply of CBD parking and, in some instances, to direct construction of new spaces to areas on the CBD periphery. Most of the

91

policies reviewed are directed at reducing the total available supply of CBD parking, although several cities are also pursuing programs to increase short-term parking opportunities and reduce long-term parking in the CBD. Efforts to reduce total available parking are most evident in cities where there are viable alternatives to automobile commuting.

DOWNTOWN PARKING POLICES IN SELECTED NORTH AMERICAN CITIES

Several cities in both Canada and the U.S. have implemented parking management policies to manage automobile access to their downtowns. These communities have adopted various zoning and related parking control measures that address their individual circumstances. It became apparent while surveying downtown parking policies that no one approach will be universally successful. Parking is only one aspect of larger transportation management activities. It is necessary to consider other actions the cities described below have taken to understand the context of their parking policies.

In general, the surveyed communities have parking requirements in their zoning ordinances that range from one space per 95 gross m^2 (1,000 gross ft^2) of development to one space per 235 gross m^2 (2,500 gross ft^2) (the net-to-gross ratio is about 0.85). Although zoning ordinances have traditionally specified the minimum amount of parking required, more and more communities are using zoning to set maximum limits and thus control the growth of downtown parking supply. Transit's role in providing downtown access is stressed in communities seeking to limit parking supply, and several cities reported that in well-recognized transit corridors, developers voluntarily built significantly fewer parking spaces than the maximum allowable. Some communities interpreted this as the building industry's willingness to place the transportation burden on the public sector and thereby improve its return on investment. The proportion of the allowable parking spaces provided by a builder was dependent on the characteristics of the individual site; the survey of communities did not produce any conclusive generalizations about how much parking should be provided in a downtown area.

This paper reviews the parking policies in Chicago, Denver, Edmonton, Los Angeles, Montgomery County (Maryland), Portland, Seattle, and St. Paul. Table 1 summarizes the demographic, transportation, economic, and downtown parking characteristics of most of these cities.

Chicago

Chicago responded to its air quality problems by placing a ban on new parking structures in 1975 and creating zoning incentives to reduce parking provided in new buildings. Ten percent reductions in the parking required are permitted for underground parking, buildings with good transit connections, buildings with pedestrianway connections, and buildings located in the CBD. If fewer than 50 spaces are required, the developer need not provide any parking. Experience to date suggests that developers will provide the smallest amount of parking possible. Fifty-story buildings typically have as few as 100 spaces, and some CBD office towers with more than 475 m^2 (500,000 ft^2) are being built with as few as 80 to 100 stalls. With a CBD worktrip transit mode split of 80%, developers apparently are more concerned with avoiding costs than with providing parking.

Denver

Denver does not require any parking in its downtown buildings except in an urban renewal area where there is a one space to 95 m^2 (1000 ft^2) (gross) requirement. (The requirement in the urban renewal area was established in the 1960s when a larger freeway system was envisioned.) What is noteworthy about Denver is the actual rate at which parking is provided in the absence of any requirements. Denver city planning staff cited the examples in Table 2 to support their belief that developers will avoid building parking to the extent possible.

Denver CBD office space increased by 40 percent between 1970 and 1980 to a total of 3.1 million m^2 (33 million ft^2), and is expected to increase to 4.1 million m^2 (44 million ft^2) by 1985. Regional office and retail space has been growing at a slightly faster pace than the Denver CBD. A city official stated that recent CBD constructon shows that parking in or next to buildings is not necessary to encourage development. Of the 60,000 parking spaces in the CBD area, 24,000 spaces are in fringe lots serving long-term parkers. There are 1.5 parking stalls per employee in the CBD area.

Edmonton

Edmonton has linked transportation access to its parking policies. The city's objective is to reduce the growth rate of parking stalls in the CBD and to encourage alternative access modes. Edmonton has enacted an ordinance that requires developers to provide one stall per 95 gross m^2(1,000 gross ft^2) either in the building or within 120 m (400 ft) of the entrance. However, if the building has direct access to a pedestrianway, the requirement is one stall per 185 gross m^2(2,000 gross ft^2). If there is direct access to the light rail transit (LRT) system, the requirement is reduced to one stall per 2300 gross m^2 (25,000 gross ft^2).

Edmonton estimates its 1980 downtown employment at 54,000 and its total CBD parking inventory at 20,136, or an average of one stall per 2.68 employees. The city feels that it has maintained good rapport with the developers, and there is no wide-spread apprehension that these policies will create a parking shortage in the future. Edmonton metropolitan area population grew 12.2% from 1976 to 1980, and the city anticipates 80,000 CBD employees by 1986.

Los Angeles

Los Angeles developed a parking management plan that allows developers

Table 1 Comparison of downtown parking in selected North American cities

City	Regional population	Employment		CBD office space		Total
		Regional	CBD	Total ft^2	Growth	
Denver	1.4 million	N/A	93,000	33 million	11 million additional by 1985	34,000 (CBD core) 60,000 (CBD core fringe)
Edmonton	621,600	N/A	54,000	N/A	N/A	20,100
Portland	1.2 million	575,000	80,000	13.5 million	1 million/ year	38,000
Seattle	21 million	400,000	115,000	19 million	4.5 million additional by 1982	43,700
St. Paul	2.5 million	1.5 million	62,000	8 million	150,000/ year	30,000

to provide transportation alternatives in lieu of parking. The municipal zoning ordinance currently requires one space per 95 m^2 (1,000 ft^2) of development in the CBD, and one space per 46 m^2 (500 ft^2) of development in other parts of the city. Under the adopted parking management plan, developers can reduce their parking construction if they implement an effective transportation alternative to solo commuting.

The adopted parking management plan allows reductions in parking requirements provided (a) the developer provides alternatives to single-occupant automobile commuting (for example, ridesharing promotion); (b) a park-and-ride program is implemented to substitute off-site spaces for on-site requirements; and (c) preferential parking is designated on-site for

Downtown parking supply					
Surface (on-street & (off-street)	Structure	Long-term	Short-term	CBD worktrip mode split (% transit)	Zoning bylaw
36,000 (core and fringe)	24,000 (core and fringe)	N/A	N/A	24	No zoning bylaws governing parking except in an urban renewal area where 1 stall per 1,000 gross ft^2 is required.
N/A	N/A	6,400	13,700	N/A	*Minimum* 1 stall per 1,000 gross ft^2 If direct access to pedway, 1 stall per 2,000 gross ft^2 If direct access to LRT, 1 stall per 2,500 gross ft^2 Must be provided within 400 ft.
N/A	N/A	23,000	15,000	35–40	*Maximum* 1 stall per 1,000 gross ft^2 to 1 stall per 1,429 gross ft^2 depending on proximity to transit spine.
N/A	N/A	N/A	N/A	45	*Maximum* 1 space per 1,500 gross ft^2 for buildings where at least 80% of gross floor area is office space. 1 space per 1,200 gross ft^2 for buildings where less than 80% of gross floor area is office space. Principal use parking structures (i.e., those buildings used for parking only) and surface lots are prohibited.
10,000	20,000	N/A	N/A	35	No zoning bylaws governing parking for office development.

high-occupancy vehicles. The developer is responsible for developing the transportation alternatives.

Performance standards included in contractual agreements between developers and the city are an important part of the adopted plan. These performance requirements are intended to ensure adherence to the agreed-upon contractual agreement and may include on-site monitoring to ascertain that solo driving has been reduced. The city hopes that reducing the costs of providing parking facilities will encourage ridesharing programs operated by developers and employers.

Montgomery County

Montgomery County, Maryland is a suburban area north of Washington, D.C., with a population of approximately 600,000. In response to a deficiency of shopper and employee parking, four parking lot districts were established, corresponding to the county's business areas. These parking lot districts are economically self-sufficient units designed to meet the parking needs of the business areas.

Funding for the districts is provided by an ad valorem parking lot district tax on office and other developments that do not provide the two spaces per 95 m² (1,000 ft²) required by the zoning ordinance. The tax is levied only against the value of the proportion of the building not used for parking. The county feels that the ad valorem ordinance enhances development because it is cheaper for the developer to pay the tax than to build parking. Additional funding for the parking districts is obtained from parking fees, enforcement fines, and income from investments and bond issues.

Most of the long-term parking is provided in off-street facilities, and the short-term parker is served by on-street and off-street facilities. Each parking lot district is designed to be financially self-sufficient. Surplus funds are used for new programs and capital projects.

Table 2 Selected relations between numbers of parking spaces and building size and ratio of parking space to gross size in Denver

Parking spaces	Building size (gross m² (ft²))	Ratio of parking space to gross m² (ft²)
175	74,000 (800,000)	1/425 (4,571)
400	59,000 (630,000)	1/146 (1,575)
600	76,000 (820,000)	1/127 (1,367)
325	39,000 (421,000)	1/120 (1,295)
80	19,000 (205,000)	1/238 (2,563)
100	15,000 (157,000)	1/146 (1,570)
134	60,000 (650,000)	1/451 (4,851)

Portland

In response to Federally mandated clean air requirements, Portland, Oregon implemented coordinated transit and parking policies designed to discourage downtown automobile traffic and promote transit usage. The city is directing high-density development to its main transit corridor and freezing the number of allowable downtown parking spaces at the 1973 level of 38,870 (including on- and off-street parking).

Portland currently has 1.3 million m^2 (13.5 million ft^2) of downtown office space, and the supply of office space is increasing at a rate of about 200 thousand m^2 (two million ft^2) per year. Downtown employment is about 80,000, and Portland has 2.06 employees for each downtown parking space. Of a total of 38,870 parking spaces, approximately 15,000 are short term (the city controls about 10,000 spaces), which reflects the city's policy of promoting short-term parking.

Portland's zoning ordinance sets a maximum limit on allowable parking that ranges from one space per 95 gross m^2 (1,000 gross ft^2) to one space per 133 gross m^2 (1,429 gross ft^2), depending upon the proposed building's proximity to transit. The City Planning Department also reviews each application for its impact on the parking freeze policy and on preservation of the ceiling. To date, the city believes that downtown development has not been deterred by these restrictions. CBD employment has increased by 10,000 since the program was adopted in 1975, and there has been a greater proportional increase in CBD development than in suburban development. The policy has caused no concern to date, apparently due to a doubling of transit ridership and the net contribution of usable spaces to the total allowable number. Parking in surface lots that no longer exist or in on-street spaces lost as a result of traffic improvements is credited to the total allowable supply.

Initially, the parking management program encountered substantial resistance from developers. In a recent review, the city concluded that this resistance has largely dissipated as developers realized that they were being equitably treated and that the reduced parking requirements were saving them money. Developers are apprehensive about what actions the city might take once the ceiling is reached, but they also recognize that the LRT, scheduled to open in 1985, could be an important factor in reducing parking demand. A representative of the Portland Building Owners and Managers Association (BOMA) indicated that Portland's policies were successful so far but that a mechanism for change should be available if these policies do create serious problems in the future.

Portland's experience since adopting a maximum zoning ordinance indicates that most developers provide less than the allowable parking. Outside the transit corridor, the maximum limit is one space per 95 m^2 (1,000 ft^2); however, several buildings have provided one space per 110 m^2 (1,200 ft^2) and one site provided one space per 186 m^2 (2,000 ft^2). On the transit corridor, one example was cited of one space per 186 m² (2,000 ft²), another of one space per 220 m² (2,400 ft²), and a third of no parking at all. Smaller projects farther away from transit, where developers provide the maximum allowable parking, are exceptions to this trend.

Seattle

Like Portland, Seattle adopted parking restrictions in response to Federal clean air requirements. Seattle's zoning ordinance prohibits principal use parking garages (in other words, buildings dedicated to parking only) and parking lots in the downtown core. It also sets a maximum allowable rate of one space per 140 gross m² (1,500 gross ft²) for CBD developments where 80% or more of the gross floor area is office space. The maximum limit for CBD developments with less than 80% office space is one space per 110 gross m² (1,200 gross ft²). The city requires that 30 to 40% of the allowable parking be reserved for carpools and vanpools.

Allowable limits for the area surrounding the office core are one space per 140 gross m² (1,500 gross ft²) where 80% of the gross floor area is office space, and one space per 185 gross m² (2,000 gross ft²) where less than 80% of the gross floor area is for office use. Principal use parking garages and parking lots are allowed in the CBD periphery if the city determines that the additional automobiles attracted to these facilities will not adversely affect the nearby traffic flow or exceed the street capacity. The parking supply in recent developments indicates that parking is actually provided at a rate substantially lower than the amount allowed. Seattle estimates that one space per 230 gross m² (2,500 gross ft²) is actually being provided, and developers are not eager to provide more, for economic reasons. Developers have voiced strenuous objections to the 30 to 40% of parking set aside for carpoolers, however. They argue that this requirement does not reflect actual travel behavior and hurts their competitive position with repect to older buildings that are free of this restriction.

The total CBD parking inventory in Seattle declined from 44,642 spaces in 1976 to 43,264 spaces in 1978, largely because of redevelopment activities and the ban on principal use parking. With CBD employment approximately 114,200, parking averages one space per 2.64 employees. Seattle expects an additional 400 thousand m² (4.5 million ft²) of office development by 1982, for a total of 2.2 million m² (23.6 million ft²).

St. Paul

To promote downtown retail and commercial activity, St. Paul operates a program that allocates over half of CBD parking to short-term use and provides fringe parking for long-term parkers. To achieve these objectives, the city uses pricing, a fringe parking shuttle bus, and its Skywalk system to create an integrated set of parking incentives and disincentives. St. Paul has no parking requirements or limitations in its zoning law.

To encourage short-term parking in the CBD, the city set the following rate structure at city-owned facilities and at private lots participating in the city's program:

$0.25 per ½ hour for the first 3 hours;

rate increases (increment depends upon location) for parking after the first 3 hours, resulting in a total daily rate as high as $8.00/day; and

free parking during evening shopping hours.

Private operators participate on a voluntary basis, and the city reimburses them for their foregone parking fees. These private operators are still allowed to set special long-term rates; only the short-term parking fees are fixed. Several of the short-term parking structures are connected to the Skywalk system (the largest in the U.S.), which St. Paul feels has been well received and well used.

Long-term parking is encouraged in the fringe lots by attractive long-term rates of $1/day or $20/month and by providing free shuttle bus service during peak hours to the CBD at five-minute headways east/west and 10-minute headways north/south. Most of the fringe lots are located on vacant city-owned land. Two private lots are also used as fringe lots, and the city receives $.25 from each dollar collected to help pay for the shuttle bus service. The operations and capital expenses of the entire shuttle bus and parking program are self-sufficient and financed through parking revenues and half the meter receipts.

Developers initially opposed these policies, but opposition has decreased as buildings have been successfully leased (the overall occupancy rate is 93%). There are 62,000 employees and 30,000 total parking spaces in the CBD, for an average ratio of 2.06 employees per stall. The parking supply consists of 20,000 long-term parking spaces and 10,000 short-term spaces. Industry and warehousing are important functions in St. Paul, and office space occupies only 750 thousand m² (8 million ft²) in the downtown area.

PLANNING AND IMPLEMENTING OFF-STREET SUPPLY TACTICS

The types of tactics of particular interest to cities are

changes in zoning requirements for parking (for example, minimum space requirements, maximum space requirements, joint use of parking, reduced requirements for developments near transit facilities);

constraints on the growth in parking supply (for example, ceilings on supply, reductions in parking requirements through high occupancy vehicle (HOV) and transit incentives, restrictions on principal use parking facilities);

preferential parking for HOV's, handicapped, and small vehicles in off-street parking facilities; and

construction and management of peripheral parking to reduce long-term parking demand in the CBD.

The private sector typically builds, owns, and operates most of the off-street parking facilities in activity centers (in other words, CBD's, office parks), although there are notable exceptions. Consequently, the government agencies' role in providing CBD parking is predominantly developing and applying rules and standards regulating the amount, location, and type (for instance, lot or garage) of parking, and the amenities and facilities to be provided to protect public health and welfare (lighting, ventilation, and fire protection).

Assessment of Existing Parking Systems

Some of the off-street supply tactics, particularly those involving parking ceilings, freezes, or major changes in zoning requirements, may generate considerable controversy. There is limited experience with such tactics, and it is difficult to predict accurately the economical, developmental, environmental, and transportational impacts of such tactics.

There is concern in most communities as to how changes in parking policies will affect the economic viability and development potential of activity centers such as the CBD, or major office and retail areas outside the CBD. The viability of such centers is important to a community's tax base and, therefore, proposed government policies affecting such activity centers should be studied carefully and objectively. Consequently, it is important to analyze and evaluate such tactics comprehensively, even if qualitatively, and to address important issues raised by affected interests.

In many jurisdictions where zoning and supply constraint tactics have been implemented, there was and is broad-based community sentiment to reduce traffic congestion, improve transit ridership, reduce air pollution and other undesirable environmental impacts, and promote an economically and culturally strong downtown area.

An essential step in evaluating changes in off-street parking policies (such as zoning changes or freezes) is to determine the characteristics and adequacy of the existing parking system, and the likely characteristics and adequacy of the system in the future, assuming current parking policies. This step should include compiling accurate information on the existing supply, location, type (such as ownership), usage, and prices of parking within activity centers.

Selection of Tactics

Based on the results of the problem assessment, planners should be able to identify changes to existing off-street supply programs or new tactics for promoting activity center development and economic objectives. Table 3 shows the applicability of selected off-street supply tactics to alleviate activity center problems. The advantages and disadvantages of various off-street parking supply tactics are described below and summarized in Table 4.

Minimum and Maximum Parking Requirements

Most communities have zoning codes that specify the number of parking spaces to be provided per unit (for example, 95 m² (1,000 ft²), dwelling unit) and type of development (office, retail, hotel, or industrial). Some communities specify the minimum and others specify the maximum number of spaces required per unit of development. The use of minimums or maximums is important in controlling off-street parking supply. A community that wishes to constrain supply can set maximum (in other words, "build no more than") parking requirements at a low level to achieve this objective. Conversely, if inadequate parking supply is available for certain uses (e.g., retail), minimum (in other words, "build at least") parking space requirements can be set at a high level to promote additional supply.

Aside from specifying parking requirements in terms of minimums and maximums, many jurisdictions should review their parking space zoning requirements in terms of public transit, carpool/vanpool, and other transportation programs designed to increase modal split and vehicle occupancies, particularly for work trips. Zoning requirements can be set to restrict parking supply, which will probably increase the price of parking. Both of these effects may encourage transit ridership, carpooling, and vanpooling. Gasoline availability and price increases may also cause reductions in parking demand over time. Changed parking requirements in a zoning code are likely to have long-term rather than short-term impacts on supply, as such impacts would be felt as new development or redevelopment occurs over time.

Joint Use of Parking Facilities

This tactic is intended to lessen duplication and improve the utilization of existing and new parking facilities. Two or more nearby developments would meet local zoning requirements by constructing fewer total parking spaces (probably in a single facility) than would normally be required if each development were treated separately. Several conditions typically must be met for this tactic to be feasible:

the proposed joint parking facility should be close—say, within 460 m (1,500 ft)—to each participating development;

the time periods during which each development would use the parking facility should not overlap or conflict; and

there should be a legally enforceable agreement between each participating developer to ensure that the parking facility is built and operated in accordance with local zoning requirements.

Table 3 Applicability of off-street supply tactics to selected problems in major activity centers

Tactics Off-street parking supply in activity centers	Provide adequate supply of short term parking

Expand or restrict off-street supply in CBD and activity centers*
  Zoning requirements
    Minimum requirements
    Maximum requirements
    Joint use	

Constrain normal growth in supply
  Maximum ceiling (i.e., freeze) on CBD spaces
  Reduced minimum parking requirements through HOV
    and transit incentives
  Restrict principal use parking facilities	

Construct new lots and garages	×
Change mix of short and long-term parking*	×
Restrict parking before or during selected hours of the day	×

Preferential parking*
  Carpool/vanpool parking
  Handicapped parking
  Small vehicle spaces	

For example, a joint use parking facility may be feasible where theaters or sports arenas, which attract evening and weekend travel, are built near an office development that experiences its peak parking demands on weekdays between 8 a.m. and 6 p.m. The key element of this example is that the temporal distribution of parking demand for these developments not overlap, and consequently, that the parking supply in the joint use facility could serve both developments. This would eliminate the need for a duplicate parking supply.

This tactic provides an incentive to developers to reduce costs associated with meeting municipal parking requirements while allowing the development of more revenue-producing space in their projects. Duplicative parking can eliminate spaces that serve travelers with different temporal parking patterns (daily work-trip parkers vs. evening theater or sports parkers). The land freed by such a tactic can be developed for employment and revenue-producing purposes that benefit citizens and municipalities. Further, the tactic might encourage multipurpose projects, increasing activities during the evening hours in downtown areas oriented toward office buildings.

This tactic has limitations. There are relatively few instances where *no*

Text continued on page 110.

Selected problems				
Provide adequate supply of long term parking	Encourage efficient use of existing supply	Reduce highway congestion in peak periods	Promote economic development	Conserve energy and reduce air pollution
		X	X	X
		X	X	X
	X		X	
		X		X
		X	X	X
		X		X
X	X	X	X	X
		X		X
	X	X		X

Table 4 Characteristics of selected off-street parking management tactics

Tactic	Jurisdiction	Agency	Area
Expand or restrict supply in CBD and activity centers			
Zoning requirements			
Maximum and no minimum parking requirements	Portland, Ore.	Planning commission	CBD
	San Francisco	City Planning commission	CBD
	Seattle	Department of buildings	CBD
Joint use	Los Angeles	Planning commission	Entire city
	Montgomery County, Md.	Division of parking	Suburban CBD
	Portland	Planning comission	CBD
Constrain normal growth in supply	Palo Alto	Department of planning and community environment	Entire city
Maximum ceiling (i.e., freeze) on CBD supply	Boston	Boston air pollution control commission	CBD

Operating characteristics	Compliance	Impacts
No minimum required parking Maximum allowed parking for retail or office development is 1 space per 1,000 ft^2	Development review process	This action in conjunction with other tactics has resulted in 1 space per 1350 ft^2 being provided for new developments
No minimum required parking Limits parking to 7% of the gross floor area	Development review process	Moderate growth in private off-street parking has occurred in contrast to high growth in downtown office and retail space
No minimum required parking Depending on the zone and utilization. Maximum allowed parking ranges from 1 space per 1,000 ft^2 to 1 space per 2,000 ft^2	EIS review	Parking supply is growing in areas further from the retail core and decreasing closer in.
Would allow developments within 1500 ft. to share parking if demand patterns do not conflict	Land covenant Performance bond	Proposed action
Spaces rented by local college for use by students	Parking patrol checks for valid stickers	Student parking impacts have been reduced
City has agreed to increase number of short-term spaces in city garage if developer reduces number of off-street spaces provided Code allows developers to share parking	Development review process	Development under construction
Allows reduction of up to 20% for developers without conflicting demand patterns	Development review process	
Limit on the total number of allowable commercial spaces. Freeze does not apply to free employee and customer parking	Development review process	Development has not been hindered

(continued)

Table 4 Characteristics of selected off-street parking management tactics

Tactic	Jurisdiction	Agency	Area
	Portland	Planning commission	CBD
Reduced minimum parking requirements through HOV and transit incentives	Arlington, Va.	Zoning administration	Entire county
	Chicago	Zoning administration	CBD
	Los Angeles	Planning commission	Entire city
	Palo Alto	Department of planning and community environment	Entire city
Restrict principal use parking facilities	Chicago	Zoning administration	CBD
	San Francisco	Planning commission	CBD
	Seattle	Department of buildings	CBD

Operating characteristics	Compliance	Impacts
Limit on the total number of allowable parking spaces by sector	Development review process	Ceiling has not been reached. Tactic has encouraged parking in desired sectors. Development has not been hindered.
Developers located near rail rapid transit station may provide approximately 70% of required parking	Development review process	Should reduce commuter parking impacts
Required parking is reduced if developer meets certain conditions concerning transit stations	Development review process	There are 1000 fewer spaces in CBD since 1975 A 110 story building (Sears Tower) constructed with 150 spaces
Parking requirements would be reduced if developer provides HOV and transit incentives Developer would be allowed to substitute on-site spaces for off-site park-and-ride spaces Developer would be able to reduce required parking by 1.5 space for each space reserved for HOV's	Land covenant Development review process Developer would contribute monies for park-and-ride facility development and transit shuttle services	Proposed actions
Allows up to 20% reduction in required parking if transit and HOV incentives are employed	Development review process Legal agreements	Several new developments have agreed to institute HOV incentives
Prohibits construction of principal use parking facilities	Development review process	The number of parking spaces has decreased by 1,000 since 1975 Number of long-term parkers has increased
New principal use parking facilities require conditional use review	Development review process	
New parking lots are prohibited. New parking structures are prohibited in most of CBD.	Development review process	No new principal use facilities have been built since 1976. Economics is a major factor.

(continued)

Table 4 Characteristics of selected off-street parking management tactics

Tactic	Jurisdiction	Agency	Area
Construct new municipally owned parking facilities			
CBD	Baltimore	Baltimore City	CBD
	Montgomery County, Md.	Division of parking	Suburban CBD's
	Portland, Ore.	Downtown development commission	Retail core of CBD
Neighborhood shopping districts	Los Angeles	City DOT	Various neighbor-hoods
	San Francisco	Parking Authority	Various Neighbor-hoods
Carpool/vanpool preferential parking	Alexandria, Va.	Alexandria	CBD
	Los Angeles	City of Los Angeles	At city facilities
	Montgomery County, Md.	Division of parking	Suburban CBD's
	San Francisco	California DOT	Fringe of CBD

Operating characteristics	Compliance	Impacts
New facilities for tourists and shoppers are in capital improvement plan	Not applicable	Facilities are planned and under construction
New parking structures have been constructed to meet long-term and short-term demand	Not applicable	Employers and shoppers are encouraged to work and shop in these suburban CBD's
Recently completed 492 space garage with a 752 space garage under construction. Designed for short-term use only 60¢ per hour, merchant stamp program	Not applicable	Merchants pleased by increased supply of short-term parking
Over 7000 spaces in over 100 facilities have been provided	Not applicable	Program has increased attractiveness of shopping districts
Began program to increase the number of available short-term spaces	Not applicable	Merchants are supportive. Made less impact on surrounding neighborhoods
Reserves spaces for city employee carpools of 3 or more persons City vehicles are also available to carpools	Applications are cross checked	15 pools in program
Free reserved spaces are proposed for city employees	——	Proposed action
55 spaces are reserved for carpools of 3 or more. Cost is $16 per month versus normal fee of $24 per month.	Vehicles must arrive with 3 or more occupants	There are 48 pools in the program
40% of under freeway lots are reserved for vanpools Fee is $10 per month versus normal fee of $60 per month	Vanpools are certified	Program begun (1979)

(continued)

Table 4 Characteristics of selected off-street parking management tactics

Tactic	Jurisdiction	Agency	Area
	Seattle	Commuter pool	CBD and fringe of CBD

conflicts exist in the parking hours for two or more developments. The developments must be in close proximity; otherwise the long walking distance to one or both developments will inconvenience parkers. Enforcement of the joint use agreement through a land covenant or performance bond may discourage the execution of such an agreement. This tactic can be implemented by revising the zoning code. However, to be effective, considerable care must be exercised in defining the criteria for joint use, and in specifying the legal and financial mechanisms that developers must follow to enforce the agreement over time. If either or both of these items are perceived by developers and others as too rigid, this tactic may not be used.

Ceiling and Freeze on Parking Supply

Ceilings and freezes are major actions taken to control parking supply. A ceiling sets an upper limit on the parking supply within a geographic area, a limit equal to or larger than the existing parking supply. Conversely, a parking freeze limits the future parking supply in a geographic area to the number of spaces available at the time the freeze is put into effect.

There are several significant factors that must be considered in planning and implementing a ceiling or freeze on parking: the types of parking covered; the geographic area affected; provisions for reviewing and approving proposed parking facilities; and provisions for "banking" parking supply converted to other uses.

Reduce Parking Requirements through HOV and Transit Incentives

This tactic aims to reduce vehicular travel to, and congestion in, major activity centers by encouraging travelers to park at remote locations and use carpools, vanpools, and transit to reach their place of employment. This tactic differs from conventional park-and-ride tactics in several important respects. A municipality would construct park-and-ride facilities in suburban parts of the municipality. The municipality would then encourage developers

Operating characteristics	Compliance	Impacts
219 spaces under a freeway are reserved for 3+ carpools at $5 per month 1,000 spaces in stadium lot are available to poolers of of 3+ for free	Carpools must be certified and are audited	Freeway lot is full Stadium lot has low utilization 40% of carpoolers formerly used transit

and employers to purchase such spaces as an alternative to building spaces within major activity centers. The charge to the developers and employers would be the unit development cost per space to acquire the remote parking supply. Regulations governing this tactic should be documented in a municipality's zoning code.

The participating developers and employers would be required to support transportation services (carpools, vanpools, or public transit) to link the lots with the place of employment. To ensure that these links are provided, it may be necessary to require performance bonds or execute covenants on the property in question.

Providing remote parking for transit, carpools, and vanpools would promote HOV travel, particularly among single occupant auto drivers, and thus could reduce congestion. The developer can use more of his project for office, retail, or other purposes, which could increase the project's profitability. Developers will also save capital costs for constructing parking facilities.

Care must be taken in selecting sites for such park-and-ride lots, in operating the lots, and in supporting transit services. It will be necessary to locate lots where they will serve employees of the specific firms that have purchased park-and-ride lot spaces. These commuting patterns may change over time. Therefore, facilities must be located where a stable market of employees is likely to be found.

Keys to developer/employer participation in this type of effort will include

the role of and cost to the developer/employer in promoting and finan-cially supporting carpool, vanpool, and transit service programs;

the type of legal agreements (for example, performance bonds, land covenants) required by the municipality;

the savings in parking facility capital costs to the developer; and

the ease of leasing space under the provisions of the parking substitution program.

These are difficult issues, but they are critical to the overall success of the project.

It is a particularly important municipal responsibility to develop timely and cost-effective park-and-ride facilities that can be acquired by the private sector. If the planning and construction of such spaces are not coordinated with private sector schedules, the results of this tactic may be jeopardized. Municipal staff, capital, and operating budgets will have to be structured to meet this need.

Restrict Principal Use Parking Facilities

A number of cities, such as Chicago, San Francisco, and Seattle, have restricted the development of principal use parking facilities. Both Chicago and Seattle have prohibited the development of principal use parking facilities in all or most of their CBDs. In San Francisco, proposed new principal use parking facilities must undergo a conditional use review.

These restrictions are generally intended to restrict growth in parking supply, especially parking that is not part of a development project within these cities.

It should be noted that this tactic may not be applicable in many jurisdictions with inadequate parking or in those that rely heavily on the private parking industry to build and operate such facilities.

Preferential Parking

Considerable interest has been generated in providing preferential parking in off-street parking facilities to promote certain social, energy conservation, and other objectives. Reserving convenient parking spaces for the handicapped is a practice that is increasing in many parts of the country. Government and private employers are increasingly providing preferential parking for carpools and vanpools, a practice that readily complements carpool and vanpool programs sponsored by such employers.

There is little evidence, however, that the private parking industry has implemented preferential parking tactics for carpools and vanpools. Several factors may contribute to this. Reserving spaces for carpools and vanpools may cause a loss in revenue if the spaces are not fully utilized, and such spaces may require rules to identify carpools and additional supervision. These types of problems are likely to be overcome through proper coordination between the public sector and the private parking industry.

CONSIDERATIONS IN APPLYING OFF-STREET SUPPLY TACTICS

Several factors should be considered in using off-street parking supply management tactics. First, parking management tactics can be effective in alleviating some but not all transportation problems either within individual municipalities or across an urban area. Such tactics frequently should be planned and implemented in conjunction with other transportation system management (TSM) tactics to help achieve local, regional, and national transportation, energy, economic, and environmental objectives. It should be noted that parking management tactics are not limited to actions restricting passenger vehicles. Rather, they include many actions intended for the more effective use of roadway capacity, management of parking supply, and/or encouragement of the economic growth of activity centers while promoting transportation, environmental concerns, energy conservation, and other community objectives.

Second, parking management tactics can frequently be implemented quickly and inexpensively, which is important to local governments. Many of the on-street, off-street, pricing, marketing, and enforcement tactics involve developing new ordinances (such as, zoning or enforcement), or modifying existing ordinances, and do not entail large increases in staffing or costs.

Third, parking management tactics are frequently planned, implemented, and operated by local governments, transit authorities, and/or state departments of transportation. In many situations, local governments are the lead agencies because of the highly localized and often politically sensitive impacts of such measures. Nevertheless, it is important that such planning be supportive of both the transportation improvement program (TIP) of the affected metropolitan planning organization (MPO), and adopted regional transportation plans and policies. MPOs can and do play an important role in identifying and promoting the use of parking management tactics and programs to encourage the urban area's goals and objectives.

Fourth, the highly localized and potentially significant nature of the impacts associated with many tactics makes it extremely important (1) to encourage business, residential, governmental, and other interests to participate in planning such tactics; and (2) to use accurate, current data on parking demand and supply for the study area in question. If either of these items is neglected, the credibility of the recommended parking management program may be jeopardized. Another potentially serious constraint in planning and implementing parking management tactics is institutional conflict between various local, regional, and State agencies. These conflicts are common and should be accounted for in planning, implementing, and operating parking management measures.

Fifth, a frequently overlooked but critical element affecting the successful operation of parking management tactics is having an effective parking enforcement program. On-street parking tactics require strict enforcement if they are to be successful.

Sixth, although this paper has endeavored to present "best current practice," it does have several limitations. Most importantly, the suggested procedures and practices should be tailored to the needs and problems of each urban area or municipality. Without this tailoring, strict adherence to the procedures described may undermine the success of the parking management program.

ACKNOWLEDGEMENTS

This paper is based in part on studies undertaken by Peat, Marwick, Mitchell & Co. for the City of Calgary and for the Federal Highway Administration under Contract No. DOT-FH-11-9537. The authors gratefully acknowledge the constructive comments provided by Messrs. Dan Bolger and Malcolm Brown of the City of Calgary and Wayne Berman of the Federal Highway Administration. Any errors or omissions are, of course, the sole responsibility of the authors.

REFERENCES/BIBLIOGRAPHY

DiRenzo, J.F., Cima, B., and Barber E., 1981
STUDY OF PARKING MANAGEMENT TACTICS, prepared by Peat, Marwick, Mitchell & Co., for the Federal Highway Administration, Washington, D.C. (Volume 3).
DiRenzo, J.F., Cima, B., and Barber E., 1980
STUDY OF PARKING MANAGEMENT TACTICS, prepared by Peat, Marwick, Mitchell & Co., for the Federal Highway Administration, Washington, D.C. (Volume 1 and 2).

Peat, Marwick, Mitchell & Co., 1981
PARKING POLICIES FOR DOWNTOWN CALGARY, prepared for the City of Calgary, Washington, D.C., June.

Response of the Elderly and Handicapped to Living in a Barrier-Free Tall Building

Gilda Moss Haber

INTRODUCTION

The number of elderly people (aged 65 and over) in the U.S. and in the other advanced countries (North America, Japan, Europe, Australia, New Zealand, and the Soviet Union) is rapidly and dramatically increasing. In 1960 the total population of these countries was 944,937,000. The number of people 65 and over was 80,249,000, which constituted 8.5% of the population. In 1975 the total population in the advanced countries was 1.1 billion, of whom 128,631,000, or 11.3%, were aged 65 and over. In 2000 we expect the total population of the advanced countries to be 1.3 billion, of whom 167,193,000, or 13.2%, will be 65 and over. Between 1960 and 2000 there will be an increase of 86,884,000 of people aged 65 and over (Ross, 1982).

This phenomenon of the rapid growth of the elderly is not limited to the more developed countries. Because of the spread of improved public health measures and medicine, the age span of those in the underdeveloped countries, or the Third World, is also increasing. In 1960 the total population of the Third World was 2,081,598,000, and that of the population aged 65 and over was 77,591,000, or 3.7% of the total population. In 1980 the total population of the Third World was 3,284,341,000, and that of those aged 65 and over was 128,913,000, or 3.9% of the population. In 2000 the total population of the Third World is expected to be 4,927,045,000, and that of those aged 65 and over, 228,732,000, or 4.6% of the population.

The increase of those aged 65 and over between 1960 and 2000 in the underdeveloped countries will be 151,141,000. When this is added to the increase over the same time period in the developed countries, there will be 238,025,000 more people aged 65 and over in 2000 than there were in 1960. These figures were derived by compilation from a United Nations report on population (1980) and from Soldo (1980).

In the developed countries, meanwhile, the younger age groups are decreasing, with a similar change expected later on in the Third World. People are having fewer children and living longer. All this leaves an ever increasing population aged 65 and over.

Formerly, the elderly lived with married children or vice versa, or alone in their own homes. Family patterns in the developed countries have changed to an emphasis on the nuclear family composed of only two parents. Often only one parent and the one or two children of a previous marriage make up the nuclear family, because of increasing divorce rates.

If the elderly are left alone in apartments or houses it may be too expensive or too much work for them to manage alone. Stairs often become a problem. But it is not necessary for most of the elderly to live in institutions, as about 95% of them are able to live fairly independently and want to do so, in the American tradition of independence.

Given the increase in the number of aged and the trend away from their being housed with family or in institutions, what are some of the ways in which this burgeoning population can be successfully housed?

In this time of spiraling inflation in land and building costs, the answer has been found, in more and more instances, in the use of high-rise apartment houses suited particularly and built especially for the aged and handicapped. This arrangement, with some minor modifications in design, promises to be one of the most successful solutions to the veritable population explosion among the over-65 population of the world.

PAST LITERATURE

Nahemow, Lawton, and Howell (1977) observe that there are now many multistory units for the elderly in a number of countries, but that there has been almost no research on the performance of tall buildings for the elderly and handicapped. (In using the term "tall buildings," we are referring to the definition used by the *Standard Building Code*, namely buildings of seven stories and over, the height beyond which firefighters cannot easily reach

(Southern Building Code Congress International, 1982). A computer search for literature in this field confirmed this, as virtually nothing has been found written on the subject since 1976. However, a summary of such literature as does exist follows. Research on the elderly's use of tall buildings has been used as a basis for the present study on Revitz House.

Sommer (1970) notes that the elderly are usually retired and have much time on their hands. Therefore attention should be paid, in building design, to spaces for their social life.

About 85% of the elderly are widows living alone. Studies show (McBride, 1961) that women are more gregarious than men, accentuating the need for socializing space among them.

Pastalan et al. (1970) and, independently, Newman (1973) observed that tall buildings work well for the elderly provided they are separated clearly from children and juveniles. Smaller children often irritate the elderly, although they may make exception for their own grandchildren. Newman (1973) and Haber (1980b) both found that where juveniles live near the elderly, they tend to prey on the elderly, robbing them of money and often knocking them down.

Haber (1976) found that those who had had experience living in tall buildings, or working in them, were more accepting of tall buildings than those who had not had these experiences. Thus Haber (1980b) found that the younger and more educated among the elderly accepted tall buildings more than the older (over 81) residents.

Newman (1973) found that the elderly living in tall buildings often had fears for their safety. He suggests design considerations for improving their safety.

Haber (1980b) found that the elderly and handicapped often had difficulty in walking, or problems with teenagers, or problems with getting on and off buses. Hence shopping was problematic for them. Many requested, therefore, a small shop within the building stocked with staples. This idea, however, contradicted the theory of some designers for the aged, who purposely placed some facilities such mailboxes *outside* the building to encourage the elderly to go outside.

The problem of transportation for the elderly remains, since it is often too hard for them to get into normal buses, and most have either never driven or no longer drive. Economics may also be a factor in their not having a car, since many elderly people live on reduced incomes.

PROFILE OF REVITZ HOUSE

The present study deals with a Maryland suburban apartment house, four years old, a brick construction 11 stories high, built for the express purpose of housing the elderly and handicapped. There were 250 residents in four types of apartments: single, single handicapped, double for married couples, and double handicapped for handicapped couples. Residents paid according to their means, the top rent being $650 a month. This included a hot meal at dinnertime each day. The building was Federally subsidized by the U.S. Department of Housing and Urban Development under Section 236 dealing with housing for families and the handicapped. It was administered by a board of directors composed of volunteers from the area. The building was located in a beautiful suburban setting overlooking rolling green fields yet with shopping centers nearby. The building was also located near a community center which offered instruction in crafts, a theater, concerts, an art gallery, a library, and other recreation.

The handicapped apartments were designed for wheelchair residents, even though not all handicapped occupants were wheelchair cases. Sinks, lights, and cupboards were all low, within the reach of wheelchair occupants. There were bars around the commodes and shower nozzles were hand held. All apartments, for the nonhandicapped and the handicapped, had emergency pulls next to the bed, connecting to the front desk. Residents hung white cards outside their doors to indicate when they were in. If such a card was not withdrawn in the day, a staff member would check on the occupant to see if he or she needed help.

The average age of the residents was 81. However, those who answered the questionnaire were often younger, since the sample was composed of 63% "younger" (65–80) and 37% "older" (those 81 and over). Nineteen percent of the sample were men and 81% were women. Fifty-three percent of the men and 31% of the women had handicaps, according to their answers to the questionnaire. The men's handicaps were largely those of the heart, hearing and vision; those of the women had usually to do with walking. Since many of the women were older, it would appear that there is a relationship between age and ambulatory difficulties. This affected their access to the outside world.

Seventy-two percent of the sample was widowed, 17% still married and living with their spouses, 9% had never married and, like the widowed, lived alone. Sixty-two percent of the sample had high school educations, 38% had some college, a college degree or postgraduate training. Eighty-five percent of the residents typified themselves as middle class. Thus they fairly well represented the average Americans of their age group.

METHOD

This building was selected because it seemed to house an average elderly population, and because the management and staff were cooperative and helpful in arranging for the survey. Residents were asked to participate in a study on living in tall buildings. Many residents did not think of Revitz house as a tall building, and asked staff and the author what tall buildings had to do with them.

On the designated evening the author arrived with refreshments, crucial to the participation of the group, and about 50 people arrived and filled out the questionnaire after the purpose of the study was explained to them. Some needed help due to visual or other handicaps. The apartment numbers of those who came to the meeting were listed, and after the end of the meeting, the remaining questionnaires were distributed under the doors of those who had not attended the meeting. They were asked to return their questionnaires to the front office and informed that the author would return in a week to answer questions or give help where needed. Another 42 persons left filled questionnaires at the front desk, and when the author returned for the promised visit, another eight questionnaires were filled out. This led to a total of exactly 100. The staff indicated that this was a very good response for these residents.

FINDINGS

In the main, residents were very happy with the building. Over 80% responded positively when asked a series of questions as to whether they liked or did not like various features of the building, such as its location, environment, height, the floor they were on, the lobby and cafeteria, their own apartments, and whether they thought the building was safe or offered them enough quiet and privacy.

More women responded favorably than men, and the handicapped and older residents were even more satisfied than younger people and the nonhandicapped. While women liked the esthetic aspects of the building more often, such as the scenery around the building, more men than women approved of practical things like the quiet and privacy of the building. This is in line with an earlier study by Haber (1976) where men, responding to the question, "what do you like or dislike about this room," answered mainly that they liked the comfortable chairs and the fact that the shades could be drawn to darken the room for movies. The women of the group, like the women at Revitz House, responded to esthetics of the room, the color or the elegant design of the furniture. In other words, the women of both studies are interested in esthetics and pleasing appearance. The men, more pragmatic, want performance and the provision of creature comforts.

When the sample at Revitz House was asked what they thought of tall buildings, whether they liked them or not, 33% said they liked tall buildings, 67% that they did not, although later the majority said that they were quite happy living at Revitz House. As we noted earlier, many did not see Revitz House as a tall building. When asked, 66% agreed that tall buildings were good for apartments and 93% that they were good for office buildings. It should be taken into account that this group of people grew up around the turn of the century when there were very few tall buildings such as we know them today. It is to be expected, then, that they are more conservative toward tall buildings than younger people. As remarked earlier, Haber (1980b) found the younger members of this elderly sample, and those more educated, to be more accepting of tall buildings than the older and less educated residents of the study. We can expect, then, an increasing acceptance of tall buildings by the future elderly who, like most of us, have grown up among tall buildings.

When asked whether tall buildings were good for the elderly, 75% of the Revitz House sample said that they were, and 59% agreed that they were good for the handicapped.

There were some objections by a number of residents to sharing the building with the handicapped. The response may be due to the idea among many older citizens and the handicapped that one needs to be near to the ground floor in case of any emergency. In cases where evacuation of the elderly and handicapped has been urgent, however, Haber (1978, 1980a) found that "horizontal evacuation," namely staying on the same floor as the fire, behind a solid door, worked as well or better than evacuating people through smoke filled areas to go to lower floors or outside. All those in one large fire in a nursing home who stayed behind their doors right next to the fire survived, while those who wandered out into the corridor to go downstairs were overcome by smoke and perished. Admittedly, the concept of horizontal evacuation is difficult to explain and accept for frightened people, surrounded by smoke and fire. Ideally it should be done *before* any emergency, but is rarely done for fear of frightening residents about possible fires.

Neighborhood

Revitz House is set in a beautiful suburban environment with a view of rolling green grass from most of the windows of the building. Many residents expressed gratitude at being able to live in such a setting. Apparently it conformed to their first choice of neighborhood. Although most residents of Revitz House had grown up in the city, 80% of them chose the suburbs over a rural area, a small town, or a city, as their first choice. This choice, however, might have been due to their satisfaction in living at Revitz House in its suburban setting.

Although Revitz House is in a suburb, it is nevertheless near a community house having many activities for the elderly in addition to those provided by Revitz House itself. The choice of site was also motivated by the fact that many of the married children of Revitz House lived within commuting distance of it. Thus residents of the house could live independently yet still be in touch with their families.

The residents were also asked, to check on Newman's idea that the elderly wanted to be separated from children, whether they preferred to live with people their own age only, with adults of mixed ages, or with adults and children. Fifty-three percent chose to live with adults of mixed ages, although 24% wanted to live where there were children. The other 20% wanted to live with people of their own age only. Thus Newman's concept seems to be borne out, since 77% of the residents wanted to live with people of different ages. Of those who selected living with children, we do not know how many were thinking solely of their own grandchildren.

Building Height and Floor Height

In response to the question, "Do you like tall buildings?" 33% answered positively and 67% negatively. However, 85% said they either liked living in Revitz House very much, or that it was O.K. Apparently they feared the idea of tall buildings, but liked living in their building, which they did not consider a tall building. In dealing with the elderly and handicapped, who have little experience in tall buildings, we might want to choose another term for a tall building that would convey excellence and prestige rather than height.

Further corroboration of the idea that the residents were comfortable in a tall building, without recognizing that it was a tall building, came from the fact that 70% were satisfied with the floor they were on. A sizeable number of these came from people on upper-level floors and were among those who had said they did not like tall buildings. Twenty-four percent wanted to move to a lower floor. However, this was not only due to a fear of height. Among these were some handicapped who preferred to be lower, and some wanted to be on lower floors for a religious reason: they were orthodox Jews, to whom it was forbidden to ride in any vehicle, including elevators, on the Sabbath; hence their desire to be able to get downstairs on foot.

A phenomenon noted by Newman (1973), and found in about 20% of our responses, was the expressed wish of some respondents that the handicapped be housed on lower floors. This was less a concern for their welfare than because some elderly found that seeing the handicapped was "depressing" for them, and they wanted the handicapped segregated from the rest of the residents. This brings up ethical considerations as well as practical ones. Segregating the handicapped, even though it might be advantageous to them, is a little like the Jim Crow laws, which segregated Blacks from Whites. Furthermore, the handicapped were among those most pleased with the existing arrangements in the building. Should the nonhandicapped be spared "depressing" sights, such as people in wheelchairs, people with walkers, and the deaf and blind? As far as we know, no one has discussed this problem or consulted the handicapped concerning their attitudes to the proposition of segregating them; but one can hardly expect them to like the idea.

Security

Newman (1973) found that the elderly in tall buidings often did not feel safe, but we did not at all find this to be the case at Revitz House. Eighty-five percent of the respondents said that they felt safe (from interlopers) in the building. This was possible for three suggested reasons. (a) The stairway between the lobby and the lower level, where the dining room was situated, was not open to the public or even to residents except when the staff opened it. This reduced the possibility of interlopers entering the building. (b) There was always a security guard on duty from 5 p.m. to 8 a.m., seven days a week. (c) The building was in a low crime area. And as already observed, there was no harassment from teenagers, because there was no high school in the neighborhood.

Elevators

In this, as in earlier studies on tall buildings by Haber (1977, 1980b), elevators were a sore point for residents of tall buildings. In bad neighborhoods they are often the sites of crime. In good neighborhoods they are simply frustrating. According to the residents of the three studies, there are never enough elevators except in the high-rises occupied by people with high incomes and therefore presumably in well maintained buildings. In buildings occupied by lower income people, as the 1977 study showed, there are vociferous complaints about the elevators. Such elevators as there are in buildings occupied by lower income people are always "breaking down" or "too slow" or "too crowded." The complaints at Revitz House included all these. Two small elevators were not enough for 250 people, particularly when everyone had to use them to get to the dining hall in the basement, or when they were using the room for a social activity.

A further complaint of some residents was that the handicapped slowed the elevator by taking a long time to get in and out, and that they increased the crowding of the elevator with wheelchairs and walkers. The healthy aged often asked for a separate elevator to be used for the ill and the dead, so that they might not be brought through the public areas of the building. Again we must ask whether it is legitimate to ask that distressing sights be confined to private areas. This separate elevator, however, was also recommended for moving furniture so that normal passengers would not be held up for long periods.

Meeting Places: The Lobby and the Social Hall

As Sommer (1970) observed, since the elderly are retired, they have plenty of time and interest in social life, particularly the women. Thus the building for the elderly should provide adequate socializing areas. Two such areas are the lobby and the social hall.

The lobby was approved of by 86% of the respondents, more so by the elderly over 81 than by the younger residents. This is probably because the older residents are less mobile (most of the women's handicaps were ambulatory), they get out less often, and therefore they rely more on meeting people in the building for their social contacts. The lobby was often used by people as a place to meet by those who did not invite people to their apartments, because a host would normally be expected to serve refreshments to visitors in his apartment. This might be a strain on a host's budget. Furthermore, meeting in the lobby reduced housekeeping, both in preparing and in cleaning up after refreshments had been served. Thus the lobby was an important meeting place.

The second major area for socializing was the dining room in the lower level. Residents complained that the dining room was used also as social hall, so that evening meetings could not begin until dinner had been cleared away at about 8:30 p.m. Since the elderly tend to go to bed early, a meeting might have to be rushed to finish in time.

In exploring social life, we found that 90% of the people 81 and over knew most of the residents by sight, and only 81% of those 65 to 80 did so. This was probably due to the greater amount of time the older group spent in building, underscoring the need for meeting places.

We also found that while those with a high school education had more friends than those with a college education, the latter group was visited by friends and visited friends more often than the high school educated group. Most of the residents, except those from far out of town, were visited by, or visited, their relatives at least once a week.

Apartments

Apartments were designed with a view to providing a barrier free environment, as proposed by the Architectural and Transportation Compliance Board (1977). Over 80% of the residents were satisfied with their apartments. More of the older residents, the handicapped, and women were satisfied with their apartments than were the younger, the male, and those without handicaps. A few said that their apartments were too small.

Shopping

Residents were asked whether shopping was convenient to them. Only 60%, a low percentage compared to that on other questions, answered positively, because although there was a small shopping area within two or three blocks and many residents could have walked to it, the only access was by means of a path through the grass. The elderly are highly conscious of brittle bones that are likely to break if they fall. Thus the residents of Revitz House avoid this path and cannot use the shopping center. There is another and larger shopping center, also within walking distance, but to reach this one it is necessary to cross a four-lane highway. It is difficult even for younger and faster people to get across such a large road before the light changes; for the elderly and handicapped it represents an impossible obstacle. Moreover, for reasons to be discussed later, many of the elderly cannot get up the steps of a bus. For all these reasons, accessibility to shops is severely limited for many of the elderly and handicapped. Yet going shopping is a highlight in the lives of many elderly and handicapped, and thus ought to be made possible and even encouraged.

Transportation

Thirty percent of the sample said they still kept and drove cars. These residents had little difficulty in getting around. One man, however, pointed out that the parking lot was no longer kept clear of ice in winter, as it had been formerly, which often made the parking lot too hazardous to use. Again, fear of falling curtailed trips to the outside in icy weather.

There was public transportation, and there were so-called Elderbuses that ran from the house twice a week. However, residents had to be able to mount the steps and to maintain seating on the bus in spite of carrying a cane and/or packages. Those who could neither walk nor use a bus to get to the store had to wait until a volunteer or a relative took them by car to the store. Failing this they could only ask people going to bring back small amounts of food.

This, then, concludes the main findings derived from the questionnaire administered to the residents of Revitz House. Some suggestions follow for future design based on the information derived from this and previous studies. Such design considerations often involve small changes, but could significantly improve the quality of living for the increasing number of those over 65.

DESIGN SUGGESTIONS

Neighborhood

Since so many residents chose the suburbs as a place to live, it might be well to site tall buildings for the aged and handicapped in suburban areas. The greenery around Revitz House was appreciated so much that landscaping might also be consciously included in the design of tall buildings for the elderly and handicapped.

Residents of Revitz House mainly preferred to live with adults of different ages; their second choice was to live with people their own age. This suggests designing buildings for housing adults but not children. Since juveniles tend to gang up on the elderly, a tall building for the latter should be built a healthy distance from high schools or should have a separation between the elderly and the juveniles.

Building Height

Since respondents answered negatively to liking tall buildings in general, but positively to living at Revitz House which is a tall building, one suggestion is to change the name of such buildings when dealing with the elderly. Such terms as "Majestic," "King Size," and "Queen Size" for buildings might give an impression of excellence and splendor without producing a sense of impersonality and excessive height. Another idea is to educate the elderly who are going to live in tall buildings about their advantages and safety. This may, however, involve more work with less chance of success than changing the name used for a tall building.

Security

While security measures at Revitz House seem to be quite adequate, other ways need to be explored for improving security without sacrificing mobility.

Elevators

Residents in all three studies carried out by the author complained about the elevators: they were too few, too slow, too small, and always breaking down. If at all possible, more elevators should be put into tall buildings for the elderly and handicapped; this population needs elevators more than younger and nonhandicapped people. There is a need to examine the belief of some nonhandicapped elderly that the handicapped should use separate elevators. Should we protect the sensitivities of the healthy or side with the freedom of movement of the handicapped? No one yet has asked the handicapped what they think of this situation. Perhaps they would dislike being segregated, and even prefer to be a part of nonhandicapped society. This possibility should not be ignored.

Meeting Places

Since meeting places for socialization figure so importantly in the life of the elderly, adequate provision should be made for a pleasant, comfortable lobby. Seating should be face-to-face, side-to-side, or cater-cornered, which Sommer (1969) notes are positions most conducive to interaction. The dining room should not double as a social hall unless this is necessary for economic reasons. If it is possible to have one room for each activity, this might be the most useful design. Some, however, argue that rooms should be multi-purposed. In this particular study, the opposite seems to be called for.

Apartments

A second emergency pull should be put in the bathroom for elderly and handicapped residents, as this is the location of many bad falls.

Shopping

A number of residents of all three studies suggested that a small shop containing staples be included in the design of a tall building for the aged and handicapped. This shop could be run by volunteer residents, as is the cafeteria at Revitz House. There is frequently a gift shop in buildings for the aged or infirm, so why not a grocery shop in buildings for the elderly and handicapped? Any profit made could be put back into the building.

Transportation

Buses with electrically moveable steps or a moving platform in the back could be a part of the equipment considered necessary when a tall building is designed for the elderly and handicapped. Or, underground passes between the building and nearby shopping centers might be provided for the elderly. An elevator would take the rider down to the underground pass, and there one could either walk or ride a moving belt; at the other end another elevator would take one up to ground level again. Such belts already exist in Washington D.C., connecting many government buildings to each other.

EPILOGUE

One month after the findings of this study were written, the author called for a meeting with residents of Revitz House to inform them of the findings and to verify that they represented resident feelings.

Residents at this meeting concurred on all points with our findings and agreed that they represented their points of view. They agreed that they loved the neighborhood and its open space (most of them had grown up in cities). They were satisfied with their floor level and likewise with security measures. They were very dissatisfied with the size of the elevators and wanted more of them; and they wanted separate ones for the handicapped, sick, or dead, or for moving furniture.

They agreed that the dining room should not double as a social hall because if it did they could not begin a social activity until the dining hall was cleared of dishes.

They were satisfied with their apartments but concurred that shopping was a problem for many of them because of the grass path to one, and the four-lane highway that had to be crossed to reach the other. They were highly enthusiastic about having a small store with staples inside the building. The manager agreed to help them begin it, if they could find residents willing to staff it voluntarily. (This may be a problem, as it is not easy to get volunteers to commit themselves for a regular activity.)

Two points bear specific mention. Some elderly complained of having to live with the handicapped when they had been promised, before they moved in, that the building was for the elderly who could look after themselves. However, some of the residents making these objections, including one indomitable lady who walked with a cane, were themselves somewhat handicapped. Apparently this lady did not consider herself handicapped although she admitted she could no longer walk, as she had previously, to the major shopping center. All efforts to get residents to define what they meant by a handicap failed. We asked if handicapped meant people in a wheelchair and were told, "no." This answer *might* have been given because a resident who attended the meeting was in a wheelchair.

A further factor is that with age, or by age 80 or more, there was a statistically significant increase in handicaps. All residents could expect, therefore, to develop handicaps, but this apparently does not occur to those complaining about the handicapped.

Thus the study was felt to represent the attitudes of residents of Revitz House toward tall buildings. We should keep in mind that most of the changes, except for more elevators, were probably easily achieved and that 80% of the residents liked living in Revitz House, a tall building.

The fact that a considerable number of residents responded both to the questionnaire and to the meeting also brought out the social functions of a tall building. This would not be the case where elderly persons lived with their children or where elderly persons lived alone.

Acknowledgment

The author wishes to thank Ms. Linda Freniere, Managing Director, Ruth

Rice, R.N., M.A., and Ms. Ruth Kerbel, Social Worker, all at Revitz House, for cooperation and assistance in carrying out this study. We especially thank the residents for their participation.

REFERENCES/BIBLIOGRAPHY

Architectural and Transportation Barriers Compliance Board, 1977
  RESOURCE GUIDE TO LITERATURE ON BARRIER-FREE ENVIRONMENTS, Architectural and Transportation Barriers Compliance Board.

Gutman, R., Ed., 1972
  PEOPLE AND BUILDINGS, Basic Books, New York.

Haber, G. M., 1976
  MALE AND FEMALE RESPONSE TO A COLLEGE CLASSROOM (unpublished).
Haber, G. M., 1977
  THE IMPACT OF TALL BUILDINGS ON USERS AND NEIGHBORS, Human Response to Tall Buildings, Dowden, Hutchinson & Ross, Stroudsburg.
Haber, G. M., 1978
  HUMAN BEHAVIOR IN FIRE DEPENDING ON TYPE OCCUPANCY: HEALTH CARE, PENAL AND LEISURETIME OCCUPANCIES, Second International Seminar on Human Behavior in Fire Emergencies, U.S. Department of Commerce.
Haber, G. M., 1980a
  HUMAN BEHAVIOR IN FIRE IN TOTAL INSTITUTIONS: A CASE STUDY, Fires and Human Behavior, John Wiley & Sons, Ltd., New York.
Haber, G., M., 1980b
  PILOT STUDY ON RESPONSE OF THE ELDERLY TO LIVING IN TALL BUILDINGS (unpublished).

MacBride, et al., 1961
  SOCIAL PROXIMITY EFFECTS ON GALVANIC SKIN RESPONSE IN ADULT HUMAN, Journal of Psychology, pp. 153-7.

Nahemow, L., Lawton, M., Powell, and Howell, S. C., 1977
  ELDERLY PEOPLE IN TALL BUILDINGS: A NATIONWIDE STUDY, Human Response to Tall Buildings, Dowden, Hutchinson & Ross, Stroudsburg.
Newman, O., 1973
  DEFENSIBLE SPACE, Collier Books, New York.
Newman, O., 1976
  DESIGN GUIDELINES FOR CREATING DEFENSIBLE SPACE, National Institute of Law Enforcement.

Pastalan, L., Carson, A., and Daniels, H., Eds., 1970
  SPATIAL BEHAVIOR OF OLDER PEOPLE, University of Michigan, Ann Arbor.

Ross, J., ed., 1982
  INTERNATIONAL ENCYCLOPEDIA OF POPULATION, Vols. I and II, The Free Press.

Soldo, B. J., 1980
  AMERICAN ELDERLY IN THE 1980's, Population Bulletin, Vol. 35, No. 4, November.

Sommer, R., 1969
PERSONAL SPACE, Prentice Hall, Englewood.
Sommer, R., 1970
SMALL GROUP ECOLOGY IN INSTITUTIONS FOR THE ELDERLY, Spatial Behavior of Older People, University of Michigan, Ann Arbor.
Southern Building Code Congress International, 1982
STANDARD BUILDING CODE, Southern Building Code Congress International Incorporated.
Spengler, J. J., 1978
FACING ZERO POPULATION GROWTH, Duke University Press, Durham.

Systems and Concepts

Introductory Review

Walter P. Moore, Jr.

This work compiles some of the latest thoughts on the design of systems and concepts currently used in tall buildings. It comes at a time when the large amount of design and construction of tall buildings in the United States is slowing down. Much has happened in a relatively short time, and it is very important that the current state-of-the-art techniques be updated and published. This is the best, indeed the only, viable way for designers to stay at the threshold of innovation and design technology.

It is also a time to look ahead and to try to anticipate what will happen in the immediate future. While tall building construction is slowing down in the United States, it is certainly not dormant. Also, we are probably on the threshold of an explosion of tall buildings outside the United States. The next generation of super tall buildings will probably occur in the Far East. As these tall buildings begin appearing there and around the world, a great body of new knowledge on systems and concepts will emerge. It will incorporate the differing needs, customs, and local conditions of the particular countries involved into the basic information previously collected in the Monograph and earlier updates.

Service systems will be developed to respond to the local cultures. Structural systems and foundation systems will continue to be refined as our knowledge of wind and earthquake engineering improves. Certainly more attention and effort need to be devoted to the development of innovative and economical construction techniques in the tall building process. Also, the work required in developing suitable cladding systems is far from complete, as was clearly

131

demonstrated by the damage resulting from the hurricane that struck downtown Houston in August of 1983. The importance of interior partitions and ceilings must not be forgotten. The performance of different types of partitions and ceilings during tall building movement due to wind, earthquake, or gravity loading will probably have the most noticeable effect on the acceptance of a tall building by the general public. More knowledge is required about the way these systems affect the behavior of the building, most notably in the way of damping. Finally, environmental design as it influences building climatology will become a greater problem in the future.

The greatest efforts for the future should be directed toward modification of our current design concepts toward the general trend of tall buildings outside the United States and Canada. The beginning of this trend is contained in Gregorian's paper on the serviceability criteria and structural systems available in the design of tall industrial buildings. Many significant differences in approach are discussed. Although some tall industrial buildings are built in the United States and Canada, their more extensive application is probably in the Far East, notably in Hong Kong.

At the Tall Buildings Conference in Sofia, Bulgaria in October, 1983, the emphasis was on prefabricated building systems for tall residential projects. Housing is probably the type of building project most in demand throughout the world, so we need information on the design and construction of high-rise apartments built from precast concrete pieces made in the factory. Experience in both Western and Eastern Europe will prove quite valuable. The study of industrialized prefabricated buildings will be of great interest in the immediate future.

It is the hope of the committees involved in the work of the Systems and Concepts Group that our task will continue to receive support from around the world. In that way we can continue to collect and disseminate state-of-the-art information that the design and construction professions can use with confidence.

Seismic Design of Composite Tubular Buildings

Hal Iyengar
Mohammad Iqbal

INTRODUCTION

In the last twenty years, several structural systems have been developed to minimize cost premiums for building height. These include tubular, tube-in-tube, and bundle-tube systems involving reinforced concrete and structural steel construction (Khan, 1974). It has also been found that one of the most effective ways to minimize costs in tall building construction is through composite or mixed steel-concrete construction, in which the most desirable attributes of each material are utilized and the disadvantages eliminated. In this process, elements of concrete systems, such as the shear walls and punched framed tubes, have been recognized as efficient elements to resist wind forces and to provide lateral rigidity. The use of these elements with simple structural steel framing, especially for floor framing, offers advantages of economy and speed. The object of combinations has been to utilize the rigidity of concrete for lateral load resistance, and the lightness and spannability of steel for floor framings. As the construction methodology of such mixing of systems was established and accepted by the construction industry, their use became widespread, which spurred further refinements and developments.

(Iyengar, 1977; Iyengar, 1979; and Iyengar and Iqbal, 1982). Thus mixed steel-concrete systems gained popularity and acceptance as viable alternatives to both structural steel and reinforced concrete buildings. In current practice, it is almost customary to offer three choices—steel, concrete, and composite systems—for cost and system evaluations for a high-rise building. Since there are numerous types of suitable members in both reinforced concrete and structural steel, a variety of practical combinations can be derived that serve and meet the overall structural performance criteria.

Resistance to wind has been the prime consideration in the composite system design since, until recently, tall buildings were mostly built in nonseismic areas. In recent years, however, there has been a growing interest in using the efficient structural systems developed for wind resistance to build tall earthquake-resistant structures economically.

A framed tube system consists of closely-spaced exterior columns tied at each floor level with deep spandrel beams, thereby creating an effect of a hollow concrete tube perforated by window openings. From a structural point of view, the tubular system combines the behavior of a flexural cantilever, such as a slender shear wall, with that of a beam-column frame. The overturning under lateral load is resisted by the tube form causing compression and tension in the columns, while the lateral shear is resisted primarily by the frames on the two sides of the building parallel to the direction of lateral loads. This is illustrated in Fig. 1. In modern tubular buildings, limiting lateral drift controls design more often than the strength requirements. And, it is considered necessary to keep a proper balance of stiffnesses between spandrels and columns so that these elements are efficiently utilized to provide lateral stiffness.

From a seismic perspective, a framed tube can be designed to act as a three-dimensional ductile moment frame wherein the exterior columns and spandrel beams are the elements resisting the seismic and the tributary vertical loads. Designing strong columns and weak beams is considered essential to the survival of a ductile frame subjected to strong ground motion (Selna et al., 1980). There are four major considerations that are fundamental to the design of ductile moment frame columns and beams:

1. The columns in each story are designed to resist story shear.

2. At any joint, column flexural strength is greater than the beam flexural strength.

3. Spandrel beams are designed to meet strength and ductility requirements for resistance to vertical and lateral loads. Beam stiffnesses are provided to meet drift requirements for the framed tube.

4. Column reinforcement detailing must prevent brittle shear and compression failure.

Little information is available on the feasibility of framed tubular build-ings in seismic regions. There is a concern that the framed tube systems with deep spandrels may not meet the strong-column weak-beam requirement and that plastic hinging in beams may preceed the column hinge formation, thereby adversely affecting structural stability.

This paper examines this issue and presents a rational approach of a composite tubular building in seismic regions. First, the design and con-struction considerations in nonseismic areas are reviewed briefly. Then, seismic considerations and a design approach using inelastic time-history analysis are described. It is followed by a design case study of a 43-story

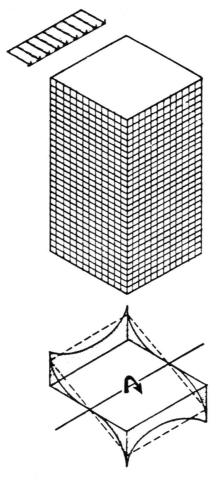

Fig. 1 Effect of shear lag in a tubular building

composite tubular building subjected to the ground motion of the 1940 El Centro (E–W component) earthquake. Further design guidelines are given at the end.

COMPOSITE TUBULAR SYSTEMS

The composite tubular system combines the exterior concrete framed tube with simply-supported, nonrigid steel framing on the interior. All the lateral resistance is derived from the exterior framed tube (Fig. 1). Exterior concrete framed tubes are highly efficient for use in the mixed form. The framed tube is formed by close spacing of columns with wide columns and deep beams giving the appearance of a punched wall. Generally, 30 to 40% of the punched tube wall is covered with columns and beams. The column spacings may vary from 6 ft (2 m) to about 15 ft (5 m), depending on member proportions. As with shear walls, the framed tubes are versatile in terms of possible shape modulations. The continuity and rigidity at the joints are obtained from the natural monolithic character of concrete. This type of punched tube wall can be constructed with gang forms or slip-forming techniques. Architecturally, concrete of the vertical and horizontal surfaces of the tube can be molded to any reasonable shape to bring the desired articulations and can be exposed, if desired. An exterior framed tube, therefore, performs the dual function of being a structure and a building enclosure. Figure 2 shows an elevation of a 37-story composite tubular system that typifies the basic character of an exterior tube. The punched-tube wall generally results in a reduction of glass area on the facade and, therefore, offers savings in perimeter air systems because of reduced heating and cooling loads. Another advantage of the closely spaced column form of the framed tube relates to simplification of window wall details. Since each window is framed all around by tube elements, window glazing is directly attached to the members by simple gasket details. Concrete framed tube systems can be effective up to 100 stories or more in nonseismic regions.

The general arrangement, shown in plan form in Fig. 3, indicates a framed tube on the periphery and steel floor framing and columns on the interior. All interior framing has nonrigid types of connections designed for gravity force only. Composite metal decks with composite steel beams or trusses are used for floor framing as in a steel structure. A typical cross-section of the spandrel beam and exterior column (Fig. 3) shows that steel beams are connected to small-size steel columns that are incorporated into the vertical members of framed tube. These steel columns can be used to permit the steel construction to advance ahead of the concrete components. The floor diaphragm is attached by dowelling the deck unit into exterior columns and beams.

When the composite tubular system was introduced in the mid-1960s, many initial applications were simple prismatic rectilinear shapes, such as those shown in Figs. 2 and 3. But the ability of the exterior concrete tube to conform to various exterior shapes makes it a versatile system and has promoted its use for other shapes. The inherent large torsional stiffness of the exterior framed tube form makes it acceptable for some asymmetry. In fact, the system can be used to create almost free-form shapes as long as the asymmetry is reasonable.

The exterior composite tube represents the simplest concept, and it allows for advance erection of structural steel. Construction coordination is generally

Fig. 2 Gateway III, Chicago

simpler because of concrete construction outside or on the periphery of steel construction. However, the rigid discipline of the exterior structure does not allow for exterior profile modifications.

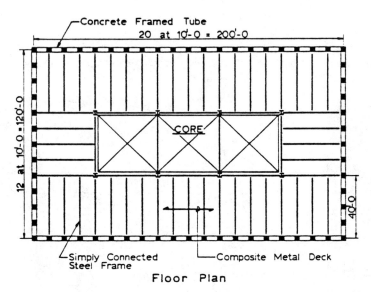

Floor Plan

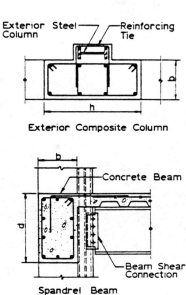

Fig. 3 Composite framed tube, floor plan and details

ANALYSIS AND DESIGN

Lateral load analysis generally involves only the framed tube and neglects the nominal participation of the steel part. The lateral loads are resisted by the entire three-dimensional tube, and induce both axial force and bending moment in columns. A preliminary analysis of such structures can be made by estimating the cantilever and shear frame forces. In this analysis, considerable judgment will have to be exercised to allow for the inefficiencies associated with a perforated tubular wall as opposed to a solid wall. A detailed discussion on estimation of cantilever effectiveness of tubes is presented by Khan and Amin (1973); this is useful as a practical guide.

For wind loads, the final structural analysis of the framed tube can be performed by utilizing three-dimensional frame analysis programs that consider column axial deformations. The effect of large widths and depths of members in terms of stiffness contribution should be included. This can be done by adjusting the member properties by ratio of clear span to center line span for beams and columns, or by separate evaluation of a one-story model with finite element analysis. Similarly, a more refined analysis can be performed by use of the finite element approach on a panelized model of the punched tube.

Preliminary design of the tubular buildings can be done using code-specified static forces (ICBO, 1980 and ATC, 1978). The code-specified forces are smaller than dynamic forces, which would be induced if the structure were to respond elastically to moderate-to-strong earthquakes. This is intended to produce ductile structures. In the final design phase, a time-history method is quite desirable. General-purpose computer programs are available to perform three-dimensional elastic time-history analysis. The calculation of inelastic response of two-dimensional reinforced concrete frames has also become possible by using realistic models of reinforced concrete behavior under cyclic loading. The Takeda "decreasing stiffness" model (Takeda, Sozen and Neilsen, 1970) of the hysteretic loop shown in Fig. 4 is one example. This model idealizes the moment–rotation relation of reinforced concrete members subjected to reversing loads. This model has been included in the computer program DRAIN-2D, developed to determine 2-D (planar) structural response to ground motions (Kanaan and Powell, 1975). Recent studies have shown that plastic (or yield) moment levels significantly affect the structural behavior of reinforced concrete walls and frames (Derecho et al., 1979 and Fintel and Ghosh, 1980). It is pointed out that present code seismic provisions do not account for the effect of yield moment explicitly. A design method that properly considers yield level explicitly would provide flexibility in designing for a range of yield level values and thereby would permit the engineer to control the locations and sequence of plastic hinge formations. The approach has been used in a case study of a symmetrical 31-story shear wall-frame building (Fintel and Ghosh, 1980).

From a structural point of view, a framed tube differs from a shear wall-frame system in one important aspect. In the framed tube, there is a three-dimensional interplay of forces under lateral loading, whereas the force distribution is generally planer in frame-shear wall type buildings. Khan and Amin (1973) showed that behavior of a framed tube can be reasonably represented by an assembly of two plane frames, representing web and flange frames of the tube. The frames are so connected that the web frame resists the entire lateral shear and the flange frame provides axial restraint to the corner column. In order to cut down computer cost and memory requirements, the entire flange can be represented by a single column having the properties of the flange frame. By using this equivalent plane frame, the Takeda "decreasing stiffness" model for reinforced concrete, and a computer program such as DRAIN-2D, the inelastic time-history analysis of a composite framed tube can be performed. The following example summarizes the design procedure for a 43-story composite tubular building.

DESIGN EXAMPLE

The seismic design considerations for a 43-story composite tubular building are presented here. The plan dimensions are 36.6 by 61.0 m (120 by 200 ft), as shown in Fig. 3.

Prior to carrying out a detailed seismic analysis, the building was designed to withstand the gravity and static wind forces. The three-dimensional model used for static analysis is shown in Fig. 5A. The top drift under wind was limited to $H/500$. The salient building data, along with structural criteria, is summarized in Table 1. The exterior columns and spandrel beams were designed to withstand the combined gravity and wind loads.

For inelastic time-history analysis, an equivalent plane frame (Fig. 5B) was used. Both web and flange frames of the framed tube are represented in the

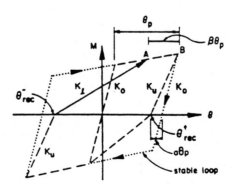

Fig. 4 Modified Takeda model *(Kanaan and Powell, 1979)*

equivalent frame. The properties of flange frame were so proportioned that equivalent frame behavior corresponded closely with the 3-D tubular model. As Fig. 6 shows, the lateral drift and spandrel beam moments for both 2-D and 3-D models compare very well. Both models also showed similar vibrational characteristics. The first three modes and periods of vibration are shown in Fig. 7.

Then, following the currently accepted practice, two levels (or intensities) of seismic input were defined for the dynamic analysis:

1. Design earthquake: ⅔ intensity of the first 10 s of the 1940 El Centro E–W component.

2. Maximum earthquake: full intensity of the first 10 s of the 1940 El Centro E–W component.

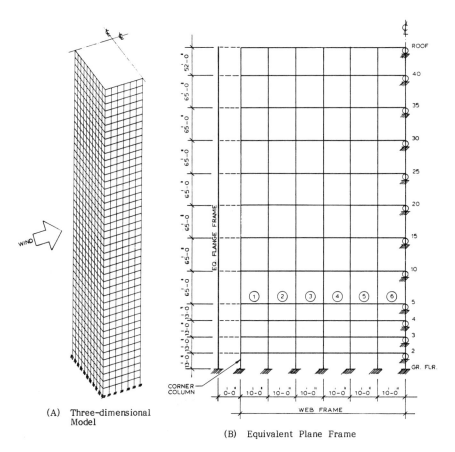

(A) Three-dimensional Model

(B) Equivalent Plane Frame

Fig. 5 Analytical models of the 43-story composite tubular building

Table 1 Design example: composite tubular system

Number of stories	43	Office live load	2400 Pa (50 lb/ft²)
Building height	170 m (559 ft)	Partition load	958 Pa (20 lb/ft²)
Average wind pressure	1915 Pa (40 lb/ft²)	Translatory period	5 s
Lateral drift	0.33 m (13.2 in.)	Torsional period	1.5 s
Floor-plan dimensions	See Fig. 3		

Slab
    50 mm (2-in.) composite metal deck with 83 mm (3¼ in.), 4000-psi structural lighteight concrete topping
Steel floor framing
    W21×44, A36 typical composite-steel at 3.09 m (10 ft) centers
Exterior framed-tube dimensions

Floors	h	d	b	f'_c (kPa) (psi)
0–10	0.9 m (36 in.)	.84 m (33 in.)	0.51 m (20 in.)	(35) 5000
10–20	0.9 m	.84 m	0.51 m	(35) 5000
20–30	0.9 m	.84 m	0.41 m (16 in.)	(28) 4000
30–42	0.9 m	.84 m	0.3 m (12 in.)	(28) 4000

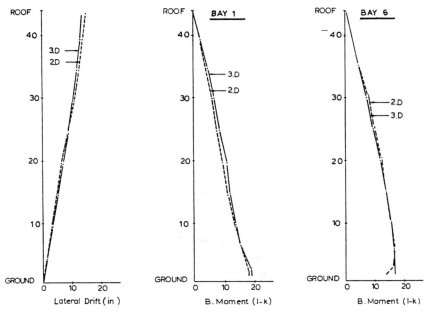

Fig. 6 Comparison of 2-D and 3-D computer model results

The choice of the 1940 El Centro E–W component as input motion is based on a parametric study by Derecho et al. (1979), which shows that the El Centro E–W Component (Fig. 8) is the most critical input motion for the building. The selection of input motion intensity and duration are based on the authors' judgment and are consistent with current practices. The structural design criteria to be applied with these two earthquakes is that stresses in the framed tube will not exceed yield moment in the design earthquake, but that ductility as high as 10 will be accepted in the spandrels in the maximum earthquake. The exterior columns would not yield in either case. Response of the building only in short direction is presented here.

Figure 9A shows the drift along the building height. The top drift increases with an increasing earthquake intensity. The effect of inelasticity on drift is, however, negligible. This is in conformity with previous studies reported in literature. The time-histories of top drift, nodal rotations, and spandrel beam moments are shown in Figs. 9B through 9D. It may be noted that local high beam moments attenuate when the member is allowed to yield and thereby dissipate its energy. The results of dynamic analyses with an earthquake having 1.25 times the 1940 El Centro (E–W) are plotted in Figs. 9A through 9D to give the reader an idea of the amplification in structural response due to an increase in earthquake intensity. Figure 10 shows the

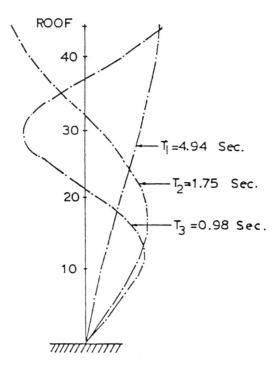

Fig. 7 Modes of vibrations

variation in the spandrel beams along the building height. Several dynamic moment sets are plotted for comparison. The static moments are also shown. Table 2 shows the ductility requirements in various beam bays when the composite tubular system is subjected to full intensity of the 1940 El Centro E–W component. Most of the beams remained elastic. The maximum ductility demand is noted to be 7.0, which is lower than the specified limit of 10. The hysteretic loop of a spandrel beam with a ductility demand of 1.41 is shown in Fig. 11.

Similar analysis can be made when the earthquake acts parallel to the long faces of the structure.

The analysis results indicate that plastification is limited only to the areas indicated. Suitable detailing in reinforced concrete can then be applied to these areas to accommodate such plastification. It should be recalled that confinement reinforcement and full plastic shear reinforcing will be required at the joints and in the members. The above reinforcing requirement can be relaxed in areas that are elastic. This in itself is of great benefit, since provision of confining reinforcing and full plastification shear reinforcing is cumbersome and often physically not possible. The authors feel that this type of analysis needs to be continued further to modulate member proportions to induce plastification in desirable areas. In exterior concrete tubes, such areas can be two middle bays on each facade. This type of design

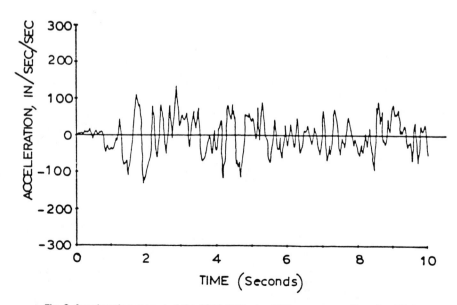

Fig. 8 Acceleration record of the 1940 El Centro E-W component *(Derecho, 1979)*

refinement is currently being studied and will be reported in due course. Using the inelastic dynamic analysis method, it is possible to control the sequence and location of the plastic hinge formation.

In addition, further design considerations are necessary in seismic design of tall buildings. It is customary to assume that an earthquake will act in the direction of the principal axes of the structures and in one direction at a time.

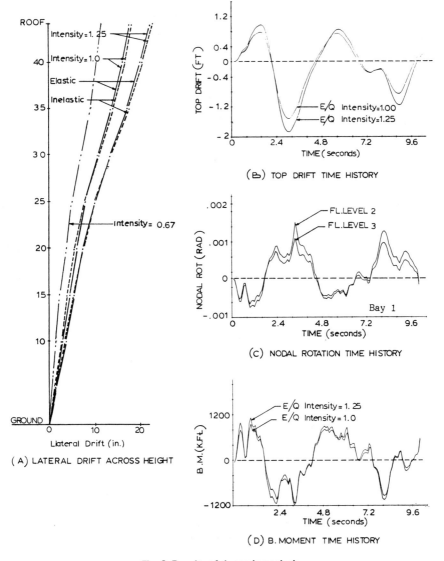

Fig. 9 Results of dynamic analysis

Table 2 Ductility demand in spandrel beams

Floor Level	Yield moment (k-ft)	Reinf. ratio (%)	Bay[a] 1	Bay 2	Bay 3	Bay 4	Bay 5	Bay 6
41–roof	252	0.33	E[b]	E	E	E	2.83	2.83
36–40	252	0.33	E	E	2.19	6.4	6.0	5.92
31–35	420	0.50	1.38	1.71	2.24	6.1	4.43	4.48
26–30	560	0.66	1.57	2.0	E	7.0	3.64	4.07
21–25	700	0.83	1.49	3.71	3.4	2.66	2.4	3.54
16–20	840	1.0	E	E	E	3.62	1.74	2.14
11–15	980	1.17	E	E	E	E	E	E
6–10	1120	1.33	E	E	E	E	E	E
5	1120	1.33	E	E	E	E	E	E
4	1120	1.33	E	E	E	E	E	E
3	1120	1.33	1.13	1.45	E	E	E	E
2nd	1120	1.33	1.41	E	E	E	E	E

[a] See Fig. 5B for beam bay location
[b] E = Elastic
[c] 1 k-ft = 1.36 kNm

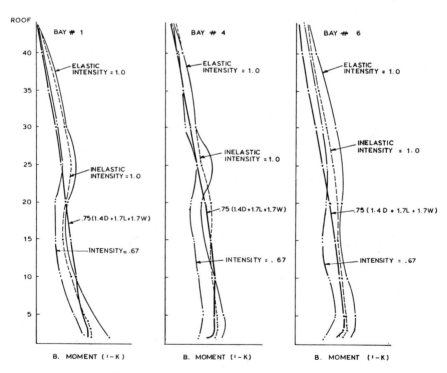

Fig. 10 Spandrel beam moments in composite tubular building

However, it must be kept in mind that earthquakes do not necessarily strike in the principal directions. Therefore, yielding of spandrel beams in both short and long faces may begin simultaneously. Moderate beam ductilities can be achieved using vertical stirrups; however, diagonal reinforcement may be necessary where ductility requirements are relatively high (Paulay and Binney, 1974). Care should be taken to design corner columns with low axial compression and biaxial bending. Beam-column joint design requires special attention. The work of ACI Committee 352 (1976) is a good guide. Current code provisions for confining steel are based on rather arbitrary assumptions. A more logical approach for the determination of the required amount of transverse steel would be based on ensuring a satisfactory moment-curvature relation. Moment-curvature analyses for column sections for monotonic flexure are currently available (Park and Paulay, 1975).

CLOSING REMARKS

Great advances have been made in the last 20 years in minimizing the premium for building height. One of the most effective ways to cut costs in tall buildings is through composite or mixed steel-concrete construction, whereby the advantages of both reinforced concrete and structural steel constructions are utilized and their disadvantages eliminated. Similar advances have been made in determining the response of complex structures to strong ground motion. The three-dimensional elastic time-history analysis and the two-dimensional inelastic time-history analysis for reinforced concrete structures are now cost-effective and are currently being used in design practice. This paper summarizes an investigation on the design of a 43-story composite tubular building subject to the full intensity of the 1940 El Centro E–W Component acting parallel to short faces of the building. Further design refinements are currently being studied and will be reported in due course.

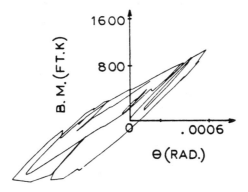

Fig. 11 M-θ relationship of a beam

REFERENCES/BIBLIOGRAPHY

ACI Committee 352, 1976
RECOMMENDATIONS FOR DESIGN OF BEAM-COLUMN JOINTS IN MONOLITHIC REINFORCED
CONCRETE STRUCTURES, ACI Journal, July.

Applied Technology Council, 1978
TENTATIVE PROVISIONS FOR DEVELOPMENT OF SEISMIC DESIGN REGULATIONS FOR BUILD-
INGS, Applied Technology Council, ATC 3-06, Washington, D.C.

Derecho, A. T., Ghosh, S. K., Iqbal, M., and Fintel, M., 1979
STRENGTH, STIFFNESS AND DUCTILITY REQUIRED IN REINFORCED CONCRETE STRUCTURAL
WALL FOR EARTHQUAKE RESISTANCE, ACI Journal, Vol. 76, No. 8, August, pp. 875-896.

Fintel, M. and Ghosh, S. K., 1980
SEISMIC RESISTANCE OF A 31-STORY SHEAR WALL-FRAME BUILDING USING DYNAMIC
INELASTIC RESPONSE HISTORY ANALYSIS, (Proceedings of the Seventh World Conference on
Earthquake Engineering, September 1980) Istanbul, Turkey.

International Conference of Building Officials, 1980
UNIFORM BUILDING CODE, 1980 Edition, Whittier, California.

Iyengar, H. S., 1977
STATE-OF-THE-ART-REPORT ON COMPOSITE OR MIXED STEEL-CONCRETE CONSTRUCTION
FOR BUILDINGS, ASCE, New York.

Iyengar, H. S., 1979
MIXED STEEL-CONCRETE HIGH-RISE SYSTEMS, Handbook of Composite Construction Engineering, Van Nostrand Reinhold, New York.

Iyengar, H. S. and Iqbal, M., 1982
COMPOSITE CONSTRUCTION, Building Structural Design Handbook, John Wiley & Sons,
New York.

Kanaan, A. E. and Powell, G. H., 1975
A GENERAL PURPOSE COMPUTER PROGRAM FOR INELASTIC DYNAMIC RESPONSE OF
PLANE STRUCTURES, Earthquake Engineering Research Center, Report No. 73-22, University
of California, Berkeley, California.

Khan, F. R., 1974
NEW STRUCTURAL SYSTEMS FOR TALL BUILDINGS AND THEIR SCALE EFFECTS ON CITIES,
(Proceedings of Symposium on Tall Buildings held at Vanderbuilt University, November 1974),
Nashville, Tennessee.

Khan, R. F., and Amin, N. R., 1973
ANALYSIS AND DESIGN OF FRAMED TUBE STRUCTURES FOR TALL CONCRETE BUILDINGS,
American Concrete Institute, Publication SP-36, Detroit, Michigan.

Park, R. and Paulay, T., 1975
REINFORCED CONCRETE STRUCTURES, John Wiley and Sons, Inc., New York.

Paulay, T. and Binney, J. R., 1974
DIAGONALLY REINFORCED COUPLING BEAMS OF SHEAR WALLS, American Concrete Institute, Shear in Reinforced Concrete, Publication SP-42, pp. 579-598.

Selna, L., Martin, I., Park, P., and Wyllie, L., 1980
STRONG TOUGH CONCRETE COLUMNS FOR SEISMIC FORCES, Journal of the Structural
Division, ASCE, Vol. 106, No. ST8, August.

Takeda, T., Sozen, M. A. and Neilsen, N. N., 1970
REINFORCED CONCRETE RESPONSE TO SIMULATED EARTHQUAKE, Journal of the Structural
Division, ASCE, Vol. 96, No. ST12, December, pp. 2257-2573.

Structural Systems

An Update

Hal Iyengar

Recent structural systems for high-rise buildings are strongly influenced by evolving architectural forms and esthetics. The traditional rectilinear forms of the 1950s and 1960s have given rise to buildings of different shapes that respond to the site geometry, urban planning criteria, and visual impacts of the varying vertical profile. Often, the vertical modulation of shape may be due to a need to create floors of different shapes and sizes to optimize rental revenue. The horizontal modulation of shapes may be a result of contextual relationship to urban grid and massing with respect to other buildings. All these influences produce buildings that are nonprismatic and often asymmetric. In addition, because of increased costs of structures, there is a growing incentive to evolve optimum structural systems.

The family of structural systems that are based on the tubular concept is the type of system most widely used today and likely to be used in the future. Even though initial forms were rectilinear, the rigidity and efficiency of the system for wind forces and the adaptability to create different shapes have been responsible for their broad appeal. Previous systems, such as the plane frame, shear wall, vertical truss, and belt truss-outrigger truss are also in use, but less frequently than before.

The tubular system was introduced in the mid-1960s with the DeWitt-Chestnut Apartment Building in Chicago (Fig. 1). The framed tube is formed by closely spaced perimeter columns and deep spandrel beams, giving the appearance of a punched tube. This results in a system that behaves like a cantilever fixed at the ground and subjected to wind

Fig. 1 De Witt-Chestnut apartment building

forces. The interior floor framing was a concrete flat plate with random arrangement of columns to suit the apartment layout. There have been many examples of this tubular system application for office and apartment buildings, with column spacings ranging from 3 ft 4 in. to 15 ft. Some versions have included an interior shear wall tube for additional stiffness as a *tube-in-tube* system.

The need for vertical modulation in a logical fashion has created a new type of tubular structure based on clustering or bundling smaller tubes, each of which can rise to a different height. This is typified by the One Magnificent Mile Project, a 57-story concrete structure in Chicago. The free-form structure is composed of three hexagonal, reinforced concrete framed tubes with the highest tube at 57 stories and the others at 49 and 22 stories each (Fig. 2). The arrangement of tubes and their orientation were determined from the site configuration and the need to optimize exposure and views to Lake Michigan. The lower 20 stories, which have all three tubes, are occupied by commercial and office space, while the upper stories are devoted to apartments (Figs. 3 and 4). The floor system is a reinforced concrete, flat slab system in both office and apartment floors. The structure for the tubular lines involves columns at

Fig. 2 One Magnificent Mile *(Courtesy; Jim Hedrich, Hedrich-Blessing)*

close centers and deep spandrel beams. The high structural efficiency combined with the improved construction method utilizing mechanized gang forms makes this system cost-effective. The interior framed tube lines are similar to the exterior ones and are constructed similarly.

The moldability of the reinforced concrete tubular system is further illustrated by the First Canadian Centre Project in Calgary, which involves an L-shaped site. Given a significant corner in downtown Calgary, the visual impact of a sculpted form was desirable in addition to the diagonal office orientation for mountain and city views. The concept involves two towers, one facing each side of the L-shaped site, and a 12-story banking pavilion, as shown in Fig. 5. The towers are 64 and 43 stories. The structural system for this parallelogram shape with truncated and reentrant corners is based on a reinforced concrete, tube-in-tube system with steel and concrete floor framing,

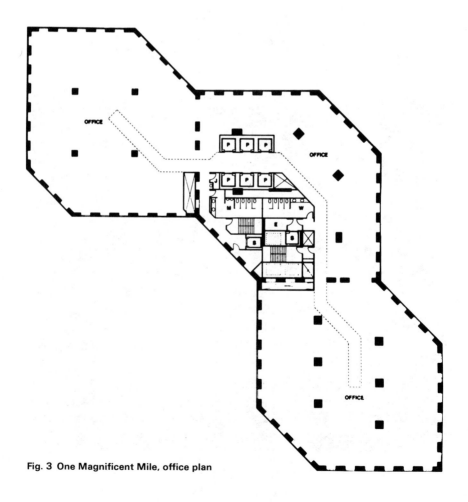

Fig. 3 One Magnificent Mile, office plan

as shown in Fig. 6. The perimeter framed tube is formed by a combination of perimeter wall elements at truncated and reentrant corners connected with beam-column framed tube elements, all working within the discipline of the exterior tube. The inner tube supplies the additional stiffness required. In spite of the unusual form, the high efficiency of the system is indicated by the following quantities for the high tower: concrete, 0.61 ft^3/ft^2; reinforcing steel, 3.73 psf; and structural steel, 4.34 psf. There have been other applications with this type of structural system in the 50- to 75-story range.

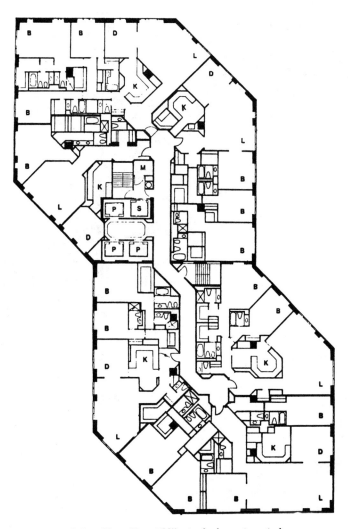

Fig. 4 One Magnificent Mile, typical apartment plan

In steel structures, the bundled tube system of the Sears Tower, Chicago, has brought about a new form of structure. Here the bundled tube was composed of square modules 75 ft × 75 ft, and nine components were lumped together as shown in Fig. 7 to form the total system. The intention was not only to create a powerful structural system but also to create vertical modulation

Fig. 5 First Canadian Centre

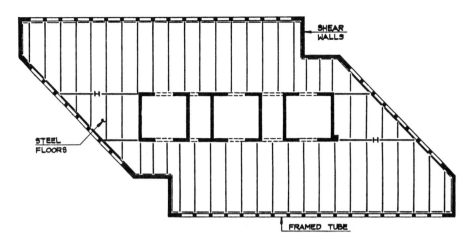

Fig. 6 First Canadian Centre floor plan

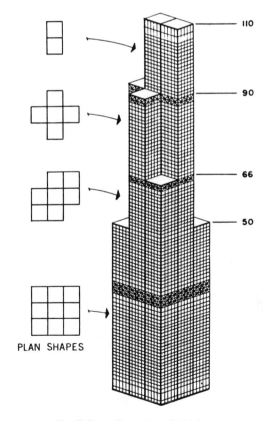

Fig. 7 Sears Tower, bundled tube

in a logical fashion. The concrete clustered tubular system of the One Magnificent Mile Project is a derivative of the bundled tube system. Considerable latitude exists in the form of each tube, which allows for various shapes.

Two recent examples of the application of the bundled tube concept are worth noting. One is the Crocker Center Project in Los Angeles, which involves two towers, 57 and 47 stories tall. The site conditions, together with considerations for a sculpted form, resulted in a shape outfitted with a square tube and a triangular tube, as shown in Fig. 8. A column spacing of 16 ft was selected for the tubular system. A significant advantage of the bundled tube system is its enormous torsional resistance, which is helpful in absorbing torsional lateral forces due to asymmetry. In this case, the torsional loads were generated by both wind and seismic forces.

The 75-story, 296-m (970-ft) tall Allied Bank Tower recently completed in Houston, Texas is another example of bundled frame tube applications. The shape is formed by two quarter circle tubes placed antisymmetrically about the middle tubular line (Figs. 9 and 10). The column spacings are 15 ft with the usual "tree" type construction. The system also uses two vertical trusses in the core that are connected to the exterior tube by outrigger and belt trusses. Significant improvement in tubular behavior is obtained because of the participation of the trusses. This system, therefore, embodies elements from the framed tube, bundled tube, and truss systems with belt and outrigger trusses. The truss system provided another transverse frame linkage in the curvilinear part to improve its shear lag characteristics.

Current structural systems often borrow elements from various previous systems if they can be utilized efficiently and if a combination can be derived to suit the needs of the project. Combinations may involve framed tubes of

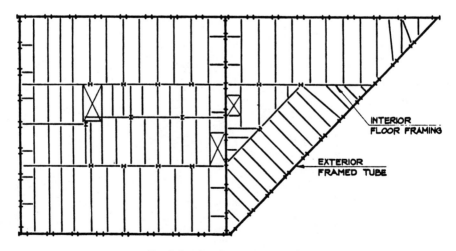

Fig. 8 Crocker Center framing plan

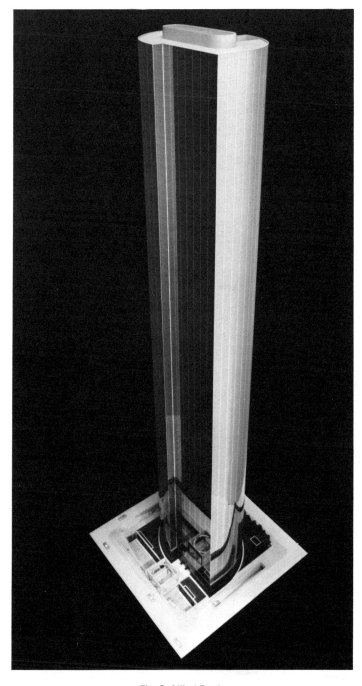

Fig. 9 Allied Bank

various shapes, vertical trusses, belt trusses, tube-in-tubes, braced tubes, and bundled tube systems. A variety of systems can be created with this methodology. In fact, the combination may involve reinforced concrete components and structural steel for a variety of mixed steel-concrete systems, such as the composite tubular and concrete core braced steel systems.

Framed tube member proportions involve wide members for both beams and columns. In structural steel, the joints need to be welded for rigidity and the members built up for larger widths. The formation of a prefabricated framed tube "tree" element, where all welding can be done in the shop in a horizontal position, has made the steel frame tube practical and efficient. The "trees" are then erected by bolting at mid-span of the spandrel with minimum welds for column splices. Construction speed resulting in 2 stories a week can occur if "trees" are used, as shown in Fig. 11.

A recent improvement in steel framed tube construction in the 40- to 50-story range utilizes 36, 33 and 30 in. rolled beams as columns. The conventional 14W series columns are not efficient as frame tube columns, and deeper depths are required. The use of deeper beam shapes as columns makes built-up members unnecessary. This alone has made application of steel framed tubes for medium height buildings in 40 to 50 stories economically viable. The Sixty State Street Project (Figs. 12 and 13) in Boston is a 45-story office tower that was configured to suit the site and to preserve sight lines from existing neighboring tall buildings. The result was practically a free-form

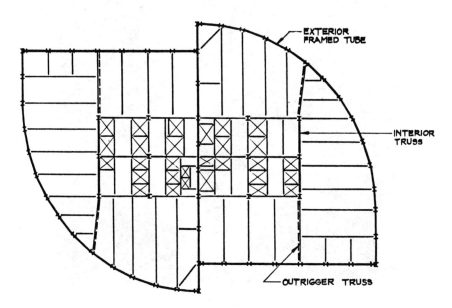

Fig. 10 Allied Bank floor framing plan

shape. The exterior framed tube uses columns at 10 ft center based on a "tree" type erection unit. All interior framing is simply connected. The system uses a structural steel quantity of 18 psf.

The Sixty State Street Project represents the flexibility available in exterior tubular systems that has given architects and planners new freedom in integrating sight lines, ground level activities, form, and esthetics.

Energy-conservative high-rise designs are beginning to emerge, impacting architectural form and, consequently, its structure. One such example is the 33 West Monroe Building in Chicago. The 1,000,000 ft² office space is contained in a building envelope of 210 ft × 180 ft by 27 stories. This squat form was evolved to reduce the window wall proportion in relation to floor area, resulting in significant energy conservation. This concept also incorporates interior stacked atriums to use large interior spaces effectively as well as to create varying floors within the atrium, as shown in Fig. 14. This simplified structure involves less cost for height. Perimeter moment frames are sufficient to provide adequate rigidity. The atriums are contained within the interior column grid and are framed with simple beam framing, as is all interior framing. The structure was so efficient that it required only 14 psf of structural steel. Simpler structural solutions in concrete are also emerging with this concept, which utilizes exterior frames and flat slab framing.

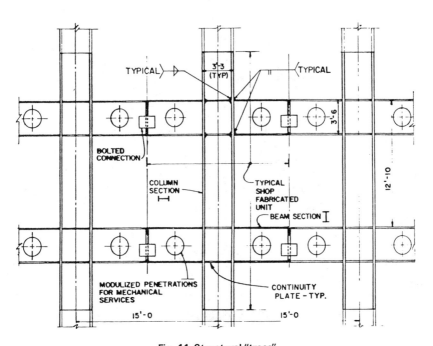

Fig. 11 Structural "trees"

Fig. 12 Sixty State Street *(Courtesy; Ezra Stoller)*

The 33 West Monroe Building involves three stacked atriums with some floors covering the entire floor area. A vertical extension of this concept can involve many such stacked atriums, creating a tall mega-structure. The large exterior dimensions required for this concept offer enormous opportunity to use different forms of tubular systems. One may utilize a framed tube concept or an exterior diagonalized system, such as that of the John Hancock Center in Chicago or a super-frame concept which frees atrium areas from the exterior structure.

Future high-rise structures will involve a variety of forms and shapes. They will demand considerable flexibility for creating exciting habitable spaces, perhaps involving multiple uses. Simple and efficient solutions are possible integrating concepts involving rational structural logic.

ACKNOWLEDGMENT

A version of this paper also appeared in the November, 1982 issue of *Building Design & Construction*, ©Cahners Publishing Company.

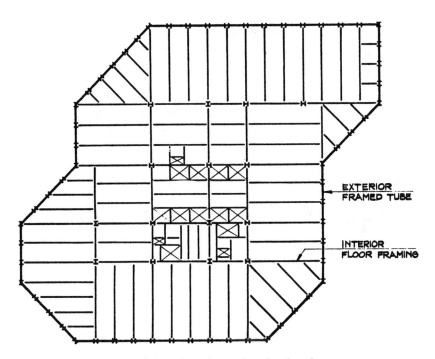

EXTERIOR
FRAMED TUBE

INTERIOR
FLOOR FRAMING

Fig. 13 Sixty State Street, floor framing plan

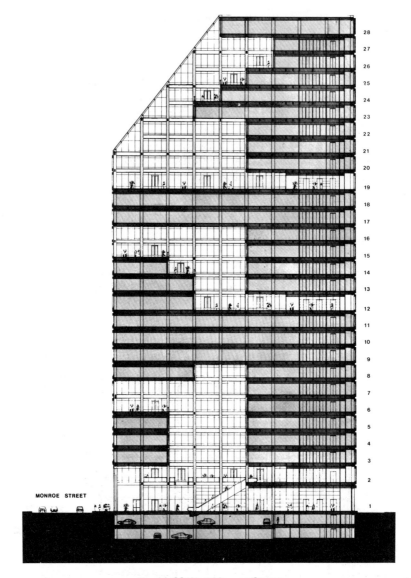

Fig. 14 33 West Monroe Street

Structural Systems Selections in High-Rise Buildings

Joseph P. Colaco

INTRODUCTION

The design of high-rise buildings requires the creative talents of a knowledgeable team of professionals. This team consists of the owner, the architect, the engineers, and the contractor. Each member of the team brings specialized knowledge and creativity to bear on the design of the building.

The process generally begins with an initial meeting between the owner and the architect to set up the program requirements. The next step is generally a meeting with the entire team to consider what alternatives should be studied for the construction of the project. Each member of the team, based on his experience and creativity, discusses his ideas within his own discipline. The outcome is a work program called "value-engineering." The aim is to develop different designs for the construction of the project.

VALUE ENGINEERING

In structural engineering, there are three major techniques in constructing a high-rise building. They are: structural steel, reinforced concrete, and a composite (both steel and concrete). Within each of these structural techniques there are a very large number of choices that can be considered. Some of these are eliminated because of the building program; some, because of labor availability; and some, because of owner preference. The result of the early meetings is to reduce the number of viable options. These are then studied in detail so that the most effective one will be selected. From a structural engineering standpoint, at least two options are studied in any project. The maximum number of options the author has studied on a project is sixteen; the details of this study are discussed in this paper.

EVALUATION CRITERIA

The evaluation criteria for a structural system are

1. Economics

2. Construction time

3. Construction risk

4. Integration of architectural and structural needs

5. Integration of structural and mechanical needs

6. Material and labor availability and skills

7. Future flexibility.

It is extremely important that a fair comparison be made of each system, and that an evaluation be made of the factors in other disciplines (architectural, mechanical, etc.) that are affected by the particular structural system under study. In general, for example, a structural steel system will require slightly larger beam depths, and therefore require larger floor-to-floor heights than a concrete system. The increase in floor-to-floor height impacts all the vertical elements within the building, and has to be value-engineered as well. A further example is that the smaller column sizes in a steel frame, as opposed to a concrete structure, have a beneficial effect on the leasability of the space. This fact has to be evaluated.

PROJECT DESCRIPTION

The project described here is a 30-story office building. The plan dimensions are 150 ft by 150 ft with the four corners chamfered. The owner and the architect decided that an aluminum and glass curtainwall would be used as the exterior of the building. It was further decided that all the floors would have the same plan dimensions. The main variables needing investigation were the following:

1. Construction materials: Steel, concrete, and composite.

2. Span: Whether to clear span between the core and the exterior columns or to provide a row of interior columns.

3. Exterior column spacing: This was varied from 15 ft to 30 ft in different schemes.

The project design was started in early 1977. The unit prices used by the contractor are given in Table 1.

Estimated costs include the entire structural cost of the building, including the foundation but excluding the contractor's overhead and profit. The cost of the foundation in the steel schemes was estimated at $1.00/ft² and for the concrete schemes was $1.50/ft². Further, an analysis was conducted to price the difference in floor-to-floor height. It was determined that for every inch increase in floor height, the cost premium was 3.5¢/ft². In the following studies, Scheme C-1 was used as the base for floor heights since it had the lowest height of any scheme.

It should be noted that the following schemes only address the first cost of the structure. Construction times and the costs of the time premium were separately evaluated by the contractor.

Table 1 Unit price of structural materials for a 30-story office building

Material	Unit price
Concrete	
Normal weight	$37/cu yd
Light weight	$42/cu yd
Slab finishing	15¢/ft²
Reinforcement	
A615-Grade 60	24¢/lb
Welded wire fabric	15¢/ft²
Concrete Forming	
Pan joist slabs	$1.20/ft²
Flat slabs with drop panels	$1.20/ft²
Flat plate	$1.05/ft²
Special beams for slab system	$1.20/ft²
Beam forms	$1.50/ft²
Column forms	$2.00/ft²
Wall forms	$1.10/ft²
Structural Steel	
ASTM 572-50	$800/ton
ASTM A36 (including shear connectors)	$750/ton
Metal Deck (2" non-cellular	65¢/ft²
Spray-on fireproofing	65¢/ft²

STRUCTURAL SCHEMES

The following are the schemes that were studied for this particular building:

Scheme S-1

This scheme is shown in Fig. 1 and is a steel scheme with exterior columns set 25 ft on centers. The lateral resisting system consists of cross-bracing in both directions in the core and a welded perimeter frame. Interior columns were provided at 13 ft from the center line of the exterior columns. The summary of the analysis is shown in Fig. 1. The cost of this scheme was $8.54/ft² plus a premium of $0.53/ft² because of additional floor height. The relative cost is therefore $9.07/ ft².

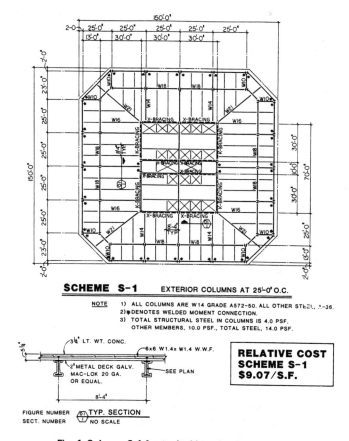

SCHEME S-1   EXTERIOR COLUMNS AT 25'-0" O.C.

NOTE   1) ALL COLUMNS ARE W14 GRADE A572-50. ALL OTHER STEEL, A-36.
2) ♥ DENOTES WELDED MOMENT CONNECTION.
3) TOTAL STRUCTURAL STEEL IN COLUMNS IS 4.0 PSF.
   OTHER MEMBERS, 10.0 PSF., TOTAL STEEL, 14.0 PSF.

RELATIVE COST SCHEME S-1 $9.07/S.F.

FIGURE NUMBER   TYP. SECTION
SECT. NUMBER   NO SCALE

Fig. 1 Scheme S-1 for typical low-rise framing plan

Scheme S-2

This scheme was very similar to Scheme S-1 except that the exterior columns were changed to 30 ft on centers and the floor framing ws turned. The cost was $8.74/\text{ft}^2$ plus $0.53 premium for floor height, for a total of $9.27/\text{ft}^2$.

Scheme S-3

This scheme is shown in Fig. 2. The exterior columns are spaced at 20 ft on centers, and there are no interior columns between the core and the outside wall. A stub–girder system was used to clear span the 40 ft and 45 ft dimensions between the core and the exterior. The wind resisting system was the same as in Scheme S-1. The cost of the scheme was $9.12/\text{ft}^2$ and the premium for floor height was $0.42. Hence, the relative cost was $9.54/\text{ft}^2$.

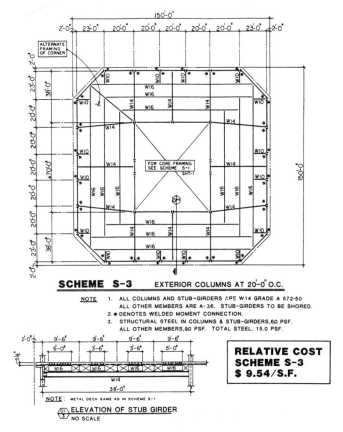

SCHEME S-3   EXTERIOR COLUMNS AT 20-0" O.C.

NOTE   1.   ALL COLUMNS AND STUB–GIRDERS ARE W14 GRADE A 572-50
ALL OTHER MEMBERS ARE A-36. STUB-GIRDERS TO BE SHORED.
2. ✦ DENOTES WELDED MOMENT CONNECTION.
3.   STRUCTURAL STEEL IN COLUMNS & STUB-GIRDERS, 6.0 PSF.
ALL OTHER MEMBERS, 9.0 PSF. TOTAL STEEL, 15.0 PSF.

**RELATIVE COST
SCHEME S-3
$ 9.54/S.F.**

NOTE : METAL DECK SAME AS IN SCHEME S-1

ELEVATION OF STUB GIRDER
NO SCALE

Fig. 2 Scheme S-3 for typical low-rise framing plan

Scheme S-4

In this scheme, the exterior columns are placed at 25 ft on centers and no interior columns were used between the core and exterior wall. Simple span composite floor beams were spaced at 8 ft-4 in. on centers between the core and the outside. The cost of this scheme was $9.47/ft² plus a premium of $0.63/ft² for increase in floor height, for a relative cost of $10.10/ft².

Scheme S-5

This is a steel scheme with exterior columns at 20 ft and 30 ft on centers. This scheme is shown in Fig. 3. Composite floor beams were spaced at 10 ft on centers as opposed to 8 ft-4 in. on centers for Scheme S-4. All other details are similar. The relative cost of this scheme was $9.18/ft².

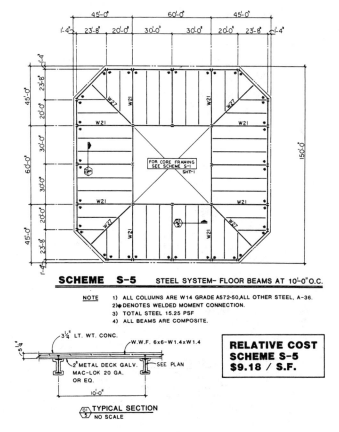

SCHEME S-5   STEEL SYSTEM– FLOOR BEAMS AT 10'-0" O.C.

NOTE   1) ALL COLUMNS ARE W14 GRADE A572-50,ALL OTHER STEEL, A-36.
2) ✷ DENOTES WELDED MOMENT CONNECTION.
3) TOTAL STEEL 15.25 PSF
4) ALL BEAMS ARE COMPOSITE.

RELATIVE COST SCHEME S-5 $9.18 / S.F.

TYPICAL SECTION
NO SCALE

Fig. 3 Scheme S-5 for typical low-rise framing plan

Scheme S-6

This steel floor scheme shown in Fig. 4 is similar to Scheme S-5 with the same exterior column spacing. However, the floor beams are mostly placed at 15 ft on centers and a 3 in. metal deck was used as opposed to 2 in. metal deck. Also, the floor beams are changed to high-strength steel, A572-50, and penetrations were made in the beams for the mechanical ducts to go through, thereby reducing floor-to-floor height. This scheme had a cost of $8.26/ft^2 plus $0.18/ft^2 for floor height premium, for a total of $8.44/ft^2.

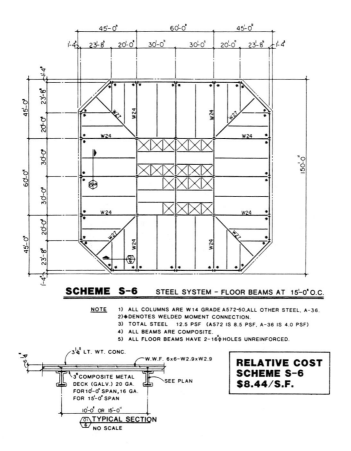

SCHEME S-6　　STEEL SYSTEM – FLOOR BEAMS AT 15'-0" O.C.

NOTE　1) ALL COLUMNS ARE W14 GRADE A572-50,ALL OTHER STEEL, A-36.
2) ◆DENOTES WELDED MOMENT CONNECTION.
3) TOTAL STEEL　12.5 PSF　(A572 IS 8.5 PSF, A-36 IS 4.0 PSF)
4) ALL BEAMS ARE COMPOSITE.
5) ALL FLOOR BEAMS HAVE 2-16"φ HOLES UNREINFORCED.

3¾" LT. WT. CONC.
W.W.F. 6x6-W2.9xW2.9
3" COMPOSITE METAL DECK (GALV.) 20 GA. FOR 10'-0" SPAN, 16 GA. FOR 15'-0" SPAN
SEE PLAN
10'-0" OR 15'-0"
TYPICAL SECTION
NO SCALE

**RELATIVE COST
SCHEME S-6
$8.44/S.F.**

Fig. 4 Scheme S-6 for typical low-rise framing plan

Scheme S-7

This was similar to Scheme S-2 but the core was modified to 60 ft × 60 ft. The core bracing was much more efficient. The cost of this scheme was $7.73/ft² plus $0.53 premium for floor height, for a total of $8.26/ft². This scheme was later abandoned for architectural reasons.

Scheme C-1

This is a concrete flat slab scheme shown in Fig. 5. In this scheme, the exterior columns are placed at 25 ft on centers and a row of interior columns is placed 15 ft from the exterior glass wall. Shear walls were placed in the core. Three options were considered for the floor framing system, namely 11 in. thick mild steel flat plate, 8 in. thick post-tensioned flat plate, and 9 in. flat slab with drop panels. These three were evaluated and the 9 in. flat slab was chosen. This scheme had the lowest floor-to-floor height, and the relative cost was $7.57/ft².

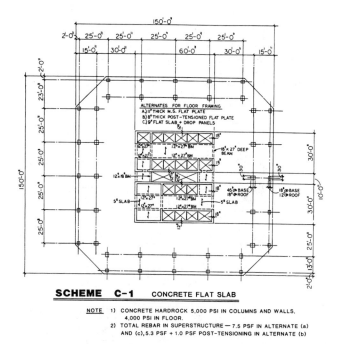

SCHEME C-1   CONCRETE FLAT SLAB

NOTE   1) CONCRETE HARDROCK 5,000 PSI IN COLUMNS AND WALLS,
            4,000 PSI IN FLOOR.
         2) TOTAL REBAR IN SUPERSTRUCTURE — 7.5 PSF IN ALTERNATE (a)
            AND (c), 5.3 PSF + 1.0 PSF POST-TENSIONING IN ALTERNATE (b)

**RELATIVE COST
SCHEME C-1
$7.57/S.F.**

Fig. 5 Scheme C-1 for typical low-rise framing plan

Scheme C-2

This was a concrete scheme with exterior columns at 30 ft on centers and a row of interior columns 15 ft back from the center line of the exterior columns. The interior columns are also placed at 30 ft on centers. Girders connected the corresponding interior column with the exterior column and the core. The core detail was very similar to that shown in Scheme C-1. Pan joists spanning 30 ft were used to frame between the girders. Three options were developed for spacing of the pans, namely 3 ft spacing, 5 ft spacing, and 6 ft spacing. The relative cost of this scheme was $7.70/ft^2.

Scheme C-3

This is a concrete beam and slab system shown in Fig. 6, designed to utilize flying forms. The exterior columns were removed and a row of columns was placed 15 ft back from the glass line. These columns were spaced at 15 ft on

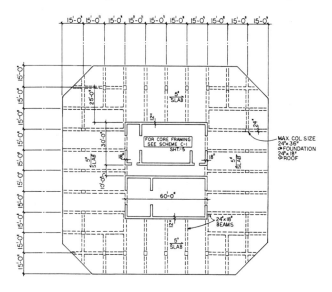

SCHEME C-3   CONCRETE BEAM AND SLAB SYSTEM

NOTE   1) CONCRETE HARDROCK 5,000 PSI IN COLUMNS AND WALLS,
4,000 PSI IN FLOORS.
2) TOTAL REBAR IN SUPERSTRUCTURE IS 6.8 PSF.

**RELATIVE COST
SCHEME C-3
$7.32/S.F.**

Fig. 6 Scheme C-3 for typical low-rise framing plan

centers. Concrete shear walls were placed in the core as in the two previous schemes. The relative cost of this scheme was $7.00/ft² plus a height premium for depth of $0.32/ft², giving a relative cost index of $7.32/ft².

Scheme C-4

This scheme is shown in Fig. 7. This is a concrete scheme with concrete shear walls in the core and exterior columns spaced at 20 ft on centers. There are no interior columns between the glass line and the core walls. The clear span between the core and the exterior columns was framed with concrete haunched girders and a one-way slab system. The relative cost was $7.39/ft² plus a premium for depth of $0.25/ft², to give a relative cost index of $7.64/ft². An additional premium of $0.04/ft² was needed to reduce the column size in this scheme to 30 in. by 30 in. for the sixth floor and above, bringing the total cost index to $7.68/ft².

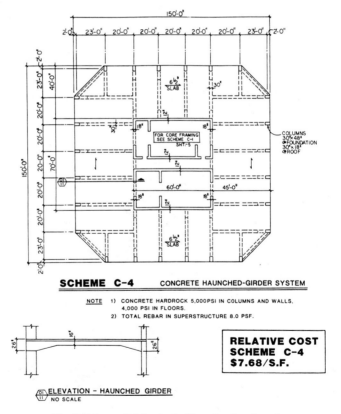

SCHEME C-4   CONCRETE HAUNCHED-GIRDER SYSTEM

NOTE   1) CONCRETE HARDROCK 5,000PSI IN COLUMNS AND WALLS.
4,000 PSI IN FLOORS.
2) TOTAL REBAR IN SUPERSTRUCTURE 8.0 PSF.

RELATIVE COST SCHEME C-4 $7.68/S.F.

ELEVATION – HAUNCHED GIRDER
NO SCALE

Fig. 7 Scheme C-4 for typical low-rise framing plan

Scheme C-5

This is a concrete scheme shown in Fig. 8. It is a concrete system utilizing pan joist construction. There are concrete shear walls in the core, and the exterior columns are at 25 ft on centers. There are no interior columns between the glass line and the core walls. The span between the shear wall core and the exterior column and spandrel system utilizes a one-way pan joist system using 24 in. deep pans and a 4½ in. slab. The relative cost of this scheme was $7.52/ft² plus a premium for depth of $0.70/ft², giving a relative cost of $8.22/ft².

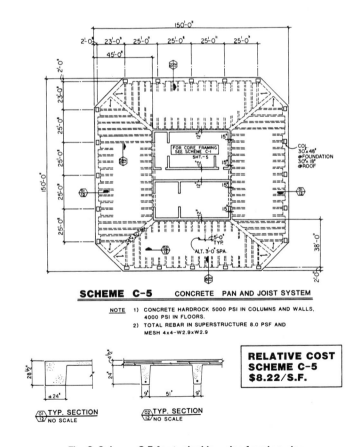

SCHEME C-5 CONCRETE PAN AND JOIST SYSTEM

NOTE 1) CONCRETE HARDROCK 5000 PSI IN COLUMNS AND WALLS, 4000 PSI IN FLOORS.
2) TOTAL REBAR IN SUPERSTRUCTURE 8.0 PSF AND MESH 4x4-W2.9xW2.9

RELATIVE COST
SCHEME C-5
$8.22/S.F.

01 TYP. SECTION NO SCALE
02 TYP. SECTION NO SCALE

Fig. 8 Scheme C-5 for typical low-rise framing plan

Scheme C-6

This is a concrete scheme with exterior columns at 15 ft on centers. There is a row of interior columns at 15 ft and 20 ft from the exterior columns. A one-way beam and slab system framed the floor. The rest of the details were similar to Scheme C-4. The relative cost was $7.19/ft^2 plus a premium for depth of $0.31/ft^2, giving a relative cost index of $7.50/ft^2.

Scheme C-7

This is a concrete scheme with exterior columns at 15 ft on centers with no interior columns. The rest of the scheme is similar to Scheme C-6. The relative cost was $7.38/ft^2 plus a premium for depth of $0.52/ft^2, for an overall relative cost of $7.90/ft^2.

Scheme M-1

This scheme is a composite scheme shown in Fig. 9. The exterior composite columns are spaced at 15 ft on centers. There is a row of interior columns spaced 15 ft from the exterior wall. The interior columns were spaced at 30 ft on centers as shown in the figure. The relative cost of this scheme is $8.60/ft^2 plus a premium for depth of $0.46/ft^2, for a relative cost index of $9.06/ft^2.

Scheme M-2

This scheme is also a composite scheme similar to Scheme M-1 in all respects, except there are no columns between the core and the outside column line. The relative cost of this scheme was $9.34/ft^2 plus a premium for depth of $0.75/ft^2, giving a total relative cost index of $10.09/ft^2.

The studies indicated that of all the schemes considered, C-3, a concrete scheme with no exterior columns, had the lowest relative cost of $7.32/ft^2. However, based on an overall evaluation on the project needs, Scheme S-6, which had a relative cost index of $8.44, was selected for the project. This was because construction time savings and other considerations far outweighed the cost savings.

CONCLUSIONS

It is obvious from this study that there are several variations in structural systems that need to be studied, and that they provide a wide range of cost differentials. The value-engineering of these schemes is extremely important and is, in the author's judgment, the only way to arrive at an intelligent solution to the selection of the structural system for a high-rise building.

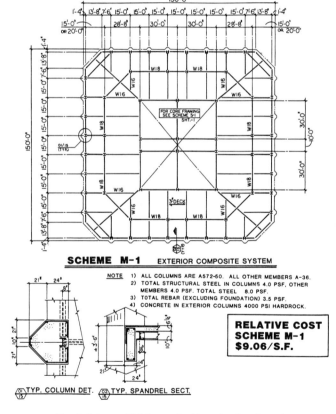

SCHEME M-1   EXTERIOR COMPOSITE SYSTEM

NOTE 1) ALL COLUMNS ARE A572-50. ALL OTHER MEMBERS A-36.
2) TOTAL STRUCTURAL STEEL IN COLUMNS 4.0 PSF, OTHER MEMBERS 4.0 PSF. TOTAL STEEL 8.0 PSF.
3) TOTAL REBAR (EXCLUDING FOUNDATION) 3.5 PSF.
4) CONCRETE IN EXTERIOR COLUMNS 4000 PSI HARDROCK.

**RELATIVE COST
SCHEME M-1
$9.06/S.F.**

TYP. COLUMN DET.   TYP. SPANDREL SECT.

Fig. 9 Scheme M-1 for typical low-rise framing plan

Industrial Tall Buildings

Zareh B. Gregorian

Tall buildings provide efficient use of land for commercial and residential purposes. Industrial buildings, such as power plants, refineries, and mills, can also be tall buildings, and thus experience the same kinds of problems as commercial and residential tall buildings. In fact, because of the functions and irregular shapes of industrial buildings, the problems and solutions are more complicated than for other buildings.

The five-volume monograph published by the Council on Tall Buildings and Urban Habitat (Council on Tall Buildings, 1978-1981) has provided a valuable reference on residential and commercial tall buildings. Little information, however, has been gathered on industrial tall buildings. To overcome this problem, the specialty area "Industrial Tall Buildings" is being addressed.

This paper presents a brief outline and comparison of the major factors affecting the structural design of residential and commercial tall buildings and of industrial tall buildings. Its intent is to enable structural engineers to coordinate existing research on both types of buildings and to provide a path for documenting future research.

HOW TALL IS A TALL BUILDING?

The question "How tall is a tall building?" cannot simply be answered with a number. Instead, a building, whether residential, commercial, or industrial, is considered to be a tall building if it has the height-related design problems associated with tall buildings.

In residential and commercial tall buildings, the problems associated with height depend on the structural system, wind, earthquake, deflection, human comfort, stability, vertical communication facilities, and many other factors. Combined, these elements produce the overall criteria that establish whether a building has to be treated with the more careful structural design considerations and tools appropriate to a tall building.

All these factors are also important in industrial tall buildings. Other major factors of importance are stability during and after construction, heavy loadings on upper stories, limited deflections, machinery comfort, and operability of electrical and mechanical equipment during wind, tornados, and earthquakes. Most of these factors can cause severe problems, even when the building is only a few stories high.

DESIGN CONCEPTS AND STRUCTURAL SYSTEMS

Proper functioning, safety, comfort, economy, material availability, erection procedures, and energy use are major features that lead to a proper design concept and structural system to be used for a conventional tall building.

Central concrete or steel shear cores capable of withstanding lateral loads and providing stability for a structure with peripherical columns provide large open spaces for office buildings. Bundled tube structures are efficient for taller buildings, providing both the open space required and the resistance to lateral forces that become more significant as the building height increases.

Rigid frame structures with shear walls or braced systems are also used when a conventional function is required. Large braced frames on the periphery of buildings are used for interior space freedom, when the bracing does not obscure the exterior view and appearance of the building.

The main factors that must be considered in the design of conventional tall buildings are function, stability, safety, and economy. While these considerations are also important in industrial buildings, the dominating factors are different.

The proper functioning of equipment is of major importance in industrial tall buildings. The bracing used must not interfere with necessary openings. Most of the time the lateral load resisting system must be independent of contributions from lateral load resistance of floor framing to enable parts of the existing floor to be removed during the service life of the structure. The system must be capable of carrying unevenly distributed heavy loads both resting on the floor and hanging from columns on girders at different elevations.

The cladding problem is not a major issue for industrial tall buildings, except in some special cases where the structure has to be airtight and able to undergo expansion when excessive interior pressures build up during an accident.

Spacing of bays in an industrial building are not equal; the size of adjacent bays may differ by a factor of five. Floor systems are not continuous at one elevation, and irregular patterns exist in horizontal planes. Irregular split levels are very common, and numerous setbacks can be found in industrial tall buildings.

With these irregular patterns of loading, framing and bracing systems in the conceptual and structural design of such tall buildings are much more complicated than those of conventional tall buildings.

STEEL OR CONCRETE INDUSTRIAL TALL BUILDINGS, USE OF HIGH STRENGTH STEELS, PRECAST CONCRETE CONSTRUCTION

Steel structures are in general more feasible than concrete structures for industrial tall buildings that need flexible horizontal floor and vertical spaces. The steel structure can be rearranged easily to conform with new functions required during the lifetime of the structure. Also, rigid type framing systems are not commonly used for industrial buildings; thus reinforced concrete cast in-place structures, which are mainly rigid systems, are not normally used.

Commercial and residential buildings are generally of a regular shape; as a result, only a few sizes of precast modules are needed to construct a precast reinforced conventional tall building. Industrial buildings, on the other hand, are not modular, and numerous types of precast elements are needed to accomodate a variety of heights, spans, and loading conditions. Therefore, except in typical one-story warehouse type structures or in some symmetrical structures such as cooling towers, the use of precast concrete structures is not feasible for industrial tall buildings.

When the size of columns and girders becomes important, as is often the case with industrial tall buildings, the use of high-strength steels instead of ordinary steels could be both technically and economically feasible. The use of high strength steels also facilitates transportation and construction when heavily loaded columns and long span girders are used.

MOVING LOADS, VIBRATIONS, FATIGUE PROBLEMS, AND EFFECTS ON HUMAN COMFORT

In most conventional tall buildings, live loads are assumed to be uniformly distributed over the surfaces of the floor areas. The worst conditions of gravity moments introduced in beams and columns occur when alternate spans are loaded. This is an important issue for the top stories of a high building, where the gravity loading alone, without taking into account the effect of wind and earthquake lateral loads, is a major factor.

In industrial tall buildings, live loads may not be uniformly distributed. In addition, heavy moving loads are very common. These loads can be either crane loads, or loads moved over certain floor areas, thus producing complicated loading patterns.

The fatigue caused by mechanical equipment vibrations is of major importance. Provisions are made to eliminate the vibration problems. In some cases careful studies are necessary to determine the frequency range of such vibrations to assure that it does not coincide with the natural frequency and thus result in severe resonance conditions that might interfere with the functioning of mechanical equipment. Such problems exist in ordinary tall buildings only in cases where the mechanical floor is placed at higher floors or for very tall buildings where vortex shedding can produce resonance.

Deformations occur in tall structures when subjected to wind and earthquake loading. Drift limitations are established by various codes. The Applied Technology Council (1978) recommends a value of

$$\varDelta = 1 \pm [(H - 20)/10]\,(0.5)$$

where H is in feet and delta is in inches.

A deflection index of 0.0015 to 0.0035 is recommended for commercial, and 0.0010 to 0.0025 for residential, buildings. (Gaylord and Gaylord, 1979)

Several design provisions limit the drift. These include using tubular structural systems, braced tubes on the periphery of the structure, heavy braced portions at the lower stories of structures, and, in recent years, mechanically controlled dampers.

Replaceable viscoelastic energy-dissipative dampers are used in the twin towers of the World Trade Center in New York (Fig. 1). To control deflections in tall structures, tuned mass dampers (Fig. 2) are used in the John Hancock Tower in Boston (Wiesner, 1979) and the Citicorp Center Building in New York (McNamara, 1977).

Research is also being done on the control of movement of a structure through the use of active tendon systems installed between adjacent floors (Yang, 1982) (Fig. 3).

Human comfort is an important design criterion for both conventional and industrial tall buildings. Much general research has been done on motion due to static and dynamic forces, human perception and tolerance to motion, and psychological responses. The movement of furniture and fixtures has been categorized, and the human response to motion has been studied using motion simulators. By implementing various design criteria such as human comfort, maximum acceleration, threshold exceedance, storm occurrence, and drift ratio criteria, conclusions can be drawn on the criteria's effectiveness, and needs for future research can be specified. In industrial buildings, machinery functioning becomes important. Excessive deflections, caused either by mechanical equipment vibrations or by wind or earthquake motions, will interfere with the proper functioning of the equipment.

Furthermore, a study of human comfort in industrial tall buildings from the kinesiological, psychological, and physiological points of view can be applied to conventional tall buildings. A study of persons working in industrial buildings might reveal how a person exposed to extensive motion during his work period can tolerate the motion but cannot tolerate motions of much less magnitude for much shorter periods when staying in a tall building. The results of such a study could help educate people who live in tall structures.

WIND DESIGN

The wind design is a major factor that dominates many aspects of the structural and architectural design of tall buildings. The multidirectional forces acting on windward–leeward sides and roof of the structure are resisted by proper framing and bracing of shear wall or shear core systems.

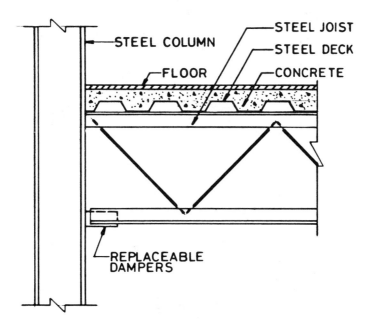

Fig. 1 Viscoelastic energy dissipative dampers

Most conventionally shaped buildings do not have openings on elevations around the periphery of the structure, although research is underway on providing some openings on top stories of tall structures to minimize the effect of vortex shedding.

Cladding also is a major consideration in conventional tall buildings. Glass walls are desirable from the architectural standpoint. If proper design is not used for these features, serious problems may arise during the lifetime of the building.

Considerable research exists on conventional tall buildings. Much of this research could be applied to industrial tall buildings.

For various functional reasons, partially closed or totally open spaces are common features of industrial tall buildings. This creates special problems, but the solutions of these are rarely discussed in the research literature. The special bracing systems that are used are more important than those systems used in conventional tall structures.

To scatter the load to several column lines, bracing is placed in several bays

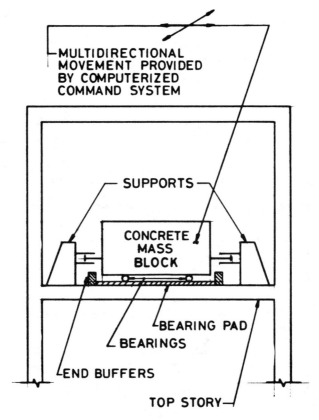

Fig. 2 Tuned mass dampers

on different floors (Fig. 4). This may not be desirable from the architectural point of view. Also, if the braced lines are in interior spans, the flexibility of the interior is decreased. Due to relatively large spans and story heights, single bracing capable of taking both tension and compression forces is used instead of X bracing. The system of scattered bracing provides a much more even distribution of lateral loads and could be a better economical and technical solution than bracing one or two bays all along the height of a structure (Fig. 5).

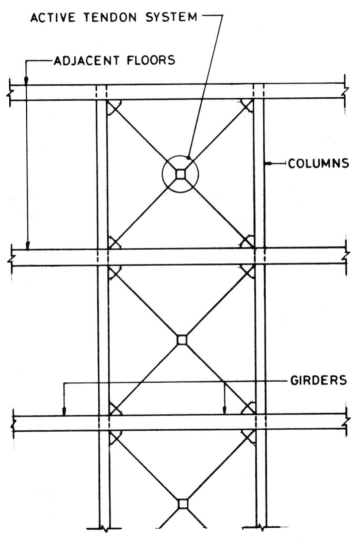

Fig. 3 Active tendon system installed between adjacent floors

Another major feature in industrial buildings is the enclosure criterion. Depending on the proportion of the enclosed area, the building is handled either as an enclosed or as an unenclosed structure. If less than 10% of the area is enclosed, the building is usually treated as an open structure. In open structures wind load acting on structural members and mechanical equipment is taken into account (ASCE Structural Division, 1962). In some cases equipment such as boilers, silos, and turbines, with large areas exposed to wind pressure, exist within the structure. The wind loads transferred to supports of such equipment and to the lateral load resisting system of the structure then become important.

The effect of the side suctions occurring at corners of structures is also of considerable importance and is treated as a local wind effect problem. ANSI (1982) provides general information on wind design of structures.

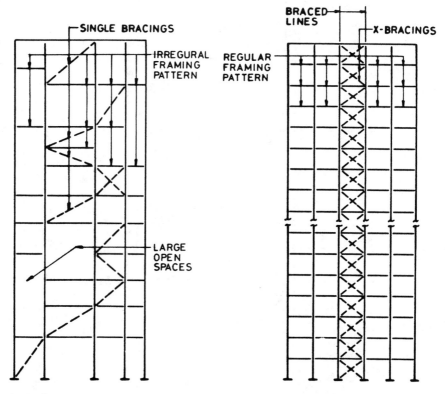

Fig. 4 Industrial tall buildings with irregular bracing systems

Fig. 5 Conventional tall building with regular bracing systems

EARTHQUAKE LOADING AND RESPONSE

Earthquake design of residential and commercial buildings is less complicated than the earthquake design of industrial buildings. One of the reasons is the symmetrical shape in plan and uniformity in story height of conventional buildings. The uniform distribution of dead and live loads throughout the structure also simplifies design.

In industrial tall buildings, the shape of the structure is not symmetrical and the load distribution is not uniform. Heavy equipment loading exists on different levels, and resonance problems become significant and affect the operability of the mechanical equipment. Sometimes huge equipment like turbines, boilers and silos, which weigh thousands of tons, are hung or placed on different levels. Using proper dynamic modeling, special analysis, and time-history ground acceleration records, the forces acting on different parts of structures can be calculated (Blume et al., 1961; Newmark and Rosenblueth, 1971; Applied Technology Council, 1978). The structure and soil interaction and the damping value are important, and provide more accurate data on the structural behavior of the building during earthquake motions. By special computer programming, the amplified response spectra can be developed for mechanical equipment (Fig. 6), and by using information about the natural frequency of equipment, the amplified acceleration acting on such equipment can be calculated and resonance zones identified, and the operability of equipment investigated for such amplified accelerations.

The preparation of the seismic model, taking into account lumped mass systems (Biggs, 1964; Rosenblueth, 1980; NRC, 1972), which account for eccentricities in plan of stories, is not a simple procedure, and does not produce ideal results. However, with some modifications, the above procedure could be applied to residential and commercial tall buildings, and the results incorporated with code values for design purposes.

By assuming the floor weights as lump masses at different elevations and columns and connecting the masses as stick members, the acceleration at each level of the structure can be calculated and human comfort can be investigated. This problem cannot be solved by simple code applications.

This overall design approach will become simple if the geometry of the structure is kept simple and symmetry is maintained throughout the structure.

DEFLECTION AND STABILITY PROBLEMS DURING CONSTRUCTION AND SERVICE LIFE OF THE BUILDING

In residential and commercial tall buildings the deflection problem is of utmost importance during the service life of the building. As discussed previously, excessive deflections may cause serious problems for the partitions, claddings, and glass exterior of buildings, and may also cause human discomfort.

In industrial tall buildings the governing factor is the deflection limit that will cause malfunctioning of mechanical equipment. The cladding problem is not significant, because most industrial buildings have lightweight metal sidings. Also, the stability of commercial and residential tall buildings is not significant when compared with that of industrial ones. In conventional tall buildings, only a few bays are left open for tower crane operations; in industrial tall buildings, large areas have to be left open for installation of massive equipment, thus creating major construction stability problems.

TEMPERATURE EFFECTS AND EXPANSION PROBLEMS

Changes in environmental temperatures produce common problems in both conventional and industrial buildings. Greater fluctuation results in more serious problems. The temperature change in certain parts of industrial buildings can be very great during the operation and service period of such structures, causing severe structural problems if proper attention is not given to the subject. Much research exists on the effect of such severe temperature changes in industrial tall buildings. This research can be applied to residential and commercial buildings when the temperature changes during the lifetime of the structures are considerable.

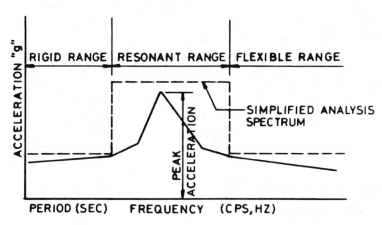

Fig. 6 **Amplified response spectra by time-history** *(output of structure could be used as input for equipment)*

FIREPROOFING

The fire problem is not a major issue in industrial tall buildings. Very little attention is given to the problem of protecting both the occupants and the building, compared to what is being done in commercial and residential tall buildings. The problem is insignificant in industrial buildings for two reasons; first, there is comparatively little material to burn; second, there is enough space and volume for people to move around and evacuate the building in case of fire. Therefore smoke inhalation, which is a major cause of loss of life in fires in conventional buildings, becomes an unimportant issue in industrial tall buildings. Some coatings are used on steel members in some parts of the steel structures, and generally preventive measures are taken in accordance with fire-safety-related codes such as U.B.C. (ICBO, 1979). Sprinklers are seldom used except in office areas of tall industrial buildings. Fire problems are localized and only affect limited portions of the structures.

Precautionary measures are taken when fuels are stored and fire could start as the result of oil spray by hydraulic rupture. Also precaution is taken on coal conveyor structures.

ARCHITECTURE OF INDUSTRIAL TALL BUILDINGS, APPEARANCE, AND BLENDING WITH THE ENVIRONMENT

The architectural features of commercial and residential tall buildings are dominating factors, both in the sociological and other human-related aspects, and in the structural design of such buildings.

A lot of effort is put into blending new structures with the existing environment in terms of both function and appearance. Height limitations, volume sizes, and materials used for the facade contribute a lot to proper blending criteria. Examples of these types of buildings include several buildings in Dacca, the second capital of Pakistan (Komendant, 1975), the Bu Ali Sina University, and the Iran Center for Management Studies in conjunction with Harvard University. In all these projects, careful study has been conducted to match the buildings with the environment from several human, technical, and geographical aspects.

In industrial tall buildings, this problem is also important, especially if a structure is built in the middle of a residential area. Although the architecture of industrial buildings is dominated by the mechanical functions of the structure, a proper architectural design will diminish many problems and will provide a better siting.

ENVIRONMENTAL EFFECT, NOISE, AND POLLUTION PROBLEMS

Industrial tall buildings are generally built on specifically selected sites. Because large pieces of land are used for such buildings, noise and pollution issues become less important. Major problems arise when such buildings are built in thickly settled residential areas. Vibration, noise, and pollution could cause severe problems for the community where such buildings are built.

Research has been conducted on eliminating or minimizing these problems in industrial tall buildings. This research could be used in commercial and residential tall buildings when a specific problem of similar nature arises. Such research can contribute a great deal to specific problems of commercial and residential tall buildings, and research on commercial and residential tall buildings in certain aspects can be of great help to designers of industrial tall buildings.

REFERENCES/BIBLIOGRAPHY

ANSI A58. 1-82, 1982
    AMERICAN NATIONAL STANDARD BUILDING CODE REQUIREMENTS FOR MINIMUM DESIGN
    LOADS IN BUILDINGS AND OTHER STRUCTURES, Section 6, American National Standards
    Institute, Inc., New York.
Applied Technology Council, 1978
    TENTATIVE PROVISIONS FOR THE DEVELOPMENT OF SEISMIC REGULATIONS FOR BUILD-
    INGS, ATC 3-06, NSF 78-8, Applied Technology Council Associated with Structural Engineers
    Association of California, Palo Alto, California.
ASCE Structural Division, 1962
    WIND FORCES ON STRUCTURES, Paper No. 3269, ASCE, New York, pp. 1124-1198.

Biggs, J. M., 1964
    INTRODUCTION TO STRUCTURAL DYNAMICS, McGraw-Hill Book Company, New York.
Blume, J. A., Newmark, N. M., and Corning, L. H., 1961
    DESIGN OF MULTISTORY REINFORCED CONCRETE BUILDINGS FOR EARTHQUAKE MOTION,
    Portland Cement Association, Skokie, Illinois.

Council on Tall Buildings, 1978-1981
    PLANNING AND DESIGN OF TALL BUILDINGS, A MONOGRAPH, 5 volumes, ASCE, New York.
Council on Tall Buildings, Committee 36, 1981
    MOTION PERCEPTION AND TOLERANCES, Chapter PC-13, Volume PC of the monograph on
    Planning and Design of Tall Buildings, ASCE, New York.

Gaylord, Jr., E. H. and Gaylord, C. N., 1979
    STRUCTURAL ENGINEERING HANDBOOK, 2nd Edition, McGraw-Hill Co., New York.

ICBO, 1975
    UNIFORM BUILDING CODE (UBC), International Conference of Building Officials, Whittier,
    California.

Komendant, A. E., 1975
    18 YEARS WITH ARCHITECT LOUIS I. KAHN, Aloray Publisher, Englewood, New Jersey.

McNamara, R. J., 1977
TUNED MASS DAMPERS FOR BUILDINGS, Journal of the Structural Division, ASCE, Vol. 103, No. ST9, September, pp. 1785-1795.

Newmark, N. M., and Rosenblueth, E., 1971
FUNDAMENTALS OF EARTHQUAKE ENGINEERING, Prentice Hall Inc., Englewood Cliffs, New Jersey.

NRC, 1972
NONLINEAR STRUCTURAL DYNAMIC ANALYSIS FOR CATAGORY I STRUCTURES, NUREG/CR-1161, URS, John A. Blume and Assoc., Engineers, New York.

Rosenblueth, E., Ed., 1980
DESIGN OF EARTHQUAKE RESISTANT STRUCTURES, John Wiley and Sons, New York—Toronto.

Wiesner, K. B., 1979
TUNED MASS DAMPERS TO REDUCE BUILDING WIND MOTION, Reprint 3510, ASCE Convention Exposition, Boston, Massachusetts, April, 1979.

Yang, J. N., 1982
CONTROL OF TALL BUILDINGS UNDER EARTHQUAKE EXCITATION, Journal of the Engineering Mechanics Division, ASCE, Vol. 108, No. EM5, October, pp. 833-849.

Foundation Systems

Deep Foundations — Caissons and High Capacity Piles

Clyde N. Baker, Jr.

INTRODUCTION

There have been many developments in caisson and high-capacity pile design and construction over the past ten years, since the Planning and Design of Tall Buildings, the First International Conference held at Lehigh University, August 21–26, 1972. The Monograph, a five-volume compendium of tall building information published from 1978 to 1981, which developed from that conference, presents a comprehensive review on trends and developments in types of piles and caissons and in knowledge of foundation behavior up to that time.

This paper deals with developments that have assumed importance since the Conference, and is heavily influenced by the author's personal experiences (which carries a decidely U.S. perspective and, in the case of caissons, a decidedly Chicago perspective). The developments covered include

1. In-situ testing for best soil property information to use in design

2. Testing and instrumentation to facilitate caisson construction

191

3. Use of large diameter, very high bearing belled caissons on both cohesive and noncohesive soil

4. Use of very high capacity friction piles and caissons

5. Increased use of dynamic measurements during pile driving.

IN-SITU TESTING; USE OF THE MENARD PRESSUREMETER

The Need for Improved Soil Property Measurements

Conventional deep foundation design considers both bearing capacity and settlement, making sure that there is an adequate factor of safety against failure and that predicted settlement is tolerable. Most bearing capacity theories use the equation

$$q_{ult} = CN_cS_1 + \bar{q}N_q + \tfrac{1}{2}\gamma BN_\gamma S_2$$

where

q_{ult} = ultimate bearing capacity,
γ = unit weight,
S = shape factor,
C = cohesion,
$\bar{q}$ = effective overburden pressure,
B = width, and
N_c, N_q, and N_γ = bearing capacity factors that vary with the different theories.

For soils with significant friction angle, the N_q term represents the determining factor. Figure 1 shows the wide range of N_q values that are possible at a given friction angle for different bearing capacity theories. The possible range is almost 10 to 1. Fortunately, bearing capacity usually does not turn out to be the determining consideration, but rather settlement. Traditionally, settlement predictions were based on consolidation tests performed on laboratory samples or were estimated from Standard Penetration Resistance data (blow count) correlated with past experience. The former procedure involves all the problems with obtaining truly undisturbed samples and the latter procedure has all the problems of correlating a dynamic test with a possible erratic energy input with desired static soil parameters.

Principles of the Menard Pressuremeter

Figure 2 is a schematic rendering of the pressuremeter, showing a radially expandable probe that is lowered into the bore hole and expanded radially against the sides of the bore hole walls, measuring soil deformation and pressure. With this data, it is possible to compute a modulus, limit pressure, creep pressure, and shear strength. Principles of pressuremeter theory and

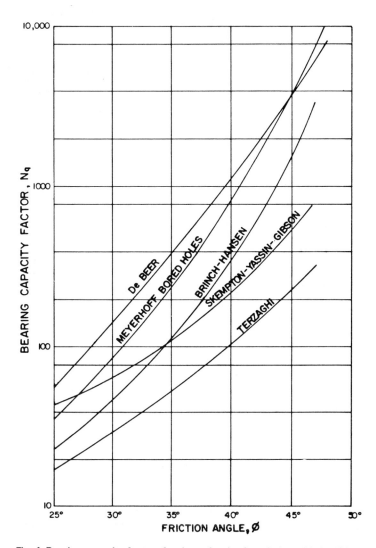

Fig. 1 Bearing capacity factors for deep circular foundations *(Vesic, 1967)*

operation are described in by Sol-Soils 26 (1975); NRCC (1975); Lucas and DeBussy (1976); Baguelin et. al. (1978); and Gambin (1979).

Figure 3 depicts pressuremeter results showing change in probe volume versus pressure. The so-called pseudoelastic range is the straight line portion of the plot up to the point where the plot curves and creep is noted. Creep is defined as the increase in volume change as each load increment is maintained from 30 s to 1 min. In the author's practice, following the procedures outlined in Sol-Soils 26 (1975) has yielded relatively reliable results in granular deposits, preconsolidated soils, and residual soils. The pressuremeter has been particularly useful in helping to determine values of horizontal subgrade reaction modulus and P-Y curves to utilize in beam on elastic foundation computer programs for predicting lateral deflection and bending stresses for piles and caissons subject to horizontal loads.

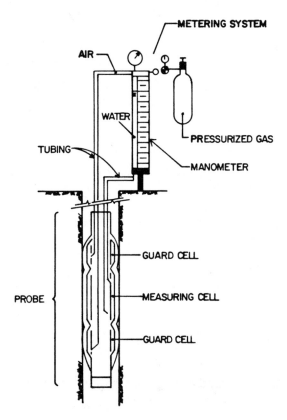

Fig. 2 Schematic diagram showing pressuremeter in a borehole *(Menard, 1975)*

Other In-Situ Testing Developments

In addition to the Menard pressuremeter, other in-situ testing devices useful in determining soil modulus information include the self-boring pressuremeter, the Dutch cone, and the dilatometer. They are all described in the references.

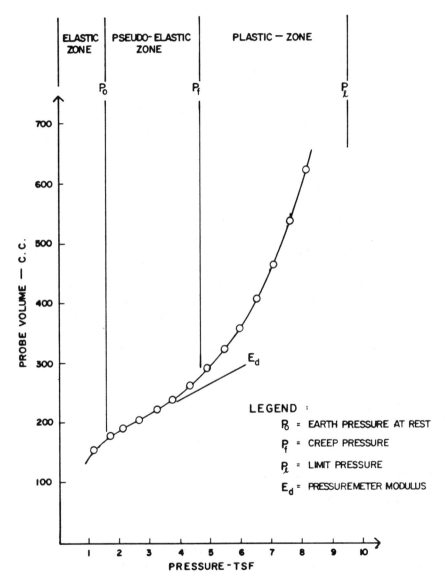

Fig. 3 Typical pressuremeter curve *(Menard, 1975)*

It is anticipated that there will be increasing use in coming years of in-situ testing equipment to determine soil deformation properties directly.

TESTING AND INSTRUMENTATION TO FACILITATE CAISSON CONSTRUCTION

In recent years, more attention has been paid to testing and instrumentation to facilitate caisson construction with a minimum of detrimental adjacent ground movement. From the experience of the author, the primary causes of ground movement adjacent to caisson construction are clay squeeze and excessive water pumping. Experience gained on a number of Chicago caisson projects where ground movements were measured have been summarized in Lukas and Baker (1978). With regard to clay squeeze, the conclusion was reached that squeeze will typically occur when the ratio of overburden pressure to clay shear strength exceeds 6. When the ratio is in the range of 6 to 8, the squeeze may be slow and not noticeable. Where the ratio is in the range of 8 to 10, the squeezing is much faster and may be observed as the hole is being drilled. Complete collapse typically occurs when the ratio exceeds 10.

On major projects in the Chicago area where deep excavations and large caissons are planned, inclinometers are normally installed at the perimeter of the site to monitor any lateral ground movement. The inclinometers can be used not only to detect lateral movement in the softer clay zones but also to detect any movement in fine silt and sand zones due to water pumping. Figure 4 shows the inclinometer data indicating both lateral movements in the clay zones and movement in the deeper water-bearing silt layer that occurred as a result of heavy water pumping from the nearby rock caissons on a major downtown office tower. All the reported movements occurred during the extended caisson construction time that was required because of the water problems and rock removal problems. Because of this observed silt movement, the City of Chicago typically sets water pumping limits for a contractor during rock caisson construction. As a result of these water pumping limits, considerable work has been done utilizing grouting to minimize water problems. Baker et. al. (1982) describe a number of such projects.

LARGE DIAMETER, HIGH BEARING PRESSURE BELLED CAISSONS ON COHESIVE AND NONCOHESIVE SOIL

Because of the high cost of rock caisson foundations in the Chicago area, there have been increasing economic pressures to put taller and heavier buildings on belled caissons in soil above the rock. The Chicago soil profile includes a dense clayey hardpan stratum underlain by a very dense cohesionless silt stratum that is water-bearing and typically under an artesian head. In recent years, buildings in the 59 to 75-story range with column loads as high as 18,000 kips have been supported on belled caissons on these layers. Three typical case histories are summarized in Table 1. The maximum allowable bearing pressure and the compressibility and deformation properties of the supporting stratum were determined in each case by in-situ pressuremeter

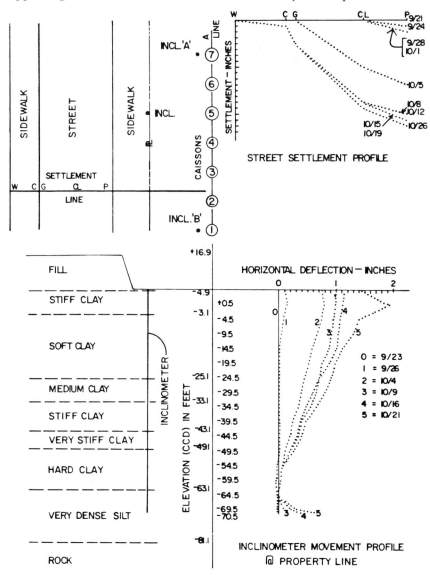

Fig. 4 Inclinometer movement profile at property line

testing. Where measured settlements were taken, they agreed very well with predicted settlements. It is interesting to note that the highest bearing pressures were utilized on the cohesionless very dense silt deposit, because the in-situ testing confirmed the extremely high capacity and modulus of the material in its confined state. The dense silt layer had not previously been utilized as a bearing stratum in Chicago because of the typical artesian head condition. In the past several years, the deep water table has been lowered, permitting construction directly on the layer.

Use of such high bearing pressures on unreinforced belled caissons has raised concern for the development of possible excess tensile stress in the bell. Theoretical studies and laboratory testing on model caissons in the unconfined state indicate tensile stresses sufficient to crack the concrete, contrary to observed field experience where no such problems have been recorded. Research is currently underway on measurement and testing of actual belled caisson installations to determine the effects of confinement and the maximum bell angles that should be used for the highest loading conditions.

USE OF HIGH-CAPACITY FRICTION CAISSONS

It has been common practice in certain parts of the United States, such as the Southwest and California, to use caissons or drilled shafts designed on the basis of side friction. Much research has been completed on how the load distributes to the soil in side friction, and many designs are based on an alpha (or adhesion) factor, which is the ratio of the ultimate friction per unit area divided by the shear strength of the soil. The work of Dr. Lymon Reese is noteworthy in this area. However, until recently, maximum caisson or shaft loads designed on this basis have been on the order of 3,000 kips.

Table 1 Comparison of predicted and measured building settlements

Building	Profile below bearing level[a]	Bearing pressure in TSF	Column load (tons)	Predicted settlement (inches)	Measured settlement (inches) Range	Average
75-story RC tower	15' clayey hardpan over 25' very dense silt over limestone bedrock	14.5	8000	2.00	1.69–2.19	1.94
50-story steel	25' very dense silt over limestone bedrock	20	2000	0.5	none reported	
50-story steel	15' clayey hardpan over 20' very dense silt over limestone	12	2000	0.56	.48–.54	0.5

[a]Bearing level typically is 80+' below ground surface

The author is aware of several recent projects in the United States where so-called drilled caissons have been socketed into rock and the load carried primarily in side friction and column loads being as high as 10,000 kips. These projects have involved load testing and/or instrumentation and have generally confirmed that load sheds in the rock in general acccordance with the theory of elasticity, with faster load shedding where the rock modulus is high with regard to the concrete, and slower load shedding where the rock modulus is low relative to the concrete. This is shown theoretically by Gill (1970) in Fig. 5. Gill has also shown theoretically that these load shedding trends are only moderately affected by seams in the rock.

Figure 6 shows an instrumented rock caisson on a 57-story high-rise office tower in Chicago, where the caisson extended approximately 2 diameters into the rock. The design was based on end bearing, and the penetration into the rock was required because of fissures and seams in the rock and the inability to achieve a water seal with the casing. The casing was grouted in with a cement

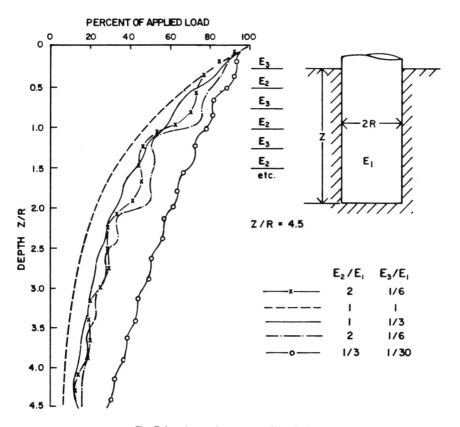

Fig. 5 Load transfer curves *(Gill, 1970)*

grout. Carlson strain cells and stress cells were installed at the top of the grouted section and at the base of the caisson, respectively, to determine the load that reached the bearing level. Measurements on the cells were taken throughout the building construction. Figure 7 shows the load distribution in the rock socket. Only 4% of the load reached the bottom of the caisson with the remainder carried out in side friction. The details of this project are indicated by Bushell and Baker (1981).

On another project, caissons for a 152.4 m (500 ft) tall cooling tower for a nuclear power plant were extended through 12.2 m (40 ft) of a soft chert conglomerate rock (where Standard Penetration Resistance values ranged from approximately 50 per 0.305 m (1 ft) to more than 100 per 25.4 mm (1 in.)) and ended on limestone or sandstone. Instrumentation was installed in one caisson to determine how much load reached the bottom of the caisson. Figure 8 shows that out of a 3,000 kip load, 0% reached the bottom with the entire 3,000 kip load taken out in side friction in the chert conglomerate.

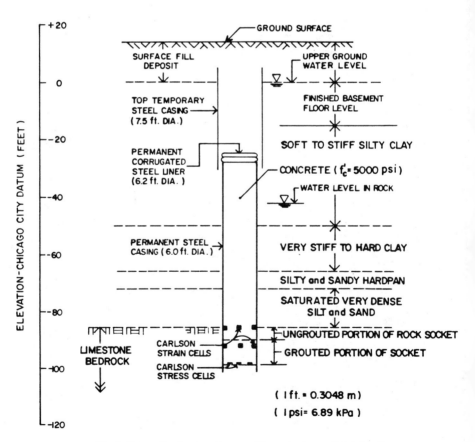

Fig. 6 Generalized subsurface profile and caisson G-3.1 detail

On a current (1983) project in Cleveland, Ohio, a 47-story office tower is being supported on 73.2 m (240 ft) deep caissons extended through glacial soils into a shale. Because of gas problems immediately above the shale, the design is based on penetrating the shale sufficiently to carry the full design load in socket friction. Column loads as large as 10,000 kips are involved, and socket penetration into the competent shale up to 4.9 m (16 ft) is anticipated. An instrumented caisson load test is planned.

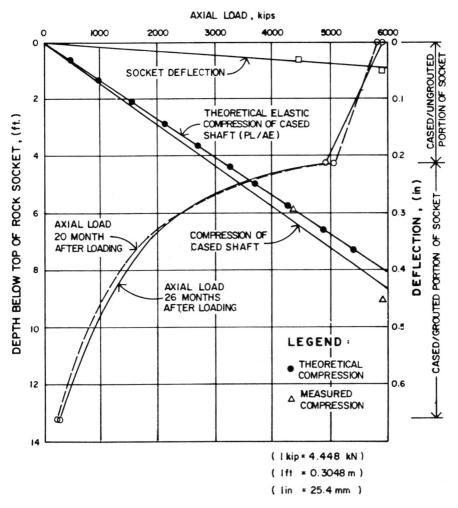

Fig. 7 Load distribution and load deflection curves for caisson G-3.1

USE OF HIGH-CAPACITY FRICTION PILES

Over the past ten years, there has been increasing use of higher-capacity piles. This appears to be particularly true where deposits are deep and it is possible to base designs in large part on side friction and utilize higher than normal stress levels in the steel. Most building codes still limit stress levels in steel piles to 36% of the yield but no more than 82,740 kPa (12,000 psi) unless justified by detailed engineering analysis. However, the 50-story First Wisconsin Center in downtown Milwaukee is supported on 89-pound, 356 mm (14 in.) H-section piles using Grade 60 steel and based on a 250-ton design. This results in a theoretical steel stress level of 131,000 kPa (19,000 psi). The piles

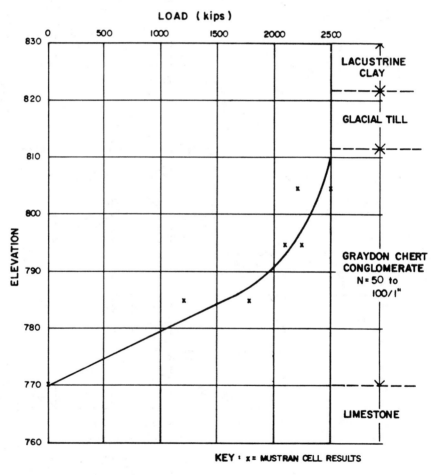

KEY : x = MUSTRAN CELL RESULTS

Fig. 8 Instrumented cooling tower foundation

extended approximately 51.8 m (170 ft) deep and approximately 15.2 m (50 ft) into dense granular soils. Extensive load testing was performed in advance of construction to confirm the high stress level used in the design.

An atypical code is that used in New Orleans, where deep friction piles are the standard foundation design and where the code permits utilizing up to 50% of the yield strength of the steel. A 12.7 mm (0.5 in.) wall thick, 508-mm (20-in.) pipe driven open ended to depths of 73.2 m (240 ft), has safely carried a 380-ton design load. It would appear that where extensive alluvial deposits exist, there will continue to be increasing pile loads utilized by driving larger-diameter and longer-friction piles, with the marketplace determining the most cost effective system.

INCREASED USE OF DYNAMIC MEASUREMENTS DURING PILE DRIVING

Over the last ten years, there has been increased use of dynamic measurements taken during pile driving, led by George Goble and Frank Rausche and their associates at Case Western Reserve University. A firm started by them, Pile Dynamics, Inc., now sells equipment all over the world for taking and analyzing dynamic measurements. A schematic representation of the equipment is shown in Fig. 9. Force measurements are taken with strain transducers and velocity measurements with low output impedance quartz crystal accelerometers. Each blow from the pile hammer can be recorded on an analog magnetic tape and can be recreated in the laboratory. It can then be processed automatically by converting the analog signal to digital form and storing only the important part of the record. These measurements can be used for calculating hammer energy delivered to the pile and for back-calculating hammer efficiency to plug into a desired wave equation. Experience has indicated that actual hammer efficiency may vary significantly from the manufacturers rated hammer efficiency, and this may significantly affect pile capacity predictions based on wave equation analysis. Measuring of hammer efficiency can be particularly important for pile driving on a batter, where the effect of the batter can be much more than that predicted by geometry only. On a recent major pile testing program for a nuclear power plant cooling tower, it was observed that the average hammer efficiency when driving on a 3:1 batter was approximately 50%, compared to an average hammer efficiency of 70% when driving vertical.

Concurrently with development of the Case Goble Pile Analyzer, the Case Pile Wave Analysis Program (CAPWAP) was developed. With CAPWAP, it is possible to predict the load distribution along a pile under design load or test load. The soil forces for each discreet pile element in the embedded zone must be estimated: the static resistance R_u, the quake q, and the damping j. In the CAPWAP analysis, a reasonable assumption is made regarding the soil parameters, and the motion of the pile is input using the measured top acceleration as the boundary value. The theoretical wave equation curves are compared with the observed measured curves, the soil parameters are modified, and another iteration is made to improve the match. When good agreement is reached, the true capacity and load distribution have been achieved.

Over the past ten years, thousands of piles have been tested using dynamic measurements and the Case Pile Analyzer method, and good agreement has been reached with static load tests provided that proper account has been taken of ground freeze. For best results, the load test pile should be retapped with dynamic measurements made following the load test.

It is anticipated that increasing use will be made of dynamic measurements in the future, as equipment is made available and utilized by more and more companies and organizations.

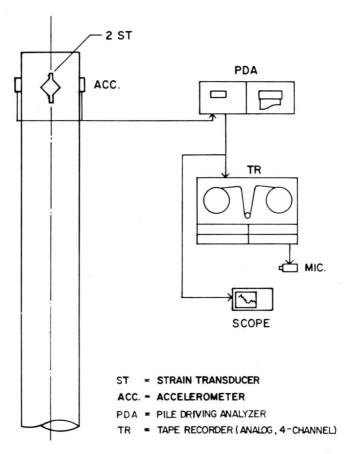

ST = STRAIN TRANSDUCER
ACC. = ACCELEROMETER
PDA = PILE DRIVING ANALYZER
TR = TAPE RECORDER (ANALOG, 4-CHANNEL)

Fig. 9 Schematic of instrumentation *(Goble, 1980)*

Figure 10 shows the results of a large number of static load tests and CAPWAP capacity predictions summarized by Pile Dynamics, Inc.

Figure 11 shows the correlation of the capacity predicted using hammer efficiencies determined by dynamic measurements combined with the wave equation analysis and compared to static load tests on a large cooling tower project in which the writer was recently involved.

CONCLUSIONS

In-situ testing developments have led to better soil property determination, and the trend towards taller and heavier buildings has led to higher caisson design capacities. Instrumentation on actual caissons has demonstrated high load capacity in side friction when socketed into material that has varied on different projects from soft to hard rock. Load shedding in these cases has agreed reasonably with the theory of elasticity.

High capacity driven piles in the range of 250 to 380 tons have successfully supported tall buildings. The most cost effective use seems to be those

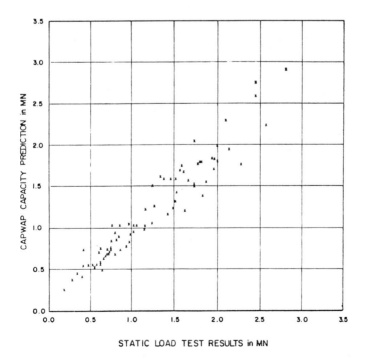

STATIC LOAD TEST RESULTS in MN

Fig. 10 CAPWAP and static load test capacity correlation *(Goble, 1980)*

situations in which soil conditions are adverse for caissons, and where the piles are very long and carry the major portion of their load in side friction.

The trend towards taller and heavier buildings will undoubtedly accelerate the use of even higher-capacity caissons and piles.

REFERENCES/BIBLIOGRAPHY

Baguelin, F., Jezequel, J. F., and Shields, D. H., 1978
    THE PRESSUREMETER AND FOUNDATION ENGINEERING, Trans Tech Publications.
Baker, C. N., Echevarria, F. A., and Cnaedinger, J. P., 1982
    USE OF GROUTING IN CAISSON CONSTRUCTION, ASCE Specialty Conference, February, New Orleans, Louisiana.
Baker, C. N. and Khan, F., 1971
    CAISSON CONSTRUCTION PROBLEMS AND CORRECTION IN CHICAGO, Journal of the Soil Mechanics and Foundation Division, ASCE, Vol. 97, No. SM2, February, pp. 417-440.

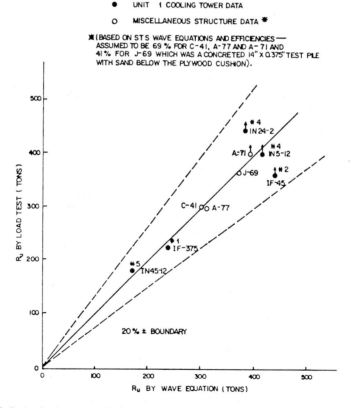

Fig. 11 R_u by load test vs. R_u by wave equation *(unit 1 cooling tower and miscellaneous structure data)*

Bauer, G. E., 1980
THE MEASUREMENT AND ANALYSIS OF LOAD TRANSFER FROM A CAISSON TO ITS ROCK SOCKET, International Conference on Structural Foundations on Rock, (Proceedings of Conference held in Sydney, Australia), pp. 235-240.

Bushell, T. D. and Baker, C. N., 1981
DISCUSSION OF CAISSON SOCKETED IN SOUND MICA SCHIST, BY KOUTSOFTAS, Geotechnical Journal, ASCE.

Cunningham, J. A. and Robbins, J. R., 1974
ROCK CAISSONS FOR THE NORTHERN BUILDING IN CHICAGO'S LOOP, (Proceedings of Conference held in Bangkok, Thailand), ASCE-IABSE.

Ellison, R. D., D'Appolonia, E., and Thiers, G. R., 1971
LOAD DEFORMATION MECHANISM FOR BORED PILES, Journal of the Soil Mechanics and Foundation Division, ASCE, Vol. 97, No. SM4, April.

Freeman, C. F., Klajnerman, D., and Prasad, G. D., 1972
DESIGN OF DEEP SOCKETED CAISSONS INTO SHALE BEDROCK, Canadian Geotechnical Journal, Vol. 9, No. 1, February, pp. 105-114.

Gambin, M., 1979
CALCULATIONS OF FOUNDATIONS SUBJECTED TO HORIZONTAL FORCES USING PRESSUREMETER DATA, Sol-Soil 30/31.

Gill, S. A., 1970
LOAD TRANSFER MECHANISM FOR CAISSONS SOCKETED INTO ROCK, Ph.D. Thesis, Northwestern University, Evanston, Illinois.

Gill, S. A., 1980
DESIGN AND CONSTRUCTION OF ROCK CAISSONS, International Conference on Structural Foundations on Rock, (Proceedings of Conference held in Sydney, Australia), pp. 241-252.

Goble, G. G., Rausch, F., and Likins, G. E., 1980
THE ANALYSIS OF PILE DRIVING—A STATE-OF-THE-ART, Seminar on the Application of Stress Wave Theory on Piles, June 4-5, Stockholm, Sweden.

Goehr, P. M. and Hustad, P. A., 1979
INSTRUMENTED DRILLED SHAFTS IN CLAY SHALE, ASCE Symposium on Deep Foundations, October 25, 1979, Atlanta, Georgia.

Horvath, R. G., Kenney, T. C., and Trow, W. A., 1980
RESULTS OF TESTS TO DETERMINE SHAFT RESISTANCE OF ROCK-SOCKETED DRILLED PIERS, International Conference on Structural Foundations on Rock, (Proceedings of Conference held in Sydney, Australia), pp. 349-361.

Horvath, R. G., 1978
FIELD LOAD TEST DATA ON CONCRETE-TO-ROCK BOND STRENGTH FOR DRILLED PIER FOUNDATIONS, Publication 78-07, Department of Civil Engineering, University of Toronto, Toronto, Canada.

Ladanyi, B. and Domingue, D., 1980
AN ANALYSIS OF BOND STRENGTH FOR ROCK SOCKETED PIERS, International Conference on Structural Foundations on Rock, (Proceedings of Conference held in Sydney, Australia) pp. 363-373.

Lukas, R. G. and Baker, C. N. 1978
GROUND MOVEMENT ASSOCIATED WITH DRILLED PIER INSTALLATIONS, ASCE Spring Convention and Exhibit, Preprint No. 3266, Philadelphia, Pennsylvania.

Lukas, R. G. and DeBussy, B., 1976
PRESSUREMETER AND LABORATORY TEST CORRELATIONS FOR CLAYS, Geotechnical Division, ASCE, No. GT9, September.

Menard, L., 1975
THE MENARD PRESSUREMETER—INVESTIGATION AND APPLICATION OF PRESSUREMETER TEST RESULTS, Sol-Soils 26.

National Research Council of Canada, 1975
    CANADIAN MANUAL ON FOUNDATION ENGINEERING, Associate Committee on the National
    Building Code, National Research Council of Canada, Ottawa.

Osterberg, J. O. and Gill, S. A., 1973
    LOAD TRANSFER MECHANISM FOR PIERS SOCKETED IN HARD SOILS OR ROCK, (Pro-
    ceedings of 9th Canadian Symposium on Rock Mechanics held in Montreal, Quebec, November,
    1973), pp. 235-262.
Osterberg, J. O., 1968
    DRILLED CAISSONS DESIGN, INSTALLATION, APPLICATION, Chicago Soil Mechanics Lecture
    Series, Department of Civil Engineering, Northwestern University, Evanston, Illinois.

Pells, P. J. N., and Turner, R. M., 1979
    ELASTIC SOLUTIONS FOR THE DESIGN AND ANALYSIS OF ROCK-SOCKETED PILES, Canadian
    Geotechnical Journal, Vol. 16, No. 3, August, pp. 481-487.

Reese, L. C. and O'Neil, M. W., 1969
    FIELD TESTS OF BORED PILES IN BEAUMONT CLAY, ASCE Annual Meeting, Preprint No. 1008,
    Chicago, Illinois.
Reese, L. C. and Wright S. V., 1977
    DRILLED SHAFT MANUAL, Two Volumes, Implementation Package 77-21, U. S. Department
    of Transportation, Office of Research and Development, Washington, D.C.
Rosenberg, P. and Journeaux, N. L., 1976
    FRICTION AND END BEARING TESTS ON BEDROCK FOR HIGH CAPACITY SOCKET DESIGN,
    Canadian Geotechnical Journal, Vol. 13, No. 3, August, pp. 324-333.

Sanglerat, G., 1972
    THE PENETROMETER AND SOIL EXPLORATION, Elsevier Publishing Company, Amsterdam.
Schmertmann, J. H., 1975
    THE MEASUREMENT OF IN-SITU SHEAR STRENGTH, 6th PSC, ASCE, Vol. 2, pp. 57-138.

Vesic, A. S., 1967
    ULTIMATE LOADS AND SETTLEMENT OF DEEP FOUNDATIONS IN SAND, Proceedings Sym-
    posium: Bearing Capacity and Settlement of Foundations, (Conference held at Duke University
    in Durham, North Carolina), pp. 53-68.
Vogan, R. W., 1977
    FRICTION AND END BEARING TESTS ON BEDROCK FOR HIGH CAPACITY SOCKET DESIGN:
    DISCUSSION, Canadian Geotechnical Journal, Vol. 14, pp. 156-158.

Woodward, R. J., Gardner, W. S., and Greer, D. M., 1972
    DRILLED PIER FOUNDATIONS, McGraw-Hill Book Company, New York.

Energy Conservation

Handling the Energy
Impact of the Electronic
"Office of the Future"

Gershon Meckler

The ingenuity of building system designers will be seriously tested over the next 10 to 20 years by the rapid spread of electronic office equipment, as major heat gains are experienced in office buildings. A clash is developing between the drive to reduce building energy consumption, and the need to pour new quantities of energy into productivity-raising new machines. Without corresponding gains in the efficiency of air conditioning systems to handle this increased heat, building energy consumption will jump back up to—and beyond—pre-1970s levels.

REDUCING SYSTEM LOAD . . . OR INCREASING
SYSTEM EFFICIENCY

Since the oil embargo of 1973, advances in building energy use have come mainly from reducing the load on the air conditioning system, rather than increasing the efficiency of the system in handling its load. Load control has stemmed from (a) energy-conscious building envelope design to reduce solar heat gain, (b) reduced lighting levels and improved lighting design to cut the interior heat from lights, and (c) better energy management (operation patterns and practices) to reduce consumption directly.

The improvements are impressive. In new energy-conscious office buildings the heat load has dropped some 40% from pre-1970s standards. Without comparable advances in the future, however, the electronic revolution will cancel this gain entirely in new office buildings; and older buildings—most of the existing stock—will find it difficult to compete in the real estate market.

Where will the advances come from? It will not be possible to cut the surge in energy consumption by reducing the electronic equipment load, since this load represents a direct investment in higher productivity. It is unlikely that we can squeeze significant additional savings out of other load factors. Instead, efforts must shift to a new frontier—increasing the thermodynamic efficiency of the total system. Savings in this area will transform waste into productivity, by taking energy salvaged from environmental systems and applying it to the new requirements of the electronic office.

The focus will be on thermodyamically rational integration of building systems, and the incorporation of renewable energy sources and usable waste heat, for maximum net savings of purchased energy. Significant and often dramatic savings are possible, since design generally has not been approached from a total system, thermodynamic perspective. System efficiency has usually implied the fine-tuning of machinery rather than, for example, developing new concepts for efficient heat removal. Before exploring design approaches and examples, a brief look at the problem is in order.

SCOPE OF CHANGE: THE ELECTRONIC OFFICE

Major shifts in the structure of the American economy and workforce are driving us rapidly into the electronic future. A majority of American workers are now engaged in the information business—processing, retrieving, evaluating, exchanging, or applying information. These office workers received 60% of the $1.3 trillion paid for wages, salaries, and benefits in the United States in 1980, and the percentage is expected to grow (Salmons, 1982). Further, within the office environment some 92% of costs are "on the floor"—tied up in salaries. Pressures to increase productivity from this 92% investment are powerful; and the new wave of productivity improvements is the shift from paper to electronic operations. Without any doubt, a massive transformation is on the way.

According to William Kistler, Staff Architect with IBM Corporation, which employs 165,000 office workers, "The electronic office of the future has arrived, and it's going to keep on arriving for a long time to come" (Kistler, 1982). "Certainly the trend is toward one-man, one-station offices in the near future," confirms Dr. Walter Baer, Director of Advanced Communications Technology for Times Mirror Corporation. "I would guess that by the decade's end companies will be planning for more computer work stations than parking spaces" (Baer, 1982). The Continental Illinois National Bank & Trust Company, a leader in applying the new technology, already has some 3,000 work stations compared with a total workforce of 12,000 (Salmons, 1982). And Vincent E. Giuliano of Arthur D. Little, Inc. projects that by 1990 there will be some 38 million terminal-based work stations, not counting possibly 34 million home terminals (Giuliano, 1982).

Experts see the big productivity boom coming at the white collar level, by way of such electronic support as prompt information retrieval (text, graphics, data, audio, video), computer-assisted writing and drawing, scheduling and management systems, electronic mail, video conferences, and more. Professionals, managers, and executives will personally use computer terminals for interactive, retrieval, and communication functions that will directly support creative, analytical, and decision-making activities. They literally will have libraries of specialized information at their fingertips; and since "information is power," competitors will not lag far behind. For example, Baer believes that "videotext . . . an information retrieval center complete with color and graphics" will be a feature of most professional work stations by 1990.

Booz, Allen & Hamilton, Inc. concluded, after a year-long study of the status and potential of office automation in fifteen large U.S. organizations, that "within five years knowledge workers could save an average of 15% of their time through more highly automated support" (Poppel, 1982). The actual timetable may be in doubt, but the revolution is not.

IMPACT ON THE OFFICE ENVIRONMENT

Introducing the new electronic equipment into existing buildings reveals problems of heat gain, glare and reflections, crowding, inadequate wiring, and inappropriate office furniture. These problems define the new challenges for architects, planners, interior designers, and engineers in relation to the design of new buildings as well as the renovation and retrofit of older office buildings that must adapt to avoid obsolescence. Design that does not explore and resolve these problems is inadequate design. If not faced now, the needs will have to be met at greater expense in the near future.

A difficulty facing all categories of building designers is the uncertainty among clients as to how rapidly, how extensively, and where they will introduce the new equipment. To some extent this is unavoidable; the technology is changing so rapidly that change will be an ongoing process in offices for the foreseeable future. This points to a highly significant consideration for all designers: Flexibility to handle the introduction of new technology becomes a supreme value in new or newly renovated office buildings.

TAKING THE HEAT

Heat from terminals and other electronic equipment is a particularly challenging problem because it can have a major impact on capital costs (the size of air conditioning equipment and distribution ductwork); energy consumption and therefore annual operating costs; space required for mechanical equipment, distribution ductwork, and floor-ceiling space between floors; and people's comfort and therefore productivity. Tables 1 and 2 summarize the heat gain from introducing the new office equipment into (1) current energy-conscious buildings and (2) existing buildings designed to pre-1970 standards. The number used for building heat gain from electronic equipment in the relatively near future is 13 Btu/ft^2/hr. This assumes one computer terminal of a currently standard type per work station of around 100 ft^2.

Table 1 Heat gain, current and projected, in energy-conscious office buildings of the 1970s and 1980s

	Heat gain (Btu/ft^2/hr)	
Heat gain component	Current standard office (Electric typewriters)	Near future — 1980s-90s (Computer terminals)[a]
People	2.5	
Lighting	6.8	
Building envelope	10.0	
Office equipment	1.7	13.0
Total heat gain	21.0 Btu	32.3 Btu
% increase in total gain	Base	54%

[a]Equipment heat increases by factor of 8. Total internally generated heat gain (excluding perimeter gain through envelope) more than doubles

Table 2 Heat gain, current and projected, in pre-1970s office buildings

	Heat gain — Btu/ft^2/hr	
Heat gain component	Current standard office (Electric typewriters)	Near future — 1980s-90s (Computer terminals)[a]
People	2.5	
Lighting	13.6	
Building envelope	15.0	
Office equipment	1.7	13.0
Total heat gain	32.8 Btu	44.1 Btu
% increase in total gain	Base	34%

[a]Equipment heat increases by factor of 8. Total internally generated heat gain (excluding perimeter gain through envelope) increases 61%

These numbers are derived from actual requirements for an air conditioning system developed in 1976 by the author and constructed in Baltimore, Maryland for the Social Security Administration (SSA) Metro West facility. The SSA, for practical reasons a pioneer in heavy use of computer terminals, specified that 300,000 ft^2 of the 786,000 ft^2 complex be capable of handling 13 Btu/ft^2/hr. This established the capacity and size of central plant equipment. However, since the precise location of the terminals was unknown, in effect the entire facility had to be able to handle the heat concentrations; that is, the distribution network had to be capable of handling the maximum load throughout the facility. This challenge—to incorporate a high degree of heat-handling flexibility at a competitive cost—will face all office designers in coming years. An overview of the SSA design solution, which was selected because it had the lowest life cycle cost among designs satisfying all General Services Administration specifications, is included later in this paper.

In the past, heat from office equipment typically has been a small percentage—around 5%—of a building's total heat gain from both internal sources (people, lights, office equipment) and solar gain through the building envelope. With the spread of computer terminals in the foreseeable future, heat from office equipment will increase eightfold, from 1.7 Btu/ft^2/hr to 13 Btu/ft^2/hr. This represents a jump from 5% to 29% of total heat gain in a typical office building designed to pre-1970 standards (Table 2). Assuming current energy-conscious building design (Table 1), the jump would be from 8% to 40% of the total heat gain.

By the year 2000 the total building heat load may be 55% larger. Will energy consumption grow proportionately? Will the space consumed by air conditioning equipment, distribution ductwork and fan horsepower grow accordingly? What are the implications for costs and for the viability of existing buildings? And what are the alternatives?

COST FACTORS

Energy costs have climbed so high during the past decade that total energy operating costs over the life of a building now equal the building's initial capital costs. Owners are finding new ways to pass these costs along to building users.

Annual energy costs will continue to rise, independent of international or inflationary pressures, as the use of electronic equipment increases. In a highly competitive market, the efficiency with which a building uses energy to minimize the utility bill will be increasingly important.

There are two components to the new energy cost rise: (1) energy to power the equipment; and (2) energy to remove the heat generated by the equipment. The first cost is unavoidable. The second cost can be reduced by increasing the overall efficiency of building systems in handling the heat load. Using typical methods, the energy cost of removing heat from the new equipment is two to three times the cost of powering the equipment. This variable cost component can be decreased up to 50%, saving as much as a third of the total cost of powering/cooling the equipment. On the basis of cost alone, pressures will mount to apply thermodynamic design techniques and incorporate all cost-effective energy sources to reduce ongoing operating costs. As the following section explains, energy cost is not the only pressure at work.

ARE EXISTING BUILDINGS OBSOLETE?

As computer terminals and other electronic equipment spread rapidly and become indispensible to a viable modern operation, they will be introduced into existing buildings as well as new ones. But in most of the current stock of office buildings—those built prior to the 1970s or designed to pre-1970 standards—adoption of the new equipment will be severely limited by (a) the cooling capacity of the existing air conditioning systems and (b) the lack of space for system expansion. If these buildings are to remain competitive— and they must—they will at some point require innovative retrofit of building systems. More efficient systems, that require less space and energy for a given quantity of work, will be urgently needed as older buildings struggle to handle the heat surge and stay in the mainstream of the business office community.

The standard response to a heavier load on the air conditioning system is simply to increase proportionately the capacity and size of the system's machinery and distribution ductwork. This response to the coming heat rise would pose serious if not insurmountable problems in terms of cost and space. Tables 1 and 2 indicate the magnitude of the problem. To house the electronic office of the near-future, older buildings will have to handle a 35% rise in the building's heat load; in newer buildings designed to more energy-conserving standards, the heat rise will be around 55%.

In many cases extra space is not available for significantly enlarged machinery in central plant areas, or for enlarged ductwork in the floor-to-ceiling areas between floors. In any case, office building space is a valuable commodity in major cities, where much of it is concentrated. If they can avoid it, owners will not shift sizable chunks of space from income-producing office area to accommodate larger air conditioning components.

As a result there will be a powerful demand for new concepts that (a) increase the overall efficiency of heat removal systems so that less purchased energy—less refrigeration energy and less fan horsepower—is required for a given amount of cooling; and (b) minimize the quantity of air that must be distributed from a central plant, and thus minimize the size of ductwork.

In addition to streamlining the air conditioning systems, lighting systems will have to be updated. Those installed during the 1950s and 1960s, when electric utilities were promoting high footcandle levels, produce twice as much heat as current state-of-the-art systems.

The lighting change and innovative retrofit of air conditioning systems are the two major elements of an upgrade that could carry these buildings through to the years 2030–2050, when they will need total revamping in ways we cannot quite predict. (For example, they may need adaptation to a largely solar-based economy.)

NOT WHETHER TO INNOVATE BUT HOW

As office heat grows into a real threat to older buildings, it will take a fundamental rethinking of the air conditioning process—and the application of innovative design concepts—to prevent a comparable rise in the space and energy consumed by heat removal systems. If this need is not addressed, the consequences will include

1. A major rise in building energy use, quite possibly wiping out the past decade's progress in reducing this total;

2. A corresponding rise in annual energy costs based on quantity consumed, on top of any unit price rises due to inflation and supply or international problems;

3. A diversion of much-needed funds from direct productivity investments;

4. Serious hardship for marginal office users as well as building owners facing a shift of income-producing space to the air conditioning system.

Even without the looming problem of office heat, more energy-efficient buildings are both desirable over the short run to cut costs, and essential over time to reduce dependence on declining fossil fuels. Clearly the question is not whether, but how, to innovate.

HANDLING THE IMPACT—THERMODYNAMIC EFFICIENCY

With the aim of reducing net purchased energy consuption, building designers will turn increasingly to a new frontier of energy efficiency—a total, integrated systems approach guided by overall thermodynamic efficiency (Meckler, 1983a). Specific materials, components, subsystems, energy sources, and concepts of energy efficiency will be used or not based on their contribution to an integrated master plan. A key measure of the plan's success will be the facility-wide coefficient of performance (COP)—the ratio of the work done (in other words, meeting the owner's design requirements) to the quantity of purchased energy used to accomplish the work. Improvements in materials and components will continue to provide incremental energy savings; but comprehensive energy-integrated systems design appears to be the principal largely untapped source of significant national energy savings in building design.

This approach requires a total building, total energy flow perspective. It looks first at the givens, particularly at (a) available energy sources, both purchased and alternative, and their cost and temperature level; and (b) specific design requirements including architectural and environmental. It attempts to use the first (energy sources) to achieve the second (design objectives) in the most energy-efficient, cost-effective way. Methods include thermodynamic techniques, alternative energy sources, task cooling, systems integration, and objective evaluation of alternative designs.

Efficiency requires the application of thermodynamic design techniques. A vivid and important example is high-temperature cooling. Based on the Second Law of Thermodynamics, the temperature level of a cooling or heating medium should be as close as possible to the final conditioned temperature; that is, heating should be done at the lowest temperature possible, and cooling at the highest temperature possible. Purchased energy use is reduced, clearly, when nonrefrigerated cooling tower water can be used for cooling, in place of chilled water. Purchased energy is also reduced (and the COP improved) when chilled water can perform a given cooling task at an elevated temperature. An example is the SSA facility, where all sensible cooling is done with 55°F (instead of 42°F) chilled water.

Efficiency requires the application of both First and Second Law thermodynamic techniques. The First Law relates to the quantity of energy used, without regard to its work potential (temperature level). A system can operate efficiently based on the First Law (minimizing the quantity required) but inefficiently according to the Second Law (for example, a lower-than-necessary temperature level for cooling). The aim is to optimize thermodynamic efficiency based on both First and Second Laws for the facility as a whole.

Alternative energy sources such as solar energy and recoverable waste heat can significantly improve a building's COP (requiring less purchased energy for given results); they should be incorporated whenever their use reduces a facility's total life cycle costs as well as improving its COP. Site-derived renewable energy will be an increasingly important factor as the technology evolves and experience with it grows.

A cost-effective practical example is the use of solar energy in the cooling process—in contrast to the more familiar solar heating—in the Washington, D.C. Veterans Administration Hospital, where it is expected to reduce annual utility costs by about 30%. In an integrated design developed by the author, dehumidification (latent cooling) is separated from temperature control (sensible cooling). Dehumidification, which typically is a significant portion (up to 40%) of a chiller's cooling load, is handled instead by a moisture-absorbing desiccant solution (Meckler, 1983b). The drying process (desiccant regeneration) is powered by low-temperature solar energy (130–140°F), which is available from flat plate collectors during a high percentage of the cooling season. In this design, a cogenerator will provide backup heat. When operating to supply engine heat for desiccant regeneration, it simultaneously generates electricity to drive the central chiller, which handles a reduced cooling load (sensible only) at a significantly improved COP.

Task cooling will be a favored technique in the future office with heat-generating electronic equipment. In many applications there will be a net improvement in COP when task cooling handles local "hot spots" without burdening the background air handlers. Individual work station fans and controls may increase physical (and perhaps psychological) comfort.

Systems integration is the practical technique for combining components in the most efficient way, guided by thermodynamic concepts and available energy sources and heat sinks. Systems integration, as defined here, is more than just the physical coordination of separately designed subsystems. It identifies the functional and energy flow interfaces of all building sub-systems—architectural, structural, heating, cooling, ventilating, lighting, acoustical, fire-safety, interior design, and others. It integrates these functional interfaces to permit the direct interaction of system energies when the result is a net reduction in the total system's purchased energy use. Systems integration thus is a technique for interrelating all components and subsystems so they become functionally supportive elements of a single energy-integrated system.

This approach uses components to do as many jobs as possible. For example, one component may become a functional part of two subsystems, eliminating an unnecessary duplication of energy consumption, or an unnecessary energy lead penalty of one subsystem on another. Appropriate integration permits subsystems to operate in their most efficient ranges, use the waste of one to augment another, incorporate renewable resources, and use the lowest-costing, most readily available utility energy.

Most efficient and cost-effective are tightly integrated selective energy systems with alternative operating modes. The alternative modes use available energy sources and systems in different combinations at different times, to respond most efficiently to varying environmental conditions (both internal and external) as well as to changes in utility price structure.

Alternative designs are developed and then measured, evaluated, and compared through modeling techniques including an integrated energy and life cycle cost analysis. This provides a rational methodology for (a) evaluating dynamic interacting cost/energy parameters, and (b) trading capital cost against total costs that bear on the choice of energy-efficient components in the design, construction, and operation of facilities.

ONE SOLUTION: SSA-METRO WEST

The Social Security Administration–Metro West complex in Baltimore, Maryland, designed in 1976, is the first prototype of the electronic "office of the future." It exemplifies many of the problems of these office buildings — and some of the solutions appropriate for retrofit projects as well as new buildings. (Fig. 1).

The facility is very large — 786,000 ft² of conditioned space with long distribution runs. SSA projected the use of computer terminals in approximately 40% of the space. In this 40% the heat gain from electronic equipment would be 13 Btu/ft²/hr (eight times the previous standard for office equipment). The catch was that the future location of the terminals was unknown at the time and subject to changing space use. The central refrigeration plant could be sized for a specific total load; but the distribution system could not be tailored to the varying loads in different parts of the building. Due to the unspecified location of the heat concentrations, the distribution network had to be able to handle the maximum load throughout the facility.

A major challenge was to meet these requirements for flexibility without installing expensive, maximum-capacity ductwork throughout the large

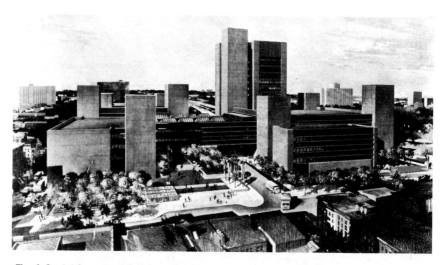

Fig. 1 Social Security Administration-Metro West, Baltimore, Maryland. Energy integrated HVAC system designed for prototype electronic "office of the future."

facility. At SSA-Metro West the use of desiccant dehumidification permitted a particularly appropriate solution that produced the lowest life-cycle bid. Central plant dehumidification in a desiccant conditioner, with terminal sensible cooling, achieved significant savings in distribution costs as follows (refer to the Fig. 2 system diagram).

Desiccant absorption dries the air very deeply, so it was possible to reduce primary-air distribution to the minimum quantity of outside air required for ventilation—0.1 cfm/ft^2—and to reduce ductwork size and fan horsepower proportionately. That quantity of primary air, dried to 31 grains/lb (grains of moisture/lb of dry air), takes care of the internal humidity load. Additional space was saved by integrating the floor structural system and the air distribution system, as shown in Fig. 3. Primary air flows through selected cells in the cellular steel floor deck, to be tapped wherever needed. One direct result was a 30% reduction in the floor-ceiling spaces between occupied floors.

Sensible cooling is then handled at fan-coil terminals, which recirculate room air and cool with coils circulating 55°F chilled water. With this system it was possible to acheive the needed *flexibility for changing space use by installing modular piping throughout the facility. Additional fan-coil units can be plugged in when and where more cooling capability is needed.* The chilled-water return piping also functions as the fire sprinkler system, reducing total piping costs (Meckler, 1982).

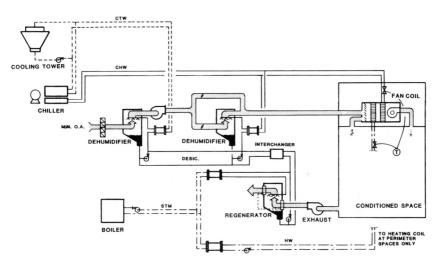

Fig. 2 Central desiccant dehumidification with terminal sensible cooling at SSA-Metro West, Baltimore, Maryland. Minimum ventilation quantity of outside air is dried very deeply (31 grains/lb), permitting minimum primary air distribution, ductwork size, and fan power. Fan-coil terminals mix primary with recirculated air and cool (at 55°F) or heat sensibly.

With a large latent cooling load, and an unusually large sensible cooling load due to heat from electronic equipment, the size and efficiency of the refrigeration plant was also a major cost concern. Desiccant dehumidification permitted a 33% reduction in the *size* of the refrigeration equipment (compared with a conventional system), based on the shift of a major part of the latent cooling load from the chiller to the desiccant system. The *efficiency* (COP) of chiller operation was improved also, by 20%, based on higher-temperature cooling (55°F). Consequently, 20% less utility energy is required for a given amount of sensible cooling. In addition, a chilled-water thermal storage tank permits a shift of electric utility demand from day to night, when rates are cheaper.

REFERENCES/BIBLIOGRAPHY

Baer, W., 1982
   TELECOMMUNICATIONS, Facilities Planning News, July.

Giuliano, V., 1982
   THE MECHANIZATION OF OFFICE WORK, Scientific American, September.

Kistler, W., 1982
   PLANNING FOR THE ELECTRONIC OFFICE, Facilities Planning News, July.

Meckler, G., 1982
   ENERGY-INTEGRATED FIRE PROTECTION SYSTEMS, Proceedings of the Conference on Energy Conservation and Firesafety in Buildings, (Conference held in Washington, D.C., June 1981), National Academy Press.

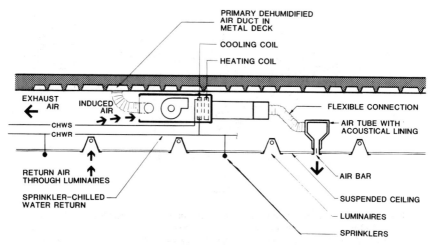

Fig. 3 Integrated floor structural system/air distribution system. Primary air flows through selected cells in the cellular steel floor deck, to be tapped wherever needed.

Meckler, G., 1983a
TECHNIQUES FOR ENERGY-EFFICIENT INTEGRATIONS OF DESICCANT DEHUMIDIFICATION,
Proceedings of the 2nd International Conference on Building Energy Management, (Conference
held at Iowa State University, May 31-June 3).

Meckler, G., 1983b
THERMAL WINDOW SYSTEM REDUCES HEATING AND COOLING LOADS, ASHRAE Journal,
February, pp. 37, 39, 41.

Poppel, H., 1982
WHO NEEDS THE OFFICE OF THE FUTURE? Harvard Business Review, November-December.

Salmons, S., 1982
THE DEBATE OVER THE ELECTRONIC OFFICE, The New York Times Magazine, November 14.

Urban Services and the Infrastructure

Lynn S. Beedle

One of the key factors in the viability of the tall building—both for business and for residence—is the adequacy of the urban services. While this is true for any building, it is particularly important for the high-rise—and becomes more so with each step taller.

Broadly speaking, urban services are those functions that serve the city—they serve the people who live there and those who visit. These people need mobility, and this means a transportation network: sidewalks, streets, buses, stations, and an access system that suitably interfaces with the building. People also need drinking water, and this means a water supply system: dams (or wells), distribution systems, outlets, drinking faucets and taps.

At the Council on Tall Buildings and Urban Habitat's second international conference (Council on Tall Buildings, D. Sfintesco, ed. 1978–1980), a session was held on the subject of urban services, with two aspects particularly identified, the technological and the social. In retrospect, it would perhaps have been better to categorize the urban services as functional and social, and to replace the term *technological* by the current term, *infrastructure*. In such a context, infrastructure may be thought of as the physical manifestation of the urban services, whether functional or social.

This note will identify the urban services and categorize the resulting infrastructure.

223

URBAN SERVICES: FUNCTIONAL

Functional services include things like transportation, water supply, sanitation systems, delivery of food and other services, and fire protection. In other words, they are the services that give the city life and maintain it. The major functional urban services are identified in Table 1.

In existing cities, the functional problem is the failure to keep services up with the growth of population. In the suburbs, the problem is the high cost of providing these services at considerable distance (and, for new suburbs, in a short time). In new communities, the problem is to anticipate the extent of future growth.

URBAN SERVICES: SOCIAL

Social services include welfare, health, recreation, education, counseling, and the like. These factors are of major significance in the social and cultural viability of a city. They vary considerably from country to country and within a country. The social services are included in Table 2.

These services are perhaps more important in the consideration of high-rise housing than they are in office buildings, although some have an important place in both.

Table 1 Urban services: functional (the services that are required to give a city life, to sustain and maintain it, and to enable it to meet the needs of the people)

Transportation
   Pedestrian, automobile, bus, streetcar
   and subway, railroad, aircraft, water
   transport, harbors, waterways, parking
   facilities
	Housing
	   Individual, multi-family, dormitory,
	   spontaneous

Water Supply
   Domestic, industrial, service
	Employment (commercial, business, and
	   industrial)
	   Construction, business, manufacturing,
	   processing

Sanitation
   Waste disposal (solid and liquid),
   storm water runoff
	Government
	   City hall, community center

Energy supply
   Gas, electricity, coal, nuclear, gasoline
	Service industry
	   Maintenance, repair

Communication
   Mail, telephone, telegraph, telex,
   computer
	Labor force
	Food supply
	Fire protection
	Space for development
	   Land, air rights

THE INFRASTRUCTURE

The infrastructure is more than highways, bridges, and roads. It is the entire physical system that makes possible the delivery of services, meeting the functional and social needs of the city or town. Table 3 describes the infrastructure system, in general following the sequence of Tables 1 and 2, and attempting to identify the physical systems that correspond to the indicated urban service. The list goes considerably beyond the usual public works (involved essentially with the first four items in Table 3) and includes the entire spectrum, whether public or private.

Major attention has been directed to the problems of the infrastructure, starting in 1981–1982 in the United States. Although there had been prior studies in the 1970s on the subject, it was not until the books of Peterson (1983) and Choate and Walter (1981) began to receive attention that the public at large became aware of how serious the problem was. Over the next 10 years, the money required to restore highways, water systems, bridges, and other public facilities is estimated to range from $500 billion (Morgan Guarantee & Trust) to $3 trillion (Choate and Walter, 1981).

The United States Congress took action in 1983 to begin to remedy some of the infrastructure problems through the enactment of an additional 5¢ per gallon tax on gasoline, the proceeds of which would be used to upgrade streets, highways, and bridges. The full attention of both the private and the public sector, however, will be needed before any real progress can be made.

Conferences and workshops have highlighted the problem (NRC, 1983). The American Society of Civil Engineers has given it major attention (ASCE/NSF, 1983 and 1984). *Engineering News Record* has featured the problem in a major series (1983). *Professional Engineer* (1982) has featured a cover story on the topic, and *Time* (1983) gave it major coverage. (A few additional articles dealing with the topic are contained in the bibliography.)

It is increasingly evident, then, that the problem exists. For the United States, the correction of infrastructure deficiencies is essential for appropriate growth. Tall building planning and design must now, more than ever, consider the urban services. Ruchelman's book on the World Trade Center (1977) tells of the effort to examine in a comprehensive way the transportational aspects of the infrastructure problem.

Table 2 Urban services: social, economical, cultural, political (the services that make the city attractive, viable, safe, and secure)

Health care	Cultural activities
Security, control, crime prevention	Entertainment
	Religious observance
Education	Welfare
Recreation	Counselling

Table 3 The infrastructure (the physical systems that make possible the delivery of the identified urban services . . . what it takes in the way of facilities to meet human expectations)

Transportation	
Roads	Airports
Bridges	Terminals and Stations
Tunnels	Interfaces
Interstate	Waterways
Pedways	Harbors
Parking facilities	Ports and docks
Buses (and servicing)	Canals
Busways	Locks
Taxi fleets	
Railways	
Street car and rail transit equipment	
Water Supply	
Dams	Reservoirs
Wells	Pumping stations
Storage tanks	Water mains
Pipelines	Aqueducts
Treatment plants	
Sanitation	
Sewer lines	Trash containers
Sewage treatment plants	Storm water runoff system
Waste disposal sites	Emergency clean-up equipment
Power and Energy Supply	
Gas storage tanks	Gasoline storage system
Gas lines	Gasoline distribution system
Electricity power plants, power lines,	Pipelines
transformer stations	Oil storage facilities
Nuclear power plants	Electric transmission lines
Coal handling facilities	
Communication	
Post offices	Television (cable, transmission)
Telephone facilities	Microwave relay stations
Telex, telegraph facilities	Newspaper printing plants
Computer networks	Broadcast stations
Housing	
Single-family homes	Public housing
Multi-family homes	Spontaneous developments (squatters)
Dormitories	Housing for the elderly
Employment (commercial, business, and industrial)	
Office buildings	Warehouses
Industrial plants (manufacturing,	Shops, stores, and banks
material processing)	
Government Services	
City halls	Community centers

Service Industry	
Spare parts supplies	Repair services
Maintenance facilities	

Labor Force	
Employment placement services (offices)	Labor halls

Food Supply	
Food distribution centers	Agricultural land
Markets	Restaurants
Delivery systems	

Fire Protection	
Fire stations	Fire hydrants
Fire apparatus	Building fire protection systems

Space for Development	
Land	Air rights

Health Care	
Hospitals	Rest homes
Medical centers	Ambulance and emergency services

Security, Control, and Crime Prevention	
Police stations	Correctional institutions
Security fleets (auto)	Courts of law

Education	
Schools (public and private)	Libraries
Colleges and universities (public and private)	

Recreation	
Parks	Gymnasiums and health clubs
Community centers	Sports arenas
Theatres, halls, and auditoriums	

Cultural Activities	
Museums	Music centers
Art museums	

Entertainment	
Theaters	Concert halls
Parks (attractions industry)	Night clubs

Religious Observance	
Churches, synagogues, mosques	Campsites

Welfare	
Distribution centers (office)	

Counseling	
Counseling centers (office)	

Communities just beginning to grow skyward should not repeat the mis-
takes made in older cities. Future planning must take into account the following points.

If a comprehensive inventory of facilities is not in force, one should be
prepared. Data forms should be compatible, at least for cities within the
same country or region.

Inspection schedules should be established, with specific guidelines as
to how those inspections should be made.

Criteria of adequacy need to be established. Standards and other performance criteria must be indicated.

The appropriate levels of maintenance need to be specified.

Regulations must be instituted to be sure that the standards are adhered
to and that the maintenance program is carried out.

The infrastructure maintenance program should be tied to the development and comprehensive planning program for the city and for the
region.

Public awareness programs may be needed, and certainly both private
and public resources must be focused for capital investment and for
maintenance support.

REFERENCES/BIBLIOGRAPHY

ASCE/NSF, 1984
   WORKSHOP TO DETERMINE RESEARCH NEEDS RELATED TO THE NATION'S INFRASTRUC-
   TURE. (Proceedings of a Conference held at Warrenton, VA, April 26-27, 1984), American Society
   of Civil Engineers/National Science Foundation.

Choate, P. and Walter, S., 1981
   AMERICA IN RUINS: BEYOND THE PUBLIC WORKS PORK BARREL, Technical Report, Council
   of State Planning Agencies, Washington, D.C.
Constructor, 1982
   A REPORT TO THE NATION: WHY AMERICA MUST REBUILD, November, pp. 18-43.
Council on Tall Buildings, D. Sfintesco, ed., 1978-1980
   2001: URBAN SPACE FOR LIFE AND WORK, (Proceedings of Conference held in Paris, France,
   November, 1977), CTICM, Paris 4 Volumes, (In English and French).

Engineering News Record, 1983
   ENR SPECIAL REPORT: INFRASTRUCTURE, Engineering News Record, selected issues, April-
   June.

National Research Council, 1983
    SYMPOSIUM ON THE ADEQUACY AND MAINTENANCE OF URBAN PUBLIC UTILITIES, (Proceedings of a conference held at Warrenton, VA, February 25-26, 1983), National Research Council, Ottawa, Canada.
National Research Council, 1984
    PERSPECTIVES ON URBAN INFRASTRUCTURE, National Research Council, Ottawa, Canada.
National Society of Professional Engineers, 1982
    R_X FOR AMERICA'S AILING INFRASTRUCTURE, *Professional Engineer*, Vol. 52, No. 4, Winter.

O'Day, K., 1983
    ANALYZING INFRASTRUCTURE CONDITION—A PRACTICAL APPROACH, *Civil Engineering/ASCE*, April, pp. 39-42.

Peterson, G. E., 1983
    FINANCING THE NATION'S INFRASTRUCTURE REQUIREMENTS, Paper prepared for conference sponsored by NAS/NAE, February.

Ruchelman, L. I., 1977
    THE WORLD TRADE CENTER: POLITICS AND POLICIES OF SKYSCRAPER DEVELOPMENT, Syracuse University Press, Syracuse, New York.

TIME, 1983
    THE REPAIRING OF AMERICA, *Time*, January 10, pp. 12-15.

U. S. News and World Report, 1982
    TO REBUILD AMERICA—$2.5 TRILLION JOB, *U. S. News & World Report*, September 27, pp. 57-61.

Criteria and Loading

Introductory Review

Alan G. Davenport

This section on criteria and loading includes papers on areas of structural engineering that both now, and at the time of preparation of the original Monograph volume, *Tall Building Criteria and Loading*, were rapidly developing. The application of probabilistic methods to questions of reliability and safety was one such area. This has had a profound effect on the thinking in structural design. It has been part of the impetus given to load and resistance factor design (or limit states design). The use of statistical methods has now spilled over into most of the areas of structural loading.

A good example of this is provided in the article by Corotis on the application of stochastic approaches to live loads. This report demonstrates the important linkages with the new codes.

The article by Derecho refers to a number of areas of growing importance. One of these is the controlled development of plastic hinges both to improve ductibility and to increase the energy dissipation. The development of this seemingly magical property of damping with significant power for reducing vibration amplitude is now attracting increased attention.

Jensen's report on fire safety again touches on a question of great importance and increasing public concern. Excellent research has been carried out in the past decades, and the current efforts to put this knowledge into practice is clearly important.

The fourth contribution is on the imperfections of precast frame elements. This is a load-related phenomenon because of its amplifying influence on the gravity loads through the P-delta effect. The careful documentation by

Pawlowski and his colleagues of the measurements provides a useful source of information on a subject that has not received much attention.

The developments presented here only begin to scratch the surface of recent activity in the field of tall building criteria and loading. Work continues world-wide. A number of significant papers on wind loading, for example, were presented at the Fifth International Conference on Wind Engineering, held at the Gold Coast, Australia in April 1983.

The spotlight is now shifting to other areas of growing importance. The entire question of quality control is in need of improved understanding, to ensure that tall buildings are well formulated, well designed, and well built, and that they function well. The techniques for quality control that have been expanding rapidly in other fields are likely to make their impact in the near future.

Live Loads: A Stochastic Process Approach

Ross B. Corotis

LIVE LOAD DETERMINATION

Live loads have traditionally been treated in design as time-independent. Implicit recognition of the uncertain nature of live loads has been reflected by the use of a higher load factor than that used for dead loads, and by the use of a live-load reduction factor. The introduction of more realistic probabilistically based load models has led to a reassessment of live loads.

Most building codes and national model codes derive their live load requirements from the American National Standard, *Minimum Design Loads for Buildings and Other Structures* (ANSI, 1982). Loads of particular interest in tall building design are offices (2400 Pa or 50 psf), private and public rooms (2100 Pa or 40 psf and 4800 Pa or 100 psf, respectively) in hotels and multifamily residences, fire exitways and stairs (100 psf), corridors above the first floor (same as area served), and balconies (100 psf).

Figure 1 illustrates a typical simplified model of the live load process. In this model, the sustained load is assumed to be constant for the duration of a single occupancy. The occurrence of a new occupant in a given space then creates a new sustained load. Unusual loading situations, such as those related to remodeling or high concentrations of people, are treated as a second stochastic process superimposed on the sustained load. Figure 1 shows such extraordinary loads as short duration, high intensity events.

The conceptual framework for a stochastic live load process was reported by Peir and Cornell (1973) and later refined by McGuire and Cornell (1974) and Ellingwood and Culver (1977). The use of these concepts in design criteria, however, has only recently been implemented, by incorporation in the American National Standards Institute (ANSI) A58.1-1982, *Minimum Design Loads for Buildings and Other Structures* (ANSI, 1982).

SUSTAINED LIVE LOADS

Extensive review of all available major live load surveys has been used to establish the characteristics of a sustained load (Chalk and Corotis, 1980). This consists of the mean and standard deviation of an arbitrary-point-in-time sustained load. This load is a function of floor area (Harris et al., 1981) and is in a probability distribution form (Gamma distribution). Consideration of the sustained load process over the economic lifetime of a building involves an assumption of an exponential duration for each sustained load, and correlation of successive loads (independent). This last assumption is based on an analysis of actual load survey data from the National Bureau of Standards (Corotis and Jaria, 1979).

EXTRAORDINARY LOAD

Extraordinary loads are an important part of the total load process. Unfortunately, it is more difficult to obtain data on extraordinary loads than on sustained loads. During some load surveys, interviews have been conducted to determine prior history of personnel overcrowding. This information can be combined with engineering judgment and load models to calibrate a multiple extraordinary load model (Harris et al., 1981). Such a model uses alternative sources of occurrence (such as relocation of furniture into one

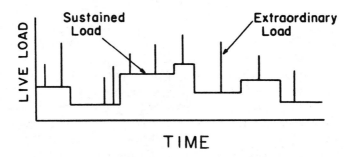

Fig. 1 Floor load history with one sustained and one extraordinary load process

room while adjacent rooms are being remodeled, crowding of people during parties, overcrowding during fire or other emergencies) to assign extra-ordinary load intensity (as a function of floor area), duration, and occurrence.

For example, the extraordinary load E_1 might refer to a remodeling load. Its statistics are chosen such that the load for a given area equals the total weight of furnishings (the sustained load) for that area, implying that fur-niture from an equal-sized area is moved in during remodeling. The rate of occurrence of E_1 would typically be once every 4–10 years, except in the case of renter-occupied buildings, in which case remodeling generally occurs when the space is vacant, so there is no E_1 load. The mean duration for E_1 might be taken as 2 weeks. The extraordinary load E_2 represents crowding during planned activities. This is the concept used by McGuire and Cornell (1974) and Ellingwood and Culver (1977) and leads to the statistics in Table 1, with mean duration typically of 6 hr. A final extraordinary load E_3 represents overcrowding due to emergencies. This load has the same basic statistics as E_2, but the magnitude might be scaled up by a factor of 2–3, and the average frequency of occurrence decreased to about once every 10 years (apartments, hotels) or once every 50 years (offices). The average duration for E_3 is about 15 minutes. All extraordinary load magnitudes are modeled as Gamma, the duration can be taken as either uniform or exponential, and the occurrence is Poisson.

Table 1 Live load statistics *(ANSI A58.1, 1982)*

Occupancy or use	Survey load m_s (lbf/ft^2)[a]	σ_s[a] (lbf/ft^2)	Transient load m_t[a] (lbf/ft^2)	σ_t[a] (lbf/ft^2)	Temporal constants τ_s[b] (years)	v_e[c] (per year)	T[d] (years)	Mean maximum load[a] (lbf/ft^2)
Office buildings								
Offices	10.9	5.9	8.0	8.2	8	1	50	55
Residential								
Owner occupied	6.0	2.6	6.0	6.6	2	1	50	36
Renter occupied	6.0	2.6	6.0	6.6	10	1	50	38
Hotels								
Guest rooms	4.5	1.2	6.0	5.8	5	20	50	46
Schools								
Class-rooms	12.0	2.7	6.9	3.4	1	1	100	34

[a] For 200-ft^2 reference area, except 1000 ft^2 for schools
[b] Duration of average sustained load occupancy
[c] Mean rate of occurrence of transient load
[d] Reference period

COMBINED LOAD PROCESS

By using the modeling assumptions for the sustained and extraordinary load processes, it is possible to derive a complete load process model for a given floor area. Traditionally, design has been concerned primarily with maximum loads. By using the load process statistics, it is possible, either through simulation or through analytical means, to derive maximum load information as a function of floor area and economic lifetime. Unfortunately, there is a general lack of statistically significant data for most occupancy types. Therefore, the selection of design live loads based purely on these statistical models is somewhat premature. The use of these models does, however, lead to a better understanding of the stochastic nature of the actual live load process, an appreciation of load sensitivity to various physical components, and an assessment of how design loads relate to the likelihood of occurrence during the lifetime of the structure.

For selected common occupancy types, statistics of the basic load processes have been included in the Appendix of the 1982 ANSI load standard. These have been intended to help the structural engineer develop a feel for the source of the design loads, and as an aid in facing unusual load situations not explicitly covered in the load standard. Table A4 from the ANSI standard is shown here as Table 1. It is interesting to note that in general, the mean of the lifetime maximum total load is close to the present design load. This means that design loads, developed primarily through historical experience and limited field data, without the benefit of formal stochastic theories, approximate the maximum load expected over the economic lifetime of the building.

To overcome the shortage of sufficient detailed data for the stochastic models in formulating design loads, an alternative source of input was introduced. The so-called Delphi method has been used for the minimum uniformly distributed live loads in the 1982 ANSI standard. The procedure is summarized in the next section.

THEORY OF THE DELPHI METHOD

In structural engineering, the use of traditional frequentist probabilistic methods is often limited by the scarcity of data and the uniqueness of design situations. Then the role of subjective probability becomes essential. The Delphi method is a highly structured form of communication used to gather unbiased subjective input from multiple sources (Ludlow, 1975).

The first step in conducting a Delphi is the selection of a panel of experts. The people on this panel should each have expertise in the area being addressed, should be relatively independent of each other in the source of their experience, and, if the weighting of opinions is not included, should have approximately comparable values of experience.

Once a panel is selected, opinions on the subject under investigation are solicited from the individuals, but no communication is permitted among members of the panel. Information is sent to a Delphi communicator, who statistically summarizes the information. The communicator then returns this statistical summary to all panel members, thus maintaining anonymity of individual responses. This prevents the distortion of response caused by deference to persons of perceived dominant reputation or personality.

Panel members review the statistical summary of responses and then are asked to respond again. The process continues until the responses either converge or stabilize with irreconcilable differences.

APPLICATION OF THE DELPHI METHOD

To apply the Delphi method to the selection of live loads, a panel of twenty-five of the most prominent practicing structural engineers in the United States was selected (Corotis et al., 1981). First, engineers throughout the United States were solicited for names of the most highly respected engineers in their geographical regions. From these names the panel was selected. Then, all members of the panel were sent a table of the current live load provisions and asked to confirm the existing values or select new ones. A histogram of values was constructed for each occupancy type and recycled back to the panel.

For two uses, there is significant disagreement with current practice. For office corridors above the first floor (previously 3900 Pa or 80 psf), the first Delphi round elicited 17 responses (9 at 2400 Pa or 50 psf, 1 at 3600 Pa or 75 psf, 4 at 3900 Pa or 80 psf, and 3 at 4800 Pa or 100 psf). For corridors not serving public rooms in hotels (previously 3900 Pa or 80 psf), first-round results were 9 at 1900 Pa (40 psf), 1 at 3600 Pa (75 psf), 4 at 3900 Pa (80 psf), and 1 at 4800 Pa (100 psf).

A second round led to results that were convergent in all cases.

A discussion of these Delphi results may be found elsewhere (Corotis et al., 1981). The principal changes affecting tall buildings are the reduction of the loading of office corridors (other than stairs and exitways) above the first floor to the same load as the area served (50 psf) and the reduction of the loading of corridors serving private rooms in hotels and multifamily residences to the same as the area served (40 psf). These changes have direct and important implications in the case of tall office and residential buildings.

LIVE LOAD REDUCTION

The reduction of unit-area live load with an increase in supported area can be extremely important in the design of tall buildings. The final design of a building with an efficient wind-resisting system is dictated significantly by the gravity load provisions. The concept of live load reduction is based primarily on observed load surveys conducted in the 1920s, and was first proposed in the late 1930s. This principle, which is based on the assumption that large areas are unlikely to be simultaneously heavily loaded, is a stochastic one. The provisions that existed until the 1982 ANSI A58.1 standard were based purely on the surveyed sustained load and deterministic principles.

With the introduction of a stochastic live-load process model, it is possible to introduce area-dependent statistics for both sustained loads and extra-ordinary loads. The lifetime load process statistics can then be computed as functions of floor area. This procedure has been followed for a variety of occupancy types. Because the mean of the lifetime maximum total load provides a good approximation to the current unreduced design live load provisions, a live load reduction provision was derived such that for any area the design load is the mean lifetime maximum total load. Such a live load reduction provision is easy to implement and is a reasonably close approximation to past practice (ANSI, 1972).

A simple live load reduction multiplier has been derived. It multiplies the unreduced design live load whenever the influence area exceeds 400 ft^2 (37 m^2). Based on an approximate fit, primarily to office occupancy data (Chalk and Corotis, 1980; Harris et. al., 1981), the following multiplier has been adopted for the 1982 ANSI standard:

$$0.25 + \frac{15}{\sqrt{A}},$$

in which A is the influence area in square feet. (The influence area differs somewhat from the concept of tributary area used previously (ANSI, 1972), and may be visualized as the area over which a simplified influence surface is nonzero. As Fig. 2 illustrates, for example, this is the four surrounding bays for an interior column and the two adjacent bays for an interior girder. It was first shown by McGuire and Cornell (1974) that this area has a more consistent probabilistic basis for live load reduction than tributary area.)

There is the restriction here that the reduced live load be not less than 50% of the unreduced design live load for members receiving load from a single floor, and 40% otherwise.

SUMMARY

Over the past ten years a general understanding of live loads as temporal and spatial stochastic processes has been achieved. Such processes permit a realistic approach to load duration and load combination. The use of these concepts has helped in producing the revised design loads and the Appendix in the 1982 ANSI load standard.

Refinements to the load process model and additional data will undoubtedly lead to improved physical modelling of the actual live load processes in buildings.

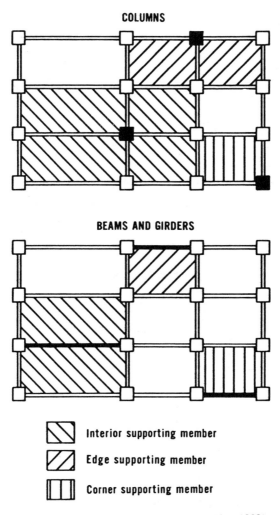

Fig. 2 Illustration of influence areas *(ANSI A58.1, 1982)*

REFERENCES/BIBLIOGRAPHY

ANSI, 1972
BUILDING CODE REQUIREMENTS FOR MINIMUM DESIGN LOADS IN BUILDINGS AND OTHER STRUCTURES, ANSI A58.1-1972, American National Standards Institute, New York.

ANSI, 1982
MINIMUM DESIGN LOADS FOR BUILDINGS AND OTHER STRUCTURES, ANSI A58.1-1982, American National Standards Institute, New York.

Chalk, P. L. & Corotis, R. B., 1980
PROBABILITY MODEL FOR DESIGN LIVE LOADS, Journal of the Structural Division, ASCE, Vol. 106, No. ST10, Proc. Paper 15753, October, pp. 2017-2033.

Corotis, R. B., Fox, R. R. and Harris, J. C., 1981
DELPHI METHODS: THEORY AND DESIGN LOAD APPLICATION, Journal of the Structural Division, ASCE, Vol. 107, No. ST6, Proc. Paper 16322, June, pp. 1095-1105.

Corotis, R. B. and Jaria, V., 1979
STOCHASTIC NATURE OF BUILDING LIVE LOADS, Journal of the Structural Division, ASCE, Vol. 105, No. ST3, Proc. Paper 14441, March, pp. 493-510.

Ellingwood, B. R. and Culver, C. G., 1977
ANALYSIS OF LIVE LOADS IN OFFICE BUILDINGS, Journal of the Structural Division, ASCE, Vol. 103, No. ST8, Proc. Paper 13109, August, pp. 1551-1560.

Harris, M. E., Corotis, R. B., and Bova, C. J., 1981
AREA-DEPENDENT PROCESSES FOR STRUCTURAL LIVE LOADS, Journal of the Structural Division, ASCE, Vol. 107, No. ST5, Proc. Paper 16266, May, pp. 857-872.

Ludlow, J., 1975
DELPHI INQUIRES AND KNOWLEDGE UTILIZATION, The Delphi Method, Techniques and Applications, (H. A. Linstone and M. Turoff, eds.) Addison-Wesley, Reading, Mass., pp. 102-123.

McGuire, R. K. and Cornell, C. A., 1974
LIVE LOAD EFFECTS IN OFFICE BUILDINGS, Journal of the Structural Division, ASCE, Vol. 100, No. ST7, Proc. Paper 10660, July, pp. 1351-1366.

Peir, J-C., and Cornell, C. A., 1973
SPATIAL AND TEMPORAL VARIABILITY OF LIVE LOADS, Journal of the Structural Division, ASCE, Vol. 99, No. ST5, Proc. Paper 9747, May, pp. 903-922.

New Developments in Earthquake Loading and Response

Arnaldo T. Derecho

It may seem odd to discuss earthquakes in Chicago, where except for sensitive structures like nuclear reactors, very little if any consideration has been given to the earthquake-resistant design of buildings and other structures. Several authorities, however, have allowed as much as a one-in-four chance of a great earthquake occurring near the New Madrid fault in southeastern Missouri, near the southern tip of Illinois, before the year 2000 (EERI, 1982). It may be recalled that during the two-month period from December 16, 1811 to February 7, 1812, three major shocks rocked this region. This earthquake has been estimated to be the largest that has occurred in the continental United States. It temporarily reversed the direction of the Mississippi River and created an eight-mile-long lake (Reelfoot Lake).

Figure 1 shows the approximate area affected by the New Madrid earthquake of 1811 in relation to the area affected by the 1906 San Francisco earthquake. The 1811 New Madrid and the 1906 San Francisco earthquakes were both shallow-focus earthquakes in that their foci or hypocenters occurred within 60 km of the earth's surface. A major reason for the greater area affected by the New Madrid earthquake, apart from its having been of greater magnitude, is the lower anelastic attenuation of seismic waves in the Midwestern and Eastern regions of the country for frequencies in the range of 0.1 to 25 Hz when propagating in the upper 20 kilometers of the earth's crust, compared to the Western United States or most neotectonic regions of the earth (Nuttli, 1981).

An interesting anecdote associated with the great New Madrid earthquake relates to so-called "earthquake Christians" (EERI, 1982). As a result of the 1811–1812 earthquake, the membership of the Methodist Church in the affected area was reported to have increased by approximately 50% during the year. This compared with an increase of 1% for the rest of the nation during the same period. One account reported that after the first shock, the citizens of Louisville subscribed $1,000 to build a church. The project, however, languished for lack of further support when the first series of tremors subsided. After a second violent shock occurred, another $1,000 rattled the collection plates. The campaign for funds once more lagged when the shocks subsided. The third major shock quickly brought in another $1,000.

While this cycle of religious conversion and apathy may seem only mildly amusing in our less superstitious times, it is worth noting that today's interest

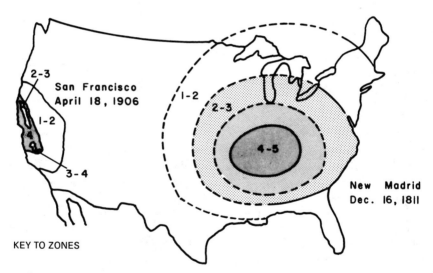

KEY TO ZONES

1. The disturbance was felt only by people in certain circumstances; the sensation was like a passing truck.
2. Felt by nearly everyone; the sensation was like a truck striking a building. Some dishes were broken, some plaster cracked.
3. Damage was slight, but the disturbance was felt by everyone. It moved some heavy furniture and damaged some plaster.
4. The disturbance caused considerable damage to poorly built or badly designed structures.
5. All buildings and bridges destroyed. Landslides occurred along river banks.

Fig. 1 Relative areas affected by 1906 San Francisco and 1811–1812 New Madrid Earthquakes (Nuttli, 1972)

and concern with providing for safety against earthquakes follows almost the same trend. A disaster appears to be necessary to generate sufficient interest and funding to carry out needed research and improvement of existing facilities.

As most are aware, the subject of earthquake loading and response is a broad field that has absorbed the efforts of geologists, geophysicists, and engineers of various specializations. A number of excellent papers treating different aspects of earthquake loading and response have appeared in the literature during the last two decades. The more significant were summarized in *Tall Building Criteria and Loading* (Volume CL) of the 5-volume monograph issued by the Council on Tall Buildings and Urban Habitat (1978-1981), as well as in Volume Ib of the earlier 5-volume *Proceedings of the 1972 International Conference on Planning and Design of Tall Buildings* (Joint Committee on Tall Buildings, 1973), which served as the basis for the monograph series.

This paper focuses on a few selected topics on the subject of earthquake loading and response, aimed at providing a rough overview of this complex subject. The choice of topics has necessarily been influenced by the author's limitations, and therefore relate mainly to structural engineering aspects of the subject.

EARTHQUAKE LOADING

In discussing earthquake loads on structures, attention is generally limited to the inertial forces associated with dynamic response of structures to the passage of seismic waves through the ground on which these structures stand.

The effects of soil instability, such as occurred in Niigata, Japan during the June 1964 earthquake, or in the Turnagain Heights area in Anchorage, Alaska during the March 1964 earthquake, although involving major problems in themselves, are not included in this discussion.

EARTHQUAKE PREDICTION

Central to the subject of earthquake loads is the determination of the likelihood of occurrence of earthquakes. The problem of prediction relates mainly to estimating the probability of occurrence of a major shock, the general location of the earthquake focus, the type of faulting, and the probable magnitude of the earthquake in terms of energy release.

During the past decade, some successes have been recorded in predicting the occurrence of mostly minor earthquakes. The successful prediction of a 7.3-magnitude earthquake in Haicheng (Liaoning province), China in February, 1975 is credited with saving several hundred thousand lives.

The principal geophysical basis of earthquake prediction is the so-called dilatancy effect. This is the change in velocity of P-waves transmitted through rock masses due to the presence of fine cracks produced by high stresses, such as would occur near a potential slippage zone. Other earthquake precursors, such as changes in the elevation and tilt of the ground, the local magnetic field, the electrical resistance of the earth, the radon (a radioactive gas) content of groundwater, and even erratic animal behavior, have aided in forecasting earthquake occurrence. However, much still remains to be done to establish major earthquake prediction on a firm, reliable basis.

CHARACTER OF GROUND MOTION AT SITE

Apart from the problem of predicting the time of occurrence and location of earthquakes, there is a need to establish reliable estimates of earthquake risk for specific geographical areas to serve as bases for design. Of major interest is the character of the expected ground motion at particular locations as well as its relative frequency of occurrence. A number of approaches have been used to estimate the character of ground shaking at a site, including "seismic site evaluations" that account to some degree for such items as seismic history, expected earthquake magnitude, and transmission path characteristics. The most commonly used basis for determining seismic loading for design purposes, however, is a seismic risk map showing the geographical distribution of expected seismic activity. The seismic risk map, found in the Uniform Building Code (ICBO, 1982) which is used as a basis for determining the magnitude of the design lateral forces, is an example of this type of map.

Alternatively, this type of information can be presented in the form of isoacceleration maps corresponding to 50- or 100-year recurrence intervals. Because of the many uncertainties involved in estimation of the character of ground motion at a site, a probabilistic approach has been found to be most appropriate in dealing with this subject. The effective peak acceleration and velocity-related acceleration maps given in the Applied Technology Council's *Tentative Provisions for the Development of Seismic Regulations for Buildings* (1978), based on the work of Algermissen and Perkins (1976), are rendered in this form. This method of estimating the intensity of probable earthquakes in a particular area on the basis of historical records is sometimes called the statistical method of predicting earthquakes.

The estimation of seismic risk has been based mainly on historical records of earthquakes and long-term measurements of seismic activity and crustal movements. Historical records of intensity and estimates of associated rates of strain release form the basis of seismic regionalization maps of the United States and Canada. These maps indicate contours of expected maximum ground acceleration or a related quantity corresponding to specific recurrence intervals or return periods. Because of meager data and the need to exercise judgment in the interpretation of such data, some inconsistencies are bound to arise. For example, seismic regionalization maps for the United States and Canada, produced by different groups, show contiguous regions with widely different expected seismicity.

With better record keeping and a more comprehensive data base, more reliable seismic regionalization maps should result.

Factors Affecting Character of Ground Motion — The analysis and design of a particular structure will depend on the character of the expected ground motion at the site. Ground motion is most conveniently presented by plots of the time-wise variation of acceleration components along three mutually perpendicular directions. The motion in each direction is usually characterized by three parameters, namely, intensity, duration, and frequency content. Intensity is a measure of the amplitude of the acceleration pulses, duration refers to the length of time in which large-amplitude pulses occur, and frequency content indicates the frequency range in which the dominant wave components of the motion occur.

The motion at a particular site is affected by a number of factors, among the more important of which are the magnitude and focal depth of the earthquake, the epicentral distance, transmission path characteristics, regional and local geology, and local soil conditions.

The type of fault along which sudden slippage occurs, whether strike-slip, normal thrust, or shallow-angle thrust, is thought to have an effect on the character of the ground motion close to the fault. At a distance of several miles from the fault, the ground motion generated by these three major types of faults has been observed to have very similar characteristics during the strong acceleration phase. However, in the long-period phase following the strong acceleration phase, the normal thrust fault has been known to produce stronger long-period motions. This is significant in relation to tall buildings, which have a relatively longer natural period of vibration.

It is known that the high-frequency components of seismic waves tend to attenuate more rapidly with distance than the longer-period waves. Thus, short-period structures tend to be excited more near the epicenter, while long-period structures tend to respond more strongly to the long-period waves that are transmitted over larger distances. From this it follows that for a given large earthquake, the area affected by ground shaking, potentially damaging to long-period high-rise buildings, is much greater than the area affected by ground motions potentially damaging to short-period single-story structures. On the other hand, small earthquakes are potentially more damaging to one-story structures located near the epicenter than to tall buildings.

The regional geology or nature of the ground through which seismic waves are transmitted, in other words, the transmission path, affects the character of the waves that reach a particular site. Field observations have indicated that virtually all soil deposits tend to amplify the underlying rock accelerations when the motions are of low intensity. However, for high-intensity motions, which can produce overstressing of the overlying soil, attenuation of the rock accelerations generally occurs. This attenuation is greater for deep and soft soil deposits than for shallow stiff soils.

Local geology may also influence the nature of the ground motion at a particular site. The shape of a particular soil deposit may impart a distinct or predominant period of vibration to the soil mass. For example, on what was once Lake Texcoco, where Mexico City now stands, the accumulated body of sedimentary deposits has been known to exhibit dominant periods of vibration in the 1.8 to 3.0 sec range when excited by waves from the Acapulco region, some 260 km away.

EARTHQUAKE RESPONSE

The response of a structure to earthquakes can be thought of as consisting of two elements: the first being the dynamic response itself, with its associated forces and deformations, and the second relating to the behavior of the structure under earthquake excitation, with particular reference to its capacity to resist the induced forces and deformations. These two aspects of response will be discussed in conjunction with the general problem of design for earthquake resistance.

EARTHQUAKE-RESISTANT DESIGN OF BUILDINGS

It is well known that, for most materials in common use, it is generally uneconomical to design conventional buildings to resist strong earthquakes within the elastic range, such as we now do for gravity and wind loading. The accepted practice is to allow some members in a building to be stressed in the inelastic range during the strong earthquakes that may occur once or twice in the life of the structure.

Once it is accepted that under severe earthquakes, there must be allowed some degree of inelastic response, the design problem becomes that of providing a structure where the critical elements have the required strength and deformation capacity. This means that a member must be able to maintain its strength while being subjected to a reasonable number of inelastic cycles of deformation of specified amplitude. Thus ductility is often defined as a measure of the maximum amplitude of deformation that can be sustained by a member a given number of times without significant loss of strength.

Damage Control — Initially, the primary concern in designing buildings for strong earthquakes was for life safety, in other words, the prevention of collapse. More recently, however, it has become increasingly obvious that buildings that house facilities essential to post-earthquakes operations — such as hospitals, power plants, fire stations, and communication centers—must be designed not just to prevent collapse but to be able to remain operational after a major earthquake. This means that such buildings should suffer a minimum of damage. Thus damage control has been added to life safety as a second design criterion.

Often, damage control becomes desirable from a purely economic point of view. The extra cost of preventing severe damage to the nonstructural components of a building, such as partitions, ceilings, and elevators and other mechanical systems, may be justified by the savings realized through the continued use of a building after a strong earthquake.

DETERMINING EARTHQUAKE DEMAND AND STRUCTURE CAPACITY

Whether dealing with concrete, steel, or some other material, the immediate design problem becomes that of determining how much strength and deformation capacity is required. In addition, there is the problem of determining a minimum lateral stiffness of the structure to limit interstory distortions and hence damage to the building.

Numerical estimates of earthquake demands are most conveniently obtained by dynamic inelastic analysis of appropriate models. Structure capacity, on the other hand, can be established reliably only by testing large-size specimens under realistic loading conditions. Figure 2 shows a coupled shear wall specimen being tested under slowly reversed loading simulating earthquake response.

A major distinction between designing for earthquakes and the usual approach to wind design is the interdependency of stiffness, strength, and deformation demand. Thus the question of how much deformation capacity is required cannot be answered without knowing the natural period of vibration of the structure (particularly as affected by stiffness) and the strength that the structure can develop or is designed to provide. Results of dynamic inelastic analyses show that for a given stiffness and mass distribution and a design earthquake of specified intensity, the lower the strength or yield level, the greater the ductility demand. As might be expected, the less the stiffness (for the same mass), or the longer the period of vibration of the structure, the larger the maximum displacements under a given earthquake.

On the basis of this observation, it is to be expected that structures built of materials that lack ductility must have more strength built into them so as to avoid ductility demands beyond the capacity of the material (see Fig. 3). This is essentially what the codes do. For materials or structural configurations that are known to be relatively less ductile, large base shear coefficients are specified, that is, relatively higher strengths or yield levels are to be provided. Theoretically, then, structures made of brittle materials would have to be

Fig. 2 Testing of reinforced concrete coupled wall specimen under slowly reversed cyclic loading simulating earthquake response *(Courtesy: Construction Technology Laboratories, PCA)*

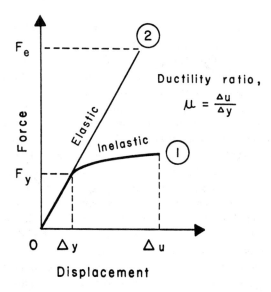

Fig. 3 Interdependency between required strength and available ductility

designed so that they respond to the design earthquake within the elastic range of the material, with no inelastic deformation allowed.

Lateral Stiffness—Lateral stiffness of tall buildings under wind is usually determined on the basis of a drift limitation, particularly as affected by human perception of motion. In designing for earthquakes, the criteria determining lateral stiffness are usually damage control and stability, with damage control generally governing.

Damage control principally involves limiting interstory distortions to acceptable levels. The maximum permissible interstory displacement will depend on the maximum tolerable deformation of the most critical component in the structure. This may involve considerations of glass breakage, partition damage, or mechanical equipment malfunction. An effective means of stiffening a building against lateral displacements is through the use of shear walls or vertical trusses (Fig. 4). Often, the tolerable displacement of building components can be increased by proper detailing. For example, deep rubber mounting gaskets for glass panels and supporting channels, along which partition walls may freely move, have been used. Similar attention to detail for doors and mechanical equipment may be desirable, not only to increase

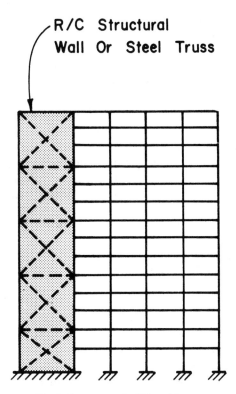

R/C Structural Wall Or Steel Truss

Fig. 4 Truss- or wall-stiffened frame

the maximum tolerable interstory distortion or reduce the required lateral stiffness but also as a means of increasing the margin of safety against malfunction.

INELASTIC DYNAMIC RESPONSE

Most tall buildings in high seismic risk areas are now analyzed by some combination of elastic (time-history) dynamic analysis and modal super-position using elastic response spectrum data. It is recognized, however, that certain aspects of the actual inelastic response are not accurately reflected in the results of a linearly elastic analysis. This is particularly true if significant inelasticity develops in the actual structure. Two important features of inelastic response that are not accounted for in an elastic analysis are (1) the amplitude and distribution of local inelastic deformations in members, and (2) the interdependency of the criticality of a given input motion, especially with respect to frequency characteristics, and the extent of yielding (or the change in "effective period") of the structure.

The local inelastic deformations become difficult to determine from an elastic analysis because when the model is linearly elastic throughout the response, the magnitude of deformation in members is always proportional to overall displacement. However, when inelasticity develops early in a member, there is a tendency for the inelastic deformation to increase more rapidly in that member than in other less stressed members. The relatively weaker member tends to attract most of the inelastic deformation.

It will be noted with the second feature that because of the change in effective period of vibration accompanying yielding, an input motion that is critical for an elastic structure (with fixed period) may not be critical for a yielding structure. For example, a shift in the effective period of a yielding structure into the range of dominant frequency components of an input motion could produce a response significantly greater than might be inferred from an elastic analysis.

THE CONCEPT OF CONTROLLED ENERGY
DISSIPATION IN SELECTED MEMBERS

In designing a structure to resist earthquakes, it is essential that the stability of the structure be maintained throughout the response and after the earthquake. This means that attention must be focused on elements vital to the overall stability of the structure. If yielding is to be allowed or expected in some members of a structure, it would be desirable, from this standpoint, to proportion the elements in the structure such that yielding occurs in the secondary members rather than in the primary elements. This concept underlies the "strong-column weak-beam" design requirement for moment-resisting frames found in codes.

This concept, when carried far enough, has led to proposals where all of the inelasticity is confined to the base of a tall structure while the rest of the structure remains essentially elastic during the response. This is basically an extension of the "structural fuse" concept to shock isolation.

Other applications of the structural fuse concept include coupled walls and eccentric truss connections. In reinforced concrete coupled walls incorporating this concept, the coupling beams are designed to dissipate most of the input energy by yielding. The presence of the stiff coupled walls limits the interstory displacements in attached frames so that the inelastic deformation in the frame members is significantly reduced. The work of Paulay in New Zealand has led to diagonally reinforced coupling beams (Fig. 5), which exhibit a more stable hysteresis loop under cyclic reversed loading, and hence greater energy-dissipation capacity, than conventionally reinforced beams (Paulay, 1981).

In steel, Popov and his associates at the University of California Berkeley have shown that an effective energy-dissipative mechanism can be designed into a truss by making the joints eccentric (Roeder and Popov, 1977) (Fig. 6) so that a short segment in the secondary web member absorbs most of the input energy in flexural yielding.

Closely related to the eccentric truss joint, but this time applied to reinforced concrete moment-resisting frames, is the "off-column plastic hinge". Figure 7 shows one detail of such a hinge. The object of having the plastic hinge in the beam form away from the column is to spare the beam–column joint, and hence the column, from the large disruptive forces associated with hinging in the beam close to the face of the column.

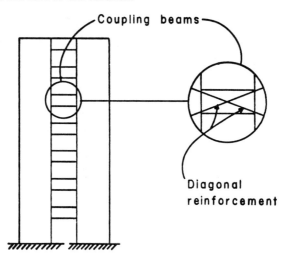

Fig. 5 Diagonally reinforced coupling beams in coupled wall structure

EARTHQUAKE DAMAGE OBSERVATIONS

There are numerous lessons learned from observations of earthquake damage over the years. Among these, one feature bears re-emphasizing because it has recurred in a number of cases in recent years. The object lesson here has to do with discontinuities in geometry and stiffness in the lateral-load-resisting system.

It is recognized that discontinuities, even under static loading, tend to magnify the forces acting on members in the immediate vicinity of the discontinuity. Under dynamic conditions, these magnified forces lead to increased ductility demands in the weaker members close to the discontinuity.

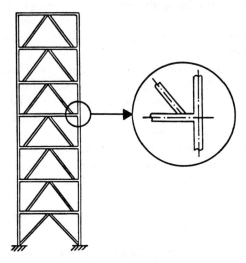

Fig. 6 Eccentrically framed joints in steel truss

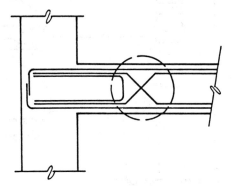

Fig. 7 Off-column hinging region in beam

Serious damage has resulted from discontinuities built into a structure without sufficient allowance for the significant increase in forces associated with their presence. During the 1971 San Fernando earthquake, there was a substantial shift of the upper floors of the Olive View Hospital with respect to the ground floor. This was caused primarily by the interruption of the walls in the upper stories below the second floor level so that in the first story, the lateral-load-resisting system consisted mainly of columns.

Unintended discontinuities have also been known to result in serious distress. A common example occurs when infill walls that have a height less than the story height are introduced between columns of a frame that are designed on the assumption of having an unsupported length equal to the full story height (Fig. 8). Figure 9 shows one such case, where 0.61 m (2 ft) lengths of columns between infill panels and a massive roof failed in shear, causing the entire roof to collapse. The same distress, but with less serious consequences, can occur in beams, as shown in Fig. 10.

CURRENT WORK

Based on a review of recently published literature, continuing work in the general area of earthquake loading and response appears to be directed along the following lines of investigation:

Maintenance and extension of seismic monitoring arrays for gathering data on crustal movements, as well as recording earthquake ground motions and developing techniques for predicting earthquake occurrence.

Development of more refined analytical models for analyzing three-dimensional inelastic response, including soil-structure interaction effects,

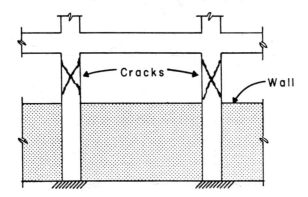

Fig. 8 Column height shortened by subsequent addition of wall

Fig. 9 Shear failure in segment of shortened column

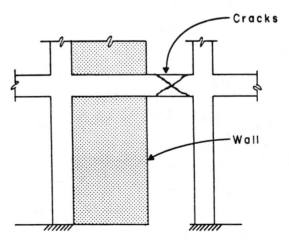

Fig. 10 Beam span shortened by subsequent addition of wall

as well as models for predicting the character of ground motions as a site from given or known source and transmission path characteristics.

Investigation of the merits of simplified analytical models for dynamic analysis as bases for design and critical evaluation of current analysis techniques.

Testing of large-scale models of structural systems in shaking tables or under slowly reversed cyclic loading.

Testing of elements and development of data for design of specific structural types, materials or details.

REFERENCES/BIBLIOGRAPHY

Algermissen, S. T. and Perkins, D. M., 1976
  A PROBABILISTIC ESTIMATE OF MAXIMUM ACCELERATION IN ROCK IN THE CONTINGUOUS UNITED STATES, U.S. Geological Survey Open File Report, 76-416.
Applied Technology Council, 1978
  TENTATIVE PROVISIONS FOR THE DEVELOPMENT OF SEISMIC REGULATIONS FOR BUILD-INGS, ATC 3-06, NBS Special Publication 510, June, 514 pp.

Council on Tall Buildings, 1978-1981
  PLANNING AND DESIGN OF TALL BUILDINGS, A Monograph, 5 volumes, ASCE, New York.

EERI, 1982
  THE NEW MADRID FAULT, Earthquake Engineering Research Institute Newsletter, Vol. 16, No. 4, July, pp. 48-49.

ICBO, 1982
  UNIFORM BUILDING CODE, 1982 Ed., International Conference of Building Officials, Whittier, CA.

Joint Committee on Tall Buildings, 1972
  PLANNING AND DESIGN OF TALL BUILDINGS, (Proceedings of ASCE-IABSE International Conference held at Lehigh University, August 1972), ASCE, New York, (5 volumes).

Nuttli, O. W., 1972
  MAGNITUDE, INTENSITY AND GROUND MOTION RELATIONS FOR EARTHQUAKES IN THE CENTRAL UNITED STATES, Proceedings of International Conference on Micro-zonation for Safer Construction—Research and Application, Seattle, WA, Vol. 1, pp. 307-318.
Nuttli, O. W., 1981
  SIMILARITIES AND DIFFERENCES BETWEEN WESTERN AND EASTERN EARTHQUAKES AND THE CONSEQUENCES FOR EARTHQUAKE ENGINEERING, Proceedings of Conference on Earthquakes and Earthquake Engineering—the Eastern United States, Knoxville, TN, September, Vol. 1, pp. 25-51.

Paulay, T., 1981
  DEVELOPMENTS IN THE SEISMIC DESIGN OF REINFORCED CONCRETE FRAMES IN NEW ZEALAND, Canadian Journal of Civil Engineering, Vol. 8, pp. 91-113.

Roeder, C. W. & Popov, E. P., 1977
  INELASTIC BEHAVIOR OF ECCENTRICALLY BRACED STEEL FRAMES UNDER CYCLIC LOAD-INGS, EERC Report No. 77-18, College of Engineering, University of California, Berkeley, August.

Fire

High-Rise Fire Safety
How Much Real Progress?

Rolf Jensen

INTRODUCTION

Important changes have occurred over the past 10 years in systems design (sprinkler, fire alarm and supervisory, and smoke control), fire detectors, and the requirements of codes. The major contributors to high-rise fires as evidenced by the additional accumulated fire record, and the related contributing factors, have not changed. Specifically, fires still happen because:

Concentrations of combustible loading cover a large area without a suppression system or without adequate barriers.

There are open or nearly open vertical shafts such as poke-throughs from floor to floor, elevator hoistways, expansion or seismic joints, or HVAC or plumbing penetrations.

Exterior facades offer a continuous path for a fire to propagate from floor to floor.

Structures poorly built have violations of basic rules of fire safety or codes such as inadequate exits, combustible interior finish, or no fire alarms.

FIRE RECORD AND EXPERIENCE

The overall fire experience in high-rise buildings is better than in most other occupancies. For example, the National Fire Protection Association's five-year analysis of over 2.3 million fires reports that the total number of fires in *low-rise and high-rise* apartments, hotels, offices, and banks was 56,940 or 2.4%. In a 1972 study of fires in New York City, of 1,400 fire deaths that occurred in the preceding five years, only 6 deaths occurred in high-rise buildings. These were in 3 different fires, none of which was in a fully occupied building during office hours.

The National Commission on Fire Prevention and Control regularly reports the fire loss statistics in the United States. One of these reports shows 11,840 fire deaths reported, 7,570 fire deaths in buildings, 6,600 deaths in residential occupancies, and 970 deaths in commercial and industrial buildings. Analyzing these numbers, it is found that

64% of all fire deaths occurred in buildings.

87% of the fires in buildings occurred in residential occupancies, nearly all of which were in one and two-family dwellings.

8% of all fire deaths occurred in commercial and industrial buildings.

Clearly, our major life safety fire problem is residential, mostly in one and two-family dwellings.

In a study of probability of accidental deaths, Otway et al. (1970) determined the probability of death by fire per person per year to be 4.0×10^{-5}. Otway calculated the probability of being struck by lightning to be 5.5×10^{-7}. Following the same procedure used by Otway, Harrison (1974) calculated the probability of being killed in a high-rise fire to be 6.0×10^{-8}. From this probability analysis, it is clear that the probability of being killed in a high-rise fire is less than the probability of being struck by lightning.

A 1975 analysis of 124 major high-rise fires is given in Table 1. The principal causes were highly combustible interior finishes, unprotected vertical openings, inadequate exits, unprotected exits, delay in detection and alarm, and human error. These basic causes, with the exception of delays in detection and alarm and in human error, are mostly controlled by the requirements of existing building codes in the U.S., and have been for many years. In the nineteen fires in other countries having major life loss, traditional fire protection requirements were violated in each case.

An examination of fire records for ignition source shows that the fire causes are smoking and matches, electrical, heating and cooking appliances, incendiary, or unknown.

THE CAUSES OF FIRES IN HIGH-RISE BUILDINGS ARE THE SAME AS THE CAUSES IN ANY OTHER TYPE OF BUILDING. Table 2 comes from an analysis of 56 major high-rise fires in the U.S. between 1973 and 1983 (see the Appendix). It shows:

The highest life loss rate is in hotels (28.6 per fire), followed by apartments (2.0 per fire), followed by office buildings (0.5 per fire).

Our large life-loss fires are in *non*-sprinklered buildings.

Code violations are involved in all the large life-loss fires.

High-rise fire safety programs other than sprinklers are not effective; i.e., major losses still happen in buildings without sprinklers, regardless of other fire safety features.

Table 3 comes from NFPA FIDO statistics (covering all reported fires). It shows hotels at 2.95 deaths per fire, apartments at 0.73 deaths per fire, and offices at 1.82 deaths per fire. This drops to 0.05 for offices if the 1974 San Paulo, Brazil fire is omitted and to 1.24 for hotels if the Seoul, Korea and Manila, Philippines fires are omitted. In both studies the relative order is about the same. Note that other occupancies such as hospitals, schools, and dormitories are very low.

The NFPA data also shows the record clearly for sprinklered buildings; it is nearly perfect.

SUMMARY

An interesting observation that can be drawn from these fire record studies is that our experience has not changed substantially during this century. When there is a significant and identifiable fire load and occupant load in a building (whether high-rise or low-rise) and the building does not contain an adequate automatic suppression system, the potential exists for a tragic fire. When the building additionally has fundamental weaknesses such as have been described herein, there is a great probability that major property damage or loss of life will occur. What is substantially different today is that these tragedies get much faster and broader media attention, which increases public awareness and the pressure for a regulated solution. Further, it is

Table 1 Analysis of high-rise fire deaths in the U.S. and other countries

	U.S.	Other countries
Number of fires	105	19
Number of deaths	129	497
Average deaths/fire	1.23	26.2

perceived that we have the technology to build in a fire-safe manner without an excessive economic burden. This has led to expensive regulation, with little concern for benefits derived for the money spent.

CODES & REGULATIONS

In 1970 there were four model building codes and numerous state and municipal building codes in the United States. The four model building codes were the Uniform Building Code published by the International Conference of Building Officials (ICBO, 1973 and 1976), the BOCA Basic Building Code published by the Building Officials and Code Administrators International, Inc. (BOCA, 1970, 1973 and 1981), the Standard Building Code published by the Southern Building Code Congress International, Inc. (1973 and 1981), and the National Building Code published by the American Insurance Association (1976). In 1970 none of these codes contained special provisions for high-rise buildings.

Beginning in 1973 the first of the special high-rise provisions appeared in Section 1807 of the Uniform Building Code as "Special Provisions for Group F Division 2 Office Buildings and Group H Occupancies." Group H occupancies are hotels and apartment houses. A similar requirement was included in the 1973 supplement to the BOCA Basic Building Code as Section 432, in the 1976 edition of the Standard Code as Section 506, and in the 1976 edition of the National Building Code as Section 520. The BOCA and Standard Building codes applied these provisions to offices, hotels and apartment buildings. The National Building Codes applied these provisions to all high-rise buildings.

All the codes defined high-rise buildings or tall buildings as those having human occupancy more than six stories or 23m (75 ft) above the average grade. The initial approaches (Uniform and BOCA) provided for compartmentation and sprinkler options. Components of the fire safety system for the compartmentation option included areas of refuge, fire alarms, fire detectors, voice alarm systems, voice communication systems, central control

Table 2 High-rise fire record: major fires 1973 to 1983

Occupy	No. Fires	Spread			Fatalities		Injuries	
		Room	Floor	More	Total	Rate	Total	Rate
Office	19	6	7	6	10	0.5	359	18.9
Apartment	20	7	8	5	40	2.0	33	1.7
Hotel	17	2	6	9	486	28.6	1198	70.5

stations, smoke control, elevator recalls, standby power and light, special exit provisions, and protection of spandrels. When the building was sprinklered with supervised valves and two-source water supplies, certain reductions were permitted in other fire protection requirements, including a 1-hour fire resistance rating reduction, omission of occupant hose lines, increase in allowable exit travel distance, omission of spandrel protection, and omission of areas of refuge if stairwells were pressurized. Sprinklers were recognized as means of accomplishing smoke control. Details varied somewhat among the several codes.

When the Standard Building Code and National Building Code versions appeared in 1976, the former mandated the use of automatic sprinklers for buildings greater than twelve stories or 46m (150 ft), and the latter mandated sprinklers for buildings more than five stories and 23m (75 ft).

Numerous local codes have been written containing high-rise requirements—some mandating that these requirements be applied to all building occupancies and some mandating that they be applied starting at heights as low as three stories. No attempt will be made to discuss such regulations in this paper.

CURRENT CODES

Currently the model codes that are generally used are the 1982 Uniform Building Code, the 1982 Standard Building Code, and the 1981 BOCA Basic Building Code. All three codes still permit both sprinklered and compartmentation options. A 1983 supplement to BOCA mandates the use of sprinklers for buildings twelve stories or 46m (150 ft) in height or greater. When the building is sprinklered, the codes generally permit a reduction in fire resistance rating for the basic structure, corridors, shafts, and doors, as well as the omission of occupant hose on standpipe systems, increase in exit travel distance to 92m (300 ft), omission of smokeproof enclosures, omission of spandrel protection, omission of fire dampers, and omission of operable windows otherwise required for smoke relief.

		Number of buildings having			
Det.	HVAC	Sprinklers	Compartment	Doors Open	High Combustible Load
2	4	0	3	—	—
7	0	0	20	9	—
4	0	0	17	4	4

In the compartmentation option, there must be two or more areas of refuge for each floor having more than 1400m² (15,000 ft²), with each area having at least one enclosed exit and one elevator, or a single elevator lobby with a vestibuled fire-resistant enclosure. Exterior openings must have flame barriers, compartmentation walls must be 2-hour fire-resistance rated, and a manual fire alarm must be provided.

In addition, for all buildings, smoke detectors are required in mechanical, electrical, transformer, telephone, and elevator machine rooms, and at each connection to a vertical return duct. There must be a voice alarm system arranged for one-way announcements, a separate fire department two-way communication system, a central control station, smoke control systems, automatic elevator recall, emergency standby power for all the required systems, automatic unlocking for any locked stairway doors, and a stairway communication system.

Required smoke control may be accomplished by panels or windows that can be opened remotely from the fire floor, by the building's mechanical system (if the building is sprinklered) or by any other method that can be proved effective by a test.

Smokeproof enclosures are required for at least one stairwell, or all exit stairwells may be pressurized when the building is sprinklered. All elevators other than those on the main entry level must have lobbies separated from the remainder of the building by 1-hour fire-resistance rated construction. In the overall, the trend in the codes is from a compartmentation or automatic sprinkler option to both. Current trends are to mandate the use of sprinklers while also requiring smoke control and other systems common to the compartmentation option.

SMOKE CONTROL AND REMOVAL

There do not appear to have been substantial technical changes in the definition of the smoke control and smoke movement problem in the past 10

Table 3 Death rates per incident in high-rise buildings (NFPA systems), U.S. and foreign, 1971 to 1982

Occupancies	Sprinklered	Nonsprinklered	Overall
Educational (200–240)	None	0.0	0.0
Hospitals (330–339)	0.0	0.07	0.07
Apartments (420–429)	None	0.73	0.73
Hotels/Motels (440–449)	0.0	2.95	2.81
Dormitories (460–469)	0.0	0.07	0.06
Offices (590–599)	0.0	1.82	1.70
Overall (100–649)	0.03	1.30	1.24

years. The factors affecting smoke movement still are pressure differentials between the upper and lower levels of the building due to stack effect, movement by air handling systems, wind-caused pressure differentials, and the pressure differential caused by the fire itself.

Much publicity has been directed at smoke as the principal cause of fire-related deaths. Concurrently little attention has been given to work by Zikria (1972) in his studies on inhalation injuries in fires (Jensen, 1973) or by Berl and Halpin (1977 and 1978) in their analyses of fire-induced injuries and fatalities (ICBO, 1973 and 1976). Both show that the primary problem is carbon monoxide. If one is to avoid lethal concentrations of carbon monoxide, flaming combustion must be ended, i.e. the fire must be extinguished.

Regardless, codes still require smoke control systems, and designers must create systems that meet test acceptance requirements for the installed system. None of the codes specifically defines how the tests are to be conducted or what constitutes an acceptable performance. All the tests currently conducted are done with cold smoke bombs and measure only the ability of installed mechanical systems to move air. Such tests are not currently formulated to evaluate how smoke will move in a building under real fire conditions.

EXITING

While the methods for evaluation of people movement (in other words, timed exit analysis) have existed for over 30 years, they are not described in the codes and are rarely used. In general the best treatment of the subject is contained in Fruin's book, *Pedestrian Planning and Design* (1971), though there have been notable studies by several others. Exit analyses conducted by Fruin's methods verify that complete egress in a high-rise fire is impractical. Thus some system must be devised to defend exposed people who must remain where they are. This supports the compartmentation and automatic sprinkler design options. It does not support many of the existing code requirements for alarm systems to initiate people movement except to the extent that notification is needed to avoid panic and either to inform people that the sprinklers have the fire under control or that they should move to an area of refuge when they are endangered by the fire. Bryan's recent studies (1982) on the actions of people in the MGM Grand fire support this.

COMMUNICATIONS AND ALARM SYSTEMS

System design has changed somewhat during the past decade, mostly because of significant improvements in electronic equipment and computer or microprocessor-based control systems. Much hardware now required by codes has evolved because of the technology rather than a documented need. The performance and design characteristics of the system have evolved as a response to the code requirements.

With respect to detectors, there has been a strong trend to the use of smoke detectors. The first single-station smoke detectors appeared in the early 1970s and have gone through extensive design improvement and cost reduction in the past decade. Current detectors are far more sensitive than those available in the 1970s, because of a significant change in UL testing standards that occurred in 1979. In fact, those detectors currently on the market may be excessively sensitive and in the long run produce undesirable, unwanted (false) alarms. Intense pressure among manufacturers of this equipment to reduce prices for greater market penetration has also reduced quality. Further, there is a real need to evaluate the extent to which smoke detectors can live with the environment in the areas where they are currently being required by codes, such as mechanical rooms, and whether they are needed at all when a building is sprinklered.

EXTINGUISHING SYSTEMS

Extensive changes have occurred in the design and fabrication methods used for automatic sprinkler systems in the period since 1972.

In the period up to 1972 most systems were sized by a pipe schedule; today they are usually hydraulically calculated to determine pipe sizing. Currently, systems are piped in loops and grid networks to achieve better hydraulic balance and significantly greater flow with smaller pipe sizes. Pipe sizing 100-mm (4-in.) and greater was commonplace 10 years ago, but today it is rare.

Extensive changes in fabrication methods have also occurred. Ten years ago most systems used threaded fittings; today most are welded or use grooved fittings. Light-weight pipe is now being used, and plastic pipe is expected to come into the picture shortly. Water requirements have been significantly lessened, and if the standards that require large amounts of water for the standpipes are reduced consistent with the need in sprinklered buildings, further economic gains will be made.

Ten years ago it was difficult to justify economically a sprinkler system in a high-rise building on a cost/benefit analysis, but today it is easier. The installed cost of a system has increased less than 25% during a decade when inflation overall has been 250%.

Sprinklers have become smaller in size and have been developed with greater performance characteristic variations. Currently there are quick-response and residential sprinklers available, as well as sprinklers that cover large areas for applications such as hotel rooms and apartments. With the code-mandated requirements for supervision of valves and power supplies, the reliability of the systems has been greatly improved. Further, the fire record of success in sprinklered high-rise buildings is impressive (see Table 4).

STANDPIPES

From a practical standpoint, the only change that has occurred in stand-pipes is that occupant hose is now typically omitted in buildings containing combined spinkler–standpipe systems. Fire department and occupant-use water supply requirements for combined sprinkler–standpipe systems were reduced for a few years in the early 1970s but have been subsequently increased again. Today the installation standards still require excessive volumes of water supply for combination sprinkler-standpipe systems.

The water used by the fire department from such systems can be supplied from their pumpers in all cases when the building is less than 122m (400 ft) in height, and for higher buildings when the fire department has pumping equipment having pressure capability to reach greater heights. Thus pumps are sized as if all water that comes from the standpipe must be pumped by the building pumps, and the contribution that will come from fire department pumpers is ignored. Yet the fire department uses no water until they are on-scene with their pumpers.

Standpipe designs in the early 1970s were largely limited to zone heights of 84m (275 ft). The evolution of reliable pressure regulating valves and pressure control valves has now permitted standpipe systems to be installed with zone heights as great as 427m (1400 ft). This eliminates the need for high-level storage and cuts down on the total number of pumps required.

SYSTEMS CONCEPT OF DESIGN

In the original report written in 1972, the hope was expressed that with the then new systems concept of design we could apply state-of-the-art knowledge to the solution of the high-rise fire problem and all fire problems without excesses or misapplications. While there was a flurry of activity in the evolution of these methods in the early 1970s, that activity has become dormant. Still, the capability exists for the fire load to be defined by fire growth modeling techniques and for systems to be designed as responses to the fire load. Certain people are still working in this direction, notably Nelson at the National Bureau of Standards and Fitzgerald at Worcester

Table 4 Hard-to-find sprinkler experience

Chicago Marriott	Guest room	1 Head
Crown Center, K.C.	Linen storage	1 Head
Mid-Americas Plaza, Dallas	Office	1 Head
Montreal Marriott	Washroom	1 Head
Regency Hyatt, Houston	Guest room	1 Head

Appendix: Fire record data

Building	Location	Date	Height	Year built	Cause	Spread[a]
One New York Plaza Office	New York, NY	8/70	50	1970		
Educational	Madison, WI	10/70	7		Arson	
College dormitory	Berkley, CA	10/70	8		Arson	
Office	New York, NY	12/70	47			
Hotel	Tuscon, AZ	12/70	11		Arson	
Apartment	New York, NY	12/70	33			
Office	Los Angeles, CA	3/71	21		Unknown	
Office	Nashville, TN	7/71	28			
Hotel	New Orleans, LA	7/71	17		Arson	2
Apartment	Parma, OH	11/71	8		Accid.	3
Hotel/Office	Seoul, Korea	12/71	21	1970	Unknown	3
Office	Montreal, P.Q.	1/72	10			2
Office/Mercantile	Sao Paulo, Brazil	2/72	31	1961		3
Hotel	New York, NY	3/72	14	1930	Accid.	2
Hotel/Office	Osaka, Japan	5/72	7	1932	Smoking	
Office/Apartment	New Orleans, LA	11/72	16	1968	Arson	3
Office/Apartment/ Mercantile	Chicago, IL	11/72	100		Arson	3
Apartment	Atlanta, GA	11/72	11	1972		2
Hyatt Regency Hotel	Rosemont, IL	4/73	10			
Pima County Admin. Bldg.	Tucson, AZ	6/73	11	1969	Arson	3
Resort Center	Isle of Man, BI	8/73	8	1971	Accid.	3
Office Bldg.	Toronto, Canada	11/73	43		Incend	3
Apartment	Cicero, IL	2/76	9	1973	Elec.	1
High-rise office	Indianapolis, IN	5/76	11		Smoking	2
Apartment	Roanoke, VA	6/76	6		Smoking	1
Department	Cincinnati, OH	10/76	10		Elec.	1
Office	Los Angeles, CA	11/76	32	1964	Arson	3
Apartment	Fort Worth, TX	3/77	11		Unknown	2
Hotel	Manila, Philippines	11/77	10	1958	Smoking	3
Hotel	Kansas City, MO.	1/78	6	1868–87	Unknown	3
Dormitory	Fitchburg, MA	4/78	10	1971–73	Unknown	1
Apartment	Brochton, MA	5/78	10		Smoking	1
Apartment	Pawtucket, RI	6/78	8		Elec.	1
Office	Chicago, IL	8/74	80		Suspect. arson	2
Hotel	Virginia Beach, VA	9/74	11	1973		2
Office	Los Angeles, CA	11/74	15	1970	Accid.	2
Apartment	Poughkeepsie, NY	1/75	18		Smoking	2
Motel	Peoria, IL	2/75	9	1966–67	Smoking	1
Apartment	Chicago, IL	2/75	29	1956	Unknown	3
Office	New York, NY	2/75	12			3
Office	New York, NY	2/75	110			3

Unprotected Vertical opening	Fatalities	Injuries	A.S.	Standpipes	Auto detectors	Alarm	Comments
	2		None	None	Yes	Yes	$10 million damage
	1						$1.5 million damage
	0			Yes		Yes	
	3			Yes	Yes		$2.5 million damage
	28		None	Yes		None	$1.5 million damage
	0						$10,000 damage
	0			Yes			$378,000 damage
	0					Yes	
	6		None	Yes		Yes	Room door open
	0						Under construction
Yes	163	60		Yes	Heat	Yes	Combustible finish
Yes	5						Combustible interior finish
Yes	16	375		Yes	None	None	Combustible interior finish
	4			Yes		Yes	
Yes	118	69		Yes		Yes	
	6		None	Yes	None		
No	0	0		Yes	Heat	Yes	Compartmentation
	11			Yes		Yes	
	0	2		Yes	Yes		
	0	0	None	Yes		Yes	$565,000 damage
	50	50				Yes	
Yes	0	0		Yes	Yes	Yes	$½ million damage
	8			Yes	Yes	Yes	
	0	0	None	Yes	Yes	Yes	$700,000 damage
	4	12		Yes	No	Yes	
	0	0	A.S.			Yes	$3,000 damage
	0			Yes	Yes	Yes	$3.6 million damage
	4	0		Yes	Heat	Yes	No door closer
Yes	47			No		Yes	
Yes	20	9	No	Yes	No	Ineff.	
		2	No	Yes	Heat	Yes	
	0	0	No	Yes	Heat	Yes	Door closers $12,000 damage
Yes	0	4	No	Yes	No	Yes	No door closers
			No				
	1	31				Local	
	0	0					
		0	None		None		
	0	12	None	Yes	Heat	Yes	
	1	2	None	Yes		No	
		213			Yes	Yes	
					Smoke		

(continued)

Appendix: Fire record data

Building	Location	Date	Height	Year built	Cause	Spread[a]
Hotel	Seattle, WA	3/75	15	1932	Arson	3
Apartment	Albany, NY	3/75	14	1974	Smoking	2
Office	New York, NY	4/75	110		Arson	1
Office	New York, NY	7/75	34	1972	Smoking	1
Office	Boston, MA	10/75	39	1975	Smoking	1
Apartment	Tallahassee, FL	10/75	12		Unknown	1
Apartment	Boston, MA	12/75	19		Smoking	
Apartment	Dallas, TX	12/75	21	1966	Unknown	2
Hospital	New Orleans, LA	7/79	10	1972	Arson	1
Hospital	California	7/79	7		Elec.	
Apartment	Charleston, WV	8/79	13		Accid.	2
Dormitory	Oklahoma	12/79	12		Arson	
Apartment	Arlington County, VA	2/80	12	1965	Smoking	3
Office	Maryland	4/80	6		Elec.	
Hospital	Montreal, Canada	5/80	12	1908	Incend.	
Office	New York, NY	6/80	42		Smoking	2
Hotel	Las Vegas, NV	11/80	23	1970	Elect.	3
Hotel	California	12/80	12		Elect.	1
Hotel	Toronto	1/81	23	1971	Accid.	2
Hotel	Las Vegas, NV	2/81	30	1969–79	Incend.	3
Hotel	Boston, MA	3/81	7	1961		2
Hotel	Evanston, IL	3/81	8	1924	Arson	2
Office	New York, NY	10/81	52		Arson	2

[a]1, confined to room of origin; 2, spread to floor of origin; 3, spread to other floors

Unprotected Vertical opening	Fatalities	Injuries	A.S.	Standpipes	Auto detectors	Alarm	Comments
	0	0		Yes		No	
Yes	2	15		Yes	No	Yes	
No	0	0	Yes	Yes	Yes	Yes	
	0	1	No	Yes	Smoke	Yes	
	0	0	No	Yes			
	0	0					
	1			Yes	Smoke	Yes	
	2	0		Yes	No		$315 million damage
Yes	0	4	None	Yes	Smoke	Yes	Compartmented $200,000 damage
Yes	0	0	None		No		
		0			Smoke	Yes	$175,000 damage
			None			Yes	$170,000 damage
			None	Yes	Yes	Yes	No door closers $1 million damage
			None			Yes	
Yes	0	0	None	Yes	No	Yes	
	0	137					Compartmented
Yes	85	600	No	Yes		Yes	Combustible furnish
	0	0				Yes	
Yes	6	67		Yes	Heat & smoke	Yes	
	8	348	No	Yes	Partial smoke	Yes	Combustible furnish & finish
	0		No	No	No	Yes	In process of updating alarm & detection, combustible finish, no door closers on room doors.
	0	0	No	Yes	Smoke	No	$200,000 damage emergency lights
	0	8		Yes			Firewalls

Polytechnic Institute. Further, the development of the FS-3 method of calculating fire resistance by Law (1979) of Ove/Arup & Partners, Ltd. in London is an important contribution to designed fire protection.

Continued evolution of these methods, as well as more objective evaluation of our fire record and experience to determine how well our design concepts and systems are working, should yield more rational and precise solutions for future fire safety design.

One fact is clear. If we are to avoid fire disasters, whether high-rise or low-rise, we must extinguish the fire before it reaches an intolerable size.

REFERENCES/BIBLIOGRAPHY

American Insurance Association, 1976
   NATIONAL BUILDING CODE, American Insurance Association, New York.

BOCA, 1970, 1973, and 1981
   BOCA BASIC BUILDING CODE, BOCA, Homewood.
Berl, W. G. and Halpin, B.M., 1978
   HUMAN FATALITIES FROM UNWANTED FIRES, Johns Hopkins University, Applied Physics Laboratory, Baltimore.
Berl, W. G. and Halpin, B. M., 1977
   AN ANALYSIS OF FIRE-INDUCED INJURIES AND FACILITIES, Johns Hopkins University, Applied Physics Laboratory, Baltimore.
Bryan, J. L., 1982
   HUMAN BEHAVIOR IN THE MGM GRAND HOTEL FIRE, NFPA Fire Journal.

Fruin, J., 1971
   PEDESTRIAN PLANNING AND DESIGN, Metropolitan Association of Urban Designers and Environmental Planners, New York.

Harrison, G. A., 1974
   THE HIGH RISE FIRE PROBLEM, National Bureau of Standards, Washington, D.C.

ICBO, 1973 and 1976
   UNIFORM BUILDING CODE, International Conference of Building Officials, Whittier, California.

Jensen, R. H., 1973
   MEANS OF FIRE FIGHTING AND SAFETY DEVICES, Planning and Design of Tall Buildings, (Proceedings of Conference held at Lehigh University, August, 1972), ASCE, Vol. IB-8, New York.

Law, Margaret, 1979
   FIRE SAFE STRUCTURAL STEEL—A STEEL DESIGN GUIDE, American Iron and Steel Institute, Washington, D.C.

Otway, H. J., Baker, J., Thomas, W. N., and Marshall, M. R., 1970
   A RISK ANALYSIS OF THE OMEGA WEST REACTOR, University of California, Los Alamos Scientific Laboratory, Los Alamos.

Southern Building Code Congress, 1976 and 1982
   STANDARD BUILDING CODE, Southern Building Code Congress, Birmingham.

Zikria, B. A., 1972
   INHALATION INJURIES IN FIRES, Columbia, University College of Physicians & Surgeons, New York.

Influence of the Imperfections of Precast RC Frame Elements on the Overall Safety of Tall Buildings

Zbigniew Pawłowski
Wiesław Rokicki
Ryszard Kowalczyk

INTRODUCTION

Erecting multistory buildings from prefabricated reinforced concrete elements has been the trend in recent years in Poland. The quality and accuracy of prefabricating and assembling precast elements has therefore become a significant factor in this type of structure.

Despite constant improvement in prefabrication work, in the application of stiff molds, and in the permanent supervision of the assemblage work by optical (theodolite) measurement services, observed imperfections in the erected structures substantially exceed the assumed tolerances. These imperfections influence the load-carrying capacity of the structure and, as a consequence, diminish the safety margin of the building. They also make more difficult the evaluation of initial eccentricities for proper calculation and dimensioning of columns.

This paper presents the results of investigation of imperfections in assembled columns of prefabricated reinforced concrete skeleton structures, the analysis of deviations of the column axis from vertical axis, and the analysis of displacement in joints.

Investigations were carried out on several 18- to 24-story buildings. The structural system consisted of cast-in-place reinforced concrete core and precast reinforced concrete framework. The framework was assembled from one- or two-story high columns with 0.30 by 0.60 m cross-sections and pin-connected spandrel beams. The layout of the building is given in Fig. 1.

The measurements were carried out on 324 columns in arbitrarily chosen rows. Deviations of column tops from the vertical axis in two perpendicular directions, together with displacement in joints, were measured.

THE MAGNITUDE OF DEVIATIONS

The measurements of column deviations from the vertical axis were carried out on each floor to within an accuracy of $\pm$ 2 to 3 mm (theodolite). The measured values for each row and each floor are given in Figs. 2 and 3.

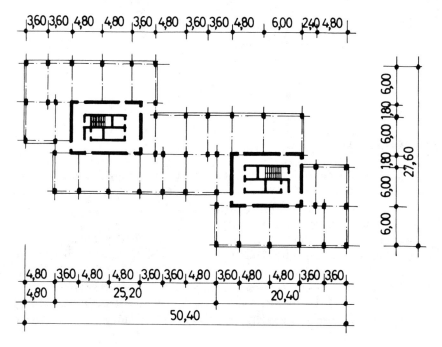

Fig. 1 Building layout

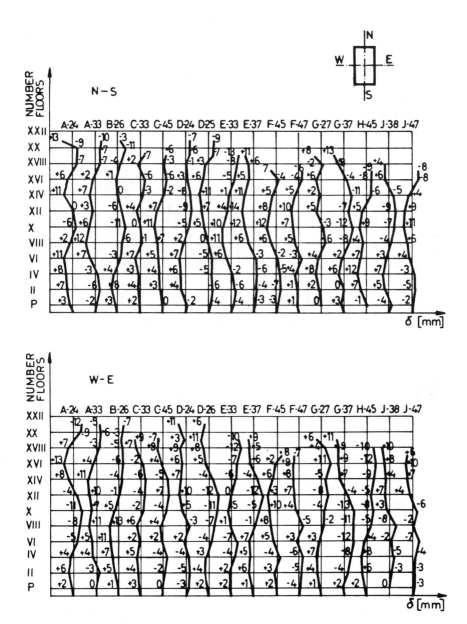

Fig. 2 Results of measurements of column deviations for a 21-story building

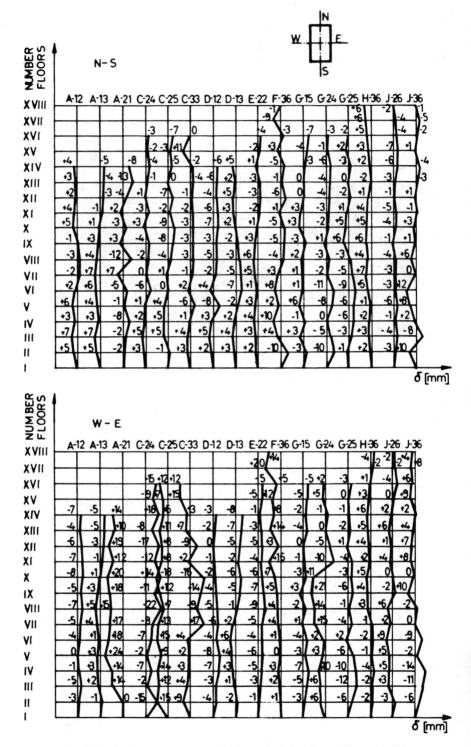

Fig. 3 Results of measurements of column deviation for an 18-story building

274

The histograms of the results and approximations by normal (Gaussian) distribution are illustrated in Figs. 4 and 5, where n = number of measurements, $\overline{X}$ = a mean value of displacement, and δ = standard deviation.

Displacement of the column top δ_i, resulting from deviation of the column axis from the vertical axis, has been chosen as the parameter. These deviations can occur in both directions, which theoretically means that they can have either a positive or a negative value, and that the deviation has to be treated as an arbitrary parameter.

In the frame structure under consideration, displacements in two perpendicular directions (along symmetry axes of column cross-sections), and rotation with respect to the vertical axis, are both possible.

Only relative displacements of the column head from the bottom of the next-floor column have been analyzed. The differences in the columns' horizontal displacements in the joints have been designated as $\Delta\delta_i$.

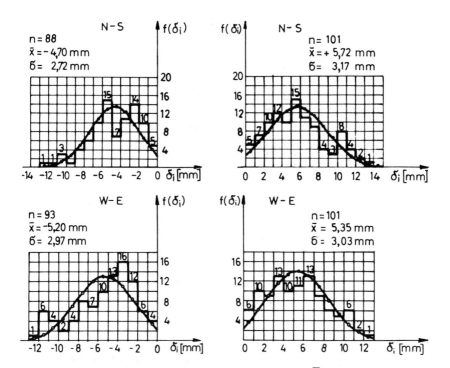

Fig. 4 Histograms of the measured displacements, mean values $\overline{X}$ and standard deviation δ for a 21-story building

ANALYSIS OF RESULTS

The designate δ_i is encumbered with some error, because the measurements have been carried out on randomly chosen rows of columns.

Applying the statistical analysis for evaluation of measured data, and taking into account a 95% probability level, the values of the δ_i for columns in two buildings (in two perpendicular directions) are given in Table 1.

Similarly, Table 2 gives the values of horizontal displacements of columns $\Delta\delta_i$ in joints.

The magnitude of deformations of the building frame depend on imperfections in the production of the precast elements, the heterogeneity of the material properties, and the quality of the assemblage. This magnitude is considered in calculations by the application of the initial eccentricities.

The Polish building code does not define any values for evaluation of these initial eccentricities. For comparison only, the values of the eccentricities applied in wall systems can be used. These values are given in Table 3. In this Table the deviation for columns in the SBO system (treated as a wall system), as well as the results of investigations, are assembled. Analysis of the results has shown that the errors in the assemblage of columns do not depend

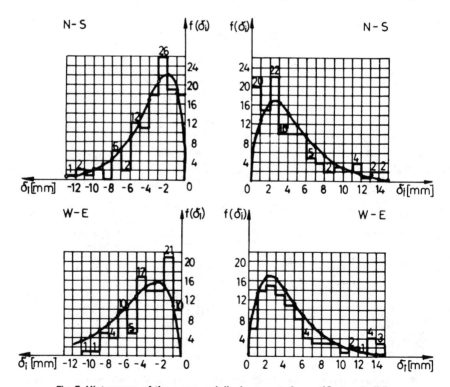

Fig. 5 Histograms of the measured displacements for an 18-story building

on the dimensions of the columns. Observations of both buildings have confirmed this conclusion.

The mean values of deviation δ_i of the column tops with regard to the vertical axis did not exceed 12 to 13 mm. Thus taking into account the measurement error of ± 2 to 3 mm, it can be assumed that the technological displacements should not exceed the value of 15 mm, provided the assembly work is of good quality.

INFLUENCE OF COLUMN DEFORMATIONS ON THE SAFETY COEFFICIENT

The investigations were carried out on buildings in which structural systems were composed of a central reinforced concrete core and an external prefabricated frame. Because the stiffness of the core was much greater than that of the columns, the bending moments resulting from the horizontal displacements of floor slabs are very small.

This allows one to calculate the columns as eccentrically loaded. The influence of measured deformations on the safety of the structure was small and did not exceed 2.5% of the global load capacity.

Table 1 Column top displacements δ_i (mm) in two perpendicular directions: NS and WE

	Building No. 1		Building No. 2	
	N–S	W–E	N–S	W–E
Positive values	11.9	11.3	11.2	10.8
Negative values	10.0	11.0	9.4	13.1

Table 2 Column horizontal displacements in joints $\Delta\delta_i$ (mm)

	Building No. 1	Building No. 2
Plane N–S	11.5	9.65
Plane W–E	9.5	11.6

Table 3 Initial eccentricities (mm) given by Polish code for wall systems and values resulting from investigations

	Codes			Deviations in the assembladge of SBO columns	Results of investigation
Plane N–S	20	13.8	12	20	11.9
Plane W–S	10	–	12	10	13.1

Structural Design of Tall
Steel Buildings

Introductory Review

William McGuire

The contributions to the Steel Buildings section of the second Monograph update are of two types: summaries of recent development in particular areas, and reports of recent research.

In the first category is Iffland's valuable review of the latest pertinent literature on the stability of steel structures. Similarly, Karnikova, Marek, Pirner, Skaloud, and Tichy report on the way limit states (load and resistance factor) design is being applied in Czechoslovakia. The paper by Lui and Chen contains a new column design equation that accounts for both residual stress and initial imperfections. But it, too, is particularly noteworthy for its general summary of advances in column design.

On the construction rather than the design side are the papers of Chen and Lui on connections, Iyengar on mixed construction in the United States, and Sato on Japanese developments in the same medium. Each of these papers is a report of significant recent progress in its area.

The research contributions are those of Arciszewski and Jayachandran. The former reports on the use of unhomogeneous Markov chains for the determination of wind bracing types. The latter summarizes analytical studies of the earthquake resistance of eccentrically braced tall buildings.

Decision-Making
Parameters and Their
Computer-Aided Analysis
for Wind Bracings

Tomasz Arciszewski

INTRODUCTION

There is a growing interest in high-rise decision making. A number of research programs on it and related matters have already been completed, (Arciszewski and Pancewicz, 1976; Moser, 1978; Council on Tall Buildings, Committee 28, 1981), are in progress (Arciszewski, 1980), or have been recently proposed (Mutunayagam, 1980 and 1981).

In the design of a tall building, structural decision making regarding wind bracing is a major, strategic part of the design. A model of the structural behavior and formal characteristics of the proposed bracing is considered here and decision-making parameters are essential elements of it.

Wind bracing in a steel skeleton structure can be described by a set of qualitative and quantitative decision-making parameters. Qualitative parameters describe the structural form of a bracing. These parameters concern its incommensurable properties such as the kind of material used, as well as certain measurable properties of discrete character that are decisive from the structural point of view. Quantitative parameters concern detailed dimensions of the bracing, its specification, weight, costs, and the like and usually can be treated as continuous variables.

When the design of a wind bracing is considered, two main phases can be distinguished: structural shaping and detailed design. The first phase has a qualitative character, while the second has a quantitative one. Structural shaping is understood here as a process of decision making—the determination of the structural form of bracing and regarding qualitative parameters. Structural decisions are based upon the appraisal of feasible solutions (Arciszewski and Brodka, 1978; Arciszewski and Lubinski, 1978). In some cases, however, decision making is called appraisal. Then not only representation, measurement, and evaluation of solutions but also their modification are included in the process of appraisal (Markus, 1974; Bridges, 1975; Maver, 1980). Detailed design concerns quantitative parameters, their analysis and optimization. This paper deals with structural shaping, when qualitative parameters and their feasible states are presented in the form of a morphological field. Its computer-aided analysis by means of nonhomogeneous Markov chain is proposed for the determination of wind bracing types.

QUALITATIVE PARAMETERS

The structural shape of a wind bracing can be described by a number of qualitative parameters of discrete character. Each parameter has a certain finite number of feasible states. The type of bracing is assumed to be defined by a compatible combination of feasible states, when for all parameters one state only is taken at a time. Such an approach is usually called *typology by coverings* (Goralski, 1975). As a result of analysis of existing types and current trends in structural shaping of wind bracings (Khan, 1971; Lubinski and Kwiatkowski, 1972; Council on Tall Buildings, Committee 3, 1980), nine qualitative parameters have been found to describe a bracing accurately enough from the structural point of view. These parameters are mainly for a symmetrical bracing in a symmetrical three-bay skeleton structure. The wind was assumed to act on the plane a, perpendicular to the plane β, which is called the *main plane of bracing*, where the bracing considered, when flat, is located (Fig. 1). The parameters discussed are introduced under the following terminology.

Core: A system of interacting frames (steel or concrete), trusses, bar discs, or reinforced concrete discs, located in different planes, usually in the central part of the building. It can also be a monolithic reinforced concrete shell or a steel spatial bar girder called a frame tube.

Vertical truss: A truss with parallel chords situated vertically in the main plane of bracing (Fig. 1).

Horizontal truss: A truss with parallel chords situated horizontally in the main plane of bracing (Fig. 1) or in a plane parallel to it.

Transverse horizontal truss: A truss with parallel chords situated horizontally in the plane perpendicular to the main plane of bracing (Fig. 1).

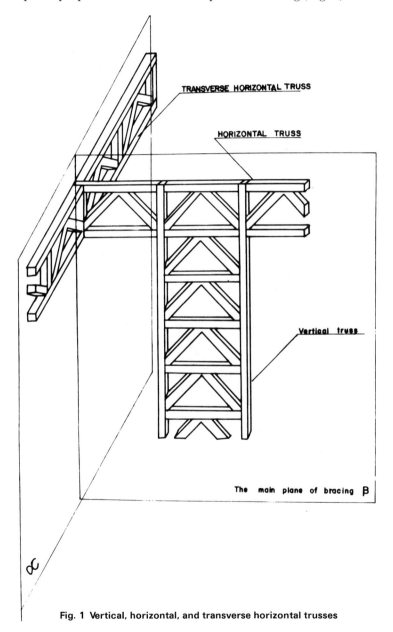

TRANSVERSE HORIZONTAL TRUSS

HORIZONTAL TRUSS

Vertical truss

The   main plane of bracing β

Fig. 1 Vertical, horizontal, and transverse horizontal trusses

Horizontal truss system: A spatial truss grid composed of horizontal and transverse horizontal trusses (Fig. 2).

External elements: Structural members situated in external walls.

External joints: Structural joints of external elements.

Bottom external joints: External joints between external elements and the foundation.

The following qualitative parameters have been found.

    A. Static character of joints.

    B. Number of bays entirely occupied by bracing.

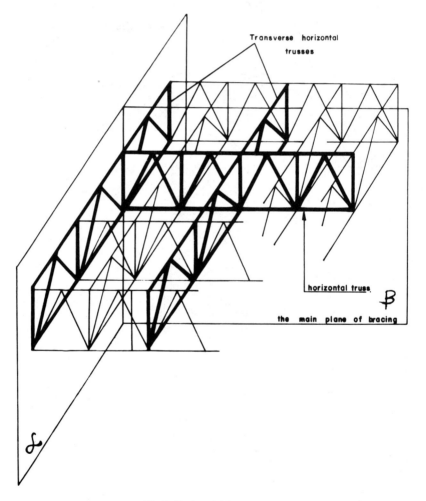

Fig. 2 Horizontal truss system

C. Number of vertical trusses.

D. Number of horizontal trusses.

E. Number of horizontal truss systems.

F. Material for core used.

G. Number of cores.

H. Structural character of external elements.

I. Static character of bottom external joints.

The static character of joints is described by two parameters (A and I). The first one is general and pertains to all joints in the case when the bottom external joints are of the same character as the rest. Then these two parameters are identical. Otherwise the bottom external joints are additionally described by the parameter I.

A bracing may entirely occupy a different number of bays from their bottom to the top; this is described by the second parameter, B. For all parameters, their feasible states have been determined, assuming certain structural limits regarding the complexity of the wind bracing. It was assumed that the number of horizontal trusses or horizontal truss systems (parameters D and E) should not exceed three. A morphological approach, (Zwicky, 1969; Arciszewski and Kisielnicka, 1977) has been used to present parameters as well as their feasible states, and a proper morphological table was called a *typologic table*. In its rows, successive parameters and their feasible states are specified. (Table 1). Such a typologic table has been used in a further morphological analysis of qualitative parameters and subsequently for a wind bracing typology.

IDENTIFICATION AND FORMAL TYPOLOGY

An initial formal typology attempt for wind bracings has been presented in Lubinski and Kwiatkowski (1972) and Arciszewiski (1975). Here the proposed approach is applied for a family of frame bracings only, used as an example. A family of bracings is understood as a set of bracings having at least one common feasible state for their qualitative parameters. Frame bracings are usually defined as bracings with mostly rigid joints. In this case all such bracings are described by a typologic table (Table 2) consisting of all feasible states covering structural properties of bracings under consideration.

The traditional analysis of parameters starts with the known, simplest type of frame bracing, when a set of feasible states, identifying this bracing, is determined. Next, this set is investigated by successive changes of single feasible states, determining the compatability of new sets and identifying other, more complex frame bracings. As result of such a systematic analysis of the typologic table, a large number of types can be obtained. To present these types in the form useful for structural purposes, a morphologic tree called a *typologic development tree* should be used (Fig. 3).

The simplest types are situated on the lowest, bottom level of the tree, while more complicated ones are positioned above. The position of a bracing depends on its relative complexity to the simplest type, measured by their morphological distance and expressed by the number of different feasible states identifying both types. The distance between two types situated on adjacent levels is two, while for these on the same level it is one. For all branches of the tree, morphological distances from the simplest type grow along branches upwards and for all levels rightwards, thereby representing a double hierarchy structure of the typologic development of bracings.

An individual type is identified by means of a set of feasible states (formal typology by coverings) as well as by a code denotation determining its position. In this denotation the first symbol stands for the bracing family, the second for the branch of the tree; successive digits enable the detection of the

Table 1 General typologic table

Parameters		Feasible states				
Number	Symbol	Decision-making parameters	1	2	3	4
1	A	Static character of joints	Rigid	Hinged	Rigid and hinged	
2	B	Number of bays entirely occupied by bracing	1	2	3	
3	C	Number of vertical trusses	0	1	2	3
4	D	Number of horizontal trusses	0	1	2	3
5	E	Number of horizontal truss systems	0	1	2	3
6	F	Material for core used	0	Steel	Reinforced concrete	
7	G	Number of cores	0	1	2	3
8	H	Structural character of external elements	0	Columns and beams	Cables	Bar discs
9	I	Static character of bottom external joints	0	Rigid	Hinged	Rigid and hinged

development route for this type. The construction of the typologic development tree for frame bracing starts from the single, rigid frame (F1—Table 2). The bracing may occupy a variable number of bays, and this number is asumed to be the second qualitative parameter B (Table 2), which has feasible states 1, 2, and 3. The set of feasible states describing this first, elementary type is to be considered. When only the second parameter is analyzed and its states changed, two new types (F2 and F3) are obtained with morphological distance one and therefore situated on the same bottom level of the tree; they are called *basic types*. These three types establish the bases for all individual branches of the tree. To construct these branches, sets of feasible states identifying basic types are to be analyzed. When the same two feasible states (here of parameters A and D) are identically changed for all basic types, three new types of more complex structural character are obtained to be situated on the higher, second level of the tree. These are flat bracings with a single horizontal truss, situated on the top. When for all obtained types only the

Table 2 Typologic table for frame bracing

	1	2	3	4
A	●		●	
B	●	●	●	
C	●			
D	●	●	●	●
E	●	●	●	●
F	●	●		
G	●	●	●	●
H	●	●		●
I	●	●		

feasible state of parameter D (the number of horizontal trusses) is to be changed, then the next two bracings for each branch can be found with two or three horizontal trusses. Such types should be situated as their predecessors on the second level, since their morphological distances are one, and they should be situated symmetrically to them.

More complicated spatial bracings, situated on level three, can be derived when two feasible states for parameters D and E are changed in sets identifying bracings on the lower, second level. In structural terms it means the substitution of flat trusses by spatial horizontal truss systems. For all branches, spatial bracings have the same unit morphological distance and therefore are on the same third level. Bracings called frame tubes, positioned on the fourth level of the tree, are to be obtained directly from basic types. It can be simply done by changing feasible states for parameters F and G (Table 2) in the case of the left branch, while for the remaining two branches, states for parameters F, G, and H must be changed. Further evolution of frame tubes leads to more advanced *tube in tube* bracings situated on the same fourth level (morphological distance from frame tube is one) or to the most advanced *tubular system* bracings positioned on the top, fifth level.

This typologic development tree represents a simple structural evolution when tradition, experience, and prejudices strongly affect the whole process of analysis. The total number of feasible types considered is significantly reduced to known or slightly modified bracings only. In some cases, however, a more creative approach to structural shaping is required.

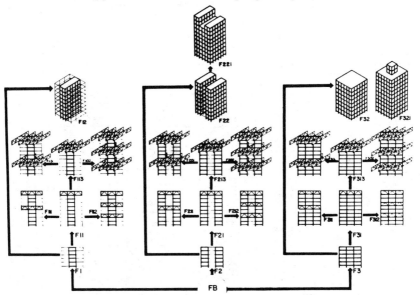

Fig. 3 Typologic development tree for frame bracings (graphical presentation)

COMPUTER-AIDED MORPHOLOGICAL APPROACH

The construction of a typologic development tree as described in the previous section is in fact a systematic search of the morphological field with all its limitations. Such a field, however, can be a subject of a computer-aided advanced morphological analysis by means of nonhomogeneous Markov chain (Eisen and Eisen, 1975).

The application of a morphological approach means here the elimination of tradition and personal preference and makes the process more creative. However, the basic requirements of this approach must be satisfied.

1. The field to be analyzed should be complete in structural terms; all existing bracings should be covered by it.

2. Existing limitations regarding contradictions between individual feasible states should be temporarily suspended.

3. The determination of a bracing type should be unbiased. Therefore a set of feasible states identifying it is to be randomly generated. Such a generation could be compared to a walk through the morphological field from its first row to the last one. For each row, representing a consecutive parameter, only one feasible state is randomly selected and included in the set, which identifies the complete solution, a new bracing type.

4. Structural assessment of feasible states combinations, being obtained successively during the walk through the field, should be delayed until the end of the process.

5. Final structural assessment should be performed only when a complete new bracing is generated. Then it can be accepted or rejected, if the combination of feasible states identifying this bracing is incompatible from the structural point of view.

The morphological field discussed in Section 2 has been constructed as the result of comprehensive studies on structural shaping of wind bracings. Therefore it seems justifiable initially to assume that the first requirement is met. Remaining requirements will be completely satisfied when a nonhomogeneous Markov chain as a model of a morphological analysis is applied. Results of an unbiased morphological analysis may be described by a sequence of independent, identically and uniformly distributed random variables $X_1, X_2, X_3, \ldots, X_n, \ldots, X_r$, where r is the total number of parameters considered. Such a sequence is a stochastic process with x trials. This process is a nonhomogeneous Markov chain, when the following three conditions are met.

1. It is a sequence of r consecutive trials (r is finite), and each trial has m possible outcomes called states (m is finite). The random variable $X_n = i$ if and only if for the nth trial the ith state is selected ($n = 1, 2, \ldots, r$).

2. $P(X_n = i \mid X_{n-1} = i, X_{n-2} = i, \ldots) = P(X_n = i \mid X_{n-1} = i)$ (1)

The left side of this equation is a conditional probability of the event $X_n = i$, given that following events occur: $X_n - 1 = i, X_{n-2} = i, \ldots, X_1 = i$. The right side is a conditional probability of the same event, given that the predeceding event $X_{n-1} = i$ occurs only.

3. $P(X_{n+1} = j \mid X_n = i) \neq P(X_n = j \mid X_{n-1} = i)$ (2)

The left expression represents the conditional probability of the event $X_{n+1} = j$, given that the event $X_n = i$ occurs, while the right one is the conditional probability of the predeceding event $X_n = j$, given that $X_{n-1} = i$.

When a given morphological field is considered, a maximum number of entries, including possible intermediate empty entries, is m for the most numerous single row of this field. It can be then formally assumed that each trial has m possible outcomes, called states. For some rows in the field, states may include feasible states as well as certain outcomes representing empty entries, or states that will never occur. It is convenient, however, to make the size of all rows in the field uniform and to assume that it is m.

The analysis is a sequence of $r - 1$ random transitions performed successively between adjacent rows. It starts from the first row, when for the variable X_1 its absolute probabilities at time 1 are randomly generated and their complete and ordered set, called the absolute probability vector at time 1, is to be determined so that

$$p_j(1) = P(X_1 = j) \tag{3}$$

$$p(1) = \{p_1(1), p_2(1), \ldots, p_k(1), \ldots, p_m(1)\}, \tag{4}$$

where

$P(X_1 = j)$ is the probability of the event $X_1 = j$;

$p_j(1)$ is the absolute probability at time 1;

$p(1)$ is the absolute probability vector at time 1;

m is the total number of states.

This first trial is also called the initial trial, while its results are initial probabilities and the initial probability vector.

The next step of the analysis is the transition from the first to the second row; the absolute probability vector at time 2, for the random variable X_2, is calculated as

$$p(2) = p(1) \, T_1^{(1)}, \tag{5}$$

where

$p(2)$ is the absolute probability vector at time 2;

$p(1)$ is the absolute probability vector at time 1 or the initial probability vector;

$T_1^{(1)}$ is the one-step randomly generated transition matrix for the first transition, second trial.

All subsequent transitions are performed in the same manner and may be described in general by

$$p(n) = p(n-1) \, T_{n-1}^{(1)}, \tag{6}$$

$$p(n) = \{p_1(n), P_z(n), \ldots, p_k(n), \ldots, p_m(n)\}, \tag{7}$$

where

$p(n)$ is the absolute probability vector at time n;

$p(n-1)$ is the absolute probability vector at time $n-1$;

$T_{n-1}^{(1)}$ is the one-step randomly generated transition matrix for the $n-1$ transition, nth trial;

n is the number of a trial, $n = 1, 2, 3, \ldots, r$;

r is the number of parameters or rows in the field, the total number of trials.

The one-step transition matrix $T^{(1)}{}_{n-1}$ is a square $m \times m$ matrix with entries $p_{ij}^{n-1}(1)$, which are called one-step transition probabilities and are defined as

$$p_{ij}^{n-1}(1) = P(X_n = j \mid X_{n-1} = i), \tag{8}$$

$$T_{n-1}^{(1)} = \{p_{ij}(1)\}, \tag{9}$$

where

$p\,(X_n = j \mid X_{n-1} = i)$ is the condition probability of the event $X_n = j$, given X_{n-1} is in the state i;

i, j are 1, 2, ... , m;

m is the size of the transition matrix.

Since in an ideal morphological analysis there are no relations between states of adjacent rows, transitions between them should be purely random. In the general case, individual rows may have different numbers of feasible states because certain entries, intermediate or last, may be empty. That makes not all transitions possible, which must be reflected in the form of a transition matrix. It may have zero-rows and zero-columns corresponding to empty entries in the pre-transition row and in the post-transition row respectively. Such a matrix should be called a modified stochastic matrix, since for zero-rows sums of entries are not equal to unity. For the whole analysis, all individual transition matrices should be different as well as independently and randomly generated.

When this stochastic process is completed, a set $P = \{p(1), p(2), \ldots, p(n), \ldots, p(r)\}$ of probability vectors is obtained and thus discrete distribution functions for all random variables X_n $(n = 1, 2, \ldots, r)$ are known. Then a final selection of feasible states should be made and three different decision criteria applied:

1. Absolute probability maximum value,

2. Expected value, and

3. Random value.

In the first case a combination of feasible states with highest values of absolute probabilities for consecutive rows is selected as the final choice for a given analysis.

To apply the second criterion (Meredith et. al., 1973), for all X_n $(n = 1, 2, \ldots, r)$ expected values are to be calculated by

$$EX_n = \sum_{k-1}^{m} k p_k(n), \tag{10}$$

where

EX_n is the expected value of random variable X_n

$p_k(n)$ is the absolute probability at time n

m is the total number of states.

Each calculated expected value EX_n ($n = 1, 2, \ldots, r$) is to be rounded up to the closest integer that determines the chosen feasible state for this nth trial. If the selected state is impossible (empty entry), the whole analysis is to be repeated.

The third criterion requires random numbers $D_n \in \{0, 1\}$ ($n = 1, 2, \ldots, r$) to be generated for each of r trials. For the nth trial, the kth state is selected in the following condition is satisfied:

$$\sum_{L=1}^{k-1} p_L(n) < D_n < \sum_{L=1}^{k} p_L(n), \tag{11}$$

where

$P_L(n)$ is the absolute probability at time n;

D_n is a randomly generated number.

In this case the selection of an unfeasible state is impossible because the probability of its occurrence is zero.

A computer program in BASIC for use with a desk-top computer (the HP-85) has been prepared for the above-described process. The program begins by the arbitrary determination of the starting feasible state for the first row of the field, although its completely random run is also possible. Figure 4 shows the flowchart of the program. The application of this program is promising, although results so-far obtained are not sufficient for sound statistical conclusions. About 3% of the combinations of feasible states obtained are compatible. A bracing type F211 has been rediscovered (Fig. 3), while a new type of bracing (Fig. 5) seems to be quite interesting.

A spatial steel frame is proposed as its core. Two horizontal truss systems, situated at the top of the building and one story above the ground level respectively, support rigid frames connected with the core. This solution is similar to the traditional concrete structures of tall buildings, but a (controversial) steel core substitutes for a concrete core.

CONCLUSIONS AND FUTURE DIRECTIONS

This approach to the formal typology of bracings is effective and relatively simple. The typologic table and typologic development tree should be useful tools for structural shaping of wind bracings. This method of decision making is for use mainly in the shaping of bracing, but it could be also

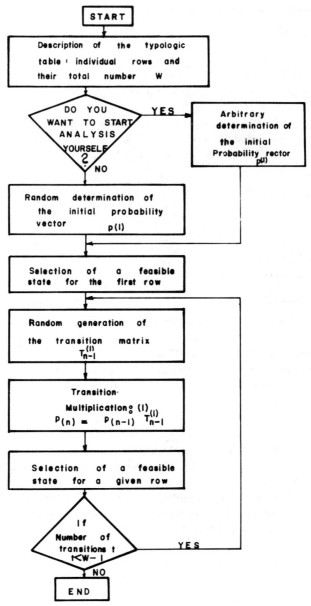

Fig. 4 Flow-chart for the computer program prepared

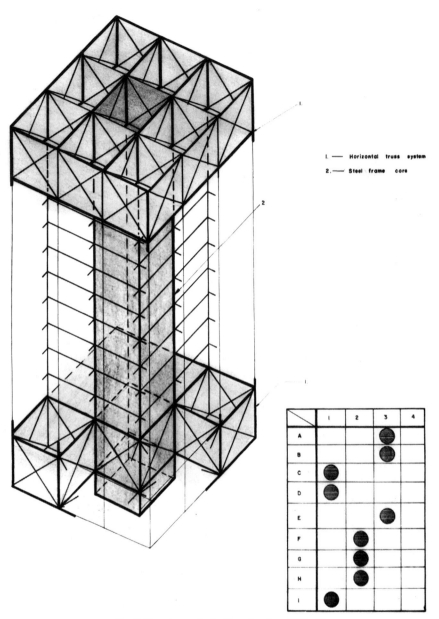

Fig. 5 New type of wind bracing (see Table 1)

applied to other problems of high-rise decision making. Initial results of its application seem to be promising, although the effectiveness of the method would be significantly increased if certain basic contradictory combinations of feasible states were not allowed. That would mean, however, the introduction of limits on analysis, which could unintentionally eliminate some unexpected solutions and would reduce the heuristic character of the presented approach. But some limits are desirable; their range, which most likely will depend on the purpose of a given analysis, should be investigated.

Future research should be concentrated on the development of multicriteria appraisal methods to assess and compare obtained wind bracings. This is the most important part, from the structural point of view, of the whole process of high-rise decision making.

ACKNOWLEDGMENTS

Many long and fruitful discussions with members of the Heuristic Section of the Polish Cybernetic Society, with friends from the Department of Metal Structures of the Warsaw Technical University, and with colleagues from the Decision-making Parameters Committee of the Council on Tall Buildings and Urban Habitat resulted in this paper. A final part of the research on decision–making parameters was financially supported by the University of Nigeria, which support is also gratefully acknowledged.

REFERENCES/BIBLIOGRAPHY

Arciszewski, T., 1975
    WIND BRACING OF TALL BUILDINGS IN THE FORM OF BELT TRUSS SYSTEMS (in Polish),
    Ph.D. Thesis, Warsaw Technical University, Warsaw, Poland.
Arciszewski, T., 1980
    STUDIES ON HIGH RISE BUILDINGS IN THE DEVELOPMENT OF NIGERAN URBAN CENTERS.
    HIGH RISE DECISION MAKING. Research Report, University of Nigeria, Nsukka, Nigeria.
Arciszewski, T. and Brodka, J., 1978
    TECHNICAL QUALITY OF STRUCTURAL SOLUTION APPRAISAL METHOD (in Polish), Journal
    of Invention and Rationalization, Vol. 1, pp. 29-33.
Arciszewski, T. and Kisielnicka, J., 1977
    MORPHOLOGICAL ANALYSIS (in Polish), Problem, Method, Solution. Techniques of Creative
    Thinking, PWN Publishing House, Warsaw, Poland.
Arciszewski, T. and Lubinski, M., 1978
    METHOD OF ANALYSIS AND APPRAISAL OF A STRUCTURAL SYSTEM (in Polish) (Proceedings
    held at the Warsaw Technical University, 1978), Vol. 1, Warsaw, Poland, pp. 35-57.
Arciszewski, T. and Pancewicz, 1976
    AN APPROACH TO THE DESCRIPTION OF WIND BRACING CHARACTERISTICS IN SYSTEMS
    SKELETON STRUCTURES (in Polish), (Proceedings held at the Wroclaw Technical University,
    1976), Vol. 20, Wroclaw, Poland, pp. 7-19.

Bridges, A. H., 1975
    THE INTERACTION OF DESIGN AND PREFORMANCE VARIABLES, ABACUS Occasional Paper
    No. 41, Strathclyde University, Great Britain.

Council on Tall Buildings, Committee 3, 1980
    STRUCTURAL SYSTEMS, Chapter SC-1, Volume SC of the Monograph on Planning and Design
    of Tall Buildings, ASCE, New York.
Council on Tall Buildings, Committee 28, 1981
    PHILOSOPHY OF TALL BUILDINGS, Chapter PC-1, Volume PC of Monograph on Planning and
    Design of Tall Buildings, ASCE, New York.

Eisen, M. M. and Eisen, C. A., 1973
    PROBABILITY AND ITS APPLICATIONS, Quantum Publishers, New York.

Goralski, A., 1975
    METHODS OF SOLVING PROBLEMS SPACE (in Polish), (Proceedings of the 2nd Conference
    on Heuristic Methods held in Warsaw, Poland, 1975), Warsaw, Poland, pp. 7-10.

Khan, F. R., 1971
    CURRENT TRENDS IN THE CONSTRUCTION OF TALL BUILDINGS MADE OF REINFORCED
    CONCRETE AND STEEL (in French), Annales ITBTP, No. 281.

Lubinski, M. and Kwiatkowski, J., 1972
    STATICAL AND STRUCTURAL SYSTEMS OF TALL STEEL BUILDINGS, (Proceedings of the
    Regional Conference on the Planning and Design of Tall Buildings in Warsaw, 1972), Warsaw,
    Poland, Vol. 1, pp. 141-165.

Markus, T. A., 1974
    THE APPRAISAL OF BUILDINGS AS A TOOL FOR RESEARCH AND DESIGN, (Proceedings of
    the Congress "The Impact of Research on the Built Environment" in Budapest, Hungary, 1974),
    Budapest, Hungary, pp. 105-108.
Maver, T. W., 1980
    APPRAISAL IN DESIGN, Design Studies, Vol. 1, No. 3, pp. 160-165.
Meredith, D. D., Wong, K. M., Woodhead, R. W. and Wortman, R. H., 1973
    DESIGN AND PLANNING OF ENGINEERING SYSTEMS, Prentice-Hall, New Jersey.
Moser, M., 1978
    TALL BUILDING DECISION-MAKING PARAMETERS, Fritz Laboratory Report No. 444.3, Lehigh
    University, Bethlehem, Pennsylvania.
Mutunayagam, N. B., 1980
    DECISION PROCESSES FOR TALL BUILDINGS—A POSITION PAPER, Occasional Paper, Virginia
    Polytechnic Institute and State University, Blacksburg, Virginia.
Mutunayagam, N. B., 1981
    HIGH RISE BUILDING DECISION MAKING IN THE NIGERIAN CONTEXT—A PROSPECTUS FOR
    RESEARCH Occasional Paper, Virginia Polytechnic Institute and State University, Blacksburg,
    Virginia.

Zwicky, F., 1969
    DISCOVERY, INVENTION, RESEARCH THROUGH THE MORPHOLOGICAL ANALYSIS, Mac-
    millan, New York.

Recent Developments in Stability of Steel Buildings

Jerome S. B. Iffland

INTRODUCTION

There have been major advances in the state of the art in the field of stability of steel buildings since the publication of *Developments in Tall Buildings 1983* (Council on Tall Buildings, 1983). Progress has been made in the stability of individual columns, stability of two-dimensional frames, stability of three-dimensional frames, approximate stability solutions for special types of framing, and stability under dynamic and repeated load. In addition, progress in selected special topics including research needs is worth noting. These individual subjects are discussed herein.

STABILITY OF INDIVIDUAL COLUMNS

The subject of individual columns has received much recent attention. New maximum-strength column curves have been proposed both for pin-ended columns and for restrained columns. There have been at least two additional proposals for replacing multiple column curves with single column equations.

299

The subject of beam-columns has received considerable attention, and as usual there have been many studies of selected types of individual columns.

Maximum Strength of Pin-Ended Columns

Hall (1981) has developed an empirical maximum-strength column curve based on statistical studies and the use of regression analysis. The strength in the elastic range is represented by a hyperbola whereas the strength in the inelastic range is represented by straight lines. A comparison of Hall's column curve to ones by the Canadian Standards Association (1974) and Galambos and Ravindra (1973) is shown in Fig. 1. In commenting on Hall's column curve, Shen and Lu (1982) emphasized that the strength of steel columns is influenced significantly by the manufacturing process and that the use of a single set of design formulas for columns manufactured by different processes may result in designs with inconsistent margins of safety.

End-restrained Steel Columns

Numerous investigators have continued to study real columns, in other words, columns with initial crookedness, residual stresses, and end restraint. These have included work by Chen (1980) with discussions by Bjorhovde (1981), Tarnai (1981), and Chen (1982); Lui and Chen (1981); Shen and Lu

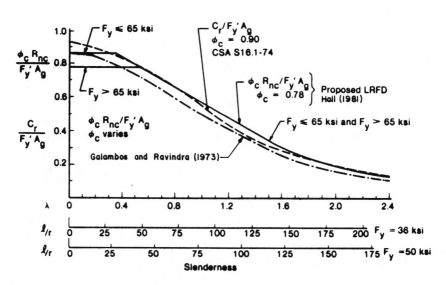

Fig. 1 Comparison of three column strength criteria

(1981); Jones et. al. (1982); Sugimoto and Chen (1982); and Lui and Chen (1982). All these studies show conclusively that consideration of end restraint results in an increase in the maximum load capacity and a reduction in overall column deflection. Residual stresses and initial crookedness have a destabilizing effect on columns, whereas end restraint can provide a stabilizing effect. The combined effect of these factors was studied systematically by Shen and Lu (1981). There is considerable empirical and theoretical support for including the effect of end restraint in a basic column formula. Based on the combined work of the references cited, Lui and Chen (1982) proposed such a curve to be used in conjunction with appropriate values of the effective length factor K wherein all three factors (residual stress, geometrical imperfections, and end restraints) that influence the ultimate strength of centrally loaded columns with simple end connections of the restraining beams can be taken into account in a limit state design. The curve proposed is SSRC Curve 2 (Johnson, 1976) as modified by Rondal and Maquoi (1979) so that it can be represented by a single equation. Figure 2 shows a comparison of SSRC Curve 2 and the Rondal and Maquoi approximation. Also shown in Fig. 2 are the recommended K values to be used with this curve to account for the beam with simple end connections end restraint. The procedure is not presently applicable to fixed-end beams or beams with substantial end restraints.

Simplified Multiple Column Curves

Rotter (1982) has taken the Rondal and Maquoi (1979) approximation to SSRC Curve 2 (Johnston, 1976) and, by the use of modifying functions, adapted it to SSRC Curves 1 and 3. By the use of these modifying factors, all column designs can be covered by a single table containing stresses and values of the modifying functions. With this approach, it is possible to provide smooth transitions between one curve and another and to place some column sections between the existing SSRC curves if desired. The modifying factor is a modified nondimensional slenderness ratio.

Finzi and Zandonini (1982) have studied three different approaches and adapted them to both the five multiple column curves of ECCS (1976) and the three multiple column curves of SSRC (Johnston, 1976). In all three approaches the authors have used the highest multiple column curve as the reference curve, since for both ECCS and SSRC this curve essentially depends only on the initial out-of-straightness. The first approach utilizes modified slenderness ratios, whereas the second and third methods utilize modified radii of gyration determined from the modified slenderness ratio. The third method was recommended because it has evident physical meaning. Modified radii of gyration can be tabulated with the section design properties for each cross-section, which results in a simple design approach.

Beam-Columns

   Ballio and Campanini (1981) have addressed the problem of defining the
value of the equivalent moment to be used in beam–column interaction
equations. They have studied approximately 1000 cases with different
slenderness ratios, section properties, and loadings. The beam-columns have
no transverse end displacements and are loaded both by end moments and by
intermediate transverse loads. The initial geometric imperfection conformed
to the ECCS (1976) stability curves. Residual stresses were taken as equal for
all beams of equal sections. In all calculations the loading procedure consisted
of applying bending moments to the beam-columns and then increasing
axial load until the ultimate load was reached. The study concluded that it is
very difficult to establish better methods of design than those presently
adopted by various codes. The results were so diverse that a simple presentation is impossible. The study did suggest clarification and modification of
existing criteria where they appear incomplete when transverse forces are
present or inexact when axial loads are modest and end moments only are
applicable.

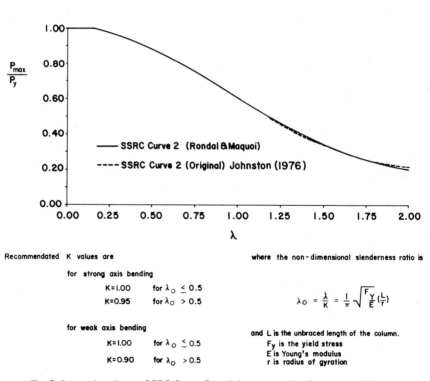

Recommendated K values are

for strong axis bending

$K = 1.00$ for $\lambda_0 \le 0.5$
$K = 0.95$ for $\lambda_0 > 0.5$

for weak axis bending

$K = 1.00$ for $\lambda_0 \le 0.5$
$K = 0.90$ for $\lambda_0 > 0.5$

where the non-dimensional slenderness ratio is

$$\lambda_0 = \frac{\lambda}{K} = \frac{1}{\pi}\sqrt{\frac{F_y}{E}}\left(\frac{L}{r}\right)$$

and L is the unbraced length of the column.
F_y is the yield stress
E is Young's modulus
r is radius of gyration

Fig. 2 Approximation to SSRC Curve 2 by Johnston and by Rondal and Maquoi

The American Institute of Steel Construction's tentative LRFD specification (AISC, 1982) includes new interaction equations for the design of beam-columns. Both doubly and singly symmetric members in flexure and tension and doubly and singly symmetric members in flexure and compression are treated. Equations for the latter are shown in Fig. 3. As can be noted, the problems of column stability and frame stability have been separated. The equations are general, but they can be considerably simplified in many cases. The format permits the use of a P-Delta design procedure. Grundy (1980) has also studied use of the beam-column formulas and has suggested a similar separation of amplification factors.

Individual Columns of Special Types

There are a number of studies associated with special types of columns. These include a study of collapse loads of laced columns by Svensson and Kragerup (1982); an experimental study of thin-web welded columns by Avent and Wells (1982); the strength and behavior of fabricated tubular columns subjected to external pressure by Toma, et al. (1982); and buckling of pretwisted columns by Tebedge (1982). A parametric investigation of circular and rectangular hollow sections subject to both axial load and uniaxial bending moments by Virdi (1981); an investigation of stayed columns with initial imperfections by Wong and Temple (1982); and a study of the interaction between local buckling and column buckling for cold formed light gage steel sections by Hancock (1981) are also included. With respect to cold formed light gage members, Springfield (1982b), in a discussion of Hancock's work, has noted that the present methods of handling stiffened and unstiffened elements are in greater error than the column curves, and that the stiffened element approach becomes increasingly unconservative with an increase in flat width ratio and overall slenderness ratio. The opposite is apparently the case for unstiffened elements.

STABILITY OF TWO-DIMENSIONAL FRAMES

Associated with the interest in end restraint on individual columns is research focusing on the stability analyses of frames with flexible connections. Among several investigations, two studies are cited. Moncarz and Gerstle (1981) investigated steel frames with nonlinear connections. They directed their attention to the connection response and concluded that an assumption of linear response of flexible connections is reasonable and gives a good prediction of bare-frame response. Ackroyd and Gerstle (1982) made a parametric study of frames with flexible connections in the elastic range to assess the validity of existing design philosophies. Both studies conclude that the assumption of rigid connections underestimates building drift and that the current procedures for designing buildings with flexible connections can result in buildings with excessive drift. While analytic methods are available for considering flexible connections in frame stability, data is needed on connection flexibility, especially of bolted joints.

$$\frac{P_u}{\phi_c P_n} + \frac{8}{9}\left[\frac{M^*_{ux}}{\phi_b M_{nx}} + \frac{M^*_{uy}}{\phi_b M_{ny}}\right] \leq 1.0 \text{ for } \frac{P_u}{\phi_c P_n} \geq 0.2 \qquad (1)$$

$$ \qquad\qquad\qquad\qquad\qquad\qquad\qquad\qquad\qquad (2)$$

$$\frac{P_u}{2\phi_c P_n} + \frac{M^*_{ux}}{\phi_b M_{nx}} + \frac{M^*_{uy}}{\phi_b M_{ny}} \leq 1.0 \text{ for } \frac{P_u}{\phi_c P_n} < 0.2$$

where

$$M^*_u = B_1 M_{NT} + B_2 M_{LT},$$

$$B_1 = \frac{C_m}{1 - \dfrac{P_u}{P_e}} \geq 1$$

$$B_2 = \frac{1}{1 - \Sigma P_u \left(\dfrac{\Delta_{OH}}{\Sigma HL}\right)}$$

M_{NT} = required flexural strength in member assuming there is no lateral translation in the frame, in in.-kips.

M_{LT} = required flexural strength in member as a result of lateral translation of the frame only, in in.-kips.

P_e = $A_g F_y / \lambda_c^2$, where λ_c is the slenderness parameter considering effective length

ΣP_u = required axial load strength of all columns in a story, kips

Δ_{OH} = translational deflection on the story under consideration, in.

ΣH = Sum of all story horizontal forces producing Δ_{OH}, kips.

L = Story height, in.

P_n = nominal axial strength considering effective length

C_m = coefficient depending on column end moment ratios

Fig. 3 Interaction equations for symmetric members in flexure and compression

In the field of analysis considering stability effects, Grundy and Wathen (1972) have presented a procedure for assessing frame–shear wall interaction considering four types of second–order destabilizing effects. These are axial shortening of the columns, shear deformation of the columns, stability effects on column and sway stiffness, and gusset effects or size effects in beams and columns.

STABILITY OF THREE-DIMENSIONAL FRAMES

Schmidt et al. (1981) have studied the influence of joint eccentricity and rigidity on the load capacity of a space truss subassemblage. They concluded that although large joint eccentricities reduced subassemblage stiffness and peak load capacity, the continuity of the chords largely offset these reductions even when bolted joint details were used. They also concluded that the stiffness of such systems is highly sensitive to member and joint imperfections including joint slip at bolts.

Oran (1981) has summarized the stability behavior of both perfect and imperfect elastic systems and has suggested procedures for obtaining highly accurate approximate solutions.

APPROXIMATE STABILITY SOLUTIONS FOR
SPECIAL TYPES OF FRAMING

Coull et al. (1982) have extended earlier work in simplified analysis of tube structures to bundled-tube structures. By replacing the discrete structure by an equivalent multicell tube with orthotropic panels and by making reasonable simplifying assumptions regarding the stress distribution in the structure, a simple closed form solution is obtained. The theory agreed reasonably with values obtained from tests on a model two-cell structure. A satisfactory approximate analysis is essential to assessing stability of the structure.

STABILITY UNDER DYNAMIC AND REPEATED LOAD

There are several investigations into stability under dynamic and repeated load that are worth noting. Gillies and Shephard (1981) have developed a computer program enabling prediction of time-history response of three-dimensional frame structures to earthquake ground motion applicable to completely general structural geometry. The results of a study on a six-story building demonstrate that the response based on an equivalent planar frame assumption is modified significantly when account is taken of concurrent earthquake effects.

Popov and Black (1981) have studied steel struts under severe cyclic loadings, with the goal of developing an approach for design of these struts as used in braced buildings. An important conclusion is that effective slenderness ratios appear to be the single most important parameter in determining hysteretic behavior. Toma and Chen (1982) have studied cyclic analysis of fix-ended steel beam-columns and developed analytical solutions for tubular steel columns. The solutions compare favorably with test results by others.

STABILITY OF STRUCTURES OF MIXED STEEL-CONCRETE CONSTRUCTION

No work is being reported under this topic for this paper.

SPECIAL TOPICS

Rack Structures

Springfield (1982c) has prepared a study on the stability of rack structures. He has compared several second-order approaches including iterative second-order analysis, the negative cross-sectional brace method, the frame amplification factor, and the Euler type amplification factor applied to frames. One conclusion is that utilizing P-Delta forces is an effective method of ensuring structural stability for rack structures.

Research Needs

Bjorhovde (1980) has prepared a comprehensive summary of research needs for the SSRC's Committee on Research Priorities. Discussions of this paper by Pillai (1981), Sherman (1981), Springfield (1982a), and Massonnet and Maquoi (1981) among others provide substantial contributions to the original paper.

REFERENCES/BIBLIOGRAPHY

AISC, 1982
    TENTATIVE SPECIFICATION FOR LOAD AND RESISTANCE FACTOR DESIGN, FABRICATION AND ERECTION OF STRUCTURAL STEEL FOR BUILDINGS—SECTION 2.6, MEMBERS UNDER COMBINED STRESS, TORSION, AND COMBINED STRESS AND TORSION, Unpublished Draft, June, pp. 1-2.

Ackroyd, M. H. and Gerstle, K. H., 1982
BEHAVIOR OF TYPE 2 STEEL FRAMES, Journal of the Structural Division, ASCE, Vol. 108, No. ST7, Proc. Paper 17207, July, pp. 1541-1556.

Avent, R. R. and Wells, S., 1982
EXPERIMENTAL STUDY OF THIN-WEB WELDED H-COLUMNS, Journal of the Structural Division, ASCE, Vol. 108, No. ST7, Proc. Paper 17209, July, pp. 1464-1480.

Ballio, G. and Campanini, G., 1981
EQUIVALENT BENDING MOMENTS FOR BEAM-COLUMNS, Journal of Constructional Steel Research, Vol. 1, No. 3, May, pp. 13-23.

Bjorhovde, R., 1980
RESEARCH NEEDS IN STABILITY OF METAL STRUCTURES, Journal of the Structural Division, ASCE, Vol. 106, No. ST12, Proc. Paper 15926, December, pp. 2425-2442.

Bjorhovde, R., 1981
DISCUSSION OF END RESTRAINT AND COLUMN STABILITY, BY WAI F. CHEN, Journal of the Structural Division, ASCE, Vol. 107, No. ST8, Proc. Paper T6410, August, pp. 1696-1700.

Canadian Standards Association, 1974
CSA STANDARD S16.1-1974, STEEL STRUCTURES FOR BUILDINGS—LIMIT STATE DESIGN, Canadian Standards Association, Rexdale, Ontario, Canada, December, pp. 1-114.

Chen, W. F., 1980
END RESTRAINT AND COLUMN STABILITY, Journal of the Structural Division, ASCE, Vol. 106, No. ST11, Proc. Paper 15796, November, pp. 2279-2295.

Chen, W. F., 1982
CLOSURE TO END RESTRAINT AND COLUMN STABILITY, Journal of the Structural Division, ASCE, Vol. 108, No. ST5, Proc. Paper 17236, August, pp. 1929-1933.

Council on Tall Buildings, 1983
DEVELOPMENTS IN TALL BUILDINGS—1983, an update of Monograph on the Planning and Design of Tall Buildings, Hutchinson Ross Publishing Co., Stroudsburg, Pennsylvania.

Council on Tall Buildings, Group SB, 1979
STRUCTURAL DESIGN OF TALL STEEL BUILDINGS, Volume SB of Monograph on Planning and Design of Tall Buildings, ASCE, New York.

Coull, A., Bose, B., and Ahmed, A., 1982
SIMPLIFIED ANALYSIS OF BUNDLED-TUBE STRUCTURES, Journal of the Structural Division, ASCE, Vol. 108, No. ST5, Proc. Paper 17065, May, pp. 1140-1153.

ECCS, 1976
MANUAL ON STABILITY OF STEEL STRUCTURES, ECCS Committee on Stability, European Convention for Structural Steelwork.

Finzi, L. and Zandonini, R., 1982
A SIMPLIFIED APPROACH FOR PREDICTING THE BUCKLING STRENGTH OF CENTRALLY COMPRESSED MEMBERS, Journal of Constructional Steel Research, Vol. 2, No. 1, January, pp. 10-21.

Galambos, T. V. and Ravindra, M. K., 1973
TENTATIVE LOAD AND RESISTANCE FACTOR DESIGN CRITERIA FOR STEEL BUILDINGS, Civil Engineering Department, Washington University, No. 18, St. Louis, Missouri.

Gilles, A. G. and Shephard, R., 1981
POST-ELASTIC DYNAMICS OF THREE-DIMENSIONAL FRAMES, Journal of the Structural Division, ASCE, Vol. 107, No. ST8, Proc. Paper 16432, August, pp. 1485-1501.

Grundy, P. and Wathen, G. R., 1972
FRAME-SHEAR WALL INTERACTION, Civil Engineering Transactions, The Institute of Engineers, Vol. CE14, No. 1, April, pp. 102-108.

Grundy, P., 1980
COMPUTING AND USING EFFECTIVE LENGTH IN PORTAL FRAME DESIGN, Civil Engineering Research Report No. 4/1980, Department of Civil Engineering, Monash University, Clayton, Victoria, Australia.

Hall, H., 1981
    PROPOSED STEEL COLUMN STRENGTH CRITERIA, Journal of the Structural Division, ASCE, Vol. 107, No. ST4, Proc. Paper 16198, pp. 649-670.
Hancock, G. J., 1981
    INTERACTION BUCKLING IN I-SECTION COLUMNS, Journal of the Structural Division, ASCE, Vol. 107, No. ST1, Proc. Paper 15978, January, pp. 165-179.

Johnston, B. G., Ed., 1976
    GUIDE TO STABILITY DESIGN CRITERIA FOR METAL STRUCTURES, John Wiley and Sons, Inc., New York.
Jones, S. W., Kirby, P. A., and Nethercot, D. A., 1982
    COLUMNS WITH SEMIRIGID JOINTS, Journal of the Structural Division, ASCE, Vol. 108, No. ST2, Proc. Paper 16855, February, pp. 361-372.

Lui, E. M. and Chen, W. F., 1981
    STRENGTH OF H-COLUMNS WITH SMALL END RESTRAINTS, Structural Engineering Technical Report No. CE-STR-38, Purdue University, West Lafayette, Indiana,
Lui, E. M. and Chen, W. F., 1982
    END RESTRAINT AND COLUMN DESIGN USING LRFD, Structural Engineering Technical Report No. CE-STR-82-24, Purdue University, West Lafayette, Indiana.

Massonnet, C. E. and Maquoi, R. J., 1981
    DISCUSSION OF THE RESEARCH NEEDS IN STABILITY OF METAL STRUCTURES, BY REIDAR BJORHOVDE, Journal of the Structural Division, ASCE, Vol. 107, No. ST9, Proc. Paper 16481, September, pp. 1885-1889.
Moncarz, P. D. and Gerstle, K. H., 1981
    STEEL FRAMES WITH NONLINEAR CONNECTIONS, Journal of the Structural Division, ASCE Vol. 107, No. ST8, Proc. Paper 16440, August, pp. 1427-1441.

Oran, C., 1981
    DISCUSSION OF ELASTIC INSTABILITY OF UNBRACED SPACE FRAMES, BY ZIA RAZZAQ AND MOOSSA M. NAIM, Journal of the Structural Division, ASCE, Vol. 107, No. ST5, Proc. Paper 16218, May, pp. 1020-1022.

Pillai, S., 1981
    DISCUSSION OF RESEARCH NEEDS IN STABILITY OF METAL STRUCTURES, BY REIDAR BJORHOVDE, Journal of the Structural Division, ASCE, Vol. 107, No. ST11, Proc. Paper 16616, November, pp. 2299-2300.
Popov, E. P. and Black, G., 1981
    STEEL STRUTS UNDER SEVERE CYCLIC LOADING, Journal of the Structural Division, ASCE, Vol. 107, No. ST9, Proc. Paper 16497, September, pp. 1857-1881.

Rondal, J. and Maquoi, R., 1979
    SINGLE EQUATION FOR SSRC COLUMN-STRENGTH CURVES, Journal of the Structural Division, ASCE, Vol. 105, No. ST1, Proc. Paper 14276, January, pp. 245-250.
Rotter, M. J., 1982
    MULTIPLE COLUMN CURVES BY MODIFYING FACTORS, Journal of the Structural Division, ASCE, Vol. 108, No. ST7, Proc. Paper 17194, July, pp. 1655-1669.

Schmidt, L. C., Morgan, P. R., and Phang, P. W., 1981
    INFLUENCE OF JOINT ECCENTRICITY AND RIGITY OF THE LOAD CAPACITY OF A SPACE TRUSS SUBASSEMBLAGE, Journal of Constructional Steel Research, Vol. 1, No. 4, September, pp. 16-22.
Shen, Z. Y. and Lu, L. W., 1981
    ANALYSIS OF INITIALLY CROOKED, END RESTRAINED STEEL COLUMNS, Fritz Laboratory Report No. 471.2, Lehigh University, Bethlehem, Pennsylvania.

Shen, Z. Y. and Lu, L. W., 1982
   DISCUSSION OF PROPOSED STEEL COLUMN STRENGTH CRITERIA, BY DANN H. HALL,
   Journal of the Structural Division, ASCE, Vol. 108, No. ST5, Proc. Paper 17045, May, pp.
   1194-1195.
Sherman, D. R., 1981
   DISCUSSION OF RESEARCH NEEDS IN STABILITY OF METAL STRUCTURES, BY REIDAR
   BJORHOVDE, Journal of the Structural Division, ASCE, Vol. 107, No. ST11, Proc. Paper 16616,
   November, pp. 2301-2302.
Springfield, J., 1982a
   DISCUSSION OF RESEARCH NEEDS IN STABILITY OF METAL STRUCTURES, BY REIDAR
   BJORHOVDE, Journal of the Structural Division, ASCE, Vol. 108, No. ST2, Proc. Paper 16834,
   February, pp. 488-490.
Springfield, J., 1982b
   DISCUSSION OF INTERACTION BUCKLING IN I-SECTION COLUMNS, BY GREGORY J. HANCOCK,
   Journal of the Structural Division, ASCE, Vol. 108, No. ST2, Proc. Paper 16834, February, pp.
   493-494.
Springfield, J., 1982c
   STUDY OF RACK STRUCTURES, PART II—STABILITY Carruthers & Wallace Limited, Toronto,
   Canada.
Sugimoto, H. and Chen, W. F., 1982
   SMALL END RESTRAINT EFFECTS ON STRENGTH OF H-COLUMNS, Journal of the Structural
   Division, ASCE, Vol. 108, No. ST3, Proc. Paper 16941, March, pp. 661-681.
Svensson, S. E. and Kragerup, J., 1982
   COLLAPSE LOADS OF LACED COLUMNS, Journal of the Structural Division, ASCE, Vol. 108,
   No. ST6, Proc. Paper 17179, June, pp. 1367-1384.

Tarnai, T., 1981
   DISCUSSION OF END RESTRAINT AND COLUMN STABILITY BY WAI F. CHEN, Journal of the
   Structural Division, ASCE, Vol. 107, No. ST11, Proc. Paper 17180, June, pp. 1385-1399.
Tebedge, N., 1982
   BUCKLING OF PRETWISTED COLUMNS, Journal of the Structural Division, ASCE, Vol. 107, No.
   ST11 Proc. Paper 16616, November, pp. 2292-2293.
Toma, S. and Chen, W. F., 1982
   CYCLIC ANALYSIS OF FIXED-ENDED STEEL BEAM-COLUMNS, Journal of the Structural Division,
   ASCE, Vol. 108, No. ST6, Proc. Paper 17180, June, pp. 1385-1399.
Toma, S., Chen, W. F., and Finn, L. D., 1982
   EXTERNAL PRESSURE AND SECTIONAL BEHAVIOR OF FABRICATED TUBES, Journal of the
   Structural Division, ASCE, Vol. 108, No. ST1, Proc. Paper 16797, January, pp. 177-194.

Virdi, K. S., 1981
   DESIGN OF CIRCULAR AND RECTANGULAR HOLLOW SECTION COLUMNS, Journal of
   Constructional Steel Research, Vol. 1, No. 4, September, pp. 35-45.

Wong, K. C. and Temple, M. C., 1982
   STAYED COLUMN WITH INITIAL IMPERFECTIONS, Journal of the Structural Division, ASCE,
   Vol. 108, No. ST7, Proc. Paper 17217, July, pp. 1623-1640.

Dynamic Response of Eccentrically Braced Tall Buildings to Earthquakes

P. Jayachandran

INTRODUCTION

The dynamic response analysis of 10-, 20-, and 40-story tall buildings with eccentrically braced frames (EBF) subjected to factored values of El-Centro-type and computer simulated earthquakes are briefly described herein. Companion concentrically braced frames (CBF) and moment-resisting frames (MRF) were also analyzed for the same earthquakes to compare the relative efficiency of the EBF for strength, stiffness and energy dissipation capacity.

DYNAMIC RESPONSE OF BRACED FRAMES

The linear and inelastic dynamic analysis of the braced frames were accomplished using a revised version of the computer software ANSWERS and DRAIN-2D, with refined post-buckling truss elements and shear yielding beam elements included to model the braces and the eccentric girder elements.

311

The geometric stiffness matrix $[K_g]$ was included in the dynamic analysis for all elements. Original stiffness proportional damping of 5% was used for all modes. The earthquake excitations of factored El Centro (N–S) and computer simulated earthquakes as nonstationary stochastic processes were utilized in the analyses. The sections of 10-, 20-, and 40-story buildings are shown in Figs. 1, 2, and 3 respectively. Belt-trusses were included in the 20- and 40-story buildings to simulate the effects of mechanical levels often present in such buildings. These frames were designed with gravity and lateral loads specified according to the American National Standards Institute (ANSI-A58.1, 1972) and the Applied Technology Council Provisions for Seismic Loadings (ATC, 1978).

The lateral displacements at various story levels for the 10-story EBF and MRF are shown in Fig. 4 for a large factored El Centro earthquake (1.42g). This shows that the EBF is extremely stiff in resisting large earthquakes, even though the moment-resisting frames were approximately 25–30% heavier than the eccentrically braced frames. The concentric braced frames were

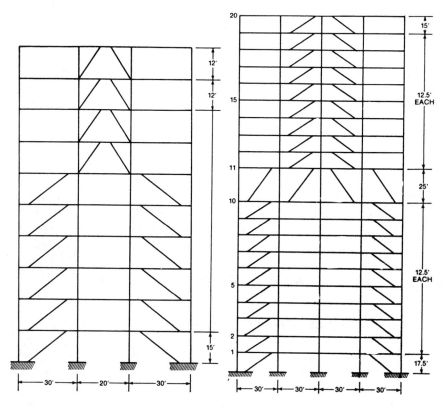

Fig. 1 10-story eccentrically braced frame   **Fig. 2 20-story eccentrically braced frame**

approximately 18–20% heavier than the EBF. The maximum story drifts for the EBF and the MRF for the large factored El Centro earthquake are shown in Fig. 5. The relative efficiency of the EBF is clearly seen, with the MRF exhibiting almost three times the story drift at mid-height. Also, the EBF develops fairly uniform story drift values, thus resulting in excellent energy dissipation at several levels of the building. The EBF has increasing story drifts toward the lower 20% of the height.

The time-history of displacements at levels 10, 8 and 6 are presented in Fig. 6 for the factored El Centro earthquake (1.42g). The influence of higher modes can be seen with fundamental translational modes giving larger values. The maximum displacements at roof were in the range of 15 to 16 in. (381 to 406 mm). The responses to simulated earthquakes were of the same order of magnitude but showed more high frequency components (Jayachandran, 1982). The maximum lateral displacements of the EBF, CBF, and MRF are shown in Fig. 7, for a factored El Centro earthquake (0.5g) after 8s of response. This shows that the EBF is more efficient in drift control than the CBF, or the MRF, exhibiting lower drifts at roof level. The CBF does show

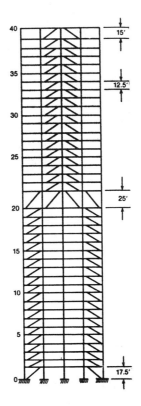

Fig. 3 40-story frame

slightly smaller displacements at lower levels, but it is about 18.9% heavier than the EBF. However, the MRF develops large lateral displacements (2 to 3 times) at various levels, mainly because of the P-Delta effects and column-girder deformations; also, the MRF is heavier than the EBF system by about 30% in this case. This clearly illustrates the strength and stiffness characteristics of EBF relative to the MRF or CBF systems.

The maximum values of story drift for EBFs, CBFs, and MRFs are shown in Fig. 8 for the factored El Centro earthquake with 0.5g maximum accelerations. The story drifts show a trend of relatively uniform drift variation for the EBF, with a slight increase at the lower 25% of the height of building.

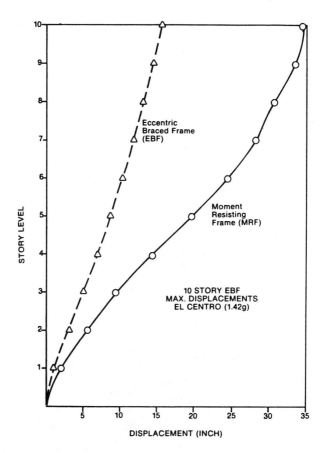

Fig. 4 Displacements for eccentrically braced frames and moment-resisting frames

However, the CBF story drift values are much larger (2 to 3 times) at the upper three levels and show random variation in the lower seven levels. The moment-resisting frame shows drifts increasing towards mid-height, with values of 2 to 3 times the drifts of the EBF and CBF. These drift values would cause extensive nonstructural damage resulting in more costly repair after moderate and large earthquakes. These results do show that the EBF is extremely efficient in drift control, even though the CBF and MRF are heavier than the EBF by about 18–30% in structure weight.

The time-history response of the 20-story EBF is shown in Fig. 9. The response shown for the 20-story EBF is due to a factored El Centro earthquake of 1.42g maximum accelerations. The maximum displacement at roof level was 27.8 in. (706.1 mm) due to this excitation and had smaller values for simulated earthquakes. The maximum values of vertical floor displacements were of the order of 1.73 in. (43.9 mm) at level 20 and 1.67 in. (42.4 mm) at level 16 for the 20-story EBF. These deformations are likely to cause excessive

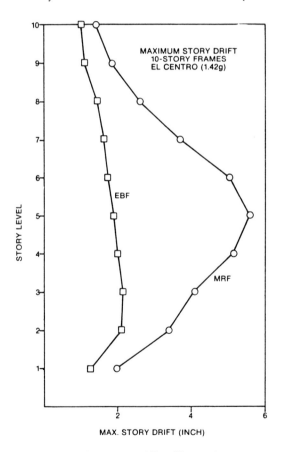

MAXIMUM STORY DRIFT
10-STORY FRAMES
EL CENTRO (1.42g)

EBF

MRF

STORY LEVEL

MAX. STORY DRIFT (INCH)

Fig. 5 Maximum story drifts, 10-story frames

damage to floor slabs after a large earthquake, necessitating later repair. The MRF for the 20-story building was heavier than the EBF by 25% and developed large plastic deformations after about 7 s of response, and yielded when subjected to only 0.5g maximum acceleration due to an El Centro earthquake. The response of the MRF is presented in Fig. 10.

The time-history response of the 40-story EBF is presented in Fig. 11 for a factored El Centro earthquake of 0.5g maximum accelerations. The response was mainly in the fundamental modes with contributions from at least ten normal modes. The maximum lateral displacements were of the order of 38.3 in. (972.8 mm) at the roof level, which occurred at about 6 s of response. The maximum values of vertical displacements at floor levels were 2.99, 2.67, 2.25 and 1.44 in. (75.9, 67.8, 57.2 and 36.6 mm) at levels 40, 30, 20, and 10 respectively, due to the El Centro earthquake (0.5g maximum). The maximum values observed for the floor displacements suggest the cracking of floor slabs and substantial damage to the floor system after large earthquakes. However, brace and column stress levels remained within acceptable values. Thus the 40-story EBF exhibits a very stiff system with members sized for strength and drift limits.

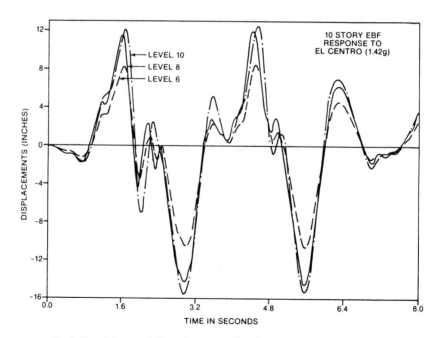

Fig. 6 Time-history of displacements, 10-story eccentrically braced frame

SUMMARY OF RESULTS

The dynamic response of 10-story eccentrically braced frames shows that the EBF is an extremely stiff structural system with excellent energy-absorbing capacity to resist the effects of large earthquakes. The eccentric split K-braced system used in the 10-story EBF performed well under large earthquakes; the eccentric girder element developed large axial forces in addition to the shear yielding type of hinging mechanism. Also, the eccentric K-bracings in this frame forced some inelastic activity in the columns, where the bracings connect to column–girder joints. In the 10-story EBF system, the girder inelastic deformations were reduced somewhat when the brace members sizes were reduced.

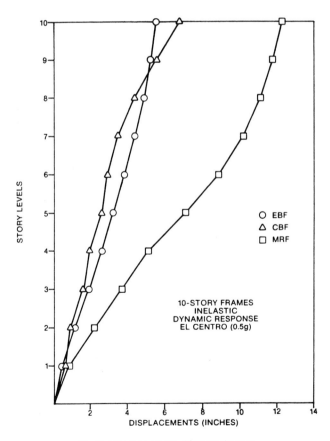

Fig. 7 Displacements, 10-story frames

The EBF system showed relatively smaller lateral displacements and more uniformly distributed story drifts than the companion CBF or MRF systems. The MRF was flexible but showed good energy absorbing characteristics. The CBF, however, showed less ductility because some of its braces buckled under large earthquakes. The CBF and MRF were also heavier than the EBF by about 18–30% in weight, suggesting cost savings in using the EBF in earthquake-resistant design.

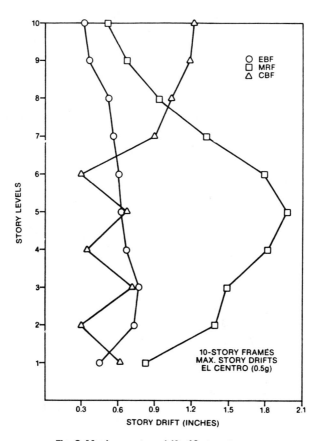

Fig. 8 Maximum story drift, 10-story frames

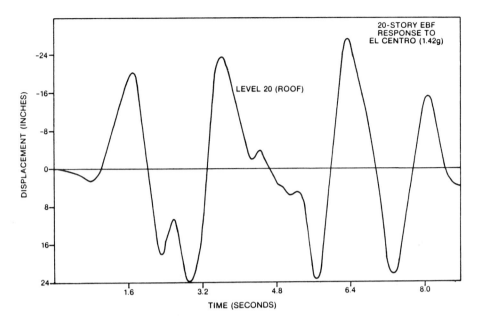

Fig. 9 Time-history of displacements, 20-story eccentrically braced frames

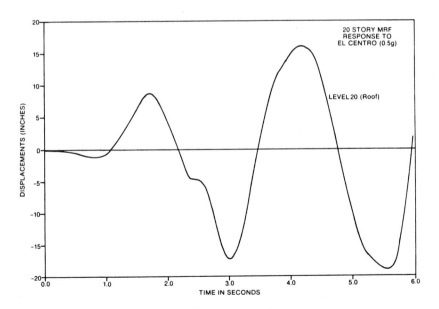

Fig. 10 Response of 20-story moment-resisting frames

320   Stability

The dynamic response of 20- and 40-story EBFs shows that the single inclined eccentric bracing system is excellent for displacements giving large stiffness values, as well as being efficient for energy absorption during large earthquakes. The EBF systems studied herein do develop large vertical displacements at some floor levels during large earthquakes. This will cause considerable cracking of floor slabs and partitions resulting in some non-structural damage, which should be repaired at some cost after large earthquakes. Also, a simple method for computer simulation of earthquakes using Fast Fourier Transforms was developed, which is useful in the calculation of dynamic response of braced frames.

REFERENCES/BIBLIOGRAPHY

ANSI A58.1, 1972
   AMERICAN NATIONAL STANDARD BUILDING CODE REQUIREMENTS FOR MINIMUM DESIGN
   LOADS IN BUILDINGS AND OTHER STRUCTURES, American National Standards Institute, Inc.,
   New York.
ATC, 1978
   TENTATIVE PROVISIONS FOR THE DEVELOPMENT OF SEISMIC REGULATIONS FOR BUILDINGS,
   Applied Technology Council NBS Special Publication 510, U.S. Government Printing Office,
   Washington D.C.

Jayachandran, P., 1982
   DYNAMIC RESPONSE OF ECCENTRICALLY BRACED TALL BUILDINGS TO EARTHQUAKES,
   NSF Research Report, Worcester Polytechnic Institute, Worcester, Massachussetts, June, pp.
   1-100.

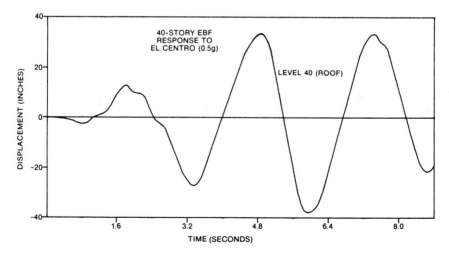

Fig. 11 Response of 40-story eccentrically braced frames

Kanaan, A. and Powell, G. H., 1973
    DRAIN-2D, GENERAL PURPOSE COMPUTER PROGRAM FOR INELASTIC DYNAMIC RESPONSE
    OF PLANE STRUCTURES, Report No. UCB/EERC-73/6, University of California, Berkeley,
    California.

Maison, B. F. and Popov, E. P., 1980
    CYCLIC RESPONSE PREDICTION FOR BRACED STEEL FRAMES, Journal of the Structural
    Division, ASCE, Vol. 106, No. ST7, July, pp. 1401-1479.

Nilforoushan, R., 1973
    SEISMIC BEHAVIOR OF MULTISTORY K-BRACED FRAME STRUCTURES, Ph.D. Thesis in Civil
    Engineering, University of Michigan, Ann Arbor, Michigan, pp. 1-168.

Peyrot, A. H., Saul, W. E. and Jayachandran, P., 1975
    ANSWERS, A STRUCTURAL ANALYSIS SOFTWARE FOR STATIC AND DYNAMIC ANALYSIS,
    University of Wisconsin, Madison, Wisconsin.
Popov, E. P., Takanashi, K. and Roeder, C. W., 1976
    STRUCTURAL STEEL BRACING SYSTEMS: BEHAVIOR UNDER CYCLIC LOADING, Report No.
    UCB/EERC-76-17, University of California, Berkeley, California.

Roeder, C. W. and Popov, E. P., 1977
    INELASTIC BEHAVIOR OF ECCENTRICALLY BRACED STEEL FRAMES UNDER CYCLIC LOADINGS,
    Report No. UCB/EERC-77/18, University of California, Berkeley, California.

Saul, W. E., Jayachandran, P. and Peyrot, A. H., 1976
    RESPONSE TO STOCHASTIC WIND OF N-DEGREE TALL BUILDINGS, Journal of the Structural
    Division, ASCE, Vol. 102, No. ST5, May, pp. 1059-1076.

Generalized Column Equation — A Physical Approach

E. M. Lui
W. F. Chen

INTRODUCTION

One of the most important structural elements in a building frame is the column. As a result, the study of the behavior and strength of centrally loaded columns in framed structures has never diminished over the years. Because strength and stability share an equal importance in affecting column behavior, a valid analysis or design procedure must be geared towards the satisfaction of both criteria.

Since the development of the Euler column formula in 1744, a considerable amount of research has been done theoretically and experimentally on centrally loaded columns. The result of these two centuries of research has led to the identification and understanding of all important factors that influence the behavior and strength of these columns: (1) the magnitude and distribution of residual stresses; (2) the initial out-of-straightness; and (3) the end conditions of the column.

Although a large amount of theoretical and experimental data are available in the literature, the column design formula contained in the present specification (AISC, 1978) acknowledged explicitly only the effect of residual

323

stresses in its development. No consideration is given to the detrimental effect of initial out-of-straightness on column strength. Realizing that perfectly straight columns are rarely encountered in real life, a variable factor of safety varying from 1.67 at $L/r = 0$ to 1.92 for $L/r > C_c$ ($C_c = \sqrt{2\pi^2\,E/F_y}$, (where E is the modulus of elasticity and F_y is the yield stress of material) was introduced into the design formula to account for the harmful effect of initial out-of-straightness and other imperfections such as load eccentricity and material nonhomogenity. A variable factor of safety was used under the presumption that the effect of initial out-of-straightness is more pronounced as the slenderness ratio (L/r) increases and that as the slenderness ratio exceeds C_c, this detrimental effect remains constant.

To account for end conditions, the concept of effective length was introduced. However, it should be remembered that the effective length factors K currently in use for the design of columns are based on the conditions that the column be elastic and that joint rotation and translation be either fully realized or nonexistent. In reality, no perfectly pin-ended or fix-ended column exists. The actual end conditions lie somewhere between these two extreme conditions. Furthermore, under the combined action of high axial thrust and bending moment, yielding or plastification of some of the fibers of the column may result. The assumption that the column is fully elastic may not be valid in some cases. Realizing that there are discrepancies between the theoretically assumed and the actual conditions, the K factors recommended for design are usually slightly higher than their theoretical counterparts.

Although the use of a variable factor of safety and an increased K factor are not without justification, the numbers chosen are not based on a rigorous analytical approach. Because of the empirical or semiempirical nature of the current approach, it is not possible to incorporate explicitly in the design process all the information and factors known to affect column strength and stability. This shortcoming may not be important as long as allowable stress design is used. However, with the current trend in design philosophy changing from an allowable stress approach to a limit states approach, the consideration of all factors that are known to affect column behavior and strength becomes vital. This is because in a limit state approach to design, the structural elements are designed to their limit of usefulness. Thus all factors that may influence the behavior and strength of these structural elements must be considered with equal emphasis.

The upcoming limit states approach to design is called the Load and Resistance Factor Design (LRFD). The development of the LRFD method is based on first-order probabilistic theory. The safety factor (referred to as safety index in LRFD) has definitive theoretical substantiation. The use of one column curve to represent the strength of all steel columns is obviously undesirable since it will give inconsistent margins of safety for columns made by different manufacturing processes and steel grades. A more appropriate approach is to use multiple column curves. A set of column curves is used to predict the strength of different types of columns. Each column curve will then be representative of a particular group of columns. This approach, although theoretically sound, is not very practical, since a designer will not know in advance the size and type of columns to be used and will therefore find it difficult to pick the appropriate column curve for the design. This problem can be alleviated by providing the designer with column tables. Since only discrete data can be listed in the tables, interpolation of the data may be necessary. This approach is not suitable for computer-aided design.

The first part of this paper summarizes the theory and background behind the development of some steel column curves currently in use or proposed in the United States and Europe. Against the background of this information, a new column equation integrating the merits of all these column design curves is proposed in what follows. This proposed equation is then compared with the current column formulas to show the validity of the present approach.

CURRENT COLUMN DESIGN FORMULAS

The derivation of the present column design formulas can be related to either the bifurcation (eigenvalue) approach or the stability (load-deflection) approach.

Bifurcation Approach

In the bifurcation approach, the load corresponding to the state where stable equilibrium is possible for the column in the straight and slightly bent position is calculated using the linear column theory. A linear differential equation was written for the column in a slightly bent configuration and the solution to the characteristic equation of this differential equation gives

$$P_E = \frac{\pi^2 EA}{\left(\frac{KL}{r}\right)^2}, \tag{1}$$

where

P_E = Euler load;

E = modulus of elasticity;

A = cross-sectional area;

KL = effective length of the column;

r = radius of gyration of the cross section.

The essential feature of this equation is that the critical load is expressed as a function of material property (E), cross sectional geometry (A, r) and slenderness ratio (L/r). In other words, all these factors are identified as the key parameters that will influence the behavior and strength of an elastic column.

Equation 1 was derived by Euler in 1744 under the assumption that the column is perfectly straight and ideally pinned at the ends (in other words, $K = 1$). The load is applied along the centroidal axis, the member is fully elastic, and the material obeys Hooke's Law. This formula works well for long columns as long as the axial stresses in the member remain below the proportional limit. When the axial stress reaches the proportional limit, yielding will occur, and the load-carrying capacity of a partially yielded column with the full yielding capacity of the cross section (P_y) will fall below the Euler load at low slenderness ratios. Thus the Euler load will be unconservative for short columns.

Figure 1 shows a plot of the normalized Euler load P_E/P_y with a yielding cutoff. The solid line shows the load that controls for a given nondimensional slenderness $\lambda = (1/\pi) \sqrt{F_y/E} \ (KL/r)$.

Test results on a number of columns indicate that the buckling load for columns of intermediate slenderness falls significantly below those given by the solid curve in Fig. 1. In the early investigations, it was concluded that this reduction in strength was due primarily to the presence of residual stresses incurred during the manufacturing process.

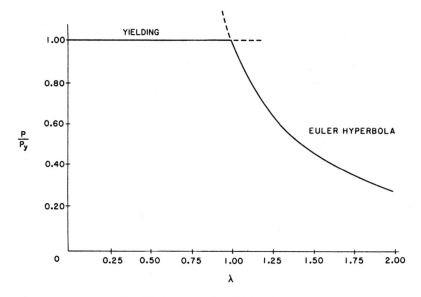

Fig. 1 Euler curve with yielding cutoff

Figure 2 shows the stress–strain (σ–ϵ) relationship for mild structural steel obtained from a coupon test (dashed line) and a stub column test (solid line). The σ–ϵ curve for the coupon test of a mild structural steel can be represented schematically by an elastic–perfectly plastic picture, since a coupon is free of residual stress. All its fibers remain elastic until the applied stress reaches the yield strength, after which plastic flow will occur. In contrast, the σ–ϵ curve for the stub column curve shows a gradual yielding. This is because the fibers that have compressive residual stress will yield first, followed by the fibers with tensile residual stress as the applied stress is increased. Thus yielding is a gradual but not a simultaneous process, as in the case of a coupon.

The slope of the stress–strain curve of the stub column is called the tangent modulus E_t. To account for residual stress, Eq. 1 can be modified by replacing E by E_t (Bleich, 1952):

$$P_t = \frac{\pi^2 E_t A}{\left(\dfrac{KL}{r}\right)^2},\tag{2}$$

in which P_t is the tangent modulus load.

Since P_t is a function of E_t, and E_t reflects the influence of residual stress, the use of the tangent modulus load takes into account the effect of material nonlinearity.

In lieu of a stub-column test, the tangent modulus load can be determined

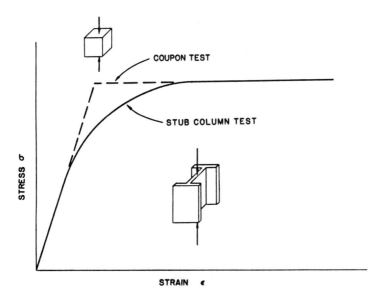

Fig. 2 Stress-strain relationship for steel

analytically by assuming a residual stress pattern. According to the ideas that (1) the axial load and bending moment increase simultaneously when the critical load has just been passed and (2) no strain-reversal occurs as the column buckles, only the elastic core of the cross section will be effective in carrying the applied force (Shanley, 1947). Thus the tangent modulus load can be written as

$$P_t = \frac{\pi^2 E A \left(\dfrac{I_e}{I}\right)}{\left(\dfrac{KL}{r}\right)^2} \tag{3}$$

in which I_e is the moment of inertia of the elastic part of the cross-section (Huber and Beedle, 1954). The ratio I_e/I depends on the residual stress distribution, the cross sectional shape, and the axis of buckling of the column.

For hot-rolled wide-flange shapes, the residual stress distribution lies somewhere between the linear and the parabolic type, as depicted in Fig. 3. Using an idealized I-section (in other words, I-section with negligible web thickness), the ratio I_e/I can easily be evaluated (Salmon and Johnson, 1980).

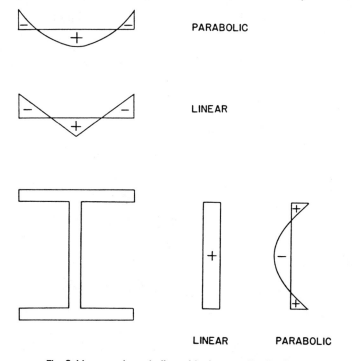

PARABOLIC

LINEAR

LINEAR   PARABOLIC

Fig. 3 Linear and parabolic residual stress distributions

The results of the tangent modulus loads correspond to a linear and parabolic residual stress distribution of an idealized I-section buckle about the strong and weak axis, as shown in Fig. 4 (Salmon and Johnson, 1980). It can be seen that the tangent modulus load depends on the residual stress distribution and the axis of buckling of the column.

Based on these curves as well as on the test results of a number of small and medium-size hot-rolled wide-flange shapes of mild structural steel with $F_y = 33$ ksi (228 MN/m^2), the Column Research Council (CRC) recommended in the second edition of the Guide (Johnston, 1973) a parabola proposed by Bleich (1952) to approximate column strength in the inelastic range:

$$F_{cr} = F_y - B\left(\frac{KL}{r}\right)^2 \tag{4}$$

B was chosen to be equal to $F_y/4\,\pi^2 E$ so that the parabola merges with the Euler curve at $F_{cr} = 0.5F_y$. The slenderness ratio corresponding to $F_{cr} = 0.5F_y$ is designated as C_c, in which

$$C_c = \sqrt{\frac{2\,\pi^2 E}{F_y}} \tag{5}$$

Thus for columns with slenderness ratios less than or equal to C_c, the CRC curve assumes the shape of a parabola (Eq. 4), and for slenderness ratio exceeding C_c, the CRC curve is the Euler hyperbola:

$$F_{cr} = \begin{cases} F_y\left[1 - \dfrac{(KL/r)^2}{2C_c^2}\right] & \left(\dfrac{KL}{r} \le C_c\right) \\[3ex] \dfrac{\pi^2 E}{\left(\dfrac{KL}{r}\right)^2} & \left(\dfrac{KL}{r} > C_c\right) \end{cases} \tag{6}$$

Equation 6 expresses the CRC curve in stress form. The corresponding load form in terms of the nondimensional slenderness ratio λ is

$$\frac{P}{P_y} = \begin{cases} 1 - 0.25\lambda^2 & (\lambda \le \sqrt{2}) \\[2ex] \lambda^{-2} & (\lambda > \sqrt{2}) \end{cases} \tag{7}$$

The CRC curve as represented by Eq. 7 is also plotted in Fig. 4 together with the other tangent modulus curves. It can be seen that it does provide a compromise between strong and weak axis bending in the inelastic range.

The CRC curve divided by a variable factor of safety of

$$\frac{5}{3} + \frac{3}{8}\frac{(KL/r)}{C_c} - \frac{1}{8}\left(\frac{KL/r}{C_c}\right)^3$$

in the inelastic range ($F_{cr} \geq 0.5F_y$) and a constant factor of safety of 23/12 in the elastic range ($F_{cr} < 0.5F_y$) gives the present AISC curve, which is contained in the present AISC Specification (1978) for the design of steel columns (Fig. 4).

Stability Approach

In the bifurcation approach, the column is assumed to be perfectly straight and only the critical load corresponding to the point of bifurcation of equilibrium is obtained. In contrast, the stability approach takes into consideration that the column can have initial geometrical imperfections and that the complete load-deflection curve starting from initial loading to

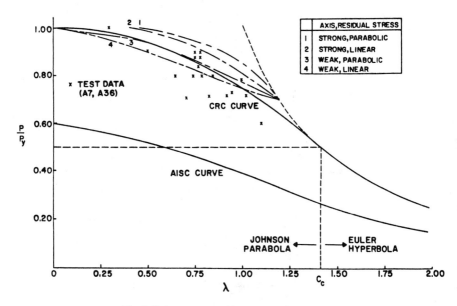

Fig. 4 Column curves (theoretical, CRC, AISC)

final failure is traced by numerical techniques. The maximum load-carrying capacity of the column is obtained from the peak point of this load-deflection curve.

This type of analysis is much more complicated than the bifurcation approach and is made possible by computer technology (hardware and software), a sizeable amount of experimental data, and new concepts and development in beam-column theory (Chen and Atsuta, 1976, 1977).

Realizing that perfectly straight columns are rarely encountered in real life, researchers investigated theoretically and experimentally the strength and stability of initially-crooked imperfect columns (Bjorhovde, 1976; Sfintesco, 1976). It is evident from the results of these studies that the strengths of different types of steel columns due to different manufacturing and fabrication processes, different sizes and steel grades, and different axes of bending may vary considerably, so that more than a single design curve may be desirable.

Based on a computer model developed for a geometrically imperfect column of initial out-of-straightness $0.001L$ at mid-height and actual measured values of residual stresses, Bjorhovde (1972) developed a set of three multiple column strength curves based on the total of 112 columns investigated. Each of these curves is representative of the strength of a related category of columns. Included in these categories are hot-rolled and cold-straightened members, wide-flange and box shapes, as well as round bars and members composed of welded plates.

The Structural Stability Research Council (SSRC) in its third edition of the SSRC Guide (1976) presents these three curves along with the former CRC curve.

The expressions for the three SSRC curves are

(Curve 1)

$$\frac{P_{max}}{P_y} = \begin{cases} 1 \text{ (yield level)} & (0 \le \lambda \le 0.15) \\ 0.990 + 0.122\lambda - 0.367\lambda^2 & (0.15 \le \lambda \le 1.2) \\ 0.051 + 0.801\lambda^{-2} & (1.2 \le \lambda \le 1.8), \\ 0.008 + 0.942\lambda^{-2} & (1.8 \le \lambda \le 2.8) \\ \lambda^{-2} \text{ (Euler buckling)} & (\lambda \le 2.8) \end{cases} \quad (8a)$$

(Curve 2)

$$\frac{P_{max}}{P_y} = \begin{cases} 1 \text{ (yield level)} & (0 \le \lambda \le 0.15) \\ 1.035 - 0.202\lambda - 0.222\lambda^2 & (0.15 \le \lambda \le 1.0) \\ -0.111 + 0.636\lambda^{-1} + 0.087\lambda^{-2} & (1.0 \le \lambda \le 2.0), \\ 0.009 + 0.877\lambda^{-2} & (2.0 \le \lambda \le 3.6) \\ \lambda^{-2} \text{ (Euler buckling)} & (\lambda \ge 3.6) \end{cases} \quad (8b)$$

(Curve 3)

$$\frac{P_{max}}{P_y} = \begin{cases} 1 \text{ (yield level)} & (0 \le \lambda \le 0.15) \\ 1.093 - 0.622\lambda & (0.15 \le \lambda \le 0.8) \\ -0.128 + 0.707\lambda^{-1} - 0.102\lambda^{-2} & (0.8 \le \lambda \le 2.2) \\ 0.008 + 0.792\lambda^{-2} & (2.2 \le \lambda \le 5.0) \\ \lambda^{-2} \text{ (Euler buckling)} & (\lambda \ge 5.0) \end{cases} \quad (8c)$$

These equations were obtained by curve fitting a parabola or hyperbola to the designated characteristic column curves that are the arithmetic mean curves of the three divided categories. Thus each curve is represented by nine or ten coefficients, which are somewhat cumbersome to use. Furthermore, the lack of smooth transition from one curve to another means that there will be a jump in strength for some columns which may be very close to one another. This is not desirable.

An attempt to avoid the use of multiparameters to define the SSRC curves was proposed by Rondal and Maquoi (1979). The model of an imperfect centrally loaded bar subjected to an axial force P and an amplified moment M was used. The ultimate strength was defined as the state when initial yielding occurs at the most highly stressed fiber of the column. The following equation could then be written.

$$\frac{P}{P_y} = \frac{1 + \eta + \lambda^2}{2\lambda^2} - \frac{1}{2\lambda^2}\sqrt{(1 + \eta + \lambda^2)^2 - 4\lambda^2}, \qquad (9)$$

in which η is the imperfection parameter expressed as

$$\eta = \alpha(\lambda - 0.15), \qquad (10)$$

where

$$\alpha = \begin{cases} 0.103 \text{ (SSRC Curve 1)} \\ 0.293 \text{ (SSRC Curve 2)} \\ 0.622 \text{ (SSRC Curve 3)} \end{cases} \qquad (11)$$

A plot of the SSRC curves using Eqs. 8a–c, Eqs. 9 to 11 is shown in Fig. 5. They are almost identical.

The analysis of geometrically imperfect columns was also carried out extensively in Europe, where a series of over 1000 columns were tested in several countries. The data obtained were analyzed using a computer model. A probabilistic approach based on an initial crookedness of $0.001L$ at mid-height was used in evaluating the experimental strength of the columns (Sfintesco, 1976). The result was the development and adoption of the

European multiple column curves of the European Convention for Constructional Steelwork (ECCS). At present, there are five ECCS curves in use. Column strength values are, however, given in tabulated form rather than in mathematical form.

To this end, Maquoi and Rondal (1978) proposed the use of Eq. 9 to approximate the strength of these ECCS curves. The imperfection parameter η used for these curves is

$$\eta = \alpha(\lambda - 0.20), \tag{12}$$

in which

$$\alpha = \begin{cases} 0.125 \text{ (ECCS Curve } a_0) \\ 0.206 \text{ (ECCS Curve a)} \\ 0.339 \text{ (ECCS Curve b)} \\ 0.489 \text{ (ECCS Curve c)} \\ 0.756 \text{ (ECCS Curve d)} \end{cases} \tag{13}$$

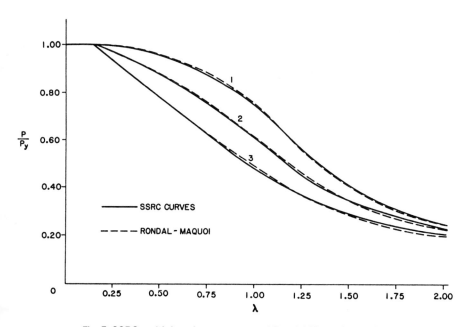

Fig. 5 SSRC multiple column curves and Rondal-Maquoi equation

Recently, Maquoi (1982) has suggested modifying the α values for the ECCS curves shown in Eq. 13 and redefining the imperfection parameter η in terms of the yield strength F_y in addition to the slenderness ratio λ so that smooth transition from one curve to the other is possible for steel of higher grade.

A plot of the ECCS curves using Eqs. 9, 12, and 13 is shown in Fig. 6. ECCS curves a_0, b and d are very comparable to SSRC curves 1, 2 and 3 respectively.

Note that the SSRC curves and the ECCS curves were developed based on the stability approach using the maximum or ultimate strength concept rather than the bifurcation concept as discussed previously. These curves are more representative than the CRC curve because they consider not only geometrical imperfections explicitly in their development but also the vast differentiation of column strength due to the variability in manufacturing processes. The rather different intention of usage also renders those multiple column curves more appropriate for use in a limit states design approach.

Although the SSRC curves and the ECCS curves are more accurate than the CRC curve in representing column strength, it should be remembered that all these multiple column curves were developed assuming an initial out-of-straightness at mid-height of 0.001L. A common question posed is whether these multiple column curves are applicable if the initial crookedness is not 0.001L. Furthermore, although both residual stresses and initial crookedness were taken into consideration in the development of these multiple column

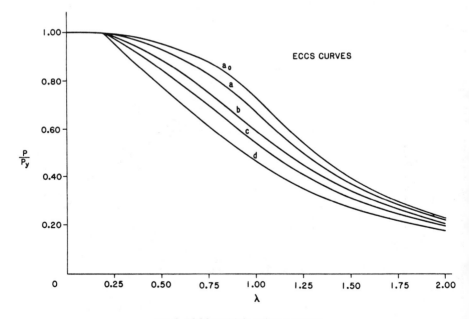

Fig. 6 ECCS multiple column curves

curves, these factors are not clearly identified in the column equations. Therefore, it is the intent of this article to present a column equation that will explicitly identify the factors that influence column strength so that the analyst or designer can have better insight into the column problem.

CRITERIA FOR COLUMN DESIGN EQUATIONS

Before we proceed to the derivation of the column equation, the criteria for such an equation will be discussed. A good and valid column design equation should be realistic in nature, versatile in application, simple to use, and comparable to existing column formulas.

A clear physical identification of factors that influence the strength of columns should be incorporated in the derivation of any column equation. It is well known that residual stresses and initial out-of-straightness have a detrimental effect on the strength and stability of columns. Therefore, any material nonlinearity and geometric imperfection should be considered. Material nonlinearity is reflected in the tangent modulus E_t, which is the slope of the stress–strain curve of a stub column test. Geometrical imperfection can be represented by an initial crookedness at mid-height. This initial crookedness will contribute to the P-Delta effect, resulting in an amplified moment that affects stability. In addition, the column equation should include parameters such as area or radius of gyration to reflect the geometry of the cross section. Finally, different end conditions resulting from the columns being framed into the structural system should also be considered.

The column equation should be versatile in the sense that it can be used for a vast number of columns rather than just a specific category of column. It should also be flexible enough to allow for further updating or revision that is deemed necessary in the future, when the characteristics of new materials, geometry, and end conditions are redefined in later years.

Simplicity in use is also important, should the formula appeal to designers. It should also be adaptable to programming so that computer-aided design can be carried out.

Last but not least, any newly derived column equation should be comparable with other existing column formulas. Through many years of practice, existing column design formulas have become cornerstones to designers. Therefore, compatibility between new and existing formulas is essential to enhance the acceptance of a new formula for general use.

DERIVATION OF COLUMN EQUATION

The derivation will follow a beam-column approach. The essential characteristic of a beam-column is that the additional moment arises from the

P-Delta effect. The physical model used here is shown in Fig. 7. The imperfect column has an initial out-of-straightness of δ_i at mid-height. Upon application of an axial force P, a magnified moment M will be induced at mid-height of the column. As a column problem, the ultimate strength is said to have been reached when the axial force P equals the tangent modulus load P_t. As a beam problem, the ultimate strength is said to have been reached when the magnified moment equals the average flow moment M_m. The average flow moment is depicted in Fig. 8. This moment lies between M_{yc} (the yield moment adjusted for the present of axial force) and M_{pc} (the plastic moment adjusted for the present of axial force). It was first used by Chen and Atsuta (1976) in approximating the ultimate strength of beam-columns.

Thus the ultimate strength of this beam-column model is said to have been reached when

$$\frac{P}{P_t} + \frac{M}{M_m} = 1. \tag{14}$$

Since M, the magnified moment, can be expressed as

$$M = \frac{P\delta_i}{1 - \frac{P}{P_E}}, \tag{15}$$

where P_E is the Euler load, substitution of Eq. 15 into Eq. 14 yields

$$\frac{P}{P_t} + \frac{P\delta_i}{(1 - \frac{P}{P_E})M_m} = 1. \tag{16}$$

The flow moment can be expressed as the product of the plastic section modulus Z and an average flow stress $\bar{\sigma}_y$:

$$M_m = Z\bar{\sigma}_y \tag{17}$$

The flow stress is such that $\sigma_y/f \le \bar{\sigma}_y \le \sigma_y$, in which f is the shape factor of the cross-section.

Thus Eq. 16 can be rewritten as

$$\frac{P}{P_t} + \frac{P\sigma_i}{(1 - \frac{P}{P_E})Z\bar{\sigma}_y} = 1 \tag{18}$$

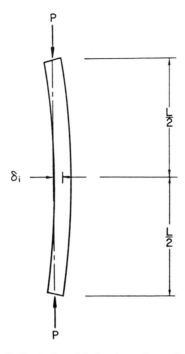

Fig. 7 Physical model of an imperfect column

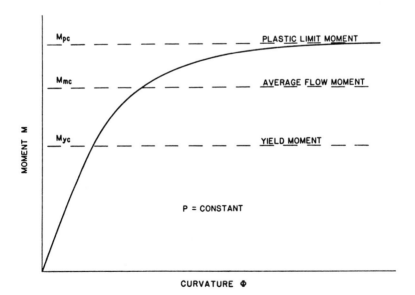

Fig. 8 Schematic representation of average flow moment M_m

or

$$\left(\frac{P}{P_y}\right)\left(\frac{P_y}{P_E}\right)\left(\frac{P_E}{P_t}\right) + \frac{P\delta_i}{\left(1-\frac{P}{P_y}\frac{P_y}{P_E}\right)\left(\frac{Z}{S}\right)S\left(\frac{\overline{\sigma}_y}{\sigma_y}\right)\sigma_y} = 1, \qquad (19)$$

where S is the elastic section modulus.

Defining

$$\hat{E} = \frac{E}{E_t} = \frac{P_E}{P_t}, \qquad (20)$$

$$f = \frac{Z}{S}, \qquad (21)$$

$$\hat{\sigma}_y = \frac{\overline{\sigma}_y}{\sigma_y} \qquad (22)$$

and realizing that

$$\frac{P_y}{P_E} = \lambda^2, \qquad (23)$$

where

$$\lambda = \frac{1}{\pi}\sqrt{\frac{F_y}{E}}\left(\frac{KL}{r}\right),$$

Eq. 19 can be written as

$$\left(\frac{P}{P_y}\right)\lambda^2\hat{E} + \frac{P\delta_i}{\left(1-\frac{P}{P_y}\lambda^2\right)f\hat{\sigma}_yS\sigma_y} = 1 \qquad (24)$$

or

$$\left(\frac{P}{P_y}\right)\lambda^2\hat{E} + \frac{\left(\frac{P}{P_y}\right)}{\left(1-\frac{P}{P_y}\lambda^2\right)}\hat{\eta} = 1, \qquad (25)$$

in which

$$\hat{\eta} = \frac{\delta_i A}{f\hat{\sigma}_y S} \tag{26}$$

is the imperfection parameter.

Solving Eq. 25 for P/P_y gives

$$\frac{P}{P_y} = \frac{\hat{\eta} + (1 + \hat{E})\lambda^2 - \sqrt{[\hat{\eta} + (1 + \hat{E})\lambda^2]^2 - 4\hat{E}\lambda^4}}{2\hat{E}\lambda^4}, \tag{27}$$

which is the proposed generalized column design equation.

The maximum load that a column can carry is a function of $\hat{\eta}$, $\hat{E}$, and λ. Any column curve can be generated using this equation, provided that the parameters $\hat{\eta}$, $\hat{E}$, and λ are known.

Now, expressing the initial crookedness δ_i of a column as a fraction of the column length L,

$$\delta_i = \frac{L}{\gamma}, \tag{28}$$

and realizing that

$$S = \frac{I}{c} = \frac{Ar^2}{c}, \tag{29}$$

where c is the distance from neutral axis to extreme fiber and r is the radius of gyration, Eq. 26 can be written as

$$\hat{\eta} = \frac{cL}{\gamma f\hat{\sigma}_y r^2}, \tag{30}$$

or in terms of λ (with $K = 1$ for pin-ended column),

$$\hat{\eta} = \pi \sqrt{\frac{E}{F_y}} \left(\frac{1}{\gamma}\right)\left(\frac{1}{f}\right)\left(\frac{c}{r}\right)\left(\frac{\lambda}{\hat{\sigma}_y}\right) \tag{31}$$

Note that this imperfection parameter reflects the effects of yield stress (F_y), geometrical imperfection (γ), axis of bending (f), cross-sectional shape (c and r) and slenderness ratio (λ) on the load-carrying capacity of columns.

The average flow stress $\bar{\sigma}_y$ depends on the degree of plastification of the cross-section and is a function of the load level and column types. Since, for a column, the degree of plastification depends on the load level and the load level is a function of the slenderness ratio of the column, this flow stress can therefore be thought of as a function of the slenderness ratio λ. If λ is very large and P/P_y is very small, the problem will resemble a beam problem and the plastic limit moment M_{pc} will govern the ultimate state, so $\overline{\sigma}_y$ approach σ_y. On the other hand, if λ is very small, P/P_y will approach unity, the problem will resemble an axially loaded short column problem, and the yield moment M_{yc} will govern the ultimate state, so $\overline{\sigma}_y$ will approach $\overline{\sigma}_y/f$ where f is the shape factor.

Based on this argument, the following expression for the flow stress is proposed:

$$\overline{\sigma}_y = (\frac{1}{\beta\lambda^2 + f})\sigma_y. \tag{32}$$

The constant β can be determined from experiments or from calibration against existing column curves.

Substitution of Eq. 32 into Eq. 31 (with $\sigma_y = F_y$ and $\sigma_x = \overline{\sigma}_y/\sigma_y$) gives

$$\hat{\eta} = [\pi\sqrt{\frac{E}{F_y}}(\frac{1}{\gamma})(\frac{1}{f})(\frac{c}{r})](\beta\lambda^3 + f\lambda). \tag{33}$$

It can be seen clearly that the imperfection parameter decreases as λ and c/r decrease and as F_y, γ, and f increase. This observation agrees with the following general experimental facts:

The load-carrying capacity of a column increases as the slenderness decreases.

The column curves for light and medium columns are relatively higher than those of large and heavy shapes.

The column has greater strength if manufactured using a higher grade of steel.

The column strength increases as the initial out-of-straightness decreases.

The column is stronger upon bending about its strong axis ($f = 1.12$ for hot-rolled wide-flange shapes) than about its weak axis ($f = 1.55$).

For a given column, the terms inside the brackets of Eq. 33 are known, so it can be written in general form as

$$\hat{\eta} = \hat{a}\lambda^3 + \hat{b}\lambda. \tag{34}$$

The modulus ratio $\hat{E}$ can be evaluated if the tangent modulus E_t is known either from an experimental or from a theoretical approach. Recall that the tangent modulus is the slope of the nonlinear stress–strain curve. This nonlinearity is due to material for aluminum columns and to residual stresses for steel columns. Thus this modulus ratio will reflect material nonlinearity and imperfections.

For simplicity, this modulus ratio is taken to be the ratio of the Euler curve to the CRC curve:

$$\hat{E} = \frac{E}{E_t} = \frac{P_E}{P_{CRC}} = \begin{cases} \dfrac{4}{(4 - \lambda^2)\lambda^2} & (\lambda \leq \sqrt{2}) \\ \\ 1 & (\lambda > \sqrt{2}) \end{cases} \tag{35}$$

To sum up, the generalized column curve is expressed as

$$\frac{P}{P_y} = \frac{\hat{\eta} + (1 + \hat{E})\lambda^2 - \sqrt{[\hat{\eta} + (1 + \hat{E})\lambda^2]^2 - 4\hat{E}\lambda^4}}{2\hat{E}\lambda^4}, \tag{27}$$

where

$$\hat{\eta} = \hat{a}\lambda^3 + \hat{b}\lambda \tag{34}$$

$$\hat{E} = \begin{cases} \dfrac{4}{(4 - \lambda^2)\lambda^2} & (\lambda \leq \sqrt{2}) \\ \\ 1 & (\lambda > \sqrt{2}) \end{cases} \tag{35}$$

COMPARISON OF PROPOSED EQUATION WITH EXISTING DESIGN FORMULAS

The versatility and validity of the proposed equation is demonstrated by comparing it with the current design formulas.

CRC Curve

The CRC curve was developed for a perfectly straight column, so $\delta_i = 0$. In other words, γ will approach infinity (Eq. 28). As γ approaches infinity, $\hat{\eta}$ will approach zero by Eq. 33. Setting $\hat{\eta} = 0$ in Eq. 27 and using Eq. 35 yields

$$\frac{P}{P_y} = \begin{cases} 1 - 0.25\lambda^2 & (\lambda \leq \sqrt{2}) \\ \lambda^{-2} & (\lambda > \sqrt{2}) \end{cases},$$ (36)

which is the expression for the CRC curve.

Thus by setting $\hat{\eta} = 0$, the proposed equation reduces to the CRC formula.

Rondal-Maquoi Mathematical Expression for SSRC and ECCS Multiple Column Curves

The Rondal–Maquoi mathematical expression was developed by assuming that the ultimate strength is reached when yielding occurs at the most severely stressed fiber, that is when

$$\frac{P}{P_y} + \frac{M}{M_y} = 1.$$ (37)

By setting $P_t = P_y$ and $M_m = M_y$, Eq. 16 can be written as

$$\frac{P}{P_y} + \frac{P\delta_i}{(1 - \frac{P}{P_E})M_y} = 1$$ (38)

or

$$\frac{P}{P_y} + \frac{P\delta_i}{(1 - \frac{PP_y}{P_y P_E})M_y} = 1.$$ (39)

Substitution of $M_y = S\sigma_y$ and defining $\eta = \delta_i A/S$ gives

$$\frac{P}{P_y} + \frac{\frac{P}{P_y}}{1 - \frac{P}{P_y}\lambda^2}\eta = 1.$$ (40)

Solving for P/P_y yields

$$\frac{P}{P_y} = \frac{(1 + \eta + \lambda^2) - \sqrt{(1 + \eta + \lambda^2)^2 - 4\lambda^4}}{2\lambda^2},$$ (41)

which is equivalent to Eq. 9. Thus by setting $P_t = P_y$ and $M_m = M_y$, the proposed equation reduces to the Rondal–Maquoi mathematical expression (Maquoi, 1982).

Based on the above discussions, the proposed equation can be thought of as a generalized equation integrating the CRC formula and the Rondal–Maquoi expression for multiple column curves.

The proposed formula can also be used to represent the existing multiple column curves through calibration. By using values of $\hat{a}$ and $\hat{b}$ shown in Table 1, for example, the SSRC and ECCS multiple column curves can be closely approximated.

Figures 9 and 10 show these approximations. Good correlation between the actual curves and the proposed equation is generally observed.

FURTHER STUDIES OF THE PROPOSED EQUATION

Column with Initial Imperfection Other Than 0.001L

An immediate use of the proposed column equation is to generate column curves for columns with initial out-of-straightness at mid-height other than the value 0.001L.

Referring to Eq. 33, $\hat{\eta}$ is inversely proportional to γ. The coefficients $\hat{a}$ and $\hat{b}$ in Eq. 34 and Table 1 were generated for columns with $\gamma = 1000$. Thus, for example, if γ is now equal to 500, the coefficients $\hat{a}$ and $\hat{b}$ will be double. Using this argument, three column curves [ECCS a_0, a, b (Fig. 11)] are generated. These curves are generated because the residual stresses for columns represented by these curves can be closely approximated by the CRC. (Recall that the term $\hat{E}$ in Eq. 35 was obtained by normalizing the elastic modulus E by the tangent modulus E_t derived from the CRC curve.)

Comparable results are obtained upon comparison with the same column curves generated using the approach recommended by Maquoi (1982).

As a further illustration, two column curves corresponding to the strong and weak axis bending of a hot-rolled wide-flange shape are generated. The column is a W12 × 65 shape with an initial crookedness of 0.002L at mid-height. Material and geometric properties are given in Table 2.

The numerical values for $\hat{a}$ and $\hat{b}$ for this column were obtained by first evaluating β (Eq. 33) from the values $\hat{a}$ and $\hat{b}$ shown in Table 1 for a typical hot-rolled wide-flange column that is represented by SSRC Curve 2. The properties of this representative column are given in Table 3.

The values of β for strong axis and weak axis buckling were found to be −0.378 and −0.308 respectively. These values were then used in conjunction with the material and geometric properties of the W12 × 65 section to evaluate $\hat{a}$ and $\hat{b}$ using Eq. 33.

Figure 12 shows a plot of the two column curves generated by the proposed equation and the same curves generated using a computer model (Sugimoto and Chen, 1982). Good agreement is generally observed.

Other Residual Stress Distributions

The effect of residual stresses is reflected in the modulus ratio defined in Eq. 20. For columns with residual stresses other than linear or parabolic, Eq. 35 may not give an appropriate representation of $\hat{E}$. To obtain an appropriate value for $\hat{E}$, the tangent modulus E_t has to be found.

Table 1 Values of $\hat{a}$ and $\hat{b}$ to approximate SSRC and ECCS multiple column curves

Curve	$\hat{a}$	$\hat{b}$
SSRC 1	0.002	−0.001
SSRC 2	−0.036	0.159
SSRC 3	−0.092	0.453
ECCS a_0	0.002	0.007
ECCS a	−0.007	0.057
ECCS b	−0.021	0.148
ECCS c	−0.035	0.256
ECCS d	−0.053	0.454

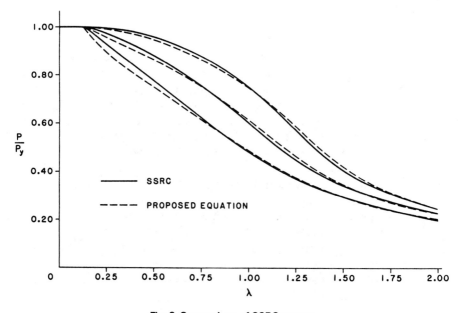

Fig. 9 Comparison of SSRC curves

Table 2 Material and geometric properties for strong and weak axis bending of a hot-rolled, wide-flange shape

	Strong axis	Weak axis
E	30000 ksi	30000 ksi
F_y	36 ksi	36 ksi
γ	500	500
f	1.101	1.515
c/r	1.148	1.987
$\hat{a}$	−0.071	−0.072
$\hat{b}$	0.208	0.361

Table 3 Properties of representative column

	Strong axis	Weak axis
E	30000 ksi	30000 ksi
F_y	36 ksi	36 ksi
γ	1000	1000
f	1.12	1.55
c/r	1.176	2.000

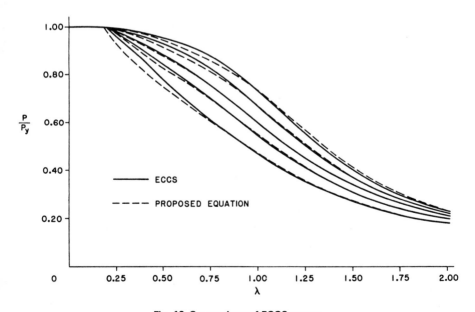

Fig. 10 Comparison of ECCS curves

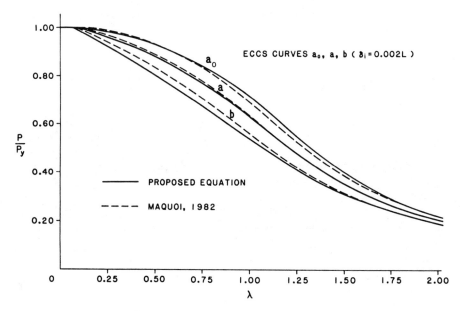

Fig. 11 ECCS curves a_0, a, b ($\delta_i = 0.002L$)

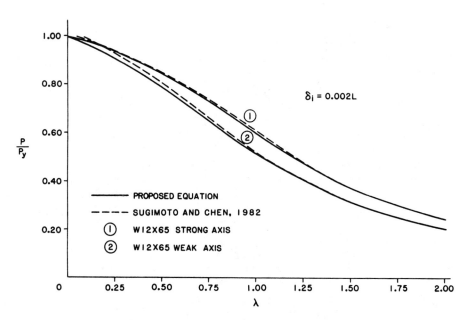

Fig. 12 Comparison of proposed equation with computer model

For steel columns, E_t can be determined theoretically by Eq. 3 as EI_e/I or experimentally by stub column tests.

For aluminum columns, residual stress has virtually no effect, and the nonlinearity of the stress–strain curve is due primarily to material property. For a given type of aluminum alloy, the nonlinear stress–strain relationship can be closely approximated by the Ramberg–Osgood (1943) three parameter law

$$\epsilon = \frac{\sigma}{E} + 0.002(\frac{\sigma}{\sigma_{0.2}})^n, \tag{42}$$

where E is the elastic modulus, $\sigma_{0.2}$ is a 0.2% offset yield stress, and n is the hardening parameter.

The modulus ratio $\hat{E}$ is obtained from Eq. 42 by differentiation:

$$\hat{E} = \frac{E}{E_t} = E\frac{d\epsilon}{d\sigma} = 1 + 0.002n\frac{E}{\sigma_{0.2}}(\frac{\sigma}{\sigma_{0.2}})^{n-1}. \tag{43}$$

Thus Eq. 43 can be used in place of Eq. 35 for aluminum columns.

COLUMN WITH LOAD ECCENTRICITY

The physical model for a column with load eccentricity is shown in Fig. 13. The difference between a column with a load eccentricity e and one with an initial crookedness δ_i is that the expression for moment magnification factor changes somewhat. Figure 14 shows a comparison of these two moment magnification factors.

Based on a numerical study, the authors found that the magnification factor for load eccentricity can be closely represented by the approximation

$$\Delta = \sec\frac{\pi}{2}\sqrt{\frac{P}{P_E}} \approx \frac{1 + 0.25(\frac{P}{P_E})}{1 - \frac{P}{P_E}}. \tag{44}$$

This approximation is plotted in Fig. 14. It can be seen that an excellent agreement is obtained.

The failure criterion for an eccentrically loaded column has the form

$$\frac{P}{P_t} + \frac{Pe\sec\frac{\pi}{2}\sqrt{\frac{P}{P_E}}}{M_m} = 1. \tag{45}$$

Using Eq. 44 and Eq. 17, we obtain

$$\frac{P}{P_t} + \frac{Pe[1 + 0.25(\frac{P}{P_E})]}{(1 - \frac{P}{P_E})Z\bar{\sigma}_y} \tag{46}$$

or

$$(\frac{P}{P_y})(\frac{P_y}{P_E})(\frac{P_E}{P_t}) + \frac{Pe[1 + 0.25(\frac{P}{P_y})(\frac{P_y}{P_E})]}{(1 - \frac{P}{P_y}\frac{P_y}{P_E})(\frac{Z}{S})S(\frac{\bar{\sigma}_y}{\sigma_y})\sigma_y} = 1, \tag{47}$$

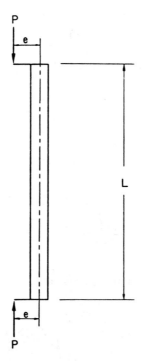

Fig. 13 Physical model for a column with load eccentricity *e*

or

$$\left(\frac{P}{P_y}\right)\lambda^2\hat{E} + \frac{\left(\dfrac{P}{P_y}\right)[1 + 0.25\left(\dfrac{P}{P_y}\right)\lambda^2]}{\left(1 - \dfrac{P}{P_y}\lambda^2\right)}\,\overline{\eta} = 1, \qquad (48)$$

where

$$\overline{\eta} = \frac{eA}{f\hat{\sigma}_y S}. \qquad (49)$$

Solving Eq. 48 for P/P_y gives

$$\frac{P}{P_y} = \frac{\overline{\eta} + (1 + \hat{E})\lambda^2 - \sqrt{[\overline{\eta} + (1 + \hat{E})\lambda^2]^2 - 4[\hat{E}\lambda^4 - 0.25\overline{\eta}\lambda^2]}}{2(\hat{E}\lambda^4 - 0.25\overline{\eta}\lambda^2)}. \qquad (50)$$

Equation 50 can be used to generate column curves for columns with load eccentricity.

COLUMNS WITH INITIAL CROOKEDNESS AND LOAD ECCENTRICITY

The ultimate strength of the column shown in Fig. 15 is

$$\frac{P}{P_t} + \frac{P\delta_i}{\left(1 - \dfrac{P}{P_E}\right)M_m} + \frac{Pe\sec\dfrac{\pi}{2}\sqrt{\dfrac{P}{P_E}}}{M_m} = 1. \qquad (51)$$

Following the same procedure as before, the nondimensional load P/P_y can be expressed as

$$\frac{P}{P_y} = \frac{q - \sqrt{q^2 - 4p}}{2p}, \qquad (52)$$

in which

$$p = \hat{E}\lambda^4 - 0.25\overline{\eta}\lambda^2;$$
$$q = \hat{\eta} + \overline{\eta} + (1 + \hat{E})\lambda^2.$$

$\hat{E}$, $\hat{\eta}$, and $\bar{\eta}$ are defined as before. Note that if $\bar{\eta} = 0$, Eq. 52 reduces to Eq. 27, and if $\hat{\eta} = 0$, Eq. 52 reduces to Eq. 50.

EXTENSION TO BEAM-COLUMN AND FRAME ANALYSIS

Although the generalized column equation was developed for a pin-ended column, it can be used in conjunction with the effective length factor K for columns with other end conditions or with the K-nomographs for columns in frames.

The proposed equation can also be used as the end points for beam-column interaction equations.

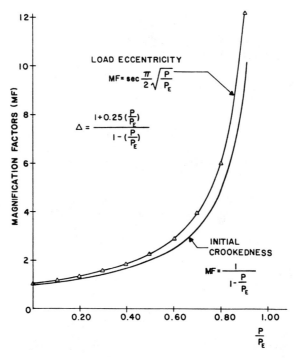

Fig. 14 Comparison of moment magnification factors for an initially-crooked and an eccentrically-loaded column

SUMMARY AND CONCLUSIONS

Conventional column analysis includes the use of the eigenvalue approach or the stability approach. The former approach pertains to perfectly straight columns, whereas the effect of residual stresses can be accounted for by the use of the tangent modulus concept. The latter approach can be used for columns with residual stresses as well as initial crookedness, but it requires much more computational effort. In this paper, a generalized column equation capturing all essential features of these two approaches was developed based on a physical model.

The proposed column design equation can be used to generate column curves for columns with different residual stress distribution, with different initial crookedness, and with or without load eccentricity. In the proposed approach, the effect of residual stress is reflected in the modulus ratio $\hat{E}$, whereas the effect of crookedness is reflected in the γ term. In addition, the effect of other parameters such as yield stress, axis of bending, column size, and cross sectional shape are all explicitly identified in the imperfection parameters $\hat{\eta}$. For columns with load eccentricity, the same approach can be used to develop a similar column equation.

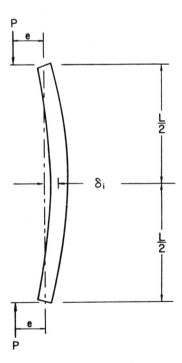

Fig. 15 Physical model for a column with initial crookedness δ_i and load eccentricity e

The validity of the present approach is demonstrated by comparing it with other existing column formulas. The present formula is therefore recommended for general use.

REFERENCES/BIBLIOGRAPHY

American Institute of Steel Construction, 1978
    SPECIFICATION FOR THE DESIGN, FABRICATION AND ERRECTION OF STRUCTURAL STEEL FOR BUILDINGS, American Institute of Steel Construction, Chicago.

Bjorhovde, R., 1972
    DETERMINISTIC AND PROBALISTIC APPROACHES TO THE STRENGTH OF STEEL COLUMNS, Ph.D. Dissertation, Lehigh University, Bethlehem, Pennsylvania.
Bleich, F., 1952
    BUCKLING STRENGTH OF METAL STRUCTURES, McGraw-Hill, New York.

Chen, W. F. and Atsuta, T., 1976
    THEORY OF BEAM-COLUMNS: IN PLANE BEHAVIOR AND DESIGN, Vol. 1, McGraw-Hill, New York.
Chen, W. F. and Atsuta, T., 1977
    THEORY OF BEAM-COLUMNS: SPACE BEHAVIOR AND DESIGN, Vol. 2, McGraw-Hill, New York.

Huber, A. W. and Beedle, L. S., 1954
    RESIDUAL STRESS AND THE COMPRESSIVE STRENGTH OF STEEL, Welding Journal, December, pp. 589s-614s.

Johnston, B. G., Ed., 1973
    GUIDE TO DESIGN CRITERIA FOR METAL COMPRESSION MEMBERS, 2nd Edition, John Wiley, New York.
Johnston, B. G., Ed., 1976
    SSRC GUIDE TO STABILITY DESIGN CRITERIA FOR METAL STRUCTURES, 3rd Edition, John Wiley, New York.

Maquoi, R. and Rondal, J., 1978
    ANALYTICAL EXPRESSIONS FOR THE NEW EUROPEAN COLUMN CURVES (Formulation Analytique des nouvelles courbes europeenes de flambement), Construction Metallique, No. 1.
Maquoi, R., 1982
    SOME IMPROVEMENTS IN THE BUCKLING DESIGN OF CENTRALLY LOADED COLUMNS (Proceedings of the Structural Stability Research Council), pp. 8-14.

Ramberg, W., and Osgood, W. R., 1943
    DESCRIPTION OF STRESS-STRAIN CURVES BY THREE PARAMETERS, NACA Technical Note No. 902.
Rondal, J. and Maquoi, R., 1979
    SINGLE EQUATION FOR SSRC COLUMN-STRENGTH CURVES, Journal of the Structural Division, ASCE, Vol. 105, No. ST1, January, pp. 247-250.

Salmon, S. G. and Johnson, J. E., 1976
    STEEL STRUCTURES: DESIGN AND BEHAVIOR, 2nd Edition, Harper & Row, New York.
Sfintesco, D., Ed., 1976
    ECCS MANUAL ON THE STABILITY OF STEEL STRUCTURES, 2nd Edition, ECCS, Paris.
Shanley, F. R., 1947
    INELASTIC COLUMN THEORY, Journal of the Aeronautical Sciences, Vol. 14, No. 5.
Sugimoto, H. and Chen, W. F., 1982
    SMALL END RESTRAINT EFFECTS ON STRENGTH OF H-COLUMNS, Journal of the Structural Division, ASCE, Vol. 108, No. ST3, Proc. Paper 16941, March, pp. 661-681.

Recent Developments in
Structural Connections

W. F. Chen
E. M. Lui

INTRODUCTION

Understanding the behavior of the connection as a structural element or as an integral part of a structural system is imperative for the following reasons. First, from the viewpoint of analysis and design, there is a trend towards a new design philosophy. In this philosophy, now known as limit states design, the structural element or system is designed to its limit of usefulness. As a result, all factors that may influence the behavior of the structure, from the beginning of loading to its ultimate strength, have to be considered. Since structural connections are basic elements in a structural steel frame, the behavior of these connections will undoubtedly affect the behavior of the frame. Therefore, to have a valid limit states design, it is essential to consider the effect of connections on the behavior and strength of a structure.

Further, construction costs can be reduced if more understanding of the behavior of various types of connections is available. For instance, in designing moment-resisting beam-to-column connections, a noticeable reduction in fabrication and erection costs can be achieved if bolting can be used to replace welding. Economic advantage can also be realized in the design of columns with simple end restraints. Rather than designing such columns as if their ends were pinned, the effective length concept can be used, which may enable a designer to select a lighter section.

The study of the behavior of connections can be related to three basic categories:

1. The effects of connections on columns;

2. The effects of connections on frames;

3. The effects of connections on the steel bracing system.

These categories will be discussed in the following sections.

THE LITERATURE ON THE STATE OF THE ART

Since the publication of the Monograph volume on the Structural Design of Tall Steel Buildings, Volume SB, by the Council on Tall Buildings and Urban Habitat (1979), significant advances have been made in the behavior of the connection, both as a structural element and as an integral part of a structural system. These advances have been reported in the ASCE state-of-the-art report on beam-to-column building connections edited by Chen (1980). The papers contained in this report are grouped in three parts:

A. Connection details, which includes the work by Rentschler et al. (1980); Mann and Morris (1980); and Yura et al. (1980);

B. Connection as a structural element, which includes papers by Tarpy (1980); Chen and Patel (1981); Krawinkler and Popov (1982); and Kato (1982);

C. Connection in frames, which includes work by Ackroyd and Gerstle (1982); Jones et al. (1982); Moncarz and Gerstle (1981); and Witteveen et al. (1982).

World literature on the analyses and performance of rigid and semirigid joints as individual structural elements and as parts of structural systems can be found in the recent volume edited by Howlett et al. (1981). Readers should refer to the above volumes to get up-to-date knowledge on recent advances on connection behavior and design.

CONNECTION ECONOMICS

The cost of a structural system accounts for more than 30–40% of the total construction cost of an average building. Of this 30–40%, the fabrication and erection costs of the structural elements account for well over 75%. Thus any saving in fabrication and erection can considerably reduce the cost of construction. Since connection is an essential element in a structural steel frame, a reduction in its fabrication and erection cost will undoubtedly cut the cost of the construction.

Some of the measures that an engineer or designer can consider in reducing cost are as follows:

1. Avoid using fully welded connections when partially welded or bolted connections would be adequate.

2. Avoid use of full or partial penetration welds where a fillet weld would be adequate.

3. Avoid overdesign of connections.

4. Design details must be practical. Ease of fabrication and erection should be considered when designing the connections.

5. Design details prepared for the fabricator should be complete and without ambiguity.

6. Consider the stabilizing effect of end restraint from beam-to-column connections in designing columns.

7. Consider using eccentrically braced systems to resist lateral forces so that the use of complicated moment-resisting beam-to-column connections can be avoided in moment-resisting frames. In addition, by using eccentrically braced systems, the difficulties encountered in forcing the center lines of beams, columns, and braces to one common work point as in concentrically braced frames can be avoided.

It should be emphasized that personal judgement and experience should prevail in all engineering work. First consideration should be given to the safety and serviceability of the building. Some case studies of connection economics can be found in the paper by Holesapple (1982).

THE EFFECTS OF CONNECTIONS ON COLUMNS DESIGN

Since the publication of the paper "End Restraint and Column-Stability" by Chen (1980), followed by discussions by Bjorhovde (1981) and Tarnai (1981), numerous papers on the study of end-restraint columns have been reported. Investigators have continued to study columns with initial crookedness, residual stresses, and end restraint. These have included the work by

Vinnakota (1981); Lui and Chen (1983a and 1983b); Shen and Lu (1981); Jones et al. (1982); Sugimoto and Chen (1982); Chapuis and Galambos (1982); and Razzaq (1983). All these studies show conclusively that consideration of end restraint results in an increase in the maximum load-carrying capacity and a reduction in overall deflection of columns. This phenomenon is shown in Fig. 1, where the nondimensional load-mispan deflection curves for a W10 × 29 column restrained at both ends by simple web cleats fastened with A325 bolts are plotted. The four solid curves are theoretical load-deflection curves of the end-restrained column generated numerically by Sugimoto and Chen (1982) using the tangent stiffness method, by Jones et al. (1982) using the finite element method, and by Vinnakota (1981) using the finite difference method. The fourth solid curve is a test curve from actual test results by Bergquist (1977). The dashed curve corresponds to the load-deflection curve of the same column with its ends pinned. It is evident from the figure that the end-restrained column provides more strength and less deflection than its pin-ended counterpart.

The amount of increase of maximum load-carrying capacity of a column due to small end restraint from connections depends on a number of factors. Some of the important ones are as follows:

1. The rotational stiffness of the connection;

2. The magnitude of the initial out-of-straightness of the column;

3. The axis of bending and slenderness ratio of the column;

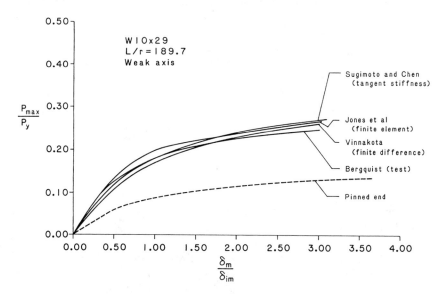

Fig. 1 Comparison of analytical and experimental load-deflection curves

4. The magnitude and distribution of residual stresses over the cross-section of the column; and

5. The flexibility of beam that connects to the column.

In general, the maximum load-carrying capacity of the column increases as the rotational stiffness of the connection increases (except at very low slenderness ratios when yielding is the primary cause of failure). The increase in load-carrying capacity is more noticeable at high slenderness ratios. An increase in the magnitude of inital crookedness has a detrimental effect on the strength-increasing effect of end restraint. The strength increasing effect of end restraint is more pronounced in weak axis bending than in strong axis bending. Residual stress has little or no effect on column strength at high slenderness ratios, when compared with initial crookedness and end restraint.

A systematic study was done by Lui and Chen (1983a) of nonsway steel columns of hot-rolled wide-flange shapes and flame-cut H-shapes with initial mid-height out-of-straightness of $0.001L$. In this investigation, end restraints are provided by four simple beam-to-column connections (Fig. 2): single-web angles, double-web angles, header plate, and top and seat angles. No lateral loads or end eccentricities are present, but both strong and weak axis bending is considered. Five types of residual stress distributions conformable to the experiments reported by researchers at Lehigh University, and several different steel grades, are used in the study. A total of 83 end-restrained column curves were generated and compared with the corresponding pin-ended column curves, from which a relationship between the effective length factor K and the end restraint parameter a was developed. The determination of K and a are shown schematically in Figs. 3 and 4. In these figures, P_y is the yield load, λ is the nondimensional slenderness ratio $(1/\pi)\sqrt{F_y/E}\,(L/R)$, and M_{pc} is the plastic moment capacity of the column section considering the effect of axial load. The relationship between K and a is shown in Fig. 5. The significance of this simple relationship is that the effective length concept in structural stability analysis, with which most structural engineers and designers are familiar, can be used in the design of columns with modest end restraint. This approach has been further developed and refined for practical use by Lui and Chen (1983b), and by Bjorhovde (1984).

A systematic study of end-restraint initially crooked columns, including the effect of eccentricities, is reported by Shen and Lu (1981). The maximum load-carrying capacity of a column may increase or decrease depending on whether the eccentricity is in the direction, or opposite to the direction, of the initial out-of-straightness of the column.

The investigation of initially crooked end-restrained columns is also reported by Razzaq (1981, 1983) in which design concepts and procedures are recommended.

THE EFFECTS OF CONNECTIONS ON FRAMES

Early work on the effects of moment-resisting connections on frames is reported by Becker (1975); Fielding et al. (1972); and Kato (1982). Attention is given to the shear capacity of the panel zone and to the effect of panel zone shear deformation on the strength and stiffness of the entire frame. It was demonstrated theoretically and experimentally by these researchers that the strength and stiffness of the structural frame is dependent on the shear capacity of the panel zone. By proper stiffening of the panel zone, the strength of the frame and resistance to drift can be increased.

Subsequent analytical and experimental studies on flange moment-resisting connections under static loading are reported by Huang et al. (1973); Regec et al. (1973); Standig et al. (1976); Parfitt and Chen (1976); Chen and Patel

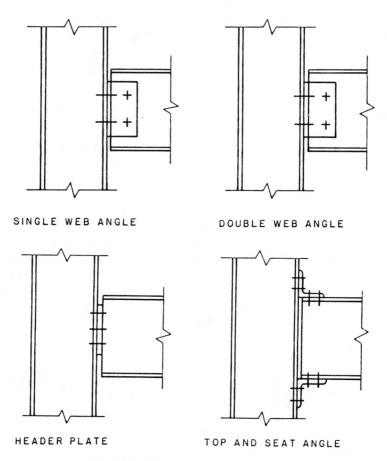

SINGLE WEB ANGLE   DOUBLE WEB ANGLE

HEADER PLATE   TOP AND SEAT ANGLE

Fig. 2 Simple beam-to-column connections

(1981); and Patel and Chen (1985). The studies on web moment-resisting connections are reported by Rentschler and Chen (1975); Chen and Rentschler (1976); Rentschler (1979); Rentschler et al. (1980); Patel and Chen (1982); and Rentschler et al. (1982). It is concluded that as far as flange moment connection is concerned, bolted connections will give comparable moment capacities and ductilities with welded connections. However, bolt slip at or

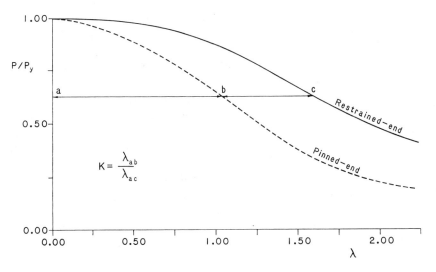

Fig. 3 Effective length factor *K*

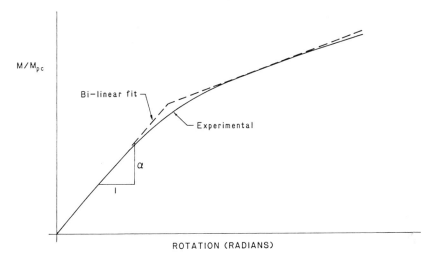

Fig. 4 End restraint parameter α

near the working load condition reduces the elastic stiffness of bolted connections. This reduction in elastic stiffness may have a significant effect on frame stability.

It was found that most web moment connections fail prematurely and give inadequent ductilities that make them undesirable for use in plastic and seismic-resistant design. Suggestions to avoid premature failure of these web connections are reported by Driscoll and Beedle (1982). Experimental research is now underway at Lehigh University to test the validity of these suggestions.

Recent studies on the behavior of flexible connections on the stability analysis of frames include works by Moncarz and Gerstle (1981) and Ackroyd and Gerstle (1982). The former paper concerns the investigation of the behavior of steel frames with nonlinear connections, whereas the latter report deals with the parametric study of frames with flexible connections in the elastic range to assess the validity of existing design philosophies. Both studies lead to the conclusion that the current design specification assuming rigid joints (Type 3 construction) underestimates building drift, and that current procedures for designing buildings with flexible connections (Type 2 construction) may result in buildings with excessive drift.

The study of connections on frame stability under cyclic loading are reported by Popov and Pinkney (1968); Krawinkler et al. (1971); Popov and Stephen (1972); Krawinkler (1978); and Popov and Bertero (1980). To enable the frame to absorb and dissipate large amounts of energy, ductility of the connections is very important in seismic-resistant design.

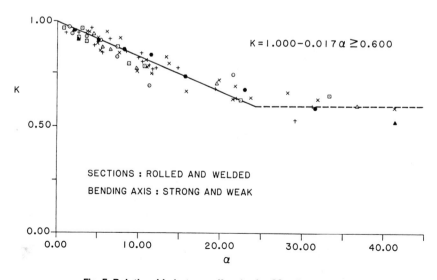

Fig. 5 Relationship between K and α for 83 column curves

ECCENTRICALLY BRACED FRAMES

Eccentrically braced frames are frames in which the center lines of braces are deliberately offset from the points of intersection of the centerlines of the beams and columns. In an eccentrically braced frame, one component of the axial force in the brace is transferred through shear in the beam.

It is pointed out by Popov (1982) that to have an effective eccentrically braced configuration, it is essential to have a kinematic collapse mechanism such that each brace is connected to at least one beam link that can undergo large relative displacements between its ends. A beam link is short beam segment between braces or between a brace and a column. Because of this requirement, beam web buckling due to high shear force is expected. Therefore the need for web stiffeners is inevitable. Criteria for the length of beam links and the spacing of the stiffeners are given by Popov (1982).

An eccentrically braced frame has the advantage over a moment-resisting frame in that for a comparable ductility requirement, beam sizes are smaller and expensive details of doubler plates in panel zones are avoided. In comparison with a concentrically braced frame, an eccentrically braced frame does not have the problem of significant decrease in brace capacities due to repeated buckling under severe cyclic loading. Since the shear capacity of a beam link can be predicted accurately, a brace of sufficient strength can be selected to prevent it from buckling.

Another advantage of an eccentrically braced frame is that by deliberately offsetting the brace, expensive connection detailing, resulting from forcing all the center lines of braces, beams, and columns to pass through one common point, can be avoided. Thus it leads to a more economical design.

A properly designed eccentrically braced frame is very stiff at light and moderate lateral loads but very ductile at high loads. This enables the frame to absorb and dissipate large amounts of energy under severe earthquakes.

The papers of Popov (1981), Popov and Manheim (1981), and Popov (1982) hold more thorough discussions on this subject.

REFERENCES/BIBLIOGRAPHY

Ackroyd, M. H., and Gerstle, K. H., 1982
   BEHAVIOR OF TYPE 2 STEEL FRAMES, Journal of the Structural Division, ASCE, Vol. 108, No. ST7, Proc. Paper 17207, July, pp. 1541-1556.

Becker, E. R., 1975
   PANEL ZONE EFFECT ON THE STRENGTH AND STIFFNESS OF STEEL RIGID FRAMES, Engineering Journal, AISC, First Quarter, Vol. 12, No. 1, pp. 19-29.
Bergquist, D. J., 1977
   TESTS ON COLUMNS RESTRAINED BY BEAMS WITH SIMPLE CONNECTIONS, Report No. 1, American Iron and Steel Institute Project No. 189, Department of Civil Engineering, The University of Texas at Austin, Texas, January.

Bjorhovde, R., 1981
DISCUSSION OF END RESTRAINT AND COLUMN STABILITY, BY WAI F. CHEN, Journal of the Structural Division, ASCE, Vol. 107, No. ST8, Proc. Paper 16410, August, pp. 1696-1700.

Bjorhovde, R., 1984
EFFECT OF END RESTRAINT ON COLUMN STRENGTH—PRACTICAL APPLICATIONS, Engineering Journal, AISC, Vol. 21, No. 1, pp. 1-13.

Bjorhovde, R. and Chen, W. F., 1983
BEHAVIOR OF COLUMNS—A COMPREHENSIVE TREATMENT, W. H. Munse Symposium Volume on Metal Structures—Research and Practice, ASCE, May 17.

Bjorhovde, R. and Chen, W. F., 1983
DESIGN CRITERIA FOR END RESTRAINED COLUMNS, (Proceedings of the International Colloquium on Stability of Metal Structures held in Paris, France, November 16-17, 1983).

Chapuis, J. and Galambos, T. V., 1982
RESTRAINED CROOKED ALUMINUM COLUMNS, Journal of the Structural Division, ASCE, Vol. 108, No. ST3, Proc. Paper No. 16937, March, pp. 511-524.

Chen, W. F., Huang, J. S., and Beedle, L. S., 1974
RECENT RESULTS ON CONNECTION RESEARCH AT LEHIGH, Proceedings of the Regional Conference on Tall Buildings, Bangkok, January, pp. 799-814.

Chen, W. F. and Rentschler, G. P., 1976
TESTS AND ANALYSIS OF BEAM-TO-COLUMN WEB CONNECTIONS, Proceedings of the ASCE Specialty Conference on Method of Structural Analysis, held at the University of Wisconsin-Madison, August 22-25, pp. 957-976.

Chen, W. F., Ed., 1980
BEAM-TO-COLUMN BUILDING CONNECTIONS: STATE-OF-THE-ART, Preprint 80-179, ASCE Spring Convention, Portland, Oregon, April 14-18, 260 p.

Chen, W. F., 1980
END RESTRAINT AND COLUMN STABILITY, Journal of the Structural Division, ASCE, Vol. 106, No. ST11, Proc. Paper 15796, November, pp. 2279-2295.

Chen, W. F. and Patel, K. V., 1981
STATIC BEHAVIOR OF BEAM-TO-COLUMN MOMENT CONNECTIONS, Journal of the Structural Division, ASCE, Vol. 107, No. ST9, Proc. Paper No. 16512, September, pp. 1815-1838.

Chen, W. F. and Lui, E. M., 1984
EFFECTS OF CONNECTION FLEXIBILITY AND PANEL ZONE SHEAR DEFORMATION ON THE BEHAVIOR OF STEEL FRAMES, (Proceedings of the ING/IABSE Seminar on Tall Structures and Use of Prestressed Concrete in Hydraulic Structures held in Srinagar, India, 1984).

Chen, W. F. and Lui, E. M., 1985
BEAM-TO-COLUMN MOMENT RESISTING CONNECTIONS, Chapter 6, Vol. 4, Framed Structures in Developments in the Stability and Strength of Structures, R. Narayanan, ed., Applied Science, United Kingdom.

Council on Tall Buildings, Committee 43, 1979
CONNECTIONS, Chapter SB-7, Volume SB of Monograph on Planning and Design of Tall Buildings, ASCE, New York, pp. 485-575.

Driscoll, G. C. and Beedle, L. S., 1982
SUGGESTIONS FOR AVOIDING BEAM-TO-COLUMN WEB CONNECTION FAILURE, Engineering Journal, AISC, First Quarter, Vol. 19, No. 1, Chicago, pp. 16-19.

Fielding, D. J., Chen, W. F., and Beedle, L. S., 1972
FRAME ANALYSIS AND CONNECTION SHEAR DEFORMATION, Fritz Engineering Laboratory Report No. 333.16, Department of Civil Engineering, Lehigh University, Bethlehem, Pennsylvania, January, 102 p.

Fielding, D. J. and Chen, W. F., 1973
STEEL FRAME ANALYSIS AND CONNECTION SHEAR DEFORMATION, Journal of the Structural Division, ASCE, Vol. 99, No. ST1, January.

Holesapple, J. C., 1982
    THE FABRICATOR/DESIGNER CONNECTION, Civil Engineering, ASCE, November, pp. 64-68.
Howlett, J. H., Jenkins, W. M., and Stainsby, R. Eds., 1981
    JOINTS IN STRUCTURAL STEELWORK, John Wiley & Sons, New York.
Huang, J. S., Chen, W. F., and Regec, J. E., 1971
    TEST PROGRAM OF STEEL BEAM-TO-COLUMN CONNECTIONS, Fritz Engineering Laboratory
    Report No. 333.15, Lehigh University, Bethlehem, Pennsylvania, July.
Huang, J. S., Chen, W. F., and Beedle, L. S., 1973
    BEHAVIOR AND DESIGN OF STEEL BEAM-TO-COLUMN MOMENT CONNECTIONS, WRC Bul-
    letin No. 188, October.
Huang, J. S. and Chen, W. F., 1973
    STEEL BEAM-TO-COLUMN MOMENT CONNECTIONS, ASCE National Structural Engineering
    Meeting, San Francisco, April 9-13.

Jones, S. W., Kirby, P. A., and Nethercot, D. A., 1982
    COLUMNS WITH SEMIRIGID JOINTS, Journal of the Structural Division, ASCE, Vol. 108, No.
    ST2, February, pp. 361-372.

Kato, B., 1982
    BEAM-TO-COLUMN CONNECTIONS RESEARCH IN JAPAN, Journal of the Structural Division,
    ASCE, Vol. 108, No. ST2, Proc. Paper No. 16852, February, pp. 343-360.
Krawinkler, H., Bertero, V. V., and Popov, E. P., 1971
    INELASTIC BEHAVIOR OF STEEL BEAM-TO-COLUMN SUBASSEMBLAGES, EERC Report 71-7,
    Earthquake Engineering Research Center, University of California, Berkeley, California.
Krawinkler, H., 1978
    SHEAR BEAM-TO-COLUMN JOINTS IN SEISMIC DESIGN OF STEEL FRAMES, Engineering
    Journal, AISC, Vol. 15, No. 3, pp. 82-91.
Krawinkler, H., and Popov, E. P., 1982
    SEISMIC BEHAVIOR OF BEAM-TO-COLUMN CONNECTIONS AND JOINTS, Journal of the
    Structural Division, ASCE, Vol. 108, No. ST2, Proc. Paper No. 16865, February.

Lui, E. M. and Chen, W. F., 1983a
    STRENGTH OF H-COLUMNS WITH SMALL END RESTRAINTS, The Journal of the Institute of
    Structural Engineers, Vol. 61B, No. 1, March, pp. 17-26.
Lui, E. M. and Chen, W. F., 1983b
    END RESTRAINT AND COLUMN DESIGN USING LRFD, Engineering Journal, AISC, Vol. 20, No.
    1, First Quarter, pp. 29-39.
Lui, E. M. and Chen, W. F., 1984
    SIMPLIFIED APPROACH TO THE ANALYSIS AND DESIGN OF COLUMNS WITH IMPERFEC-
    TIONS, Engineering Journal, AISC, Second Quarter, Vol. 21, No. 2.

Mann, A. P. and Morris, L. J., 1980
    LACK OF FIT IN END-PLATE CONNECTIONS, Spring Convention, ASCE, April, Portland, Oregon,
    pp. 21-45.
Moncarz, P. D. and Gerstle, K. H., 1981
    STEEL FRAMES WITH NONLINEAR CONNECTIONS, Journal of the Structural Division, ASCE,
    Vol. 107, No. ST8, Proc. Paper 16440, August, pp. 1427-1441.

Parfitt, J. and Chen, W. F., 1976
    TESTS OF WELDED STEEL BEAM-TO-COLUMN MOMENT CONNECTIONS, Journal of the
    Structural Division, ASCE, Vol. 102, No. ST1, Proc. Paper 11854, January, pp. 189-202.
Patel, K. V. and Chen, W. F., 1982
    NONLINEAR ANALYSIS OF STEEL BEAM-TO-COLUMN WEB CONNECTIONS, Structural Engi-
    neering Report CE-STR-82-7, School of Civil Engineering, West Lafayette, Indiana.

Patel, K. V. and Chen, W. F., 1985
ANALYSIS OF A FULLY BOLTED MOMENT CONNECTION USING NONSAP, Computers and Structures, Vol. 19.
Popov, E. P. and Pinkney, R. B., 1968
BEHAVIOR OF STEEL BUILDING CONNECTIONS SUBJECTED TO INELASTIC STRAIN REVERSALS, AISI Bulletin Nos. 13 and 14, November.
Popov, E. P. and Stephen, R. M., 1972
CYCLIC LOADING OF FULL-SIZE STEEL CONNECTIONS, AISI Bulletin, No. 21, February.
Popov, E. P. and Bertero, V. V., 1980
SEISMIC ANALYSIS OF SOME STEEL BUILDING FRAMES, Journal of the Engineering Mechanics Division, ASCE, Vol. 106, No. EM1, February, pp. 75-95.
Popov, E. P. and Manheim, D. N., 1981
ECCENTRIC BRACING OF STEEL FRAMES IN SEISMIC DESIGN, (Transactions from the 6th International Conference on Structural Mechanics in Reactor Technology, held in Paris, France, August, 1981), Vol. K(b), K13/8.
Popov, E. P., 1981
RECENT RESEARCH ON ECCENTRICALLY BRACED FRAMES, Structural Engineers of California, (Proceedings of Conference held in Coronado, California, September, 1981).
Popov, E. P., 1982
SEISMIC STEEL FRAMING SYSTEMS FOR TALL BUILDINGS, Engineering Journal, AISC, Third Quarter, Vol. 19, No. 3, pp. 141-149.

Razzaq, Z., 1983
END RESTRAINT EFFECT ON STEEL COLUMN STRENGTH, Journal of the Structural Division, ASCE, Vol. 109, No. ST2, February, pp. 314-334.
Razzaq, Z. and Chang, J. G., 1981
PARTIALLY RESTRAINED IMPERFECT COLUMNS, (Proceedings of the International Conference on Joints in Structural Steelwork held at Teesside Polytechnic, U.K., April, 1981).
Regec, J. E., Huang, J. S., and Chen, W. F., 1973
TEST OF A FULLY WELDED BEAM-TO-COLUMN CONNECTION, WRC Bulletin No. 188, October.
Rentschler, G. P. and Chen, W. F., 1975
TEST PROGRAM OF MOMENT-RESISTANT STEEL BEAM-TO-COLUMN WEB CONNECTIONS, Fritz Engineering Laboratory Report No. 405.4, Lehigh University, Bethlehem, Pennsylvania.
Rentschler, G. P., 1979
ANALYSIS AND DESIGN OF STEEL BEAM-TO-COLUMN WEB CONNECTIONS, Ph.D. Dissertation, Department of Civil Engineering, Lehigh University, Bethlehem, Pennsylvania.
Rentschler, G. P., Chen, W. F., and Driscoll G. C., 1980
TESTS OF BEAM-TO-COLUMN WEB CONNECTIONS, Journal of the Structural Division, ASCE, Vol. 106, No. ST5, Proc. Paper 15386, May, pp. 1005-1022.
Rentschler, G. P., Chen, W. F., and Driscoll, G. C., 1982
BEAM-TO-COLUMN WEB CONNECTION DETAILS, Journal of the Structural Division, ASCE, Vol. 108, No. ST2. Proc. Paper 16880, February, pp. 393-409.

Shen, Z. Y. and Lu, L. W., 1981
ANALYSIS OF INITIALLY CROOKED, END RESTRAINT STEEL COLUMNS, Fritz Engineering Laboratory Report No. 471.2, Lehigh University, Bethlehem, Pennsylvania.
Standig, K. F., and Rentschler, G. P., and Chen, W. F., 1976
TESTS OF BOLTED BEAM-TO-COLUMN MOMENT CONNECTIONS, WRC Bulletin No. 218, August.
Sugimoto, H. and Chen, W. F., 1982
SMALL END RESTRAINT EFFECTS ON STRENGTH OF H-COLUMNS, Journal of the Structural Division, ASCE, Vol. 108, No. ST3, Proc. Paper 16941, March, pp. 661-681.

Tarnai, T., 1981
DISCUSSION ON END RESTRAINT AND COLUMN STABILITY, BY WAI F. CHEN, Journal of the Structural Division, ASCE, Vol. 107, No. ST11, Proc. Paper 16616, November, pp. 2292-2293.

Tarpy, T. S., 1980
BEAM-TO-COLUMN END PLATE CONNECTIONS, Spring Convention, ASCE, April, Portland, Oregon.

Vinnakota, S., 1981
EFFECT OF IMPERFECTIONS ON PLANAR STRENGTH OF RESTRAINED BEAM-COLUMNS, SSRC-TG23 Report, May, pp. 1-33.

Witteveen, J., Stark, J. W. B., Bijlaard, F. S. K., and Zoetemeijer, P., 1982
WELDED AND BOLTED BEAM-TO-COLUMN CONNECTIONS, Journal of the Structural Division, ASCE, Vol. 18, No. ST2, Proc. Paper 16873, February, pp. 433-455.

Yura, J. A., Birkemore, P. C. and Ricles, J. M., 1980
BEAM WEB SHEAR CONNECTIONS—AN EXPERIMENTAL STUDY, Journal of the Structural Division, ASCE, Vol. 108, No. ST2, Proc. Paper 16848, February, pp. 311-325.
Yura, J. A., Frank, K. H. and Cayes, L., 1981
BOLTED FRICTIONS WITH WEATHERING STEEL, Journal of the Structural Division, ASCE, Vol. 107, No. ST11, Proc. Paper 1664, November, pp. 2071-2087.

Load and Resistance Factor (Limit States) Design in the Field of Metal Structures

Irena Kárníková
Pavel Marek
Mirŏs Pirner
Miroslav Škaloud
Milík Tichý

INTRODUCTION

The method of Load and Resistance Factor Design (LRFD), sometimes called limit states (LS) design, was introduced in the field of metal structures about fifteen years ago, and has recently received increased attention in Czechoslovakia. There is a need to deal with various obscurities and contradictions in the application of this method, from the viewpoint of fundamental rules as well as terminology, definitions, and links with the theory of loading or design models. The development of specifications led to an international conference in Carlsbad (CSVTS, 1981). This paper analyzes the results of the conference proceedings as well as the discussions that followed.

APPLICATION OF THE LRFD METHOD FOR METAL STRUCTURES

Contribution of the LRFD Method

As opposed to an earlier method of allowable stresses, the main contribution of the LS method is the comprehensive concept of equally reliable criteria of carrying capacity and serviceability, as well as the employment of mathematical, statistical, and probability models for the formulation of these conditions. The LRFD method includes in one basic scheme elastic as well as plastic design, static as well as dynamic response, and limitation of serviceability.

Method of Extreme Values

In Czechoslovak ČSN specifications, the present interpretation of the LRFD method is based upon the so-called method of extreme values (sometimes designated as the "first level" theory of reliability) with the minimum carrying capacity characterized by comparing it with the most unfavorable values of the load-effect; serviceability is characterized by comparing the "average" load-effect with the values limiting serviceability and performance capability of the structure. The method based on extreme values will serve to formulate the conditions of reliability for some time, even if the theoretical models of reliability are also being elaborated for methods of higher levels. The transition to the higher-level methods should be preceeded by a complete mastery of the practical applications of the first level, in specifications as well as in common design practice.

Loading and its Effects

The contemporary conception of load data presentation within specifications can be challenged by numerous comments. Should preconditions to a clear formulation of reliability and the corresponding criteria of carrying capacity and serviceability be established, the specifications must include such characteristics of loading as are generally indispensable for determining the history of the effects of load. These should describe the *response* of the structure during its total lifetime with respect to all crucial criteria, such as the spectrum of stress-ranges for the fatigue criterion. Emphasis should be placed upon the difference between *loading*, a phenomenon independent of the structure that it affects, and *the response to load of the structure*, which is described, for instance, by the history of stress, deformation, acceleration, or other variables of reliability as it relates to carrying capacity and serviceability in proportioning structures and their elements.

Theoretical and Experimental Models

To define the response of the structure, various theoretical and/or experimental models are to be used. The development of these models, giving an increasingly accurate picture of the actual behavior of the structure, together with the improvement of computers, makes it possible to include the influence of imperfections, unhomogeneities, complexities of loading, and other variables in the analysis of the structural response. Even the most perfect application of a model, however, does not substitute for the condition of reliability in LS of carrying capacity or serviceability. The models only make it possible to determine those characteristics of response that enter individual conditions in accordance with their substance. It is necessary to make certain that the level of computation models corresponds to the level of input variables and preconditions (Kristek et al., 1983).

LIMIT STATE OF CARRYING CAPACITY

General

The structure must be designed and assessed so that it will be able to transfer the most unfavorable effects of load without losing its capability of fufilling its function properly over its lifetime of service. The definitions of the most unfavorable values of the load effects, and similarly the definitions of minimum carrying capacity, are based either on statistical analysis of the random variables for the quantile chosen, a semiprobability approach, or possibly on a deterministic qualified estimate corresponding to experience and the like. With the increasing knowledge of random variables, the above definitions should be derived with increased precision according to the theory of reliability.

The LS of carrying capacity are examined according to the character of the individual conditions of reliability (see the following) for the defined most unfavorable effects of loading, expressed, for example, by the extreme value of stress or strain (strength) or by the stress-range spectrum, and so on (Table 1).

In view of the nature of reaching the carrying capacity of metal structures, individual conditions of reliability and the criteria can be included in the main groups determined in the Czechoslovak specifications ČSN 73 0031-77, which are generally valid for all building structures. The structures must fulfill all the equivalent conditions of load carrying capacity, as it is not always clear in advance of proportioning members which conditions will be critical in the design of the structure.

In the next text, LS of carrying capacity are divided into groups, consistently emphasizing the specific character of individual conditions and criteria valid for metal structures. The difference among individual conditions of reliability consists on one hand of the mechanism of reaching carrying capacity, and on the other of the characteristics of the response to load of the structure, which must be introduced into the conditions of reliability.

Stability of Position

The condition of stability of position serves to ensure the reliability of the structure and its components to resist overturning, lifting, or shifting in bearings and so on (Table 1, CC-I). In current cases, this LS is assessed primarily for the extreme values of the effects of load, for both maximum and minimum values.

Strength

Carrying capacity is defined in case of strength criterion with respect either to the first-order theory (simple strength) or to the second-order theory (stability strength) and from all other problems considering the equilibrium on a deformed structural system (Table 1, CC-IIa and CC-IIb). Next, the elastic as well as elastoplastic range of structural response may be considered. (In the area of metal structures, with the conscious use of plastic reserves, it is possible to define the reaching of strength from "below," from the elastic zone, or from "above," through an adequate reduction of the value of load corresponding to collapse (Marek, 1983; Marek et al., 1979).)

Simple Strength.   The assessment of simple strength is based upon determining such a level of the design carrying capacity (CC-IIa, Table 1). This excludes not only the complete failure from the defined extreme effects of load (failure of a tension bar, joint, etc.), but also the emergence of such permanent or total elastic-plastic deformations, which must be regarded as unacceptable with respect to the long-term performance of the structure. (This is the case of assessment of criteria different from the criteria of deformation in the group of limit states of serviceability.)

"Stability" (Second-Order Theory) Strength.   For a long time, stability phenomena were regarded as an independent LS (Table 1, CC-II6). In the original view of their substance, the object of examination was an "ideal" structure without initial geometrical or physical imperfections, while carrying capacity was inferred from the load at the emergence of the bifurcation of equilibrium. Following actual structures, and laboratory testing verifying and improving initial preconditions, led to recognizing a contradiction between the above idealized concept of stability and the actual behavior. One of the main causes of the contradiction is the unavoidable presence of initial imprefections, which replaced the phenomenon of sudden deflection with a gradual, more or less monotonous increase in the deformation of bars or plates (webs, chords, shells) from the outset of loading. This type of failure is quite similar to failure at reaching simple strength except for the difference in the deformation rate. LS is identified with the achievement of the design strength in the most exposed locality and/or with the achievement of the admissible elastic or elasto-plastic strains and/or deformations (local or total). However in the analysis it is necessary to employ the second-order theory.

Stability strength is usually connected with the extreme value of gradually increasing load which, however, is not generally valid, especially in the case of dynamic response.

Incremental Collapse

In the case of utilization of plastic reserves, carrying capacity may be related to exceeding the premissible permanent deformations in the cases where the criterion of shake-down is not fulfilled (Table 1, CC-III). It is the increase in elastic-plastic deformations in the criterion of strength that corresponds to the history of loading.

Low-Cycle Fatigue

In cases when in the history of loading, corresponding plastic reversals in some parts of the structure occur, it is necessary to assess the condition of reliability from the standpoint of low-cycle fatigue (Table 1, CC-IV). The response to load must be expressed by the number and magnitude of plastic reversals over the total lifetime, the criterion being the strength in low-cycle fatigue. In this case it is defined for a definite material by an acceptable number of cycles of alternative plastification of a definite extent (that is, according to the Manson–Coffin law).

High-Cycle Fatigue

In case of significant time-dependant response, the culmination of fatigue damage is mainly related to the initiation and propagation of fatigue cracks. The condition of reliability from the standpoint of high-cycle fatigue incorporates the characteristics of the response expressed, for example, by the spectrum of stresses in an investigated locality over the lifetime of the structure (Table 1, CC-V). The most unfavorable effects of load are defined by the extreme values of response, such as the "extreme spectrum." The criterion does not depend on the design strength of the material but is based upon the relationship for high-cycle fatigue. This is determined, for instance, by S–N curves established from experimental results for the chosen quantile. The relationship between the characteristic of the most unfavorable response and strength in high-cycle fatigue must be expressed in dependence on crucial variables as related to the mechanisms of the cumulation of fatigue damage. This differs in steel ropes, composite profiles, thin-walled profiles, and the like.

Brittle Fracture

Structural damage through brittle fracture such as a rapidly propagating crack may appear without previous warning. The LS of damage through fracture is assessed by the condition of reliability, which incorporates, on the one hand, the response to loading expressed by stresses, loading rate, temperature, and so on, and on the other hand, material properties, defects, and other imperfections of the structure such as residual stresses. Brittle fracture may appear even under very low load.

Table 1 Limit states of carrying capacity and corresponding conditions of reliability

Limit states	Indication	Description of loading
Stability of position	CC-I	Extreme (highest and lowest) value
Strength (Simple stability)	CC-IIa CC-IIb	Extreme values of load with regard to their simultaneous occurrence, dynamic response of the structure, etc.
Shake-down	CC-III	History of loading, including extreme values of loads
Low-cycle fatigue	CC-IV	History of loading
High cycle fatigue	CC-V	History of loading
Brittle fracture	CC-VI	Extreme values, loading rate, environment, etc.
Combinations	CC-VII	With regard to the individual case

Additional Remarks and Combinations

The above enumeration of LS is not wholly complete. A considerable decrease in reliability can also occur with combinations of the above individual conditions (Table 1, CC-VII). For instance, a structural element fulfills both the condition of low-cycle fatigue and the condition of high-cycle fatigue. The two corresponding types of damage, however, are not independent. The alternative plastifications may speed up the damage considerably by high-cycle fatigue. Similarly, the risk of damage may considerably increase in structures exposed simultaneously to high-cycle fatigue and to stress leading to brittle fracture.

In metal structures the rheological properties of material are usually not very marked. Only in some cases (steel at higher temperatures, composite steel and concrete structures, friction joints, and the like) is it necessary to take into account the dependence of strain upon time, and the corresponding response history.

Conditions of reliability with respect to carrying capacity	
Description of response	Criterion of carrying capacity
Extreme effects (highest and lowest)	Safety (>1.0) against the loss of stability of position
Stresses or deformations corresponding to extreme loads, including dynamic response, etc.	Design strength, allowable local or total deformations, allowable relative plastic deformations, etc.
History of elastic–plastic strains corresponding to the history of loading	Shake-down criterion
Number and range of plastic reversals	Criterion of Manson–Coffin, Serensen, etc.
Spectrum of stress ranges, etc.	S–N curves, etc.
Stress, loading rate and response, temperature, etc.	Design value K_{IC} for given material, etc.
According to the particular case	

Characteristics of Load and Response

Table 1 clearly presents the characteristics of load and response necessary for the assessment of carrying capacity according to individual conditions CC-I to CC-VII. The existing arrangement of values and data on loading, for example in the ČSN 73 0035, is primarily concerned with the condition of strength (CC-I). To make certain that the specifications of loading correspond to the comprehensive character of the conditions of reliability according to Table 1, it is necessary gradually to complete these specifications with data that (while using appropriate theoretical or experimental models) permit the determination of the characteristics of response needed for the verification of the conditions of reliability CC-I to CC-VII.

LS OF SERVICEABILITY

Generally

Metal structures shall be designed to withstand not only loading in terms of LS of carrying capacity (see Section 3) but also the demands of operation and performance and serviceability at common service load and its effects. Some serviceability limitations with respect to human comfort, operation of machinery, and the like, have already been included in many specifications (Ministry of Public Health of Czechoslovakia, 1977). Permissible criteria are acceleration, deformations, rotations, etc.

It is clear that in the list of the LS of serviceability, effects of loading are assessed differently from the effects incorporated into the conditions of reliability in regard to carrying capacity. Presented here are characteristics of reliability conditions for metal structures serviceability.

Classification of LS of Serviceability

Table 2 presents the basic groups of LS of serviceability common to all metal structures. Group SA-V, concerned with operational noise of the structure, is added as compared to specifications ČSN 73 0031.

The determination of loading input effects and of the criteria formulating reliability conditions of structure serviceability are generally very individual. It depends on the function, purpose, user demands, protection against equipment damage and so on. Therefore, relevant regulations in the design specifications can only be partly formulated qualitatively and quantitatively.

Table 2 classifies the reliability conditions of serviceability into groups according to the impact on human comfort, on building, machinery or other technological equipment.

Loading and Response from the Standpoint of Serviceability

LS of serviceability are often, in a simplified way, regarded as the effects of load (response) corresponding to the *average* working load. Generally, it is necessary to contemplate the relationship between load and the actual serviceability criterion in the framework of a definite project (for example, following agreement with the user). This is because the *current* operational load and corresponding effects may, with respect to functional demands, correspond to load intensities differing considerably from the working load. The working load itself (as defined in ČSN 73 0035) does not enter into the design when the design values are to be used for carrying capacity conditions, as well as serviceability, where the load-factor 1.0 is presently usually prescribed. This value, however, may be gradually replaced in the future with values smaller or larger than 1.0, depending on the nature of the case.

Conditions of Reliability (see Table 2)

Human Comfort (SA-I, SA-V). This criterion is expressed by (1) an allowable acceleration of motion expressing the admissible dynamic response to load (horizontal and vertical vibration and the like); (2) an allowable deformation (esthetic and psychological effect); and (3) an allowable level of noise caused by the structure in operation.

Table 2 Limit states and conditions of reliability in relation to serviceability of metal structures

Indication	Conditions of reliability of limit states of serviceability for metal structures		
	Requirement	Effects of load	Criterion
SA-I	Human comfort	Effects of "average" loading (or load corresponding to the usual required function) characterized by deformation, acceleration, etc.	Allowable deformations, allowable accelerations, etc.
SA-II	Excluding or limiting the damage of building fittings		
SA-III	Ensuring the required function of machinery and other mechanical equipment		
SA-IV	Gas-tightness and water-tightness	Individually according to the character of the structure and the performance conditions. See Hygienic Regulations (Ministry of Public Health, 1977)	
SA-V	Limiting noise caused by the operation of the structure		

Some criteria are presented, for instance, in hygienic regulations (Ministry of Public Health of Czechoslovakia, 1977), and in standards for designing steel structures (ČSN 73 1401). Often the limiting values must be established by the structural designer following agreement with the user, the designer of the machinery, or others.

Protection against Damage to Building Equipment (SA-II). Load effects must not damage partitions, glass, ceilings, or other parts of the building; therefore, it is necessary to take into consideration current unfavorable static as well as dynamic effects of load and adequately formulated criteria.

Operation of Machinery and Equipment (SA-III). Both static and dynamic operational effects must not reach values that would disturb the operation and function of equipment supported by the structure. The limits of static deformation and dynamic response must be determined by the equipment designer, and/or by the user, with respect to sensitivity, fail-safety, and the like. In formulating reliability conditions of serviceability, it is also necessary to account for the temporal use of the structure (continuous or occasional, public or private, and so on).

Gas-Tightness and Water-Tightness (SA-IV). The effects of loading on the gas- or water-tightness in pools, pressure vessels of reactors, and other equipment depends upon the tightness of screws, rivets, or weld joints, and on other structural details, and should be proved through testing.

Reduction of Noisiness (SA-V). Noisiness caused by the structure in operation, as in the case of box-girder bridges in urban areas, should be assessed and the conditions of serviceability determined.

SUMMARY AND CONCLUSIONS

Further development of the LRFD of metal structures is enhanced by the following findings:

Type of Probability Method

In the development and practical application of the LS method in the field of metal structures, the design procedure and assessment will probably continue to be based upon the so-called first-level theory of reliability (in other words on the method of extreme values). This method should be elaborated upon regarding the whole comprehensive system of conditions of reliability as well as of criteria both for carrying capacity and for serviceability before a higher-level theory of reliability can be introduced to the standards.

Loading and Response

The conditions of reliability of limit states carrying capacity as well as serviceability incorporate values and characteristics of the loading response of the structure (effects of load) expressed by the history of stress or strain, acceleration and the like. The values of load—a phenomenon generally independent of the structure upon which it acts—are not incorporated into proportioning and assessing directly. But they do, through theoretical or experimental models, permit the determination of static or dynamic and elastic or elastic–plastic response. The loading and design specifications of structures should be gradually completed with the data necessary to determine the response of a structure, especially as it relates to carrying capacity and serviceability (Tables 1 and 2).

Conditions of Reliability

In proportioning metal structures, a comprehensive set of equivalent conditions of reliability in terms of carrying capacity and serviceability should be provided. It is possible then to specify the main conditions of reliability as presented in Table 1. Similarly, it is also possible to classify the conditions of reliability in terms of serviceability (Table 2).

It is the designer's task to consider all conditions and to determine the crucial conditions for proportioning the structure by means of elimination.

In the further development of standards and regulations for structural steel design, including specifications of loading, the conditions and criteria presented in Tables 1 and 2 should be considered.

Application of the Theory of Reliability

In defining the most unfavorable effects of load and minimum carrying capacity in terms of the limit states of carrying capacity and serviceability, as well as the average effects of load, the theory of probability, statistics, and so on should be increasingly employed. Due to the complexity of the problems involved and to the lack of data, definitions are still often based on a deterministic estimate, or experience. With improvement of design methods and corresponding specifications, it is necessary to analyze and supplement information on crucial random variables.

ACKNOWLEDGMENT

This paper was published in Czech in *Stavebnicky casopis*, October, 1983, VEDA, Bratislava, and in English in the Proceedings of the International Conference on Steel Structures, *Design Limit States of Steel Structures* 1983/84, VUT, Brno.

REFERENCES/BIBLIOGRAPHY

ALFA, 1981
Inzenyrske stavby, Vol. 2, Bratislava (In Czech or Slovak).

CSVTS DT, 1981
LIMIT STATES OF THE METAL BUILDING STRUCTURES (in Czech), (Proceedings of Conference held in Carlsbad, April), Vol. 1 to 5.

Kristek, V., Marek, P., and Pirner, M., 1983
ON THE RELATIONSHIP OF THEORETICAL MODELS AND CRITERIA IN DESIGNING STEEL STRUCTURES (in Czech), Building Journal (in preparation).

Marek, P., 1983
LIMIT STATES OF THE METAL BUILDING STRUCTURES (in German), Bauverlag, Berlin.
Marek, P., Faltus, F., Mrazik, A., and Skaloud, M., 1979
PLASTICITY OF STEEL STRUCTURES (in Czech), Building Journal, Vol. 10.
Ministry of Public Health of Czechoslovakia, 1977
HYGIENIC REGULATIONS OF THE MINISTRY OF PUBLIC HEALTH, Provision No. 13/1977 Digest, from 13.1.1977, Vol. 37.

SNTL, 1980
POZEMNI STAVBY, Vol. 12, Prague (in Czech).

VITKOVICE, 1980
BULLETIN OF TECHNOLOGY, STEEL STRUCTURES, Volume 4, Ostrava (in Czech).

Recent Developments in Composite High-Rise Systems

Hal Iyengar

Steel–concrete composite systems for tall buildings involve combining structural steel and reinforced concrete components in the same building. By their integral action, these components resist all the wind and gravity forces of the high-rise system. The key to this system lies in combining the most efficient component of either structural steel or reinforced concrete systems to establish an optimum composite of the two.

Developments in reinforced concrete and structural steel high-rise building systems in the 1960s and 1970s set the stage for mixed steel–concrete types of systems. The object of the combination was to utilize the rigidity of concrete for lateral load resistance and the lightness and spannability of steel for floor framings. Elements of concrete systems, such as the shear wall and punched framed tubes, were recognized as efficient in resisting wind forces and providing lateral rigidity. The inherent rigidity of concrete, its ability to be molded to different sizes and shapes, its high modulus of elasticity with high strength, and its ability to form monolithic joints between beams and columns, are all attributes that make it particularly suited for use in elements that contribute to lateral stiffness in tall buildings. If it is no longer necessary for structural steel to serve this function, steel can instead be used for simple framing elements, interior/exterior columns, and other such gravity framings. Then the steel–concrete combination can offer considerable advantages of economy and speed.

Mixed systems in the 1960s and early 1970s were simply applied to conventional high-rise office buildings that were in vogue at the time. The buildings were generally rectilinear in shape, and the mixed form (either exterior tubular system or core braced system) was offered as an alternate design. Mixed systems were selected in many instances where the contractor was able to handle the coordination of construction. As the construction methodology of such mixing of systems was established and accepted by the construction industry, their use became widespread, spurring further refinements and developments.

In current practice, it is usually customary to offer three alternatives, steel, concrete, and composite systems, for cost and system evaluations for any particular high-rise building.

The following descriptions will illustrate this particular new trend in the use of mixed systems.

COMPOSITE TUBULAR SYSTEM

In principle, the composite tubular system combines a reinforced concrete framed tube on the exterior of the building, with simple steel framing on the interior. The framed tube is formed by wide columns placed at close centers with deep beams creating a punched wall appearance. In this system, the exterior reinforced concrete tube resists all lateral forces of wind, and the interior, consisting of simple steel column–beam framing, resists only the gravity loads of the interior of the building. Also, in these applications, the building shape is rectilinear.

The advantages of this system are:

1. The reinforced concrete tube is the most efficient element for resisting wind forces.

2. The structural steel quantity is reduced to 30–40% of that required in an equivalent steel building.

3. Expensive rigid connections for steel are eliminated.

4. Interior floor spans and core planning are rendered more efficient with steel framing. Longer spans are possible with lightweight members.

5. The speed of construction is equivalent to that of a steel building, in spite of the use of concrete on the exterior tube.

6. The exterior framed tube in concrete can make buildings up to 80 stories more economical. Since the exterior is field-cast concrete, it

can be molded to various shapes of buildings more readily. Further, large facade coverage by reinforced concrete reduces the glazed area, reduces the heating–cooling loads, and simplifies stone or masonry cladding and window wall details.

Apart from being an efficient structural system, the composite tubular system has allowed considerable latitude in shaping buildings and creating different massing for different expressions.

FIRST CANADIAN CENTRE, CALGARY

The First Canadian Centre consists of two towers and a 10-story banking pavilion located in an L-shaped site in downtown Calgary. The two towers are 64 and 43 stories, the latter of which is under construction. A sculpted form that would provide diagonal vistas to mountains and the city was highly desirable for this prominent corner site. The result was a two-tower concept, each one facing a street. Each tower is similarly shaped as a parallelogram with truncated and reentrant corners. Figure 1 shows the variation in vertical heights, as well as the siting of the towers and the banking pavilion. The cores are located in the center of the floor plate in the lower portion of the building and at the exterior wall in the upper part.

The structural concept is based on a tube-in-tube concept involving an exterior reinforced concrete framed tube and an interior shear wall core tube. Economic evaluation indicated that the floor framing be made of concrete in Tower I and structural steel in Tower II.

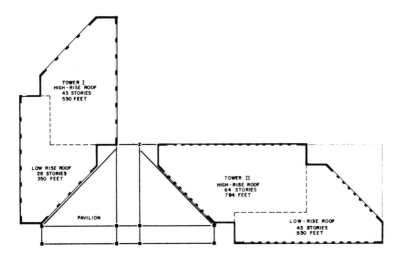

Fig. 1 First Canadian Centre: Siting of the tower

Figures 2 and 3 show the framing plan for the taller tower. Figure 2 is for the lower portion of the tower, and Fig. 3 is for the upper portion. The tube system on the exterior is a combination of framed tube with beams and columns and solid walls at the corners. The structural essence of the concrete framed tube wall is that of a bearing wall. As such, the punched wall and solid wall are both compatible parts of the system. In this system, the solid walls are used in the corners to complete the exterior form of the framed tube, and also to provide continuity for transmission of forces around the corners. The columns are provided at 2.95m (9ft 8in.) centers along the flat faces and along the diagonal lines. The column width is 0.91m (36 in.) and the spandrel beam depth 0.99m (39 in.). The thicknesses of columns, beams and walls vary from bottom to top. The interior shear wall core is provided around core elements and follows the variation of the core over the height. The floor framing involves 0.71m (28 in.) deep composite steel trusses at 2.95m (9ft. 8 in.) centers with a 51mm (2 in.) composite metal deck. The trusses are fabricated with tubular shapes and the general triangular configuration allows for transmission of HVAC ducts. The details of the truss are shown in Fig. 4. In terms of construction, shear walls are built first using step forms, followed by the exterior framed tube on a floor-by-floor basis. The steel trusses are then erected in typical fashion using a corbel detail at the exterior walls and at shear walls as shown in Fig. 4. The structural quantities were 0.186 m^3/m^2 (0.61 ft^3/ft^2) of concrete for the exterior and interior concrete tubes, 179 Pa (3.73 psf) of reinforcing steel, and 208 Pa (4.34 psf) of structural steel.

Extensive systems studies were performed to select the optimum. The systems were steel framed tube, composite tube-in-tube, and shear wall core braced steel frame. The shape was highly inefficient for the steel system, and

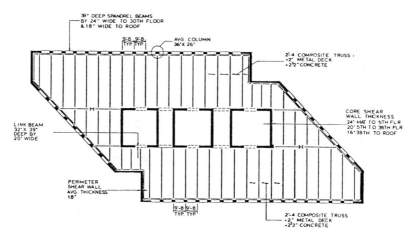

Fig. 2 First Canadian Centre: Structural floor plan, lower portion

steel quantities of the order or 1149 Pa (24 psf) were involved. The concrete core wall braced system, even though more efficient than the steel system, still involved about 766 Pa (16 psf) of structural steel. An all-concrete system for Tower II was ruled out because of weight and foundation difficulties. The logical and most effective solution was the composite tube-in-tube system.

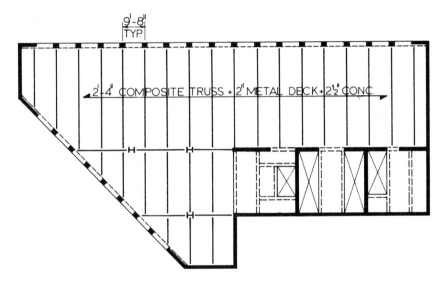

Fig. 3 **High-rise floor framing plan, Tower II**

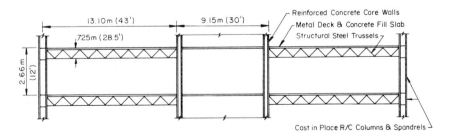

Fig. 4 **First Canadian Centre: Truss detail**

SOUTHEAST FINANCIAL CENTER, MIAMI

The Southeast Financial Center, completed in 1984, is a high-rise office development in downtown Miami. It consists of a 53-story office tower reaching 222 m (730 ft) above grade and is the tallest building in Miami. The project also includes a 14-story Annex Building housing the Banking Hall, parking, and support facilities. The site has views to the east over Bay Front Park, and as such, a design requirement was to orient the office toward the east and provide a dramatic profile modification at the top floors to optimize vistas (Fig. 5). From the office efficiency point of view, a floor area of 1858 to 2323 m^2 (20,000 to 25,000 ft^2) with a 12.2 m (40 ft) column free exterior span was desirable.

Design wind load comparisons revealed that the tower wind loads would be twice that of Houston and four times that of Chicago. Therefore an extremely rigid and efficient wind resistive structural system was required. In addition, a more massive structure would alleviate potential difficulties with foundation uplift. A composite bundled tube system was selected over others as being the most appropriate to meet the criteria. The bundled tube is composed of an approximately rectangular tube and a stepped triangular tube (Fig. 6). The common wall between the two tubes is made up of solid walls and beam-column arrangement. The provision of this interior frame line was essential to improve the tubular efficiency. The 64m (210 ft) long straight facade on the west is relieved by a V-shaped wall intersection connecting the tubes. This vertical notch expresses the tubes and also provides a relief for the broad expanse of tubular expression. The interior 12.2 m (40 ft) spans and core framing are framed with nonrigid, simple steel members. The use of the concrete composite tube had the following advantages:

1. Development of extreme rigidity and strength provided optimum wind resistance.

2. Massiveness of concrete eliminated potential uplift difficulties.

3. Concrete was more natural in being molded to this unusual space.

4. Provision of wall and framed tube elements simplified load flow to various parts of the tubular system.

5. The stone cladding attachment to concrete was simpler and more beneficial than strong-back systems for steel structures.

The use of structural steel framing on the interior had the advantages of flexibility, possibility of in-floor electrical distribution, and speed.

Structural solutions using only structural steel were extremely inefficient for this shape. Steel requirements were high and consequently not cost effective.

Fig. 5 Southeast Financial Center: Elevation

In summary, the Southeast Financial Center represents a logical application that exploited the rigidity and massivity of concrete to the fullest.

CONCRETE CORE BRACED SYSTEM

The composite tubular system, though efficient for exterior shaping, retains its basic character—that of a punched wall. Often, the structural demands of the tubular form are too great when it meets the ground with respect to flexibility for open spaces and planning ground level access and facilities. The dense grid of the tubular structure also presents architectural difficulties when flush, glazed, crystalline exterior forms are desired.

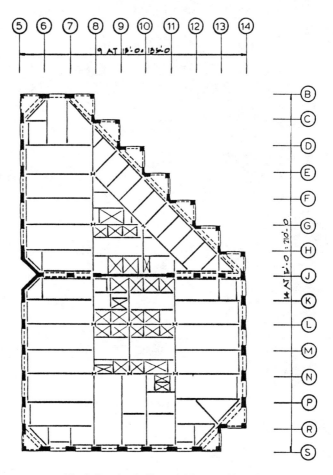

Fig. 6 Southeast Financial Center: Floor plan

In these instances, a structure that is concentrated in the core of the building for wind resistance affords flexibility of framing on the exterior. A logical mixed combination here is a concrete shear wall core, which resists all the wind forces, and simple steel framing for floors and exterior columns.

This form has been commonly used during the last 15 years for various applications in the United States and elsewhere.

Initial systems were constructed utilizing step-form techniques, whereby the core would be advanced three or four floors ahead of the exterior steel by forming one floor at a time. Recent use of individually adjustable slip-form jacks makes slip-form techniques practical for building applications. In this process, the core would be slip-formed in its entirety in a short period of time prior to the erection of the steel. Floor beam connection details and attachments have to be suitably planned to accommodate slip-forming.

As contrasted to this sequence, a system that would permit construction of structural steel first, in advance of core wall construction, is used where concrete core construction in advance presents labor and trade coordination difficulties.

TOWER 49, NEW YORK

The 44-story Tower 49 structural system in New York is based on a composite core braced steel system. In essence, concrete shear walls in the building core provide a major portion of the lateral resistance to wind forces. The core braced system offers flexibility in forming the exterior shape by concentrating major structural resistance at the center of the building. The exterior shape

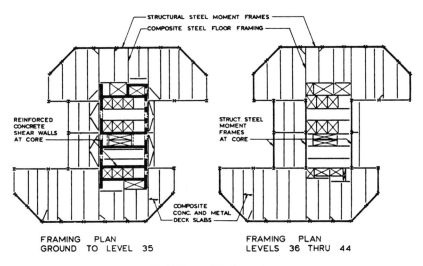

FRAMING   PLAN
GROUND   TO LEVEL 35

FRAMING   PLAN
LEVELS   36 THRU 44

Fig. 7 Tower 49: Floor plan

was determined from site considerations, to create a faceted crystalline form. The concrete core is augmented by fascia moment frames on two sides of the building, while the entire resistance is provided by the core in its long direction, as shown in Fig. 7. An economic study resulted in the elimination of the core above the 35th floor. All the wind resistance above this level is provided by the moment frame. The system involved 670 Pa (14 psf) of structural steel.

For effective erection of structural steel, the system was conceived on the basis of constructing the steel frame first, which would later be infilled with shear walls. The framing in the core and the core columns was detailed to suit construction of the shear walls with respect to the forming inside a steel frame and the subsequent form removal and movement. This construction sequence alleviates some of the difficulties related to differential speed of steel and concrete construction.

The floor framing involves composite beams of 3.05m (10 ft.) on centers. All interior framing is simply connected.

CONCLUSIONS

Recent developments indicate that composite or mixed steel–concrete systems offer a real alternative to steel or concrete systems. In many applications, mixed systems show a distinct advantage in cost effectiveness and architectural-structural effectiveness. Newer mixed forms and additional refinements will undoubtedly occur in the future at an accelerated pace.

Mixed Construction

New Composite Structural Systems for High-Rise Buildings

Kuniaki Sato

OUTLINE OF DEVELOPMENT

Background of Development of Technique in Japan

The development and increased use of steel-framed buildings in Japan during the last 20 years have constituted a remarkable phenomenon. Statistically speaking, it was in the latter half of the 1960s that construction starts for steel-framed structures overtook those for reinforced concrete structures in terms of floor area (Fig. 1).

There are two possible reasons for this phenomenon. One is the natural environment of Japan: since it is both an earthquake country and lies in the path of typhoons, steel-frame construction is suited for meeting Japan's severe structural requirements. The time period when steel-framed structures increased greatly in number corresponded to the high-growth period of the Japanese economy. Even in the tradition-bound building sector, which had been said to be a labor-intensive industry, it was a time when, as with other fields of industry such as electrical equipment, chemicals, machinery and automobiles, increased productivity and thoroughgoing quality control were pursued.

The second reason for the marked increase in steel-framed construction was the emergence of a number of structural forms more readily able to meet the needs for improved construction productivity These structural forms were a result of increased technical exchanges and joint research and development between various engineering fields. As a consequence, steel-framed construction has come to be used not only for high-rise buildings but also for many middle- and low-rise buildings. In particular, steel-framed structures are now being used for almost all projects that have short construction periods (Fig. 2).

Development of the HISPLIT System

High earthquake resistance and high wind resistance are prerequisites for buildings in Japan. Consequently, effective use must be made of structural steel, which is comparatively expensive, in building production to achieve the goals of improved safety, ease of work execution, and economy.

Factory fabrication cost is related to the number of fabrication steps and the cost will be decreased as the number of fabrication steps is reduced, while qualilty will be stabilized through more concentrated quality control. The part of a steel-framed structure requiring the largest number of fabrication steps is the connection between each beam and column. Moreover, even at a

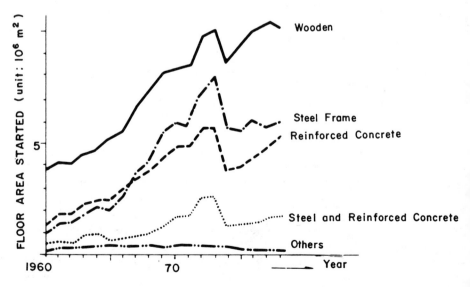

Fig. 1 Annual construction starts by structural type

fabricating plant a fairly high level of engineering control is required; otherwise, not only the tolerances but also the structural strength of the connection will be greatly affected.

The author, taking note of this last point, has developed a method of simplifying the fabrication and construction of beam-to-column connections while maintaining their mechanical performance. The construction method is to assemble joints by simple tightening of bolts at the jobsite using connection parts mass-produced at the factory (Fig. 3). This method is called the (KM) HISPLIT System from the name of Hitachi Metals, Ltd., the

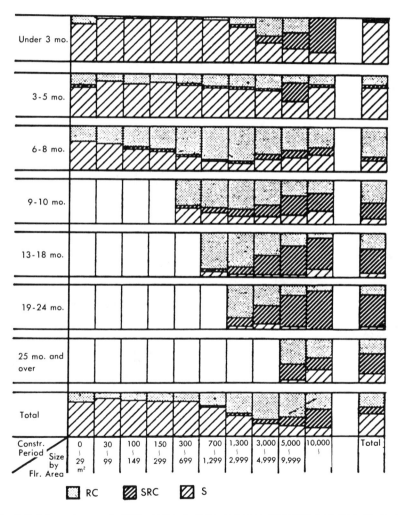

Fig. 2 Reinforced concrete (RC), steel and reinforced concrete (SRC), and steel structures (S) in Japan by construction period and by size

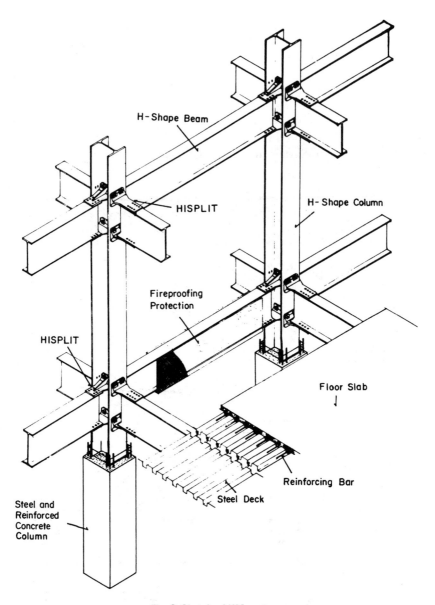

Fig. 3 Sketch of KM system

codeveloper and the maker of the connectors. Since its development in 1973, this system has been used on more than 450 projects, not only in Japan but also in the U. S., Germany, and the Near and Middle East.

The HISPLIT connecting hardware is made of cast steel or is stamp-forged. These manufacturing methods allow stresses to be smoothly transferred. The mechanical properties of the HISPLIT are as shown in Table 1. The HISPLIT shapes are standardized according to the number of bolts needed for connecting to the flanges of the columns. The various shape dimensions are given in Fig. 4.

KM System

The types of building structures which may be considered are reinforced concrete structures, steel-framed structures, masonry structures, and wooden structures. Each of these types has advantages and disadvantages from the standpoints of both the construction method and mechanics. For example, a reinforced concrete structure is strong against compressive forces, and its flexural and shear strengths can be controlled by the arrangement of reinforcement; but many steps are required for construction, and the completed building has considerable weight. In contrast, a steel-framed structure is light and since the greater part is fabricated at the factory and the work at the jobsite consists only of erection, construction efficiency is improved and quality control is easier than for reinforced concrete. But the cost is generally high.

In view of this situtation, a structural form that incorporates the most desirable features of these two types was developed. Steel structure was selected for the basic framework to take advantage of the desirable features of steel: high productivity and lightness; reinforced concrete was utilized to make a composite structure of structural steel and reinforced concrete at columns, which must carry large compressive forces. Light-weight steel beams of long spans were used for freedom in spatial planning, while floor slabs were made of reinforced concrete. This effective combination of the

Table 1 Mechanical properties of HISPLIT

	HISPLIT	
	kg/mm²	1000 psi
Tensile strength	Not less than 49.0	Not less than 69.7
Yield point	Not less than 28.0	Not less than 39.8
Elongation (%)	Not less than 23.0	
Impact value	Not less than 2.8 kg · m/cm²	Not less than 130.7 lb · foot/in²
Bending 180°		OK

development techniques accumulated over many years is called the Kajima Mixed Structure System, or the KM system (Fig. 3).

The KM System makes possible a reduction of more than 30% of the total building weight compared with that of a conventional reinforced concrete structure. Since its construction efficiency corresponds to that of steel-frame construction, during the last three year period it has been applied to more than twenty buildings such as offices, factories, and schools. Moreover, the steel quantities required are greatly reduced compared with those of an all steel-frame structure, which substantially reduces costs (Fig. 5).

As previously stated, Japan is an earthquake country and is situated in a zone through which typhoons pass. In countries where conditions are less

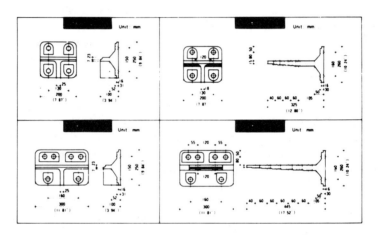

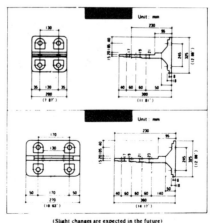

(Slight changes are expected in the future)

Fig. 4 Examples of HISPLIT dimensions

severe, the KM System will offer even more advantages than it does in Japan. That is, it is believed that significant advantages can be provided for the client from a comprehensive viewpoint since interior spaces of large spans are made possible with respect to spatial planning, while foundation and ground preparation work is reduced through lightening of dead load, and construcion periods are shortened.

VERIFICATION OF RELIABILITY OF FRAMEWORK

Technological development is the act of producing a new effect through the effective combination of technologies accumulated in the past, and it may be said that the essential point in development lies in the manner of combining. Meanwhile, a new material may be invented, but for it to be of worth, we must have three things: the technology to produce the material, the theoretical background making possible design using the material, and the technology to apply the material. However, since these technologies will have been developed based on social needs, influencing each other out of necessity, the interrelationships of technologies will have great significance.

Hints for technological development are hidden inside problems that should be solved in the course of routine daily work. In effect, leads to development may be found in extraction of problematic points and in contemplating counter-measures.

This article describes the set-ups and methods provided for verifying the reliability of the KM System prior to its introduction in society. It is centered on the HISPLIT framing system for structural steel, which may be said to be the very basis of the KM System.

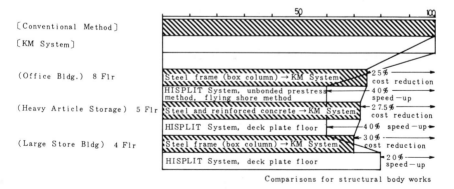

Comparisons for structural body works

Fig. 5 Sample comparisons of cases in Japan

Set-up for Quality Assurance

To put a newly developed technology into practice, all ambiguous points must be clarified. A building, once it has been designed and constructed, cannot be redone.

Accordingly, a set-up for quality assurance of the kind shown in Fig. 6 is normally followed. First, needs for which the situation must be improved or developments must be made are analyzed to give birth to an idea. Next, the theoretical basis of the idea is subjected to a desk study referring to existing literature and its validity is evaluated. At this time, comparisons are made with existing technologies, or studies are made as to where problems lie using techniques such as FMEA (Failure Mode and Effect Analysis). If the theoretical validity is recognized, an advance is made to the step of experiments, trial fabrication for confirmation, and evaluation from the stand-point of reliability. The next step is implementation.

What must be noted in the series of operations for quality assurance is that a method that takes advantage of the FMEA technique is adopted for deciding on the kind of experiment to be conducted (Fig. 6, Table 2).

FMEA is one of the reliability engineering techniques used by NASA in the U. S. for quality assurance in its successful launching of moon rockets. The FMEA technique is considered an extremely effective means for quality assurance of a new technology and is producing good results in many industrial fields in Japan such as electronics and precision machinery.

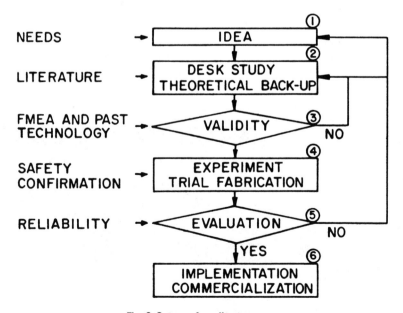

Fig. 6 Set-up of quality assurance

Reliability Block Diagram and the FMEA Chart

Utilization of the FMEA technique begins first of all with preparation of a reliability block diagram (Fig. 7).

When carrying out FMEA on a certain system, it is necessary to grasp thoroughly what kinds of subsystems it is composed of, how one subsystem is tied to another subsystem, and what components are combined in each subsystem. A reliability block diagram is suitable for grasping the structure of such a system.

Figure 7 shows a reliability block diagram of the KM System. As illustrated, the KM System consists of the six subsystems of foundation, column base, column, joint, composite beam, and wall. Each subsystem may again be divided into components, subassemblages, or parts. Whether or not a component is to be further divided is decided by the analysis level. To take a known component with which there is no technical problem and break it up further into parts for FMEA does not have very much meaning.

In FMEA, the designed system, subsystems, and components (or parts) are broken up into designated analysis levels, and these are assembled in the form of a reliability block diagram. The respective functions are clarified for each block, failure modes are listed, evaluations are made of the effects of these failures on the components, subsystems, or systems, and the measures to be taken for reliability assurance are decided. The FMEA chart consists of the series of operations in tabulated form; FMEA may be accomplished by making entries in the order indicated by the table.

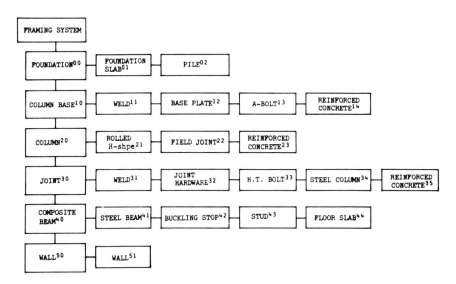

Fig. 7 Reliability block diagram (see Table 2)

Table 2 FMEA chart

MAIN SYSTEM: KM SYSTEM   SUBSYSTEM: JOINT [30]

Block No.	Name	Function	Failure Mode	Estimated Cause
31	WELD	Stress transfer between hardware and structural steel beam	Rupture Slag inclusion Cracking Poor penetration	Bevel shape Poor skill of welder Work environment Welding material (rod) Base metal
32	JOINT HARDWARE (HISPLIT)	Transfer of beam stress to column by bolt	Bending Rupture Distortion	Shape Dimension accuracy Dimension accuracy Material, strength Welding method Shape
33	H.T. BOLT	Stress transfer between hardware and column (tension connection)	Rupture	Material strength Defective tightening Hole misalignment Work environment Excessive load
34	STEEL COLUMN	Carrying of part of column stress	Bending of flange Buckling during erection Web rupture Web bending	Insufficient plate thickness Material strength Insufficient slenderness ratio Insufficient plate thickness Ditto
35	REINFORCED CONCRETE	Carries most of joint stress	Failure Shear Splitting Rupture of reinforcing bar (hoop reinforcement)	Defective placement Defective formwork Defective curing Defective mixing Encasement of joint hardware Insufficient steel quantity Defective reinforcing Poor strength

Evaluation				Responsibility Phase				Remedial Measure
C1	C2	C3	C1 C2 C3	Maker	Design	Constr.	Maint.	
5	3	2	30	o	o			Adoption of J-bevel
	4	4	80			o		Examination of fabricating procedure, product inspection, ultrasonic flaw detection test
	4	3	60			o		Ditto
	1	4	20	o				Examination of manufacturing procedure
	1	4	20	o				Mill sheet
4	2	4	80		o			Analysis and confirmation test
	2	3	18	o				Product precision standard
5	2	3	30	o				Ditto
	2	4	40	o				Comparative test with SM50A, mill sheet
3	4	3	36			o		Examination of fabricating procedure, product inspection
	3	4	36		o			Testing, improvement of jigs
5	1	4	20	o				Mill sheet
	3	3	45		o	o		Use of special bolt
	4	1	20			o		Examination of installation procedure
	2	3	30			o		Ditto
	2	3	30				o	Preparation of special specifications, preparation of use standards
4	3	4	48		o			Confirmation of restraining effect of concrete (confirmation test)
	1	4	16	o				Mill sheet
4	3	3	36		o			
5	3	4	60		o			Confirmation of restraining effect of concrete, preparation of design standards, (confirmation test)
4	3	4	48		o			Ditto
5	3	2	30		o	o		Simplification of joint
	3	3	45			o		Improvement of end form
	2	2	20			o		
	2	3	30	o				Examination of mix proportions, failure tests of specimens
	3	3	45		o			
5	3	4	60		o			Adoption of Kajima Hoop, confirmation test
	4	3	60			o		Reinforcement inspection
	1	4	20	o				Mill sheet

Table 2 gives the example of a joint from among the FMEA of the KM System. The evaluation point score of the degree of influence of failure, as shown in Table 3, is expressed by the geometric product of the seriousness of the effect of failure (C1), the estimated frequency of cause occurrence (C2), and the possibility of discovering failure (C3). For all those components that have high evaluation points and failure possibilities for which counter-measures have not been established, reliabilities are confirmed by experiments.

Structural Experiments

As previously described, for all the problems extracted by FMEA that had been given high evaluation points, but for which no counter-measures (in particular those adequate for quality assurance) had been established, reliabilities were confirmed through structural experiments. The items tested for reliability assurance of the KM System may be listed as follows:

Foundation experiments, experiments for trial fabrication
  (1) Basic physical and chemical experiments on the material for HISPLIT
  (2) Investigation and research on configurations, dimensions and tolerances for HISPLIT
  (3) Experiments on weldability of HISPLIT

Basic mechanical experiments
  (4) Experiments on mechanical configurations and effects of HISPLIT
  (5) Comparative experiments between uniform-thickness SPLIT TEE and HISPLIT

Table 3 Evaluation procedure

C1	Seriousness of Effect of Functional Failure	
	Leads to collapse	5
	Large deformation produced	3
	Little effect	1
C2	Estimated Frequency of Cause Occurrence	
	Can occur frequently	5
	Can occur at times	3
	Seldom occurs	1
C3	Possibility of Discovery	
	Great effort needed for discovery	5
	Can be discovered	3
	Is readily discovered	1

(Note) The figures 4 and 2 may be used for interpolation between 5 and 3, and 3 and 1.

Experiments for confirmation as structure

    (6) Experimental study on out-of-plane bending of column flange

    (7) Various comparative experiments on connections between columns and beams

    (8) Beam-to-column joint experiments considering high-rise buildings

    (9) Experiments on beam-to-column joints composed of steel and reinforced concrete

   (10) Experiments on steel and reinforced concrete using H-shapes

Experiments for confirming the performance on floor slabs

   (11) Experiments on strength of stud connectors for composite beams

   (12) Strength tests of floor slabs using deck plates

   (13) Fire resistance tests of floor slabs using deck plates

   (14) Experiments on floor slabs with unbonded prestress

Outlines of items (6), (7), (8), and (10) will now be described.

Study on Out-of-Plane Bending of H-Shape Flange (6).   Along with analyses by yield line theory, tension tests were performed on specimens made by joining HISPLIT by bolts to H-shape flanges. The purpose of this study was to obtain a formula for calculating out-of-plane bending of column flanges.

Full-size Experiments on Steel Beam-to-Column Joints (7), (8).   Repetitive loading tests were carried out with the purpose of confirming the structural safety of beam-to-column joints using HISPLIT. There were five specimens in Series A (steel frames of middle- and low-rise buildings) and three in Series B (steel frames for high-rise).

Experiments on Steel and Reinforced Concrete Columns Using H-Shapes (10).   Lateral-load tests were conducted on column members with the purpose of developing steel and reinforced concrete columns of superior earthquake resistance and ease of work execution that use a smaller quantity of steel. These objectives were achieved by using a type of column that contains structural steel inside and uses high-strength concrete outside. The test specimens were column models of approximately half-scale. Ten specimens, as shown in Table 4, were used.

Conclusions

The results of the studies conducted on the KM System described above are summarized as follows:

    1. The separation load of the HISPLIT connection including a tapered effect, can be evaluated by

$$T_a = n\frac{a(1 + k^2)}{1 + ak^2}Pa, \qquad (1)$$

where

T_a is the allowable tensile strength of the HISPLIT connection;
a is $a/1$ (see Fig. 8);
n is the number of bolts in the connection;
k is the thickness ratio of the middle part to the edge of the T-stub
  flange; and
Pa is the allowable tensile strength of the bolt.

2. HISPLIT connections were found to have stable restoring force characteristics as moment-resisting connections and to possess strengths, rigidities, and ductilities superior to those of ordinary welded connections.

3. Lateral stiffener plates can be eliminated from a column because of the stiffening effect of HISPLIT attachments, provided the allowable tensile force on the column flange of an all steel frame structure satisfies the equations in Tables 5a–c.

4. Even in the case of HISPLIT without a beam web joint, the bending moment and shear force could be transferred completely from beam to column through the T-stub web of HISPLIT alone. The structural performance of the whole connection was satisfactory.

Table 4 Specimens

No.	Designation	Section	Steel Cross Section	Hoop Type	Loading Direction	Axial Force* $\times$BDF$_c$
1	KS-L-2				Strong axis	0.2
2	KS-L-4		H$_B$ − 175 × 175	Kajima	" "	0.4
3	KS-L-6		× 12 × 12	Spiral	" "	0.6
4	KS-L-4Y				Weak axis	0.4
5	KS-L-4XY	Main bar: 12-D22 (SD35)			Diagonal (45°)	0.4
6	KS-S-2				Strong axis	0.2
7	KS-S-4		H$_B$ − 150 × 150	Kajima	" "	0.4
8	KS-S-6		× 9 × 9	Spiral	" "	0.6
9	T-L-4		H$_B$ − 175 × 175		Strong axis	0.4
10	T-L-6		× 12 × 12	Tie hoop	" "	0.6

*Concrete strength: $F_c = 300$ kg/cm^2

Table 5a Design equations for determining allowable tensile force T for out-of-plane bending of column flange, no horizontal column stiffener

4-Bolt Type	$T_a = 4 \cdot Z \cdot f_{b1} \left\{ \dfrac{d}{b} + \dfrac{\sqrt{4c^2 + 4ca - a^2}}{b} \right\} + 4B_a \cdot \dfrac{b-a}{b}$

$$d \leqq 2a_o \qquad T_a = 4 \cdot Z \cdot f_{b1} (\sqrt{\dfrac{16c}{a_o} - 9} + \dfrac{2d}{a_o})$$

$$d > 2a_o \qquad T_a = 4 \cdot Z \cdot f_{b1} (\sqrt{\dfrac{16c}{a_o} - 9} + 4\sqrt{\dfrac{2d}{a_o} - 4})$$

6-Bolt Type

$$T_a = 2 \cdot Z \cdot f_{b1} \left\{ \sqrt{\dfrac{16c}{a_{o1}} - 9} + \sqrt{\dfrac{16c}{a_{o2}} - 9} + 8\sqrt{(\dfrac{2d}{a_{o2} - a_{o1}})^2 + 1} \times \sqrt{\dfrac{a_{o2}}{a_{o1}}} \right.$$
$$\left. - \dfrac{16d}{a_{o2} - a_{o1}} \right\}$$

$$T_a = 2 \cdot Z \cdot f_{b1} \left\{ \sqrt{\dfrac{16c}{a_{o2}} - 9} + \sqrt{\dfrac{16c}{a_{o3}} - 9} + 8\sqrt{(\dfrac{2d}{a_{o3} - a_{o2}})^2 + 1} \times \sqrt[4]{\dfrac{a_{o3}}{a_{o2}}} \right.$$
$$\left. - \dfrac{16d}{a_{o3} - a_{o2}} \right\} + 2B_a \cdot \dfrac{a_{o3} - a_1}{a_{o3}}$$

$$T_a = 2 \cdot Z \cdot f_{b1} \left\{ \dfrac{2d}{b} + \dfrac{\sqrt{4c^2 + 4ca_2 - a_2^2} + \sqrt{4c^2 + 4ca_3 - a_3^2}}{b} \right\}$$
$$+ 2 \cdot B_a \cdot \dfrac{3b - (a_1 + a_2 + a_3)}{b}$$

8-Bolt Type

$$d \leqq 2a_o \qquad T_a = 4 \cdot Z \cdot f_{b1} (\sqrt{\dfrac{16c}{a_{o1}} - 9} + \dfrac{2d}{a_{o1}})$$

$$d > 2a_o \qquad T_a = 4 \cdot Z \cdot f_{b1} (\sqrt{\dfrac{16c}{a_{o1}} - 9} + 4\sqrt{\dfrac{2d}{a_{o1}} - 4})$$

$$T_a = 4 \cdot Z \cdot f_{b1} (\sqrt{\dfrac{16c}{a_{o2}} - 9} + \dfrac{2d}{a_{o2}}) + 4B_a \cdot \dfrac{a_{o2} - a_1}{a_{o2}}$$

$$T_a = 4 \cdot Z \cdot f_{b1} (\dfrac{d}{b} + \dfrac{\sqrt{4c^2 + 4ca_2 - a_2^2}}{b}) + 4B_a \cdot \dfrac{2b - (a_1 + a_2)}{b}$$

Notes: B_a: allowable tensile force per high tension bolt

Z: section modulus per unit length for out-of-plane bending of column flange
($= 1/6\ c^t f^2$, $c^t f$: thickness of column flange)

f_{b1}: allowable bending stress for out-of-plane bending of column flange
(long term: $f_{b1} = F/1.3$, short term: 1.5 times long term)

m_a: out-of-plane allowable bending moment per unit length of column flange
($= 1/6\ c^t f^2 \cdot f_{b1}$)

m_a': out-of-plane allowable bending moment per unit length of reinforcing plate
($= 1/6\ t_2^2 \cdot f_{b1}$, t_2: thickness of reinforcing plate)

Table 5b Design equations for determining allowable tensile force T for out-of-plane bending of column flange, with horizontal column stiffener

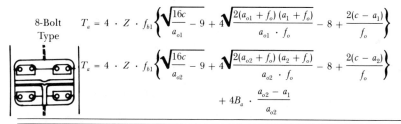

4-Bolt Type

$c - a \leq 2f_o$

$$T_a = 4 \cdot Z \cdot f_{b1}\left\{\sqrt{\frac{16c}{a_o} - 9} + 4\sqrt{\frac{2(a_o + f_o)(a + f_o)}{a_o f_o}} - 8 + \frac{2(c - a)}{f_o}\right\}$$

$c - a > 2f_o$

$$T_a = 4 \cdot Z \cdot f_{b1}\left\{\sqrt{\frac{16c}{a_o} - 9} + 4\sqrt{\frac{2(a_o + f_o)(a + f_o)}{a_o f_o}} - 8 + 4\sqrt{\frac{2(c - a)}{f_o}} - 4\right\}$$

6-Bolt Type

$$T_a = 2 \cdot Z \cdot f_{b1}\left\{\sqrt{\frac{16c}{a_{o1}} - 9} + \sqrt{\frac{16c}{a_{o2}} - 9} + 4\sqrt{\frac{2(a_{o1} + f_{o1})(a_1 + f_{o1})}{a_{o1} \cdot f_{o1}}}\right.$$

$$\left. + 4\sqrt{\frac{2(a_{o2} + f_{o2})(a_2 + f_{o2})}{a_{o2} \cdot f_{o2}}} + \frac{2(c - a_1)}{f_{o1}} + \frac{2(c - a_2)}{f_{o2}} - 16\right\}$$

$$T_a = 2 \cdot Z \cdot f_{b1}\left\{\sqrt{\frac{16c}{a_{o2}} - 9} + \sqrt{\frac{16c}{a_{o3}} - 9} + 4\sqrt{\frac{2(a_{o2} + f_{o2})(a_2 + f_{o2})}{a_{o2} \cdot f_{o2}}}\right.$$

$$\left. + 4\sqrt{\frac{2(a_{o3} + f_{o1})(a_3 + f_{o1})}{a_{o3} \cdot f_{o1}}} + \frac{2(c - a_2)}{f_{o2}} + \frac{2(c - a_3)}{f_{o1}} - 16\right\}$$

$$+ 2B_a \cdot \frac{a_{o3} - a_1}{a_{o3}}$$

8-Bolt Type

$$T_a = 4 \cdot Z \cdot f_{b1}\left\{\sqrt{\frac{16c}{a_{o1}} - 9} + 4\sqrt{\frac{2(a_{o1} + f_o)(a_1 + f_o)}{a_{o1} \cdot f_o}} - 8 + \frac{2(c - a_1)}{f_o}\right\}$$

$$T_a = 4 \cdot Z \cdot f_{b1}\left\{\sqrt{\frac{16c}{a_{o2}} - 9} + 4\sqrt{\frac{2(a_{o2} + f_o)(a_2 + f_o)}{a_{o2} \cdot f_o}} - 8 + \frac{2(c - a_2)}{f_o}\right\}$$

$$+ 4B_a \cdot \frac{a_{o2} - a_1}{a_{o2}}$$

Notes: B_a: allowable tensile force per high tension bolt

  Z: section modulus per unit length for out-of-plane bending of column flange
  ($= 1/6\ c^tf^2$, c^tf: thickness of column flange)

  f_{b1}: allowable bending stress for out-of-plane bending of column flange
  (long term: $f_{b1} = F/1.3$, short term: 1.5 times long term)

  m_a: out-of-plane allowable bending moment per unit length of column flange
  ($= 1/6\ c^tf^2 \cdot f_{b1}$)

  $m_a{}'$: out-of-plane allowable bending moment per unit length of reinforcing plate
  ($= 1/6\ t_2^2 \cdot f_{b1}$, t_2: thickness of reinforcing plate)

Table 5c Design equations for determining allowable tensile force T for out-of-plane bending of column flange, reinforcement by fish plate inside column flange (no welding)

4-Bolt Type	

$$T_a = 4 \left(\sqrt{\frac{4c}{a_0} P^2 - (P + Q)^2} + \frac{d}{a_0} P \right)$$

$$T_a = 4 \left(\frac{\sqrt{4c^2 m_a Q + (4c - a)am_a^2}}{b} + \frac{d}{b} m_a \right) + 4 B_a \frac{b - a}{b}$$

6-Bolt Type

$$T_a = 2 \left(\sqrt{\frac{4c}{a_{02}} P^2 - (P + Q)^2} + \sqrt{\frac{4c}{a_{01}} P^2 - (P + Q)^2} + 8 \sqrt{\left[\left(\frac{2d}{a_{02} - a_{01}} \right)^2 + 1 \right] Q} \right.$$

$$\left. \times \sqrt{\frac{a_{02}}{a_{01}} \frac{P}{2} + \frac{m_a'}{2} + \frac{16d}{a_{02} - a_{01}} Q} \right)$$

$$T_a = 2 \left\{ \sqrt{\frac{4c}{a_{03}} P^2 - (P + Q)^2} + \sqrt{\frac{4c}{a_{02}} P^2 - (P + Q)^2} + 8 \sqrt{\left[\left(\frac{2d}{a_{03} - a_{02}} \right)^2 + 1 \right] Q} \right.$$

$$\left. \times \sqrt{\frac{a_{03}}{a_{02}} \frac{P}{2} + \frac{m_a'}{2} - \frac{16d}{a_{03} - a_{02}} Q} \right\} + 2B_a \frac{a_{03} - a_1}{a_{03}}$$

$$T_a = 2 \left(\frac{\sqrt{4c^2 m_a Q + (4c - a_3)a_3 m_a^2}}{b} + \frac{2d}{b} m_a + \frac{\sqrt{4c^2 m_a Q + (4c - a_2)a_2 m_a^2}}{b} \right)$$

$$+ 2B_a \frac{3b - (a_1 + a_2 + a_3)}{b}$$

8-Bolt Type

$$T_a = 4 \left(\sqrt{\frac{4c}{a_{01}} P^2 - (P + Q)^2} + \frac{d}{a_{01}} P \right)$$

$$T_a = 4 \left(\sqrt{\frac{4c}{a_{02}} P^2 - (P + Q)^2} + \frac{d}{a_{02}} P \right) + 4B_a \frac{a_{02} - a_1}{a_{02}}$$

$$T_a = 4 \left(\frac{\sqrt{4c^2 m_a Q + (4c - a_2) a_2 m_a^2}}{b} + \frac{d}{b} m_a \right) + 4B_a \frac{2b - (a_1 + a_2)}{b}$$

Notes: B_a: allowable tensile force per high tension bolt

Z: section modulus per unit length for out-of-plane bending of column flange
($= 1/6 \, c^t f^2$, $c^t f$: thickness of column flange)

f_{b1}: allowable bending stress for out-of-plane bending of column flange
(long term: $f_{b1} = F/1.3$, short term: 1.5 times long term)

m_a: out-of-plane allowable bending moment per unit length of column flange
($= 1/6 \, c^t f^2 \cdot f_{b1}$)

m_a': out-of-plane allowable bending moment per unit length of reinforcing plate
($= 1/6 \, t_2^2 \cdot f_{b1}$, t_2: thickness of reinforcing plate)

5. In case of a HISPLIT connection in the weak-axis direction of an all steel-frame column, the elastic rigidity of the subassemblage was about one-fourth of that of a strong-axis connection. This weak-axis connection is feasible for use as a semirigid connection.

6. With steel and reinforced concrete columns carrying large axial forces, the respective hysteresis curves were close to being spindle-shaped, indicating good properties regardless of structural steel quantities. Flexural strength was still maintained even at the large deformation of 0.25 rad, and it was verified that the system is quite practical.

These studies have dealt with the structural aspects of the HISPLIT System, which is characterized by the use of mass-produced cast steel attachments. This connection system is applicable not only to steel structures but also to composite (steel and reinforced concrete) structures. It has already been adopted in more than 400 actual building frames, making an important contribution to the rationalization of steel frame construction.

EXAMPLES OF IMPLEMENTATION AND TRIAL DESIGNS

The Building Standards Law of Japan was revised in 1963 because of the necessity for high-rise urban redevelopment and because of the progress achieved in earthquake-resistant design technology. In effect, the height limit of 31 m (112 ft) for buildings was abolished, and it became possible to construct high-rise buildings.

The first of these was Kasumigaseki Building in Tokyo (1968) (Fig. 9). Since then more than 100 high-rise buildings have been constructed of which the tallest is the Sunshine 60 building (Fig. 10). Except for five earthquake-resistant

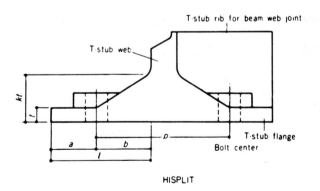

HISPLIT

Fig. 8 Dimensions of T-stub

high-rise buildings of reinforced concrete structure (developed independently by Kajima), almost all the high-rise buildings in Japan are of steel-frame structure. The reasons, as described earlier, are the high productivity inherent in steel-frame structure and the high earthquake-resistance and superior wind-resistance obtained with this type of structure.

The types of beam-to-column connections used frequently in high-rise structures in Japan, the required quantities of steel, and the construction periods are analyzed in the remainder of this paper.

Fig. 9 Kasumigaseki Building

**Connection System for Structural Steel and
Steel Weight Required**

To increase the earthquake resistance and wind resistance of high-rise buildings such as those in Japan, it will be effective to utilize walls. However, such resistance can also be obtained by rigidly connecting the columns and beams. Figure 11 compares the U.S. and Japan and indicates the relationships between required quantities of steel and numbers of stories of high-rise buildings. In Japan, the relatively low steel requirements despite earthquake-resistant designs are attributable to the design methods for beam-to-column connections and structural planning methods including shear walls.

When beam-to-column joints are rigidly connected, vertical deflections due to floor loads are decreased. In cases of long spans, this will be extremely effective in an earthquake-free country.

Fig. 10 Sunshine 60

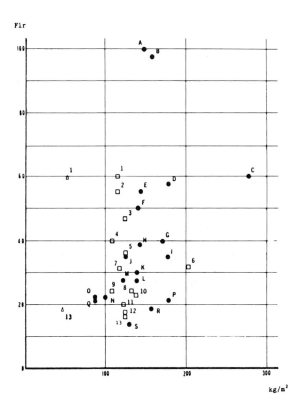

Fig. 11 Relation of steel weight required per unit area and number of stories

The types of rigid connections between columns and beams normally used in Japan are shown in Fig. 12. As indicated in (a), (b) and (c), the method of welding beam ends to columns is mechanically effective for rigid connections. However, this method requires a high technical level including good quality control to assure reliable welding. Figure 12 (d) shows the simplest type of connection, the HISPLIT System. This is the connection method adopted for the Akasaka Prince Hotel in Tokyo, which will be described next. The structural steel frame of the KM System incorporates the HISPLIT connection system. Since it will suffice to consider only lateral rigidity against the

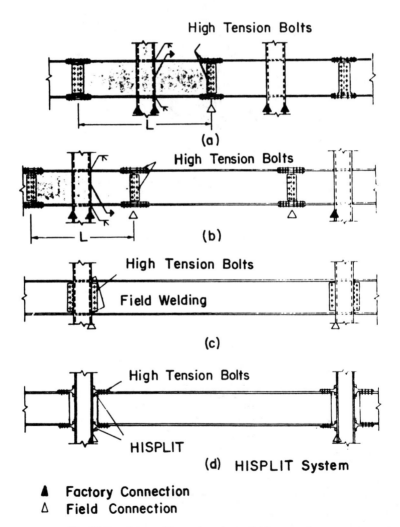

Fig. 12 Four types of beam-to-column rigid connections

external lateral wind force in an earthquake-free country, making composite columns of H-shapes and reinforced concrete, as in the KM system, means that large compressive (stress) forces can be carried. When designing floor structures, it is easy to secure the necessary degree of fixation against bending moment at the end of a beam, so that this system is especially suited to high-rise buildings having long spans.

An Example of Implementation

Let us consider the steel framing system of the new high-rise Akasaka Prince Hotel in Tokyo (Fig. 13). Designed by Kenzo Tange and built by the Kajima Corporation over a period of 3 years, it has a typical floor area of 1,485 m² (16,000 ft²), a total floor area of 67,485 m² (726,410 ft²), and 39 stories above ground, and 2 stories underground. Its height is 139.8 m (127.9 ft) above ground level, with a typical story height of 3.2 m (10.5 ft). Its second basement floor is of reinforced concrete and it first basement floor up to the second floor is of reinforced concrete encased steel. The third floor and above is a steel structure of the HISPLIT System. The exterior finish is an aluminum curtain wall with mirror glass. The structural materials used are concrete (approx. 25,000 m³ [32,700 yd³]); reinforcing steel (approx. 2,800 ton); structural steel (approx. 8,500 ton); and HISPLIT T-Stub (approx. 500 ton).

The most attractive feature of this hotel is the V-shaped building plan consisting of two wings. This plan is reflected conspicuously in the exterior elevation, which is the essence of modern architecture. But the unusual shape of this plan posed some perplexing problems for the structural engineer. Two of the problems are briefly described below:

The first was to design a structural system that would minimize stresses and deflections of the building structure against earthquake and wind forces in all directions to ensure a high degree of safety during earthquakes and storms. The goal was not to spoil residential comfort in this 761-room hotel, even under such circumstances.

The second was to develop a construction method for the steel frame to simplify the connections of this complicated structural framing in three directions. The construction method must also serve to raise productivity of fabrication at the factory, to simplify erection at the jobsite, and to ensure a high degree of quality control with minimum effort.

The solutions are now described.

The structural system employed in this building is a combination of a rigid steel frame (4.0 m (13 ft) bay × 4.0 m (13 ft) bay) and precast concrete shear walls (slitted shear walls) located at the central core portion and at the end of each wing to minimize the torsional deflection of the building.

The slitted shear walls mentioned above, in the case of this building, bear 30 to 50% of the horizontal forces due to earthquakes and storms. The safety of

Fig. 13 Akasaka Prince Hotel

this structural system against earthquakes and storms was studied and confirmed in detail by means of a three-dimensional elastoplastic analysis program developed by the Kajima Corporation.

The construction method of the steel frame employed in this building is a method of prefabrication by means of HISPLIT T-Stubs at rigid column-beam connections (Fig. 14).

Steel fabrication at the factory was reduced to a minimum using simplified connection details, and at the same time the erection speed at the jobsite was raised dramatically.

This HISPLIT T-Stub was designed to be of ideal shape and dimensions to raise joint efficiency close to the maximum; it was manufactured by Hitachi Metals, Ltd. on a mass-production basis to meet the great demand from middle- and low-rise steel-frame buildings presently existing in Japan. It is needless to say that a great deal of study for theoretical analysis and full-size strength tests was carried out to confirm the strength and ductility of this type of connection. Outside of Japan, this construction method was employed in the project of the trade center building in the GDR (the Internationales Handels- und Einkaufszentrum) of 25 stories above ground and one basement story.

Features of the Work Schedule for a High-rise Building

When the construction periods of 45 projects recently undertaken by Kajima Corporation are analyzed according to the number of stories in each building, a trend is seen, as shown in Fig. 15. Urban areas in Japan are generally confined and jumbled, with parking areas and machinery rooms provided underground in many cases. The number of basement floors is normally two or three. Consequently, the construction periods of underground structures vary greatly depending on not only spatial planning but

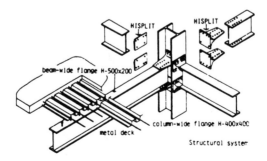

Fig. 14 Structural system for Akasaka Prince Hotel

also the siting conditions including ground strata. Regarding stories above
ground, the efficiencies of cranes are determined by the floor plan of the
building, so the relationships between scale and construction period cannot
be simply described. The distribution over a wide range is due to such a
reason. Further, it may be seen that efficiencies are relatively good for
high-rise buildings of 30 stories and over.

Figure 16 gives a standard work schedule chart for a steel-frame high-rise
building in Japan. The interrelationships of the various activities can be
understood from this figure. What greatly influences the construction period
is the structural steel work. It should be noted that the schedule for finishing
the next work step is almost parallel to the gradient for the structural steel

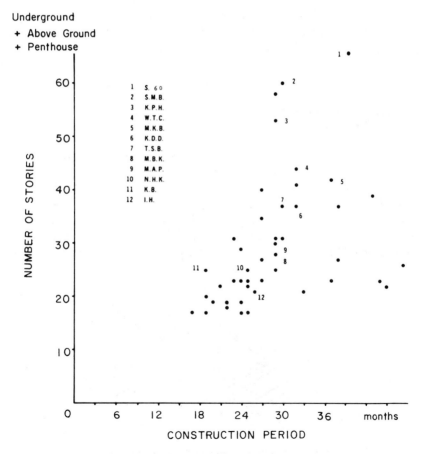

Fig. 15 Construction periods

work. The construction periods for the excavation, underground structure, and structural steel work can be estimated by the following. The excavation time in months is given by

$$\frac{V}{30v}, \tag{2}$$

where V is the volume of soil excavation and v is the volume of soil excavated per day. The time of construction of the underground structure is 1 month per story. The time in months of structural steel erection is given by

$$(1 + \frac{nd}{30}\alpha + 1.5), \tag{3}$$

STORY

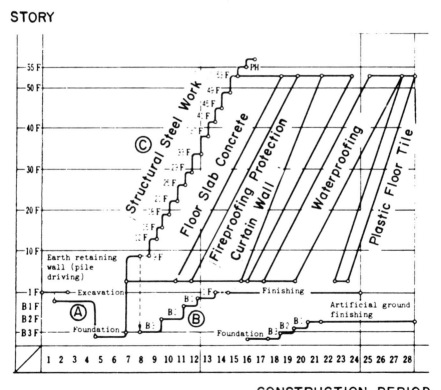

CONSTRUCTION PERIOD

Fig. 16 Typical work schedule

where n is the number of stories, d is the net number of days required for construction per story, and a is the conversion factor for the number of calendar days required.

The construction of a high-rise building is divided into three periods. Figure 17 is a conceptual drawing of the above. With the initial stage consisting of preparations, earth retaining, excavation, and foundation work as Phase I, the structural steel work as Phase II, and the stage from finishing after completion of the structural steel work until completion of exterior works and delivery as Phase III, the results shown in Table 6 are obtained.

Of these, Phase II, the structural steel work, holds the key to the construction period of the entire project.

When the HISPLIT System is used for erection of structural steel, there is no welding to be done at the jobsite. The number of bolts used is extremely small, so that it is possible to shorten the time required for erection. According to the records up to this time, the speed of erection is increased 20 to 40% in the case of this system, and the number of days required per story, the value of a (Eq. 3), may be expected to be lowered (Fig. 18 and 19). Based on the above, it may be seen that this method further contributes to speeding up the entire project compared with conventional steel structure. And since there is no welding on the jobsite, the precision of erection can be improved.

Table 6 Actual construction periods

| | Number of stories | | |
Building*	Underground	Above ground	Penthouse
Kasumigaseki	3	36	3
International Telecommunications Center	3	32	2
Shinjuku Mitsui	3	55	1
Sunshine 60	3	60	3
Akasaka Prince Hotel	2	39	—

*All buildings in Tokyo

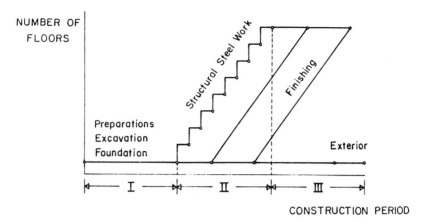

Fig. 17 Conceptual diagram of work schedule

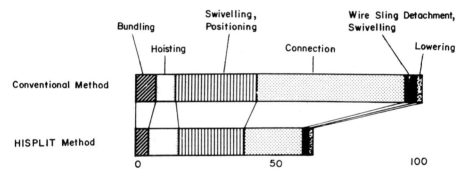

Fig. 18 Comparison of erection times required for HISPLIT and conventional methods
(connecting 20-m span beam to column)

Hgt	Floor Area (m²)		Construction period (mo.)			Completion
m	Total	Typical floor	I	II	III	
147	165,692	3,505	15	13	11	1968
153	123,803	2,916	13	11	11	1974
212	179,956	2,480	8	10	12	1974
226.3	248,605	3,105	14	11	25	1978
138.9	69,948	1,498	12	9	12	1982

REFERENCES/BIBLIOGRAPHY

Architectural Institute of Japan, 1972a
  RECOMMENDATION FOR DESIGN AND PRACTICE OF HIGH STRENGTH BOLTED CONNEC-
  TIONS (in Japanese), Architectural Institute of Japan, Japan.
Architectural Institute of Japan, 1972b
  STANDARDS FOR DESIGN OF STEEL STRUCTURES (in Japanese), Architectural Institute of
  Japan, Japan.

Kato, B. and McGuire, W., 1973
  ANALYSIS OF T-STUB FLANGE-TO-COLUMN CONNECTIONS, Journal of the Structural Division,
  ASCE, Vol. 99, No. ST5, May.

Sato, K. and Tomita, A., et al., 1981
  EXPERIMENTAL INVESTIGATION ON T-STUB CONNECTIONS USING CAST STEEL (Part VI) (in
  Japanese), A. I. J. Research Report, Japan.
Sato, K. and Toyama, K., et al., 1974
  EXPERIMENTAL INVESTIGATION OF T-STUB CONNECTIONS USING CAST STEEL (Parts I and
  II) (in Japanese), A. I. J. Research Report, Japan.
Sato, K. and Toyama, K., et al., 1975
  EXPERIMENTAL INVESTIGATION ON T-STUB CONNECTIONS USING CAST STEEL (Part III) (in
  Japanese), A. I. J. Research Report, Japan.
Sato, K. and Toyama, K., et al., 1976
  EXPERIMENTAL STUDY ON BEAM-TO-COLUMN CONNECTIONS USING CAST STEEL T-STUBS,
  Report No. 23, Kajima Institute of Construction, Japan.
Sato, K. and Yamada, S., et al., 1977
  EXPERIMENTAL INVESTIGATION OF T-STUB CONNECTIONS USING CASE STEEL (Part V) (in
  Japanese), A. I. J. Research Report, Japan.

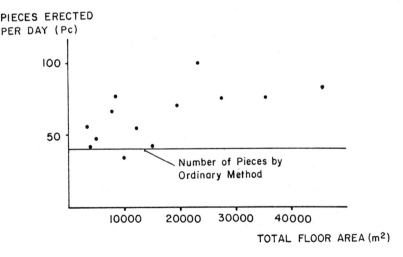

Fig. 19 Pieces erected per day by HISPLIT system

Structural Design of Tall Concrete and Masonry Buildings

Introductory Review

Ignacio Martín

The structural design of tall concrete and masonry buildings continues to advance, and this advance is reflected primarily in a better knowledge of the lateral loads that tall buildings must resist, simpler and more accurate methods of analysis, simpler and more effective detailing of reinforcement, better quality concrete, and more efficient construction methods.

This second Monograph update volume, *Advances in Tall Buildings*, reflects advances in the design of tall concrete and masonry buildings in analysis, design, and use of high-strength materials. The papers on analysis in the volume discuss simplified methods of analysis including the use of shear walls combined with frame structures. These papers discuss methods of analysis that reflect the behavior of buildings. The mutual influence of analysis and design in tall buildings, in the proper frame of the nature of lateral loads and behavior of materials, is now receiving the necessary attention from designers and researchers.

The engineering profession is getting simultaneously two new codes dealing with seismic design: the final draft of the *CEB Model Code for Seismic Design of Concrete Structures*, October 1983, and Appendix A in the new *ACI Building Code Requirements for Reinforced Concrete* (ACI 318-83). These documents reflect the present knowledge of seismic loads, behavior of concrete structures under seismic loads, and detailing to improve this behavior. It should not come as a surprise that this volume includes papers dealing with these subjects in their application to the design of actual buildings.

There have been recent structural building failures that should receive the attention of those involved in development and construction. These failures have focussed attention on the need for proper detailing and supervision during construction. To prevent these failures from occurring in the future, the concerted effort not only of the contractors and designers but also of the owners, government officials, and consumers is necessary.

High-strength concrete is particularly effective in tall concrete buildings. None of the failures mentioned can be traced to the use of high-strength concrete, but a thorough knowledge of the material properties and short- and long-term behavior of this material, as well as the quality control and methods of construction to be used in tall buildings, are a present-day concern of tall building designers and builders.

In accordance with the present state of the art, the contents of *Advances in Tall Buildings* are responsive to the concerns of those involved in tall concrete and masonry building design and construction.

Laterally Loaded Asymmetric Shear Buildings: Planar Analysis

A. Rutenberg
M. Eisenberger

INTRODUCTION

The lateral load analysis of asymmetric building structures usually requires a full three-dimensional (3-D) computer procedure. In such cases the size of the problem is often larger than can be handled by in-house computers, or too costly to be analyzed by the 3-D options of standard general computer programs. Therefore, it is often necessary to reduce the size of the problem by neglecting less significant degrees of freedom, for instance normal bending and torsion of columns and beams, and by taking advantage of the particular structural and geometric features of the building.

The shear building, namely a building structure whose lateral force–displacement curve is shear dependent, lends itself to such a treatment. This type of structure is a very popular model among design engineers, mainly for the preliminary analysis of planar and 3-D framed structures, and among research workers for behavioral and parametric studies. It is popular because it models the behavior of framed structures quite realistically, and because it is a near coupled structural system, it lends itself to story-by-story analysis, that is, vertical uncoupling. Nevertheless, analysis of even this type of structure by hand methods is tedious and time consuming, particularly for the asymmetric 3-D case.

This paper describes a simple procedure for the analysis of laterally loaded asymmetric shear buildings consisting of assemblages in two perpendicular directions, by means of plane frame computer programs. The approach is based on two analogies: one is between the behavior of a laterally loaded shear building and an axially loaded plane frame, and the other is between the torsion of a bar and the bending of a rotationally constrained cantilever. The first analogy, which has already been described in an earlier paper (Rutenberg, 1980), could not model walls or frames with finite torsional rigidity or oriented at a right angle to the direction of excitation. In the present paper this restriction is removed, thus permitting more realistic modeling. The proposed model is also a realistic representation for low-rise structures with shear walls of low aspect ratio. The large lateral stiffness of squat shear walls requires that the in-plane flexibility of the floor slabs be considered. As is well known, many efficient 3-D programs (for example in Wilson, 1975) are incapable of doing this. However, with the proposed approach it is possible to examine the flexibility of certain floor slab systems, even when only the capability of handling plane frames is available. Another advantage of the approach is that it can easily account for P-Delta effects.

ANALOGOUS PLANE FRAME

The *axial* displacement curve of an elastic bar loaded axially along its length is similar in shape to the *lateral* displacement curve of a shear beam when the same system of forces is applied laterally, assuming, of course, equivalent end conditions. This analogy is shown schematically in Fig. 1. Therefore, the shear rigidity of a plane frame or shear wall can be replaced by an equivalent axial rigidity of a column. Similarly, it is possible to replace the twist about a vertical axis of an elastic bar in pure torsion by the rotation about a horizontal axis of a series of rotationally constrained vertical cantilevers having equivalent flexural rigidities, as shown in Fig. 2. It is thus seen that by assigning specified axial and flexural properties to the equivalent columns, shear and lateral displacements are transformed into axial compression and displacements respectively, whereas torque and twist about a vertical axis are transformed into bending moment and rotation about a horizontal axis respectively. Thus in both cases a planar representation is obtained.

Floor slabs are modeled as continuous beams supported on the equivalent columns. When the floors can be assumed to be rigid in their own plane, very high values of flexural and shear rigidities should be assigned to the equivalent beams. However, the analogy's ability to model flexible floor slabs should be used with some care. When floors are rectangular in plan, which is the case this paper considers, their aspect ratio between adjacent frames or shear walls is likely to be low. Therefore, the assumption of plane sections, which is made in standard plane frame programs, is likely to lead to some errors.

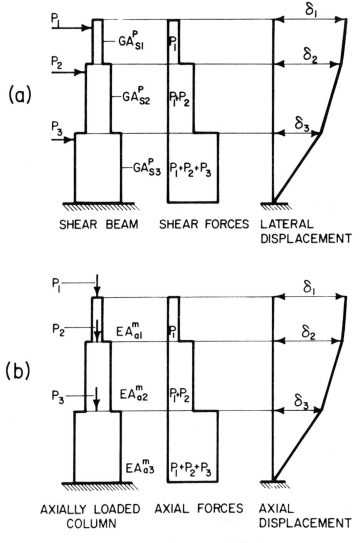

Fig. 1 Analogy between shear and axial displacements

These may become significant when the torsional contribution of frames perpendicular to the direction of excitation is considered.

To illustrate the analogy, Fig. 3 shows a simple structural system composed of three frames in the direction of excitation (Nos. 1, 2, 3) and two frames in the perpendicular direction (Nos. 4, 5). Replacing the shear rigidities of frames 1, 2, and 3 by axial rigidities, the torsional rigidities of frames 4 and 5 by flexural rigidities, and the lateral forces W_1 and W_2 by equal vertical forces yields the model in Fig. 3c. Note that the floor slabs were assumed to be rigid and thus modeled as rigid continuous beams. Also note that with this assumption, the torsional rigidity of frames 4 and 5 can be combined and allocated arbitrarily to any column. This, evidently, is a more economical procedure. It is only for illustrative purposes that the vertical cantilever is shown as a separate member.

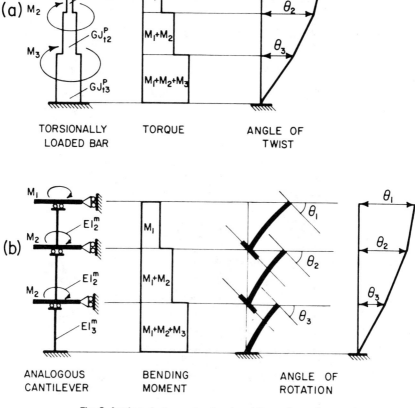

Fig. 2 Analogy between torsional and flexural rotations

It will be observed that, when the floors are rigid, all shear carrying assemblages can also be lumped into a single equivalent column, and all the torsional resistance (not only that of members oriented at a right angle to the direction of force) can be lumped into one equivalent constrained cantilever. These two can further be merged into a single member located at the shear (or rigidity) center of the story, as shown in Fig. 4. However, it is evident that this further reduction of the model requires additional manual work. Therefore, if used as a computer oriented model, it is much more suitable for dynamic response calculations and parametric studies than for static analysis.

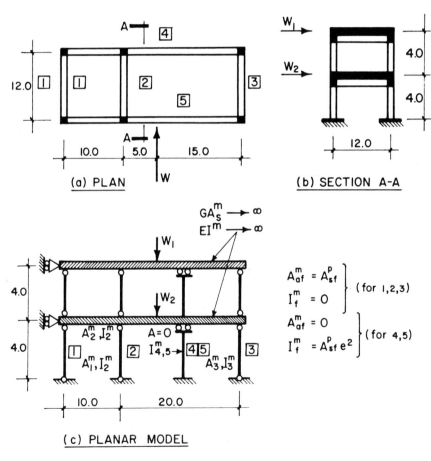

Fig. 3 Two-story structure and its analogous frame

The procedure can be implemented in the following stages:
1. Evaluate the cross-sectional area A_a^m of the equivalent columns modeling shear members. For a shear wall system, replace the shear area of the wall A_{sw}^p by A_{aw}^m using the expression

$$A_{aw}^m = \frac{A_{sw}^p}{2(1+\nu)} \tag{1}$$

in which ν = Poisson's ratio. Note that Young's modulus E remains unchanged in the model. For multistory frames, first compute the approximate story stiffness A_{sf}^p using standard procedures (for example in Cheong-Siat-Moy, 1974). For a story with m columns:

$$A_{sf}^p = \frac{12}{h^2} \sum_i^m \frac{I_c}{1+2\psi}, \tag{2}$$

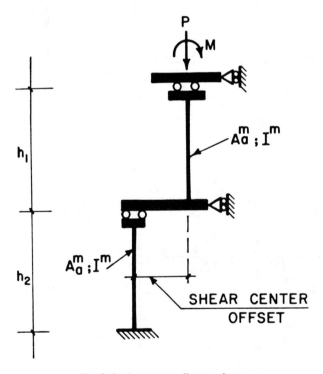

Fig. 4 Analogous cantilever column

in which

$$\psi = \frac{I_c}{h} [\overset{n}{\underset{j}{\Sigma}} \frac{I_b}{L_b}]^{-1},$$ (3)

h is the story height, I_c is the column inertia, I_b is the beam inertia, and n is the number of beams framing into the column ($n \leq 2$). For the top and bottom stories, modify Eq. 2 as follows (Cheong-Siat-Moy, 1974): for the top story,

$$A_{sf}^p = \frac{12}{h^2} \overset{m}{\underset{i}{\Sigma}} \frac{I_c}{1 + \psi},$$ (2a)

and for the bottom story, assuming fixed column bases,

$$A_{sf}^p = \frac{12}{h^2} \overset{m}{\underset{i}{\Sigma}} \frac{I_c (3 + \psi)}{3 + 4\psi}.$$ (2b)

$$\text{Replace} \qquad A_{sf}^m = A_{sf}^p.$$ (4)

2. To consider P-Delta effects, modify the equivalent area A_a^m to read

$$A_{a\Delta}^m = A_a^m - \gamma \frac{N}{E},$$ (5)

in which $A_{a\Delta}^m$ is the modified cross-sectional area, N is the factored gravity load tributary to the frame under consideration, and γ is the correction factor to account for the deviation of the deflected curve from a straight line (Rutenberg, 1981).

3. Evaluate the equivalent inertia I^m of the vertical cantilever modeling torsional stiffness. For shear walls, compute the contribution to torsional rigidity of walls perpendicular to the plane of action by

$$J_{tw}^p = A_{sw}^p e^2 + J_{tow}^p$$ (6)

in which J_{tw}^p and J_{tow}^p are the torsional constants about the center of rotation and about the member's own axis respectively, and e is the eccentricity of the wall from the axis of rigidity. Then replace J_{tw}^p by I_w^m using the expression

$$\frac{I_w^m = J_{tw}^p}{2(1 + \nu)}$$ (7)

For multistory frames, use Eq. 2 to evaluate the lateral stiffness A_{sf}^p of all the frames whose line of action is perpendicular to the direction of excitation. Then use Eq. 8 to obtain the flexural rigidity I_f^m of the model:

$$I_f^m = A_{sf}^p e^2 \qquad (8)$$

Remember to assign zero axial rigidity to the vertical cantilevers resisting torsion only.

4. For rigid floor slabs lump all torsional rigidities into an equivalent cantilever and assign its properties and end conditions to any arbitrary column. As noted above, the whole system may be lumped into an equivalent vertical member if so desired (Fig. 4). When floor flexibility is considered by assigning finite stiffness to equivalent horizontal beams, the location of the vertical cantilever along the floor beams should match their position in plan. Evidently, this proposal is not very meaningful when frames are wide and extend over a sizable part of the floor length.

5. Let the lateral forces and lateral inertia (for dynamic analysis) act vertically, disregarding real vertical forces.

6. Solve model plane frame for vertical displacements and internal forces.

7. The resulting axial forces in columns are the lateral shear forces in shear carrying walls or frames.

8. The resulting flexural moment in vertical cantilever beams is the contribution to torque of perpendicular assemblages. When these assemblages are lumped, distribute moments among participating assemblages in proportion to their torsional rigidities.

9. Vertical settlements are lateral displacements. Rotations about a horizontal axis are rotations about a vertical axis.

10. Shear forces and moments in horizontal floor beams are their counterparts in floor slabs. Note, however, that this is a very crude approximation, since strength of materials assumptions are often not satisfied; also, walls and frames have finite lengths, so that the lateral displacements of perpendicular assemblages due to rotation depend on the particular points in plan wherein they are assumed to be located.

NUMERICAL EXAMPLE

The simple two-story framed structure shown in Fig. 3 was chosen for this example. The floor slabs were assumed rigid in their plane, a realistic assumption even for low-rise framed buildings (Shepherd and Donald, 1967), although not necessarily so for shear wall buildings (Rutenberg, 1980). The analogous frame and its loading are given in Fig. 3c. Member properties are listed in Table 1 and in Table 2.

Two analyses were carried out: (1) an "exact" analysis using a 3-D computer program, and (2) an approximate analysis based on the proposed analogy, using the transformation formulae given in the preceding section. The results are shown in Table 3. The small disagreement between the two sets of results should not be interpreted to suggest that the proposed analogy models shear behavior only approximately; as explained earlier, the modeling is accurate within our engineering framework. It rather reflects the limitations of the shear building *per se* to model the response of low-rise framed structures with moderate girder-to-column stiffness ratios.

SUMMARY AND CONCLUSIONS

A planar model for the lateral force response of asymmetric shear buildings has been presented. It is based on the analogy between a shear beam and an axially loaded column and on the analogy between a twisted bar and a bent cantilever beam. Since shear dependence is assumed, the approach is applicable to relatively wide multistory frames and to low-rise shear walls systems. Compared with three-dimensional procedures, this approach does not entail the costly need to consider degrees of freedom of minor significance such as member torsion about its own axis (although this can be approximately accounted for quite easily in the present approach) and warping and transverse bending of columns and walls. Although that capability has not been explored

Table 1 Two-story framed structure: member properties

Member	FRAMES: I in m^4				
	1, 3	2		4, 5	
Columns	0.0036	0.0054	0.0004	0.0014	0.0004
Beams	0.0150	0.0500	0.0150[a]		0.0500[b]

$E = 2 \times 10^4$ kN/mm^2; [a]short span; [b]long span

Table 2 Analogous frame: member properties

Floor	COLUMNS: A_{af}^m in m^2; I_f^m in m^4		
	A_{af}^m		I_f^m
	1, 3	2	4 + 5
Upper	0.00314	0.00612	0.110
Lower	0.00342	0.00627	0.110

in this paper, the approach permits considering—albeit approximately—the effect of inplane floor flexibility (Rutenberg, 1980). This represents an advantage over some efficient 3-D computer procedures for multistory buildings, which usually ignore this effect.

The analysis can be performed by means of standard plane frame programs, and the internal forces in columns of framed structures can be computed manually. Moreover, the analogy should be particularly suitable for engineering offices with in-house computing facilities of limited capability, where reduction in the size of problems is an important consideration, and minor modifications in existing programs, to incorporate the early and final stages of the analysis, can easily be carried out. Because of its economy and simplicity of application, it can also become a useful research tool.

Table 3 Comparison of results: lateral displacements and shear forces

Floor	Analysis	Frames: displacements in mm			
		1	2	3	4, 5
Upper	S.F.	6.01	7.51	10.50	0.90
	A.F.	5.73	7.11	9.87	0.83
Lower	S.F.	3.53	4.33	5.90	0.48
	A.F.	3.77	4.65	6.43	0.53

S.F. = space frame; A.F. = analogous frame

REFERENCES/BIBLIOGRAPHY

Cheong-Siat-Moy, F., 1974
   CONTROL OF DEFLECTION IN UNBRACED STEEL FRAMES, (Proceedings of the Institution of Civil Engineers in London, December, 1974), Vol. 57, Part II, London, pp. 619-634.

Rutenberg, A., 1980
   LATERALLY LOADED FLEXIBLE DIAPHRAM BUILDINGS: PLANAR ANALOGY, Journal of the Structural Division, ASCE, Vol. 106, No. ST9, pp. 1969-1973.
Rutenberg, A., 1981
   A DIRECT P-DELTA ANALYSIS USING STANDARD PLANE FRAME COMPUTER PROGRAMS, Computers and Structures, Vol. 14, No. 1-2, pp. 97-102.

Shepherd, R. and Donald, R. A. D., 1967
   THE INFLUENCE OF IN-PLANE FLOOR FLEXIBILITY ON THE NORMAL MODE PROPERTIES OF BUILDINGS, Journal of Sound and Vibration, Vol. 5, No. 1, pp. 29-36.

Wilson, E. L. et al., 1975
   THE THREE DIMENSIONAL ANALYSIS OF BUILDING SYSTEMS (Extended Version), Earthquake Engineering Research Center, Report No. EERC 75-13, University of California, Berkeley, California.

Frames: forces in kN				Applied forces in kN
1	2	3	4, 5	
27.1	81.2	51.7	3.05	160
30.8	75.1	54.0	2.28	
66.8	142.1	111.1	3.75	160
64.4	145.8	109.8	3.93	

Simplified Method of Analysis of Frame-Wall Systems

Józef Sieczkowski
Mieczysław Lubiński
Ryszard Kowalczyk
Tadeusz Nejman

INTRODUCTION

A large class of multistory buildings, which includes offices, stores, factories and parking facilities, has plans similar to those shown in Fig. 1. They are characterized by large, undivided (or divided by nonstructural light partitions only) floor spaces with columns and a limited number of shear walls or cores.

The structural schemes of such buildings are combinations of plane frames and walls as shown in Fig. 2. There are a number of methods for the analysis of such structures, presented in the references at the end of this paper. Some of them are analysis-oriented while others are more approximate and practical.

The method of analysis presented below is simple and design-oriented. The authors have adopted a two-stage solution. In the first stage, the wall and the frame are treated separately. Their horizontal flexibilities are computed under the action of the applied load divided arbitrarily between them (Figs.

433

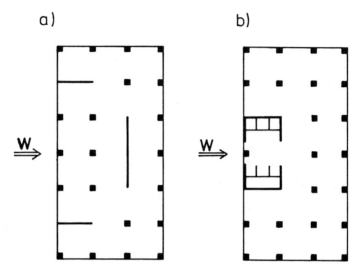

Fig. 1 Horizontal cross sections through buildings: (a) wall-frame, (b) core-frame

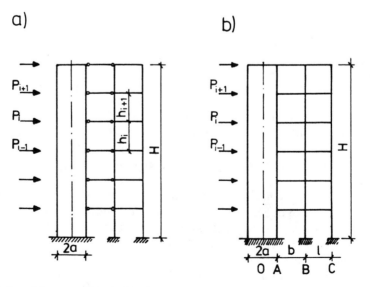

Fig. 2 A wall-frame structure: (a) pinned wall-frame connections, (b) rigid wall-frame connections

3 and 4). In the second stage, the two parts of the structure are joined by applying vectors of horizontal forces to both parts and imposing equal displacements. In the final situation, each part (that is, the frame or wall) is subjected to a vector of horizontal loads that is the sum of the external loads and the mutual reactions.

THEORETICAL MODEL

Horizontal Flexibility of the Wall

The horizontal displacements for the walls shown in Figs. 3 and 4 are obtained from the equation of the displaced axis

$$\frac{d^2 f^w}{dx^2} = \frac{1}{EI^w} \left[M(x) + \frac{EI^w}{F^w G} \alpha P(x) \right], \tag{1}$$

where

f^w = horizontal displacement of the wall;

EI^w = stiffness of the wall;

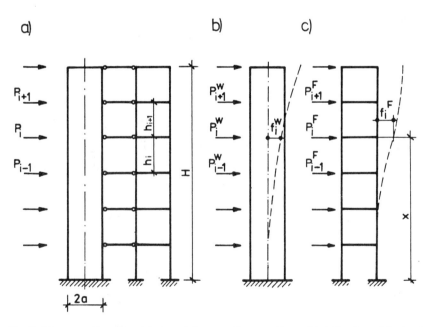

Fig. 3 A frame-wall system: (a) pinned frame-wall connections, (b) deflection of the wall, (c) deflection of the frame

F^w = area of cross section of the wall;

P = force at floor level;

α = shape factor;

G = shear modulus = $\dfrac{E}{2(1+\nu)}$; and

ν = Poisson's ratio.

For a vertical bar (Fig. 5) loaded by force P_k at the level x_k, displacements at the point i can be expressed, as follows: for $x_i \le x_k$

$$f_i^w = -\frac{P_k^w}{6EI^w} x_i^2 (3x_k - x_i) - 2(1+\nu)\alpha \frac{P_k^w}{F^w E} x_i \; ; \qquad (2a)$$

and for $x_i \ge x_k$,

$$f_i^w = -\frac{P_k^w}{6EI^w} x_k^2 (3x_i - x_k) - 2(1+\nu)\alpha \frac{P_k^w}{F^w E} x_k \; . \qquad (2b)$$

where f_i^w = horizontal displacement of the wall at level x_i.

Displacement f_i^w of the wall at the level i caused by a number of horizontal forces is the sum of the displacements caused by these forces acting separately. Thus from Eq. 2,

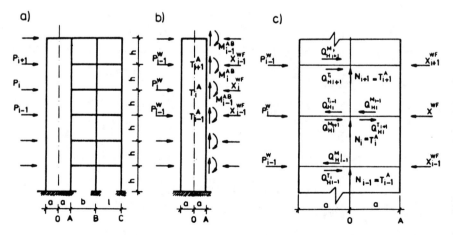

Fig. 4 A wall-frame structure: (a) rigid frame-wall connection, (b) forces acting on the wall, (c) equivalent system of forces in the wall

$$f_i^w = \frac{-1}{6EI^w} \left[\Sigma_{k=1}^{k=i-1} P_k^w x_k^2 (3x_i - x_k) + \Sigma_{k=i}^{k=n} P_k^w x_i^2 (3x_k - x_i) \right]$$

$$- \alpha \frac{2(1+\nu)}{F^w E} \left[\Sigma_{k=1}^{k=i-1} P_k^w \cdot x_k + \Sigma_{k=i}^{k=n} P_k^w x_i \cdot \right]$$

(3)

For structures of uniform floor height, for which $x_i = i \cdot h$ and $x_k = k \cdot h$, Eq. 3 can be rewritten as

$$f_i^w = \frac{-h^3}{6EI^w} \left[\Sigma_{k=1}^{k=i-1} P_k^w x k^2 (3_i - k) + \Sigma_{k=i}^{k=n} P_k^w i^2 (3k - i) \right]$$

$$- \alpha \frac{2(1+\nu)h}{F^w E} \left[\Sigma_{k=1}^{k=i-1} P_k^w \cdot k + \Sigma_{k=1}^{k=n} P_k^w \cdot i \right]$$

(3a)

The relation between the horizontal displacement of the wall axis and the horizontal loads applied can be expressed in matrix form as

$$[f^w] = [A^w] \times [P^w],$$

(4)

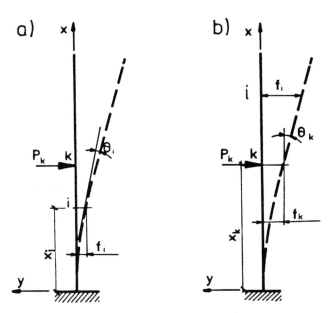

Fig. 5 Notations referring to the wall: (a) when the force acts above the relevant section, (b) when the force acts below this section

where $[A^w] = [\alpha_{ik}]$ is the flexibility matrix of the wall,

$$
\alpha_{ik} = - \begin{cases} \dfrac{h^3 i^2 (3k-i)}{6EI^{\,w}} + \alpha \dfrac{2(1+\nu)h_i}{F^w E} & \text{for } i \leq k \\[2em] \dfrac{h^3 k^2 (3i-k)}{6EI^{\,w}} + \alpha \dfrac{2(1+\nu)h_k}{F^w E} & \text{for } i > k \end{cases} , \tag{5}
$$

$$
[P^w] = \begin{bmatrix} P_1^{\,w} \\ \vdots \\ P_n^{\,w} \end{bmatrix}
$$

is the vector of horizontal forces acting on the wall, and

$$
[f^w] = \begin{bmatrix} f_1^{\,w} \\ \vdots \\ f_n^{\,w} \end{bmatrix}
$$

is the vector of horizontal displacements of the wall axis.

Horizontal Flexibility of the Frame

Horizontal displacements of the frame (Fig. 6) are computed using the equation for column cord rotation:

$$
E\psi_i^{F} = \frac{h_i \sum\limits_{k=1}^{n} P_k^{F}}{12 \sum\limits_{j=1}^{m} k_{ij}^{cF}} + \frac{\sum\limits_{j=1}^{m} k_{ij}^{cF}(\Theta_{ij} + \Theta_{i-1,j}) E}{2 \sum\limits_{j=1}^{m} k_{ij}^{cF}} \qquad \text{for } i \leq k \leq n, \tag{6}
$$

where: $k_{ij}^{cF} = I_j^{cF}/h_i$; I_j^{cF} is the moment of inertia of the jth column, m is the number of columns, and Θ_{ij} is the rotation of the $(i, j)^{\text{th}}$ beam-to-column connection. The magnitudes of the rotations were calculated assuming that the points of inflection of the beams were situated at mid-spans and those of columns at their mid-heights (with the exception of the bottom story, where they were assumed to be at the ⅔ points of the story height).

For a frame having several columns and equal story heights, (Fig. 6) the increment δ_{ik} of the horizontal deflection of the ith floor due to the horizontal load P_k at the floor k can be expressed as follows:

$$
\delta_{i,k}^{F} = \frac{P_k^{F} h^2}{12E} \left(\frac{h}{\Sigma I^{CF}} + \frac{\varsigma}{\Sigma I^{BF}} \right) \qquad \text{for } 1 < i < k
$$

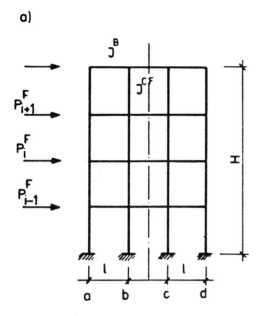

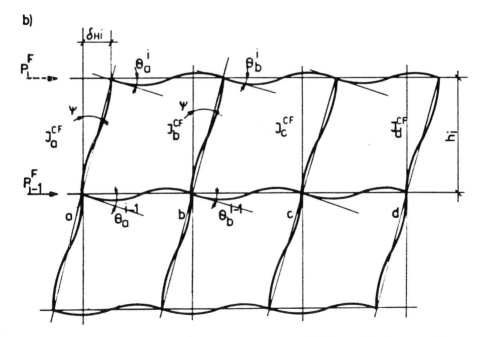

Fig. 6 Notations referring to the frame: (a) actual frame, (b) frame deflection under the action of axial forces

$$\delta^{\mathrm{F}}_{1,1} = \frac{P^{\mathrm{F}}_{1}h^{2}}{12E} \left(\frac{h}{\Sigma I^{\mathrm{CF}}} + \frac{\zeta}{6\Sigma I^{\mathrm{BF}}} \right) \qquad \text{for } i = k = 1$$

$$\delta^{\mathrm{F}}_{k,k} = \frac{P^{\mathrm{F}}_{k}h^{2}}{12E} \left(\frac{h}{\Sigma I^{\mathrm{CF}}} + \frac{3\zeta}{4\Sigma I^{\mathrm{BF}}} \right) \qquad \text{for } i = k > 1 \qquad (7)$$

$$\delta^{\mathrm{F}}_{i,k} = \frac{P^{\mathrm{F}}_{k} \cdot h^{2} \cdot \zeta}{24E \ \Sigma I^{\mathrm{BF}}} \qquad \text{for } i \geqq k + 1$$

$$\delta^{\mathrm{F}}_{1,k} = \frac{P^{\mathrm{F}}_{k} \cdot h^{2}}{12E} \left(\frac{h}{\Sigma I^{\mathrm{CF}}} + \frac{5}{12} \frac{\zeta}{\Sigma I^{\mathrm{BF}}} \right) \qquad \text{for } i = 1 < k$$

It was assumed that in the case of a force acting at the floor k, the horizontal displacements at higher floors are equal to the displacement of the $(k + 1)^{\mathrm{th}}$ floor. The total displacement of floor is obtained by the relevant summation of the increments. The relation between the horizontal displacements and the horizontal loads is expressed in matrix notation as

$$[f^{\mathrm{F}}] = [A^{\mathrm{F}}] \times [P^{\mathrm{F}}], \qquad (8)$$

where $[A^{\mathrm{F}}] = [\gamma_{j,k}]$ is the flexibility matrix of the frame and

$$\gamma_{jk} = \begin{cases} \delta_{1,1} & \text{for } j = k = 1 \\ \delta_{1,k} & \text{for } j = 1, k > 1 \\ \delta_{i,k} + \Sigma^{j}_{i=2}\delta_{i,k} & \text{for } k > 2, 1 < j < k \\ \delta_{1,k} + \Sigma^{j-1}_{i=2} \delta_{i,k} + \delta_{kk} & \text{for } j = k > 1 \\ \delta_{jk} = \gamma_{kj} & \text{for } j > k \end{cases} \qquad (9)$$

The flexibility matrix is assembled for unit forces.

THE SOLUTION OF THE WALL-FRAME SYSTEM

Solution for the Case of a Pinned Wall-Frame Connection

Frame and wall (Fig. 3) are subjected separately to external loading P^{W} and P^{F} and their resulting displacements are computed from Eqs. 4 and 8. To ensure the compatibility of displacements at each floor for the integrated system, both the frame and the wall are to be loaded by mutually opposed unknown reactions x^{WF}. The magnitude of these reactions can be calculated from the condition of equal displacements $f_i^w = f_i^F$, substituting the relations of Eqs. 3 to 9. Thus we obtain a set of linear equations in which the reactions x^{WF} are the unknowns:

$$
\begin{aligned}
[A^F] \times [P^F] + [A^F] \times [X^{WF}] &= [A^W] \times [P^W] - [A^W] \times [X^{WF}], \\
[A^F] \times [X^{WF}] + [A^W] \times [X^{WF}] &= [A^W] \times [P^W] - [A^F] \times [X^{WF}], \\
[A^F + A^W] \times [X^{WF}] &= [f^W] - [f^F].
\end{aligned}
\tag{10}
$$

The final loads acting on the frame and on the wall are the sum of the external loads and the reactions X^{WF}.

The horizontal displacement of the structure can be calculated either as the deflection of the frame or that of the wall:

$$
[A^F][X^{WF} + P^F] = f^F = f^W = [A^W] \times [P^W - X^{WF}].
\tag{11}
$$

Solution for Rigid Wall-Frame Connection

The difference between the case of pinned connections, discussed earlier, and the one discussed here is that in addition to the horizontal reactions, vertical shears as well as bending moments occur at the wall-frame connections (Fig. 4). In this system, the wall acts as a cantilever subjected to horizontal loads, vertical shears, and bending moments at the edge (or edges), all being the reactions in rigid wall-frame connection frame.

All these reactions are transferred to the wall axis and treated as pairs of forces acting on the relevant lever arms (Fig. 4c). The vertical shear has been shifted to the wall axis and a moment added:

$$
M_i^{Ti} = a T_i^A,
\tag{12}
$$

which in turn was replaced by pairs of horizontal forces Q_H^{Ti} of magnitude

$$
Q_{H,i+1}^{Ti} = Q_{H,i-1}^{Ti} = \frac{M_i^{T1}}{2h}
\tag{13}
$$

acting at $(i + 1)^{th}$ and $(i - 1)^{th}$ floor levels.

The bending moment in the rigid joint of the beams M_i^{AB} is replaced by a pair of horizontal forces:

$$
Q_{H,i+1}^{Mi} = Q_{H,i-1}^{Mi} = \frac{M_i^{AB}}{2h}.
\tag{14}
$$

Vertical force T_i^A, acting along the axis of the wall, will be neglected in further considerations, as it does not affect the magnitude of the horizontal displacement.

Shear forces T_i^{AB} and moments M_i^{AB} in the beams rigidly connected to the wall have been defined as functions of horizontal displacements.

Figure 7 illustrates the frame deformations resulting from the horizontal and vertical displacements of the wall as well as from its rotation.

The angle of rotation Θ_i^B and the moment M_i^{AB} can be expressed as functions of horizontal displacements:

$$\Theta_i^B = \frac{\dfrac{f_{i+1}-f_{i-1}}{h_i}\left[6k_c - k_B\left(1 + 3\dfrac{a}{b}\right)\right]}{12k_c + 10k_B} \quad , \tag{15}$$

$$M_i^{AB} = \frac{f_{i+1}-f_{i-1}}{h_i}2Ek_c\left[1 + \frac{3a}{2b} + \frac{6k_c - k_B\left(1 + 3\dfrac{a}{b}\right)}{12k_c + 10k_B}\right] . \tag{16}$$

The transverse force T_i^A acting tangentially on the wall is given by

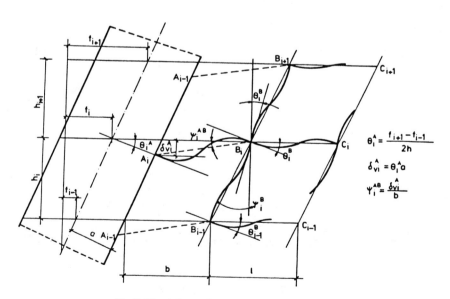

Fig. 7 The deformations of a wall-frame system

$$T_i^A = \frac{M_i^{AB} + M_i^{BA}}{b} = \frac{f_{i+1} - f_{i-1}}{h_i} \; 2E \frac{k_c}{b} \left[\frac{3}{2} + 3\frac{a}{b} + 3 \; \frac{6k_c - k_B(1 + 3\frac{a}{b})}{12k_c + 10k_B} \right] . \; (17)$$

The horizontal force X_i^W acting on the wall at the level i can be expressed as

$$X_i^W = P_i^W - X_i^{WF} - \left[(Q_{H,i}^{T_i+1} - Q_{H,i}^{T_i-1}) + (Q_{H,i}^{M_i+1} - Q_{H,i}^{M_i-1}) \right] , \qquad (18)$$

$$X_1^W = P_1^W - X_i^{WF} - Q_{Hi}^W(f). \qquad (18a)$$

Similarly, for the frame we have

$$X_1^F = P_i^F + X_i^{WF} + Q_{Hi}^F(f). \qquad (18b)$$

Using Eqs. 4 and 8 we can write

$$\begin{aligned} [A^W] \times [X^W] &= [f] \\ [A^F] \times [X^F] &= [f] \end{aligned} \qquad (19)$$

Since the displacements are equal, the set of equations (Eq. 19) must be fulfilled simultaneously for the frame and for the wall. Inserting Eqs. 18a and 18b into Eq. 19, we obtain

$$\begin{aligned} [A^W] \times [P^W] - [A^W][X^{WF}] - [A^W][Q_H^W(f)] &= [f] , \\ [A^F] \times [P^F] - [A^F][X^{WF}] + [A^F][Q_H^F(f)] &= [f] . \end{aligned} \qquad (20)$$

The unknowns are $[X^{WF}]$ and $[f]$.

In Eq. 20 we have the expressions

$$\begin{aligned} [A^W] \times [P^W] &= [f^W] \\ [A^F] \times [P^F] &= [f^F] \end{aligned} \qquad (a)$$

for the wall deflection due to $[P^W]$ and the frame deflection due to $[P^F]$ respectively.

The elements of the vector $[Q_H^W(f)]$ are functions of the unknown deflection f (e.g., the expression Q_{Hi}^W depends on the deflections f_{i-2}, f_i, f_{i+2}). In connection with this, the matrix $[A^W]$ cannot be multiplied by the vector $[Q_H^W(f)]$ because it contains unknown values. The multiplication $[A^W] \times [Q_H^W(f)]$ should be so transformed as to obtain the relation $[\eta^W] \times [f]$. This transformation cannot be carried out using matrix algebra but only by multiplying the given elements of the matrix $[A^W]$ by the relevant elements of the vector $[Q_H^W(f)]$. Subsequently these expressions should be grouped with the relation to the deflection f so as to obtain the relation $[\eta^W] \times [f]$ in which the matrix $[\eta^W]$ is the matrix $[A^W]$ suitably transformed. We deal in a similar manner with matrix $[A^F]$, which is transformed into matrix $[\eta^F]$.

As the result we obtain the expressions

$$[A^W] \times [Q_H^W(f)] = [\eta^W] \times [f],$$
$$[A^F] \times [Q_H^F(f)] = [\eta^F] \times [f]. \tag{b}$$

Substituting Eqs. (a) and (b) into Eq. 20, we obtain

$$[f^W] - [A^W] \times [X^{WF}] - [\eta^W] \times [f] = [f],$$
$$[f^F] + [A^F] \times [X^{WF}] + [\eta^F] \times [f] = [f]. \tag{20a}$$

Ordering the terms with respect to the unknowns $[X^{WF}]$ and $[f]$, we obtain

$$[A^W] \times [X^{WF}] + [\eta^W] \times [f] + [f] = [f^W],$$
$$-[A^F] \times [X^{WF}] - [\eta^F] \times [f] + [f] = [f^F]. \tag{20b}$$

Introducing the unit diagonal matrix

$$[\xi] = \begin{bmatrix} 1 & 0 & . & . & 0 & 0 \\ 0 & 1 & . & . & 0 & 0 \\ . & . & . & . & . & . \\ & & & & & \\ . & . & . & . & . & . \\ 0 & 0 & . & . & 1 & 0 \\ 0 & . & . & . & 0 & 1 \end{bmatrix}, \tag{c}$$

Equations 20b assume the form

$$[A^W] \times [X^{WF}] + [\eta^W] \times [f] + [\xi] \times [f] = [f^W],$$
$$[A^W] \times [X^{WF}] + [\eta^F] \times [f] + [\xi] \times [f] = [f^W]. \tag{20c}$$

Grouping the terms with respect to $[f]$, we obtain

$$[A^W] \times [X^{WF}] + ([\eta^W]+[\xi]) \times [f] = [f^W],$$
$$A^F \times X^{WF} + ([\eta^F]+[\xi]) \times [f] = [f^W]. \tag{20d}$$

Denoting

$$[\eta^W] + [\xi] = [\beta^W],$$
$$[\eta^F] + [\xi] = [\beta^F], \tag{d}$$

and introducing expressions (d) into Eqs. 20d, we obtain

$$[A^W] \times [X^{WF}] + [\beta^W] \times [f] = [f^W],$$
$$[A^F] \times [X^{WF}] + [\beta^F] \times [f] = [f^F]. \tag{20e}$$

As the Eq. 20e must be fulfilled for identical $[X^{WF}]$ and $[f]$, they can be written in the form

$$\begin{bmatrix} [A^W] & [\beta^W] \\ \hline [A^F] & [\beta^F] \end{bmatrix} \times \begin{bmatrix} [X^{WF}] \\ \hline [f] \end{bmatrix} = \begin{bmatrix} [f^W] \\ \hline [f^F] \end{bmatrix}, \tag{21}$$

or in short,

$$[AWF] \times \begin{bmatrix} [X^{WF}] \\ \hline [f] \end{bmatrix} = \begin{bmatrix} [f^W] \\ \hline [f^F] \end{bmatrix}. \tag{22}$$

Elements of the matrix $[AWF]$ are written

(a) Sub-matrix 1:

$AWF(i, j) = A^W(i, j)$ for $i = 1, \ldots, n, j = 1, \ldots, n,$

$AWF(i, n + k) = D(A^W(i, k + 2) - 2A^W(i, k))$ for $i = 1, \ldots, n, k = 1, 2$

$AWF(i, n + k) = D(A^W(i, k - 2) - 2A^W(i + k) + A^W(i, k + 2))$
$$\text{for}\quad i = 1, \ldots, n, k = 3, \ldots, n - 4,$$

$AWF(i, 2n - 3) = \bar{F}A^W(i, n - 1) - 2DA^W(i, n - 3) + DA^W(i, n - 5)$
$$\text{for}\quad i = 1, \ldots, n,$$

$AWF(i, 2n - 2) = \bar{F}A^W(i, n) - 2DA^W(i, n - 2) + DA^W(i, n - 4)$
$$\text{for}\quad i = 1, \ldots, n,$$

$AWF(i, 2n - 1) = -(F + \bar{F}) A^W(i, n - 1) - FA^W(i, n) + DA^W(i, n - 3)$
$$\text{for}\quad i = 1, \ldots, n,$$

$AWF(i, 2n) = FA^W(i, n - 1) + (F - \bar{F})A^W(i, n) + DA^W(i, n - 2)$
$$\text{for}\quad i = 1, \ldots, n,$$

(b) Sub-matrix 2:

$AWF(i + n, k) = A^F(i, k)$ for $i = 1, \ldots, n, k = 1, \ldots, n,$

$AWF(i + n, n + 1) = A^F(i, 1) F + A^F(i, 2)F(C - 1)$ for $i = 1, \ldots, n,$

$AWF(i + n, n + 2) = -A^F(i, 1)FC + A^F(i, 3)F(C - 1) + A^F(i, 2)F$
$$\text{for}\quad i = 1, \ldots, n,$$

$AWF(i + n, n + k) = A^F(i, k + 1)F(C - 1) + A^F(i, k)F - A^F(i, k - 1)FC$
$$\text{for}\quad k = 3, \ldots, n - 3, i = 1, \ldots, n,$$

$AWF(i + n, 2n - 2) = A^F(i, n - 1)F(C - 1) + A^F(i, n - 2)F - A^F(i, n - 3)FC$
$$+ A^F(i, n)FC \quad \text{for}\quad i = 1, \ldots, n,$$

$$AWF\,(i+n,\,2n-1)=A^{\mathrm{F}}(i,\,n-1)F-A^{\mathrm{F}}(i,\,n-2)FC+A^{\mathrm{F}}(i,\,n)F$$
$$\text{for}\quad i=1,\ldots,n,$$

$$AWF\,(i+n,\,2n)=-A^{\mathrm{F}}(i,\,n-1)FC+A^{\mathrm{F}}(i,\,n)F(1-C)\qquad\text{for}\quad i=1,\ldots,n,$$

The notation in the elements of the matrix can be found on Fig. 7:

$$F=\frac{Ek_b}{h^2}\left[2(2+\overline{C}+\frac{3a}{b})+\frac{6a}{b}(1+\overline{C}+\frac{2a}{b})\right],$$

$$\overline{F}=\frac{2Ek_b}{h^2}\left[\frac{a}{b}(\frac{3}{2}+3C+\frac{3a}{b})+(1+C+\frac{3a}{2b})\right],$$

$$D=\frac{Ek_b}{h^2}\left[\frac{a}{b}(1.5+\frac{3a}{b}+3C)+(1+\frac{3a}{2b}+C)\right],$$

$$C=\frac{6k_c-k_b\left(1+\dfrac{a}{b}\right)}{12k_c+10k_b},$$

$$\overline{C}=\frac{3k_c-k_b\left(1+\dfrac{3a}{b}\right)}{3k_c+5k_b}.$$

NUMERICAL EXAMPLES

Figure 8 shows a plane wall-frame structure, 15 stories high, with all the necessary dimensions. Other assumptions were that Young's modulus $E_c = 3 \times 10^7$ kPa$_2$ (4350 ksi), moment of inertia for the wall $I^{\mathrm{W}} = 1.07$ m^4 (124 ft^4), moments of inertia of frame columns $I^{\mathrm{CF}} = 0.00213$ m^4 (0.25 ft^4) and that for the beams, $I^{\mathrm{BF}} = 0.00137$ m^4 (0.16 ft^4). The calculations were made for the two cases 3.1 and 3.2 above, that is for pinned and rigid wall-frame connections.

The horizontal displacements of the wall-frame structure are shown in Fig. 9. The results were compared with those obtained by a standard computer program for frames, using the wide-column frame analogy. A good agreement was found by comparing the results obtained using both methods.

All computations were performed using EMC and utilizing a program written in FORTRAN for the suggested simplified method. The program is available in the Computation Center of Warsaw Technical University.

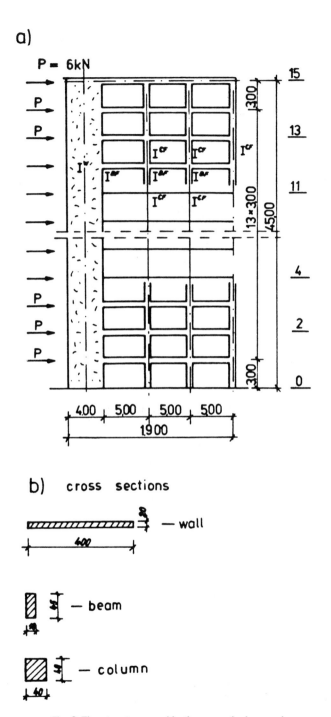

Fig. 8 The structure used in the numerical example

CONCLUSIONS

A comparative study of various methods of wall-frame structural analysis used in design practice has been carried out by Sieczkowski (1980). The method presented here allows for obtaining results accurate enough for structural design needs and for consideration of real geometrical parameters of structural elements (flat walls, angle walls) as well as their material characteristics.

The deflections of the frame wall system with pinned connections, computed using the suggested method, are approximately 8% smaller than the results obtained using the method of the wide-column-frame analogy. Similarly for the frame wall system with rigid connections, the results are 7% smaller.

The method presented allows for the solution of multistory structure design problems using small computers, because the number of unknown reactions between frame and wall is equal to the number of stories. Calculations performed on small computers with relatively small memories are considerably cheaper than those on large computers. Thus it proved economical to select a rational structural system by repeated analysis of multiple structural variants based on this method.

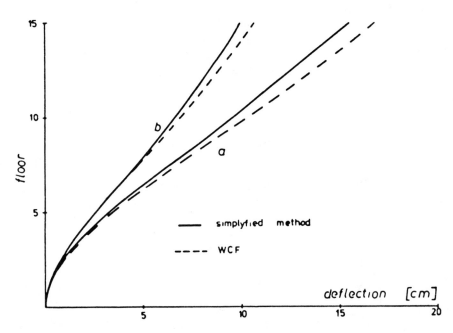

Fig. 9 Horizontal deflection diagrams: (a) for the case of pinned frame-wall connections, (b) for the case of rigid frame-wall connections

SUMMARY

This paper presents a simplified two-step method of analysis of horizontally loaded frame-wall systems. The mutual reactions between frame and wall have been selected as the unknowns. These unknowns are defined utilizing the compatibility condition of deflections of the frame and wall treated separately.

In the first step, the frame-wall system is treated as two independent systems consisting of the frame and the wall acting separately. Their flexibilities and horizontal displacements are calculated separately assuming arbitrary distribution of the horizontal load between the frame and the wall. In the second step, the cooperation of both structural systems is taken into account. The frame and wall are loaded by a set of equal and opposite forces that would make their displacements compatible.

Finally, each of these systems (frame and wall) is subjected to loading consisting of the external loading and the loading reactions between these two systems. For the computation of reactions between frame and wall, equations for each story can be written. Because of the comparatively small number of unknowns, small computers can be used for calculations. This has a significant importance for design of multistory structural systems.

REFERENCES/BIBLIOGRAPHY

Gould, P. L., 1965
    INTERACTION OF SHEAR WALL FRAME SYSTEMS IN MULTISTORY BUILDINGS, Journal ACI, Vol. 62.

Khan, F. R. and Sbarounis, J. A., 1964
    INTERACTION OF SHEAR WALLS AND FRAMES, Journal of the Structural Division, ASCE, Vol 90.
Kosicyn, B. A., 1971
    ANALYSIS OF LARGE PANEL AND FRAME BUILDINGS (Staticzeskij rascziot krupnopanielnych i karkasnych zdanij), JLS, Moscow.

MacLeod, I. A., 1970
    SHEAR WALL-FRAME INTERACTION, Portland Cement Association.

Parme, A. L., 1967
    DESIGN OF COMBINED FRAMES AND SHEAR WALLS. TALL BUILDINGS, Pergamon Press, Ltd., London.

Rosenblueth, E. and Holtz, I., 1960
    ELASTIC ANALYSIS OF SHEAR WALLS OF TALL BUILDINGS, ACI Journal, Vol. 56, No. 12.

Sieczkowski, J., 1976
    DESIGN OF CONCRETE TALL BUILDINGS (Projektowanie budynkow wysokich z betonu), Arkady Edition, Warszawa.

Sieczkowski, J., 1980
SELECTED DESIGN PROBLEMS OF TALL BUILDINGS IN CONCRETE (Wybrane zagadnienia ksztaltowania konstrukcji zelbetowych budynkow wysokich), Prace naukowe, Budownictwo zeszyt 61, W.P.W. Edition, Warsaw.
Stafford Smith, B., 1979
RECENT DEVELOPMENTS IN THE METHODS OF ANALYSIS FOR TALL BUILDINGS STRUCTURES, Civil Engineering and Works Review, Vol. 65.

Tezcan, S., 1967
ANALYSIS AND DESIGN OF SHEAR WALL STRUCTURES. Tall Buildings, Pergamon Press, Ltd., London.

Effect of Wall Stiffness and Height on Nonlinear Earthquake Response

K. E. Hodson
M. Saiidi

INTRODUCTION

It is generally known that shear walls are efficient means of providing stiffness and strength in structures subjected to severe lateral loads. The wall-frame interaction has been the subject of many experimental and analytical studies (Abrams and Sozen, 1979; Emori and Schnobrich, 1978; Fintel and Ghosh, 1979). A more recent experimental study was aimed at determining the influence of wall height on the response of frame wall buildings, through shake-table testings of three small-scale nine-story specimens (Moehle and Sozen, 1980). The wall in these specimens was discontinued at the first level in one structure, at the fourth level in another, and extended over the entire height in the third one.

The purpose of the study presented in this paper was to determine analytically the sensitivity of the overall displacement response of multistory buildings to changes in two parameters, the wall height and the elastic stiffness of the wall. The earthquake loadings used throughout the study were sufficiently strong to cause significant nonlinearity in the response.

STRUCTURES

Two groups of structures, five in each group, were used in the study. The structures were assumed to be similar to the test specimens used in Moehle and Sozen (1980) to make it possible to compare, at least qualitatively, the findings from this study with the observations made in the experimental research. Each structure was assumed to consist of two identical parallel three-span frames and a central shear wall built parallel to the frames. The frames consisted of columns with 51 mm depth and 38 mm width, and beams of 38 × 38 mm. The span length was 305 mm and height was 458 mm at the first story and 229 mm at others. The wall thickness in all structures was 38 mm, but wall height and depth varied for different structures as explained later in connection with an explanation of the longitudinal steel distribution. The shear reinforcement was assumed to be sufficiently large to avoid any shear failure.

The connection between the wall and the frames was assumed to be a hinged link with infinite axial stiffness resulting in equal displacement at each level of the wall and the frames, while preventing any transfer of moment between them. It was assumed that the mass at each level was 465 kg.

The material properties were assumed to be the same as the measured values for the test specimen with a nine-story wall (Moehle and Sozen, 1980). The concrete had a compressive strength of 34.5 MPa and a modulus of elasticity of 18,700 MPa. The yield stress of steel was 339 MPa in the wall and 399 MPa in beams and columns. The steel modulus of elasticity was 200,000 MPa.

The earthquake record used in the study was the acceleration measured during the shake-table testing of the structure with a nine-story wall (Moehle and Sozen, 1980). The time coordinate of the record was compressed by a factor of 2.5 to account for the small scale of the structures. As a result, the first 15 s of the earthquake were simulated in 6 s.

Structures with Different Wall Heights

Four structures with walls discontinued at level one, three, five, and seven, and one with a nine-story wall, were in this group. The wall width was 208 mm. Figure 1 shows a schematic view of these structures and their designations. Only one of the frames is shown in the figure. In FW9, the percent of base shear carried by the wall, based on gross section properties and triangular lateral loads with maximum at the roof, was 75% of the total base shear.

The amount and distribution of steel was assumed to be the same as those used in the experiment (Moehle and Sozen, 1980). The steel ratio was 0.88% in columns, 0.74% in beams, and the 0.9% in walls, with the ratios in beams and walls presenting the value based on steel area per face and the effective depth.

Stuctures with Different Wall Widths

Figure 2 presents the elevation view of the structures in this group. Only one of the frames is shown. The numeral in each structure's name indicates the wall width in millimeters. The width of the wall in UFFW was 208 mm. The percentage of lateral stiffness provided by the wall was 34 in UFW100, 59 in UFW150, 74 in UFFW, 82 in UFW250, and 87 in UFW300.

The provisions of the Uniform Building Code (UBC) were used to determine earthquake forces and arrive at a design that was reasonable (ICBO, 1979). Necessary modifications were made in the parameters used in UBC to account for the fact that the periods of the structures were approximately 40% of those of full-scale structures with similar configuration. It was assumed that the structures were built in zone four and had an occupancy importance factor of one. The resulting internal forces were used to design the reinforcement (Table 1).

Table 1 Reinforcement ratios (× 100) for structures with different wall widths

Element	UFW100	UFW150	UFFW	UFW250	UFW300
Beams	1.47	1.13	0.98	0.85	0.74
Columns	1.52	0.81	0.61	0.61	0.61
Walls	1.50	1.23	1.05	0.85	0.70

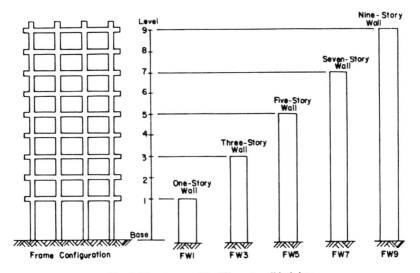

Fig. 1 Structures with different wall heights

RESPONSES

The Q-Model, a single-degree-of-freedom (SDOF) analytical model for inelastic seismic analysis of planar reinforced concrete structures, was used to determine the response histories (Saiidi and Sozen, 1981). According to the model, a multistory structure may be represented by an equivalent SDOF system with an equivalent mass mounted on a massless rigid bar which in turn is hinged to the base. The resistance against lateral displacement is provided by a nonlinear rotational spring. The properties of the equivalent SDOF systems are listed in Table 2.

Effect of Wall Height

Shown in Fig. 3 are the response histories of structures FW1-9 for a simulated El Centro, N-S, 1940 acceleration with a peak of 0.31 g. It can be seen that all the responses had the same general characteristics. No significant response was observed during the first second. Between $T = 1$ to $T = 2.5$ s large amplitudes were seen in all of the response histories. The response in the range of $T = 2.5$ and 5 s was small, but was moderate after $T = 5$ s. The effective periods were close for different curves.

To examine the effect of wall height on the maximum displacement and maximum story drift, the results for different structures were superimposed (Fig. 4). It can be seen that the maximum displacements for different structures were generally identical. Structure FW9 seems to show slightly larger

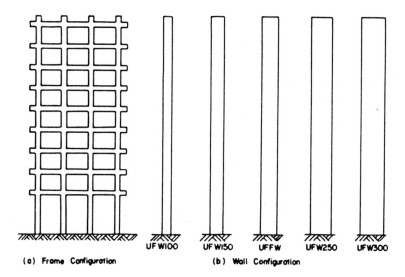

(a) Frame Configuration   (b) Wall Configuration

Fig. 2 Structures with different wall widths

Table 2 Q-model properties for different structures

Structure	Equivalent mass (kg)	Equivalent height (mm)	Yield mom. (KN-mm)	Yield disp. (KN-mm)	Post yield slope (KN-mm/mm)
FW1	3360	1643	15710	6.5	228
FW3	3260	1613	15710	6.1	182
FW5	3320	1609	16920	8.5	164
FW7	3220	1623	16920	7.2	174
FW9	3150	1620	18130	8.2	166
UFW100	3400	1544	21480	8.1	353
UFW150	3320	1594	21480	8.8	265
UFFW	3160	1632	22820	8.5	232
UFW250	3060	1664	22150	6.6	231
UFW300	3000	1678	22150	6.2	213

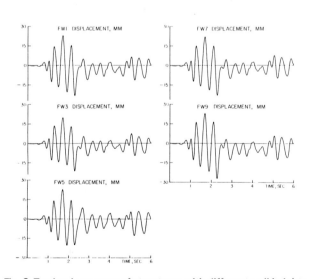

Fig. 3 Top-level response of structures with different wall heights

displacements at upper levels, but a closer inspection of the response history for FW9 (Fig. 3) indicates that this may be due to the slight shift in the response. Comparison of the maximum displacements of FW1 and FW9 shows a more uniform variation of displacements in FW9. The displacement for FW1 shows a kink at level 1 which is an indication of the abrupt change of stiffness due to the discontinued wall. Such a kink is not present in the maximum responses for FW3-7.

The drift (difference between the displacement at the adjacent floors) at the first story ranged from 2.3 mm (in FW1) to 5.2 mm (in FW9), with FW1 having the smallest drift. Structure FW1, however, experienced the largest drifts in the third and fourth stories. Among the five, structure FW3 had the most uniform distribution of drifts.

The above observations, although made for a limited number of structures and for a specific configuration, can have the following design implications. The fact that the apparent frequencies for different structures were close is an indication that the influence of shorter walls on the effective stiffness of the structures was marginal. The number of large-amplitude displacement cycles was the same in all structures. Because this number is generally representative of the number of yielding cycles experienced at critical joints, it can be concluded that detailing requirements for different structures were about the same.

Distribution of story drifts in different structures (Fig. 4) reveals that lateral deflections were controlled well, as long as the shear wall extended over approximately one-half the height of the structure. Clearly, this con-

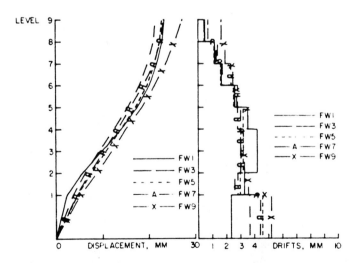

Fig. 4 Maximum response of structures with different wall heights

clusion may not be directly applicable to structures which are much shorter or taller (in terms of story numbers). What is clear, however, is that extension of the structural wall over the entire height of the structure may not be necessary.

Effect of Wall Width

Structures UFW100-300 were analyzed for the first 6 s (equivalent to 15 s in real time) of a simulated 1940 El Centro N-S record with a peak acceleration of 0.31 g. Comparison of the response histories (Fig. 5) does not show any significant variation in different curves. The only notable difference is in the number of low-amplitude cycles seen from $T = 3$ to $T = 5$ s. This difference, however, is not likely to be significant.

Figure 6 presents the maximum horizontal deflection and maximum story drifts in different structures. It is evident in the maximum deflections that structures UFW100 and UFW150 exhibited a "frame type" deflection in that the shape was bulged at lower levels. The other three structures showed about the same type of deflected shapes. The maximum deflection at levels 1

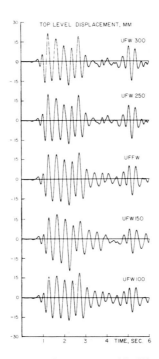

Fig. 5 Top-level response of structures with different wall widths

and 2 of these structures was approximately one-half the deflections in UFW100 and UFW150, while at the upper floors, the difference was relatively small.

The demand on maximum story drifts is an indication of joint deformations that the structure needs to accommodate without failure. By comparing the drifts for different structures, it is evident that the maximum drifts in UFFW, UFW250, and UFW300 were less critical and more uniformly distributed. Structures UFW100 and UFW150 showed smaller drifts at the upper levels and larger drifts at the lower parts.

The above observations suggest that the increse in the wall width from 203 mm (in UFFW) to 300 mm (in UFW300) did not have any pronounced effect on the response. Structures UFW100 and UFW150, in which the wall provided for 34 and 59% of stiffness respectively, experienced bulged deflected shapes resulting in relatively large story drifts at the lower levels. For these structures, it can be stated that demand on first floor joint rotation was greater (to accommodate the drift) and detailing of the joint was more critical. The problem is compounded by the significant yielding that typically occurs at the joints in lower levels of the structure; and inadequate detailing at these joints can have a more severe effect.

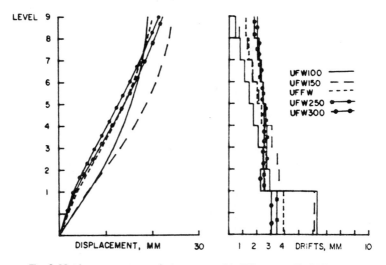

Fig. 6 Maximum response of structures with different wall widths

CONCLUSIONS

The results of the study on structures with different wall heights showed that from a structural performance viewpoint it is not necessary to extend the shear wall over the entire height of the structure. For the structures considered in this study, one-half the structural height appeared to give an optimal height (determined qualitatively). However, this conclusion is not necessarily general. A comprehensive study of several structures with different numbers of stories and different wall configurations needs to be carried out before a general quantitative recommendation about the wall height can be made.

The study on the response of structures with different wall stiffness showed that story drifts could not be controlled adequately with the use of relatively soft walls (in the study, walls that provided for about 60% or less of the lateral stiffness). Increase in the stiffness of the wall was found effective only to a certain extent. The wall that provided for 87% of the lateral stiffness appeared to control displacements to the same degree as that of the wall with 74% of total stiffness.

REFERENCES/BIBLIOGRAPHY

Abrams, D. P. and Sozen, M. A. 1979
EXPERIMENTAL STUDY OF FRAME-WALL INTERACTION IN REINFORCED CONCRETE STRUC-TURES SUBJECTED TO STRONG EARTHQUAKE MOTION, Civil Engineering Studies, Structural Research Series No. 460, University of Illinois, Urbana, Illinois.

Emori, K. and Schnobrich, W. C., 1978
ANALYSIS OF REINFORCED CONCRETE FRAME-WALL STRUCTURES FOR STRONG MOTION EARTHQUAKES, Civil Engineering Studies, Structural Research Series No. 457, University of Illinois, Urbana, Illinois.

Fintel, M. and Ghosh, S. K., 1979
DESIGN OF WALLED STRUCTURES FOR EARTHQUAKE LOADING, CSCE-ASCE-ACI-CEB International Symposium on Non-linear Design of Concrete Structures, University of Waterloo, August, pp. 441-466.

International Conference of Building Officials, 1979
UNIFORM BUILDING CODE, International Conference of Building Officials, Whittier, California.

Moehle, J. P. and Sozen, M. A., 1980
EXPERIMENTS TO STUDY EARTHQUAKE RESPONSE OF R/C STRUCTURES WITH STIFFNESS INTERRUPTIONS, Civil Engineering Studies, Structural Research Series No. 482, University of Illinois, Urbana, Illinois.

Saiidi, M. and Sozen, M. A., 1981
SIMPLE NONLINEAR SEISMIC ANALYSIS OF R/C STRUCTURES, Journal of the Structural Division, ASCE, Vol. 107, No. ST5, May, pp. 937-952.

Nonlinear Behavior and Analysis

Earthquake Resistance of Buildings Designed for Wind

Mark Fintel
S. K. Ghosh

The purpose of this investigation was to determine, through inelastic dynamic response history analysis, how much strength and/or inelastic deformability would be required in various structural members if a building proportioned for wind were to be subjected to earthquake input motions of varying intensities. It is shown that properly designed wind-resistant structures can be made to resist moderate earthquakes, if the beams are allowed to yield within the limit of acceptable damage, and if the columns and walls are strengthened somewhat to remain elastic throughout their seismic response. The additional strength required in columns and walls may be available at no extra cost, at least in the lower stories, because of the presence of gravity loads.

INTRODUCTION

In 1972 the National Science Foundation and the National Bureau of Standards initiated a cooperative program in Building Practice for Disaster

Mitigation. As a part of this program, in 1978, the Applied Technology Council (ATC), associated with the Structural Engineers Association of California, issued a state-of-the-art document entitled *Tentative Provisions for the Development of Seismic Regulations for Buildings* (referred to as ATC 3-06) (NBS, 1978). This document represents the cooperative effort of design professionals, researchers, Federal agency representatives, delegates from model code organizations, and representatives from state and local governments from throughout the United States. It is currently being reviewed by the building community under the direction of the Building Seismic Safety Council, in anticipation of its possible use as a resource document for model codes.

The ATC has chosen to represent the intensity of ground shaking at a site by two parameters: effective peak acceleration (EPA) for near earthquakes, and effective peak velocity (EPV) for distant earthquakes. The EPA and EPV are related to peak ground acceleration and peak ground velocity but are not necessarily the same as or even proportional to peak acceleraton and velocity. The EPA and EPV for a motion may be greater or smaller than the peak acceleration and velocity. Generally the EPA will be smaller than peak acceleration while the EPV will be larger than the peak velocity. The ATC report furnishes two detailed maps, one for EPA, another for EPV; each map divides the country into seven map areas. The EPA and EPV for each map area is given. The EPA ranges from 0.05 g for areas of lowest seismicity to 0.40 g for Map Area 7. The probability is estimated at 90% that the recommended EPA and EPV at a given location will not be exceeded during a 50-year period. For the purposes of discussion the EPA assigned to a map area can be considered roughly equal in magnitude to the peak ground acceleration likely to be experienced in that map area as a result of seismic events.

If and when the ATC provisions are adopted and incorporated into legal codes by the various jurisdictions around the country, some degree of seismic risk, however small, will have to be considered in the design of a structure located anywhere in the country. This will be a departure from current practice and may have significant economic repercussions. This investigation was prompted by a concern about these possible repercussions.

Table 1 shows the ATC earthquake intensities for the 40 largest metropolitan areas in the United States. More than 50% of the U. S. population lives in cities located in Map Area 1 or 2 with an effective peak acceleration of 0.05 g. Another 30% of the population lives in Map Area 3 with an effective peak acceleration of 0.10 g. Thus by far the largest volume of construction is in areas of relatively low seismicity. Structures in these areas are currently designed to resist wind; earthquake resistance is usually not considered. The purpose of this paper is to show that multistory building structures properly designed and proportioned to resist wind do possess a degree of earthquake resistance that is available at no extra cost. The performance of these structures, when subjected to moderate- to high-intensity earthquakes, is also investigated.

THE ANALYTICAL INVESTIGATION

A typical 22-story office building is first designed for gravity loads and wind. It is then subjected to inelastic dynamic response history analyses under various intensity levels of a carefully chosen earthquake input motion. In these analyses, the beams are permitted to go into the inelastic range, but the columns and the walls are kept elastic throughout their seismic response to ensure structural stability. The analyses lead to the determination of (a) the extent of inelasticity in the yielding members with increasing levels of earthquake intensity, and (b) the increase of the moments, shears, and axial forces in the elastically responding columns and walls with increasing intensities of input motion.

The Building

A specific hypothetical building configuration with a rectangular core and peripheral four-bay frames is considered (Fig. 1a). The slab system consists of one-way joists spanning between the core and the periphery and two-way waffle slabs of the same depth in the four corner bays. The 200-mm (8-in.) wide ribs of the joists and waffles are spaced 1.5 m (5 ft.) on centers.

Table 1 Seismicity of major metropolitan areas in the United States (1980)

EARTHQUAKE INTENSITIES 40 LARGEST METROPOLITAN AREAS (1980)			
56% U. S. population		30% U. S. population	14% U. S. population
Map area 1 $A = 0.05$ g	Map area 2 $A = 0.05$ g	Map area 3 $A = 0.10$ g	Map area 5 $A = 0.20$ g
Houston	Chicago	New York	Seattle
Miami	Detroit	Philadelphia	Memphis
Pittsburgh	Washington	Boston	
Minneapolis	Dallas/ Ft. Worth	St. Louis	Map Area 6
Milwaukee	Cleveland	Atlanta	$A = 0.30$ g
New Orleans	Baltimore	Phoenix	Sacramento
San Antonio	Cincinnati	Kansas City	
	Denver	Buffalo	Map Area 7
	Portland	Hartford	$A = 0.40$ g
	Indianapolis	Providence	Los Angeles
	Columbus	Albany	San Francisco
	Dayton	Honolulu	San Diego
	Louisville		
	Rochester		

The Lateral Load-Resisting System

In the E–W direction, the direction considered in this paper, the two I-segments of the core walls are coupled by beams at every floor level. The lateral load-resisting system in this direction consists of the coupled wall segments bending about their minor axes in interaction with the four-bay peripheral frames at the north and south faces of the building. The frames are connected with the core walls through the floor slabs.

Modeling for Static and Dynamic Analysis

Because of symmetry of the structural system, only half the building on either side of the E–W axis needs to be analyzed. Two structural walls, each as wide as the flange of an I-segment of the central core, and each with half the area and half the moment of inertia (about the minor axis) of an I-segment of the central core, are connected through links representing one of the two coupling beams at every floor level (Fig. 1b). These coupled walls are connected to one of the two four-bay peripheral frames on the north and south faces through flexible links at every floor level. These flexible links simulate the coupling through slabs, which transmit little bending.

The model of Fig. 1b is reduced by taking advantage of the symmetry of the frame itself. Two bays of the four-bay frame, with altered member properties for the central column stack, are connected through flexible links with a coupled wall system having half the properties of the central core in the more extended model (Fig. 1c). The static lateral loads on the reduced model should be half the corresponding loads computed for the extended model. The amounts of damping in the two models, and the dynamic excitations on them, are kept the same. The masses at every floor level of the reduced model are half the corresponding masses in the extended model.

Static Analysis for Code Wind Forces

In accordance with the Uniform Building Code, 1979 Edition, 1400–Pa (30-psf) map area wind forces are considered on the building in the E–W direction (ICBO, 1979). These wind forces are typical of the midwestern states, which include cities like Chicago, Indianapolis, Des Moines, Omaha, and Kansas City. An elastic static analysis of the lateral load resisting system under these wind forces is carried out. The resulting bending moments in the coupling beams and the spandrel beams are illustrated in Fig. 2. The strengths assigned to the beams for purposes of further analysis vary stepwise along the height of the building in accordance with standard design practice, rather than from floor to floor (Fig. 2).

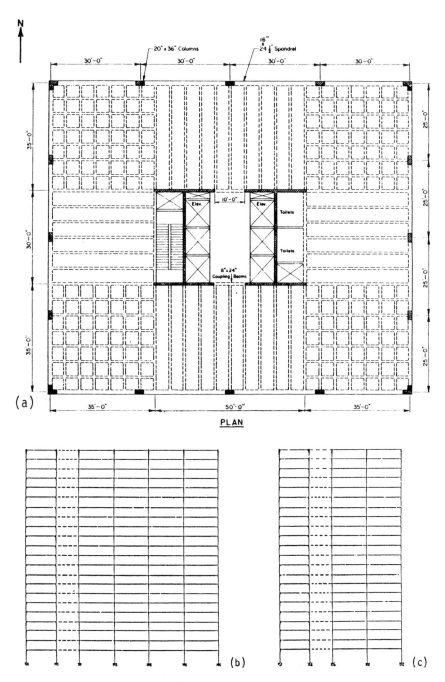

Fig. 1. Analytical model of building. Concrete strength: columns and walls, bottom 4 stories, 6 ksi; stories 5-8, 5 ksi; other columns, walls, and horizontal members, 4 ksi; specified yield strength of steel, 60 ksi

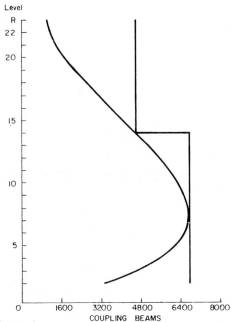

BENDING MOMENTS (in-kips)

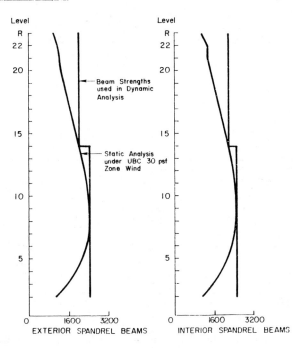

Fig. 2. Bending moments caused by factored wind forces in beams, moment capacities assigned to beams

Dynamic Analysis

Dynamic inelastic response history analysis, by the computer program DRAIN-2D, is used to determine the internal forces and inelastic deformations caused by earthquakes in the various structural members (Kanaan and Powell, 1975). DRAIN-2D accounts for inelastic effects by allowing the formation of concentrated "point-hinges" at the ends of elements where the moments equal or exceed the specified yeild moments. The moment vs. end rotation characteristics of elements are defined in terms of a basic bilinear relationship that develops into a hysteretic loop with unloading and reloading stiffnesses decreasing in loading cycles subsequent to yielding. The modified Takeda model is utilized in the program to represent the above characteristics (Takeda et al., 1970). Viscous damping in the form of a linear combination of mass-proportional and stiffness-proportional components is used. Five percent of critical damping in the fundamental and the second modes is assumed.

Definition of Ductility

The ductility discussed in this paper is based on rotations over the hinging regions of structural members. The hinging region is the length of a member over which the bending moments, while on a loading cycle, exceed the specified yield moments. Rotational ductility is defined as Θ_{max}/Θ_y where Θ_{max} is the maximum rotation, as the hinging region goes through many cycles of response, and Θ_y is the rotation corresponding to yielding. Yielding is defined as corresponding to the intersection between the initial elastic and post-yield branches of the moment-rotation diagram of the hinging region.

Input Motion

Preliminary analyses using five different input motions indicated that the 1940 El Centro E–W component is the critical input motion for the E–W direction of the structure.

Inelastic dynamic response history analyses under the chosen input motion, normalized to peak ground accelerations of 0.05 g, 0.10 g, 0.15 g, and 0.20 g, are carried out for the structure with indicated strength levels assigned to the beams, and with very high (virtually unlimited) strength levels assigned to the columns and walls. The results yield the elastic strength requirements for the columns and walls and the inelastic deformability requirements for the beams.

RESULTS OF ANALYSIS

The ductilities required in coupling beams and spandrel beams to resist earthquakes with peak ground accelerations of 0.05 g to 0.20 g are shown in Fig. 3. Hardly any ductility is required to resist a peak ground acceleration of 0.05 g. Structural response caused by an earthquake of the above magnitude is virtually elastic. The ductility requirements naturally increase with earthquake intensity. Test results indicate that the limit of available ductility may be set between 8 and 10 for slender, properly reinforced beams (span-to-depth ratio 4) (Wang et al., 1975; Ma et al., 1976). Short beams (span-to-depth ratio 2), which must be diagonally reinforced against shear failure, may have somewhat higher ductilities because of the special reinforcement (Paulay and Binney, 1974) It is thus possible for the structure under consideration to withstand a peak ground acceleration of 0.10 with little or no modification of the standard reinforcement details. A peak ground acceleration of 0.15 g requires ductilities that are at or just beyond the limit of availability. The above intensity can be withstood with minor upward adjustments in the beam strength levels, which would bring the ductilities back within available limits. A 0.20 g peak ground acceleration, however, appears to be beyond the capabilities of the wind-designed structure to withstand.

Figure 4a shows the horizontal displacements along the height of the building caused by earthquakes of varying intensity. Displacements caused by the 0.05 g earthquake are comparable to the elastic displacements caused by the factored wind forces. The displacements obviously increase with earthquake intensity, and generally explain the ductility requirements of Fig. 3.

Figure 4b shows the bending moments in the coupled wall piers caused by the earthquakes of increasing intensity. It is apparent that the 0.05 g earthquake does not require any strengthening of the walls beyond what is required by the factored wind forces. Higher earthquake intensities require progressively higher degrees of strengthening. It should be noted that, except in the top few stories, considerable excess moment capacity may be available in the walls and the columns because of minimum reinforcement requirements and because of the presence of compressive axial loads.

Figure 4c shows the axial forces in the coupled wall piers caused by earthquakes with peak ground accelerations from 0.05 g up to 0.20 g. The 0.05 g earthquake causes axial forces that are comparable to those caused by the factored wind loads. Larger earthquake intensities cause higher, but not significantly higher, axial forces.

CONCLUSIONS

Based on the limited study described it seems apparent that buildings designed to elastically resist factored wind forces that are typical of cities like

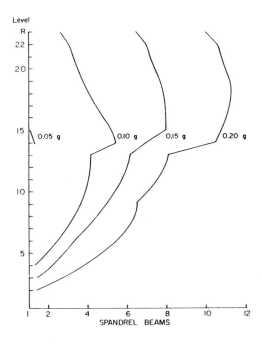

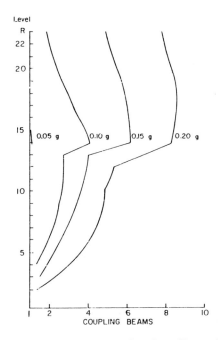

Fig. 3. Beam ductilities required by earthquakes of increasing intensity

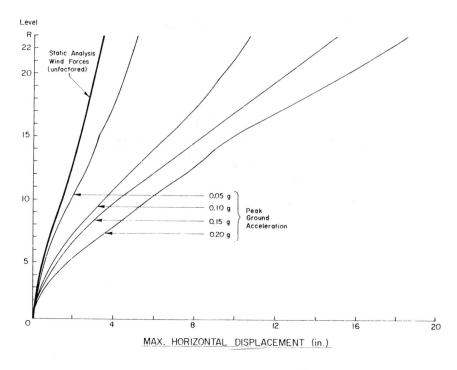

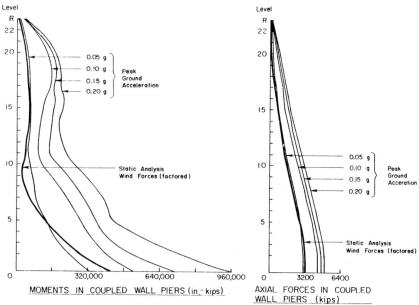

Fig. 4. Envelope values of various response quantities under earthquakes of increasing intensity

Chicago (according to the Uniform Building Code, 1979 edition) will also behave with only minimal inelasticity under an earthquake with a peak ground acceleration of 0.05 g (ICBO, 1979).

Increasing the earthquake intensity to 0.10 g causes the beams (designed for wind) to yield. The inelastic deformation capacity available in beams should be more than adequate to accommodate the extent of such yielding, provided that proper attention is paid in detailing to minimum reinforement requirements, web reinforcement, and anchorage. To prevent yeilding of the wind-designed columns and walls, their strength needs to be increased. However, the inherently available reserve moment capacity may be sufficient, except for the upper stories where the low axial forces result in a limited moment capacity.

The increase in column strength relative to the beams will assure that, during seismic response, the beams will yield before the columns and thus protect the columns against larger moments and an excessive build-up of axial forces, and will also limit the shear in the beam–column joints to that corresponding to the yield strength of the beam reinforcement. Therefore the difficult detailing requirements for ductile beam-to-column joints can be relieved. The columns need to be designed only for elastic behavior.

For acceleration levels of 0.15 g, the ductility demands in the beams are at the limit of, or just in excess of, the available ductilities. With minor upward adjustments in beam strengths, such ductility requirements can be lowered and the earthquake intensity level resisted without excessive damage or collapse.

For earthquake intensity levels approaching and exceeding a peak ground acceleraton of 0.20 g, the structure should be designed for a level of lateral forces substantially greater than that for wind.

It should be pointed out that precise limits on ductilities available in structural members can be established only in correlation with degrees of observed deformations, cracking, and damage in laboratory tests of such members. Much work still needs to be done in this area.

REFERENCES/BIBLIOGRAPHY

ICBO, 1979
    UNIFORM BUILDING CODE, International Conference of Building Officials, Whittier, California.

Kanaan, A. E. and Powell, G. H., 1975
    A GENERAL PURPOSE COMPUTER PROGRAM FOR INELASTIC DYNAMIC RESPONSE OF PLANE-STRUCTURES, Report No. EERC 73-22, University of California, Berkeley, California.

Ma, S. Y. M., Popov, E. P. and Bertero, V. V., 1976
    EXPERIMENTAL AND ANALYTICAL STUDIES ON THE HYSTERETIC BEHAVIOR OF REIN-FORCED CONCRETE RECTANGULAR AND T-BEAMS, Report No. EERC 76-2, University of California, Berkeley, California.

NBS, 1978
    TENTATIVE PROVISIONS FOR THE DEVELOPMENT OF SEISMIC REGULATIONS FOR BUILD-
    INGS, Special Publication No. 510, National Bureau of Standards, U.S. Government Printing
    Office, Washington, D.C.

Paulay, T. and Binney, J. R., 1974
    DIAGONALLY REINFORCED COUPLING BEAMS OF SHEAR WALLS, American Concrete Insti-
    tute, Publication SP-42, Shear in Reinforced Concrete, pp. 579-598.

Takeda, T., Sozen, M. A. and Nieslen, N. N., 1970
    REINFORCED CONCRETE RESPONSE TO SIMULATED EARTHQUAKE, Journal of the Structural
    Division, ASCE, Vol. 96, No. ST12, December, pp. 2557-2573.

Wang, T. Y., Bertero, V. V. and Popov, E. P., 1975
    HYSTERETIC BEHAVIOR OF REINFORCED CONCRETE FRAMED WALLS, Report No. EERC
    75-23, University of California, Berkeley, California.

Simplified Design of Slender Unbraced Columns

Albert J. Gouwens

INTRODUCTION

Current Code Procedures

The design of slender columns in unbraced frames is accomplished by applying a magnification factor to the moment or an amplification factor to the bending stress, as formulated in codes by the American Concrete Institute (ACI, 1977a) and the American Institute of Steel Construction (AISC, 1970) respectively. In the ACI code, the moment magnification factor δ is given by

$$\delta = -\frac{C_m}{1 - \dfrac{\Sigma P_u}{\phi \Sigma P_c}}, \tag{1}$$

where $C_m = 1.0$ for unbraced frames, P_u is the factored load on the column, P_c is the Euler buckling load on a column, and ϕ is the strength reduction factor. The summations are for all columns in the story.

The value of the critical buckling load P_c is determined by Euler's equation

473

$$P_c = \frac{\pi^2 EI}{(kl_u)^2},$$ (2)

where E is the modulus of elasticity, I is the moment of inertia of the column section, and l_u is the unbraced length of the column. The effective length factor k must account for the degree of restraint at the two ends of the column. Determination of k is conventionally achieved by use of alignment charts (CRC, 1966).

Due to the summation of Eq. 1, the value of P_c and thus of k must be determined for every column in the story.

In the AISC (1970) specification, the bending stress amplification factor is given as

$$\delta = \frac{C_m}{1 - \frac{f_a}{F_e'}},$$ (3)

where $C_m = 0.85$ for unbraced frames, f_a is the service load stress on the column, and F_e' is the Euler buckling stress on the column.

A simplified method of calculating the moment magnification factor δ is presented in this article. It is derived in terms of factored design loads as in Eq. 1. (Commonly used load factors are given in the ACI Code.) This method can also be applied to design procedures that are formulated in terms of allowable stresses.

Alternate Procedures

Computer programs have been developed that calculate the magnified lateral load moments by either a direct P-Delta method, as done by Gouwens (1968), or by an iterative P-Delta method, as done by Wood et al. (1976). Another form of the magnification factor is given as

$$\delta = \frac{1}{1 - \frac{\Sigma P_u \Delta_0}{\phi H_u l_u}}.$$ (4)

This equation is easily derived using the equations of Parme (1965). Substitution of his Eq. 25b into his Eq. 27 gives our Eq. 4 above. This gives nearly the same results as the computerized P-Delta techniques. One advantage of Eq. 4 is that it can be easily implemented using hand calculations.

The main advantage of Eq. 4 is that it can be used as the basis of definitions for braced frames as well as for frame instability. These are presented in the following sections. The definition for braced frames is extended to a design procedure.

A comparison of Eq. 4 with Eq. 1 shows that the value of the story's total critical buckling load may be given as

$$\Sigma P_c = H_u l_u / \Delta_0. \tag{5}$$

The physical interpretation of Eq. 5 is that the story's total critical buckling load ΣP_c is equal to the lateral stiffness of the story H_u / Δ_0 multiplied by the unbraced story height l_u.

The magnification factor, as given in Eq. 4, is equally applicable to design of steel structures using the allowable stresses, where f_a is substituted for $\Sigma P_u / \phi$ and the service lateral load is substituted for H_u. The elastic initial tangent stiffnesses should not be used in conjunction with allowable stress design; it may lead to unsafe designs. Even though the allowable stress method is used, the stiffnesses used to calculate Δ_0 must be consistent with the magnified factored load and its associated deflection.

SIMPLIFIED METHOD ADVANTAGES

Application of Eq. 4 is simpler than application of Eq. 1 because it is not necessary to calculate the Euler buckling load of all the columns in a story and the effective column length k for every column. Equation 4 uses the results of the routinely performed first-order analysis to determine the lateral stiffness of a story. Any method such as the portal method, the moment distribution method, or a general frame analysis computer program can be used to perform the first-order analysis.

A comparison of Eq. 4 and Eq. 1 with a second-order analysis computer program results for two structures are given at the end of this article. It is seen that the Eq. 4 results agree much more closely with the computer solution than do the Eqs. 1 and 2 results. For heavily loaded structures, Eqs. 1 and 2 become overly conservative and may even fail to give answers because of false indications that P is greater than P_{cr}.

UNBRACED OR BRACED?

A frequently recurring question is, "When can a column be considered a braced column?" From an absolutely theoretical point of view, the answer is that there is no such thing as a braced column. Equation 4 indicates that any structure with an applied horizontal load H_u and even a very small value of Δ_0 will have a magnification factor greater than one. The column can, therefore, never be braced in an absolute sense.

From a practical design point of view, it is reasonable to allow a preselected small amount of moment magnification or overstress. A practical definition of a braced column is one in which the moment magnification, or overstress, does not exceed the preselected small value δ_m. The maximum permissible magnified moment is denoted as the primary moment multiplied by δ_m.

DEFINITION OF A BRACED FRAME

In a braced frame, δ (given by Eq. 4) is equal to or less than δ_m. Rearrangement of terms gives

$$\frac{\delta_m}{\delta_m - 1} \frac{\Sigma P_u \Delta_0}{\phi H_u l_u} \leq 1. \tag{6}$$

This equation provides a simple, unified mathematical expression as a criterion to determine whether frames are braced. Equation 6 indicates that lightly loaded structures (small ΣP_u) or laterally stiff structures (large H_u/Δ_0) have small values of moment magnification that are necessary to achieve a braced frame in which P-Delta effects may be neglected.

Equation 6 could be further simplified by defining the maximum service load drift index $\Delta_0/l_u = 1/1000R$. The deflection at service loads is assumed to be $\Delta_0/(0.75 \times 1.7)$, where the design load factor for wind is 0.75×1.7. Assuming $\phi = 0.7$, the value of $\phi l_u/\Delta_0$ is $1000R \times 0.7/(0.75 \times 1.7) = 549R$; and Eq. 6 can be simplified to

$$\frac{\Sigma P_u}{H_u} \leq 549 \frac{\delta_m - 1}{\delta_m} R. \tag{7}$$

Equation 7 states simply that, if the ratio of the vertical to the lateral load is equal to or less than the numeric value of the expression on the right, the frame is braced. This equation is useful in making a preliminary judgment of the importance of slenderness effects in frames. When the allowable lateral displacement of a structure is more than $h/1000$, a value of R less than 1.0 should be used. When the vertical-to-lateral load ratio is known, Eq. 7 can be used to determine the maximum deflection for a braced frame.

WHICH COLUMNS ARE BRACED?

Application of Eqs. 6 and 7 to define a braced frame does not permit distinction among the individual columns which constitute the story. H_u is the total, externally applied, horizontal factored load; and ΣP_u is the total, vertical factored load in a story. Using criteria given by Eqs. 6 and 7, the story as a whole is either braced or unbraced. Not only are the flexible columns laterally supported by the stiffer columns, but when the criterion given by Eq. 6 or 7 is satisfied, the stiffer columns, even including shear walls that may occur in the story, are also laterally braced. Although this may seem illogical at first, it becomes reasonable when viewed in light of the underlying criterion used to define a braced condition. The criterion is that the magnification factor will not exceed a preselected small value δ_m and that the moments in all columns in the story, whether flexible or stiff, are magnified by a constant value of δ as given in Eq. 1. Parme (1965) shows that for a two-column rigid bent, moment magnification is nearly constant for both columns, even though their stiffnesses and load distribution vary greatly. The assumption that the magnification factor is constant for all columns is also substantiated in the section on calculations (see final section of this article) for a multistory frame with various lateral load and stiffness distributions.

C_m FOR UNBRACED FRAMES

In frames subject to sidesway, AISC Specification (1970) allows $C_m = 0.85$. The commentary gives a value of C_m as a function of axial stress as $C_m = 1 - 0.18 f_a/F'_e$. In frames subject to sidesway, ACI (1977a) specifies that $C_m = 1.0$. Neither code addresses itself to the variation of C_m as a function of the ratio of column stiffness to beam stiffness. The moment magnification factor has been shown by Parme (1965) to vary with the ratio of column stiffness to beam stiffness. C_m can be calculated using Table 3 of Parme (1965) as the table values divided by $(1 - P_u/P_c)$. Several values of C_m were calculated and are compared to the ACI (1977a) and AISC (1970) values in Table 1.

A comparison of Lines 2 and 3 in Table 1 indicate that the AISC values of C_m are based on ratios of column stiffness to beam stiffness equal to zero. A comparison of Lines 4 and 5 in Table 1 indicate that the ACI values of C_m are based on ratios of column stiffness to beam stiffness equal to infinity. Use of

Table 1 C_m values

Line	Author	f_a/F'_e or P_u/P_c			Ratio of column stiffness to beam stiffness
		0.10	0.50	0.90	
	(1)	(2)	(3)	(4)	(5)
1	AISC specification	0.85	0.85	0.85	Not specified
2	AISC commentary	0.98	0.91	0.84	Not specified
3	Parme (1965)	0.98	0.91	0.83	Zero
4	Parme (1965)	1.00	1.01	1.03	Infinity
5	ACI (1977a)	1.00	1.00	1.00	Not specified

the C_m values from Table 1, Lines 1 and 2, in structures with a large ratio of column stiffness to beam stiffness, can result in an overstress ratio from $1.00/0.85 = 1.18$ to as large as $1.03/0.84 = 1.23$. Use of the ACI values of C_m can result in a 3% overstress for stiff columns but are conservative for more flexible columns.

CHOICE OF δ_m

Selection of the maximum value of $\delta = \delta_m$ for which a frame is defined as a braced frame has not yet been established. Some considerations are given in the following section, but the final choice of a value of δ_m is left to the judgment of the engineer.

δ_m Based on Intuitive Reaction

Most engineers would agree that it is reasonable to allow in Eq. 6 at least a 5% moment magnification factor as the upper limit in determining the braced frame criteria. Using $\delta_m = 1.05$ in Eqs. 6 and 7, we obtain

$$\frac{21 \Sigma P_u \Delta_0}{\phi H_u l_u} \leq 1 \tag{8}$$

and

$$\frac{\Sigma P_u}{H_u} \leq 26.1R. \tag{9}$$

It may be that a larger value of δ_m could be justified on the basis of research or experience.

δ_m Based on Lehigh University Studies

Studies at Lehigh University (Okten et al., 1973) resulted in recommendations being given by AISC that provide that the column slenderness P-Delta effects do not need to be accounted for if (1) k is assumed to be unity in the calculation of F_a and F'_e; (2) the maximum column axial load ratio f_a/F_a does not exceed 0.75; (3) the maximum in-plane column slenderness ratio l_u/r does not exceed 35; and (4) the bare frame working load drift index does not exceed 0.004. Criterion 4 is unnecessary since it can be shown that by using the first three criteria, the maximum corresponding value of δ_m can be calculated.

Assuming $F_y = 36$ ksi (250 MPa) and $kl_u/r = 35$, it is found that $F_a = 19.58$ ksi (135 MPa).

By criterion 2, $f_a = 0.75 \times 19.58 = 14.68$ ksi (101 MPa). When $kl_u/r = 35$, as limited by criteria 1 and 3, $F_e' = 121.90$ ksi (840 MPa). The value of δ_m is then calculated as $1/(1 - f_a/F_e') = 1/(1 - 14.68/121.90) = 1.137$. This value of δ_m is determined without the use of criterion 4, limiting the drift index to 0.004. Using $\delta_m = 1.137$ in Eqs. 6 and 7, we obtain

$$\frac{8.3 \Sigma P_u \Delta_0}{\phi H_u l_u} \leq 1 \tag{10}$$

and

$$\frac{\Sigma P_u}{H_u} \leq 66.2R. \tag{11}$$

δ_m Based on Current Code Provisions

In a previous section, it was shown that values of $C_m = 0.85$ may have been used in frames with large ratios of column to beam stiffness resulting in overstress ratios of 1.18 or greater. If structures have performed satisfactorily with this magnitude of overstress, a value of $\delta_m = 1.18$ could be justified. Using $\delta_m = 1.18$ in Eqs. 6 and 7, we obtain

$$\frac{6.67 \Sigma P_u \Delta_0}{\phi H_u l_u} \leq 1 \tag{12}$$

and

$$\frac{\Sigma P_u}{H_u} \leq 83.7R. \tag{13}$$

It is not the writer's intention to recommend a limit on δ_m, but rather to enumerate the possible range and to encourage debate that will result in an acceptable consensus.

The proposed method of this article was reviewed by the Technical Activities Committee of the Chicago Chapter of the ACI. In correspondence to the Chairman of ACI Committee 318, they recommended values close to those given in Eqs. 12 and 13 (ACI, 1977b). In Eq. 12 the value 6.67 was rounded to 7. In Eq. 13 using $R = 0.4$, the value of $\Sigma P_u/H_u$ was rounded to 30.

DEFINITION OF LATERAL STABILITY

Theoretical instability occurs as $\Sigma P_u/\phi$ approaches the value of $H_u l_u/\Delta_0$. For practical considerations, as $\Sigma P_u \Delta_0/\phi H_u l_u$ has values approaching 1.0, the structure becomes very sensitive to small increases in load or deflection that may cause instability. The theoretical definition of instability gives minimal design guidance. A practical design definition of stability can be established using engineering judgment in a manner similar to the practical definition of braced frame criteria.

Neither the ACI Building Code (1977a) nor the AISC Manual (1970) contain any upper limit on the value of δ in Eqs. 1 or 3. For large values of $\Sigma P_u/\phi \Sigma P_c$ in Eq. 1, a small error in ΣP_u can cause a much larger error in δ. For example, if $C_m = 1$ and $\Sigma P_u/\Sigma P_c = 0.80$, the resulting $\delta = 5.00$. A 5% increase in $\Sigma P_u/\phi \Sigma P_c$ to a value of 0.84 results in $\delta = 6.25$, which is a 25% increase in δ. The resulting overall factor of safety would be reduced from 1.7 $\times$ 0.75/0.7 = 1.82 to 1.82/1.25 = 1.46. The assumed 5% error could be produced by changes in vertical load, lateral load, modulus of elasticity, or stiffness of the columns. It is the writer's opinion that since a 5% error in these variables is quite common, values of δ in excess of 5.00 should not be used in design. A practical design definition of instability is that δ is greater than 5.00. Such structures should be provided with additional lateral stiffness.

Figure 1 shows the relationship between axial load and the moment magnification factor as given by Eq. 1. The practical design definitions of braced frames and stable frames are also shown in the figure.

DESIGN PROCEDURES

Design of Braced Frames

Equations 6 and 7 can be used to design frames so that they can be considered braced frames. The procedure outlined below has as its objective the determination of member sizes in the frame such that the magnification factor for lateral loads δ is less than δ_m. The procedure for each story is:

1. Select a value of δ_m.

2. Calculate the vertical factored load acting above the story under consideration.

3. Calculate the lateral factored load acting above the story under consideration.

4. If the inequality of Eq. 7 is satisfied, design the members that resist lateral loads so that they limit the service load sidesway to $l_u/1000R$.

5. If the inequality of Eq. 7 is not satisfied, determine a value of Δ_0 in Eq. 6 that would satisfy the inequality, and design the members that resist lateral loads so that they limit the service load sidesway to $\Delta_0/(0.75 \times 1.7)$.

Design of Unbraced Frames

Equation 4 can be used to determine the magnified sidesway moments. The procedures given below are for a general frame problem wherein the column is slender when considered as a braced column as well as an unbraced column. In many structures, the effects of out-of-plumb erection and sidesway due to gravity are negligible, and the corresponding steps in the procedure can be eliminated. The procedure for each story is as follows.

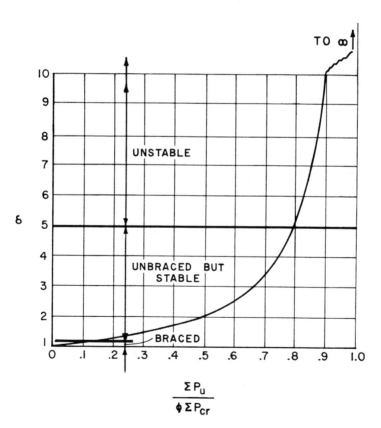

Fig. 1 Axial load vs. moment magnification factor

1. Calculate the vertical factored load acting above each column and its summation for all the columns in the story.

2. Calculate the lateral factored load acting above the story under consideration.

3. Calculate moments due to factored lateral loads and the corresponding deflection Δ_0.

4. Calculate the lateral magnification factor δ using Eq. 4.

DESIGN EXAMPLES

Example 1A: Braced One-Story Building

Problem: The structure shown in Fig. 2 has been designed for gravity loads. The loads shown are factored design loads. Determine whether the frame is braced or unbraced for a maximum service load drift of $l_u/400$, that is, $R = 0.4$.

Solution: Calculations are as follows.

$$\Sigma P_u/\phi = 1500 \times 70/0.7 = \frac{105,000}{0.7} \text{ lbs}$$

$$= 150,000 \text{ lbs}$$

$$l_u = 15 \text{ ft}$$

$$H_u = 4000 \text{ lbs}$$

$$\frac{\Sigma P_u}{H_u} = \frac{105,000}{4,000} = 26.25$$

Since $\Sigma P_u/H_u$ is less than $83.7 \times 0.4 = 33.5$, Eq. 13 indicates that the frame is braced and that sidesway moment magnification does not have to be considered. The use of Eq. 13 implies that lateral bracing must be designed to limit $\Delta_0/l_u = 0.75 \times 1.7/400 = .00319$.

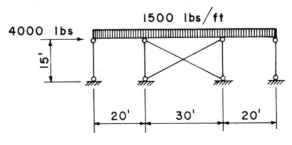

Fig. 2 Braced one-story building

Example 1B: A Braced One-Story Building

Problem: Use the same structure as in Part A of the example but reduce the lateral load H_u to 3000 lbs. Determine the area of the cross-bracing required to make this a braced frame.

Solution: Calculate the ratio $\Sigma P_u/H_u = 105{,}000/3{,}000 = 35$. On the basis of Eq. 13, the frame is unbraced. Eq. 13 is sometimes conservative, and the more rigorous Eq. 12 yields a value of the deflection index Δ_0/l_u that will produce a braced frame,

$$\frac{\Delta_0}{l_u} = \frac{\phi H_u}{6.67 \Sigma P_u} = \frac{0.7 \times 3000}{6.67 \times 105{,}000} = .003.$$

For the frame shown in Fig. 2, if the frame's joint rigidity is ignored and the cross-bracing alone is assumed to provide lateral bracing, the maximum value of primary deflection is $\Delta_0 = 0.003 \times 15 \times 12 = 0.54$ in. The corresponding cross-brace elongation is $0.54 \times 2 \sqrt{5} = 0.48$ in.

The cross-brace force is $3000 \times \sqrt{5}/2 = 3354$ lbs.

The cross-brace length is $30 \times 12 \times \sqrt{5}/2 = 402.5$ in.

The required cross-brace area is thus $3354 \times 402.5/(0.48 \times 29{,}000{,}000) = 0.097$ in². In practice, the cross-bracing would be installed in only one of several bents. If, for example, six bents were restrained by one set of cross-bracing, the required area would be $6 \times 0.097 = 0.58$ in².

Example 2: A Braced Frame Without Cross-braces

Problem: Use the same structure shown in Fig. 2 except that no cross-bracing will be provided, and the load $H_u = 3000$ lbs. Assume that the columns have fixed bases and are designed as cast-in-place concrete having a modulus of elasticity $E_c = 5{,}000{,}000$ psi. Determine the column size that will make this a braced frame.

Solution: For columns fixed at their base and hinged at their top, the maximum calculated permissible deflection is limited by Eq. 12 to

$$\Delta_0 = \frac{H_u l_u^3}{3E(\Sigma I)} \le 0.003 l_u.$$

The minimum total column stiffness that will produce a braced frame condition is thus

$$\Sigma I \ge \frac{H_u l_u^2}{3 \times 0.003 \times E} = \frac{3000 \, (15 \times 12)^2}{3 \times 0.003 \times 5{,}000{,}000} = 2160 \text{ in.}^4$$

Assuming the column's cracked section stiffness is 40% of the gross section stiffness, the minimum required stiffness can be provided by four 10×12 columns oriented for strong axis bending (ACI, 1977a). Alternatively, the stiffness can be provided by a single cantilevered 12×18 column oriented the strong way, with the three remaining columns pinned at both ends.

Example 3: A Five Story Rigid Jointed Braced Frame

Problem: For the five-story building shown in Fig. 3, it is desired to determine the member stiffnesses required such that the frame may be considered a braced frame. The bent spacing is assumed to be 20 ft. The factored loads shown approximately correspond to a wind load of 20 psf, a roof load of 30 psf, a floor load of 100 psf, and an 8-in. concrete slab of 100 psf. The modulus of elasticity of concrete is 4,000,000 psf. The maximum service load drift is 1/400 ($R = 0.4$).

Solution: On the basis of Eq. 13 alone, it appears by inspection of Column 6 in Table 2 that consideration of slenderness effects is unavoidable. An investigation using Eq. 12, however, allows the calculation of the minimum permissible story-to-story deflection as shown in Column 7 of Table 2, which, if it is not exceeded, allows the structure to be considered a braced frame. Using a preliminary assumption that the points of inflection lie at the mid-height of columns and the mid-span of beams, the values of the required column stiffnesses can be calculated.

Figure 4 shows the free body force diagram of an interior column and the calculation of the deflection assuming $E_b = 0.75E_c$ and $I_b = 0.20I_c$. The required column stiffness I_c given in Table 3, Column 3 is calculated by solving for I_c in Fig. 4c. Assuming that the stiffness of the column which accounts for yielding and cracking is 40% of the gross stiffness of the column (ACI, 1977a) the column size is calculated in Table 3, Column 4.

Table 2 Load tabulation

Story (1)	P_u (kips) (2)	ΣP_u (kips) (3)	Lateral load (kips) (4)	H_u (kips) (5)	$\dfrac{\Sigma P_u}{H_u}$ (6)	$\dfrac{\phi H_u l_u}{6.67 \Sigma P_u} = \Delta_0$ (7)
5	180	180	3	3	60.0	0.252
4	280	460	6	9	51.1	0.296
3	280	740	6	15	49.3	0.307
2	280	1020	6	21	48.6	0.311
1	280	1300	6	27	48.1	0.314

Note: 1 kip = 4.45 kN

Table 3, Column 5 shows the column size of a typical interior column based on 1% reinforcement and an average stress at minimum eccentricity of 2500 psi. A comparison of Columns 4 and 5 in Table 3 indicates that, for this structure, a small increase in the column size required for vertical load alone produces a structure that may be considered as laterally braced.

Table 3 Column size determination

Floor (1)	H_u/Δ_0 lbs/in. (2)	I_c in.^{4} (3)	Interior column size having stiffness I_c (in. × in.) (4)	Column size determined for (in. × in.) (5)
5	11,905	1728	12 × 16.3	12 × 6
4	30,405	4414	12 × 22.3	12 × 15
3	48,860	7094	12 × 26.1	12 × 24.1
2	67,524	9804	20 × 24.5	20 × 20.4
1	85,987	12484	20 × 26.6	20 × 26

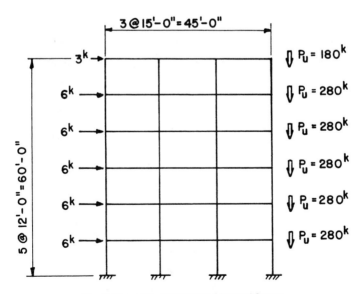

Fig. 3 Five-story rigid-jointed braced frame

SUMMARY AND CONCLUSIONS

Several simplified procedures to account for frame instability have been discussed. The information presented (1) allows a rapid determination of the moment magnification factor for each story of a building, (2) gives a single, unified mathematical expression as a practical definition of braced frames, and (3) gives a practical definition for which structures are stable. Design procedures are outlined for braced and unbraced frames.

METHOD OF CALCULATIONS

Values of δ were calculated using Eqs. 1 and 2 and were compared to the variation of δ among various columns in the story as obtained from a second-order frame analysis computer program by Gouwens (1968) with the value of δ obtained by Eq. 4. The second-order analysis program gives (1) final values of deflection; (2) moments and shears when the vertical factored loads are entered; and (3) the first-order elastic analysis values of deflections, moments, and shears when the vertical loads are entered as zero.

A comparison was also made of δ calculated by Eq. 4 to values of Δ_f/Δ_0 calculated from the results of the computer program, where Δ_f is the final deflection that occurs due to the action of both lateral and vertical loads. The structure shown in Fig. 5 was analyzed for three lateral load distributions shown as A, B, and C. The three lateral load distributions were studied to determine whether they had any effect on the variation of δ within a story.

The structure shown in Fig. 6, which contains a shear wall, was analyzed for the lateral load distribution A. The study was used to determine whether variation in column stiffness produces a variation of δ within a story. The structures were investigated for two values of vertical loads representing lightly loaded structures and heavily loaded structures.

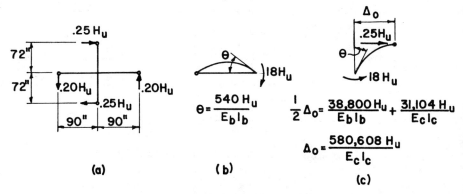

Fig. 4 Deflection of a column-beam assembly; (a) loads; (b) joint rotation; (c) mid-height column deflection

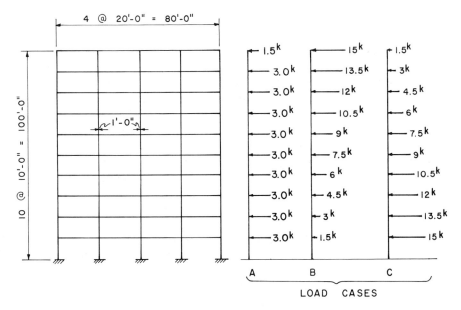

Fig. 5 Frame structure

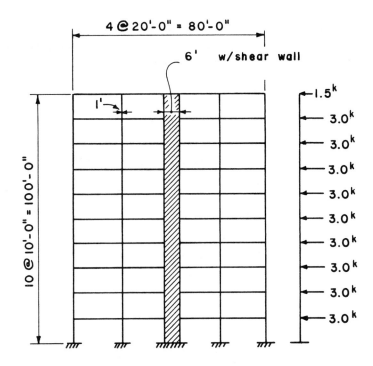

Fig. 6 Frame-shear wall structure

Table 4 shows the magnification factors calculated by Eq. 4 and the magnification factors calculated from the results of the second-order analysis computer program (see Gouwens, 1968). It also shows the values of δ as computed by Eqs. 1 and 2. The minimum and maximum values of δ for any column in the story are given in Table 4, Columns 5 and 6 respectively. Comparison of Columns 5 and 6 indicated that the moment magnification factor is nearly constant for all columns in a story. Study of Tables 4A through 4C indicate that the effect of the distribution of lateral loads on the structure is not significant. It is noted that for the heavy column load case, the value of δ by Eq. 4 are more accurate than the values of δ by Eqs. 1 and 2.

Study of Table 4D indicates that value of δ by Eq. 4 are more accurate than values of δ by Eqs. 1 and 2 even for shear wall type structures.

The ratios of δ by Eq. 4 to Δ_f/Δ_0 by the computer program in Gouwens (1968) are given in Table 5. The ratios of δ by Eqs. 1 and 2 to Δ_f/Δ_0 by the computer program are given in Table 6. A comparison of the average ratios and their standard deviation as shown at the bottom of Tables 5 and 6 indicates that Eq. 4 is much more accurate than Eqs. 1 and 2.

ACKNOWLEDGMENTS

The encouragement and review of this article by various members of the Technical Activities Committee of the Chicago Chapter of the American Concrete Institute is gratefully acknowledged.

Table 4A Comparison of δ by various methods for load distribution A on frame structure

Vertical load (1)	Story (2)	δ by Eqs. 1 & 2 (3)	δ by Eq. 4 (4)	Computer results, Gouwens (1968)		
				δ minimum (5)	δ maximum (6)	Δ_f/Δ_0 (7)
	10	1.02	1.021	0.96	1.03	1.000
	9	1.05	1.034	1.02	1.04	1.053
	8	1.08	1.052	1.04	1.06	1.051
200	7	1.11	1.070	1.06	1.08	1.068
kips	6	1.14	1.089	1.08	1.10	1.092
per						
floor	5	1.17	1.109	1.10	1.12	1.110
	4	1.20	1.129	1.12	1.14	1.131
	3	1.24	1.149	1.14	1.16	1.150
	2	1.28	1.164	1.16	1.18	1.153
	1	1.18	1.118	1.10	1.12	1.128

Table 4A Comparison of δ by various methods for load distribution A on frame structure (continued)

Vertical load (1)	Story (2)	δ by Eqs. 1 & 2 (3)	δ by Eq. 4 (4)	Computer results, Gouwens (1968)		
				δ minimum (5)	δ maximum (6)	Δ_f/Δ_0 (7)
	10	1.14	1.113	0.71	1.15	1.154
	9	1.32	1.196	1.09	1.24	1.256
	8	1.56	1.327	1.23	1.38	1.303
1000	7	1.92	1.486	1.38	1.57	1.539
kips	6	2.50	1.690	1.57	1.81	1.762
per						
floor	5	3.57	1.963	1.82	2.12	2.049
	4	6.23	2.334	2.18	2.52	2.409
	3	24.67	2.856	2.68	2.92	2.764
	2	$P_u > P_{cr}$	3.401	2.95	3.24	2.869
	1	4.24	2.119	2.03	2.36	2.432

Table 4B Comparison of δ by various methods for load distribution B on frame structure

Vertical load (1)	Story (2)	δ by Eqs. 1 & 2 (3)	δ by Eq. 4 (4)	Computer results, Gouwens (1968)		
				δ minimum (5)	δ maximum (6)	Δ_f/Δ_0 (7)
	10	1.02	1.02	1.00	1.02	1.02
	9	1.05	1.03	1.02	1.04	1.03
	8	1.08	1.05	1.04	1.06	1.06
200	7	1.11	1.07	1.06	1.08	1.07
kips	6	1.14	1.09	1.08	1.10	1.09
per						
floor	5	1.17	1.11	1.10	1.12	1.11
	4	1.20	1.13	1.12	1.14	1.13
	3	1.24	1.15	1.14	1.16	1.15
	2	1.28	1.16	1.16	1.17	1.15
	1	1.28	1.12	1.11	1.13	1.13
	10	1.14	1.09	0.98	1.12	1.19
	9	1.32	1.19	1.12	1.23	1.22
	8	1.56	1.32	1.24	1.38	1.36
1000	7	1.92	1.48	1.39	1.56	1.52
kips	6	2.50	1.68	1.57	1.80	1.72
per						
floor	5	3.57	1.95	1.82	2.10	2.02
	4	6.23	2.32	2.16	2.50	2.37
	3	24.67	2.84	2.65	2.92	2.74
	2	$P_u > P_{cr}$	3.42	2.98	3.21	2.89
	1	4.24	2.25	2.08	2.43	2.49

Table 4C Comparison of δ by various methods for load distribution C on frame structure

Vertical load (1)	Story (2)	δ by Eqs. 1 & 2 (3)	δ by Eq. 4 (4)	Computer results, Gouwens (1968)		
				δ minimum (5)	δ maximum (6)	Δ_f/Δ_0 (7)
	10	1.02	1.00	0.94	1.03	1.02
	9	1.05	1.06	1.02	1.04	1.04
	8	1.08	1.05	1.04	1.06	1.05
200	7	1.11	1.08	1.06	1.08	1.07
kips	6	1.14	1.09	1.08	1.10	1.09
per						
floor	5	1.17	1.11	1.10	1.12	1.12
	4	1.20	1.13	1.12	1.14	1.13
	3	1.24	1.15	1.14	1.16	1.15
	2	1.28	1.14	1.16	1.18	1.15
	1	1.18	1.12	1.10	1.12	1.12
	10	1.14	1.15	0.56	1.16	1.12
	9	1.32	1.28	1.06	1.26	1.21
	8	1.56	1.41	1.21	1.41	1.34
1000	7	1.92	1.58	1.37	1.60	1.50
kips	6	2.50	1.71	1.56	1.84	1.81
per						
floor	5	3.57	1.98	1.82	2.16	2.11
	4	6.23	2.36	2.21	2.55	2.46
	3	24.67	2.89	2.72	2.92	2.79
	2	$P_u > P_{cr}$	3.39	2.92	3.27	2.84
	1	4.24	2.08	2.00	2.31	2.37

Table 4D Comparison of δ by various methods for frame-shear wall structure

Vertical load (1)	Story (2)	δ by Eqs. 1 & 2 (3)	δ by Eq. 4 (4)	Computer results, Gouwens (1968)		
				δ minimum (5)	δ maximum (6)	Δ_f/Δ_0 (7)
	10	1.02	1.04	1.04	1.04	1.03
	9	1.03	1.04	1.04	1.05	1.04
	8	1.05	1.03	1.04	1.06	1.05
200	7	1.07	1.04	1.04	1.07	1.05
kips	6	1.09	1.05	1.05	1.08	1.05
per						
floor	5	1.10	1.05	1.05	1.11	1.05
	4	1.12	1.06	1.05	1.07	1.05
	3	1.14	1.05	1.05	1.05	1.05
	2	1.16	1.04	1.04	1.08	1.04
	1	1.01	1.02	1.02	1.05	1.04

Table 4D Comparison of δ by various methods for frame-shear wall structure (continued)

Vertical load (1)	Story (2)	δ by Eqs. 1 & 2 (3)	δ by Eq. 4 (4)	Computer results, Gouwens (1968)		
				δ minimum (5)	δ maximum (6)	Δ_f/Δ_0 (7)
	10	1.09	1.21	1.24	1.25	1.24
	9	1.19	1.22	1.24	1.31	1.26
	8	1.31	1.20	1.25	1.36	1.26
1000	7	1.46	1.24	1.26	1.42	1.28
kips	6	1.65	1.29	1.28	1.47	1.28
per						
floor	5	1.89	1.33	1.30	1.68	1.30
	4	2.22	1.36	1.30	1.44	1.30
	3	2.70	1.34	1.01	1.40	1.29
	2	3.42	1.25	1.24	1.51	1.26
	1	1.05	1.10	1.10	1.33	1.23

Table 5 Ratio of $\dfrac{\delta \text{ by Eq. 4}}{\Delta_f/\Delta_0 \text{ by Gouwens (1968)}}$

Vertical load (1)	Story (2)	Frame structure (Fig. 5) load case			Frame–shear wall structure (Fig. 6) load case A (6)
		A (3)	B (4)	C (5)	
	10	1.02	0.99	1.02	1.01
	9	0.98	1.00	0.98	1.00
	8	1.00	1.00	1.00	0.99
200	7	1.00	1.00	1.00	0.99
kips	6	1.00	1.00	1.00	1.00
per					
floor	5	1.00	1.00	0.99	1.00
	4	1.00	1.00	1.00	1.01
	3	1.00	1.00	1.00	1.01
	2	1.01	1.01	0.99	1.00
	1	0.99	1.00	0.99	0.98
	10	0.96	0.92	0.97	0.98
	9	0.95	0.97	0.95	0.97
	8	0.97	0.97	0.96	1.05
1000	7	0.97	0.98	0.95	1.01
kips	6	0.96	0.98	0.94	1.01
per					
floor	5	0.96	0.97	0.94	1.03
	4	0.97	0.98	0.96	1.04
	3	1.03	1.04	1.04	1.04
	2	1.19	1.18	1.19	0.99
	1	0.87	0.90	0.87	0.89
Average		0.99	0.99	0.99	1.00
Standard deviation		0.06	0.05	0.06	0.03

Table 6 Ratio of $\dfrac{\delta \text{ by Eqs. 1 and 2}}{\Delta_f/\Delta_0 \text{ by Gouwens (1968)}}$

Vertical load (1)	Story (2)	Frame structure (Fig. 5) load case			Frame–shear wall structure (Fig. 6) load case A (6)
		A (3)	B (4)	C (5)	
	10	1.02	1.00	1.00	0.99
	9	1.03	1.02	1.01	0.99
	8	1.03	1.02	1.03	1.00
200	7	0.04	1.04	1.04	1.02
kips	6	1.04	1.05	1.05	1.04
per					
floor	5	1.05	1.05	1.04	1.05
	4	1.06	1.06	1.06	1.07
	3	1.08	1.08	1.08	1.09
	2	1.11	1.11	1.11	1.12
	1	1.05	1.13	1.05	0.97
	10	0.99	0.96	1.02	0.88
	9	1.05	1.08	1.09	0.94
	8	1.20	1.15	1.16	1.04
1000	7	1.25	1.26	1.28	1.14
kips	6	1.42	1.45	1.38	1.29
per					
floor	5	1.74	1.77	1.69	1.45
	4	2.59	2.63	2.53	1.71
	3	8.93	9.00	8.84	2.09
	2	—	—	—	2.71
	1	1.74	1.70	1.79	0.85
Average		1.65	1.66	1.64	1.22
Standard deviation		1.81	1.82	1.78	0.46

REFERENCES/BIBLIOGRAPHY

ACI, 1977a
   BUILDING CODE REQUIREMENT FOR REINFORCED CONCRETE, American Concrete Institute, Detroit, Michigan.
ACI, 1977b
   MINUTES OF FEBRUARY 24, 1977 MEETING OF TECHNICAL ACTIVITIES, Committee of the Chicago Chapter of the American Concrete Institute, Detroit, Michigan.
American Institute of Steel Construction, Inc., 1970
   MANUAL OF STEEL CONSTRUCTION, with 1974 Supplement No. 3, American Institute of Steel Construction, Inc., New York.

Column Research Council, 1966
   GUIDE TO DESIGN CRITERIA FOR METAL COMPRESSION MEMBERS, 2nd Ed., Fritz Laboratory, Bethlehem, Pa.

Gouwens, A. J., 1968
LATERAL LOAD ANALYSIS OF MULTISTORY FRAMES WITH SHEAR WALLS, Bulletin AEC2, Portland Cement Association, Skokie, Illinois.

Okten, O. S., Morino, S., Daniels, J. H., and Lu, L. W., 1973
EFFECTIVE COLUMN LENGTH AND FRAME STABILITY, Fritz Laboratory Report No. 375-2, Lehigh University, Bethlehem, Pa.

Parme, A. L., 1965
CAPACITY OF RESTRAINED ECCENTRICALLY LOADED LONG COLUMNS, Symposium on Reinforced Concrete Columns, Publication SP-13, American Concrete Institute, Michigan.

Rice, P. F., and Hoffman, E. S., 1972
STRUCTURAL DESIGN GUIDE TO THE ACI BUILDING CODE, Van Nostrand Reinhold, New York.

Wood, B. R., Beaulieu, D., and Adams, P. F., 1976
COLUMN DESIGN BY THE P DELTA METHOD, Journal of the Structural Division, ASCE, Vol. 102, No. ST2, Proc. Paper 11936, February, pp. 411-427.

Lateral Drift Limitations in the Design of Tall Buildings

Ignacio Martín

DEFINITION

Lateral drift has traditionally referred to the top lateral deflection of buildings. In recent years, attention has been focused on the relative lateral drift between floors, known as story drift.

Lateral drift limitations have been imposed on concrete structures to establish a limit state of serviceability, to eliminate motion discomfort, excessive vibration, and cracking of partitions. It also avoids large secondary stresses in the structure.

The method of analysis used to compute lateral drift, the type of loading and the assumptions made in modeling the structure influence the results. Therefore, a definition of lateral drift must refer to the type of loading, the method of analysis, and the model of the structure used.

ASSUMPTIONS FOR LATERAL DRIFT CALCULATIONS

Loads

Wind loads are usually represented by static loads. Earthquake loads have also been represented by equivalent lateral static forces, which can be found in most current building codes. The equivalent static forces are used in an elastic analysis, considering the building as fixed at the base.

The lateral drift obtained from the unfactored equivalent static forces may be multiplied by an amplification factor as proposed by ATC (1978), to determine the actual lateral drift to be expected.

Method of Analysis

A dynamic or modal analysis of the structure can be made. The building is modeled as a system of masses lumped at the floor level, with each mass having one degree of freedom. Usually, the lowest three modes of vibration are determined. Lateral drift is determined, and an amplification factor is applied.

The use of modal analysis is restricted in most codes by limiting the determined period of the building to not more than the value determined by the static equivalent load method, which forces the designer to make a static analysis. This limitation also limits the savings in the cost of the structure, which makes the expense of a modal analysis a less attractive investment to the sponsor of the project.

A time-history analysis may be made of the structure, which takes into consideration the vibration applied to the structure using as a model a known earthquake and the inelastic response of the structure. The time-history analysis is more costly than a modal analysis, and its use is limited to unusual structures.

In all cases, the effect of the lateral drift introduces stresses in the structure, also known as the P-Delta effect, which must be considered in the analysis of the structure. These stresses affect the lateral drift determination.

At present, the equivalent static load analysis is the most widely used method, and therefore basic lateral drift limitations should be referred to this method af analysis. The modal and the time-history analyses will probably yield smaller lateral drifts, depending on the intensity of ground motion, and it may be necessary to use smaller lateral drift limitations when using these methods.

Modeling

The way the structure is modeled may affect the calculated lateral drift by as much as 30% (Council on Tall Buildings, 1978).

The use of the centerline dimensions of the structure or the clear length affects the results of the analysis. In general, the trend among designers is to use centerline dimensions. In the case of wide supports such as shear walls, this effect is modeled by using a very rigid haunch along the width of the support. The use of centerline dimensions lowers the computed stiffness of the structure, which increases the computed drifts. However, it covers the joint shear deformation and bar slippage at beam–column connections, which are not accounted for in the drift computations.

In reinforced concrete structures, member sections crack, reducing the stiffness of the structure. Selna (1978) has appropriately questioned the use of gross concrete sections in elastic analysis for seismic loading. The reduction of stiffness due to cracking may increase or decrease the seismic response to a given earthquake. In concrete building analysis, cracked cross-sections should be used for the determination of the stiffness parameter EI.

The contribution of the floor slab to the horizontal member stiffness continues to be a subject of debate, especially in the case of flat plate tall buildings without lateral bracing or shear walls. Freeman et al. (1980) have proposed 60% of the tributary width for the uncracked condition. For drift consideration of large amplitude motion up to the yield capacity of the structure, a 50% reduction of the gross concrete section is proposed, which lengthens the period of the structure by about 40%. Long and Kirk (1980) recommend the use of 30% of the tributary width of flat plates for the cracked condition. Vanderbilt (1981) has proposed an equivalent width analysis for flat slab multistory buildings.

The lateral drift of a building is substantially affected by the stiffness of its foundation. The lateral drift of a building may be more than doubled depending on whether it has a perfectly built-in or highly deformable soil foundation (Council on Tall Buildings, 1978). The effect of foundation flexibility must be considered when determining the lateral drift of a building.

It is a known fact that nonstructural elements contribute to the stiffness of a structure. It is very difficult to estimate the contribution of nonstructural elements, which may substantially vary from building to building. For that reason, although this contribution is acknowledged, it is usually not incorporated into design computations. Therefore, lateral drift determinations overestimate the lateral deflection because the contribution of the nonstructural elements is not accounted for.

Paulay (1981) has pointed out that magnified elastic lateral deformation cannot predict the inelastic lateral deformation for all the floors of a building, which may cause the P-Delta effect to be larger than calculated by elastic methods. Careful detailing for ductility is a safeguard against the inherent inaccuracies of analysis.

LATERAL DRIFT LIMITATIONS

Lateral Deflection

The top lateral deflection has been the limitation used by designers and some building codes to control lateral sway of buildings and its undesirable effects. The value of 1/500 has often been used (Council on Tall Buildings, 1978). Drift limitations apply to particular frames, taking torsion into account.

Story Drift

As buildings became higher and more slender, and as less cladding was used, it became necessary to study the inelastic instability of frame structures, as pointed out by Rosenblueth (1965). As a floor may become unstable, it is necessary to limit the story drift, which is the displacement of one floor relative to the floor below. The story drift limitation also restricts damage to partitions and other fragile nonstructural elements.

The 1982 Uniform Building Code (UBC) and the Recommendations of the Applied Technology Council have story drift limitations (ICBO, 1982; ATC, 1978).

The UBC limits the maximum story drift to not more than 0.005 the story height, unless it can be shown that greater drift can be tolerated. The displacement calculated by an elastic analysis following the equivalent lateral seismic load procedure is multiplied by $1/K$ to obtain the story drift, where K is a numerical coefficient that varies with the type of resisting elements. The K coefficient is 1.33 for a box system, 0.80 for a dual shear wall and ductile moment-resisting space frame, and 0.67 for a ductile moment-resisting space frame. The multiplier $1/K$ cannot be less than 1. The equivalent lateral seismic load procedure includes the effect of the soil in the calculation of the period of the building but has no provisions for the foundation rotation.

The ATC (1978) limits the story drift in accordance with the Seismic Hazard Exposure Group. For Seismic Hazard Exposure Group III, which includes buildings having essential facilities such as fire and police stations and hospitals and power stations, the maximum story drift is 0.01 the story height. For other buildings, which are included in Groups I and II, the maximum story drift is 0.015 the story height.

The lateral deflection is determined by an elastic analysis using the equivalent lateral seismic load procedure. The calculated deflection is multiplied by a deflection amplification factor that varies with the type of resisting structure. It is 4 for shear walls, 6 for ductile moment resisting frames, and 6.5 for shear walls in dual systems. The lateral deflection may be computed by taking into consideration the soil–structure interaction by means of an equation that includes the effect of the foundation rotation. The P-Delta effects on story drifts must be considered.

Table 1 shows a summary of the coefficients for interstory drift computation according to the UBC and the ATC. The two procedures are not directly comparable, but in general it may be said that the ATC procedure will yield higher values of the story drift, and that the maximum story drift limitations are more restrictive than those of the UBC.

The Comité Euro-International du Beton (CEB, 1982) has proposed an interstory drift limitation similar to the ATC drift limitation.

Building Separation

Adjoining buildings or parts of the same building should be separated as they respond to earthquake ground motion independently. The lateral deflection calculation may be used to determine the separation between buildings to avoid hammering. The ATC recommends that the separation be equal to the sum of the lateral deflection of the two units, assuming they deflect towards each other.

DRIFT CALCULATION

Drift calculations may be based on the lateral wind loads and the equivalent lateral seismic force procedure. The following items should be considered.

1. Determine the equivalent lateral load. In the case of seismic loads the equivalent lateral loads shall reflect the site location, the occupancy importance of the building, the type of structural system used, and the response (period) of the building, taking into consideration the soil conditions.

Table 1 Coefficients for interstory drift computation according to UBC and ATC

	Multiplier	Limit
UBC 1982 Sec. 2312(h)	$\dfrac{1}{K} \geq 1.0$	$0.005h_{sx}$
ATC Sec. 4.6.1, Table 3-B Sec. 3.8, Table 3-C	C_d	III $\quad 0.01h_{sx}$ I & II $0.015h_{sx}$

UBC 1982			ATC Table 3-B	
Table 23-I	K	Multiplier		C_d
Box system	1.33	1.00	Shear walls	4.0
Dual bracing	0.80	1.25	Dual shear wall	6.5
			Braced frames	5.0
Ductile-moment	0.67	1.50	Ductile	6.0
Elevated tanks	2.50	1.00	Inverted pendulum	2.5
Buildings	1.00	1.00	Moment resisting frame ordinary	2.0
Other structures	2.00	1.00	Ordinary frame	2.0

2. Use centerline dimensions.

3. Use cracked cross-section stiffness.

4. Make an elastic analysis of the structure considering it fixed at base.

5. Consider the soil structure interaction to include the foundation rotation.

6. Magnify the computed drifts by applying a deflection amplification factor to reflect the inelastic displacement of the structure.

7. Consider the P-Delta effect on the computed story drift.

8. Compare the calculated story drift with a maximum story drift.

9. For building separation, assume that the total lateral deflections of the two buildings deflect towards each other.

REFERENCES/BIBLIOGRAPHY

ATC, 1978
TECHNOLOGY PROVISIONS FOR THE DEVELOPMENT OF SEISMIC REGULATIONS FOR BUILD-INGS, ATC 3-06, NSF 78-8, NBS Special Publication 510, U.S. Government Printing Office, Washington, D.C.

CEB, 1982
SEISMIC DESIGN OF CONCRETE STRUCTURES, 2nd Draft of an Appendix to the CEB-FIP Model Code, Bulletin d'Information, No. 149, March, p. 43.
Council on Tall Buildings, Group CB, 1978
STRUCTURAL DESIGN OF TALL CONCRETE AND MASONRY BUILDINGS, Vol. CB of the Monograph on Planning and Design of Tall Buildings, ASCE, New York.

Freeman, S. A., Czarnecki, R. M., and Honda, K. K., 1980
SIGNIFICANCE OF STIFFNESS ASSUMPTIONS ON LATERAL FORCE CRITERIA, Reinforced Concrete Structures Subjected to Wind and Earthquake Forces, American Concrete Institute, Publication SP-63, pp. 437-457.

ICBO, 1982
UNIFORM BUILDING CODE, 1982 Ed., International Conference of Building Officials, Whittier, California.

Long, A. F., and Kirk, D. W., 1980
LATERAL LOAD STIFFNESS OF SLAB-COLUMN STRUCTURES, Reinforced Concrete Structures Subjected to Wind and Earthquake Forces, American Concrete Institute, Publication SP-63, pp. 197-220.

Paulay, T., 1981
DEVELOPMENTS IN THE SEISMIC DESIGN OF REINFORCED CONCRETE FRAMES IN NEW ZEALAND, Canadian Journal of Civil Engineering, Vol. 8, No. 2, pp. 97-98.

Rosenblueth, E., 1965
SLENDERNESS EFFECTS IN BUILDINGS, Journal of the Structural Division, ASCE, Vol. 91, No. ST1, Proc. Paper 4235, February, pp. 229-252.

Selna, L. G., 1978
MODELING OF REINFORCED CONCRETE BUILDINGS, (Proceedings of a Workshop on Earthquake Resistant Reinforced Concrete Building Construction held at the University of California, June, 1978), Berkeley, California.

Vanderbilt, D., 1981
EQUIVALENT FRAME ANALYSIS OF UNBRACED CONCRETE FRAMES, Significant Developments in Engineering Practice and Research-Siess Symposium, American Concrete Institute, Publication SP-72, pp. 219-246.

Column Length Changes in Ultra-High-Rise Buildings

Mark Fintel
S. K. Ghosh

A computerized procedure for prediction of elastic and inelastic column length changes, applicable to concrete, steel, and composite high-rise buildings, has been developed. Differential column length changes may cause distortion of slabs, leading to impaired serviceability, and can and should be compensated for during construction.

INTRODUCTION

Until the 1950s there were only a limited number of concrete buildings more than 20 stories high. The structures of that time had heavy cladding and masonry partitions that contributed substantially to the strength and stiffness of the buildings. Also, because of the low stress levels utilized for concrete and steel, the building frame members had sizeable dimensions, which resulted in substantial rigidity. The effects of frame distortions due to shrinkage, creep, and temperature were secondary, and could be neglected, since the capacity of the usual structure for overstress was quite high. Even wind distortions could occasionally be neglected since, although the frame was considered to provide the lateral resistance, in reality the heavy cladding resisted much of the wind.

In the late 1950s and early 1960s, the height of concrete buildings jumped from 20 to 60 stories, all in a brief period of 5 to 6 years. The increase in height was accompanied by a sharp increase in the strength of concrete and reinforcing steel, allowing reduced cross-sections and causing a reduction in the overall rigidity. The changeover from working stress design to ultimate strength design contributed further to this trend toward smaller sections. During the same period, architects introduced the use of exposed columns that are subject to thermal movements. The above changes made it necessary for the designer of high-rise buildings to consider column length changes due to

1. Elastic stresses caused by gravity loads,

2. Creep caused by gravity loads,

3. Drying shrinkage, and

4. Temperature variations of exposed columns.

All the above distortions existed in the earlier buildings; however, neglecting their effects rarely resulted in deficiencies in the serviceability of structures.

With reduced overall stiffness and with increases in height, the volume change effects became magnified and could no longer be treated as secondary considerations in design. While column length changes within a single story may be only a fraction of an inch, they are cumulative; when multiplied by a large number of stories, they amount to a number of inches. A concrete or steel structure designed and detailed to be 305 m (1000 ft) tall may, in reality, be only about 304.5 m (999 ft) tall when completed, because of shortening caused by gravity loads, and, in the case of concrete, drying shrinkage.

IMPLICATIONS OF COLUMN SHORTENING

Table 1 shows typical comparative shortenings of 80-story steel and concrete columns. It is obvious that, due to high stresses, the elastic shortening of the steel column is substantially higher than that of the concrete column. The shrinkage and creep of the concrete column, on the other hand, comprise, respectively, 36% and 28% of the total 168 mm (6.6 in.) shortening. For this example, the shortening due to creep is much smaller than that caused by shrinkage, despite the high stress level, since it may take more than a year for the lower story columns to receive all 80 load increments.

Column length changes in a multistory building have structural as well as nonstructural implications. The total amount of shortening has an effect on such nonstructural elements as pipes and elevator rails attached to the concrete, which must be detailed to allow the shortening of columns and walls to take place without being strained. Cladding details are also affected by overall changes in column lengths. The structural effects are caused by differential movements only and not by total movements; they are moments induced into the forcibly distorted slabs or beams, and the accompanying moments in the columns. The slab moments also cause load transfer to the columns that shorten less and away from the columns that shorten more. A major consequence of differential column shortenings is slab tilt, which in turn causes nonstructural partitions to rotate and to distort. The structural effects can be quite severe if the differentially shortening vertical elements are close to one another.

Two examples illustrate the possible magnitudes of deformation.

In a northern U.S. location, an average 14°C (35°F) temperature differential between a typical interior column and a partially exposed exterior column would cause an average shortening of 0.8 mm (0.0315 in.) per story, resulting in a transient movement of 32 mm (1.25 in.) at the top of a 40-story building. A creep and shrinkage strain differential of 230×10^{-6} between a heavily stressed and highly reinforced column and a more lightly stressed and lightly reinforced wall would amount to a shortening of 0.9 mm (0.035 in.) per story, resulting in a permanent distortion of 36 mm (1.40 in.) toward the top of a 40-story building. Such differential distortions could cause large frame moments (particularly in the slabs) and also slab tilt, affecting serviceability. The transient temperature movements must be limited to tolerable values through modification of column exposure, addition of insulation, or changes in the structural system. By contrast, much larger anticipated differential length changes due to elastic stresses, creep, and shrinkage can be accommodated by cambering (compensation) of formwork during construction, if the magnitudes can be predicted during design. (Cambering conventionally refers to formwork for beams and slabs that is higher at mid-span than at the edges. Here it is used to describe tilted formwork that is higher along one edge with respect to the opposite parallel edge.)

THERMAL MOVEMENTS

During the mid-1960s, structural solutions were prepared and details were suggested for dealing with the temperature movements of exposed columns

Table 1 Shortenings of an 80-Story Column *(Inches)*

	Steel	Concrete
Elastic	7.7	2.4
Creep		1.8
Shrinkage	—	2.4
TOTAL	7.7	6.6

(Fintel and Khan, 1965; Khan and Fintel, 1966 and 1968). For temperature effects due to column exposure, a methodology was developed to determine design temperatures based on geographic location and size of column; thermal gradients in the exposed column; and the resulting structural effects.

For design temperatures, maps for lowest winter and highest summer mean daily temperatures with frequencies of recurrence of once in 40 years were prepared for members less than 305 mm (12 in.) thick. For thicker members, those up to 610 mm (24 in.) thick, the use of a three-day mean temperature was suggested, to account for the time lag of penetration of ambient temperature fluctuations. A graphic approach to determining isotherms, thermal gradients, and average temperatures in exposed columns was developed, based on the approach used by hydraulic engineers in dealing with seepage through porous soils. With the thermal gradients, the consequent bowing and length changes of the columns could be determined, and hence the resulting structural effects could be determined, including the distortions of the structure.

Along with the procedure for predicting the seasonal transient column length changes, practical means were suggested for limiting such thermal movements so that they would remain within acceptable limits. Control of thermal movements can be achieved either by regulating the amount of column exposure or by insulating the columns. If these measures cannot sufficiently reduce the anticipated distortions, then slab hinging details or a different structural configuration must be chosen.

Following the initial instances in the mid-1960s of partition distress caused by thermal movements of exposed columns (Fig. 1), manufacturers improved the details of gypsum board partition assemblies, thus substantially increasing the deformability of partitions. Also, structural designers have since usually taken care either to control column exposure or to provide the necessary design details to avoid thermal distress likely to be caused by column exposure.

Observations in the 1960s showed that buildings up to 12–14 stories in height with partially exposed columns did not show distress of partitions, even in the severe Chicago climate. For buildings taller than 20 stories with exposed columns, an analysis of thermal effects is needed to predict the amount of column movement. With this information, a designer can determine whether it is necessary to incorporate special details to avoid distress of nonstructural elements.

SHRINKAGE AND CREEP MOVEMENTS

The presence of vertical reinforcement in a concrete column reduces the amount of shortening due to shrinkage and creep that would have taken place in the same column in the absence of any reinforcement. With the passage of time, shrinkage and creep cause load to be shifted from the concrete to the reinforcing steel. In a heavily reinforced column, all the load may eventually be transferred to the steel, with further shrinkage actually causing tension in the concrete. On the other hand, in columns with a very low percentage of reinforcement, all the steel may yield in compression. It is important to note that the overall load-carrying capacity is not affected by this load transfer; only the proportion of load carried by the two materials changes.

With respect to overall structural behavior, cumulative column shortening causes distortions in a structure that become quite significant with increasing height. In the late 1960s, creep and shrinkage effects in buildings in the 45- to 50-story height range were investigated, and structural solutions were published (Fintel and Khan, 1969 and 1971).

In recent years the height of concrete and concrete/steel composite structures has increased into the 70- to 80-story range. It has thus become desirable to extend the earlier solutions to cover the new heights. Also, computers are almost always used nowadays in structural engineering offices to solve problems requiring a great deal of meticulous arithmetic calculation and extensive "bookkeeping."

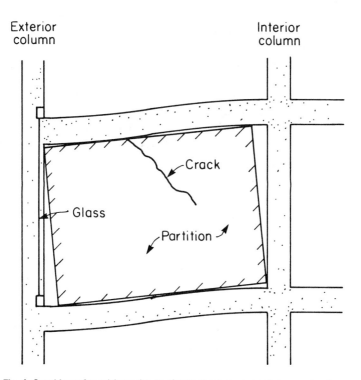

Fig. 1 Cracking of partitions due to thermal movements of exposed columns

The structural solutions for effects of shrinkage and creep that were developed in the 1960s required extensive longhand computations and summations because every story-high column segment in a multistory building is loaded in as many increments as there are stories above. At each loading increment, each column segment has new time-dependent properties (modulus of elasticity, creep and shrinkage coefficients) as well as a new transformed section size and a new ratio of reinforcement (based on transformed section). Due to this complexity, very few structures were analyzed for the effects of shrinkage and creep. Although these effects were mostly within tolerable limits for buildings in the 40- to 50-story range, there were some instances where the neglect caused performance problems.

In buildings 70 to 80 stories high, it is not only the differential column length changes due to shrinkage and creep that may be significant; the differential elastic shortenings due to gravity loads may also cause unacceptable slab tilt, particularly in structures containing both steel and concrete columns. Table 1 illustrates quite graphically that composite structures having both concrete and steel columns are especially susceptible to differential elastic column length changes. Although the total shortenings of steel and concrete columns are in the same range, their respective elastic components differ greatly from each other.

A procedure for determining elastic or inelastic column length changes in tall structures, developed earlier by Fintel and Khan (1969 and 1971), has now been updated, computerized, and made applicable to both concrete and steel, as well as to composite structures. The updated procedure (Fintel et al., 1984) considers elastic and creep shortenings due to gravity loads and separately shrinkage shortening. While elastic and creep deformations depend upon loading history, member size, and reinforcement, the shrinkage component is independent of loading and depends upon member size and reinforcement. Time and material properties, of course, are important variables in all computations of shortening.

Movements as Related to Construction Sequence

If we consider a particular slab of a multistory building, each of its supports consists of a number of single-story column or wall segments. During the construction process, each of the story-high support segments undergoes elastic shortening due to all loads applied after casting or installation of the segment. In addition, concrete and composite columns begin to shrink because of moisture loss and creep as a result of the applied compressive forces. The time of slab installation in its initial position becomes the dividing line between (1) shortenings of supports that take place up to the time of slab installation and (2) post-installation shortenings.

In cast-in-place reinforced concrete structures, the amount of support shortening before slab installation is of no importance, since compensation is usually accomplished at the time of casting of every floor slab by leveling the forms. Information is needed on how much the slab will change its position after it has been cast due to subsequent loads and subsequent volume changes. This information can then be used to adjust the level of the formwork so that in the future the slab will end up in the desired position. Depending upon circumstances, it may be decided that all the time-dependent shortening (shrinkage and creep) is to be compensated for at the time of construction. In that case, at initial occupancy the slab will still have some tilt that will gradually disappear. Or, it may be decided to compensate for only the shortening that is expected to take place within two years after construction; thus, in two years the slabs will be level, and from that time on only the remaining shrinkage and creep will cause the slab to tilt.

In structures in which columns are fabricated to exact length (steel columns, light steel erection columns that are later embedded in concrete, and precast concrete columns), the pre-installation support shortening is of consequence, since the attachments to receive the slabs are part of the fabricated columns. To assure the predetermined initial slab elevation, the pre-installation length changes of these columns need to be known and compensated for. The post-installation support shortening (elastic and inelastic) needs to be additionally considered. Or, the pre-installation and post-installation shortenings may be added to each other for compensation purposes, if the installation of slabs at predetermined initial positions is not of overriding importance.

In steel structures also, the pre-installation and post-installation shortenings can be added for compensation purposes. Although in steel structures the compensation should be made for the sum of the pre- and post-installation shortenings, it is advisable to compute them separately, since the pre-installation shortenings can also be determined in the field by measuring the levels of the column tops at the time of slab installation. On the contrary, post-installation shortenings can only be predicted analytically, and can be measured only after all the slabs above, the finishes, and the live loads have been applied.

It should be noted that compensation for column length changes to reduce or eliminate slab tilt does not eliminate slab movement or the resulting moments. In reality, compensation only changes the direction and the timing of the slab tilt; instead of the slab developing a tilt with time after it has been cast horizontally, it is constructed with an opposite tilt that gradually disappears with time, leaving the slab in a horizontal position. A structural analysis for the effects of differential support movements will yield slab moments that ought to be considered in design, remembering that, since the slab deformations take place over a period of time exceeding 30 days, at least 50% of the slab moments will "creep out."

Case Studies

Figure 2 shows pre-slab-installation and post-installation displacements of supports of an 80-story composite structure having interior steel columns and an exterior concrete beam–column system resisting the lateral forces. The shortenings of an interior steel column and an exterior composite column are shown in Figs. 2a and b respectively. Curve 'a' in Fig. 2a shows that the vertical column displacements at the various floor levels, up to the time of slab installation at those levels, increases up the height of the building,

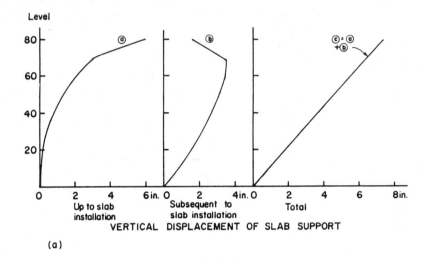

(a)

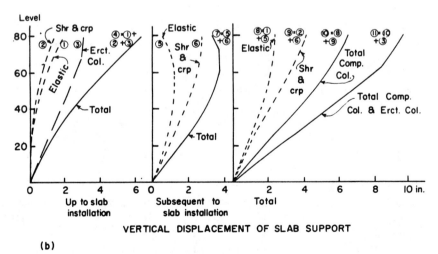

(b)

Fig. 2 Column length changes in an 80-story building with a composite steel-concrete structural system, (a) interior and (b) exterior steel columns

because the loads from each added floor shortens all the column segments below that level. The vertical column displacements at the various floor levels, subsequent to slab installation at those levels, initially increases but then decreases with increasing height (Curve 'b', Fig. 2a). This is because loads from fewer and fewer stories contribute to post-slab-installation shortenings as construction progresses towards the top of the building. At the roof level, only the mechanical bulkheads above contribute to column shortening subsequent to the installation of the roof slab. Curves '1' and '5' in Fig. 2b (showing the elastic shortening of an exterior composite column) exhibit the same trends as curves 'a' and 'b' respectively of Fig. 2a. The computed inelastic shortenings of the exterior columns are based on assumed moderate values of shrinkage and creep coefficients (Fig. 2b). Light erection columns are embedded in the peripheral concrete columns. Their elastic shortenings prior to embedment become part of the total differential shortenings between exterior and interior columns (Fig. 2b). Figure 3a shows the differential shortenings at the various floor levels between the interior steel and the exterior composite columns considered in Fig. 2. The differential shortenings up to and subsequent to the installation of slabs at the various floor levels are presented separately. In accordance with earlier discussion on composite structures, the pre-installation and post-installation differential shortenings have been added for compensation purposes and are presented in Fig. 3b. The values shown on the right side of Fig. 3b are needed to detail the columns for fabrication, so that after all loads have been applied, and shrinkage and creep have taken place, the slabs will be horizontal. For this particular case, it is suggested that at every 10th story the interior column lift be shortened as shown on the compensation curve.

If no prediction of differential movements is made during design, the corrections are usually made during construction. Every, say, ten floors, the elevations of column tops are measured and shims of proper thickness are inserted, so that all columns of the new lift start at the same elevation. This somewhat costlier procedure, however, does not account for the differential length changes that will occur after the slabs are installed.

Figure 4 shows computed shortenings of an exterior column and an interior shear wall of a 70-story reinforced concrete office building. The deformations that occur before the casting of a slab are of no consequence, since the formwork for each slab is usually installed horizontally; thus the pre-slab-installation differentials are automatically compensated for. Only the post-slab-installation deformations (right side of Fig. 4b) may need compensation, if the predicted amount is more than can be tolerated. In the case of this 70-story building, the maximum post-installation differential is expected to be 27 mm (1.05 in.) for high values of shrinkage and creep. It may be desirable to compensate for such distortion by simply raising (tilting) the formwork along the exterior columns relative to the shear walls, so that after the anticipated elastic, creep, and shrinkage length changes of the columns have taken place, the slabs will be horizontal. For low coefficients of shrinkage and creep (Fig. 5), the maximum anticipated differential distortion is 22 mm (0.85 in.). This similarity in the magnitudes of distortion when low and high coefficients of shrinkage and creep are used in computations is due to both the column and the wall being subjected to elastic, creep, and shrinkage shortenings at the same time.

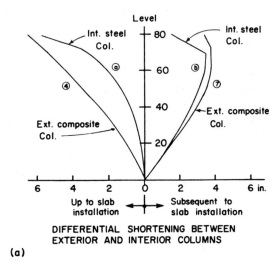

DIFFERENTIAL SHORTENING BETWEEN
EXTERIOR AND INTERIOR COLUMNS

(a)

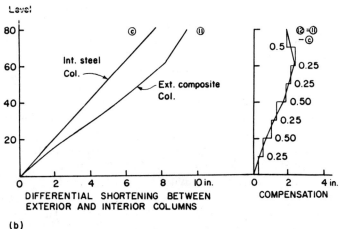

DIFFERENTIAL SHORTENING BETWEEN
EXTERIOR AND INTERIOR COLUMNS

(b)

Fig. 3 Column length changes in an 80-story building with a differential shortening between exterior and interior columns

Verification

The updated procedure for predicting column length changes is in the process of being verified against a number of measurements of actual column strains carried out over a period of up to 20 years in several tall buildings in the Chicago area. Reasonably good agreement between the predicted and the measured column strain values has been observed to date.

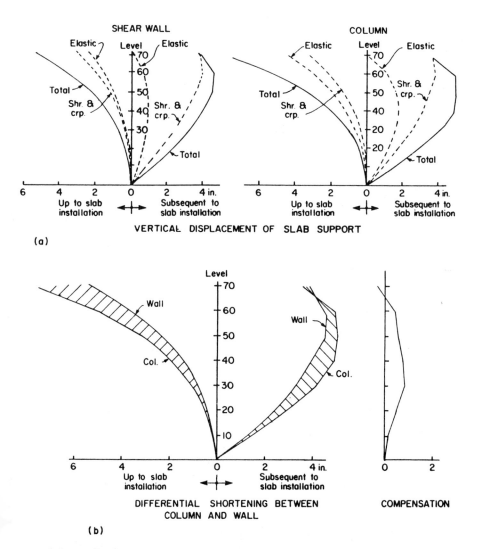

Fig. 4 Changes in the lengths of columns and shear walls in a 70-story concrete building, assuming high shrinkage and creep coefficients

CONCLUSIONS

A computerized procedure for prediction of column length changes due to elastic, creep, and shrinkage movements has been developed. The procedure is applicable to concrete, steel, and composite structures.

In high-rise buildings, the total elastic, shrinkage, and creep shortening of columns may be as high as 25 mm (1 in.) for every 24 m (80 ft) of height. The absolute amount of cumulative column shortening needs to be considered in

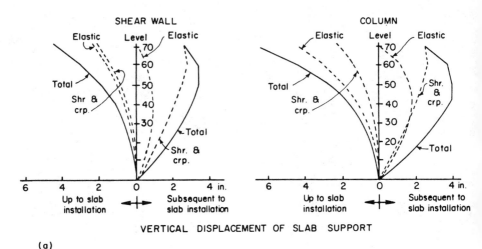

(a)

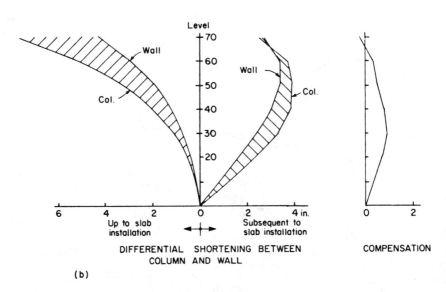

(b)

Fig. 5 Changes in the lengths of columns and shear walls in a 70-story concrete building, assuming low shrinkage and creep coefficients

the design of cladding details and in detailing elevator rails, vertical pipes, and so on. The differential shortening between adjacent columns may cause distortion of slabs, leading to impaired serviceability. The tilting of slabs due to the length changes of columns caused by gravity loads and shrinkage are permanent; they can and should be compensated for during construction.

Length changes of exposed columns due to temperature fluctuations are transient in nature, and must be limited to acceptable values.

Composite structures having both concrete and steel columns are sensitive to differential column shortenings that can be easily compensated for during construction.

Differential shortenings between concrete columns and concrete walls are only mildly sensitive to the magnitude of creep and shrinkage coefficients; the differentials can be easily compensated for during construction by adjusting (cambering) the forms.

ACKNOWLEDGMENT

This brief paper presents the highlights of research findings more extensively reported in an Engineering Bulletin to be published by the Portland Cement Association. A similar condensation of the same report has appeared in *Civil Engineering—ASCE* in 1984.

REFERENCES/BIBLIOGRAPHY

Fintel, M., Iyengar, S. H., and Ghosh, S. K., 1984
    COLUMN SHORTENING IN TALL STRUCTURES—PREDICTION AND COMPENSATION, Publication EB 108D, Portland Cement Association, Skokie, Illinois.
Fintel, M., and Khan, F. R., 1965
    EFFECTS OF COLUMN EXPOSURE IN TALL STRUCTURES—TEMPERATURE VARIATIONS AND THEIR EFFECTS, ACI Journal, Vol. 62, No. 12, December, pp. 1533-1556.
Fintel, M., and Khan, F. R., 1969
    EFFECTS OF COLUMN CREEP AND SHRINKAGE IN TALL STRUCTURES—PREDICTIONS OF INELASTIC COLUMN SHORTENING, ACI Journal, Vol. 66, No. 12, December, pp. 957-967.
Fintel, M., and Khan, F. R., 1971
    EFFECTS OF COLUMN CREEP AND SHRINKAGE IN TALL STRUCTURES—ANALYSIS FOR DIFFERENTIAL SHORTENING OF COLUMNS AND FIELD OBSERVATIONS OF STRUCTURES, Symposium on Designing for Effects of Creep, Shrinkage and Temperature in Concrete Structures, ACI Special Publication SP-27, American Concrete Institute, Detroit, Michigan, pp. 159-185.

Khan, F. R., and Fintel, M., 1966
    EFFECTS OF COLUMN EXPOSURE IN TALL STRUCTURES—ANALYSIS FOR LENGTH CHANGES OF EXPOSED COLUMNS, ACI Journal, Vol. 63, No. 8, August, pp. 843-864.
Khan, R. F., and Fintel, M., 1968
    EFFECTS OF COLUMN EXPOSURE IN TALL STRUCTURES—DESIGN CONSIDERATIONS AND FIELD OBSERVATIONS. ACI Journal, Vol. 65, No. 2, February, pp. 99-110.

Ultra High-Strength Concrete

John M. Albinger

Close communication between designers and the Chicago ready-mix industry has been an important factor in the development of new products, among them high-strength concrete. High strength in concrete has a meaning relative to the maximum utilization of materials and resources in a geographical area; in the Chicago area high-strength concrete is defined as normal-weight concrete between 41 and 96.5 MPa (6,000 and 14,000 psi).

MIX DESIGN

The designing of a high-strength concrete mixture is certainly as much of an art as a science. Because of the innumerable types and gradings of aggregates, chemistries of various cements, fly ashes, and admixtures, and the subsequent interaction of any combination of these materials, arriving at the optimum combination becomes for the most part a matter of trial and error. Certainly basic concrete technology applies, but like an artist who knows that a blend of blue and yellow makes green, one must try many combinations to attain the desired result.

Some of the basic proportioning considerations are discussed in this report. The economic advantages of using locally available materials must also be considered.

Cement

Because of varying chemical compositions of cements, their ability to perform may differ when used with various chemical admixtures and fly ashes. The selection of a cement should be based more on its performance in concrete at various ages than on mortar cubes. However, while they do not tell the whole story at the design point, mortar cubes are an important means of control after a selection has been made. The cement should have a minimum 7-day mortar cube strength of 29 MPa (4,200 psi). Once the selection has been made, limits on the physical properties should be established and submitted to the cement producers for compliance. A periodic sampling and testing program should then be initiated to ensure uniformity and comformity to the modified limits of specifications.

After the selection of the cement is made, the optimum cement content should be obtained through a series of trial mixtures in the laboratory using a single set of aggregates and at a constant slump of 65–90 mm (2½–3½ in.). The range of cement content to be considered will depend on the desired compressive strength. For all sets of materials, an optimum cement content exists over which no more strength increase is realized, and the mix becomes too sticky to handle.

Admixtures

The use of a normal set water reducer, or retarding water reducer, or a combination of these, becomes necessary to utilize efficiently all cementitious materials and to maintain the lowest practical water–cement ratio. Increased dosages over those recommended by the admixture manufacturer have been found to increase strength without detrimental effects. The use of a Type D retarding water reducer offered benefits beyond higher 56-day strengths. Varying dosages of this material helped to prevent rapid setting that might be expected from mixes containing a high amount of cement. During hot weather, this type of control is imperative. This retardation also contributes to higher late strengths. The heat of hydration of this type of concrete generates quickly and if left uncontrolled will cause high early strengths and lower ultimate strength. Factors to be considered when evaluating an admixture are cement and fly ash compatibility, water reduction, setting times, workability, time of addition, and addition rates.

Superplasticizers offer the ability to achieve higher strengths than were previously attainable. Water reductions of up to 30% are possible while maintaining a placeable consistency. A superplasticizer was instrumental in increasing our 62 MPa mix to 76 MPa (9,000 psi to 11,000 psi). These admixtures should be used in conjunction with the Type D retarder and can successfully be added at the ready mix plant and again at the job site if necessary.

Air entraining agents are not generally used because of the accompanying loss of strength. The type of application also frequently precludes their use (for example, with caissons, interior columns, and shear walls).

Fly Ash

The use of a good quality fly ash is mandatory in the production of high-strength concrete. The strength gained from the use of fly ash cannot be attained through additional cement. Normally 10% to 15% fly ash by weight of cement is used. If an ASTM Type C fly ash is being considered, greater amounts over 15% may be considered.

Micro silica is also being used in high-strength concrete, although on a limited basis. Its super fineness over $100,000 \text{ cm}^2/\text{g}$ (48,400 ft^2/lb.), in combination with its pozzolantic reactivity, offers strengths in excess of 103 MPa (15,000 psi). Some special considerations when using micro silica are availability, method of handling, finishing, and curing.

Aggregates

Careful consideration should be given to shape, surface texture, and mineralogy. Each strength level will have an optimum size aggregate that will yield the greatest compressive strength per pound of cement. To determine the optimum size for a given strength, trial batches should be made with aggregates less than 25 mm (1 in.) maximum size at varying cement contents. Our test results show that gravel concrete produces lower compressive strength and modules of elasticity than crushed stone concrete using the same size aggregate and cement content. This is probably due to the surface texture and bonding characteristics of the aggregates. At approximately 950 lbs. of cementitious material (cement and fly ash), ASTM C-33 #7 crushed stone yielded the best results, but an ASTM #67 or #8 may also be considered.

Since high-strength concrete contains an unusually high amount of cementitious material, sands that provide good finishing characteristics in regular concrete are not as necessary. Sands with a fineness modulus of around 2.5 produce concrete with a very sticky consistency, resulting in a loss of workability and lower compressive strength. Because of the extremely high percentage of cementitious material in a high-strength mixture, the recommended proportions of coarse to fine aggregates found in ACI 613 do not apply. Optimum strength and workability are achieved by increasing the coarse aggregate content.

Using these optimum strength-producing materials in trial mixes, it was found that water–cement ratios of 0.38, 0.36 and 0.34 are required to produce concrete strengths of 41 MPa (6,000 psi), 52 MPa (7,500 psi) and 62 MPa (9,000 psi) respectively. For the purpose of calculating the water–cement ratio, the weight of the fly ash is added to the cement content.

After the materials are chosen, the consistency of those materials becomes imperative. Consistency must be maintained throughout production, placement, and testing. If variations become excessive the required average strength may be unattainable.

TESTING, PLACEMENT, AND RESEARCH

In the production of high-strength concrete, many factors must be considered that are normally not important and often not specified. When cardboard cylinder molds were used, for example, a loss in compressive strength and an increase in strength variations were experienced. A significant improvement was noted when metal or plastic molds were used. Capping of cylinders must be done with extreme precision and only high-strength capping compounds may be used. All caps on high strength cylinders must be allowed to develop adequate strength and must be sounded for voids prior to testing. The time required for a capping compound to harden must be determined by evaluating the strength-producing properties of the compound. A compression machine with an adequate loading capacity must be used. The results of cylinders broken in the top 10% of a machine's capacity have shown to be more erratic. When compressive strengths of 76 MPa (11,000 psi) and over are specified, specimens other than 150 × 300 mm (6 × 12 in.) cylinders should be considered: 100 × 200 mm (4 × 8 in.), 75 × 150 mm (3 × 6 in.) cylinders or cubes.

Since the coefficient of variation or standard deviation dictates the required overdesign, all variables must be kept to an absolute minimum. As an example, if 52 MPa (7,500 psi) is the specified strength and the standard deviation is 4 MPa (581 psi) (7% C of V), the design strength would have to be 58 MPa (8,400 psi), or an overdesign of 6 MPa (900 psi). On the other hand, if the standard deviation is 8.1 MPa (1,178 psi), (13% C of V), the design strength would have to be 67 MPa (9,740 psi) or an overdesign of 15 MPa (2,240 psi). When dealing with high-strength concrete, overdesigns of this magnitude cannot be tolerated. It is obvious, therefore, that the performance of any concrete can be significantly enhanced, regardless of strength level, if variations are controlled.

When concrete arrives on the job, it should arrive at the proper slump so that the addition of water is not necessary. The contractor must understand the consequence of exceeding the specified slump and must be ready to place the concrete when it arrives. Concrete should be rejected after it is 90 minutes old unless it can be placed without the addition of retempering water. If the contractor wants to place the concrete with a pump and higher slumps are anticipated, some precautions should be taken. At times the amount of cement in a high-strength mix is optimum and, therefore, an increase in slump cannot be compensated for with additional cement. If a superplastizer is not already being used, it should be considered at this point.

Job site control must be the responsibility of the party most familiar with the performance and use of high-strength concrete, whether that is the concrete supplier, a commercial testing laboratory or a consultant. The concrete laboratory hired for testing of the concrete delivered to the job site must be competent, and one that is regularly inspected by the Cement and Concrete Reference Laboratory (CCRL). A minimum of one set of cylinders should be made for each $75m^3$ ($100 yd^3$) of concrete placed, with at least two cylinders cast for each test age; in other words 7, 28, 56, and 90 days. The 90-day cylinders should be made for back-up data. Cylinders must be cast and cured according to ASTM C-31, Section 7.3.

The basic principles of design and use of any strength concrete apply to high-strength concrete. But in high-strength concrete, variations from these established standards and specifications have a much more immediate and severe effect.

Over the past 16 years, ready mix concrete producers and engineers have researched and developed higher- and higher-strength concretes. The experience knowledge, and communication within the construction team has accomplished the task of increasing the strength of normal weight concrete from 35 MPa (5,000 psi) to 96 MPa (14,000 psi) in Chicago while strengths of lightweight concrete have increased from 35 to 55 MPa (5,000 to 8,000 psi).

In Chicago the increase of 35 to 41 MPa (5,000 to 6,000 psi) concrete in 1962 required minimal research. Fly ash, cement, and admixtures were added to the 35 MPa (5,000 psi) mix according to manufacturers recommendations to reach compressive strengths excessive of 41 MPa (6,000 psi).

In 1965, 52 MPa (7,500 psi) concrete was placed for the columns of Lake Point Tower. A carefully planned research program optimizing all ingredients in the mix established new quality control procedures for the production, delivery, handling, and placing of the concrete.

Further refinements of the 52 MPa (7,500 psi) mix enabled the production of 62 MPa (9,000 psi) concrete placed in the Mid Continental Plaza Building in 1972. In 1976, 76 MPa (11,000 psi) concrete was delivered for test columns in the River Plaza Project to continue instrumentation and research on high-strength concrete. Instrumentation of two 96.5 MPa (14,000 psi) test columns at the Chicago Mercantile Exchange was successfully accomplished in spring of 1982.

Why produce higher-strength concretes? It is certainly not economical for the ready-mix supplier to invest in highly trained technicians and expensive equipment when the major market demand is for lower strength concrete. In fact, no more than 2% of the concrete we deliver is in excess of 52 MPa (7,500 psi). Promotion of high-strength concrete requires professionals capable of answering questions on properties and design. Sale of this special material is yet another problem. Development and production costs must be evaluated, and a price that the market can bear must be established. This price must be established so that the architect and structural engineer can determine the most economical method of construction.

These negative reasons for producing high strength concrete are counter-balanced by some indirect benefits to the ready-mix supplier. Through experience with high-strength concrete, the ready-mix producer is able to improve quality of the lower-strength concretes. A better understanding of concrete allows the ready-mix supplier to develop special concretes. It is a product differentiation that facilitates the sale of lower-strength concretes and improves the technical image of the company. These benefits have to be evaluated by the ready-mix company before the decision of moving from a comfortable and known low-strength market into an unknown and highly vulnerable market.

For the designer and owner, the additional job site expense for quality control, the additional care required for synchronized pouring of slabs and columns, and the problem of mushrooming around columns are minimal considerations compared with the savings in reinforcement, column forms, concrete volume; above all there is the return on larger rentable floor areas with smaller columns.

This concrete strength seems to be economically applicable mainly to high-rise construction. These high-rises may contain commercial and resi-dential spaces within the same tower.

Because only a small number of buildings are designed for over 50 stories, high-strength concrete has limited application. Consequently, high-strength concrete technology in the Chicago area has exceeded market requirements.

REFERENCES/BIBLIOGRAPHY

Bache, H. H., 1981
    DENSIFIED CEMENT/ULTRA-FINE PARTICLE-BASED MATERIALS, (Proceedings of the Second International Conference on Superplasticizers in Concrete, Ottawa, June 10-12, 1981).

Chicago Committee on High-Rise Buildings, 1977
    HIGH STRENGTH CONCRETE IN CHICAGO HIGH RISE BUILDINGS, Task Force Report #5, Chicago Committee on High-Rise Buildings, Chicago.
Cook, J. E., 1982
    RESEARCH AND APPLICATION OF HIGH STRENGTH CONCRETE USING CLASS C FLY ASH, Concrete International, Vol. 4, No. 7, pp. 72-80.

Kaar, P. H., Hanson, N. W., and Capell, H. T., 1977
    STRESS-STRAIN CHARACTERISTICS OF HIGH STRENGTH CONCRETE, Report #RD051.01D, Portland Cement Association, Skokie, Illinois.

Mattison, E. N. and Beresford, F. D., 1973
   STUDIES OF THE PRODUCTION AND PROPERTIES OF HIGH STRENGTH CONCRETE, REPORT #7, Division of Building Research, Commonwealth Scientific & Industrial Research Organization, Australia.
Mukherjee, P. K., Loughborough, M. T., and Malhotra, W. M., 1981
   DEVELOPMENT OF HIGH STRENGTH CONCRETE INCORPORATING A LARGE PERCENTAGE OF FLY ASH AND SUPERPLASTICIZERS, CANMET, Mineral Sciences Laboratories Division Report MPR/MSL 81-124, Vol. #4, Issue #2, pp. 81-86, ASTM, Philadelphia.

Perenchio, W. F. and Klieger, P., 1978
   SOME PHYSICAL PROPERTIES OF HIGH STRENGTH CONCRETE, Report #RD056.01, Portland Cement Association, Skokie, Illinois.

Shah, S. P., 1979
   HIGH STRENGTH CONCRETE (Proceedings of a Workshop held at the University of Illinois at Chicago Centre, December 1979), Report No. PB021010057, U.S. Department of Commerce, N.T.I.S., Springfield.

Wolsiefer, J., 1982
   ULTRA HIGH STRENGTH FIELD PLACEABLE CONCRETE IN THE RANGE 69 TO 124 MPA, (10,000 TO 18,000 psi), (Presented at the 1982 Annual Convention of the American Concrete Institute, Atlanta, January 1982).

Yamamoto, Y. and Kobayashi, M., 1982
   USE OF MINERAL FINES IN HIGH STRENGTH CONCRETE—WATER REQUIREMENT AND STRENGTH, Concrete International, July.

Slender Walls Research Program by California Structural Engineers

James E. Amrhein

The Structural Engineers Association of Southern California and the Southern California chapter of the American Concrete Institute have combined efforts to conduct a major research program on the vertical and lateral load capacities of tall slender walls.

Although tall, slender walls may not be generally considered as elements in high-rise buildings, they do have pertinent application in both the building and in adjunct buildings allied with tall building complexes. In high-rise buildings, entrance lobbies may extend to two or more stories in height, and slender walls may be used. Slender walls may also be used for ballrooms, convention halls, and auditoriums that could be required facilities of a tall building complex.

In past years, walls have been constructed thinner and taller, and many suggestions have been made to relax code slenderness (h/t) limits for load-bearing concrete tilt-up walls and masonry walls. However, research data were insufficient to justify such a change. Accordingly, the above organizations decided to conduct a research program to assess the capabilities of masonry of a slenderness (h/t) far in excess of present code limitations.

In February 1981, a joint task committee was organized headed by William Simpson, a consulting structural engineer in Newport Beach. The committee

525

included consulting engineers, building officials, university professors, and concrete and masonry specialists. A series of organizational planning meetings were held in which the total program was outlined and decisions were made regarding types and design of panels to be built and where to build them. Approval was obtained from the board of directors of both sponsoring organizations to conduct these tests. Ralph McLean, a structural engineer with the Fullerton firm of McLean and Schultz, Civil & Structural Engineers, accepted the post of Test Director and worked closely with the committee in setting up the test program.

A total of 32 walls were built. Thirty-one of the walls were 1.22 m (4 ft) wide and 7.52 m (24 ft 8 in.) high. Twelve walls were concrete tilt-up panels with thicknesses of 120, 145, 185, and 240 mm (4¾, 5¾, 7¼, and 9½ in.), resulting in nominal h/t ratios of 60, 50, 50, and 30 respectively. The masonry panels were 150, 200, and 255 mm (6, 8, and 10 in.) thick for nominal h/t ratios of 48, 36, and 29 respectively. One panel, built with hollow brick units, was 90 mm (3½ in.) thick and 5 m (16 ft 8 in.) high for an h/t of 55. Through the efforts of the committee and through the generosity of the industry, materials, money, time and labor were donated toward this project. An area was set aside for the research program in the yard of concrete contractors, Sanchez and Hernandez in Irwindale, California, whose facilities were made available for the project. The test walls were built on a 15 m by 30 m (50 ft by 100 ft) concrete slab cast especially for the project.

Initially, 12 tilt-up walls were cast on the slab. After 10 days, they were lifted and placed on edge adjacent to the test site. All twenty masonry panels were then built in specified locations on the slab and braced.

The walls were built on a 13 mm (half-inch) steel plate 1.2 m (4 ft) long on which was welded a half of a four-inch pipe. This detail provided a pin support and allowed full free rotation. The top of the wall was restrained by a device with a spherical roller bearing that permitted vertical movement and rotation but prevented horizontal translation. These end restraint devices eliminated fixity top and bottom and provided free rotating pin connections, which simplified testing and calculating the moments and stresses in the panel. These pinned ends are a most severe condition; an actual building wall will have some restraint or fixity at the bottom and perhaps at the top, due to bond, restraint due to reinforcing bars, and restraint due to dead load.

All walls were reinforced vertically with 13 mm (half-inch) bars Grade 60 located in the center ($d = t/2$). The tilt-up walls were reinforced with four half-inch bars, and the masonry walls were reinforced with five half-inch bars. Horizontal bars were spaced 0.6 m (2 ft) apart for the tilt-up walls and 1.2 m (4 ft) apart for the masonry.

A loading frame was designed by the committee such that an eccentric vertical load and a lateral load could be applied simultaneously to the panel (Fig. 1). A 152 × 152 mm (6 × 6 in.) steel ledger angle was bolted to the top of the panel on which the eccentric vertical load was applied. The vertical load from water-filled drums was applied through a lever system to the ledger angle.

The vertical load simulated the actual loading from the roof of the building and was varied from the initial test with 3.64 kN/m (250 lb/lin ft) and 12.52 kN/m (860 lb/lin ft). In addition, the eccentric vertical load caused a P-Delta effect, which is a consideration in wall buckling.

An air bag 1.2 m (4 ft) wide and 7.3 m (24 ft) high was placed between the wall and the loading frame. The air bag imposed a lateral load against the wall, which caused a moment in the same direction as that created by the eccentric load on the ledger angle.

The lateral deflection was measured at 11 locations on the wall: in the center and in five places vertically on each side of the center. Micrometer dial gauges were used initially for measurement of deflections in the first three inches to determine the first crack. Yardsticks, placed on the walls and read by a transit, were also used to determine the horizontal movement of the wall as the air pressure was applied. Approximately halfway through the testing program, helical variable transducers were used to measure the deflection of the wall to an accuracy of 0.5 mm (0.02 in.).

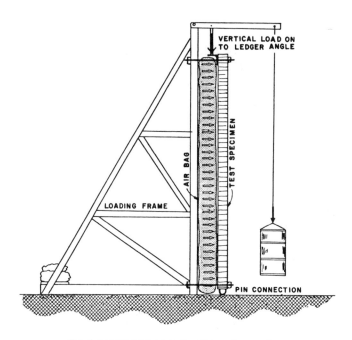

Fig. 1 Loading frame and wall specimen setup

The wall specimens exhibited high ductility under the eccentric vertical load and the lateral pressure. This expected phenomenon was observed during the first tests of the first wall (Wall #31)—a 150 mm (6 in.) concrete masonry unit (CMU) wall, reinforced with five 13 mm bars. After verifying instrumentation and procedure, the loads were increased to a maximum of 6700 Pa (140 psf) lateral pressure and an eccentric vertical load of 3.64 kN/m (250 lb/lin ft). The wall deflected a total of 600 mm (23.6 in.) and rebounded approximately 300 mm (12 in.) after removal of load.

Wall #3 was one of the next specimens tested. It deflected 490 mm (19.3 in.) under a lateral pressure of 4800 Pa (100 psf) (see Fig. 2) and rebounded to 335 mm (13.2 in.) The initial crack occurred at a lateral load of 1900 Pa (40 psf) at which point the tension stress in the mortar joint exceeded the capability of bond. The steel yielded at a lateral load of 3800 Pa (80 psf).

The vertical steel in all the panels was stressed beyond the yield stress, which provided information on the ductility properties of the masonry walls. Test results of all of the slender walls are given in Table 1. The following observations were made.

1. There was no evidence of elastic or inelastic lateral instability (buckling) in the load ranges tested.

2. The significance of the eccentric moment, applied to simulate normal load, was small.

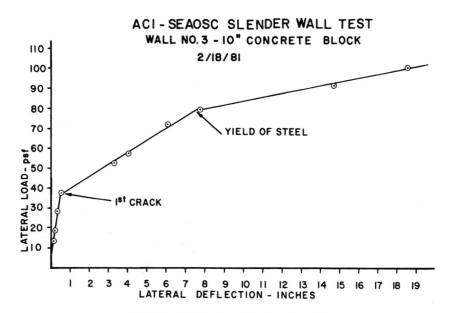

Fig. 2 Load-deflection plot of specimen 3

3. The significance of the P-Delta moment was more pronounced in the thinner panels but did not produce instability in the load ranges tested.

4. The Structural Engineers Association design procedure appears to predict adequately the yield point lateral loading. The correlation with the Structural Engineers Association design procedure yield point deflection was not as good, with concrete overpredicting, CMU adequately predicting, and brick under-predicting the amount of deflection.

5. The interaction load/moment curves provide an adequate predictive envelope for the load cases studied for both masonry and concrete.

6. The Structural Engineers Association design equations are applicable for both concrete and masonry walls.

7. The need for height-to-thickness limitations was not demonstrated in the range tested.

8. Inspection of the panels following testing revealed that in many cases, the steel location varied ±20% from the center line location specified. This can have a significant influence on moment capacity.

As a result of this program and the analysis of the test results, it is possible to learn the effects of (a) the eccentric vertical load, (b) the P-Delta effect, and (c) the capability of the walls under combined vertical and lateral loads.

The results provided satisfactory data, and code changes were made and adopted that eliminate slenderness (h/t) limits and allow walls to be built based upon the engineering calculations and capability of construction. The results of this test program were presented at the Annual Convention of the Structural Engineers Association held on September 11, 1981 in Del Coronado, California.

Figures 3 and 4 show the prisms built with the walls and several of the walls themselves during and after test. Table 1 presents the data obtained, and Fig. 2 is a load–deflection plot of specimen 3.

Table 1 Slender wall test results *(Courtesy: Structural Engineers Association of Southern California)*

Wall no.	Thickness (in.)	Material	Strength f'm psi	Actual h/t ratio
1	10	CMU	2460	30
2	10	CMU	2460	30
3	10	CMU	2460	30
4	8	CMU	2595	38
5	8	CMU	2595	38
6	8	CMU	2595	38
7	6	CMU	3185	51.2
8	6	CMU	3185	51.2
9	6	CMU	3185	51.2
10	9½	Brick	3060	30.3
11	9½	Brick	3060	30.3
12	9½	Brick	3060	30.3
13	7½	Brick	3440	38.4
14	7½	Brick	3440	38.4
15	7½	Brick	3440	38.4
16	5½	Hollow brick	6243	52.4
17	5½	Hollow brick	6243	52.4
18	5½	Hollow brick	6243	52.4
19	9½	Conc. T. U.	4000	30.3
20	9½	Conc. T. U.	4000	30.3
21	9½	Conc. T. U.	4000	30.3
22	7¼	Conc. T. U.	4000	39.7
23	7¼	Conc. T. U.	4000	39.7
24	7¼	Conc. T. U.	4000	39.7
25	5½	Conc. T. U.	4000	52.4
26	5½	Conc. T. U.	4000	52.4
27	5½	Conc. T. U.	4000	52.4
28	4¾	Conc. T. U.	4000	60.6
29	4¾	Conc. T. U.	4000	60.6
30	4¾	Conc. T. U.	4000	60.6
31	6	CMU	3185	51.2
32	3½	Hollow brick		54.9

Vertical load p.l.f.	Maximum lateral load p.s.f.	Maximum lateral deflection (in.)	Vertical reinf.	Date tested (1981)
320	102.0	7.1	5#4	3-9
860	87.3	8.0	5#4	2-25
860	102.9	19.0	5#4	2-18
860	91.5	11.2	5#4	3-10
860	81.9	10.3	5#4	3-12
320	109.2	14.8	5#4	4-21
320	62.4	17.7	5#4	4-22
320	40.0	15.9	5#4	4-30
320	49.4	11.0	5#4	5-1
320	150.8	15.6	5#4	4-20
320	164.1	16.8	5#4	4-17
320	89.4	14.6	5#4	5-11
320	59.8	19.6	5#4	5-8
320	57.2	15.9	5#4	5-7
320	78.0	14.8	5#4	5-6
320	86.6	19.3	5#4	4-15
320	86.5	17.0	5#4	4-16
320	61.6	11.1	5#4	5-4
320	88.4	9.9	4#4	5-14
320	83.2	7.0	4#4	5-12
320	88.4	12.3	4#4	4-27
320	65.0	12.2	4#4	4-28
320	60.8	11.8	4#4	4-29
860	74.0	11.8	4#4	4-14
860	53.6	13.2	4#4	3-14
860	44.7	11.1	4#4	3-18
320	51.0	12.4	4#4	3-23
320	32.2	13.0	4#4	5-5
320	35.0	19.2	4#4	5-15
320	36.4	15.2	4#4	5-14
250	140.0	23.6	5#4	12-13-81
225	56.4	17.1	3#4	6-20-81

Fig. 3 Three-and-one-half-in. hollow brick wall, 16 ft 8 in. high deflected laterally 17 in. under a 56 psf load

Fig. 4 Six-inch concrete masonry wall deflecting about 12 in.

Project Descriptions

Dearborn Park—An Urban Development

Ronald Livorsi

In 1972 a plan was developed for the City of Chicago entitled "Chicago 21." The plan was paid for by the business community and advice during its development was given by a steering committee made up of executives from the corporate community. Using the Chicago 21 plan as a base, key corporate leaders decided that the first priority should be the revitalization of the South Loop area in Chicago. These key persons were Phillip Klutznick, Chairman, Urban Development and Investment Corporation; Ferd Kramer, President of Draper & Kramer, Inc.; Tom Ayers, President and Chairman of Commonwealth Edison Corporation; John W. Baird, of Baird and Warner; Warren G. Skoning, Real Estate Vice President for Sears; and John Perkins, President, Continental Bank. The major intent of this group was to stabilize the South Loop. To be effective, they spearheaded the development of a limited-share dividend corporation, and through invitation developed a membership of 32 corporations in which, per their corporate charter, each investor was limited to a 6½% profit on his original investment.

The first action of the Corporation was to fund additional planning. Skidmore, Owings and Merrill (SOM) and Urban Investments and Development Company collaborated to provide a detailed plan for the entire Southbelt area, designated in the Chicago 21 plan as "South Loop New Town."

The plan was presented to the City for approval and received it. The Corporation obtained the purchase option of a 51-acre parcel at $7.3 million from the owner of the Chicago Bears, George Halas, who had pieced it together through purchases from seven or eight railroads that owned land in an abandoned area.

Sheldon Kantoff was selected to be the Corporation's representative, and he has served as the client on behalf of the Board. The 30-member Board is comprised predominantly of corporate CEO's and has an Executive Committee of 11 members. The Chairman of the Board is Tom Ayers and the Board President is Ferd Kramer of Draper & Kramer, Inc. Phillip Klutznick, former Secretary of Commerce, is Chairman of the Executive Committee.

FINANCE

When the emphasis narrowed to the 51-acre tract of land, the Corporation was renamed "Dearborn Park Corporation." The next step was to obtain financing. A construction loan totaling $45 million for Phase I of the project was committed by Continental Illinois Bank and Trust Company and First Federal Savings and Loan Association of Chicago (50% each). Loans for the future condominium purchasers were made available by a consortium of lenders (Table 1).

DESIGN AND MARKETING

In developing the detailed design plan for the unusual project, SOM and Urban Investments differed strongly in their concepts. SOM wanted a very futuristic and exciting new architectural style, while Urban Investments strongly felt that the project itself was enough of a departure from the norm, and that traditional architecture was called for. It was finally agreed that a measure of diversity would be good for the development, and therefore four architectural firms were hired, one for each type of housing to be included in Dearborn Park:

Table 1 Lenders providing loans for the condominium purchasers

First Federal Savings	$10,000,000
Continental	5,000,000
First National Bank of Chicago	5,000,000
Combination of Small Institutions	21,000,000
	$41,000,000

High-Rise	Gordon, Levin & Associates
Mid-Rise	Booth & Hanson
Townhouses	Hammond, Beeby and Babka
Mid-Rise Elderly	Dubin, Dubin, Black & Moutoussamy

SOM became the coordinating architect and provided the site development and landscaping plans.

The anticipated market for Dearborn Park was middle-income and young families. Accordingly, 57% of the units were designed to contain two or more bedrooms (26% are three or four bedroom units), and the remainder are one bedroom units (32%) and efficiency/studios (11%) (Tables 2a and 2b).

To prevent the possibility of units being purchased for speculation rather than actual occupancy, a requirement is made at the time of purchase that the buyer move into the unit within 60 days and must occupy the unit for two years. He cannot sell or rent the unit within the two year period. If he does, he must sell it back to the Dearborn Park Corporation at its original purchase price and an allowance for the rise in the consumer price index (CPI).

RESULTS TO DATE

Phase I contains 939 units, which entered the market during the period from July, 1979 to December, 1980 (Table 3). Dearborn Park sold more residential units during that same period than all of Chicago, which had been experiencing a trough during the previous several years. Two key elements in that success were the convenience of the location and the attractive financing available to the purchaser.

Although it is difficult to confirm a cause and effect relationship between the development of Dearborn Park and the increase in surrounding property values, there is a correlation. Property values in areas adjacent to Dearborn Park have doubled in the last few years and there has been scattered redevelopment of several nearby buildings, and ten commercial buildings have been purchased as a group and are currently being restored in a project entitled "Printing House Row." The first building completed in the project was the Transportation Building, which opened the week of November 10, 1980.

AFFIRMATIVE ACTION

As the Chicago 21 plan was totally funded by private dollars, there was no requirement to fill Federal affirmative action quotas for construction employment. However, Dearborn Park chose to set even higher standards of its own, which became part of each contract. This approach has received both City and National recognition.

Table 2a Dearborn Park: Phase I amenities

	High-rise		Mid-rise			
	Condo	Condo	Condo	Condo	Condo	Condo
Area	172924	263468	120643	8061	241286	14280
Stories	22	27	6+Garage	2+Base	6+Garage	2+Base
Units						
Studio		75				
1B	29	125			8	
2B	62	50	48		96	
3B	29		23		46	8
4B			2	4		
Total	120	250	73	4	150	8
Baths						
Full	153	254	147	8	294	16
Half	62	50	26	4	48	8
Elevators	2	3	2		4	
Garage						
Structure	31000		20994		41988	

Townhouses							
Building	1	2	3	4	5	6	7	Totals
Area	29,145	28,812	29,145	32,130	30,642	29,488	40,473	218,844
Stories	2	2	2	2	2	2	2	
Units	19	19	19	21	20	19	27	144
2B	2	3	2	2	2	5	6	22
3B	11	11	11	13	12	9	15	82
4B	6	5	6	6	6	5	6	40
Baths								
Full	36	35	36	36	38	40	54	275
Half	19	19	19	21	20	19	27	144

Table 2b Phase II amenities

	High-rise	Garden homes
Area	237,000 ft^2	36,000 ft^2
Units		
1B	122	0
2B	76	22
Baths		
Full	278	44
Half	9	22
Elevators	3 + 1 @ Garage	0
Garage	156,000 ft^2	

LOCATION

The South Loop had a poor reputation because of its missions, skid road inhabitants, and low-grade movie houses. The first marketing approach was to picture Dearborn Park as a secure and protected oasis, desirable despite its location (Fig. 1). Ultimately, the decision was made to begin all the buildings in Phase I simultaneously, which demonstrated to everyone that the project's goal was to develop a new neighborhood for its inhabitants. Security was a major design consideration, as access to the site was limited to the State Street entrance. High-rise and mid-rise buildings would be entered only by pass card or the telephone-controlled action of a resident. It is within a 10-minute walk of the downtown Chicago Loop business district. As the property values and recent restoration responded to Dearborn Park, that walk became a secure one.

PARKS

Four parks are proposed for Dearborn Park (Fig. 2). All residents will be within a block of at least one of the planned parks. Park recreational uses will include approximately 1¼ mi of continuous bicycle paths, approximately 3 mi of pedestrian walkways, eight outdoor tennis courts, two playgrounds, and family and sitting areas including chess and game tables.

PRIVATE RECREATION

Augmenting the public amenities will be private recreational amenities serving residential building groups. Each group will have its own swimming pool and clubhouse facilities, which will include game rooms, party rooms, sauna baths, and locker facilities.

Table 3 Phase I of development

Date available	Number and type of units	
July 22, 1979	120	High-rises
	144	Townhouses
	77	Mid-rises
	190	Apartments for the elderly (mid-rise)
September, 1979	79	Mid-rises
October 4, 1980	250	High-rises
December, 1980	79	Mid-rises
	939	

Fig. 1 High-rise condominiums and apartments, currently under construction, will provide housing for Dearborn Park residents that is only three blocks from the Loop, yet richly landscaped with parks, playgrounds and jogging trails. *(Photo by Lynn S. Beedle)*

Fig. 2 Dearborn Park's planned parks provide open space for recreational use. *(Photo by Lynn S. Beedle)*

The Hongkong and
Shanghai Bank Project

Jack Zunz
Mike Glover

This paper describes the development of the structural engineering concept for the new headquarters building of the Hongkong and Shanghai Banking Corporation, Hong Kong.

A general description of the structure and of the factors that have controlled its development is given. The form and scope of specialist studies and investigations that have been undertaken are reported in outline.

The building is currently under construction, with scheduled completion in 1985.

INTRODUCTION

The Hongkong and Shanghai Banking Corporation is not only Hong Kong's principal banking institution; it has developed into one of the world's major banks. Its headquarters, completed in 1935, was then the tallest building between Cairo and San Francisco. The first building in Hong Kong to be air-conditioned, its roof was designed to take "autogyros," and wiring was installed in advance of the arrival of telecasters. The building was completed in two years. At the time it was viewed as a masterpiece and an astonishing achievement, since there was no comparable building in size or technical sophistication outside of Europe or the United States. The image of the building decorates the Colony's currency as if to underline its symbolic importance (Fig. 1).

But by the middle of the 1970s the building had been outgrown, and its redevelopment was considered. In June, 1979, seven prominent architectural firms from the U.S., Australia, Hong Kong, and the United Kingdom were invited to take part in a limited competition for a design to redevelop the site occupied by the bank's headquarters, No. 1 Queens Road Central.

In October, 1979, Foster Associates were announced as the winning architects. Ove Arup & Partners, who had assisted Fosters during the competition, were appointed as civil, structural, and geotechnical engineers. This appointment was later extended to include project planning advice, fire and transportation engineering, and acoustics.

REDEVELOPMENT

The 5000 m² (53,820 ft²) site is arguably the most important site in Hong Kong, being at the head of Statue Square, the only substantial public open space in the central business district (Fig. 2). Statue Square is a major pedestrian route to the harbor waterfront and ferry services, which lie at a distance of abut 400 m (1,300 ft) from the site.

The site is roughly square in plan, bounded by roads to the north (Des Voeux Road), south (Queens Road Central), and east (Bank Street); to the west it shares a common boundary with Chartered Bank.

Fig. 1 Colony of Hongkong bank note

Redevelopment of the site is constrained by a height restriction of 178 m (584 ft) and a plot ratio of approximately 18:1. Statutory lighting angles limit the bulk of building that may be erected on any road frontage.

The facilities to be provided in the building are extensive and include the following.

1. Headquarters office accommodation including a central computer installation;

2. A multilevel banking hall around a central atrium space;

3. Security and safe-deposit vaults with secure access and unloading facilities;

4. Recreation areas, restaurant and kitchen facilities;

5. Open gardens on terraces at high levels;

6. Apartments and executive suites;

7. The potential for large swimming pool; and

8. A heliport and a multilevel viewing gallery at the top of the building.

DESIGN DEVELOPMENT

The development of the building design took place between October 1979 and January 1981, when the final concept was presented to and accepted by the Board of the Bank. Like all design development it passed through perceptive and imperceptive stages. Figure 3 indicates some of the significant milestones.

The key features of the architect's concept that have shaped the development of the structural frame can be summarized under six heads as follows.

Flexibility of Internal Planning

Flexibility of internal planning was achieved by reducing the number and size of vertical structural and servicing elements within the center of the building and providing special multilevel spaces. The size and proportion of the individual elements have been selected to reduce visual and planning obstruction. Wall elements have been discriminated against.

The design floor live loadings are greater than the statutory recommendations, principally to provide flexibility in the future arrangement of storage areas, computing facilities, and safes on the general floors. In addition, special high loading allowances have been made within the building to accommodate multiuse spaces including terraces, gardens and a swimming pool. The vertical loading for this building is estimated to be 20% higher than for a commercial building of similar proportions.

Large Open Space at Ground Level

The large open space at ground level forms a physical continuation of Statue Square and has been dedicated to public use. In recognition of this dedication the maximum plot ratio has been granted for this building. The

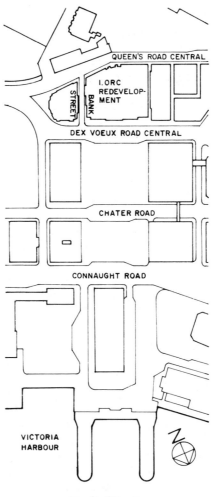

Fig. 2a Site plan

requirement to provide an open space has limited the "footprint" of the structural frame at ground level to localized tower structures to the east and west of the site.

Expressed Structural Form

A further effect of the open space has been to lead the design development towards hanging or tensile forms that, by nature of their discrete suspension structures and support towers, project a strong image of the structural form. Initial schemes considered the possibility of expressing the unclad steel framework, but the combination of fire-protection requirements and specific visual considerations around a high-quality, long-life finish ruled against their incorporation. High-performance metal cladding was identified as a universal solution at an early stage of the design development.

Integration of Structure, Services, and Architecture

The servicing concept of the building has departed from the traditional in a number of ways. The concepts that have had a significant bearing on the evolution of the structural framework are (a) vertical movement systems

Fig. 2b Aerial view

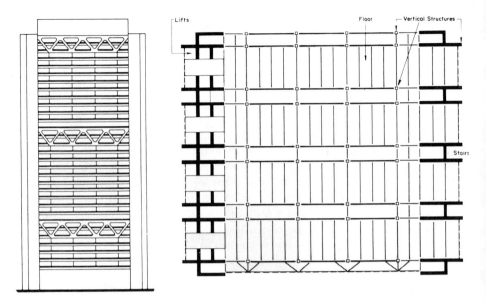

Fig. 3a Competition concept—elevation at left and typical plan at right

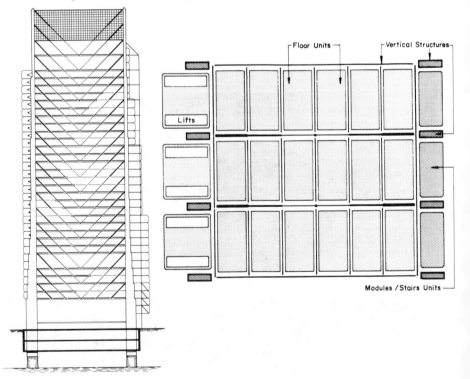

Fig. 3b Chevron concept—elevation at left and typical plan at right

provided by a combination of elevators and escalators; (b) decentralized modular services and plantrooms that consist of prefabricated, fitted out, and commissioned units completely preassembled off-site; and (c) full-access raised floors containing all servicing for light, air and communications.

Prefabricated Building

To achieve a high-quality building with a fast construction program, as many components as possible have been designed to enable prefabrication of finished products in off-site factory conditions. This concept led the design development of the structural framework toward a totally steel construction.

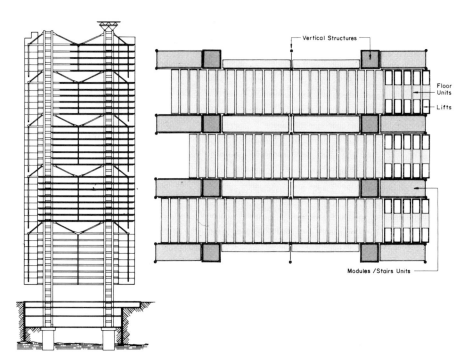

Fig. 3c Final concept—elevation at left and typical plan at right

Extendability

Statutory regulations restrict the notional shadow projection of the building development to a specified proportion of the width of road projected upon. At the initial stages of the project it was hoped that a waiver could be gained, and early design development schemes did not reflect the full implications of this restriction. Its introduction in later schemes produced the stepped north–south cross-section of the building and the setting-back of the elevation along the narrow road boundary of Bank Street. Despite this restriction, the building has been designed to provide the full area allowed by the plot ratio.

Although the statutory regulations limiting plot ratio and shadow encroachment confine the building to its proposed floor area and external geometry, all the schemes developed included the provision of infilling the multistory voids within the building envelope and also the Bank Street "set-backs" for later schemes. It is estimated that, if realized, these provisions would produce an additional 30% of floor area.

FINAL CONCEPT

The scheme comprises a rectangular plan approximately 55 × 72 m (180 × 236 ft) overall, rising 175 m (574 ft) above ground level over a 20 m (66 ft) basement extending over the full site area.

There are four levels of basements and 43 floors in the superstructure topped by a multilevel helipad structure.

The structural scheme comprises:

1. Reinforced concrete large-diameter caisson foundations;

2. Multilevel reinforced concrete basement structure within a diaphragm wall enclosure;

3. Two parallel rows of four steel masts rising from the lowest basement level to the top of the building and dividing the building horizontally into three bays of 30, 37, and 43 stories;

4. Five discrete levels of double-story height steel stability structures comprising east–west suspension trusses and north–south cross-bracings at levels 11, 20, 28, 35, and 41, dividing the building vertically into five structurally independent subbuildings;

5. Groups of steel-framed suspended floors that set back successively up the building on the east side in response to shadow restrictions;

6. Modules and stairs; and

7. Cladding and curtain walling.

STRUCTURAL BEHAVIOR

Gravity Loads

The gravity load support system is divided into five distinct zones vertically up the building by the suspension trusses. At the top of each zone the series of suspension structures span between, and cantilever beyond, the masts in the east–west direction, two per mast. Three vertical hangers (one internal and two external), suspended from each truss, support primary floor elements spanning between the hangers and the masts. The masts transmit the loading direct to the foundations. The system is illustrated in Fig. 4. The frequency of these structures is dictated by planning and not by structural considerations.

In general the suspension trusses include a tip boom between the masts. However, these are omitted for architectural reasons on the building facade frames and at the topmost zone of each mast. This significantly changes the force actions in these areas to a direct corbel action that, because of the relative flexibility of the masts under this form of loading, causes an increase in truss deflection.

Lateral Loads

The static deflected shapes of the building under wind in the two principal directions are shown in Figs. 6 and 7. It can be seen that the behavior in each direction is that of a five-story portal frame, the masts acting as the columns and the east–west suspension trusses and north–south cross-bracing as the beams. The framed structure of the masts gives a predominance of shear rather than bending deformation. The masts are restrained laterally at the highest basement level and the foundations.

STRUCTURAL COMPONENTS

Considerable development has been undertaken with the relevant subcontractors in evolving the present design. This collaboration has enabled details to be developed, combining erection and fabrication advantages with improved performance in terms of overall buildability.

The total quantity of structural steelwork is approximately 25,000 tonnes (222,000 kN), most in grades of steel equivalent to BS 4360:50D and much of this with through thickness properties.

The masts are formed by four circular tubular elements interconnected by rectangular bowtie beam elements at story height intervals of 3.9 m (12.8 ft) to form a vierendeel beam structure. The masts are 4.8 × 5.1 m (15.75 ft × 16.7 ft) center-to-center in plan.

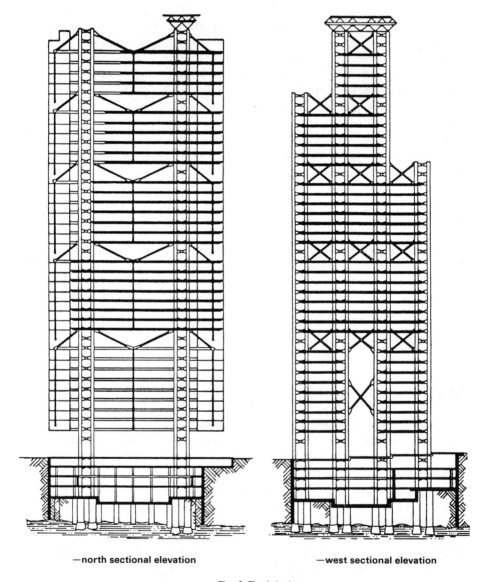

—north sectional elevation   —west sectional elevation

Fig. 4 Final design

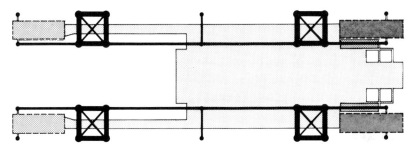

—typical one-bay office (levels 37-41)

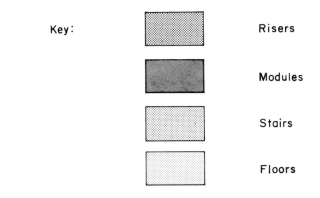

Key:

Risers

Modules

Stairs

Floors

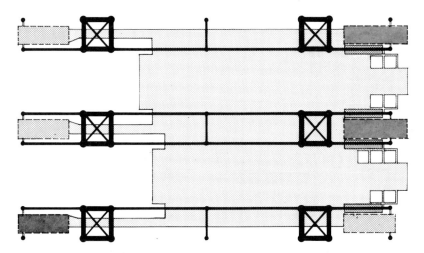

—typical two-bay offices (levels 30-35)

Fig. 4 Final design (continued)

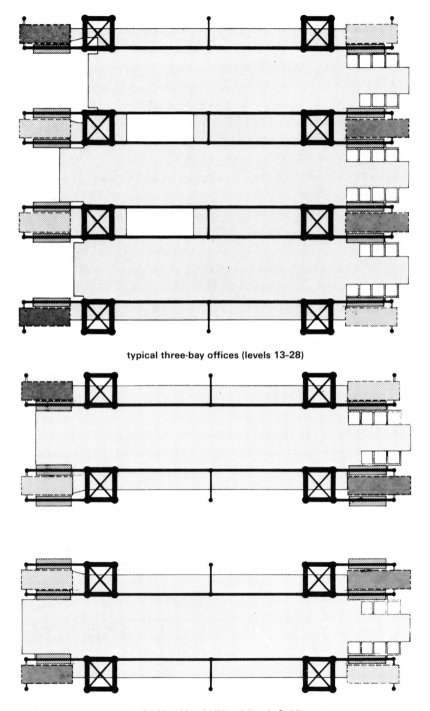

typical three-bay offices (levels 13-28)

typical banking hall level (levels 3-11)

Fig. 4. Final design (continued)

The elevational geometry of the vierendeel beams is constant throughout the height of the building; the plan geometry and diameter of the tubulars decrease up the building height to reflect the decrease in axial and
lateral loads.

The tubulars at the base of the building are typically 1400 mm (4.6 ft) in
diameter with wall thicknesses of 90 and 100 mm (3.5 and 3.9 in.). At the top of
the building they reduce to 800 mm (31.5 in.) in diameter and 40 mm (1.6 in.)

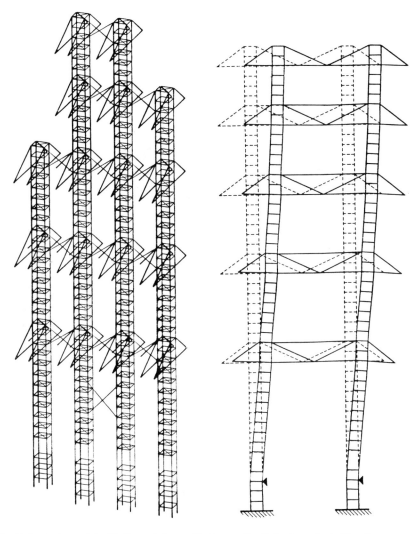

Fig. 5 Analysis model with floor plates omitted   Fig. 6 East-west wind loading
       for clarity   deflected profile

thickness. All tubulars are formed from plate by hot or cold rolling techniques. Centrifugal cast and forged elements had been considered during the early development of the project, but these have not been progressed to the final design.

The thickness of vierendeel beam flanges is generally less than 50 mm (2.0 in.), but towards the base of the building and within the suspension structure zones, these increase to 100 mm (3.9 in.). The components forming the mast elements are shown in Fig. 8.

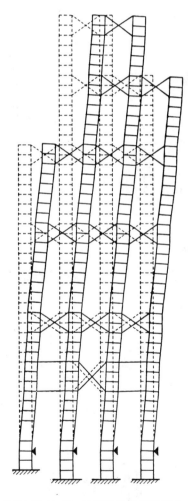

Fig. 7 North-south wind loading deflected profile

STABILITY STRUCTURES

Suspension Trusses

The suspension trusses span 33.6 m (110.2 ft) between the masts and cantilever 10.8 m (35.4 ft) beyond the masts.

The truss structures comprise rectangular elements interconnected and connected to the mast by pins passing through end lug plates into large spherical bearings located within thick gusset plates (Fig. 9).

The horizontal truss elements also provide the primary floor beams at these levels. Generally the depth of inclined elements is 500 mm (1.6 ft) and of horizontal beams 900 mm (2.95 ft).

The thicknesses of the lug and gusset plates are in excess of 100 mm (3.9 in.) and reach a maximum of 175 mm (6.9 in.) in the stability structures at the lower levels of the building. The bearings vary in size from 150 mm (5.9 in.) to 600 mm (1.97 ft) diameter; the pins are slightly smaller. The individual truss elements are formed from two thick plates spaced apart by thinner web or

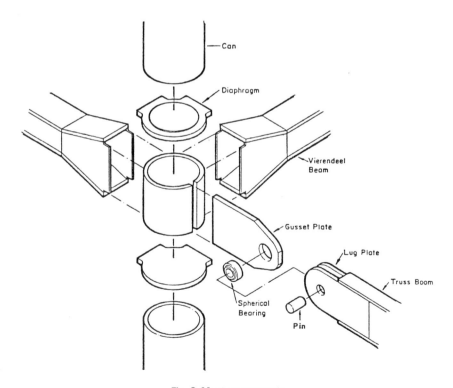

Fig. 8 Mast components

spacer plates, the thicker plates top and bottom in the horizontal elements for bending efficiency, and vertically in the inclined elements to ease connection detailing.

Schemes utilizing multiplated elements with friction grip bolt joints were researched and developed. These were not favored by the contractors because of the large number of plates and bolts involved.

Cross-bracing

The cross-bracing linking the mast in the north–south direction at suspension structure levels is located on the inner line of mast tubulars only. Their construction and size are very similar to the inclined elements of the suspension trusses, incorporating large-diameter spherical bearings within their connections to the masts.

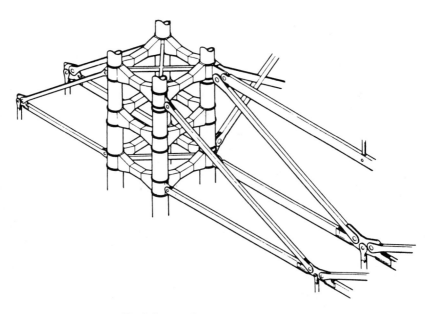

Fig. 9 Suspension structure components

Floor Structure

The detailing of the floor has been dominated by the servicing concept of a raised, full-access floor. The levels of the floor beams and concrete are governed by ceiling profiles, not by floor levels. The general arrangement of the floors at various levels of the building is shown in Fig. 4. The floor structure may be considered to be in three zones: an 11.1 m (36 ft) wide general use zone, a 5.1 m (16.7 ft) wide circulation and escalator zone, and an edge zone.

The general floor structure comprises a system of 400 mm (1.3 ft) beams at 2.4 m (7.9 ft) spacing, acting compositely with a 100 mm (3.9 in.) thick concrete slab on permanent profiled metal decking. These secondary beams span 11.1 m (36.4 ft) between 900 mm (2.95 ft) deep plate girder primary beams that span 16.8 m (55.1 ft) between the mast and central hanger. Within the circulation and edge zones is a similar arrangement of secondary beams and decking. The primary beams in the east and west zones beyond the masts support the independent service modules and staircases.

Early designs for the floor construction were developed around the principle of assembling the floor structure, services, and raised floor into completed 2.4 m (7.9 ft) wide units off-site to speed erection. But upon close analysis these solutions showed only a marginal advantage over more limited prefabrication approaches and were not adopted.

Modules and Stairs

These structurally independent elements are to be located between the primary beam structures at the east and west edges of the building for ease of erection access.

A total of 160 service modules are provided in the building. At the lower levels there are four modules servicing each floor, reducing to two at the upper levels where the building plan reduces. The maximum module size is $12 \times 3.6 \times 3.9$ m ($39.4 \times 11.8 \times 12.8$ ft), and the installation weight is typically 30 tonnes (267 kN) with a maximum of 55 tonnes (489 kN).

The vertical services are located in risers grouped in prefabricated frames two and three stories high. A total of approximately 8 km of riser frames will be provided for the building.

The structural form of the modules has been developed with the subcontractor. Monocoque stressed skin design solutions were investigated but were not developed because of the difficulty of providing the structural fire-protection requirements of one and two hours.

The module structure adopted is a simple trussed box with lightweight steel deck floors.

There are 160 stair assemblies alternating in position with the modules.

They are preassembled off-site into complete landing and stair flights 12 m (39 ft) long and attached to the floor structure in a similar manner to the modules.

Cladding and Curtain Walling

The connection details between the steelwork frame and floors and the cladding and curtain walling have been detailed to enable the latter to be erected with minimum tolerances. Movement joints are provided at each floor level to allow for structural deflections.

Three different curtain wall systems have been developed for different locations on the building elevation.

(1) Typical curtain wall for office floors comprising aluminum mullion and sill extrusions with 12 mm (0.5 in.) toughened glass. At double-height spaces the typical mullions are stiffened by adding vierendeel truss.

(2) Glass grid wall to the stairs, which comprises 12 mm (0.5 in.) toughened glass fixed to an aluminum extrusion framework using structural silicone sealant.

(3) Panel wall for the service modules and risers comprising 25 mm (1.0 in.) thick aluminum honeycomb panel fixed to an aluminum extrusion framework.

The cladding to the structural elements comprises 5 mm (0.2 in.) thick aluminum sheet fixed to extrusions at each edge that form pressure equalized joints. The finish to all exposed aluminum surfaces of the cladding and curtain wall extrusions is backed fluoropolymer coating. The cladding profiles are fixed to the structural frame over the corrosion and fire protection coatings.

The cladding shape generally conforms with the shape of the structural element enclosed but does not reflect the connection details. The cladding surfaces are continuous and precision-manufactured with a close tolerance on flatness.

PROTOTYPE TESTS

Main Frame Elements

As part of the overall quality assurance approach on this project a number of full-scale prototypes of key structural elements were fabricated, instrumented, and then loaded to destruction.

The tests were carried out using the British Steel Corporation's 1250 ton $(11.12 \times 10.3 \text{ kN})$ machine at the Britannia Works, Middlesbrough. In addition to confirming the structural design of these elements, the prototype program provided valuable information on potential problems in fabrication and erection of the production elements.

Module

A series of strength tests to destruction were carried out on floor units and individual joints within the framework, as well as a deflection test on a complete module.

Cladding

Prior to production, a full-scale prototype of each type of cladding arrangement has been carried out to 1.5 times the design wind pressure. Testing for water tightness and air leakage also have been carried out.

STRUCTURAL ANALYSIS

Analysis of the Primary Frame

The only practicable way to obtain reliable design forces for the framework was to analyze a detailed finite element model with each member included explicitly. To simplify the model and to allow accurately for the effect of the nonprismatic beam sections and the relatively large joint zones within the masts, a detailed investigation was made into the bending and shear stiffness characteristics of the column/vierendeel assembly to enable these elements to be substructured. An isometric view of the primary elements of half the model developed is shown in Fig. 5. Elements modeling the floor at each level are omitted for clarity.

This model enabled the overall force and deflection patterns of the building to be determined and detailed studies to be made.

Stability

Although the individual column elements between vierendeel beams are very stocky ($1/r > 16$), an investigation of the overall stability and force magnification of P-Delta effects of the frame was made in view of the relatively flexible vierendeel mast construction. The magnifications of around 10% were considered acceptable from a stability viewpoint.

Dynamic Analysis

The overall dynamic properties of the structure were estimated for use in conjunction with the wind engineering studies described subsequently to establish the effects of dynamic response on the peak lateral force due to wind, the perception of movement and accelerations within the building, and fatigue.

The effect of earthquakes was considered, but the seismicity of Hong Kong is low and the height of the building, combined with the relatively severe wind climate, make wind the more onerous lateral loading force.

The first mode (E–W direction) predicted by the dynamic analysis has a period of 4.5 seconds. The center of mass of the proposed building becomes progressively more offset from the shear center towards the top, because of the Bank Street set-backs, and coupled lateral torsional modes were found as expected, particularly in the N–S direction.

WIND ENGINEERING

Professor Alan Davenport of the Boundary Layer Wind Tunnel Laboratory, University of Western Ontario, was commissioned in early 1981 to carry out an extensive study of the wind effects on and around the building. The work included a fundamental reassessment of the climatology of the area involving a new and critical analysis of all available records and the calibration of wind records from specific locations in Hong Kong by using small-scale wind tunnel models. The wind regime at the site was established for all wind directions using the relevant slices of a 1 : 2500 topographical model of Hong Kong in the wind tunnel (Fig. 10). When fully assembled, the model was as large as a tennis court. The results of these tests were applied to a detailed instrumented model of the building in its surroundings for overall force, surface pressure, and environmental studies (Fig. 10).

The study shows that the application of the Hong Kong statutory wind loads and cladding pressures is conservative, particularly for this location, principally because of the sheltering afforded by the topology around the general area of the site. It is hoped that the results of the climatological research will be used to influence the loadings selected for future work.

CORROSION PROTECTION

The traditional protection scheme for external elements is to encase them within a minimum thickness of 50 mm (2.0 in.) of dense concrete. However, constructional considerations made such a solution inappropriate.

The system that has been developed and tested is based upon a polymer-modified gunite reinforced with stainless steel fibers. The proving trials have demonstrated that a thickness of 12 mm (0.5 in.) will give the required properties, low permeability in particular. Apart from site joints, the coating was intended to be applied off-site prior to erection, and in recognition of this the trials included tests of impact resistance and differential heating due to welding. Fire tests were conducted to demonstrate the stability of the material under fire load conditions.

The gunite coating has been applied to all external and main framework elements including masts and suspension structures, while the other elements have been galvanized.

FIRE ENGINEERING

The superstructure is divided into five principal compartments, which are located between the truss suspension structures. Refuge terraces are provided at the lower levels of each truss, which act as places of safety for the building occupants in the case of fire. Escape stairs are located in the outer zones of the building on the east and west elevations.

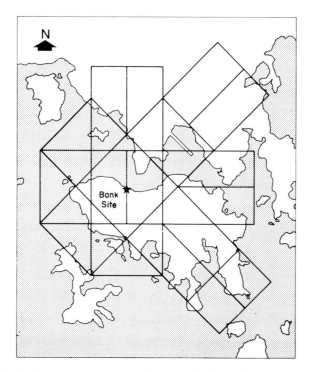

Fig. 10a Wind tunnel study—layout of topographical model for wind tunnel tests

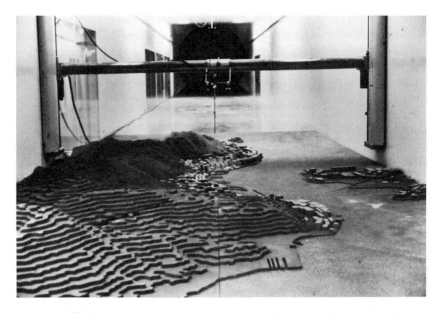

Fig. 10b Wind tunnel study—section of topographical model in wind tunnel

Fig. 10c Wind tunnel study—1: 500 scale proximity model including proposed building

The compartment sizes vary between four and eight floors. All floor areas are sprinklered in accordance with regulations to reduce the risk of fire spread within a compartment. Particular consideration has been given to smoke extraction within the banking hall, which has a full-height central atrium.

The main superstructure steel frame elements are provided with two-hour fire protection. During earlier scheme developments, the possibility of fire-protecting the main steel elements by water cooling was investigated. However, since these elements will now be clad, conventional fire protection materials have been adopted.

The main frame steel elements have been fire-protected using a ceramic fire blanket. Tests have been conducted to determine the relationship between blanket thickness and steel section size. The floor steelwork beams have been fire-protected using a board system.

The steelwork for the stairs, where the steelwork is exposed, has been protected using intumescent coatings.

SUBSTRUCTURE

The site, which is at the base of the northern slopes of Victoria Peak, has a 2 m (7 ft) incline across it. One hundred years ago the shore line cut across this site, but now after successive reclamations the shore is some 400 m (1.3 ft) further north. The geology of the site is typical of a Hong Kong harborside location, comprising 5 m (16 ft) depth of fill and marine deposits, generally over the northern part of the site, overlying granite in various stages of decomposition, to rockhead approximately 25 m (82 ft) below ground level. The stratigraphy is described in Fig. 11. Ground water level is within 2 m

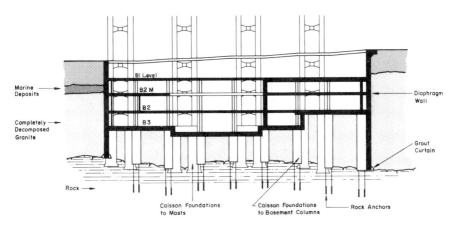

Fig. 11 Substructure section

(7 ft) of ground level on all sides of the site. A series of three site investigations has been undertaken to confirm the site geology, establish the soil
properties, and install a comprehensive array of surface and underground
monitoring stations.

The basements, which are up to 20 m (66 ft) deep, are on four levels and
house the vaults, truck loading facilities, and main plant hall, containing all
major items of plant. The basement planning reflects the superstructure
planning with vertical service distribution stairs and lifts, concentrated on
the eastern and western perimeters of the building. This planning is shown
in Fig. 12.

The basement structure comprises a perimeter diaphragm wall extending
to rock, propped by solid reinforced concrete flat slabs spanning onto columns
located on a 72 × 8.1 m (23.6 × 26.6 ft) grid. The design floor loadings are
generally 15 kN/m² with 25 kN/m² and 50 kN/m² (2.18, 3.63, and 7.25 psi) in
the safe depository and vault areas respectively.

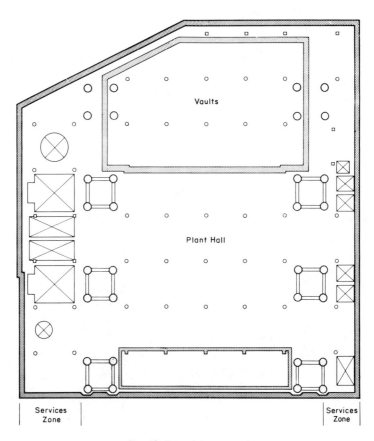

Fig. 12 Substructure plan

The columns are cased stanchions supported on 2 m (7 ft) diameter caissons founded onto the rock. The weight of the completed substructure construction is less than the potential hydrostatic uplift, and consequently a permanent rock anchor system has been adopted and incorporated into the caisson construction to maintain stability. The foundations to the superstructure masts are groups of four 3 m (9.8 ft) diameter caissons, one for each column of the mast.

Internal walls are essentially nonstructural, very high quality fair-faced blockwork. However, security requirements in vault areas dictate that many should be reinforced concrete. All exposed surfaces are to be fair-faced, and the concrete surfaces of the walls and slabs are to be lightly modeled to reflect the shuttering profiles used for them. Figure 13 shows the completed building.

Fig. 13 The Hongkong and Shanghai Banking Corporation headquarters *(Courtesy: Foster Associates, photo by Richard Davies)*

GEOTECHNICAL CONSIDERATIONS

Hong Kong has an almost automatic association with geotechnical problems. The ground conditions are difficult and highly variable. Experience has shown that a particular behavior can be expected from the completely decomposed granite that is the major subsoil constituent in this part of Hong Kong Island. The need to control and monitor ground water and the lateral movement of excavations are of paramount importance.

At an early stage, after a brief assessment of retaining wall systems, a diaphragm wall enclosure was adopted. Estimated movements were predicted using theories and computer techniques developed from our previous experience in Hong Kong. These estimates were verified by comparison with site measurements of movements during construction of Chater Road Mass Transit Station 150 m (492.1 ft) north of the site. Total vertical ground movements of the order of 50 mm (2.0 ft) were predicted.

Throughout the assessment period, different structural component forms and construction methods that give rise to the least ground movement were adopted. A key feature of this strategy was constructing the basements top-down, constructing the foundations and columns from ground level within large-diameter caissons and then casting the permanent slabs as excavation proceeds, using them as the temporary works support to the diaphragm wall.

SEA TUNNEL

Hong Kong, with its limited space and high population, has long had a water supply problem. Indeed much of its potable water is imported from China. For many years it has been commonplace to use sea-water for flushing in an effort to ameliorate the situation. In more recent years sea-water has been used as cooling water for heat exchangers with consequent savings of energy and space, an important commodity in Hong Kong.

The previous headquarters had a small sea-water pipe with an intake at Star Ferry Pier. The increased scale of the development has meant that the original system could not be reused. The final design is a 5.5 m (18 ft) diameter rock tunnel 60 m (196.85 ft) below ground, connected to an intake chamber at Star Ferry by an 11.0 m (36.1 ft) diameter shaft and to the headquarters by a 4.5 m (14.8 ft) shaft. It will provide water for the bank and future surrounding properties.

ACKNOWLEDGMENTS

Acknowledgment is given to Tony Broomhead, Alan Hart, David Thomlinson, and Mike Willford for their significant assistance with the preparation of this article.

Project Descriptions

Onterie Center

Mahjoub M. Elnimeiri

INTRODUCTION

Onterie Center is a multiuse high-rise complex located near the Lake Michigan shoreline north of the Chicago Loop. It comprises two towers, a 59-story main tower and a tapering auxiliary 12-story building (Fig. 1). The total building, with an area of 85,000 m² (920,000 ft²), is divided into five distinct areas by function (Fig. 2). On the ground floor of the main tower and the connecting low-rise building is the main public lobby and 1,860 m² (20,020 ft²) of commercial space. The parking areas occupy the basement and four floors above the lobby. Floors 6 through 10 of the tapering base as well as floors 2 through 11 of the auxiliary tower provide office space and are organized around two interior atriums.

The sky lobby at level 1 includes a health club, a swimming pool, a hospitality room, and mechanical equipment space. Levels 12 through 58 consist of one, two, and three-bedroom apartments, for a total of 593 units.

Onterie Center is the last high-rise structural project with which the late Dr. Fazlur Khan, former chairman of the Council, was involved.

STRUCTURAL FORM AND CONCEPT

Mixed-use high-rise structures demand flexibility in column spacing and core layout. Therefore, maximum structural efficiency and functional flex-

567

Fig. 1 Onterie Center, Chicago, Illinois *(Photo by Orlando Cabanban)*

ibility can be achieved by utilizing the exterior frame of the building only for the lateral force-resisting system. In Onterie Center's main tower, the entire lateral force-resisting system is achieved by closely spaced exterior columns and spandrels acting as a framed tube, coupled with infilling the window space with concrete in a diagonal pattern. These reinforced concrete infill panels act not only as diagonal braces, as in a steel high-rise structure, but as shear panels as well.

By going diagonally across the building, the infill panels will enhance both the overturning tubular behavior of the structure and its shear stiffness, which results in a much more efficient structure than if no infilling were introduced. As a result, the entire lateral stability of the building is achieved by two exterior diagonalized tubular channels located at each end of the tower

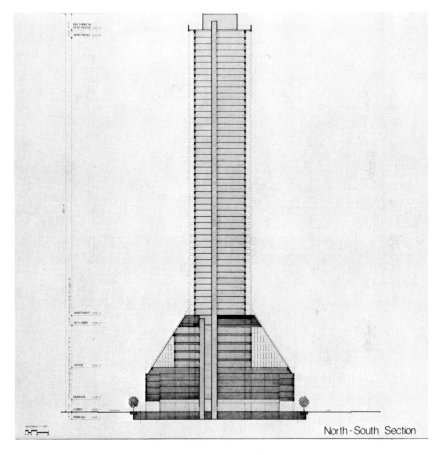

North-South Section

Fig. 2 Onterie Center North-South Section

structure. Interior columns carry gravity loads only, thus allowing more flexibility in planning the interior space and eliminating the differential creep between the core walls and adjacent columns than if a core wall had been utilized in resisting lateral loads.

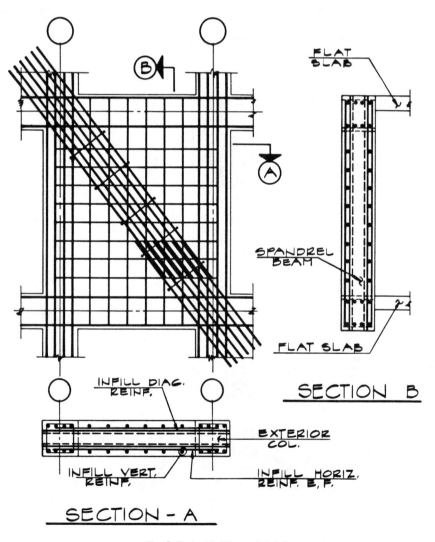

Fig. 3 Typical infill-panel detail

ANALYSIS AND DESIGN

The analysis and design of the tower was conducted utilizing Skidmore, Owings & Merrill's in-house computer capabilities. A three-dimensional computer model was used to analyze gravity and wind load cases. It was found that the lateral drift due to design wind pressures at the top of the building was well below the H/600 design limit. Over 50% of the lateral stiffness was provided by the unfilled panels; hence, the sections required for the exterior columns and spandrel beams were minimum. Exterior columns are typically 48 × 51 cm (19 × 20 in.). The infill panels have the same thickness as the columns and the spandrel beams. Typical panel reinforcement is shown in Fig. 3. The concrete cylinder strength for the exterior tube and the interior columns varies from 52 MPa (7,500 psi) at the base to 28 MPa (4,000 psi) at the top. The floor structural system is a flat slab construction with thicknesses that vary between 178 mm (7 in.) for the apartment floors to 216 mm (8.5 in.) for the commercial floors. The concrete strength for the flat slab is 35 MPa (5,000 psi). Interior column spans are about 6.71 m (22 ft) on center. Exterior columns, spandrels, and infill panels are insulated to minimize temperature deformations between perimeter and interior columns. The building foundation consists of belled bottom concrete caissons founded on the Chicago hard pan, a silty clay formation located about 24 m (78 ft) below grade level. The allowable soil pressure is approximately 1.95 MPa (40 ksf).

SUMMARY

The combination of the exterior tubular concept and diagonal shear panels introduced in Onterie Center provides a unique example in achieving a higher level of structural efficiency and creating a different architectural expression.

Project Descriptions

A Stressed-Skin Tube Tower: One Mellon Bank Center

Richard L. Tomasetti
Abraham Gutman
I. Paul Lew
Leonard Joseph

One Mellon Bank Center (OMBC), originally known as Dravo Tower, is a 54-story, 222 m (727 ft) high office building in Pittsburgh, Pennsylvania (Fig. 1). It represents the first example of a stressed-skin tube using steel plate facade panels to provide major stiffness against building drift. Advantages of this system include savings from the use of inexpensive and relatively light rolled shapes for spandrel beams, a 2323 m^2 (25,000 ft^2) gain of desirable, usable floor space along the building perimeter, a 1400 m^2 (15,000 ft^2) gain of floor space at the building core, and freedom to locate interior columns where most efficient for space planning. The 158,000 m^2 (1.7 million ft^2) project was framed using an average of 1030 Pa (21.5 psf) of steel plus 96 Pa (2 psf) for special framing considerations.

Development of OMBC can be viewed in four steps: (1) selection of the structural system; (2) design of the structural frame, using a two-step analysis; (3) treatment of special considerations in framing; and (4) development of the structural facade panels through analysis, design and detailing, and testing.

573

Fig. 1 One Mellon Bank Center, March 1983

SELECTION OF THE STRUCTURAL SYSTEM

Close cooperation between architect, engineer and developer, the interaction of project requirements, and the desire to maximize building efficiency led to the acceptance and use of innovative stressed-skin facade panels for stiffness.

The architect, Welton Becket Associates, New York, envisioned a facade with strong verticality, suggesting close column spacings along the building perimeter.

For energy conservation, only a small fraction of the facade was to have vision glass.

The building program required a relatively small tower footprint with large clear spans between perimeter and core. Thus the core had to be designed compactly and spotted precisely in its location within the footprint.

An elongated octagonal tower plan and some cantilevered projections formed eight desirable "bay window" corners on each typical floor (Fig. 2).

The developer, United States Steel Realty Development, was prepared to support the additional research, development, and testing required to bring the stressed-skin tube concept to fruition.

In high-rise construction, the bracing system used for stability and comfort under lateral loads has a major impact upon the success of the entire project. Of the various possible bracing systems considered, tubular framing was clearly preferred (Fig. 3) for five reasons. First, core bracing, using chevrons or V's, would add to core area, restrict freedom in core design, and be very inefficient due to a core height/width ratio of 20 : 1. Second, core bracing with outriggers or hat trusses to engage perimeter columns on selected floors would add to efficiency but would restrict floor usage and lock in a rigid relationship between core columns and perimeter columns. Third, plane frames would be inefficient since transverse frames would have only four columns per bent, beam spans of 14.3 m (46 ft 11 in.) and beam depth restrictions for minimal floor-to-floor height. In addition, core columns would be locked into relationships with perimeter columns. Fourth, perimeter bracing, using giant X's or V's, was incompatible with the architectural concept and presented real problems in terms of designing eight faces of three different widths, turning 45° corners, and avoiding blocking the eight "bay window" corners. Fifth, bundled-tube framing would subdivide the relatively small floors, making them undesirable from a renting standpoint. The bundled-tube concept was also found to be uneconomical for a building of this height.

Tube frame construction was selected, using closely spaced perimeter columns and stiff spandrel beams. Columns 3 m (10 ft) apart were architecturally desirable and no problem if kept narrow. However, to provide adequate stiffness, spandrel beams are commonly made as deep 3-plate sections and located

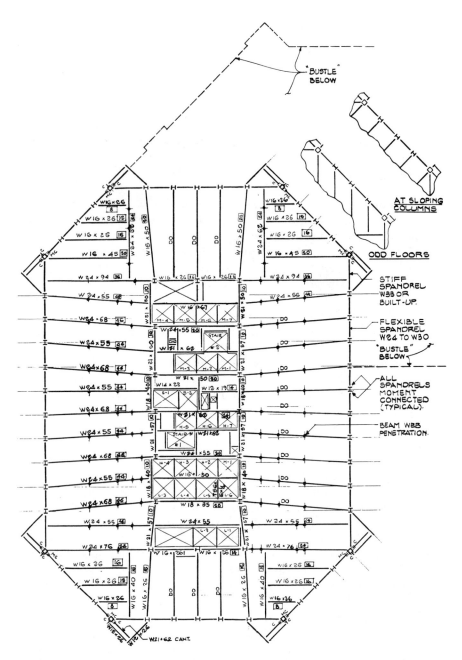

Fig. 2 Typical floor plan (even floors)

upset, so that about half the beam depth projects above the floor. This beam is usually concealed by an extra-deep windowsill, taking away valuable usable floor space (Fig. 4).

The use of facade panels for additional stiffness permitted the spandrels to be sized for strength only. In this case, rolled sections located entirely below the floor slabs proved sufficient. The rolled sections require no special fabrication and are much more economical than 3-plate "I" sections. Elimination of upset beams increases the amount of desirable, useable perimeter floor space. It also avoids blocking the "bay window" corners.

Stressed-skin facade panels with structural stiffness proved compatible with the other requirements above. The panels have a smooth exterior painted-steel face and an internal stiffening grid. The stiffeners are set back from window openings several inches to provide a lip for neoprene zipper gaskets to grip (Fig. 5), avoiding the cost and complications of window frames.

The typical panels are just under 3 m (10 ft) wide by 3 stories (11 m (36 ft)) high, and so were delivered to the site stacked flat. Vertical joints are concealed by vertical architectural column covers (Fig. 6). Horizontal joints, be-

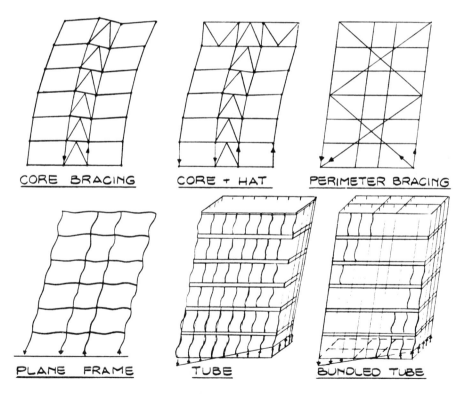

Fig. 3 Bracing systems

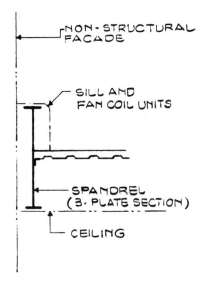

TYPICAL TUBE FRAMING

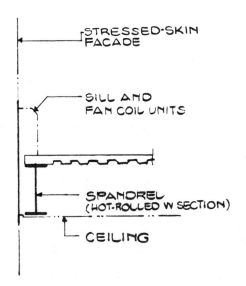

STRESSED-SKIN TUBE FRAMING
ONE MELLON BANK CENTER

Fig. 4 Typical spandrel section

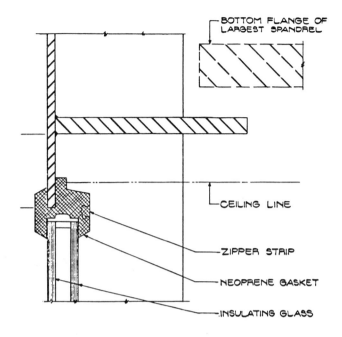

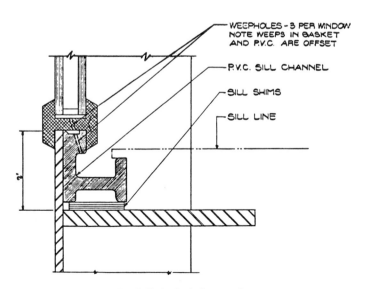

Fig. 5 Typical window section

ing typically 3 stories apart, do not break up the sense of verticality, and they minimize the number of joints and connections. Since only about 25% of the facade is glazed, sufficient steel plate remains in mullions between windows and spandrels above and below windows to provide stiffness against panel racking.

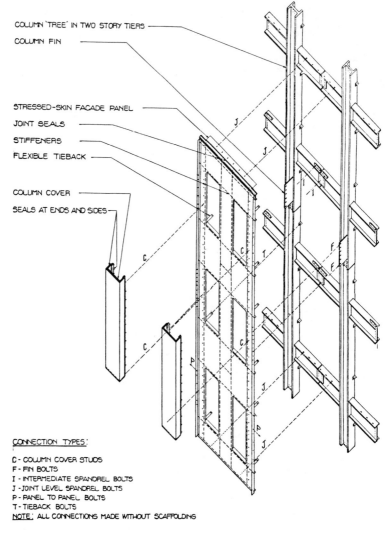

COLUMN 'TREE' IN TWO STORY TIERS
COLUMN FIN

STRESSED-SKIN FACADE PANEL
JOINT SEALS
STIFFENERS
FLEXIBLE TIEBACK

COLUMN COVER
SEALS AT ENDS AND SIDES

CONNECTION TYPES:

C - COLUMN COVER STUDS
F - FIN BOLTS
I - INTERMEDIATE SPANDREL BOLTS
J - JOINT LEVEL SPANDREL BOLTS
P - PANEL TO PANEL BOLTS
T - TIEBACK BOLTS
NOTE: ALL CONNECTIONS MADE WITHOUT SCAFFOLDING

Fig. 6 OMBC—stressed skin-tube interface

TOWER ANALYSIS AND DESIGN

The basic principle that makes the plate facade panels cost-effective is the separation of strength requirements from drift requirements. Since current U.S. building codes define required strength (wind pressure, seismic coefficients) but not wind drift, items provided only for wind drift need not be fireproofed. Thus the facade panels have the structural plate face exposed, without the expense of fireproofing or flame shields.

Since the panels cannot be counted upon for strength, a two-step analysis was performed. First, tower framing was modeled without facade panels (Fig. 7). Several trials with condensed, simplified models aided in member selection for this run. Approximately 3,000 nodes and 6,000 members were modeled

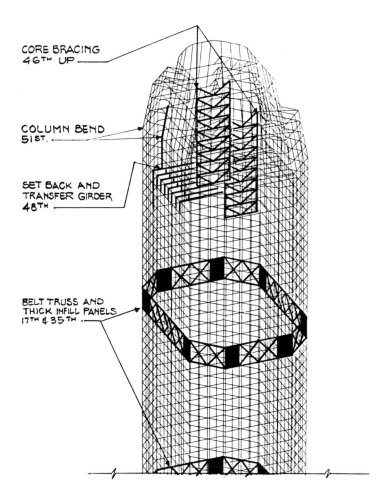

CORE BRACING
46TH UP

COLUMN BEND
51ST.

SET BACK AND
TRANSFER GIRDER
48TH

BELT TRUSS AND
THICK INFILL PANELS
17TH & 35TH.

Fig. 7 Special details of tower model (facade not shown)

using the EASE-2 computer program. The use of rigid diaphragms at each floor reduced the degrees of freedom to be solved to approximately 9,200.

Although this run was for strength, deflection was also of interest, and compatibility with panels in the second run was important. Moments of inertia for members were factored upward because members in the model use centerline spans and heights, ignoring member depths at joints. The correction factor was K^3, where K is the ratio of center length to clear length. This factor was used to simulate lateral story stiffness of a model with rigid joints of realistic size, while still using a simpler, centerline model. Because actual joints are not infinitely rigid, the clear length used for K was rounded upward. As a result, the increases in moments of inertia ($K^3 - 1$) were only about ⅔ of those that would occur using actual clear lengths. The correction factors and adjustments were recognized as approximate but sufficient for design purposes.

Loading consisted of code-required wind forces in the longitudinal, transverse, and quartering direction. Code requirements were found to be more critical than the overall wind pressures determined in wind tunnel tests at Colorado State University.

The tower model specifically included basement bracing and walls, belt bracing at levels 17 and 35 (mechanical floors), transfer girders at level 48, and supplementary bracing at levels 46 to 55. Later we will discuss these special items and the 17-story "bustle."

The second model included tower framing plus facade panels (Fig. 8). To simulate the effect of the facade panels, equivalent uniform membrane elements were established. The facade panels, being developed in parallel with the frame, were modeled using fine-mesh finite elements and racked using a 445 kN (100 k) shear force (Fig. 9).

Shear deflection of the panels was a combination of plate shear and frame action flexure of panel mullions and spandrels. While plate shear deflection is inversely proportional to face plate thickness, frame action deflection is inversely proportioned to the moments of inertia of mullions and spandrel sections. Moment of inertia is relatively insensitive to plate thickness if stiffeners, acting as flanges, hold constant. It was found that fictitious solid steel membranes 1.3 mm (1/20 in.) thick were quite close in stiffness to both 6.4 mm (1/4 in.) plate panels and 7.9 mm (5/16 in.) plate panels if panel stiffeners were constant.

Results of the two computer runs were used directly in design.

Each spandrel beam was checked for forces in each run and designed for the worst case. At this time it was determined that spandrels could be A36 steel. Using higher-strength steel and reducing spandrels further was considered undesirable, since the unclad tower was already quite limber with a drift to height ratio of $H/290$.

Perimeter columns were checked for combinations of dead and live load, overturning load, and frame bending, and were designed for the worst case.

Typically, A572 Grade 50 W14 sections sufficed, but at 45° corners (8 of 50 tower perimeter columns) built-up box sections of Grade 50 steel were required. W14 columns were used to keep within the 20 in. (508 mm) available depth in column enclosures and to avoid the expense of built-up columns.

Braces at the basement, level 17, level 35, and levels 46 to 55 were designed for the worst bracing forces plus, where applicable, additional forces induced as adjacent columns shorten under load.

Building drift with facade panels was found to be $H/590$, which was acceptable.

Foundation loads were checked for uplift using 1.3 times the worst overturning forces minus 0.9 times the minimum dead loads. Where required, columns engage concrete foundation walls via shear studs, and the walls were designed as beams to span this uplift force to locations where suffi-

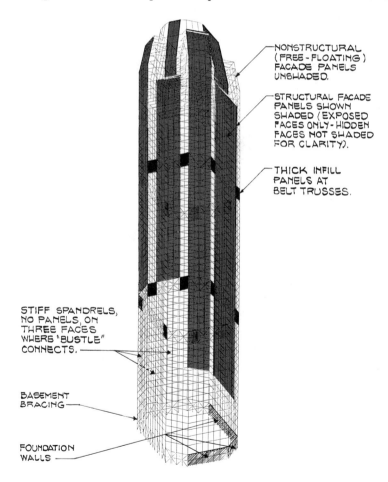

NONSTRUCTURAL (FREE-FLOATING) FACADE PANELS UNSHADED.

STRUCTURAL FACADE PANELS SHOWN SHADED (EXPOSED FACES ONLY-HIDDEN FACES NOT SHADED FOR CLARITY).

THICK INFILL PANELS AT BELT TRUSSES.

STIFF SPANDRELS, NO PANELS, ON THREE FACES WHERE "BUSTLE" CONNECTS.

BASEMENT BRACING

FOUNDATION WALLS

Fig. 8 Tower model with facade panels

cient net downward load exists. The overall foundation was checked for 1.5 times the overturning moment versus 1.0 times the minimum perimeter dead load moment.

Membrane stresses were translated directly into panel shear forces on a panel-by-panel basis. From this a table similar to a column schedule was developed, and panel thicknesses and stiffener patterns were selected to meet the load requirements (Fig. 10).

In addition, the change in shear force from panel to panel was determined. This was needed to establish the panel-to-column "fin" connection requirements, since only the change in force travels through this connection. The balance of shear travels through panel-to-panel connections. It is interesting to note that while the maximum *overall* panel shear occurs when a panel acts as a "web" of the tower tube (wind is parallel to panel face), the worst *differential* shear occurs when a panel acts as a "flange" of the tube (Fig. 11).

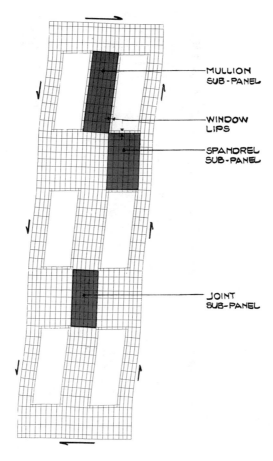

MULLION SUB-PANEL

WINDOW LIPS

SPANDREL SUB-PANEL

JOINT SUB-PANEL

Fig. 9 Racked panel (exaggerated)

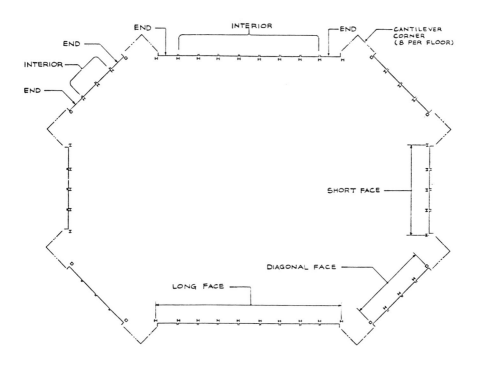

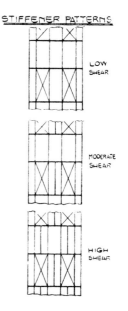

STIFFENER PATTERNS

TYPICAL PANEL THICKNESS						
LEVEL	LONG FACE		DIAGONAL FACE		SHORT FACE		CORNER
	INT.	END	INT.	END	INT.	END	
55 ROOF	P	A	R	A	P	E T	
47	¼"	¼"	¼"	¼"	¼"	¼"	
44							
41							
38							
24							¼"
	5/16"	5/16"	5/16"	5/16"	5/16"	5/16"	
6							
3							
GRADE	G	L	A	S	S		5/16"

LOW SHEAR

MODERATE SHEAR

HIGH SHEAR

Fig. 10 Tower plan

SPECIAL CONSIDERATIONS IN FRAMING

Even after the tower frame was sized and the panel system was developed (see below), special considerations in this building required special solutions.

The bustle, a low-rise, 17-story portion of the building, mirrors the tower in a perpendicular direction and is connected to it. While separating the two portions with an expansion joint would have simplified analysis, it was considered beneficial to have them solidly connected. This created three problems.

First, the portion of tower abutting the bustle cannot have facade panels attached. To compensate for this lost stiffness, very stiff 3-plate spandrel beams were used instead of more flexible hot-rolled sections. This aproach was successful, as proven by the fact that the tower model with facade panels exhibited no tendency to twist.

Second, it was considered desirable to have tower and bustle exhibit similar lateral stiffness. The bustle does not add significantly to the tower projected wind area for wind transverse to the tower, so frame action provided sufficient stiffness. For wind in the longitudinal tower direction the bustle adds considerable area. One bay of bustle interior columns was fitted with chevron braces to add its stiffness to that of perimeter frames. The bustle was fully modeled, and frame members and brace members were adjusted to "tune" lateral stiffness to match that of the tower.

Third, the potential for a split at the junction between tower and bustle was a concern. Special braces were added to provide a direct, solid line of steel between tower framing and bustle spandrels at each floor.

Complications introduced by the bustle added approximately 24 Pa (½ psf) to steel framing tonnage.

Pickups of bustle columns were handled using vierendeel action. While all 50 of the tower perimeter columns were carried to foundations, the design required that 23 of the 38 bustle perimeter columns be interrupted for driveways, loading docks, and entrances.

The perimeter frames form vierendeel trusses that act together with relatively light pickup girders to distribute loads to remaining columns. The bustle computer model was used to aid member design in these areas.

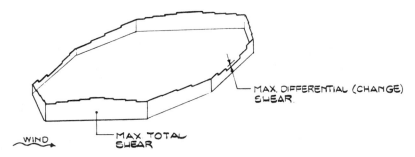

Fig. 11 Typical shear pattern for tube

Basement bracing was used on five of the eight tower faces to provide stiffness similar to the foundation walls encasing perimeter columns on the other three faces (Fig. 8). The bracing was also used to resist net uplift on some columns.

Belt trusses at double-height mechanical floors on levels 17 and 35 were required as a partial solution to the structural softness created by the architecturally desirable "bay window" corners on each floor (Figs. 2, 7, 8,). Framing across these corners must span over 5 m (15 ft), compared to 3 m (10 ft) at a typical bay. In addition, due to many local bends in the facade, and additional window openings, the panels in this bay do not add any stiffness. Thus this bay is much less stiff than typical bays, jeopardizing overall tube action.

Stiff rolled or built-up spandrels, filling the entire available space between floor slab and ceiling below, were used on each floor, but this was insufficient, and the 8 faces would tend to act more as separate frames than as an integrated tube (Fig. 12). The solution was to stitch together the faces by means of relatively thick infill plates across the corners. Sacrifice of these desirable corners could only be accepted at the mechanical floors, so 38 mm (1.5 in.) steel plates were installed there. To spread the load to the rest of the tube from these plates, X-bracing was used on each face, forming belt trusses at these two levels.

The special framing to accommodate "bay window" corners added approximately 36 Pa (¾ psf) to steel framing tonnage.

No panel stiffness was considered below level 5 because of architectural requirements for more windows near street level (Fig. 8). Built-up and upset spandrel beams were used on levels 1 to 5. These panels were isolated from the tube by means of slotted bolt holes and polyethylene washers. Similar slip details were used at non-structural panels at upper levels also.

Setbacks occur at level 12 on the bustle and level 48 on the tower as part of the architectural design (Fig. 7). Not all perimeter columns are set back at the same time. To minimize differential deflection, W36 transfer girders were

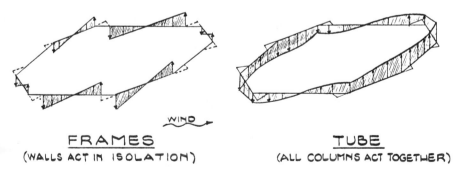

FRAMES
(WALLS ACT IN ISOLATION)

TUBE
(ALL COLUMNS ACT TOGETHER)

Fig. 12 Comparison of stress distribution in frame and in tube

used in all cases. The setbacks break the continuity of perimeter columns, and the girders act as relatively soft spring supports. To ensure adequate lateral stiffness, a stiff spine was desired. In the bustle, such a spine already existed as the chevron-braced interior bay discussed above. In the tower, two core column bays were V-braced from levels 46 to 55 plus penthouse, to act as stiffening spines, embedded two stories into the tower below the setback.

The tower models included the setbacks, girders, and bracing, supported on springs to simulate the stiffness of columns running down to grade. The bracing was found to carry ⅓ to ½ of the wind shear above level 48.

Skewed floor framing was used on typical tower floors as a result of the extremely compact core design (Fig. 2). While perimeter columns were on a 3 m (10 ft) module, core column spacing varied from 6 to 4.5 m (19 ft-9 in. to 14 ft-11 in.). In addition, to ease circulation around the core, columns were located to project into the elevator lobbies, rather than outside the core perimeter. To provide the most direct load path and the easiest and most stable erection process, floor beams were run directly from perimeter columns to core columns whenever possible, even though many such beams thus had a skewed orientation.

In addition, where perimeter columns slope (level 13 up on bustle, 51 up on tower), framing at 45° faces was turned to be perpendicular to the building face to resist large outward thrusts at the kink and the smaller inward thrusts at each floor above. Small header beams were added to maintain normal deck orientation.

The typical floor sandwich consists of 2.6 m (8 ft-6 in) high ceiling, 250 mm (10 in.) deep lights with air diffuser "boots," composite W24 A572 grade 50 beams, 18 gage and 18/20 gage 50 mm (2 in.) deep composite floor deck spanning 3 m (10 ft) in 60-40 cellular-noncellular blend with preset taps, and 2½ stone concrete fill (114 mm [4.5 in.] total). Because of the scarcity of lightweight aggregate in Pittsburgh and the need for fireproofing at trenches and taps in any case, it was determined that 63.5 mm (2½ in.) fill with spray-on fireproofing throughout was more economical than using 83 mm (3¼ in.) lightweight or 114 mm (4½ in.) stone fill with limited fireproofing.

Beam penetrations became an important design consideration. A study of the various framing alternatives for the 14.3 m (46 ft-11 in.) typical floor beams revealed that using unshored composite W24 beams with some mechanical penetrations and a 3.7 m (12 ft) floor-to-floor height was more economical than shored composite W18 beams with mechanical services below and 3.8 m (12 ft-6 in.) floor height, but only if beam penetrations could be made unreinforced or minimally reinforced. Castellated beams of 610 mm (24 in.) depth were considered but not used because supplying the required quantities of beams was a problem, and because they can sometimes be too limber for easy high-rise erection.

The use of W24 beams in lieu of shallower, lighter sections added approximately 36 Pa (¾ psf) to steel framing tonnage.

To minimize beam reinforcement, a computer program was developed that checked composite beams at penetrations for shear and for vierendeel plus overall flexural stresses. Openings were set slightly above mid-height to leave more steel in the highly stressed bottom tee and minimize overall stress. Shear was distributed to top and bottom tees in proportion to their moments of inertia. Of approximately 4000 penetrations, only 40% required reinforcement, which generally consisted of two horizontal bars at the bottom of the opening. In addition, approximately 5000 unreinforced 152 mm (6 in.) handholes were provided in spandrel beams for facade panel bolting access.

Box columns were constructed in straightforward fashion, except that due to the orientaton of flange forces applied by spandrel beams, internal stiffners had to be connected to all four column faces. This was accomplished by assembling three faces of the column and welding three edges of the stiffeners in conventional fashion, adding the last face, and then welding the stiffener's fourth edge to the last face by the electroslag process. This was considered acceptable because the column plates do not experience large tensile stresses.

Column camber was required because perimeter Grade 50 columns were controlled by combined axial and wind flexural stresses, while core Grade 50 columns were fully stressed under dead and live axial load alone. Core columns were fabricated approximately 76 mm (3 in.) longer than perimeter columns, with the adjustment (camber) distributed uniformly over the height, to compensate for differential shortening under dead load plus anticipated major partitions.

The P-Delta effect was specifically considered in column design. Wind shear moments and axial forces were factored up by $(1 + A + A^2)$, where

$$A = \frac{(\Sigma P_i)\Delta_i}{V_i H_i} \tag{1}$$

and ΣP_i is the sum of loads in *all* columns at level i; Δ_i is the lateral drift of one story at level i due to wind, without stressed-skin action; V_i is the story wind shear at level i; and H_i is the height from level i to level $i + 1$ in the same units as i.

When wind shear cumulates in a relatively linear fashion and axial load cumulates similarly, A will be relatively constant. For OMBC the critical $A = 0.14$, so a P-Delta factor of 1.16 was used. Then the columns were designed using $K = 1.0$ and $C_m = 0.85$.

In addition, the overall tube was checked for stability by idealizing it as a cantilevered column with varying load and effective moment of inertia I_e. I_e was set using $A_e d^2$ of columns, A_e being the perimeter column areas adjusted for shear lag. This was done by multiplying each perimeter column area on a level by the ratio of actual overturning force to rigid-body overturning force, and then dividing by the largest actual-to-rigid ratio of any column at that level to ensure that no column is counted as more than 100% effective. This analysis showed no problem of overall building buckling.

Compatible column stresses were considered desirable in perimeter column selection. To keep column loads on each face similar, framing to the 45° face columns changed direction on alternate floors (see Fig. 2). Rather than selecting each column to act at its full allowable combined stress, an attempt was made to keep axial stress under dead and live load at each column no more than 10% different from adjacent columns. Because vierendeel action tends to equalize stresses over adjacent columns, dramatically downsizing an understressed column will just serve to redistribute some of its load to an adjacent column, overstressing it if it were already fully loaded.

Web doubler and stiffeners were determined on a joint-by-joint basis. Due to the relatively shallow joint depth in this framing, web doublers were sometimes required, but the use of relatively stocky W14 column sections meant that stiffeners were required only rarely.

DEVELOPMENT OF THE STRESSED-SKIN FACADE PANEL SYSTEM

One Mellon Bank Center incorporates the stiffness of an innovative exterior steel plate facade to reduce building drift. The tower is 222 m (727 ft) high (see Fig. 1) and the building drift is cut in half by the use of the plate stiffening facade. The facade acts as an infill or shear diaphragm, reducing interstory drift of the building and shear lag in the tubular structural frame system of the tower, making the columns more effective in resisting overturning. To accomplish this stiffening, it was necessary to perform theoretical state-of-the-art analyses of plate buckling by classical and computer methods and to verify the analytical results by full scale testing.

This section presents the process required to develop a new structural system as a three pronged approach consisting of analysis, design and detailing, and testing.

Analysis

Description of the basic facade panel. The basic facade panel consists of a 3 m (9 ft 10⅜ in.) wide by 11 m (36 ft 4 in.) high panel covering three stories. The typical story height is 3.7 m (12 ft). There are six window openings 724 mm (2 ft 4½ in.) wide by 2 m (6 ft 7⅝ in.) high in a typical panel (see Fig. 6). Stiffeners are required on the inside of the panel to prevent plate buckling and provide out-of-plane strength for wind. These stiffeners are placed on all sides of the windows and are continuous for the height and width of the panel. The panel ideally acts as a shear diaphragm only, so connections had to be developed that would transfer shear while keeping axial forces from being transmitted into it. These aspects will be explained below.

Various support conditions were studied to determine the optimum location of the vertical connections. It was found that if the connections are alongside the windows the panels are forced by structural compatibility to act as one large panel rather than several independent panels. In effect, two 0.4 m (15 in.) wide mullions, when stitched together, have the strength and stiffness of one 0.8 m (30 in.) mullion. The thrust of the analysis was twofold: first, to determine and maximize the strength of the facade panel, and second, to determine its stiffness.

Strength Analysis. The classical analysis approach to the plate assumed that adequate stiffness would be provided from the panel stiffeners so that each subpanel could be analyzed as an independent plate simply supported at its longitudinal edges and loaded along its perpendicular edges, or width (see Fig. 9). The basic equation for plate buckling (Johnston, 1976) is

$$\tau_c = \frac{k\pi^2 E(t/b)^2}{12(1 - \nu^2)} \tag{2}$$

Where

τ_c is the critical shear stress, E is the modulus of elasticity, b is the width of the subpanel, t is the thickness, and ν is Poisson's ratio.

The constant k is 4 for uniform axial edge load and simple edge supports, $4.0 + 5.34/a^2$ for shear if $a \le 1$, $5.34 + 4.0/a^2$ for shear if $a \ge 1$, and 23.9 for bending stress; a being defined as a/b where a is the length of the subpanel.

The critical stresses are valid in the elastic range. To adjust for the inelastic range, for compressive stresses, the elastic solution was used to determine an "equivalent column" slenderness ratio (KL/r). The equivalent slenderness ratio (Johnston, 1976), for $\nu = 0.3$ would be

$$(KL/r)_{\text{equivalent}} = \frac{3.3 \, (b/t)}{\sqrt{k}} . \tag{3}$$

This equivalent column slenderness ratio was used to determine allowable compressive stresses following AISC allowable compressive stress criteria.

Allowable shear stresses can be determined elastically and also by post-elastic buckling analysis. Since visual buckling of the plate would not be desirable in the facade, only the elastic buckling solution was considered. The elastic buckling solution to web shear stress allowable has been adjusted by the AISC in their allowable shear stresses for inelastic behavior. The adjusted allowable stresses (AISC, 1980) would then be

$$F_v = \frac{F_y}{2.89} C_v \le 0.4F_y, \tag{4}$$

where in the elastic range

$$C_v = \frac{45,000k}{F_y(h/t)^2}, \tag{5}$$

and in the inelastic range

$$C_v = \frac{190}{(h/t)} \sqrt{k/F_y}. \tag{6}$$

Note that k is the shear constant previously noted in Eq. 2.

The actual state of stress in the panel is a combination of axial, bending, and shear stress. The method of combining these stresses was based on the Structural Stability Research Council recommendations (Johnston, 1976). The following interaction equation was thus used:

$$\frac{f_a}{F_a} + \left(\frac{f_b}{F_b}\right)^2 + \left(\frac{f_v}{F_v}\right)^2 \le 1.0, \tag{7}$$

where subscripts a, b, and v refer to axial, bending and shear stress respectively and f is actual stress, F allowable stress.

The key to this classical analysis was the principle that the stiffeners were fully effective, so that each subpanel defined by the stiffener grid could be checked on an individual basis for buckling. To determine whether the stiffeners were effective, two analytical techniques were used.

The first approach was to treat stiffeners from a design point of view. In this approach each stiffener was treated as a laterally unbraced flange. The rationale is provided in Lehigh University's text *Structural Steel Design* (Tall, 1974). For shallow thick-walled beams, St. Venant torsion resistance dominates. For deep, relatively thin wall beams, warping (that is, flange bending) is the main resistance. The St. Venant resistance is applicable to rolled steel sections, and warping is applicable to cold-formed steel structural members.

The panel with its stiffeners is analogous to a cold-formed structural steel member as a deep, relatively thin-walled section. Therefore the requirements of the AISI specification for the design of cold-formed steel for laterally unbraced beams were used as design criteria for the stiffeners (AISI, 1977).

As a second approach, the classical methods of analysis were confirmed by a state-of-the-art computer analysis for plate buckling. The method applied was a finite element analysis for buckling using the NASTRAN program. The goals were to verify that the subpanels would buckle before the stiffeners.

In addition, the calculated stress at which the panels and stiffeners buckle was compared to classical solutions. A simulation of the computer buckling analysis used is shown in Figs. 13 and 14.

The finite element buckling analysis is an elastic analysis and it had to be corrected to an inelastic analysis. This was done by relating the elastic stress to an equivalent slenderness ratio and then relating this equivalent slenderness ratio to an inelastic stress using the AISC compressive stress formula. Good agreement was found between the finite element buckling analysis and the classical buckling analysis. It was therefore considered acceptable to use classical analysis to size the panels.

Stiffness and Stress Analysis. Once buckling stresses for different thicknesses of panels and stiffener arrangements were determined, it was necessary to determine the state of stress in the panels and the deflection due to an arbitrary unit lateral force to be able to select the correct thickness and stiffener configuration for each actual load condition. To accomplish this, a fine-mesh finite element analysis was performed (see Fig. 9).

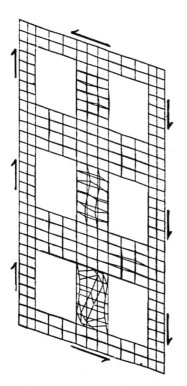

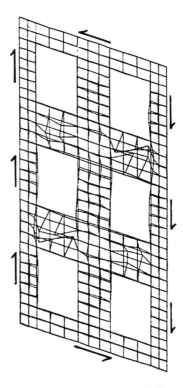

Fig. 13 Panel mullion buckling mode under shear load

Fig. 14 Panel spandrel buckling mode under shear load (only if mullions are stiffened against buckling)

A one-hundred kip unit lateral load was applied at the top of the panel and the resulting stresses and deflections determined. Boundary conditions were established to simulate "stitching" to adjacent panels where appropriate. Resulting isolines for principal stress and shear for the plate are shown in Figs. 15 and 16.

The stresses in each subpanel were then broken up into axial, bending, and shear stresses for gradually increasing increments of force. This was then checked against the capacity of the panel using classical analysis. Plate thicknesses and stiffener grids were determined to be varied in the following order, from low to high shear strength:

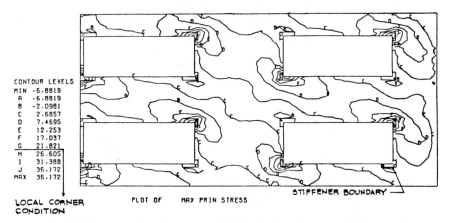

CONTOUR LEVELS
MIN -6.8819
 A   -6.8819
 B   -2.0981
 C   2.6857
 D   7.4695
 E   12.253
 F   17.037
 G   21.821
 H   26.605
 I   31.388
 J   36.172
MAX 36.172

LOCAL CORNER
CONDITION

PLOT OF   MAX PRIN STRESS

STIFFENER BOUNDARY

Fig. 15 Maximum principal stress for 100 kip horizontal shear on $5/16$ in. panel

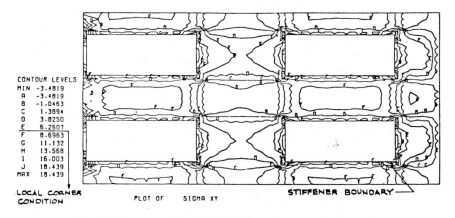

CONTOUR LEVELS
MIN -3.4819
 A   -3.4819
 B   -1.0463
 C   1.3894
 D   3.8250
 E   6.2607
 F   8.6963
 G   11.132
 H   13.568
 I   16.003
 J   18.439
MAX 18.439

LOCAL CORNER
CONDITION

PLOT OF   SIGMA XY

STIFFENER BOUNDARY

Fig. 16 Shear stress for 100 kip horizontal shear on $5/16$ in. panel

6 mm (¼ in.) plate with basic stiffeners

6 mm (¼ in.) plate with 3 added stiffeners vertically bisecting mullion subpanels

8 mm (⁵⁄₁₆ in.) plate with basic stiffeners

8 mm (⁵⁄₁₆ in.) plate with 3 added stiffeners at mullions

8 mm (⁵⁄₁₆ in.) plate with 3 mullion stiffeners plus 6 added stiffeners vertically bisecting spandrel subpanels.

The finite element analysis also provided the means of linking panel analysis to building frame analysis so that the force in the panels at each location of the building could be determined. This linkage was made by developing a solid panel "membrane" equivalent in shear stiffness to the actual perforated panel. The equivalent solid panel was then incorporated in the structural analysis of the overall building frame as an infill shear membrane. The effect of this equivalent infill membrane on the overall structure was then determined, the force induced in the infill panels was determined, and panel types were selected (see Fig. 10).

Design and Detailing

Analysis is but one of three phases in structural systems development. The second phase is the design and detailing of actual panels so that they act as assumed in the analysis.

It soon became apparent that each panel must act primarily as a shear diaphragm with respect to the structural frame and be relatively isolated against axial shortening of the frame. To accomplish this, two distinct groups of connections were necessary: panel-to-panel connections, and panel-to-frame connections. The top and bottom horizontal connections have three functions: (1) to pass horizontal shear between upper and lower panels; (2) to distribute a share of the horizontal wind shear from the frame into the panels; and (3) to relieve any vertical stress between panels due to frame shortening, thermal effects, and the like.

These functions are achieved by continuous wide horizontal plates at the top and bottom edges of the panels, which are high-strength friction bolted to the top flange of the spandrel beam about one foot away from the face as shown in Fig. 17. By having the shear plates span the one-foot distance they become flexible and act to form a stress-relieving joint.

At the vertical edges, extensive analysis showed that the most effective connection between panels occurred adjacent to the window openings. This location tends to minimize the weakening effect of the window openings. Indeed, it has the effect of forcing all mullions at a window level to carry similar shear stress. As a result, all vertical shear connections occur at windows whenever possible.

Since the panels in any one wall face act as a unit, there is little vertical shear transfer to or from the structural frame at vertical connections except at the ends of wall faces where the panels end and must unload their shear back into the structural frame. Therefore at interior vertical joints it is necessary

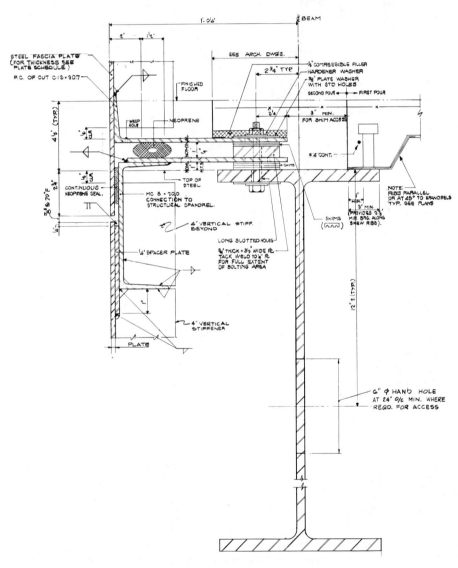

Fig. 17 Section at main horizontal joint

to connect to the structural frame only at approximately mid-height of each panel, using small connection fins.

At the end panels a larger edge stiffener is used to act as a collector of the shear force, so that although a larger force has to be transferred to the frame, bolts can still be bunched together at a mid-height location. This mid-height connection greatly limits the zone in the panel affected by the frame's axial shortening (Figs. 18 and 19).

The connection for vertical shear consists of high-strength friction bolts in holes or slots punched in outstanding legs of angle edge stiffeners. At panel-to-frame locations (mid-height) a vertical shear plate or fin projecting from the column fits in the gap between two panels. Bolts clamp panel edge angles to the fin and to each other (see Fig. 20). At panel-to-panel locations, the gap between panel edges is filled with finger shims. Bolts clamp panel to panel (see Fig. 21).

In addition to shear-transfer connections at panel edges, tiebacks are required to resist wind pressure and brace the stiffener grid against buckling. They must be stiff perpendicular to the facade but not produce substantial restraint to frame shortening. The solution was to provide horizontal flexible tieback plates from the structural frame to the ends of horizontal stiffeners of the panel at each window head and sill (Fig. 22).

The last major detail in the development of the panel was to minimize stress concentration at the corners of the window openings. Sharp corners at the openings would lead to high local stresses in the panel. Corners should be rounded to minimize this effect, but the glass should be rectangular to

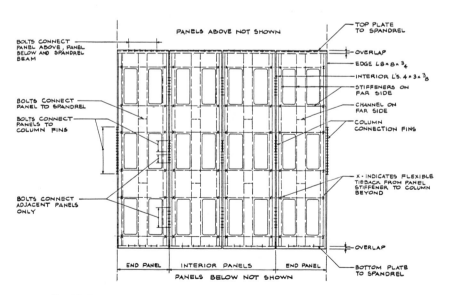

Fig. 18 Typical elevation with column covers removed, diagonal face shown

maintain economy. To accomplish these opposing goals, the corners were cut
into a "double S" shaped curve to allow both these criteria to be satisfied (Fig.
23). Since openings were cut on a numerical-controlled plasma-torch cutting
table, this potentially awkward detail was provided economically.

Testing

The last phase in the development of an innovative structural system is
testing. Testing of a full-scale prototype was done at Lehigh University's Fritz
Engineering Laboratory. The American Bridge Division of U.S. Steel
fabricated a 6 mm (¼ in.) thick test panel and a special test frame. To test for
shear, the panel-and-frame assembly was loaded diagonally. The heavy test
frame surrounding the panel acted to break this force into components, so the
frame took axial load and the panel carried shear load (Fig. 24). Observations
were recorded for in-plane and out-of-plane deformations, plate strains, and
racking deformation of the window openings.

The test panel was designed for a lateral load of 267 kN (60 kips), which
would correspond to a diagonal test load of 1000 kN (225 kips). The panel
showed nonvisible signs of incipient buckling at about 1.89 times the design

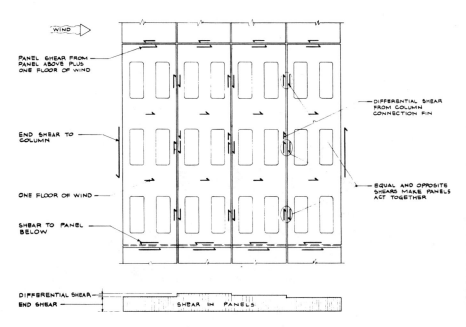

Fig. 19 Forces acting on panels

load. Visible signs of buckling occurred at 2.44 times the design load (Fig. 25). At this point the panel was exhibiting post-buckling strength. At about 3.33 times the design load the welds failed but not the panel itself.

Deformations were found to be relatively linear throughout the loading with a slight change of slope at the highest load, as seen in Fig. 26. It should be noted that only the second load path is valid, since the first load path includes bolt slippage. In general, the test showed that panel strength was in close agreement with analytical predictions. It also indicated that there was substantial reserve post-buckling strength in the panel. It further indicated that deflections were in the range anticipated and were acceptable both visually and structurally.

The development of this new structural system did not end once the structure was developed. The system had to be developed architecturally as well. The movements of the structure must be accommodated. In particular, a new sealing system had to be developed. Horizontal joints between panels are sealed using "ship lap" overlapping of panels, plus two lines of closed-cell

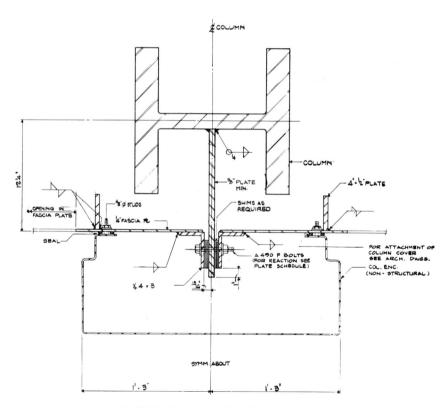

Fig. 20 Vertical connection of panels to column

sponge neoprene seals (see Fig. 17). Vertical joints are concealed and closed by separate column covers with closed-cell sponge neoprene seals along each edge (see Fig. 20). At the window, special gaskets were selected to accept the movements of the panel openings (see Fig. 5). Solid neoprene "zipper gaskets" with uncured butyl under exterior edges are used to mount double-glazed windows in window openings. The gaskets clamp around the glazing and around the panel lip. The complete sealing system was successfully tested at Construction Research Laboratory, Inc., Miami, Florida.

In addition, there are nonstructural panels in the facade that look the same as the structural panels but are isolated from the structural frame and the structural panels by slotted holes and polyethylene washers.

To protect the steel panels, a four-part coating system was used, consisting of careful sandblasting, zinc-rich primer, epoxy intermediate, and two-coat urethane finish, all shop-applied under controlled conditions.

All these elements were necessary for the successful completion of the system.

The successful testing of the prototype panel completed the development of an innovative structural system. The use of this panel allows for many positive structural benefits. The important benefits include reducing deflec-

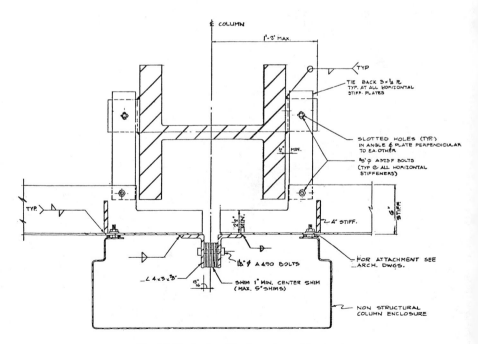

Fig. 21 Vertical connection of panel to panel

tions of the structural frame by half, allowing the structural frame to be designed for strength rather than deflection, and improving the economic efficiency of the structural tube frame system, in that less costly, normal rolled sections are used in conjunction with the facade stiffening plate system. Thus additional useable floor space is gained.

ACKNOWLEDGMENTS

We would like to acknowledge the contribution of some of the participants in this innovative system: Glen Willard, Anatol Rychalski, and Joseph Mihalik of U.S. Steel Realty Development; Henry Brennan, David Beer, Frank LaSusa, and Hugo Consuegra of Welton Becket Associates (New York); Professors

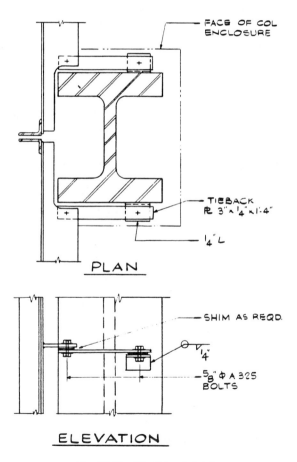

Fig. 22 Flexible tieback detail

Alexis Ostapenko and Roger Slutter of Lehigh University and Fritz Engineering Laboratory; and Manny Velivasakis and Robert DeScenza of the LZA computer department.

The owner of One Mellon Bank Center is 500 Grant Street Associates, Pittsburgh, PA.; the Developer of One Mellon Bank Center was U.S.S. Realty Development, Pittsburgh, PA; the Architect, Welton Becket Associates, New York, NY; the Structural Engineer, Lev Zetlin Associates, New York, NY; the Mechanical Engineer, Lehr Associates, New York, NY; the General Contractor, Turner Construction Company, Pittsburgh, PA; the Panel Fabricator, Calumet Industries Works, Inc., Gary, IN; and the Structural Steel Contractor and the Steel and Panel Erector, American Bridge Division, U.S. Steel, Pittsburgh, PA.

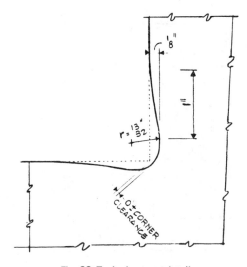

Fig. 23 Typical corner detail

Fig. 24 Panel in test machine

Fig. 25 Shadow of straightedge shows waves of buckling

REFERENCES/BIBLIOGRAPHY

AISC, 1980
    MANUAL OF STEEL CONSTRUCTION, 8th ed., American Institute of Steel Construction, New York.

AISI, 1977
    COLD-FORMED STEEL DESIGN MANUAL, American Iron and Steel Institute, Washington, D.C.

Johnston, B. G., ed., 1976
    GUIDE TO DESIGN CRITERIA FOR METAL STRUCTURES, 32d ed., Column Research Council,
    John Wiley and Sons, Inc., New York.

Tall, L. (Ed.), 1974
    STRUCTURAL STEEL DESIGN, 2nd ed., Ronald Press, New York.

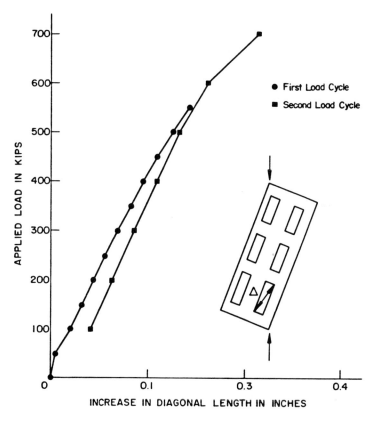

Fig. 26 Test result, window racking

Appendix

High-Rise Building Data Base

Since the inception of the Council, various surveys have been made concerning the location, number of stories, height, material, and use of tall buildings around the world. The first report on these surveys was published in the Council's Proceedings of the First International Conference in 1972. *Tall Building Systems and Concepts* (Volume SC) brought that information up to date with a detailed survey in 1980.

In 1983, changes to some of the data were reflected in *Developments in Tall Buildings 1983*, the first update volume since the Monograph.

This present document reflects changes to Table 1 that have been revealed to the Council since the publication of the first update volume.

The survey was originally based mainly on information collected from individuals in the major cities of the world. The main criterion for the selection of a city was generally its population, and another criterion was the availability of a Council member or other contact who might provide the needed information. In addition to information collected by questionnaires, data were also obtained from a few selected references.

This Appendix updates Table 1. Because the data came from so many sources, complete accuracy cannot be guaranteed. Buildings change names from time to time, and this information is sometimes slow in reaching the Council headquarters. In this sense the survey keeps its nature as a "living document."

Additions and corrections to the information presented herein are welcomed, and should be brought to the attention of headquarters staff at Lehigh University.

607

Table 1: **World's Tallest Buildings.** This is a list of the world's 100 tallest buildings. The information presented includes the city in which each building is located, the year of completion, the number of stories, the height (in meters and feet), the structural material, and the use of each building. This table originally appeared in Volume SC, *Tall Building Systems and Concepts*, and was later revised and appeared in *Developments in Tall Buildings 1983*. This present table represents the most recent information available to the Council on Tall Buildings and Urban Habitat.

Table 1   The one-hundred tallest buildings in the world

Building	City	Year Comp	No. Of Stories	Height Meters	Feet	Material	Use
Sears Tower	Chicago	1974	100	443	1454	Steel	Office
World Trade Center North	New York	1972	110	417	1368	Steel	Office
World Trade Center South	New York	1973	110	415	1362	Steel	Office
Empire State	New York	1931	102	381	1250	Steel	Office
Standard Oil (Indiana)	Chicago	1973	80	346	1136	Steel	Office
John Hancock	Chicago	1968	100	344	1127	Steel	Multiple
Chrysler Bldg.	New York	1930	77	319	1046	Steel	Office
Bank of China	Hong Kong	UC:88	71	314	1031	Mixed	Office
Texas Commerce Plaza	Houston	1981	75	305	1002	Mixed	Office
Allied Bank Plaza	Houston	1983	71	296	970	Steel	Office
Columbia Center	Seattle	UC:85	76	291	955	Steel/ Concrete	Office
American Intl. Bldg.	New York	1931	66	290	950	Steel	Office
First Bank Tower	Toronto	1975	72	285	935	Steel	Office
40 Wall Tower	New York	1966	71	283	927	Steel	Office
Dallas Main Center	Dallas	UC:85	70	281	921	Mixed	Office
Citicorp Center	New York	1977	59	280	919	Steel	Multiple
Transco Tower 2	Houston	1983	64	275	901	Steel	Office
Water Tower Place	Chicago	1976	74	262	859	Concrete	Multiple
United California Bank	Los Angeles	1974	62	262	858	Steel	Office
Transamerica Pyramid	San Francisco	1972	48	259	853	Steel	Office
RCA Rockefeller Center	New York	1933	70	259	850	Steel	Office
First National Bank	Chicago	1969	60	259	850	Steel	Office
U.S. Steel	Pittsburgh	1970	64	256	841	Steel	Office
One Chase Manhattan Plaza	New York	1961	60	248	813	Steel	Office

Table 1 The one-hundred tallest buildings in the world

Building	City	Year Comp	No. Of Stories	Height Meters	Height Feet	Material	Use
Pan American	New York	1963	59	246	808	Steel	Office
Woolworth Bldg.	New York	1913	57	242	792	Steel	Office
1 Palac Kultury I Nauki	Warsaw	1955	42	241	790	Steel/ Concrete	Office
John Hancock Tower	Boston	1973	60	241	790	Steel	Office
M.L.C. Centre	Sydney	1976	70	240	786	Concrete	Office
Commerce Court West	Toronto	1974	57	239	784	Steel	Office
Republic Bank Center	Houston	1983	56	238	780	Steel	Office
Bank of America	San Francisco	1969	52	237	778	Steel	Office
3 First National Plaza	Chicago	1981	58	236	775	Mixed	Office
I D S Center	Minneapolis	1972	57	235	772	Mixed	Office
Singapore Treasury Bldg.	Singapore	UC:86	52	235	770	Mixed	Office
One Penn Plaza	New York	1972	50	234	766	Steel	Office
Korea Ins. Company	Seoul	UC:86	63	233	764	Steel	Office
Tun Abdul Razak Bldg.	Penang	UC:85	60	232	761	Concrete	Office
Equitable Tower West	New York	UC:85	51	230	755	Steel	Office
Maine Montparnasse	Paris	1973	64	229	751	Mixed	Office
Prudential Center	Boston	1964	52	229	750	Steel	Office
Federal Reserve Bldg.	Boston	1975	32	229	750	Steel	Office
Exxon	New York	1971	54	229	750	Steel	Office
First International Plaza	Houston	1981	55	228	748	Mixed	Office
Security Pacific National Bank	Los Angeles	1974	55	226	743	Steel	Office
1 Liberty Plaza (U.S. Steel)	New York	1972	54	226	743	Steel	Office
Ikebukuro Tower (Sunshine 60)	Tokyo	1978	60	226	742	Steel	Office
Raffles City Hotel	Singapore	UC:86	70	226	741	Concrete	Hotel
20 Exchange Plaza (Citibank)	New York	1931	55	226	741	Steel	Office
Renaissance 1	Detroit	1977	73	225	739	Concrete	Hotel
World Financial Center (American Express)	New York	UC:85	51	225	739	Steel	Office
Toronto Dominion Bank Tower	Toronto	1967	56	224	736	Steel	Office
Cullen Center	Houston	1984	55	223	732	Steel	Office
Southeast Financial Center	Miami	1984	53	222	730	Steel/ Concrete	Office

609

Table 1 The one-hundred tallest buildings in the world

Building	City	Year Comp	No. Of Stories	Height Meters	Height Feet	Material	Use
One Astor Plaza	New York	1972	54	222	730	Mixed	Office
Olympia Centre	Chicago	1981	63	222	728	Concrete	Multiple
1 Mellon Bank Ctr.	Pittsburgh	1983	54	222	727	Steel	Office
Gulf Tower	Houston	1982	52	221	726	Mixed	Office
9 West 57th St.	New York	1974	50	221	725	Steel	Office
Peachtree Center Plaza	Atlanta	1975	71	220	723	Concrete	Hotel
Crocker Center	Los Angeles	1983	55	220	723	Steel	Multiple
Carlton Center	Johannesburg	1973	50	220	722	Concrete	Office
Detroit Plaza Hotel	Detroit	1977	73	219	720	Concrete	Hotel
Republic Plaza	Denver	1983	56	219	718	Steel/ Concrete	Office
One Shell Plaza	Houston	1971	50	218	714	Concrete	Office
First International Bldg.	Dallas	1973	56	216	710	Steel	Office
Hopewell Centre	Hong Kong	1980	65	216	709	Concrete	Office
Shinjuku Center	Tokyo	1979	54	216	709	Steel	Office
Terminal Tower	Cleveland	1930	52	216	708	Steel	Office
Union Carbide Bldg.	New York	1960	52	215	707	Steel	Office
General Motors	New York	1968	50	214	705	Steel	Office
PEMEX Bldg.	Mexico City	1984	52	214	705		Office
Metropolitan Life	New York	1909	50	213	700	Steel	Office
Atlantic Richfield Plaza A	Los Angeles	1972	52	212	699	Steel	Office
Atlantic Richfield Plaza B	Los Angeles	1972	52	212	699	Steel	Office
One Shell Square	New Orleans	1972	51	212	697	Steel	Office
500 Fifth Avenue	New York	1931	58	212	697	Steel	Office
Shinjuku Mitsui Bldg.	Tokyo	1974	55	212	696	Steel	Office
I B M Building	Chicago	1973	52	212	695	Steel	Office
Shinjuku Mitsui	Tokyo	1974	55	211	692	Steel	Office
4 Allen Tower	Houston	1983	50	210	689	Steel	Office
Marine Midland	New York	1966	52	210	688	Steel	Office
55 Water Street	New York	1972	53	209	687	Steel	Office
Chemical Bank Trust Bldg.	New York	1964	50	209	687	Steel	Office
Three Allen Center	Houston	1980	50	208	685	Steel	Office
Capital National Bank Plaza	Houston	1980	50	209	685	Steel	Office
One Houston Center	Houston	1978	46	208	681	Mixed	Office
Chanin Bldg.	New York	1929	55	207	680	Steel	Office
Minneapolis City Center	Minneapolis	1983	51	207	679	Steel/ Concrete	Office
Gulf-Western Bldg.	New York	1970	44	207	679	Steel	Office
Southern Bell Bldg.	Atlanta	1981	46	206	677	Concrete	Office

Table 1   The one-hundred tallest buildings in the world

Building	City	Year Comp	No. Of Stories	Height Meters	Feet	Material	Use
United Banking Center	Denver	1984	50	206	676	Mixed	Office
Metropolitan Tower	New York	1909	50	206	675	Steel	Office
Georgia Pacific Tower	Atlanta	1982	52	205	671	Steel	Office
Lincoln Bldg.	New York	1930	55	205	673	Steel	Office
McGraw-Hill Bldg.	New York	1972	51	204	670	Steel	Office
1633 Broadway	New York	1972	48	204	670	Steel	Office
Bank of Oklahoma Tower	Tulsa	1976	50	203	667	Steel/ Concrete	Office
Shinjuku Nomura Bldg.	Tokyo	1978	53	203	666	Steel	Office
Trump Tower	New York	1983	68	202	664	Concrete	Multiple

Nomenclature

A36. Structural steel with yield strength of 36,000 pounds per square inch, per ASTM standard.

A572 Grade 50. Structural steel with yield strength of 50,000 pounds per square inch, per ASTM standard.

Allowable stress design or working stress design. A method of proportioning structures such that the computed elastic stress does not exceed a specified limiting stress.

Altitude angle of sunlight. The angle of the sunlight beam from the ground level measured in the vertical plane passing through the sunlight beam.

Arbitrary-point-in-time load. Loading on the structure at any instant in time.

Azimuth angle of sunlight. The horizontal angle of sunlight beam measured on the ground from the meridian line.

Bay window. A window projecting from the wall between columns or buttresses.

Beam link. Beam segment between braces, or between a brace and a column.

Bent. A plant framework of beam or truss members that support a floor or roof and the columns that support these members.

Boot. A concealed hood over a light fixture.

Building standard. A document defining minimum standards for design.

Bundled tube. A structural system in which structural framed tubes are arranged or bundled together so that common walls of contiguous tubes are combined into single walls, thereby forcing compatibility of stresses at the interface of such contiguous tubes. In a bundled tube, individual tube elements may be terminated at any appropriate level.

Bustle. A low projection from a tall building.

Calibration. A process of adjusting the parameters in a new standard to achieve approximately the same reliability as exists in a current standard or specification.

Castellated beam. Beam fabricated by cutting through the web of the beam with a profile burning machine, separating the two halves, moving one half along the other until the "teeth" of the castellations coincide and tack welding the two halves together. Deep penetration welding is then used to weld both sides of the web.

Center length. Distance along one member between intersections of centerlines of perpendicular members.

Central business district. The key commercial area inside most modern U.S. cities.

Chevron. An inverted "V" in appearance.

Code. Building code, a legal document providing design citeria for buildings in a particular jurisdiction.

Coefficient of variation. The ratio of the standard deviation to the mean of a random variable.

Community development. The process of upgrading community conditions primarily in its physical aspects.

Core. That portion of a building that includes elevator, stairs, mechanical shaft and toilets, often centrally located.

Creep. The slow time-dependent change in dimensions of concrete under a sustained load, primarily in the direction in which the load acts. It is a dimensionless quantity having units of strain.

Dead load. The actual weight of the structural elements. (This is a gravity load.)

Differential. Difference or change between two values.

Doubler. A plate welded to or parallel to a web to add shear strength.

Drift. Lateral displacement due to lateral force.

Eccentrically braced frame. Frame in which the center lines of braces are offset from the points of intersection of the center lines of beams and columns.

Efficiency of use of land. The degree of achieving the maximum possible building area on a piece of land occupied by the building, on certain prerequisite conditions.

Electroslag. Welding by feeding electrode weld wire into an enclosed chamber.

Environmental loads. Loads on a structure due to wind, snow, earthquake, or temperature.

Facade. The face, and especially the principal elevation, of a building.

Factor of safety. The ratio of the ultimate strength (or yield point) of a material to the working stress assumed in design (stress factor of safety); or the ratio of the ultimate load, moment, or shear of a structural member to the working load, moment, or shear respectively, assumed in design (load factor of safety).

Failure. A condition where a limit state is reached. This may or may not involve collapse or other catastrophic occurrences.

Fin. A plate projecting from a member.

Finger shims. Thin plates slotted to slip around bolts.

First-order second-moment (FOSM) reliablity methods. Methods that involve (1) linearizing the limit state function through a Taylor series expansion at some point (first-order), and (2) computing a notational reliability measure that is a function only of the means and variances (first and second moments) of the random variables rather than their probability distributions.

Flame shield. A non-structural element that directs flames away from an exposed structural element to protect it.

Flange moment connection. Moment connection in which the beam is connected to the flange of the column.

Floor area ratio (FAR). A specified ratio of permissible floor space to lot area, in which the inducement to reduce lot coverage is an important component. The basic ratio is frequently modified by providing "bonus" or "premium" floor space for such aspects as arcades, setbacks, and plazas.

Format of design checking procedure. An ordered sequence of products of load factors and load effects that must be checked in the design process.

Hat truss. Stiff structural trusswork extending from core to perimeter at top of building.

Influence area. That area over which the influence function for load effect (beam shear, column thrust, etc.) is significantly different from zero. For columns, this is four times the traditional tributary area; for beams, twice; and for a slab, they are equal.

Limber. Flexible.

Limit states. Condition in which a structure or a part thereof ceases to fulfill one of its functions or to satisfy the conditions for which it was designed. Limit states can be classified in two categories: (1) *ultimate limit states*, corresponding to the load-carrying capacity of the structure— safety is usually related to these types of limit state; and (2) *serviceability limit states*, related to the criteria governing normal use of the structure.

Limit states design. A design process that involves identification of all potential modes of failure (limit states) and maintaining an acceptable level of safety against their occurrence. The safety level is usually established on a probabilistic basis.

Load combinations. Loads likely to act simultaneously.

Load effects. Moments, shears, and axial forces in a member due to loads or other actions.

Load factors. Factors applied to a load to express probability of not being exceeded; safety factors.

Load and resistance factor design. A design method in which, at a chosen limit state, load effects and resistances are separately multiplied by factors that account for the inherent uncertainties in the determination of these quantities.

Longitudinal. In the direction of the longer plan dimension.

Maximum load (ultimate load). Plastic limit load or stability limit load, as defined (also the maximum load-carrying capacity of a structure under test).

Mean recurrence interval (MRI). The average time between occurrences of a random variable that exceed its MRI value. The probability that the MRI value will be exceeded in any occurrence is 1/MRI.

Mullion. The horizontal or vertical member of a window wall or curtain wall system that is normally attached to the floor slab or beams, and supports the glass and/or elements of a window wall.

Neoprene. A synthetic rubber having physical properties closely resembling those of natural rubber but not requiring sulfur for vulcanization. It is made by polymerizing chloroprenes, and the latter is produced from acetylene and hydrogen chloride.

Node. A point at which subsidiary parts originate or center.

Nominal load effect. Calculated using a nominal load; the nominal load frequently is defined with reference to a probability level; e.g., 50 year mean recurrence interval wind speed used in calculating wind load.

Nominal resistance. Calculated using nominal material and cross-sectional properties and a rationally developed formula based on an analytical and/or experimental model of limit state behavior.

Outrigger. Stiff structural trusswork extending from core to perimeter at any point to distribute column loads between them.

Outstanding. Projecting from the main plane.

P-Delta effect. Secondary effect of column axial loads and lateral deflection on the moments in members.

Parking accumulation. Number of parked vehicles in a facility at one time.

Parking demand factor. Standard value for estimated parking demand generation for specified land-use measured in terms of the number of parking spaces needed at peak accumulation per unit of land-use.

Pile analyzer. Equipment for measuring and analyzing stress developed in a pile during pile driving.

Plasma torch. A jet of high-temperature ionized gas used to cut steel plate quickly and cleanly.

Point type high-rise building. A building in the shape of a slender tower.

Post-buckling. That which exists after buckling occurs.

Pressuremeter. Radially expandable probe for measuring radial soil pressure and resulting soil deformation.

Probabilistic design. A design method that explicitly utilizes probability theory in the safety checking process.

Probability distribution. A mathematical law that describes the probability that a random variable will assume certain values; either a cumulative distribution function (cdf) or a probability density function is used.

Probability of failure. The probability that the limit state is exceeded or violated.

Probability of survival. One minus the probability of failure.

Public-private partnerships. Relationships between the government and business sectors to achieve some special community purpose.

Quartering. In a diagonal direction across the building plan. Usually taken so as to provide a maximum projected face width.

R. The ratio of the total floor area of the many stories of the high-rise building to the area of land occupied by the building.

Rack. To deform a rectangle in shear by displacing one side laterally relative to the opposite side.

Reliability index. A computed quantity defining the relative reliability of a structure or structural element.

Resistance. The maximum load-carrying capacity as defined by a limit state.

Resistance factor. A partial safety factor to account for the probability of understrength of materials or structural members.

Seismic. Pertaining to earthquakes.

Shear stud. A short mild-steel rod with flattened head, welded to a steel member, to transfer shear force between steel and surrounding concrete.

Skewed. Not parallel or perpendicular.

Slab type high-rise building. A building in the shape of a vertical slab standing on the ground on its short dimension.

Spandrel. A beam spanning between columns on the exterior of a building.

Spandrel beam. A floor level beam in the face of a building, usually supporting the edges of the floor slabs.

Stocky. Heavy and thick, composed of elements with low width/thickness ratios.

Stressed skin. Material used for strength and stiffness in its own plane, as in a membrane.

Target reliability. A desired level of reliability in a proposed design method.

Tie backs. Mechanical devices for supporting sheeting, consisting of post-tensioned rods extending to anchor points in the soil surrounding the excavation or to rock.

Transit use. Percent of person trips to given area or land-use for which some form of public transportation is the travel mode.

Transverse. In the direction of the shorter plan dimension.

Tube. A structure with continuous perimeter frame designed to act in a manner similar to that of a hollow cylinder.

Tune. Adjust carefully.

Unclad. Not covered by facade.

Uncured butyl. A soft, putty-like synthetic rubber of polymerized iso-butylene.

Upset. Projecting above the surrounding level, especially above a floor.

Vierendeel action. Using a planar rectangular grid of members working in flexure to act as a truss for longer spans for loads in that plane.

W14. Nominally 14-inch deep steel section with wide flange or wide "I" shape.

Web moment connection. Moment connection in which the beam is connected to the web of the column.

Zipper gasket. A two-piece system of sealing glass to a surrounding plate or frame that uses the insertion of a hard "zipper" strip into an "H"-shaped rubber section to provide clamping action.

Zoning. The legal regulation of the use of land and buildings, in which the density of population and the height, bulk, and spacing of structures is also specified.

SYMBOLS

$$A = \text{peak ground acceleration}$$
$$A = \text{cross-sectional area}$$
$$A = \text{generalized structural load}$$
$$A = \text{area or P-factor}$$
$$A_E = \text{effective area}$$
$$A_I = \text{influence area}$$
$$A_g = \text{gross cross-sectional area}$$
$$A_n = \text{net cross-sectional area}$$
$$A_T = \text{tributary area}$$
$$a = \text{length of subpanel}$$
$$a, b, c = \text{linear dimensions}$$
$$B = \text{generalized modeling parameter}$$
$$B = \text{foundation width}$$
$$b = \text{width of subpanel}$$
$$b = \text{subscript for beams}$$
$$C = \text{base shear coefficient}$$
$$C = \text{cohesion}$$

$C_c = \sqrt{2\pi^2 E/F_y}$

C_m = coefficient applied to bending term in interaction formula

C_p = pressure coefficient

C_v = coefficient for web shear stress

c = generalized influence coefficient

c = subscript for columns

c = distance from neutral axis to extreme fiber

D = dead load intensity of load effect; D and D_n are mean and nominal values, respectively

D = maximum midday (during 8 A.M. to 6 P.M. period) parking demand for mixed-use project using shared parking concept

d = cross-sectional dimension

d = distance from neutral axis to area of interest

E = earthquake load effect; E and E_n are mean and nominal values, respectively

E = tensile modulus of elasticity

E = modulus of elasticity

$\hat{E}$ = modulus ratio (= E/E_t)

E = maximum evening (during 6 P.M. to midnight period) parking demand for mixed-use project using shared parking concept

E_1, E_2, E_3, etc. = modulus of elasticity of different materials

E_d = pressuremeter modulus

E_t = tangent modulus

E_Z = exposure factor

e = load eccentricity

F = generalized variable denoting cross-sectional parameters; F is mean value

F_A = allowable and computed axial stress

F_a = axial stress permitted in the absence of bending moment

F_b = allowable and computed bending stress

F_{cr} = critical stress

F_{Exx} = tensile strength of weld metal

F_e = Euler's buckling stress divided by a factor of safety

F_n = ten-year nominal design stress for wood

F_r = modulus of rupture

F_u = ultimate strength

F_v = allowable shear stress

F_X = cumulative distribution function (cdf) for random variable X

$\mathbf{F_y}$ = yield stress

F_{ys} = static yield stress

f = subscript denoting final deflected position

f = shape factor

f = horizontal displacement of building

$f'_c =$ 28-day concrete strength
$f_a =$ computed axial stress
$f_b =$ actual bending stress
$f_b =$ allowable and computed bending stress
$f_c =$ compressive stress
$f_m =$ compressive strength of prism tests
$f_t =$ tensile stress
$f_v =$ actual shear stress
$f_X =$ probability density function for random variable X
$f_y =$ yield stress
$f^W, f^F =$ horizontal displacement of the wall frame
$G =$ gust factor
$G =$ elastic modulus in shear $= E/2(1 - \nu)$
$g =$ generalized design function
$g(n) =$ Poisson's ratio
$g(Q) =$ angle of rotation at the node
$H =$ height of building
$H =$ number of hotel rooms
$H_u =$ lateral load multiplied by its load factors
$h =$ cross-sectional dimension
$h =$ height (depth) of plate girder web
$h =$ height of story
$h_i =$ story height between levels i and $i + 1$
$I =$ moment of inertia
$I =$ importance factor
$I =$ column cross-section stiffness corresponding to factored loads
$I_e =$ moment of inertia of elastic part of the cross-section
$I_e =$ effective overall moment of inertia
$I^W, I^{BF}, I^{CF} =$ moment of inertia of wall, beam, column
$J =$ soil damping factor
$K =$ building factor
$K =$ length correction or adjustment factor
$K =$ effective length factor
$k =$ effective length factor
$k =$ panel buckling constant
$k_b = I^{BF}/l$
$k_c = I^{CF}/h$
$L =$ length
$L =$ live load intensity or load effect; L and L_n are mean and nominal values, respectively; L_{apt} is arbitrary-point-in-time value
$L =$ length between supports
$L =$ length of column

L_0 = basic code-specified live load

l = length of beam

l_u = unbraced story height

M = bending moment

M = generalized material factor; M is mean value

M = magnified moment at mid-height of the column

M = maximum aggregate parking demand for mixed use project using single land-use parking factors

M^{AB}, M^{BC} = moments acting at the ends A, B

M_m = flow moment

M_p = plastic moment

M_{pc} = plastic moment reduced for the presence of axial force

M_u = ultimate bending moment

M_y = yield moment

M_{yc} = yield moment reduced for the presence of axial force

N_γ = bearing capacity factor = $(1.5)(N_q - 1) \tan \phi$

N_c = bearing capacity factor = $(N_q - 1) \cot \phi$

N_q = bearing capacity factor = $\tan^2(45 + \phi/2) \exp(\pi \tan \phi)$

n = hardening parameter

o = subscript for original deflected position (without P-Delta effects)

P = axial force

P = limit load

P = point load at floor level

$P1$ = reduction in midday parking demand ($M - D$) using shared parking concept

$P2$ = reduction in evening parking demand ($M - E$) using shared parking concept

P_c = Euler's critical buckling load in a column

P_E = Euler load

P_f = probability of failure

P_f = creep pressure = pressure at which increasing creep occurs

P_i = column loads at level i

P_L = limit pressure = pressure at which soil failure occurs

P_{max} = maximum load

P_0 = Earth pressure at rest

P_t = tangent modulus load

P_u = axial load in a column multiplied by its load factor

P_y = yield load

P^W, P^F = force at floor level of wall, frame

p = generalized professional factor; P is mean value

Q = generalized load effect; Q is mean value

Q = form factor

Q = effective overburden pressure

Q = shear force

q = pile tip quake

R = generalized resistance; R and R_n are mean and nominal values respectively

R = system factor

R = a factor for the maximum service load drift

R_u = pile soil resistance

r = radius of gyration

S = soil factor

S = snow load effect; S and S_n are mean and nominal values respectively

S = elastic section modulus

S_{V_0} = spectral amplification factor

S_1, S_2 = shape factors including ground and base factors

T = shear force in lintel

T = number of seats in theaters, auditoriums, etc.

T, t = time

t = cross-sectional dimensions

t = thickness of subpanel

V = coefficient of variation

V = wind velocity

V_i = story wind shear at level i

V_u = ultimate shear capacity

W = weight of structure

X = generalized parameter

X^{WF} = mutual reaction forces in wall and frame

x, y = rectangular coordinates

Z = zone factor

Z = plastic section modulus

$[A^W], [A^F]$ = flexibility matrix of the wall frame

$[K_g]$ = geometric stiffness matrix

Δ = story deflection

Δ_i = lateral drift over one story between level i and level $i + l$ (length)

$\Delta_{\delta i}$ = relative displacement of the column head from the bottom of the next floor column (horizontal displacement in the joint)

ϕ = capacity reduction factor

ϕ = soil angle of internal friction, degrees

π $\approx$ 3.142

Σ = summation for all the columns in a story

α = direction cosine

α = subpanel length-to-width ratio

α = coefficient of end restraint

β = reliability index
$\underline{\beta}$ = plasticity parameter
$\overline{\chi}$ = mean value of the displacement
δ = moment magnification factor for columns
δ_i = initial out-of-straightness
δ_{im} = initial mid-height out-of-straightness
δ_m = mid-height deflection
δ_m = maximum moment magnification factor for braced frames
δ_i = displacement of the column head resulting from deviation of the column axis from the vertical axis
ϕ = resistance factor
γ = load factor
γ = initial crookedness parameter
γ = unit weight
η = imperfection parameter
$\hat{\eta}$ = initial crookedness imperfection parameter
$\overline{\eta}$ = load eccentricity imperfection parameter
λ = slenderness parameter
λ = nondimensional slenderness ratio = $1/\pi\sqrt{F_y/E(1/r)}$
μ = number of measurements
σ = standard deviation
$\sigma_{0.2}$ = 0.2% offset yield stress
σ_{cr} = critical stress
σ_u = tensile strength
σ_y = yield stress
$\overline{\sigma}_y$ = flow stress
$\hat{\sigma}_y$ = stress ratio $(\overline{\sigma}_y/\sigma_y)$
τ_c = critical shear stress
ν = Poisson's ratio

ABBREVIATIONS

ACCD—Allegheny Conference on Community Development
ACI—American Concrete Institute
AISC—American Institute of Steel Construction
ANSI—American National Standards Institute
APM—Automated People Movers
ASTM—American Society for Testing and Materials
ATC—Applied Technology Council
BOCA—Building Officials and Code Administrators International, Inc.
BOMA—Building Owners and Managers Association
CAD—Computer-aided design

CAP—Central Atlanta Progress
CAPWAP—Case Pile Wave Analysis Program
CATS—Central Automated Transit System
CBD—Central business district
CBF—Centrally braced frames
CCRL—Cement and Concrete Reference Laboratory
CCTV—Closed circuit television
CEO—Chief executive officer
COP—Coefficient of performance
CPI—Consumer price index
CRC—Column Research Council
DPM—Downtown People Mover
DRAIN-2D—Dynamic Response Analysis of Inelastic Plane Frame Systems
    (Two-dimensional)
EBF—Eccentrically braced frames
ECCS—European Convention for Constructional Steelwork
EERI—Earthquake Engineering Research Institute
EPA—Effective peak acceleration
EPV—Effective peak velocity
FAR—Floor area ratio
FMEA—Failure Mode and Effect Analysis
GBC—Greater Baltimore Committee
GLA—Gross leasable area
HOV—High-occupancy vehicle
HUD—U.S. Department of Housing and Urban Development
HVAC—Heating, ventilating, air conditioning
ICBO—International Conference of Building Officials
KM—Kajima Mixed Structure System
LRFD—Load and resistance factor design
LRT—Light Rail Transit
LS—Limit states
MPO—Metropolitan planning organization
MRF—Moment-resisting frames
NBS—National Bureau of Standards
O&M—Operation and maintenance
SSA—Social Security Administration
SSRC—Structural Stability Research Council
TIP—Transportation improvement program
TSM—Transportation system management
UBC—Uniform Building Code
UMTA—Urban Mass Transportation Administration
VAV—Variable air volume

UNITS

In the table below are given conversion factors for commonly used units. The numerical values have been rounded off to the values shown. The British (Imperial) System of units is the same as the American System except where noted. Le Système International d'Unités (abbreviated "SI") is the name formally given in 1960 to the system of units partly derived from, and replacing, the old metric system.

SI	American	Old Metric
	Length	
1 mm	0.03937 in.	1 mm
1 m	3.28083 ft	1 m
	1.093613 yd	
1 km	0.62137 mile	1 km
	Area	
1 mm^2	0.00155 in.^{2}	1 mm^2
1 m^2	10.76392 ft^2	1 m^2
	1.19599 yd^2	
1 km^2	247.1043 acres	1 km^2
1 hectare	2.471 acres[1]	1 hectare
	Volume	
1 cm^3	0.061023 in.^{3}	1 cc
		1 ml
1 m^3	35.3147 ft^3	1 m^3
	1.30795 yd^3	
	264.172 gal[2] liquid	
	Velocity	
1 m/sec	3.28084 ft/sec	1 m/sec
1 km/hr	0.62137 miles/hr	1 km/hr
	Acceleration	
1 m/sec^2	3.28084 ft/sec^2	1 m/sec^2
	Mass	
1 g	0.035274 oz	1 g
1 kg	2.2046216 lb[3]	1 kg
	Density	
1 kg/m^3	0.062428 lb/ft^3	1 kg/m^3

SI	American	Old Metric
Force, Weight		
1 N	0.224809 lbf	0.101972 kgf
1 kN	0.1124045 tons[4]	
1MN	224.809 kips	
1kN/m	0.06853 kips/ft	
1kN/m²	20.9 lbf/ft²	
Torque, Bending Moment		
1N-m	0.73756 lbf-ft	0.101972 kgf-m
1kN-m	0.73756 kip-ft	101.972 kgf-m
Pressure, Stress		
1N/m² = 1 Pa	0.000145038 psi	0.101972 kgf/m²
1kN/m² = 1 kPa	20.8855 psf	
1MN/m² = 1 MPa	0.145038 ksi	
Vicosity (Dynamic)		
1N-sec/m²	0.0208854 lbf-sec/ft²	0.101972 kfg-sec/m²
Viscosity (Kinematic)		
1m²/sec	10.7639 ft²/sec	1m²/sec
Energy, Work		
1J = 1 N-m	0.737562 lbf-ft	0.00027778 w-hr
1MJ	0.37251 hp-hr	0.27778 kw-hr
Power		
1W = 1 J/sec	0.737562 lbf ft/sec	1 w
1kW	1.34102 hp	1 kw
Temperature		
$K = 273.15 + °C$	$°F = (°C × 1.8) + 32$	$°C = (°F - 32)/1.8$
$K = 273.15 + 5/9(°F - 32)$		
$K = 273.15 + 5/9(°R - 491.69)$		

[1]Hectare as an alternative for km² is restricted to land and water areas.
[2]1 m³ = 219.9693 Imperial gallons.
[3]1 kg = 0.068522 slugs.
[4]1 American ton = 2000 lb.   1kN = 0.1003612 Imperial ton.   1 Imperial ton = 2240 lb.

Abbreviations for Units

Btu	British Thermal Unit	kW	kilowatt
°C	degree Celsius (centigrade)	lb	pound
cc, cm^3	cubic centimeters	lbf	pound force
cm	centimeter	lb$_m$	pound mass
°F	degree Fahrenheit	MJ	megajoule
ft	foot	MPa	megapascal
g	gram	m	meter
gal	gallon	ml	milliliter
hp	horsepower	mm	millimeter
hr	hour	MN	meganewton
Imp	British Imperial	N	newton
in.	inch	oz	ounce
J	joule	Pa	pascal
K	kelvin	psf	pounds per square foot
kg	kilogram	psi	pounds per square inch
kgf	kilogram-force	°R	degree Rankine
kip	1000 pound force	s	second
km	kilometer	slug	14.594 kg
kN	kilonewton	U$_o$	heat transfer coefficient
kPa	kilopasal	W	watt
ksi	kips per square inch	yd	yard

References/Bibliography

The citations that follow include both references and a bibliography. The list includes all articles referred to or cited in the text, and it also includes a bibliography for further reading. The material is arranged alphabetically by author, followed by the year of publication. Since the citation in the text is to author and year, there will be instances in which reference is made to two different articles published in the same year by the same authors. In those instances it has been necessary to affix letters to the year to provide proper identification.

Additional bibliographies are available through the Council.

Abrams, D. P. and Sozen, M. A., 1979
EXPERIMENTAL STUDY OF FRAME–WALL INTERACTION IN REIN-FORCED CONCRETE STRUCTURES SUBJECTED TO STRONG EARTH-QUAKE MOTION, Civil Engineering Studies, Structural Research Series No. 460, University of Illinois, Urbana, Illinois.

ACI, 1977a
BUILDING CODE REQUIREMENT FOR REINFORCED CONCRETE, American Concrete Institute, Detroit, Michigan.

ACI, 1977b
MINUTES OF FEBRUARY 24, 1977 MEETING OF TECHNICAL ACTIVITIES, Committee of the Chicago Chapter of the American Concrete Institute, Detroit, Michigan.

ACI Committee 352, 1976
RECOMMENDATIONS FOR DESIGN OF BEAM–COLUMN JOINTS IN MONOLITHIC REINFORCED CONCRETE STRUCTURES, ACI Journal, July.

629

Ackroyd, M. H. and Gerstle, K. H., 1982
  BEHAVIOR OF TYPE 2 STEEL FRAMES, Journal of the Structural Division, ASCE, Vol. 108, No. ST7, Proc. Paper 17207, July, pp. 1541–1556.
AISC, 1970
  MANUAL OF STEEL CONSTRUCTION, with 1974 Supplement No. 3, American Institute of Steel Construction, Inc., New York.
AISC, 1978
  SPECIFICATION FOR THE DESIGN, FABRICATION AND ERECTION OF STRUCTURAL STEEL FOR BUILDINGS, American Institute of Steel Construction, Chicago, Illinois.
AISC, 1980
  MANUAL OF STEEL CONSTRUCTION, eighth edition, American Institute of Steel Construction, New York.
AISC, 1982
  TENTATIVE SPECIFICATION FOR LOAD AND RESISTANCE FACTOR DESIGN, FABRICATION AND ERECTION OF STRUCTURAL STEEL FOR BUILDINGS SECTION 2.6 MEMBERS UNDER COMBINED STRESS, TORSION, AND COMBINED STRESS AND TORSION, Unpublished Draft, June, pp. 1–2.
AISI, 1977
  COLD-FORMED STEEL DESIGN MANUAL, American Iron and Steel Institute, Washington, D.C.
ALFA, 1981
  INZENYRSKE STAVBY 2 (in Czech or Slovak), Bratislava, Czechoslovakia.
Algermissen, S. T. and Perkins, D. M., 1976
  A PROBABILISTIC ESTIMATE OF MAXIMUM ACCELERATION IN ROCK IN THE CONTIGUOUS UNITED STATES, U.S. Geological Survey Open File Report, 76-416.
American Insurance Association, 1976
  NATIONAL BUILDING CODE, American Insurance Association, New York.
ANSI, 1972
  BUILDING CODE REQUIREMENTS FOR MINIMUM DESIGN LOADS IN BUILDINGS AND OTHER STRUCTURES, ANSI A58.1-1972, American National Standards Institute, New York.
ANSI, 1982
  MINIMUM DESIGN LOADS FOR BUILDINGS AND OTHER STRUCTURES, ANSI A58.1-1982, American National Standards Institute, New York.
ANSI A58.1, 1972
  AMERICAN NATIONAL STANDARD BUILDING CODE REQUIREMENTS FOR MINIMUM DESIGN LOADS IN BUILDINGS AND OTHER STRUCTURES, American National Standards Institute, New York.
ANSI A58.1-82, 1982
  AMERICAN NATIONAL STANDARD BUILDING CODE REQUIREMENTS FOR MINIMUM DESIGN LOADS IN BUILDINGS AND OTHER STRUCTURES, Section 6, American National Standards Institute, New York.

Applied Technology Council, 1978
TENTATIVE PROVISIONS FOR THE DEVELOPMENT OF SEISMIC REGU-
LATIONS FOR BUILDINGS, ATC 3-06, NSF 78-8, NBS Special Publication
510, U.S. Government Printing Office, Washington, D.C.
Architectural and Transportation Barriers Compliance Board, 1977
RESOURCE GUIDE TO LITERATURE ON BARRIER-FREE ENVIRON-
MENTS, Architectural and Transportation Barriers Compliance Board.
Architectural Institute of Japan, 1972a
RECOMMENDATION FOR DESIGN AND PRACTICE OF HIGH STRENGTH
BOLTED CONNECTIONS (in Japanese), Architectural Institute of Japan,
Tokyo, Japan.
Architectural Institute of Japan, 1972b
STANDARDS FOR DESIGN OF STEEL STRUCTURES (in Japanese), Archi-
tectural Institute of Japan, Tokyo, Japan.
Arciszewski, T., 1975
WIND BRACING OF TALL BUILDINGS IN THE FORM OF BELT-TRUSS
SYSTEMS (in Polish), Ph.D. thesis, Warsaw Technical University, Warsaw,
Poland.
Arciszewski, T., 1980
STUDIES ON HIGH RISE BUILDINGS IN THE DEVELOPMENT OF NIGE-
RIAN URBAN CENTERS. HIGH RISE DECISION MAKING, Research
Report, University of Nigeria, Nsukka, Nigeria.
Arciszewski, T. and Brodka, J., 1978
TECHNICAL QUALITY OF STRUCTURAL SOLUTION APPRAISAL
METHOD (in Polish), Journal of Invention and Rationalization, Vol. 1,
pp. 29–33.
Arciszewski, T. and Kisielnicka, J., 1977
MORPHOLOGICAL ANALYSIS (in Polish), Problem, Method, Solution. Tech-
niques Of Creative Thinking, PWN Publishing House, Warsaw, Poland.
Arciszewski, T. and Lubinski, M., 1978
METHOD OF ANALYSIS AND APPRAISAL OF A STRUCTURAL SYSTEM
(in Polish), Proceedings held at the Warsaw Technical University, 1978, Vol. 1,
Warsaw, Poland, pp. 35–57.
Arciszewski, T. and Pancewicz, Z. 1976
AN APPROACH TO THE DESCRIPTION OF WIND BRACING CHARAC-
TERISTICS IN SYSTEMS SKELETON STRUCTURES (in Polish), (Proceed-
ings held at the Wroclaw Technical University, 1976), Vol. 20, Wroclaw, Poland,
pp. 7–19.
Arciszewski, T. T. and Pancewicz, Z., 1981a
ASSUMPTIONS AND RESULTS OF RESEARCH INTO THE STIFFNESS
SHAPING OF WINDBRACING IN THE FORM OF BELT TRUSS SYSTEMS
IN HIGH-RISE BUILDING STEEL STRUCTURES (in Polish), Building
Construction Engineering, No. 72, pp. 34–37.
Arciszewski, T. T. and Pancewicz, Z., 1981b
STIFFNESS SHAPING OF WINDBRACING IN THE FORM OF BELT TRUSS
SYSTEMS (in Polish), Building Construction Engineering, No. 72, pp. 49–65.

Arciszewski, T. T. and Pancewicz, Z., 1981c
EFFECTIVENESS OF HORIZONTAL TRUSSES OR HORIZONTAL TRUSS SYSTEMS IN THE WINDBRACING OF A HIGH-RISE BUILDING STEEL STRUCTURE (in Polish), Building Construction Engineering, No. 72, pp. 67–90.
Arciszewski, T. T. and Pancewicz, Z., 1981d
STIFFNESS EVALUATION METHOD OF TRUSS WINDBRACING IN A HIGH-RISE BUILDING STEEL STRUCTURE (in Polish), Building Construction Engineering, No. 72, pp. 91–102.
ASCE/NSF, 1984
WORKSHOP TO DETERMINE RESEARCH NEEDS RELATED TO THE NATION'S INFRASTRUCTURE, (Proceedings of a Conference held at Warrenton, Virginia, April 26–27, 1984), American Society of Civil Engineers/National Science Foundation.
ASCE Structural Division, 1962
WIND FORCES ON STRUCTURES, Paper No. 3269, ASCE, New York, pp. 1124–1198.
Avent, R. R. and Wells, S., 1982
EXPERIMENTAL STUDY OF THIN-WEB WELDED H-COLUMNS, Journal of the Structural Division, ASCE, Vol. 108, No. St7, Proc. Paper 17209, July, pp. 1464–1480.

Bache, H. H., 1981
DENSIFIED CEMENT/ULTRA-FINE PARTICLE-BASED MATERIALS, (Proceedings of the Second International Conference on Superplasticizers in Concrete, Ottawa, June 10–12, 1981).
Baer, W., 1982
TELECOMMUNICATIONS, Facilities Planning News, July.
Baguelin, F., Jezequel, J. F. and Shields, D. H., 1978
THE PRESSUREMETER AND FOUNDATION ENGINEERING, Trans Tech Publications.
Baker, C. N., Echevarria, F. A. and Cnaedinger, J. P., 1982
USE OF GROUTING IN CAISSON CONSTRUCTION, ASCE Specialty Conference, February, New Orleans, Louisiana.
Baker, C. N. and Kahn, F., 1971
CAISSON CONSTRUCTION PROBLEMS AND CORRECTION IN CHICAGO, Journal of the Soil Mechanics and Foundation Division, ASCE, Vol. 97, No. SM2, February, pp. 417–440.
Ballio, G. and Campanini, G., 1981
EQUIVALENT BENDING MOMENTS FOR BEAM-COLUMNS, Journal of Constructional Steel Research Vol. 1, No. 3, May, pp. 13–23.
Barton-Aschman Associates, 1974
THE CIRCULATION OF PEOPLE IN THE ST. PAUL CENTRAL AREA, prepared for the City of St. Paul Department of Public Works, March, St. Paul, Minnesota.
Barton-Aschman Associates, 1976
SKYWAYS IN MINNEAPOLIS/ST. PAUL; PROTOTYPES FOR THE NATION?, July.

Barton-Aschman Associates, 1978
TRANSPORTATION ANALYSIS OF THE PROPOSED DES MOINES SKY-WAY SYSTEM, City of Des Moines, Iowa, August.
Barton-Aschman Associates, 1981
PHASE I–STUDY DESIGN, Urban Land Institute, Washington, D.C.
Barton-Aschman Associates, 1982a
FEASIBILITY ANALYSIS AND PLAN FOR A SECOND LEVEL WALKWAY SYSTEM IN DOWNTOWN ROCHESTER, NEW YORK, City of Rochester, New York, July.
Barton-Aschman Associates, 1982b
PLAN FOR A SKYWAY SYSTEM, Milwaukee, Wisconsin, June.
Barton-Aschman, 1983
SHARED PARKING STUDY, Urban Land Institute, Washington, D.C.
Bauer, G. E., 1980
THE MEASUREMENT AND ANALYSIS OF LOAD TRANSFER FROM A CAISSON TO ITS ROCK SOCKET, International Conference on Structural Foundations on Rock, (Proceedings of Conference held in Sydney, Australia, 1980), pp. 235-240.
Becker, E. R., 1971
PANEL ZONE EFFECT ON THE STRENGTH AND STIFFNESS OF STEEL RIGID FRAMES, Engineering Journal, AISC, First Quarter, Vol. 12, No. 1, pp. 19–29.
Bergquist, D. J., 1977
TESTS ON COLUMNS RESTRAINED BY BEAMS WITH SIMPLE CONNEC-TIONS, Report No. 1, American Iron and Steel Institute Project No. 189, Department of Civil Engineering, The University of Texas at Austin, Austin, Texas, January.
Berl, W. G. and Halpin, B. M., 1977
AN ANALYSIS OF FIRE-INDUCED INJURIES & FACILITIES, Johns Hopkins University, Applied Physics Laboratory, Baltimore, Maryland.
Berl, W. G. and Halpin, B. M., 1978
HUMAN FATALITIES FROM UNWANTED FIRES, Johns Hopkins University, Applied Physics Laboratory, Baltimore, Maryland.
Biggs, J. M., 1964
INTRODUCTION TO STRUCTURAL DYNAMICS, McGraw–Hill Book Company, New York.
Bjorhovde, R., 1972
DETERMINISTIC AND PROBABILISTIC APPROACHES TO THE STRENGTH OF STEEL COLUMNS, Ph.D. Dissertation, Lehigh University, Bethlehem, Pennsylvania.
Bjorhovde, R., 1980
RESEARCH NEEDS IN STABILITY OF METAL STRUCTURES, Journal of the Structural Division, ASCE, Vol. 106, No. ST12, Proc. Paper 15926, December, pp. 2425–2442.
Bjorhovde, R., 1981a
DISCUSSION OF END RESTRAINT AND COLUMN STABILITY, BY WAI F. CHEN, Journal of the Structural Division, ASCE, Vol. 107, No. ST8, Proc. Paper T6410, August, pp. 1696–1700.

Bjorhovde, R., 1981b
DISCUSSION OF END RESTRAINT AND COLUMN STABILITY, BY WAI F. CHEN, Journal of the Structural Division, ASCE, Vol. 107, No. ST8, Proc. Paper 16937, March, pp. 511–524.
Bleich, F., 1952
BUCKLING STRENGTH OF METAL STRUCTURES, McGraw–Hill Book Company, New York.
Blume, J. A., Newmark, N. M. and Corning, L. H., 1961
DESIGN OF MULTISTORY REINFORCED CONCRETE BUILDINGS FOR EARTHQUAKE MOTION, Portland Cement Association, Skokie, Illinois.
BOCA, 1970, 1973, and 1981
BOCA BASIC BUILDING CODE, BOCA, Homewood, New Jersey.
Branbilla, R. and Longo, G., 1977
FOR PEDESTRIANS ONLY: PLANNING DESIGN AND MANAGEMENT OF TRAFFIC FREE ZONES, Whitney Library of Design.
Bridges, A. H., 1975
THE INTERACTION OF DESIGN AND PERFORMANCE VARIABLES, ABACUS Occasional Paper No. 41, Strathclyde University, Strathclyde, England.
Bryan, J. L., 1982
HUMAN BEHAVIOR IN THE MGM GRAND HOTEL FIRE, NFPA Fire Journal.
Bushell, T. D. and Baker, C. N., 1981
DISCUSSION OF "CAISSON SOCKETED IN SOUND MICA SCHIST," BY KOUTSOFTAS, Geotechnical Journal, ASCE.

CSVTS DT, 1981
LIMIT STATES OF THE METAL BUILDING STRUCTURES (in Czech), (Proceedings of Conference held in Carlsbad, Czechoslovakia April), Vols. 1 to 5.
Canadian Standards Association, 1974
CSA STANDARD S16.1-1974, STEEL STRUCTURES FOR BUILDINGS – LIMIT STATE DESIGN, Canadian Standards Association, Rexdale, Ontario, Canada, December, pp. 1–114.
Chalk, P. L. and Corotis, R. B., 1980
PROBABILITY MODEL FOR DESIGN LIVE LOADS, Journal of the Structural Division, ASCE, Vol. 106, No. ST10, Proc. Paper 15753, October, pp. 2017–2033.
Chapuis, J. and Galambos, T. V., 1982
RESTRAINED CROOKED ALUMINUM COLUMNS, Journal of the Structural Division, ASCE, Vol. 108, No. ST3, Proc. Paper No. 16937, March, pp. 511–524.
Chen, W. F. Ed., 1980
BEAM-TO-COLUMN BUILDING CONNECTIONS; STATE-OF-THE-ART, Preprint 80-179, ASCE Spring Convention, Portland, Oregon, April 14–18.
Chen, W. F., 1980
END RESTRAINT AND COLUMN STABILITY, Journal of the Structural Division, ASCE, Vol. 106, No. JST11, Proc. Paper 15796, November, pp. 2279–2295.
Chen, W. F., 1982
CLOSURE TO END RESTRAINT AND COLUMN STABILITY, Journal of the Structural Division, ASCE, Vol. 108, No. ST5, Proc. Paper 17236, August, pp. 1929–1933.

Chen, W. F. and Atsuta, T., 1976
THEORY OF BEAM-COLUMNS; IN PLANE BEHAVIOR AND DESIGN, Vol. 1, McGraw–Hill, New York.

Chen, W. F. and Atsuta, T., 1977
THEORY OF BEAM-COLUMNS; SPACE BEHAVIOR AND DESIGN, Vol. 2, McGraw–Hill, New York.

Chen, W. F., Huang, J. S. and Beedle, L. S., 1974
RECENT RESULTS ON CONNECTION RESEARCH AT LEHIGH, (Proceedings of the Regional Conference on Tall Buildings, Bangkok, Thailand, January), pp. 799–814.

Chen, W. F. and Patel, K. V., 1981
STATIC BEHAVIOR OF BEAM-TO-COLUMN MOMENT CONNECTIONS, Journal of the Structural Division, ASCE, Vol. 107, No. ST9, Proc. Paper No. 16512, September, pp. 1815–1838.

Chen, W. F. and Rentschler, G. P., 1976
TESTS AND ANALYSIS OF BEAM-TO-COLUMN WEB CONNECTIONS, (Proceedings of the ASCE Specialty Conference on Method of Structural Analysis, held at the University of Wisconsin at Madison, August 22–25), pp. 957–976.

Cheong-Siat-Moy, F., 1974
CONTROL OF DEFLECTION IN UNBRACED STEEL FRAMES, (Proceedings of the Institution of Civil Engineers in London, December, 1974), Vol. 57, Part II, London, England, pp. 619–634.

Chicago Committee on High-Rise Buildings, 1977
HIGH STRENGTH CONCRETE IN CHICAGO HIGH RISE BUILDINGS, Task Force Report #5, Chicago Committee on High-Rise Buildings, Chicago, Illinois.

Choate, P. and Walter, S., 1981
AMERICA IN RUINS: BEYOND THE PUBLIC WORKS PORK BARREL, Technical Report, Council of State Planning Agencies, Washington, D.C.

City of Chicago, 1973
CHICAGO LOOP PEDESTRIAN MOVEMENT STUDY, Pedestrian Mall Task Force, Chicago, Illinois.

Column Research Council, 1966
GUIDE TO DESIGN CRITERIA FOR METAL COMPRESSION MEMBERS, second edition, Fritz Laboratory, Bethlehem, Pennsylvania.

Comité Euro-International du Beton, 1982
SEISMIC DESIGN OF CONCRETE STRUCTURES, Second Draft of an Appendix to the CEB-FIP Model Code, Bulletin d'Information, No. 149, March, p. 43.

Committee for Economic Development, 1982
PUBLIC–PRIVATE PARTNERSHIP, AN OPPORTUNITY FOR URBAN COMMUNITIES, Committee for Economic Development, New York.

Constructor, 1982
A REPORT TO THE NATION; WHY AMERICA MUST REBUILD, Constructor, November, pp. 18–43.

Cook, J. E., 1982
RESEARCH AND APPLICATION OF HIGH STRENGTH CONCRETE USING CLASS C FLY ASH, Concrete International, Vol. 4, No. 7, pp. 72–80.

Corotis, R. B., Fox, R. R. and Harris, J. C., 1981
    DELPHI METHODS: THEORY AND DESIGN LOAD APPLICATION, Journal
    of the Structural Division, ASCE, Vol. 107, No. ST6, Proc. Paper 16322, June,
    pp. 1095–1105.
Corotis, R. B. and Jaria, V., 1979
    STOCHASTIC NATURE OF BUILDING LIVE LOADS, Journal of the Struc-
    tural Division, ASCE, Vol. 105, No. ST3, Proc. Paper 14441, March, pp. 493–510.
Coull, A., Bose, B. and Ahmed, A., 1982
    SIMPLIFIED ANALYSIS OF BUNDLED-TUBE STRUCTURES, Journal of the
    Structural Division, ASCE, Vol. 108, No. ST5, Proc. Paper 17065, May, pp.
    1140–1153.
Council on Tall Buildings, 1978-1981
    PLANNING AND DESIGN OF TALL BUILDINGS, A Monograph, 5 volumes,
    ASCE, New York.
Council on Tall Buildings, 1983
    DEVELOPMENTS IN TALL BUILDINGS—1983, an update of Monograph on
    the Planning and Design of Tall Buildings, Hutchinson Ross Publishing Co.,
    Stroudsburg, Pennsylvania.
Council on Tall Buildings, Committee 3, 1980
    STRUCTURAL SYSTEMS, Chapter SC-1, Volume SC of the Monograph on
    Planning and Design of Tall Buildings, ASCE, New York.
Council on Tall Buildings, Committee 28, 1981
    PHILOSOPHY OF TALL BUILDINGS, Chapter PC-1, Volume PC of Mono-
    graph on Planning and Design of Tall Buildings, ASCE, New York.
Council on Tall Buildings, Committee 31, 1981
    URBAN PLANNING AND DESIGN, Chapter PC-8, Volume PC of Monograph
    on Planning and Design of Tall Buildings, ASCE, New York.
Council on Tall Buildings, Committee 36, 1981
    MOTION PERCEPTION AND TOLERANCES, Chapter PC-13, Volume PC of
    the Monograph on Planning and Design of Tall Buildings, ASCE, New York.
Council on Tall Buildings, Committee 43, 1979
    CONNECTIONS, Chapter SB-7, Volume SB of Monograph on Planning and
    Design of Tall Buildings, ASCE, New York, pp. 485–575.
Council on Tall Buildings, Group CB, 1978
    STRUCTURAL DESIGN OF TALL CONCRETE AND MASONRY BUILD-
    INGS, Volume CB of the Monograph on Planning and Design of Tall Buildings,
    ASCE, New York.
Council on Tall Buildings, Group PC, 1981
    PLANNING AND ENVIRONMENTAL CRITERIA FOR TALL BUILDINGS,
    Volume PC of Monograph on Planning and Design of Tall Buildings, ASCE,
    New York.
Council on Tall Buildings, D. Sfintesco, ed., 1978–1980
    2001: URBAN SPACE FOR LIFE AND WORK, (Proceedings of Conference held
    in Paris, France, November, 1977), CTICM, Paris, 4 Volumes (in English and
    French).
Cunningham, J. A. and Robbins, J. R., 1974
    ROCK CAISSONS FOR THE NORTHERN BUILDING IN CHICAGO'S LOOP,
    (Proceedings of Conference held in Bangkok, Thailand), ASCE-IABSE.

Derecho, A. T., Ghosh, S. K., Iqbal, M. and Fintel, M., 1979
STRENGTH STIFFNESS AND DUCTILITY REQUIRED IN REINFORCED CONCRETE STRUCTURAL WALL FOR EARTHQUAKE RESISTANCE, ACI Journal, Vol. 76, No. 8, August, pp. 875–896.

DiRenzo, J. F., Cima, B. and Barber, E., 1980
STUDY OF PARKING MANAGEMENT TACTICS, prepared by Peat, Marwick, Mitchell & Co. for the Federal Highway Administration, Washington, D.C. (Volume 1 and 2).

DiRenzo, J. F., Cima, B. and Barber, E., 1981
STUDY OF PARKING MANAGEMENT TACTICS, prepared by Peat, Marwick, Mitchell & Co. for the Federal Highway Administration, Washington, D.C. (Volume 3).

Driscoll, G. C. and Beedle, L. S., 1982
SUGGESTIONS FOR AVOIDING BEAM-TO-COLUMN WEB CONNECTION FAILURE, Engineering Journal, AISC, First Quarter, Vol. 19, No. 1, Chicago, pp. 16–19.

ECCS, 1976
MANUAL ON STABILITY OF STEEL STRUCTURES, ECCS Committee on Stability, European Convention for Constructional Steelwork.

EERI, 1982
THE NEW MADRID FAULT, Earthquake Engineering Research Institute Newsletter, Vol. 16, No. 4, July, pp. 48–49.

Eisen, M. M. and Eisen, C. A., 1973
PROBABILITY AND ITS APPLICATIONS, Quantum Publishers, New York.

Ellingwood, B. R. and Culver, C. G., 1977
ANALYSIS OF LIVE LOADS IN OFFICE BUILDINGS, Journal of the Structural Division, ASCE, Vol. 103, No. ST8, Proc. Paper 13109, August, pp. 1551–1560.

Ellison, R. D., D'Appolonia, E. and Thiers, G. R., 1971
LOAD DEFORMATION MECHANISM FOR BORED PILES, Journal of the Soil Mechanics and Foundation Division, ASCE, Vol. 97, No. SM4, April.

Emori, K. and Schnobrich, W. C., 1978
ANALYSIS OF REINFORCED CONCRETE FRAME-WALL STRUCTURES FOR STRONG MOTION EARTHQUAKES, Civil Engineering Studies, Structural Research Series No. 457, University of Illinois, Urbana, Illinois.

Engineering News Record, 1983
ENR SPECIAL REPORT: INFRASTRUCTURE, Engineering News Record, selected issues, April–June.

Fielding, D. J., Chen, W. F. and Beedle, L. S., 1982
FRAME ANALYSIS AND CONNECTION SHEAR DEFORMATION, Fritz Engineering Laboratory Report No. 333.16, Department of Civil Engineering, Lehigh University, Bethlehem, Pennsylvania, January.

Fintel, M. and Ghosh, S. K., 1979
DESIGN OF WALLED STRUCTURES FOR EARTHQUAKE LOADING, (Proceedings of CSCE-ASCE-ACI-CEB International Symposium on Non-Linear Design of Concrete Structures, University of Waterloo, August), pp. 441–466.

Fintel, M. and Ghosh, S. K., 1980
    SEISMIC RESISTANCE OF A 31-STORY SHEAR WALL-FRAME BUILDING
    USING DYNAMIC INELASTIC RESPONSE HISTORY ANALYSIS, (Proceedings of the Seventh World Conference on Earthquake Engineering, September 1980), Istanbul, Turkey.
Fintel, M., Iyengar, S. H. and Ghosh, S. K., 1984
    COLUMN SHORTENING IN TALL STRUCTURES—PREDICTION AND
    COMPENSATION, Publication EB 108D, Portland Cement Association, Skokie, Illinois.
Fintel, M. and Khan, F. R., 1965
    EFFECTS OF COLUMN EXPOSURE IN TALL STRUCTURES—TEMPERATURE VARIATIONS AND THEIR EFFECTS, ACI Journal, Vol. 62, No. 12, December, pp. 1533–1556.
Fintel, M. and Khan, F. R., 1969
    EFFECTS OF COLUMN CREEP AND SHRINKAGE IN TALL STRUCTURES—
    PREDICTIONS OF INELASTIC COLUMN SHORTENING, ACI Journal, Vol. 66, No. 12, December, pp. 957–967.
Fintel, M. and Khan, F. R., 1971
    EFFECTS OF COLUMN CREEP AND SHRINKAGE IN TALL STRUCTURES—
    ANALYSIS FOR DIFFERENTIAL SHORTENING OF COLUMNS AND
    FIELD OBSERVATIONS OF STRUCTURES, Symposium on Designing for Effects of Creep, Shrinkage and Temperature in Concrete Structures, ACI Special Publication SP-27, American Concrete Institute, Detroit, Michigan, pp. 159–185.
Finzi, L. and Zandonini, R., 1982
    A SIMPLIFIED APPROACH FOR PREDICTING THE BUCKLING
    STRENGTH OF CENTRALLY COMPRESSED MEMBERS, Journal of Constructional Steel Research, Vol. 2, No. 1, January, pp. 10–21.
Fosler, S. and Berger, R. A., eds., 1982
    PUBLIC-PRIVATE PARTNERSHIP IN AMERICAN CITIES; SEVEN CASE
    STUDIES, Lexington Books, Lexington, Massachusetts.
Freeman, C. F., Klajnerman, D. and Prasad, G. D., 1972
    DESIGN OF DEEP SOCKETED CAISSONS INTO SHALE BEDROCK, Canadian Geotechnical Journal, Vol. 9, No. 1, February, pp. 105–114.
Freeman, S. A., Czarnecki, R. M. and Honda, K. K., 1980
    SIGNIFICANCE OF STIFFNESS ASSUMPTIONS ON LATERAL FORCE CRITERIA, Reinforced Concrete Structures Subjected to Wind and Earthquake Forces, American Concrete Institute, Publication SP-63, pp. 437–457.
Fruin, J. J., 1974
    PEDESTRIAN PLANNING AND DESIGN, Metropolitan Association of Urban Designers and Environmental Planners, Inc.

Galambos, T. V. and Ravindra, M. K., 1973
    TENTATIVE LOAD AND RESISTANCE FACTOR DESIGN CRITERIA FOR
    STEEL BUILDINGS, Civil Engineering Department, Washington University, No. 18, St. Louis, Missouri.

Gambin, M., 1979
  CALCULATIONS OF FOUNDATIONS SUBJECTED TO HORIZONTAL
  FORCES USING PRESSUREMETER DATA, Sol-Soil 30/31.
Gaylord, E. H. Jr. and Gaylord, C. N., 1979
  STRUCTURAL ENGINEERING HANDBOOK, second edition, McGraw–Hill
  Book Co., New York.
Gibson, P. A. and Liddicoat, N. K., 1981
  SHARED PARKING IN MIXED USE DEVELOPMENTS, Barton-Aschman
  Associates, April.
Gill, S. A., 1970
  LOAD TRANSFER MECHANISM FOR CAISSONS SOCKETED INTO ROCK,
  Ph.D. Thesis, Northwestern University, Evanston, Illinois.
Gill, S. A., 1980
  DESIGN AND CONSTRUCTION OF ROCK CAISSONS, International Con-
  ference on Structural Foundations on Rock, (Proceedings of Conference held
  in Sydney, Australia), pp. 241–252.
Gilles, A. G. and Shephard, R., 1981
  POST-ELASTIC DYNAMICS OF THREE-DIMENSIONAL FRAMES, Journal
  of the Structural Division, ASCE, Vol. 107, No. ST8, Proc. Paper 16432, August,
  pp. 1485–1501.
Giuliano, V., 1982
  THE MECHANIZATION OF OFFICE WORK, Scientific American, September.
Goble, G. G., Rausch, F. and Likins, G. E., 1980
  THE ANALYSIS OF PILE DRIVING — A STATE-OF-THE-ART, Seminar on
  the Application of Stress Wave Theory on Piles, June 4–5, Stockholm, Sweden.
Goehr, P. M. and Hustad, P. A., 1979
  INSTRUMENTED DRILLED SHAFTS IN CLAY SHALE, ASCE Symposium
  on Deep Foundations, October 25, 1979, Atlanta, Georgia.
Goralski, A., 1975
  METHODS OF SOLVING PROBLEMS SPACE (in Polish), (Proceedings of the
  Second Conference on Heuristic Methods held in Warsaw, Poland, 1975), Warsaw,
  Poland, pp. 7–10.
Gould, P. L., 1965
  INTERACTION OF SHEAR WALL FRAME SYSTEMS IN MULTISTORY
  BUILDINGS, ACI, Journal Vol. 62.
Gouwens, A. J., 1968
  LATERAL LOAD ANALYSIS OF MULTISTORY FRAMES WITH SHEAR
  WALLS, Bulletin AEC2, Portland Cement Association, Skokie, Illinois.
Gove, S. K. and Masotti, L. H., eds., 1982
  AFTER DALEY: CHICAGO POLITICS IN TRANSITION, University of Illinois
  Press, Urbana, Ill.
Grundy, P., 1980
  COMPUTING AND USING EFFECTIVE LENGTH IN PORTAL FRAME
  DESIGN, Civil Engineering Research Report No. 4/1980, Department of Civil
  Engineering, Monash University, Clayton, Victoria, Australia.
Grundy, P. and Wathen, G. R., 1972
  FRAME–SHEAR WALL INTERACTION, Civil Engineering Transactions, The
  Institute of Engineers, Vol. CE 14, No. 1, April, pp. 102–108.

Gutman, R., ED., 1972
PEOPLE AND BUILDINGS, Basic Books, New York.

Haber, G. M., 1976
MALE AND FEMALE RESPONSE TO A COLLEGE CLASSROOM (unpublished).
Haber, G. M., 1977
THE IMPACT OF TALL BUILDINGS ON USERS AND NEIGHBORS, Human Response to Tall Buildings, Dowden, Hutchinson & Ross, Stroudsburg, Pennsylvania.
Haber, G. M., 1978
HUMAN BEHAVIOR IN FIRE DEPENDING ON TYPE OCCUPANCY: HEALTH CARE, PENAL AND LEISURETIME OCCUPANCIES, Second International Seminar on Human Behavior in Fire Emergencies, U.S. Department of Commerce.
Haber, G. M., 1980a
HUMAN BEHAVIOR IN FIRE IN TOTAL INSTITUTIONS: A CASE STUDY, Fires and Human Behavior, John Wiley & Sons, Inc., New York.
Haber, G. M., 1980b
PILOT STUDY ON RESPONSE OF THE ELDERLY TO LIVING IN TALL BUILDINGS (unpublished).
Hall, H., 1981
PROPOSED STEEL COLUMN STRENGTH CRITERIA, Journal of the Structural Division, ASCE, Vol. 107, No. ST4, Proc. Paper 16198, pp. 649–670.
Hancock, G. J., 1981
INTERACTION BUCKLING IN I-SECTION COLUMNS, Journal of the Structural Division, ASCE, Vol. 107, No. ST1, Proc. Paper 15978, January, pp. 165–179.
Harris, M. E., Corotis, R. B. and Bova, C. J., 1981
AREA-DEPENDENT PROCESSES FOR STRUCTURAL LIVE LOADS, Journal of the Structural Division, ASCE, Vol. 107, No. ST5, Proc. Paper 16266, May, pp. 857–872.
Harrison, G. A., 1974
THE HIGH RISE FIRE PROBLEM, National Bureau of Standards, Washington, D.C.
Holesapple, J. C., 1982
THE FABRICATOR/DESIGNER CONNECTION, Civil Engineering, ASCE, November, pp. 64–68.
Horvath, R. G., 1978
FIELD LOAD TEST DATA ON CONCRETE-TO-ROCK BOND STRENGTH FOR DRILLED PIER FOUNDATIONS, Publication 78-07, Department of Civil Engineering, University of Toronto, Toronto, Canada.
Horvath, R. G., Kenney, T. C. and Trow, W. A., 1980
RESULTS OF TESTS TO DETERMINE SHAFT RESISTANCE OF ROCK-SOCKETED DRILLED PIERS, International Conference on Structural Foundations on Rock, (Proceedings of Conference held in Sydney, Australia, 1980), pp. 349–361.
Howlett, J. H., Jenkins, W. M. and Stainsby, R., eds., 1981
JOINTS IN STRUCTURAL STEELWORK, John Wiley & Sons, Inc., New York.

Hoyt, H., 1939
THE STRUCTURE AND GROWTH OF RESIDENTIAL NEIGHBORHOODS IN AMERICAN CITIES, Federal Housing Administration, Washington, D.C.

Huang, J. S., Chen, W. F. and Regec, J. E., 1971
TEST PROGRAMS OF STEEL BEAM-TO-COLUMN CONNECTIONS, Fritz Engineering Laboratory Report No. 333.15, Lehigh University, Bethlehem, Pennsylvania, July.

Huang, J. S., Chen, W. F. and Beedle, L. S., 1973
BEHAVIOR AND DESIGN OF STEEL BEAM-TO-COLUMN MOMENT CONNECTIONS, WRC Bulletin No. 188, October.

Huang, J. S. and Chen, W. F., 1973
STEEL BEAM-TO-COLUMN MOMENT CONNECTIONS, ASCE National Structural Engineering Meeting, San Francisco, April 9–13.

Huber, A. W. and Beedle, L. S., 1954
RESIDUAL STRESS AND THE COMPRESSIVE STRENGTH OF STEEL, Welding Journal, December, pp. 589s–614s.

ICBO, 1973 and 1976
UNIFORM BUILDING CODE, International Conference of Building Officials, Whittier, California.

ICBO, 1975
UNIFORM BUILDING CODE, International Conference of Building Officials, Whittier, California.

ICBO, 1979
UNIFORM BUILDING CODE, International Conference of Building Officials, Whittier, California.

ICBO, 1980
UNIFORM BUILDING CODE, International Conference of Building Officials, Whittier, California.

ICBO, 1982
UNIFORM BUILDING CODE, International Conference of Building Officials, Whittier, California.

Iyengar, H. S., 1979
MIXED STEEL–CONCRETE HIGH-RISE SYSTEMS, Handbook of Composite Construction Engineering, Van Nostrand Reinhold, New York.

Iyengar, H. S., 1977
STATE-OF-THE-ART-REPORT ON COMPOSITE OR MIXED STEEL CONCRETE CONSTRUCTION FOR BUILDINGS, ASCE, New York.

Iyengar, H. S. and Iqbal, M., 1982
COMPOSITE CONSTRUCTION, Building Structural Design Handbook, John Wiley & Sons, Inc., New York.

Jacobs, A. B., 1978.
MAKING CITY PLANNING WORK, American Society of Planning Officials.

Jacobs, A. B., 1980
THEY'RE LOCKING THE DOORS TO DOWNTOWN, Urban Design International, Vol. 1, No. 5, July/August.

Jayachandran, P., 1982
DYNAMIC RESPONSE OF ECCENTRICALLY BRACED TALL BUILDINGS
TO EARTHQUAKES, NSF Research Report, Worcester Polytechnic Institute,
Worcester, Massachusetts, June, pp. 1–100.
Jensen, R. H., 1973
MEANS OF FIRE FIGHTING AND SAFETY DEVICES, Planning and Design
of Tall Buildings, (Proceedings of Conference held at Lehigh University,
August, 1972), ASCE, Vol. IB-8, New York.
Johnston, B. G., ed., 1973
GUIDE TO DESIGN CRITERIA FOR METAL COMPRESSION MEMBERS,
second edition, John Wiley, and Sons, Inc. New York.
Johnston, B. G., ed., 1976
GUIDE TO DESIGN CRITERIA FOR METAL STRUCTURES, third edition,
Structural Stability Research Council, John Wiley and Sons, Inc., New York.
Jones, S. W., Kirby, P. A. and Nethercot, D. A., 1982
COLUMNS WITH SEMIRIGID JOINTS, Journal of the Structural Division,
ASCE, Vol. 108, No. ST2, Proc. Paper 16855, February, pp. 361–372.
Joint Committee on Tall Buildings, 1972
PLANNING AND DESIGN OF TALL BUILDING, (Proceedings of ASCE-IABSE
International Conference held at Lehigh University, August 1972), ASCE,
New York, 5 vol.

Kaar, P. H., Hanson, N. W. and Capell, H. T., 1977
STRESS–STRAIN CHARACTERISTICS OF HIGH STRENGTH CONCRETE,
Report #RD051.01D, Portland Cement Association, Skokie, Illinois.
Kanaan, A. E. and Powell, G. H., 1973
DRAIN-2D, GENERAL PURPOSE COMPUTER PROGRAM FOR INELASTIC
DYNAMIC RESPONSE OF PLANE STRUCTURES, Report No. UCB/EERC-
73/6, University of California, Berkeley, California.
Kanaan, A. E. and Powell, G. H., 1975
A GENERAL PURPOSE COMPUTER PROGRAM FOR INELASTIC DY-
NAMIC RESPONSE OF PLANE STRUCTURES, Earthquake Engineering Re-
search Center, Report No. 73-22, University of California, Berkeley, California.
Kato, B., 1982
BEAM-TO-COLUMN CONNECTIONS RESEARCH IN JAPAN, Journal of the
Structural Division, ASCE, Vol. 108, No. ST2, Proc. Paper No. 16852, February,
pp. 343–360.
Kato, B. and McGuire, W., 1973
ANALYSIS OF T-STUB FLANGE-TO-COLUMN CONNECTIONS, Journal of
the Structural Division, ASCE, Vol. 99, No. ST5, May.
Khan, F. R., 1971
CURRENT TRENDS IN THE CONSTRUCTION OF TALL BUILDINGS MADE
OF REINFORCED CONCRETE AND STEEL (in French), Annales ITBTP,
No. 281.
Khan, F. R., 1974
NEW STRUCTURAL SYSTEMS FOR TALL BUILDINGS AND THEIR SCALE
EFFECTS ON CITIES, (Proceedings of Symposium on Tall Buildings held
at Vanderbuilt University, November 1974), Nashville, Tennessee.

Khan, F. R. and Amin, N. R., 1973
ANALYSIS AND DESIGN OF FRAMED TUBE STRUCTURES FOR TALL CON-
CRETE BUILDINGS, American Concrete Institute, Publication SP-36, Detroit,
Michigan.

Kahn, F. R. and Fintel, M., 1966
EFFECTS OF COLUMN EXPOSURE IN TALL STRUCTURES–ANALYSIS FOR
LENGTH CHANGES OF EXPOSED COLUMNS, ACI Journal, Vol. 63, No. 8,
August, pp. 843–864.

Khan, F. R. and Fintel, M., 1968
EFFECTS OF COLUMN EXPOSURE IN TALL STRUCTURES–DESIGN CON-
SIDERATIONS AND FIELD OBSERVATIONS. ACI Journal, Vol. 65, No. 2,
February, pp. 99–110.

Khan, F. R. and Sbarounis, J. A., 1976
INTERACTION OF SHEAR WALLS AND FRAMES, Journal of the Structural
Division, ASCE, Vol. 90.

Kistler, W., 1982
PLANNING FOR THE ELECTRONIC OFFICE, Facilities Planning News, July.

Komendant, A. E., 1975
18 YEARS WITH ARCHITECT LOUIS I. KAHN, Aloray Publishers, Englewood,
New Jersey.

Kosicyn, B. A., 1971
ANALYSIS OF LARGE PANEL AND FRAME BUILDINGS (Staticzeskij rascziot
krupnopanielnych i karkasnych zdanij), JLS, Moscow.

Krawinkler, H., 1978
SHEAR IN BEAM-TO-COLUMN JOINTS SEISMIC DESIGN OF STEEL
FRAMES, Engineering Journal, AISC, Vol. 15, No. 3, Chicago, pp. 82–91.

Krawinkler, H., Bertero, V. V. and Popov, E. P., 1971
INELASTIC BEHAVIOR OF STEEL BEAM-TO-COLUMN SUBASSEM-
BLAGES, EERC Report 71-7, Earthquake Engineering Research Center, Uni-
versity of California, Berkeley, California.

Krawinkler, H. and Popov, E. P., 1982
SEISMIC BEHAVIOR OF BEAM-TO-COLUMN CONNECTIONS AND
JOINTS, Journal of the Structural Division, ASCE, Vol. 108, No. ST2, Proc.
Paper No. 16865, February.

Kriken, J. L., 1983
WHAT'S WRONG WITH SMALL PROJECTS, Urban Design Review, Vol. 6,
No. 2, 3, Spring, June.

Kristek, V., Marek, P. and Pirner, M., 1983
ON THE RELATIONSHIP OF THEORETICAL MODELS AND CRITERIA
IN DESIGNING STEEL STRUCTURES (in Czech), Building Journal (in
preparation).

Kuhnemann, G. and Witherspoon, R., 1972
TRAFFIC FREE ZONES IN GERMAN CITIES, Organization for Economic
Cooperation and Development, Paris.

Ladanyi, B. and Domingue, D., 1980
    AN ANALYSIS OF BOND STRENGTH FOR ROCK SOCKETED PIERS, International Conference on Structural Foundations on Rock, (Proceedings of Conference held in Sydney, Australia, 1980), pp. 363–373.

Land, P., 1981
    ECONOMIC GARDEN HOUSES NEIGHBORHOODS, Presented at the Chicago AIA Design Committee Seminar on Housing, Chicago, Illinois, March, 1981.

Law, Margaret, 1979
    FIRE SAFE STRUCTURAL STEEL—A STEEL DESIGN GUIDE, American Iron & Steel Institute, Washington, D.C.

Logan, D., 1977
    HOUSING AND URBANISM, The Form of Housing, Van Nostrand Reinhold Company, Cincinnati.

Long, A. E. and Kirk, D. W., 1980
    LATERAL LOAD STIFFNESS OF SLAB-COLUMN STRUCTURES, Reinforced Concrete Structures Subjected to Wind and Earthquake Forces, American Concrete Institute, Publication SP-63, pp. 197–220.

Lubinski, M. and Kwiatkowski, J., 1972
    STATICAL AND STRUCTURAL SYSTEMS OF TALL STEEL BUILDINGS, (Proceedings of the Regional Conference on the Planning and Design of Tall Buildings in Warsaw, 1972), Warsaw, Poland, Vol. 1, pp. 141–165.

Ludlow, J., 1975
    DELPHI INQUIRES AND KNOWLEDGE UTILIZATION, The Delphi Method, Techniques and Applications, Addison–Wesley, Reading, Massachusetts, pp. 102–123.

Lui, E. M. and Chen, W. F., 1981
    STRENGTH OF H-COLUMNS WITH SMALL END RESTRAINTS, Structural Engineering Technical Report No. CE-STR-38, Purdue University, West Lafayette, Indiana.

Lui, E. M. and Chen, W. F., 1983a
    STRENGTH OF H-COLUMNS WITH SMALL END RESTRAINTS, The Journal of the Institute of Structural Engineers, Vol. 61B, No. 2, March, pp. 17–26.

Lui, E. M. and Chen, W. F., 1983b
    END RESTRAINT AND COLUMN DESIGN USING LRFD, Engineering Journal, AISC, Vol. 20, No. 1, First Quarter, pp. 29–39.

Lukas, R. G. and Baker, C. N., 1978
    GROUND MOVEMENT ASSOCIATED WITH DRILLED PIER INSTALLATIONS, Preprint No. 3266, ASCE Spring Convention and Exhibit, Philadelphia, Pennsylvania.

Lukas, R. G. and DeBussey, B., 1976
    PRESSUREMETER AND LABORATORY TEST CORRELATIONS FOR CLAYS, Geotechnical Division, ASCE, No. GT9, September.

Ma, S. Y. M., Popov, E. P. and Bertero, V. V., 1976
    EXPERIMENTAL AND ANALYTICAL STUDIES ON THE HYSTERETIC BEHAVIOR OF REINFORCED CONCRETE RECTANGULAR AND T-BEAMS, Report No. EERC 767-2, University of California, Berkeley, California.

MacBride et al., 1961
SOCIAL PROXIMITY EFFECTS ON GALVANIC SKIN RESPONSE IN ADULT HUMANS, Journal of Psychology, pp. 153–157.

MacLeod, I. A., 1970
SHEAR WALL-FRAME INTERACTION, Portland Cement Association, Skokie, Illinois.

Madison, B. F. and Popov, E. P., 1980
CYCLIC RESPONSE PREDICTION FOR BRACED STEEL FRAMES, Journal of the Structural Division, ASCE, Vol. 106, No. ST7, July, pp. 1401–1479.

Malls Committee of the Institute for Transportation, 1979
PLANNING AND CONSTRUCTION OF MUNICIPAL MALLS, American Public Works Association, APWA Report No. 46, July.

Mann, A. P. and Morris, L. J., 1980
LACK OF FIT IN END-PLATE CONNECTIONS, Spring Convention, ASCE, April, Portland, Oregon, pp. 21–45.

Maquoi, R., 1982
SOME IMPROVEMENTS IN THE BUCKLING DESIGN OF CENTRALLY LOADED COLUMNS, (Proceedings of the Structural Stability Research Council), pp. 8–14.

Maquoi, R. and Rondal, J., 1978
ANALYTICAL EXPRESSIONS FOR THE NEW EUROPEAN COLUMN CURVES (Formulation analytique des nouvelles courbes européenes de flambement), Construction Métallique, No. 1.

Marek, P., 1983
LIMIT STATES OF THE METAL BUILDING STRUCTURES (in German), Bauverlag, Berlin.

Marek, P., Faltus, F., Mrazik, A. and Skaloud, M., 1979
PLACTICITY OF STEEL STRUCTURES (in Czech), Building Journal, Vol. 10.

Markus, T. A., 1974
THE APPRAISAL OF BUILDINGS AS A TOOL FOR RESEARCH AND DESIGN, (Proceedings of the Congress "The Impact of Research on the Built Environment" in Budapest, Hungary, 1974), Budapest, Hungary, pp. 105–108.

Massonnet, C. E. and Maquoi, R. J., 1981
DISCUSSION OF THE RESEARCH NEEDS IN STABILITY OF METAL STRUCTURES, BY REIDAR BJORHOVDE, Journal of the Structural Division, ASCE, Vol. 107, No. ST9, Proc. Paper 16481, September, pp. 1885–1889.

Mattison, E. N. and Beresford, F. D., 1973
STUDIES OF THE PRODUCTION AND PROPERTIES OF HIGH STRENGTH CONCRETE, REPORT #7, Division of Building Research, Commonwealth Scientific and Industrial Research Organization, Australia.

Maver, T. W., 1980
APPRAISAL IN DESIGN, Design Studies, Vol. 1, No. 3, pp. 160–165.

McGuire, R. K. and Cornell, C. A., 1974
LIVE LOAD EFFECTS IN OFFICE BUILDINGS, Journal of the Structural Division, ASCE, Vol. 100, No. ST7, Proc. Paper 10660, July, pp. 1351–1366.

McNamara, R. J., 1977
TUNED MASS DAMPERS FOR BUILDINGS, Journal of the Structural Division, ASCE, Vol. 103, No. ST9, September, pp. 1785–1795.

Meckler, G., 1982
ENERGY-INTEGRATED FIRE PROTECTION SYSTEMS, (Proceedings of the Conference on Energy Conservation and Fire Safety in Buildings (held in Washington, D.C., June 1981), National Academy Press.

Meckler, G., 1983a
TECHNIQUES FOR ENERGY-EFFICIENT INTEGRATIONS OF DESSICANT DEHUMIDIFICATION, (Proceedings of the Second International Conference on Building Energy Management, (held at Iowa State University, May 31–June 3).

Meckler, G., 1983b
THERMAL WINDOW SYSTEM REDUCES HEATING AND COOLING LOADS, ASHRAE Journal, February, pp. 37, 39, 41.

Menard, L., 1975
THE MENARD PRESSUREMETER–INVESTIGATION AND APPLICATION OF PRESSUREMETER TEST RESULTS, Sol-Soils 26.

Meredith, D. D., Wong, K. M., Woodhead, R. W. and Wortman, R. H., 1973
DESIGN AND PLANNING OF ENGINEERING SYSTEMS, Prentice–Hall, Englewood Cliffs, New Jersey.

Metropolitan Association of Urban Designers and Environmental Planners, Inc., 1973
PROCEEDINGS OF THE PEDESTRIAN/BICYCLE PLANNING AND DESIGN SEMINAR, Proceedings of Conference held in San Francisco, 1972, The Institute of Transportation and Traffic Engineering, University of California Berkeley.

Ministry of Public Health of Czechoslovakia, 1977
HYGIENIC REGULATIONS OF THE MINISTRY OF PUBLIC HEALTH, Provision No. 13/1977 Digest, from 13.1.1977, Vol. 37.

Moehle, J. P. and Sozen, M. A., 1980
EXPERIMENTS TO STUDY EARTHQUAKE RESPONSE OF R/C STRUCTURES WITH STIFFNESS INTERRUPTIONS, Civil Engineering Studies, Structural Research Series No. 482, University of Illinois, Urbana, Illinois.

Moncarz, P. D. and Gerstle, K. H., 1981
STEEL FRAMES WITH NONLINEAR CONNECTIONS, Journal of the Structural Division, ASCE, Vol. 107, No. ST8, Proc. Paper 16440, August, pp. 1427–1441.

Moser, M., 1978
TALL BUILDING DECISION-MAKING PARAMETERS, Fritz Laboratory Report No. 444.3, Lehigh University, Bethlehem, Pennsylvania.

Moudon, A. V., 1983
CITY FORM AND TALL BUILDINGS: CATHEDRALS, PALAZZI, TALL DOWNTOWNS AND TALL CITIES, Developments in Tall Buildings 1983, Hutchinson Ross Publishing Company, Stroudsburg, Pennsylvania.

Mukherjee, P. K., Loughborough, M. T. and Malhotra, V. M., 1981
DEVELOPMENT OF HIGH STRENGTH CONCRETE INCORPORATING A LARGE PERCENTAGE OF FLY ASH AND SUPERPLASTICIZERS, CAN-MET, Mineral Sciences Laboratories Division Report MPR/MSL 81-124, Vol. #4, Issue #2, pp. 81–86, ASTM, Philadelphia, Pennsylvania.

Muller, E. K., 1980
DISTINCTIVE DOWNTOWN, Geographical Magazine, Vol. 52, August, pp. 745–755.

Mutunayagam, N. B., 1980
DECISION PROCESSES FOR TALL BUILDINGS – A POSITION PAPER, Occasional Paper, Virginia Polytechnic Institute and State University, Blacksburg, Virginia.

Mutunayagam, N. B., 1981
HIGH RISE BUILDING DECISION MAKING IN THE NIGERIAN CONTEXT – A PROSPECTUS FOR RESEARCH, Occasional Paper, Virginia Polytechnic Institute and State University, Blacksburg, Virginia.

NBS, 1978
TENTATIVE PROVISIONS FOR THE DEVELOPMENT OF SEISMIC REGULATIONS FOR BUILDINGS, Special Publication No. 510, National Bureau of Standards, U.S. Government Printing Office, Washington, D.C.

Nahemow, L., Lawton, M., Powell, and Howell, S. C., 1977
ELDERLY PEOPLE IN TALL BUILDINGS: A NATIONWIDE STUDY, Human Response to Tall Buildings, Dowden, Hutchinson & Ross, Stroudsburg, Pennsylvania.

National Research Council, 1983
SYMPOSIUM ON THE ADEQUACY AND MAINTENANCE OF URBAN PUBLIC UTILITIES, (Proceedings of a Conference held at Warrenton, Virginia, February 25–26, 1983), National Research Council, Ottawa, Canada.

National Research Council, 1984
PERSPECTIVES ON URBAN INFRASTRUCTURE, National Research Council, Ottawa, Canada.

National Research Council of Canada, 1975
CANADIAN MANUAL ON FOUNDATION ENGINEERING, Associate Committee on the National Building Code, National Research Council of Canada, Ottawa.

National Society of Professional Engineers, 1982
RX FOR AMERICA'S AILING INFRASTRUCTURE, Professional Engineer, Vol. 52, No. 4, Winter.

Newman, O., 1973
DEFENSIBLE SPACE, Collier Books, New York.

Newman, O., 1976
DESIGN GUIDELINES FOR CREATING DEFENSIBLE SPACE, National Institute of Law Enforcement.

Newmark, N. M. and Rosenblueth, E., 1971
FUNDAMENTALS OF EARTHQUAKE ENGINEERING, Prentice–Hall, Inc., Englewood Cliffs, New Jersey.

Nilforoushan, R., 1973
SEISMIC BEHAVIOR OF MULTISTORY K-BRACED FRAME STRUCTURES, Ph.D. Thesis in a Civil Engineering, University of Michigan, Ann Arbor, Michigan, pp. 1–168.

NRC, 1972
  NONLINEAR STRUCTURAL DYNAMIC ANALYSIS FOR CATAGORY I
  STRUCTURES, NUREG/CR-1161, URS, John A. Blume and Assoc., Engi-
  neers, New York.
Nuttli, O. W., 1972
  MAGNITUDE, INTENSITY AND GROUND MOTION RELATIONS FOR
  EARTHQUAKES IN THE CENTRAL UNITED STATES, (Proceedings of
  International Conference on Micro-zonation for Safer Construction — Research
  and Application, Seattle, Washington), Vol. 1, pp. 307–318.
Nuttli, O. W., 1981
  SIMILARITIES AND DIFFERENCES BETWEEN WESTERN AND EASTERN
  EARTHQUAKES AND THE CONSEQUENCES FOR EARTHQUAKE ENGI-
  NEERING, (Proceedings of Conference on Earthquakes and Earthquake Engi-
  neering — the Eastern United States, Knoxville, Tennessee), September, Vol. 1,
  pp. 25–51.

O'Day, K., 1983
  ANALYZING INFRASTRUCTURE CONDITION — A PRACTICAL AP-
  PROACH, Civil Engineering/ASCE, April, pp. 39–42.
Okten, O. S., Morino, S., Daniels, J. H. and Lu, L. W., 1973
  EFFECTIVE COLUMN LENGTH AND FRAME STABILITY, Fritz Laboratory
  Report No. 375.2, Lehigh University, Bethlehem, Pennsylvania.
Oran, C., 1981
  DISCUSSION OF ELASTIC INSTABILITY OF UNBRACED SPACE FRAMES,
  BY ZIA RAZZAQ AND MOOSSA M. NAIM, Journal of the Structural Divi-
  sion, ASCE, Vol. 107, No. ST5, Proc. Paper 16218, May, pp. 1020–1022.
Osterberg, J. O., 1968
  DRILLED CAISSONS DESIGN, INSTALLATION, APPLICATION, Chicago
  Soil Mechanics Lecture Series, Department of Civil Engineering, Northwestern
  University, Evanston, Illinois.
Osterberg, J. O. and Gill, S. A., 1973
  LOAD TRANSFER MECHANISM FOR PIERS SOCKETED IN HARD SOILS
  OR ROCK, (Proceedings of Ninth Canadian Symposium on Rock Mechanics
  held in Montreal, Quebec, November, 1973), pp. 235–262.
Otway, H. J., Baker, J., Thomas, W. N. and Marshall, M. R., 1970
  A RISK ANALYSIS OF THE OMEGA WEST REACTOR, University of Cali-
  fornia, Los Alamos Scientific Laboratory, Los Alamos, New Mexico.

Pastalan, L., Carson, A. and Daniels, H., eds., 1970
  SPATIAL BEHAVIOR OF OLDER PEOPLE, University of Michigan, Ann Arbor,
  Michigan.
Parfitt, J. and Chen, W. F., 1976
  TESTS OF WELDED STEEL BEAM-TO-COLUMN MOMENT CONNEC-
  TIONS, Journal of the Structural Division, ASCE, Vol. 102, No.ST1, Proc.
  Paper 11854, January, pp. 189–202.

Park, R. E., Burgess, E. W. and McKenzie, R. D., 1925
THE GROWTH OF THE CITY: AN INTRODUCTION TO A RESEARCH
PROJECT, The City, University of Chicago Press, Chicago, Illinois, pp. 47–62.
Park, R. and Paulay, T., 1975
REINFORCED CONCRETE STRUCTURES, John Wiley and Sons, Inc., New
York.
Parme, A. L., 1965
CAPACITY OF RESTRAINED ECCENTRICALLY LOADED LONG COLUMNS,
Symposium on Reinforced Concrete Columns, Publication SP-13, American
Concrete Institute, Detroit, Michigan.
Parme, A. L., 1967
DESIGN OF COMBINED FRAMES AND SHEAR WALLS: TALL BUILDINGS,
Pergamon Press, Ltd., London.
Patel, K. V. and Chen, W. F., 1985
ANALYSIS OF A FULLY BOLTED MOMENT CONNECTION USING NON-
SAP, Computers and Structures, Vol. 19.
Patel, K. V. and Chen, W. F., 1982
NONLINEAR ANALYSIS OF STEEL BEAM-TO-COLUMN WEB CONNEC-
TIONS, Structural Engineering Report CE-STR-82-7, School of Civil Engi-
neering, West Lafayette, Indiana.
Paulay, T., 1981
DEVELOPMENTS IN THE SEISMIC DESIGN OF REINFORCED CONCRETE
FRAMES IN NEW ZEALAND, Canadian Journal of Civil Engineering, Vol.
8, No. 2, pp. 91–113.
Paulay, T. and Binney, J. R., 1974
DIAGONALLY REINFORCED COUPLING BEAMS OF SHEAR WALLS,
American Concrete Institute, Publication SP-42, Shear in Reinforced Concrete,
pp. 579–598.
Peat, Marwick, Mitchell & Co., 1981
PARKING POLICIES FOR DOWNTOWN CALGARY, prepared for the City of
Calgary, Washington, D.C., June.
Peir, J.C. and Cornell, C. A., 1973
SPATIAL AND TEMPORAL VARIABILITY OF LIVE LOADS, Journal of the
Structural Division, ASCE, Vol. 99, No. ST5, Proc. Paper 9747, May, pp. 903–922.
Pells, P. J. N. and Turner, R. M., 1979
ELASTIC SOLUTIONS FOR THE DESIGN AND ANALYSIS OF ROCK-
SOCKETED PILES, Canadian Geotechnical Journal, Vol. 16, No. 3, August,
pp. 481–487.
Perenchio, W. F. and Klieger, P., 1978
SOME PHYSICAL PROPERTIES OF HIGH STRENGTH CONCRETE, Report
#RDO56.01, Portland Cement Association, Skokie, Illinois.
Peterson, G. E., 1983
FINANCING THE NATION'S INFRASTRUCTURE REQUIREMENTS, paper
prepared for conference sponsored by NAS/NAE, February.
Peyrot, A. H., Saul, W. E. and Jayachandran, P., 1975
ANSWERS, A STRUCTURAL ANALYSIS SOFTWARE FOR STATIC AND
DYNAMIC ANALYSIS, University of Wisconsin, Madison, Wisconsin.

Pillai, S., 1981
DISCUSSION OF RESEARCH NEEDS IN STABILITY OF METAL STRUC-
TURES, BY REIDAR BJORHOVDE, Journal of the Structural Division,
ASCE, Vol. 107, No. ST11, Proc. Paper 16616, November, pp. 2299–2300.
Popov, E. P., 1981
RECENT RESEARCH ON ECCENTRICALLY BRACED FRAMES, Structural
Engineers of California, (Proceedings of Conference held in Coronado, Cali-
fornia, September, 1981).
Popov, E. P., 1982
SEISMIC STEEL FRAMING SYSTEMS FOR TALL BUILDINGS, Engineering
Journal, AISC, Third Quarter, Vol. 19, No. 3, pp. 141–149.
Popov, E. P. and Bertero, V. V., 1980
SEISMIC ANALYSIS OF SOME STEEL BUILDING FRAMES, Journal of the
Engineering Mechanics Division, ASCE, Vol. 106, No. EM1, February, pp. 75–95.
Popov, E. P. and Black G., 1981
STEEL STRUTS UNDER SEVERE CYCLIC LOADING, Journal of the Structural
Division, ASCE, Vol. 107, No. ST9, Proc. Paper 16497, September, pp. 1857–1881.
Popov, E. P. and Manheim, D. N., 1981
ECCENTRIC BRACING OF STEEL FRAMES IN SEISMIC DESIGN, (Trans-
actions of the Sixth International Conference on Structural Mechanics in
Reactor Technology, held in Paris, France, August, 1981), Vol. K(b), K13/8.
Popov, E. P. and Pinkney, R. B., 1968
BEHAVIOR OF STEEL BUILDING CONNECTIONS SUBJECTED TO IN-
ELASTIC STRAIN REVERSALS, AISI Bulletin Nos. 13 and 14, November.
Popov, E. P. and Stephen, R. M., 1972
CYCLIC LOADING OF FULL-SIZE STEEL CONNECTIONS, AISI Bulletin,
No. 21, February.
Popov, E. P., Takanashi, K. and Roeder, C. W., 1976
STRUCTURAL STEEL BRACING SYSTEMS: BEHAVIOR UNDER CYCLIC
LOADING, Report No. UCB/EERC-76/17, University of California, Berkeley,
California.
Poppel, H., 1982
WHO NEEDS THE OFFICE OF THE FUTURE?, Harvard Business Review,
November–December.
Price, B. T. et al., 1970
TRANSPORTATION SYSTEMS FOR MAJOR ACTIVITY CENTERS, Organi-
zation for Economic Cooperation and Development, April, Paris.
Project for Public Spaces, Inc. 1982
DESIGNING EFFECTIVE PEDESTRIAN IMPROVEMENTS IN BUSINESS
DISTRICTS, American Planning Association, Planning Advisory Service
Report No. 368, May.
Pushkarev, B. and Zupan, J. M., 1975
URBAN SPACE FOR PEDESTRIANS, the MIT Press, Cambridge, Massachusetts.

Ramberg, W. and Osgood, W. R., 1943
DESCRIPTION OF STRESS–STRAIN CURVES BY THREE PARAMETERS,
NACA Technical Note No. 902.

Rapoport, A., 1977
HUMAN ASPECTS OF URBAN FORM, Pergamon Press, London.

Rapoport, A., 1983
PEDESTRIAN STREET USE; CULTURE AND PERCEPTION, Streets as Public Property: Opportunities for Public/Private Interaction in Planning and Design, College of Architecture and Urban Planning, University of Washington, Seattle, Washington.

Razzaq, Z., 1983
END RESTRAINTS EFFECT ON STEEL COLUMN STRENGTH, Journal of the Structural Division, ASCE, Vol. 109, No. ST2, February, pp. 314–334.

Razzaq, Z. and Chang, J. G., 1981
PARTIALLY RESTRAINED IMPERFECT COLUMNS, (Proceedings of the International Conference on Joints in Structural Steelwork held at Teesside Polytechnic, U. K., April, 1981).

Regec, J. E., Huang, J. S. and Chen, W. F., 1973
TEST OF A FULLY WELDED BEAM-TO-COLUMN CONNECTION, WRC Bulletin No. 188, October.

Regional Plan Association, 1980
URBAN RAIL IN AMERICA: AN EXPLORATION OF CRITERIA FOR FIXED GUIDEWAY TRANSIT, Urban Mass Transportation Administration, Washington, D.C., November, p. 157.

Reese, L. C. and O'Neil, M. W., 1969
FIELD TESTS OF BORED PILES IN BEAUMONT CLAY, ASCE Annual Meeting, Preprint No. 1008, Chicago, Illinois.

Reese, L. C. and Wright, S. V., 1977
DRILLED SHAFT MANUAL, 2 vols., Implementation Package 77-21, U.S. Department of Transportation, Office of Research and Development, Washington, D.C.

Rentschler, G. P., 1979
ANALYSIS AND DESIGN OF STEEL BEAM-TO-COLUMN WEB CONNECTIONS, Ph.D. Dissertation, Department of Civil Engineering, Lehigh University, Bethlehem, Pennsylvania.

Rentschler, G. P. and Chen, W. F., 1975
TEST PROGRAM OF MOMENT-RESISTANT STEEL BEAM-TO-COLUMN WEB CONNECTIONS, Fritz Engineering Laboratory Report No. 405.4, Lehigh University, Bethlehem, Pennsylvania.

Rentschler, G. P., Chen, W. F. and Driscoll, G. C., 1980
TESTS OF BEAM-TO-COLUMN WEB CONNECTIONS, Journal of the Structural Division, ASCE, Vol. 106, No. ST5, Proc. Paper 15386, May, pp. 1005–1022.

Rentschler, G. P., Chen, W. F. and Driscoll, G. C., 1982
BEAM-TO-COLUMN WEB CONNECTION DETAILS, Journal of the Structural Division, ASCE, Vol. 108, No. ST2, Proc. Paper 16880, February, pp. 393–409.

Rice, P. F. and Hoffman, E. S., 1972
STRUCTURAL DESIGN GUIDE TO THE ACI BUILDING CODE, Van Nostrand Reinhold, New York.

Roeder, C. W. and Popov, E. P., 1977
  INELASTIC BEHAVIOR OF ECCENTRICALLY BRACED STEEL FRAMES
  UNDER CYCLIC LOADINGS, EERC Report No. 77-18, College of Engi-
  neering, University of California, Berkeley, August.
Rondal, J. and Maquoi, R., 1979
  SINGLE EQUATION FOR SSRC COLUMN-STRENGTH CURVES, Journal of
  the Structural Division, ASCE, Vol. 105, No. ST1, Proc. Paper 14276, January,
  pp. 245-250.
Rosenblueth, E., 1965
  SLENDERNESS EFFECTS IN BUILDINGS, Journal of the Structural Division,
  ASCE, Vol. 91, No. ST1, Proc. Paper 4235, February, pp. 229-252.
Rosenblueth, E., ed., 1980
  DESIGN OF EARTHQUAKE RESISTANT STRUCTURES, John Wiley and
  Sons, Inc., New York and Toronto.
Rosenblueth, E. and Holtz, I., 1960
  ELASTIC ANALYSIS OF SHEAR WALLS OF TALL BUILDINGS, Journal ACI,
  Vol. 56, No. 12.
Rosenberg, P. and Journeaux, N. L., 1976
  FRICTION AND END BEARING TESTS ON BEDROCK FOR HIGH CA-
  PACITY SOCKET DESIGN, Canadian Geotechnical Journal, Vol. 13, No. 3,
  August, pp. 324-333.
Ross, J., ed., 1982
  INTERNATIONAL ENCYCLOPEDIA OF POPULATION, Vol. I and II, The
  Free Press.
Rotter, M. J., 1982
  MULTIPLE COLUMN CURVES BY MODIFYING FACTORS, Journal of the
  Structural Division, ASCE, Vol. 108, No. ST7, Proc. Paper 17194, July, pp.
  1655-1669.
Ruchelman, L. I., 1977
  THE WORLD TRADE CENTER: POLITICS AND POLICIES OF SKYSCRAPER
  DEVELOPMENT, Syracuse University Press, Syracuse, New York.
Rutenberg, A., 1980
  LATERALLY LOADED FLEXIBLE DIAPHRAGM BUILDINGS: PLANAR
  ANALOGY, Journal of the Structural Division, ASCE, Vol. 106, No. ST9, pp.
  1969-1973.
Rutenberg, A., 1981
  A DIRECT P-DELTA ANALYSIS USING STANDARD PLANE FRAME COM-
  PUTER PROGRAMS, Computers and Structures, Vol. 14, No. 1-2, pp. 97-102.

SNTL, 1980
  POZEMNI STAVBY, Vol. 12, Prague (in Czech).
Saiidi, M. and Sozen, M. A., 1981
  SIMPLE NONLINEAR SEISMIC ANALYSIS OF R/C STRUCTURES, Journal
  of the Structural Division, ASCE, Vol. 107, No. ST5, May, pp. 937-953.
Salmons, S., 1982
  THE DEBATE OVER THE ELECTRONIC OFFICE, The New York Times
  Magazine, November 14.

Salmon, S. G. and Johnson, J. E., 1976
STEEL STRUCTURES: DESIGN AND BEHAVIOR, second edition, Harper
and Row, New York.
Sanglerat, G., 1972
THE PENETROMETER AND SOIL EXPLORATION, Elsevier Publishing Com-
pany, Amsterdam.
Sato, K. and Tomita, A. et al., 1981
EXPERIMENTAL INVESTIGATION ON T-STUB CONNECTIONS USING
CAST STEEL, Part VI (in Japanese), A. I. J. Research Report, Tokyo, Japan.
Sato, K. and Toyama, K. et al., 1974
EXPERIMENTAL INVESTIGATION OF T-STUB CONNECTIONS USING
CAST STEEL, Parts I and II (in Japanese), A. I. J. Research Report, Tokyo,
Japan.
Sato, K. and Toyama, K. et al., 1975
EXPERIMENTAL INVESTIGATION ON T-STUB CONNECTIONS USING
CAST STEEL, Part III, (in Japanese), A. I. J. Research Report, Toyko, Japan.
Sato, K. and Toyama, K. et al., 1976
EXPERIMENTAL STUDY ON BEAM-TO-COLUMN CONNECTIONS USING
CAST STEEL T-STUBS, Report No. 23, Kajima Institute of Construction,
Tokyo, Japan.
Sato, K. and Yamada, S. et al., 1977
EXPERIMENTAL INVESTIGATION OF T-STUB CONNECTIONS USING
CAST STEEL, Part V (in Japanese), A. I. J. Research Report, Tokyo, Japan.
Saul, W. E., Jayachandran, P. and Peyrot, A. H., 1976
RESPONSE TO STOCHASTIC WIND OF N-DEGREE TALL BUILDINGS,
Journal of the Structural Division, ASCE, Vol. 102, No. ST5, May, pp. 1059-1976.
Schaeffer, W. D., 1983
RENAISANCE OF OUR CITIES—A CIVIL ENGINEERING CHALLENGE,
Developments in Tall Buildings 1983, Council on Tall Buildings, Hutchinson
Ross Publishing Company, Stroudsburg, Pennsylvania.
Schmertmann, J. H., 1975
THE MEASUREMENT OF IN-SITU SHEAR STRENGTH, 6th PSC, ASCE,
Vol. 2, pp. 57-138.
Schmidt, L. C., Morgan, P. R. and Phang, P. W., 1981
INFLUENCE OF JOINT ECCENTRICITY AND RIGIDITY OF THE LOAD
CAPACITY OF A SPACE TRUSS SUBASSEMBLAGE, Journal of Construc-
tional Steel Research, Vol. 1, No. 4, September, pp. 16-22.
Selna, L. G., 1978
MODELING OF REINFORCED CONCRETE BUILDINGS, (Proceedings of a
Workshop on Earthquake Resistant Reinforced Concrete Building Construc-
tion held at the University of California, June, 1978), Berkeley, California.
Selna, L., Martin, I., Park, P. and Wyllie, L., 1980
STRONG TOUGH CONCRETE COLUMNS FOR SEISMIC FORCES, Journal
of the Structural Division, ASCE, Vol. 106, No. ST8, August.
Sfintesco, D., ed., 1976
ECCS MANUAL ON THE STABILITY OF STEEL STRUCTURES, second
edition, ECCS, Paris.

Shafi, S. S. and Dutta, S. S., 1982
URBAN LAND POLICY IN DELHI: A CRITIQUE, Presented at Seminar on Land in Metropolitan Development, Times Research Foundation, Calcutta, India, April.

Shah, S. P., 1979
HIGH STRENGTH CONCRETE, (Proceedings of a Workshop held at the University of Illinois at Chicago Center, December 1979), Report No. PB021010057, U.S. Department of Commerce, N.T.I.S., Springfield, Illinois.

Shanley, F. R., 1947
INELASTIC COLUMN THEORY, Journal of the Aeronautical Sciences, Vol. 14, No. 5.

Shen, Z. Y. and Lu, L. W., 1981
ANALYSIS OF INITIALLY CROOKED, END RESTRAINT STEEL COLUMNS, Fritz Engineering Laboratory Report No. 471.2, Lehigh University, Bethlehem, Pennsylvania.

Shen, Z. Y. and Lu, L. W., 1982
DISCUSSION OF PROPOSED STEEL COLUMN STRENGTH CRITERIA, BY DANN H. HALL, Journal of the Structural Division, ASCE, Vol. 108, No. ST5, Proc. Paper 17045, May, pp. 1194–1195.

Shepherd, R. and Donald, R. A. D., 1967
THE INFLUENCE OF IN-PLANE FLOOR FLEXIBILITY ON THE NORMAL MODE PROPERTIES OF BUILDINGS, Journal of Sound and Vibration, Vol. 5, No. 1, pp. 29–36.

Sherman, D. R., 1981
DISCUSSION OF RESEARCH NEEDS IN STABILITY OF METAL STRUCTURES, BY RIEDAR BJORHOVDE, Journal of the Structural Division, ASCE, Vol. 107, No. ST11, Proc. Paper 16616, November, pp. 2301–2302.

Sieczkowski, J., 1976
DESIGN OF CONCRETE TALL BUILDINGS (Projektowanie budynkow wysokich z betonu), Arkady Editions, Warsaw, Poland.

Sieczkowski, J., 1980
SELECTED DESIGN PROBLEMS OF TALL BUILDINGS IN CONCRETE (Wybrane zagadnienia ksztaltowania konstrukcji zelbetowych budynkow wysokich), Prace Naukowe, Budownictwo Zeszyt 61, W.P.W. Editions, Warsaw, Poland.

Soldo, B. J., 1980
AMERICAN ELDERLY IN THE 1980's, Population Bulletin, Vol. 35, No. 4, November.

Sommer, R., 1969
PERSONAL SPACE, Prentice–Hall, Englewood Cliffs, New Jersey.

Sommer, R., 1970
SMALL GROUP ECOLOGY IN INSTITUTIONS FOR THE ELDERLY, Spatial Behavior of Older People, University of Michigan, Ann Arbor, Michigan.

Southern Building Code Congress, 1976 and 1982
STANDARD BUILDING CODE, Southern Building Code Congress, Birmingham, Alabama.

Spengler, J. J., 1978
FACING ZERO POPULATION GROWTH, Duke University Press, Durham, North Carolina.

Springfield, J., 1982a
DISCUSSION OF RESEARCH NEEDS IN STABILITY OF METAL STRUC-
TURES, BY REIDAR BJORHOVDE, Journal of the Structural Division,
ASCE, Vol. 108, No.ST2, Proc. Paper 16834, February, pp. 488–490.
Springfield, J., 1982b
DISCUSSION OF INTERACTION BUCKLING IN I-SECTION COLUMNS,
BY GREGORY J. HANCOCK, Journal of the Structural Division, ASCE,
Vol. 108, No. ST2, Proc. Paper 16834, February, pp. 493–494.
Springfield, J., 1982c
STUDY OF RACK STRUCTURES, PART II – STABILITY, Carruthers & Wallace
Limited, Toronto, Canada.
Stafford Smith, B., 1979
RECENT DEVELOPMENTS IN THE METHODS OF ANALYSIS FOR TALL
BUILDINGS STRUCTURES, Civil Engineering and Works Review, Vol. 65.
Standig, K. F., Rentschler, G. P. and Chen, W. F., 1976
BOLTED BEAM-TO-COLUMN MOMENT CONNECTIONS, WRC Bulletin
No. 218, August.
Sugimoto, H. and Chen, W. F., 1982
SMALL END RESTRAINT EFFECTS ON STRENGTH OF H-COLUMNS,
Journal of the Structural Division, ASCE, Vol. 108, No. ST3, Proc. Paper
16941, March, pp. 661–681.
Svensson, S. E., and Kragerup, J., 1982
COLLAPSE LOADS OF LACED COLUMNS, Journal of the Structural Division,
ASCE, Vol. 108, No. ST6, Proc. Paper 17179, June, pp. 1367–1384.

Takeda, T., Sozen, M. A. and Nielsen, N. N., 1970
REINFORCED CONCRETE RESPONSE TO SIMULATED EARTHQUAKE,
Journal of the Structural Division, ASCE, Vol. 96, No. ST12, December, pp.
2557–2573.
Tall, L., ed., 1974
STRUCTURAL STEEL DESIGN, second edition, Ronald Press, New York.
Tarnai, T., 1981a
DISCUSSION OF END RESTRAINT AND COLUMN STABILITY BY WAI F.
CHEN, Journal of the Structural Division, ASCE, Vol. 107, No. ST11, Proc.
Paper 17180, June, pp. 1385–1399.
Tarnai, T., 1981b
DISCUSSION ON END RESTRAINT AND COLUMN STABILITY, BY WAI F.
CHEN, Journal of the Structural Division, ASCE, Vol. 107, No. ST11, Proc.
Paper 16616, November, pp. 2292–2293.
Tarpy, T. S., 1980
BEAM-TO-COLUMN END PLATE CONNECTIONS, Spring Convention, ASCE,
April, Portland, Oregon.
Tebedge, N., 1982
BUCKLING OF PRETWISTED COLUMNS, Journal of the Structural Division,
ASCE, Vol. 107, No. ST11 Proc. Paper 16616, November, pp. 2292–2293.
Tezcan, S., 1967
ANALYSIS AND DESIGN OF SHEAR WALL STRUCTURES. TALL BUILD-
INGS, Pergamon Press, Ltd., London.

Time, 1983
THE REPAIRING OF AMERICA, Time, January 10, pp. 12–15.
Toma, S. and Chen, W. F., 1982
CYCLIC ANALYSIS OF FIXED-ENDED STEEL BEAM-COLUMNS, Journal of the Structural Division, ASCE, Vol. 108, No. ST, Proc. Paper 17180, June, pp. 1385–1399.
Toma, S., Chen, W. F. and Finn, L. D., 1982
EXTERNAL PRESSURE AND SECTIONAL BEHAVIOR OF FABRICATED TUBES, Journal of the Structural Division, ASCE, Vol. 108, No. ST1, Proc. Paper 16797, January, pp. 177–194.
Turnipseed, S. P., 1982
URBAN STREET DESIGN ELEMENTS, Department of Environmental Design, Texas A & M University, for the U.S. Department of Transportation Federal Highway Administration, January.

U.S. News and World Report, 1982
TO REBUILD AMERICA—$2.5 TRILLION JOB, U.S. News & World Report, September 27, pp. 57–61.

W. V. Rouse & Co., 1980
GENERIC ALTERNATIVES ANALYSIS: FINAL REPORT, Vol. 2, U.S. Department of Transportation, UTMA, June.
Vanderbilt, D., 1981
EQUIVALENT FRAME ANALYSIS OF UNBRACED CONCRETE FRAMES, Significant Developments in Engineering Practice and Research—Siess Symposium, American Concrete Institute, Publication SP-72, pp. 219–246.
Vesic, A. S., 1967
ULTIMATE LOADS AND SETTLEMENT OF DEEP FOUNDATIONS IN SAND, (Proceedings of the Symposium on Bearing Capacity and Settlement of Foundations, held at Duke University in Durham, North Carolina), pp. 53–68.
Vinnakota, S., 1981
EFFECT OF IMPERFECTIONS ON PLANAR STRENGTH OF RESTRAINED BEAM-COLUMNS, SSRC-TG23 Report, May, pp. 1–33.
Virdi, K. S., 1981
DESIGN OF CIRCULAR AND RECTANGULAR HOLLOW SECTION COLUMNS, Journal of Constructional Steel Research, Vol. 1, No. 4, September, pp. 35–45.
Vitkovice, 1980
BULLETIN OF TECHNOLOGY, STEEL STRUCTURES, (in Czech), Volume 4, Ostrava, Czechoslovakia.
Vogan, R. W., 1977
FRICTION AND END BEARING TESTS ON BEDROCK FOR HIGH CAPACITY SOCKET DESIGN: DISCUSSION, Canadian Geotechnical Journal, Vol. 14, pp. 156–158.

Wang, T. Y., Bertero, V. V. and Popov, E. P., 1975
HYSTERETIC BEHAVIOR OF REINFORCED CONCRETE FRAMED WALLS, Report No. EERC 75-23, University of California, Berkeley, California.

Wiesner, K. B., 1979
TUNED MASS DAMPERS TO REDUCE BUILDING WIND MOTION, Preprint
3510, ASCE Convention Exposition, Boston, Massachusetts, April, 1979.
Wilson, E. L. et al., 1975
THE THREE-DIMENSIONAL ANALYSIS OF BUILDING SYSTEMS (Extended
Version), Earthquake Engineering Research Center, Report No.
EERC 75-13, University of California, Berkeley, California.
Witteveen, J., Stark, J. W. B., Bijlaard, F. S. D. and Zoetemeijer, P., 1982
WELDED AND BOLTED BEAM-TO-COLUMN CONNECTIONS, Journal of
the Structural Division, ASCE, Vol. 18, No. STG2, Proc. Paper 16873, February,
pp. 433-455.
Wolsiefer, J., 1982
ULTRA HIGH STRENGTH FIELD PLACEABLE CONCRETE IN THE
RANGE 69 TO 124 MPA (10,000 TO 18,000 psi), Presented at the 1982 Annual
Convention of the American Concrete Institute, Atlanta, Georgia, January 1982.
Wong, K. C. and Temple, M. C., 1982
STAYED COLUMN WITH INITIAL IMPERFECTIONS, Journal of the Struc-
tural Division, ASCE, Vol. 108, No. ST7, Proc. Paper 17217, July, pp. 1623-1640.
Wood, B. R., Beaulieu, D. and Adams, P. F., 1976
COLUMN DESIGN BY THE P-DELTA METHOD, Journal of the Structural
Division, ASCE, Vol. 102, No. ST2, Proc. Paper 11936, February, pp. 411-427.
Woodward, R. J., Gardner, W. S. and Greer, D. M., 1972
DRILLED PIER FOUNDATIONS, McGraw-Hill Book Company, New York.

Yamamoto, Y. and Kobayashi, M., 1982
USE OF MINERAL FINES IN HIGH STRENGTH CONCRETE – WATER
REQUIREMENT AND STRENGTH, Concrete International, July.
Yang, J. N., 1982
CONTROL OF TALL BUILDINGS UNDER EARTHQUAKE EXCITATION,
Journal of the Engineering Mechanics Division, ASCE, Vol. 108, No. EM5,
October, pp. 833-849.
Yura, J. A., Birkemore, P. C. and Ricles, J. M., 1980
BEAM WEB SHEAR CONNECTIONS – AN EXPERIMENTAL STUDY, Journal
of the Structural Division, ASCE, Vol. 108, No. ST2, Proc. Paper 16848, February,
pp. 311-325.
Yura, J. A., Frank, K. H. and Cayes, L., 1981
BOLTED FRICTIONS WITH WEATHERING STEEL, Journal of the Structural
Division, ASCE, Vol. 107, No. ST11, Proc. Paper 16644, November, pp. 2071-2087.

Zikria, B. A., 1972
INHALATION INJURIES IN FIRES, Columbia University College of Physicians
and Surgeons, New York.
Zwicky, F., 1969
DISCOVERY, INVENTION, RESEARCH THROUGH THE MORPHOLOG-
ICAL ANALYSIS, MacMillan, New York.

Indexes

Building Index

The following index enables the reader to identify the page number on which a particular building is mentioned. Numbers in italics that follow cities and buildings refer to panoramic photographic view.

Name Index

The following list cites the page number on which the indicated names are mentioned. This list includes authors, as well as other individuals or organizations named in the text.

Names followed by years refer to bibliographic citations that are included in the appendix entitled "References/Bibliography".

500 Grant Street Associates, 602
Abrams and Sozen (1979), 451
ACI (1977), 473, 477, 478, 480, 484
ACI (1983), 419
ACI Building Code, 473, 474, 480
ACI Building Code Requirements for Reinforced Concrete, 419
ACI Committee 352 (1976), 147
Ackroyd and Gerstle (1982), 303, 354, 360
Advances in Tall Building, 1, 419, 420
AISC (1970), 473, 474, 477
AISC (1978), 323, 330
AISC (1980), 591
AISC (1982), 303
AISC Commentary, 479
AISC Manual, 480
AISC Specification, 474, 479
AISI (1977), 592
Albinger, J. M., 517
Algermissen and Perkins (1976), 244
Allegheny Conference on Community Development, 20
Allen, I., 23
American Concrete Institute (ACI), 473, 477, 478, 479, 488, 519, 525, 528
American Institute of Steel Construction (AISC), 303, 330, 473, 477, 478, 591, 593
American Insurance Association, 260
American National Standards Institute (ANSI), 312
American Society of Civil Engineers (ASCE), 225
Amrhein, J. E., 525

ANSI (1972), 238
ANSI (1982), 184, 233, 234, 236, 238, 239
ANSI A58.1-1972, 312
ANSI A58.1-1982, 234, 235, 238, 239
ANSWERS, 311
Applied Technology Council (ATC), 312, 462, 498, 499
Applied Technology Council Provisions for Seismic Loading, 312
Architectural and Transportation Compliance Board (1977), 123
Arciszewski (1975), 285
Arciszewski (1980), 281
Arciszewski and Brodka (1978), 282
Arciszewski and Kisielnicka (1977), 285
Arciszewski and Lubinski (1978), 282
Arciszewski and Pancewicz (1976), 281
Arciszewski, T., 279, 281
Arthur D. Little, Inc., 211
ASCE/NSF (1983), 225
ASCE/NSF (1984), 225
ASCE Structural Division (1962), 184
ASTM, 519, 521, 613
ATC (1978), 139, 180, 185, 244, 312, 496, 498
Atlanta Chamber of Commerce, 22
Atlanta City Council, 23
Avent and Wells (1982), 303
Ayers, T., 535, 536

Baer (1982), 211
Baer, W., 211
Baguelin et al. (1978), 194

665

Subject Index

673

electronic office of the future, 209, 210, 211, 214, 218
elevators, 37, 122, 125, 126, 127
elevators and escalators, 547
employment, 224, 226
end conditions of column, 323, 324, 350
end eccentricities, 357
end movements, 302
end-restrained columns, 355, 356
end-restrained column curves, 357
end-restrained steel columns, 300, 301, 303
end restraint, 355, 356, 357, 359
energy-conscious office buildings, 210, 213, 215
energy conservations, 201–221, 575
energy-conservative high-rise design, 159
energy costs, 213, 214, 216, 217
enclosure criterion, 184
energy-dissipative mechanism, 251
energy efficiency, 215, 216
energy-integrated systems design, 216
energy load control, 209, 214, 218
energy management in office buildings, 210
energy savings, 45
energy supply, 224, 226
energy systems with alternating operating modes, 217
entertainment, 225, 227
entries, 2, 4, 8, 9, 10
environmental design, 132
environmental effect of industrial tall buildings, 188
environmental effects on pedestrian trips, 50, 57, 64
environmental improvement for pedestrians, 57
environment complexity, 7
environment of high-rise, 8
environments, 1, 3, 7, 16
equation for column cord rotation, 438
equation for plate buckling, 591
equivalent column slenderness ratio, 591, 593
equivalent lateral loads, 498, 499
equivalent static load analysis, 496
equivalent uniform membrane elements, 582, 595

esthetic integration of people mover, 65, 69, 71
estimated structural costs of building, 165
Euler buckling load, 473, 474, 475
Euler column formula, 323
Euler curve, 326, 329, 341
Euler load, 325, 326, 336
evaluation criteria for a structural system, 164
exiting in event of fire, 263
experiments for confirmation as structure, 401
experiments for confirming performance on floor slabs, 401
exposed columns, 504, 505, 506
exterior columns and spandrels, 569, 571
exterior concrete framed tube, 136, 137, 140, 144
exterior finish, 411, 414
exterior framed tube, 159, 161
exterior tubular concept, 571
external circulation systems, 62
external elements, 284
external joints, 284
external transportation, 49, 61
extraordinary loads, 233, 234, 235, 238
extrusions, 558

fabrication steps in construction, 390, 393
fabric, coarse-grained, 8
fabric, fine-grained, 8, 10
facade, 136
facade panel development, 573, 575, 577, 582, 586
facade panels, 583, 586
faceted crystalline form, 388
factory fabrication cost, 390
factory fabrication productivity, 411
Failure Mode and Effect Analysis technique (FEMA), 396, 397, 398, 399, 400
Fairlane Development, Dearborn, Michigan, 64
family of bracings, 285
family patterns, 116
fatigue caused by mechanical equipment vibrations, 180
feasible state, 282, 285, 286, 287, 288, 289, 290, 292, 293, 296

Council on Tall Buildings and Urban Habitat

Steering Group

J. Rankine	Chairman	Rankine & Hill Pty. Ltd.	Sydney
L. E. Robertson	Vice-Chairman	Robertson, Fowler & Assoc.	New York
L. S. Beedle	Director	Lehigh University	Bethlehem
G. W. Schulz	Secretary	University of Innsbruck	Innsbruck
L. W. Lu	Research Coordinator	Lehigh University	Bethlehem
D. Sfintesco	Past Chairman	C.T.I.C.M.	Lamorlaye

R. M. Aynsley	Papua New Guinea Univ. of Technology	Papua
R. T. Baum	Jaros, Baum & Bolles	New York
T. Brondum-Nielsen	Technical University of Denmark	Lyngby
I. G. Cantor	Office of Irwin G. Cantor, PC	New York
S. Chamecki	IPPUC	Curitiba
H. K. Cheng	H. K. Cheng & Assoc.	Hong Kong
F. L. Codella	Tower Tech. Ltd.	Cleveland
H. J. Cowan	University of Sydney	Sydney
C. DeBenedittis	Tishman Speyer Properties	New York
B. M. Dornblatt	B. M. Dornblatt & Assoc., Inc.	New Orleans
L. Finzi	Univesity of Milan	Milan
J. F. Fitzgerald	Joseph F. Fitzgerald & Assoc.	Chicago
G. F. Fox	Howard, Needles, Tammen & Bergendoff	New York
J. Freed	I. M. Pei & Partners	New York
Y. Friedman	Architect	Paris
M. P. Gaus	National Science Foundation	Washington, D.C.
G. He	Chinese Academy of Building Research	Beijing
J. S. B. Iffland	Iffland, Kavanagh, Waterbury, PC	New York
R. Kowalczyk	Technical University Bialystok	Bialystok
I. Martin	Capacete-Martin & Associates	San Juan
W. McGuire	Cornell University	Ithaca
W. A. Milek	Engineering and Research, AISC	Chicago
A. Moharram	Arab Consulting Engineers	Cairo
W. P. Moore	W. P. Moore & Associates	Houston
T. Naka		Tokyo
J. Newman	Tishman Research Corp.	New York
R. Y. Okamoto	Okamoto Murata AIA	San Francisco
L. Ouyang	Ouyang & Associates, Architects	Hong Kong
M. Paparoni	Consulting Engineer	Caracas
E. A. Picardi	Oxford Properties, Inc.	Toronto
G. Rahulan	Jurutera Perunding Awam Dan Strukt	Kuala Lumpur
M. Ridzuan-Salleh	Ranhill Bersekutu Sdn. Bhd.	Kuala Lumpur
W. A. Rutes	The Sheraton Corporation	Boston
P. H. Sedway	Sedway/Cooke	San Francisco
L. Shute	Turner Construction	New York
B. Thurlimann	Swiss Federal Institute of Technology	Zurich
W. Voss	Henn & Voss	Braunschweig
J. Zunz	Ove Arup Partnership	London

Editorial Committee

L. S. Beedle (Ch.), J. Rankine, L. E. Robertson, L. W. Lu, G. W. Schulz, D. Sfintesco, M. P. Gaus, R. M. Kowalczyk, D. B. Rice; *Group PC:* Y. Friedman, L. E. Robertson, A. Vernez-Moudon, C. Norberg-Schulz, W. Henn; *Group SC:* J. Rankine, W. P. Moore, H. J. Cowan, L. S. Beedle, I. Cantor; *Group CL:* A. Davenport, E. Gaylord, L. W. Lu; *Group SB:* L. Finzi, W. McGuire, C. Gaylord, M. Wakabayashi, L. W. Lu; *Group CB:* T. Brondum-Nielsen, I. Martin, J. MacGregor, I. Lyse, T. Huang; Chairman, Vice-Chairman and Editors of each committee (identified in each chapter), affiliates representing sponsors, and selected council representatives.

Professional Society Sponsors

International Association for Bridge and Structural Engineering (IABSE)
American Society of Civil Engineers (ASCE)
American Institute of Architects (AIA)
American Planning Association (APA)
International Union of Architects (UIA)